HUMANITIES

In the Ancient and Pre-Modern World

AN AFRICANA EMPHASIS

Wendell P. Jackson, General Editor

Frances Alston, Associate Editor

Linda M. Carter, Associate Editor

Lillian Dunmars Roland, Associate Editor

Front Cover: Designed by Lillian Dunmars Roland, based on a specific papyrus print produced by The Nile For Papyrus and made in Zifta, Egypt. Images taken from Dr. Roland's personal collection. All rights reserved by designer.

Back Cover: The male and female images; the hieroglyphic, hieratic, and demotic writing samples; and the cartographic color enhancements were added to the back cover by Dr. Lillian Dunmars Roland. The map is from the photographic collection of Mr. Steven Beikirch. All rights reserved by the designer and by the original map owner.

Printed in the United States of America

10 9 8 7 6 5 4 3 2 1

Please visit our web site at www.pearsoncustom.com

ISBN 0–536–02567-3

BA 990252

PEARSON CUSTOM PUBLISHING
160 Gould Street/Needham Heights, MA 02494
A Pearson Education Company

Copyright Acknowledgments

Grateful acknowledgment is made to the following sources for permission to reprint material copyrighted or controlled by them:

"Night Seven," by J.P. Clark-Bekederemo, reprinted from *The Ozidi Saga: Collected and Translated From the Ijo of Okabou Ojobolo*, 1977, Howard University Press.

"The Creator," "Lament," "Prayer to the Moon," "Lament for the Dead Mother," "Longing for Death," "Sadness of Life," "Loneliness," "Hymn to the Sun," "The Ancestors," "Song for the Sun that Disappeared Behind the Rainclouds," "Prayer Before the Dead Body," "Funeral Song," "Hymn to Lightning," "Death," "Lament," "The Moon," "The Sweetest Thing," "The Poor Man," "Invocation of the Creator," "The Almighty," "The Lazy Man," and "Three Friends," edited by Ulli Beier, 1966, reprinted from *African Poetry: An Anthology of Traditional African Poems*, by permission of Cambridge University Press. Copyright © 1996 Cambridge University Press.

"How Splendid You Ferry the Skyways," "God Is a Master Craftsman," "When Being Began Back in the Days of Genesis," translated by John Lawrence Foster, reprinted from *The Leiden Hymns in Echoes of Egyptian Voices: An Anthology of Ancient Egyptian Poetry*, 1992, University of Oklahoma Press.

"Send Him Back Hard by Your Lady's Small Window," "Ho, What She's Done to Me—That Girl," I Love a Girl, but She Lives Over There," "Whenever I Leave You, I Go Out of Breath," translated by John L. Foster, reprinted from *Love Songs of the New Kingdom*, 1974, Charles Scribner's and Sons (Macmillan).

"Proverbs I: On Ignorance and Knowledge," "Proverbs II: On Prudence," "Proverb III: On Knowing One's Place," "Proverb IV: On Endurance," "Proverb V: On Wealth," "Proverb VI: On Being Content With Oneself," "Proverbs VII: On Anger," "Proverb VIII: On Consequences," and "Proverb IX: On Women," by Alta Jablow, reprinted from *The Intimate Folklore of Africa*, 1961, Greenwood Publishing Group.

"Why the Earth Was Peopled," "The Story of Creation," "The Story of the Beginning of Things," "The Origin of Death, Lie and Truth," and "The Human Race," edited by Blaise Cendrars, translated by Margery Bianco, reprinted from *The African Saga*, 1927. Copyright © 1927 by Payson & Clark, Ltd.

"The Spider and the Mason-fly," "Spider Tries His Wives," "The Dog and the Cock," "The Elephant and the Dudu-bird," "The Elephant and the Gazelle," "Kwan the Boa and Longo the Viper," "The Spider and the Crocodile," "Souls and Spirits," "The Underworld," "The Origin of White People," and "The Origin of Jealousy" by Jan Knappert, reprinted from *Myths and Legends of the Congo*, 1971, Heinemann Educational Books.

"The Maiden Nsia," "The Jealous Husband," "The Son-In-Law," "Affection or Wealth?" "Blind Man and Lame Man, and Ingratitude," by Alta Jablow, reprinted from *The Intimate Folklore of Africa*, 1961, Greenwood Publishing Group.

"Sundiata," by Djibril Tamsir Niane, translated by G. D. Pickett, reprinted from *Sundiata: An Epic of Old Mali*, 1965, Longman Group.

"Psalm 8, Psalm 19, Psalm 23, and Psalm 137, Genesis 1-3,4, 6-9, 11, 37, 39-46, and excerpts from the Book of Job" King James Version, reprinted from *The Norton Anthology of World Masterpieces,* Expanded Edition, Vol. 1. Copyright © 1997 by W.W. Norton & Company.

"Song of Songs," edited by Alexander Jones, reprinted from *The Jerusalem Bible,* 1966. Copyright © by Darron, Longman & Todd, Ltd, a division of Random House, Inc. Used by permission of Doubleday, a division of Random House, Inc.

"Throned in Splendor, Deathless, O Aphrodite," "Like the Very Gods in my Sights Is He," and "Some There Are Who Say That the Fairest Thing Seen," by Sappho of Lesbos, translated by Richmond Lattimore, reprinted from *Greek Lyrics,* as appears in *The Norton Anthology of World Masterpieces,* Expanded Edition, Vol. 1. Copyright © 1997 by W.W. Norton & Company.

Excerpt from "Poetics," by Aristotle, edited by William David Ross, 1927, Charles Scribner's and Sons.

"The Theogony of Hesiod (English side only)," by Hesiod, translated by High G. Evelyn-White, reprinted from *The Homeric Hymns and Homerica,* 1936, Harvard University Press.

"The Fox and the Grapes," "The Ant and the Grasshopper," "The Hart, the Sheep, and the Wolf," "The Dog and His Shadow," "The Frogs Who Wanted a King," "The Lion and the Horse," and "The Rat, the Frog, and the Kite," by Aesop, selected by John J. McKendry, reprinted from *Aesop: Five Centuries of Illustrated Fables,* 1964, The Metropolitan Museum of Art.

"The Apology," by Plato, translated by F.J. Church, translation revised by Richard D. Cumming, reprinted from *Euthyphro, Apology, and Crito and the Death Scene from Phaedo*, 1948, 1956, Liberal Arts Press.

"Everyman," translated by Helen Louise Cohen, reprinted from *Milestones of the Drama,* 1940, Harcourt Brace & Company.

"Beginning and End," translated by Miguel Leon-Portilla and Grace Lobanov, reprinted from *Pre-Columbian Literatures of Mexico*, 1969, 1986, University of Oklahoma Press.

"Song of Tlaltecatzin, Cuauhchinanco," "Song of Springtime," "Song of Machuilxochitl," by Miguel Leon-Portilla, reprinted from *Fifteen Poets of the Aztec World*, 1992, University of Oklahoma Press.

"Prayer to Virachocha," edited by Pierre DuViols, translated by Jose Maria Arguedas, reprinted from *Dioses y hombres de Huarochiri*: Edicion bilingue, 1966, Francis Cairns Publications, Ltd.

Excerpt from "Popol Vuh," translated by Dennis Tedlock, reprinted from *Popul Vuh*, 1985, Simon & Schuster.

"Ikkaku Sennin: A Japanese Noh Play," by Komparu Zenpo Motoyasu, edited by James R. Brandon, translated by Frank Hoff and William Packard, reprinted from *Traditional Asian Plays*, 1972, Hill & Wang.

"It Is Other People. . .," "To Sit Silent . . ," "O Pine-Tree Standing. . .," "The Beloved Person. . .," "If Only Life-and-Death. . .," and "Many, Many Things They Bring to Mind," edited by John D. Yohannan, translated by Arthur Waley, reprinted from *A Treasury of Asian Literature*, 1956, Harper Collins Publishers.

"Teaching II: The Yoga of Knowledge and Teaching X: Divine Glory," translated by Swami Prabhavananda and Christopher Isherwood, reprinted from *The Song of God: Bhagavad-Gita*, 1972, The Vendanta Society of Southern California.

"Cease Not from Desire" (Gertrude Bell, trans.), "Light in Darkness (Arthur J. Arberry, trans.) and "O Ask Not" (H.H. trans.), edited by Arthur J. Arberry, reprinted from *Fifty Poems by Hafiz*, 1970, Cambridge University Press.

"Gilgamesh," translated by N.K. Sandars, reprinted from *The Epic of Gilgamesh*, (Penguin Classics, 1960, Third Edition, 1972). Copyright © NK Sandars, 1960, 1964, 1972.

"The Mahabharata," and "The Ramayana," by Dr. Meena Khorna, reprinted from *Beacham's Guide to Literature for Young Adults*, vol. 4, Beacham Publishing Corporation.

Contributors

Frances Alston: African Background (History and Culture), *The Divine Comedy*; Biographies of Sappho, Catullus, and Dante Alighieri

Ruth McKnight Antoine: African Music

Gerri Bates: Asian Literature, Noh Play, The Bhagavad Gita, Asian Music

***Michael Bayton:** Greek Theater, *Oedipus Rex, Antigone, The Iliad, The Odyssey*, Medieval Theater, Everyman; Biography of Homer

Nila Bowden: Biographies of Aristotle, Sophocles, and Chaucer

Linda M. Carter: *The Step-Mother* [of Terrence], *Fables* [of Aesop], American Background (Pre-Columbian History and Culture); Biographies of Aesop and Terrence

Grace K. Coffey: *The [General] Prologue of the Canterbury Tales*, "The Pardoner's Tale," "The Miller's Tale"

Caleb Corkery: Haiku

Glenn Harris: Japanese Poetry

Karl Henzy: Classical and Medieval Music

Dolan Hubbard: W.E.B. DuBois and *The World and Africa*

Edith Moss Jackson: Pre-Columbian Poetry, Pre-Columbian Art/Architecture

Wendell Jackson: Humanities Yesterday, African Art, Asian Background (History and Culture), Yoruba Gods and Goddesses, Egyptian Gods and Goddesses

Milford Jeremiah: Hebraic/Greco-Roman/Medieval Narrative

Ivan Johnson: "The Wife of Bath's Tale," "The Nun's Priest Tale"

Meena G. Khorana: *The Mahabharata, The Ramayana*

Adam Mekler: Pre-Columbian Literature

Sydney Onyeberechi: Chinese Poetry

Ralph Reckley, Sr.: The Narrative in Africa During the Middle Ages

Margaret Ann Reid: Medea; Biography of Euripides

Lillian Dunmars Roland: European Backgrounds (History and Culture), *The Theogony [of Hesiod], The Apology [of Plato]*; Biographies of Hesiod and Plato

Sylvia Saunders: *The Ozidi Saga*, African Tales and Myths, *Sundiata*

Ella Stevens: The Poetry of Sappho, The Poetry of Catullus; Biography of Virgil

Ordner Taylor: The Popul Vuh

Minnie Washington: *Book of Psalms, The Song of Songs, The Book of Job*; Biographies of King David and King Solomon

Patricia Wells: Islamic Poetry

Judy White: Ancient Poetry, Medieval Poetry, *Gilgamesh*

Annette Williams: African Poetry and Proverbs

***Michael Zeitler:** Martin Bernal's *Black Athena*, The Aeneid, Greco-Roman and Medieval Painting/Sculpture/Architecture, Archetype/Myth/Culture (The Symbolic Structure of the Human Psyche)

* Special Contributor

Dedication

To Ruthe T. Sheffey, Professor of English and Language Arts,
Whose foresight in 1971 and in years following
Has made possible at Morgan State University
the basic Humanities courses as we now know them

Contents

Preface

Since the early 1950s the Department of English and Language Arts at Morgan State University has conducted a humanities studies program. In those early days, the underlying aim of humanities studies was to expose students to European philosophy, literature, history, and art in order to enhance their liberal training as well as to prepare for graduate study those students who would take the Graduate Record Examination (G.R.E) and other graduate-level entrance tests. In the late 1960s and early 1970s, however, the humanities program expanded its canon by including in the curriculum many African-American, Native-American, African, and Asian materials. This globalization of the curriculum, which over the years has won many compliments from accrediting agencies, occurred one or two decades before the now common expansion of the literary, artistic, and philosophical canons. While building upon this tradition of intellectual diversity, this text, *Humanities in the Ancient and Pre-Modern Worlds: An Africana Emphasis,* acknowledges the fact that its primary audience will be young African-American women and men, who need to explore African-American and African intellectual traditions, so as to strengthen their understanding of themselves, of their heritage, and of their potential in the world. Through the sheer weight of readings and commentaries from this tradition, the emphasis of this volume is Africana. However, all readers will derive significant benefit from the text because of its broad scope, its inclusive point of view, and the deeper and more creative fusion that it may bring about between student readers and other peoples and cultures of the world.

Note to Instructors

With a few exceptions, this text includes all materials needed for a course on humanities in the ancient and pre-modern worlds, with an Africana emphasis.

Production difficulties prohibited the inclusion of Euripides' *Medea*, Geoffrey Chaucer's "The Miller's Tale" and "The Nun's Priest's Tale," and the *Ramayana*. Should the instructor feel strongly that one or the other of these be read, then the student will find in Appendix A appropriate biographies and/or backgrounds for these selections. The instructor may likewise find useful, desciptions of Yeruba, Egyptian, and Greco-Roman gods and goddesses (Appendix B), as well as the Morgan State University Student Evaluation Form and Course Syllabus (Appendix C).

Acknowledgments

In the early 1970s, Ruthe T. Sheffey, then chairperson of the Morgan State College Department of English, initiated an important change in the direction of the humanities studies program, from focusing primarily upon European civilization to pursuing a curriculum that was truly transcultural. The new curriculum took into account the insight, creativity, and history of African and Asian peoples. Hence, gratitude is extended to Ruthe Sheffey for her pioneering leadership and insight. Recognition also must be extended to DeLois Flemons and Jean F. Turpin and to the late Nick Aaron Ford, Harry L. Jones, and Iva G. Jones, who contributed so generously of their time, energy, and thought to the growth of the humanities program. The editors and contributors likewise appreciate numerous courtesies and encouragements from Dolan Hubbard, Chairperson of the Department of English and Language Arts; Burney J. Hollis, Dean of the College of Liberal Arts; Clara I. Adams, Vice-President for Academic Affairs; and Earl S. Richardson, University President. Particular recognition must be extended to the departmental Humanities Committee, not only for preserving the program for over 40 years without pause, but also, in the last year, for taking initiative to approve the project proposal for this text, to create guidelines for its production, and to provide other helpful suggestions and frameworks. Last, the editors acknowledge gratefully the extensive and tireless assistance of Maxine Thompson in typing and preparing significant portions of the manuscript.

The Humanities Yesterday

When modern peoples consider the humanities, they realize how much they really owe to ancient and pre-modern predecessors, who have been critical in shaping the moderns' understanding of who and what they are. The modern world has to wonder whether any of its current concepts originate from roots other than the ancient. Is it not true that moderns owe to these predecessors notions of right and wrong, beauty and repulsion, religion and science, the world and the universe of which that world is a part? The theories of government, societal organization, psychology, medicine, engineering, and mathematics come to the modern world from the brains, hearts, and experiences of the billions of souls who have appeared before the modern era—living, working, and ceasing on this tiny, incomprehensible globe. The sublime, 6,000-year-old vision of God held by the peoples of the Sudan and Egypt; the tragic view of the Greeks and Romans about fate or about those forces which complicate human life; the extremely symbolic, unifying perceptions of the Aztec, Incan, and Mayan empires of pre-Columbian America; the revolutionary affirmation of the value of the individual resonant throughout the Judeo-Christian spiritual tradition; the passionate and deeply humbling devotion of the followers of Islam; or the supreme intellectuality and philosophical insights of the Hindu and Buddhist theologians—all provide the framework of spiritual values by which modern humanity still directs its curious course. The profoundly metaphysical insights of African myths, Jewish narratives, and Hindu tales of courage and duty raise relevant questions about the balance of the pairs of opposites, the nature and reward of virtue, and the paradoxes of conduct still being explored in the philosophy, literature, and art of today. Moderns also are indebted to the ancients for other intellectual accomplishments. The stunning deductions of ancient and pre-modern humanity about the principles of science, mathematics, medicine, and proto-technology are indications of the penetration of the human intellect in general, its ability to grasp (often unaided by meaningful tools) concepts that reveal something of the workings of the mind of God. Finally, moderns have to wonder whether socio-political organization has advanced beyond inherited models. Family, group, and national structures seem much the same as they were 3,000 years ago. Nor have modern concepts of love, friendship, loyalty, honor, and courage altered much from those voiced by Egyptian or Roman or Medieval or Japanese thinkers.

The peoples of the ancient and pre-modern worlds, then, are the spiritual ancestors of modern cultures, preserving in these cultures the capacity to question, to marvel, and to feel sorrow about humans' puzzling, transient lives. These forerunners have borne the burden of being the first to discover the truths by which moderns now live and by which they measure all that they think and do. The ancient mind has given voice to the overarching purposes of human life which moderns still struggle to understand. And for these reasons alone, the modern world has to study continuously the ancient and pre-modern humanities for clues as to how today's peoples should conduct themselves and their complex affairs. In doing so, moderns are not in the least affirming that nothing more remains to be discovered, resolved, or known. The doctrine that wisdom is already exhausted cannot be accepted. But what the peoples of today should acknowledge is that recognizing past ways of facing and resolving material or spiritual conflicts empowers them to face and resolve their own. For they live and feel and think in the same way as their ancestors did. Moderns are capable of insights and behaviors as sublime or wicked as their predecessors'. Moderns have to walk in their own shoes and follow their own indeterminate steps. But they need not do so in complete, unmitigated ignorance of the amassed evidence of the past.

Today, it is common to speak of the marvels of science and to laud the wonders of a global, remarkably resilient technology and economy. But without the wisdom to employ these benefits for the best good of the peoples of the earth, nothing more awaits humanity than dazzling catastrophe or collapse. It is sad how little modern peoples have learned from this past, how carelessly they have heeded its best thinking about the nature of the human soul and the vicissitudes of its path. But the humanities extend to them the opportunity to walk with a greater light than individuals would be in a position to discover on their own. The humanities offer the only thread to unifying past, present, and future and to making the most of all that modern minds and spirits have to give.

Part I: The African Perspective

African Background: History and Culture

Africa is known as the birthplace of the human race. It is the second largest continent, and the only continent that is larger is Asia. The earliest civilization probably lived along the Nile River because the Nile River created the proper setting for a rich civilization to flourish. The ancient Africans connected the Nile River and its seasonal flooding with their religion and gods. To them, the Nile River was a mysterious force to be worshiped, and the Nile was respected as the god, Hapi. The longest river in the world, the Nile, starts almost at the center of the African continent, connects with the Mediterranean Sea, and flows into the Delta. The Delta is formed by rich soil left by the river as it empties into the sea. Some of the earliest civilizations grew up along the Nile River, communities of people who were advanced enough to live harmoniously together.

Egypt's development began in the Nile Valley. Egypt became a united state with one ruler many years after the culture appeared along the Nile. Starting in the south of the country, the civilization spread throughout the Nile Valley. Eventually, the north was conquered by the great king Menes, also called Narmer. King Menes was the first pharaoh to govern the entire Nile Valley from the first Cataract to the Delta. He built his capital city of Memphis and started the first dynasty. After King Menes, all pharaohs passed down the right to rule to their children or other relatives. The first dynasty of King Menes is dated about 3100 BCE.

The kings of Egypt were called "pharaohs," which means "great house," referring to the power and authority of the king to control the land and its wealth. The ancient Egyptians considered the pharaoh to be a god or a divine being. Many of the lesser gods were worshiped, but the ancient Egyptians considered the pharaoh to be their national god or deity.

The Egyptians were great observers of nature. It is evident that their ideas of eternal life were linked to agriculture. The people had a good idea about when to plant food crops, but they wanted to understand the mysterious cycles that gave them food and flood, life and death. The Egyptians also developed myths about gods to explain the mysteries of life. They had a rich religious life, dramatized in myths about death and rebirth, that explained the abundant growth of their vegetables and fruits. Some of these myths, centered around the Nile River, were a way for the priests to explain the flooding of the Nile River. The myths of creation held a special appeal for them.

African religion was a form of animism, in which it was thought that any representational image, whether it was carved or natural, held within it a powerful magical force. For instance, when Egyptians viewed a *uraeus* (image of the sacred asp or cobra on the headdress of rulers signifying the sovereignty of their office) in the pinnacle, they imbued the rock with all the power and meaning of whatever they understood the uraeus to be. Further, it was the apotropaic serpent from any number of the great goddesses, who were thought to be divine mothers of the king or daughters and protectresses of the king's divine "father." Interestingly, the ancient theologians, conceiving the rounded mountain, rising from the desert plain, as a great head wearing one or the other of these uraei, regarded the image as proof that the mountain was the seat of the god who gave kingship to mankind.

Early Roman history played itself out in North Africa, which came under Roman domination in 146 BC after the destruction of Carthage at the end of the Third Punic War. The resulting province comprised the territory that had been subject to Carthage in 149 BC; this was an area about 5,000 square miles, divided from the kingdom of Numida in the west by a ditch and embankment running southeast from Thabraco to Thaenae. About 100 BC the province's boundary was extended further westward, almost as far as the present Algerian-Tunisian border. The province grew in importance during the first century BC when Julius Caesar and Augustus founded a number of colonies in it. The most notable among them was the new Carthage, which became the second city in the Western Roman Empire. Augustus extended the provincial borders outward as far as the Sahara. In the west he combined the old province of *Africa Vetus* ("Old Africa") with what Caesar had designated as *Africa Nova* ("New Africa"), the old kingdom of Numidia and Mauritania. The original territory annexed by Rome was populated by indigenous Libyans who lived in small villages and had a relatively nomadic culture.

The early Africans cultivated science and the arts, including mathematics. There are two books about mathematics written by early Egyptians, namely: *Moscow Papyrus* and *Rhind Papyrus*. Both books of mathematical problems existed more than 2,000 years before the civilizations of Greece or Rome. In fact, ancient Africans developed the branch of mathematics known as geometry, meaning "earth measuring." The ancient Egyptians also knew a great deal about astrology and astronomy. They were so proficient in science that they were able to build pyramids so that their sides were aligned with certain stars and planets. Their knowledge of astronomy and observations of the skies even led the ancient Africans to the modern realization that the calendar needed to be 365/366 days, based on the number of days needed for the earth to revolve once around the sun.

Egyptians produced architecture, sculpture, and painting. For example, the Great Sphinx is one of the most famous of the architectural constructions of ancient Egyptians. No other ancient civilization was so rich in painting and sculpture. There were paintings on the walls of temples and tombs and massive carvings of statues of human beings and animals that represented the gods. Many of these paintings on the walls of ancient buildings inform the viewers of how the ancient Egyptians lived, and some of the sculptures and paintings are quite lifelike. In fact, in African art, all the creative disciplines are embraced: not only sculpture, painting, and architecture but also costume, jewelry, textiles, music, dance, literature, and poetry. What gives African art its special character is its fuctionality, which one finds an immediate interrelationship between art and other social forms. The earliest evidence of African art is provided by the engravings and paintings on rock surfaces in the Sahara spanning a period about 5,000 years to the present day.

Among the earliest known sculptures from Sub-Saharan Africa are those of the Nok culture, which flourished in the Western Sudan as early as the fifth century BC.

Wooden figurines have served a number of social roles, including funerary, ancestral, commemorative, healing, and fertility functions. Clay sculptures also appear frequently. In addition to the Nok culture pieces, terra cotta figurines, associated with pottery forms, occur on the Guinea Coast among the Akan as funerary pieces and among the Yoruba as shrine objects. They have also been found in the Western Sudan. Individuals have formed clay into domestic pottery and sculpted objects since they learned to work and smelt. The oldest Sub-Saharan center in which sculpted pottery figures have been found is the Upper Nile Valley, where Nubians produced their own art long before the Egyptians. Thus Africa is immensely diverse, and the innovations of its ancient, vibrant culture have established the foundations for which cultures flourish today.

Selected Bibliography

Asante, Molefi Kete. *Classical Africa*. Maywood, NJ: Peoples, 1994.

Eyo, Ekpo, and Frank Willett. *Treasures of Ancient Nigeria*. New York: Knopf, 1980.

Gillon, Werner. *A Short History of African Art*. New York: Penguin, 1984.

Kendall, Timothy. "Kings of the Sacred Mountain: Napata and the Kushite Twenty-fifth Dynasty of Egypt." *Sudan: Ancient Kingdoms of the Nile*. Ed. Dietrich Wildung. New York: Flammarion, 1997. 161–228.

African Drama: *The Ozidi Saga*

The *Ozidi Saga* was collected and translated from the Ijo of Okabou Ojobolo. The saga is based on the oral tradition of the people of Orua.

John Pepper Clark has spent much time researching the background of the *Saga*. He has examined three different texts of the *Saga*, and he has written a play, *Ozidi*. After observing one version of the *Saga* in the town of Orua, Clark and Frank Speed made the performance into a forty-five minute, sixteen mm. color film. In 1977, he published the *Ozidi Saga* with his English translation, alongside the storyteller Okabou's Ijo version of the epic. During the performance of the *Saga*, the story is presented over a period of seven nights. It has drama, music, mime, and ritual. The work is as much drama as it is epic.

The narrator is the storyteller-protagonist. The setting of the narrative is the city-state of Orua. The *Saga* recounts the deeds of young Ozidi after the murder of his father Ozidi. In the town of Orua, the commanding generals, who are jealous of the father Ozidi, kill him. To weaken the power of the family, the generals conspire to appoint Temugedege, the idiot brother of Ozidi, as king of Orua. Thus, the elder Ozidi is murdered, and his wife, who is pregnant, must flee to safety.

The *Saga* presents the boyhood and training of young Ozidi. As he grows up, he is guided by his mother, Orea, and his maternal grandmother, Oreame, who has special powers as a witch. Also, young Ozidi receives favor from Tamara, the female goddess. After he grows up and assumes his identity, young Ozidi's duty is to avenge the murder of his father. In an example of dramatic irony, young Ozidi falls asleep and is awakened by the three wives of his father's murderers. Not knowing who he is, the wives brag about their husbands' murder of young Ozidi's father, enabling him to identify his enemies. He kills the wives in order to provoke the husbands into fighting him. Of course, he succeeds in getting justice for wrongs done against his family. In another episode young Ozidi defeats the Smallpox King and drives him from Orua.

In Clark's play *Ozidi*, the storyteller plays both the father Ozidi and the son, as well as the idiot king, Temugedege. Clark makes some changes in his play that are different from the *Ozidi Saga*. In Clark's play, young Ozidi, by accident, kills his grandmother, Oreame. In the *Saga*, Oreame cures Ozidi of a disease, but in Clark's play, Ozidi's Mother, Orea, cures him. In the *Saga*, the community has a larger role than in Clark's play. Clark's play emphasizes Ozidi's personality. In both the *Ozidi Saga* and in Clark's *Ozidi*, there are elements of music, dance, magic, and ritual.

Selected Bibliography

Clark-Bekederemo, J. P. *Collected Plays and Poems, 1958–1988*. Washington, DC: Howard UP, 1991.

Clark, John Pepper. *The Ozidi Saga*. Trans. by Clark-Bekederemo. Nigeria: Ibadan UP and Oxford UP, 1977.

Etherton, Michael. *The Development of African Drama*. New York: Africana, 1982.

Night Seven of *The Ozidi Saga*

J. P. Clark-Bekederemo

SONG

Solo: Hear
Oh hear the wrestling within
Hear it and sally forth
Chorus: O hear it and sally forth!
Solo: Hear
Oh hear the wrestling within
Oh hear it and sally forth
Chorus: Oh hear it and sally forth
(Repeated several times)

Caller: O CITY!
Group: YES!
Caller: O CITY!
Group: YES!
Caller: IF YOU SEE GAME CAN YOU PLAY?
Group: OF COURSE, WE CAN!

SONG

Solo: Oh, yes!
Chorus: Oh, yes!
Solo: Paddles to the right
Chorus: O yes!
Solo: Paddles, to the right
Chorus: O yes!
Solo: Paddles, good people
Chorus: O yes!
Solo: Paddles, good people
Chorus: O yes!
Solo: Ijo people, paddles
Chorus: Oh yes!
Solo: Paddles, Ijo people
Chorus: Oh, yes!
(Repeated several times)

Caller: O CITY!
Group: YES!
Okabou: Indeed I told the story yesterday up to the entry of Tebekawene before we rose. It was at the scene of Tebekawene the story stopped, and we rose.
Now I'm going to take it up from there.
When I have narrated it as far as I know it, I am too well aware of tradition to go any farther.
I do not come from the seat of the gods.
Therefore I cannot properly finish the story for you.

Yes, but I'll tell you as much as I know it, I won't speak more, indeed I didn't open it, now the matter is ended.

GROUP: YES!
CALLER: NOW FOR ANOTHER MATTER!
GROUP: YES!

SONG

(Tebekawene song)
(Repeated several times)

CALLER: O CITY!
GROUP: YES!

In came Tebekawene stumping on his head, and levering himself upon his hands firmly on the ground, he somersaulted long distances.
Off into the air he flew, his head to the ground, his feet in the air.

CALLER: O CITY!
GROUP: YES!

And so Tebekawene stumped alone upon his head, hands balanced on the ground, he made incredible progress.
Vaulting, he had his head to the ground, his feet up in the air and flung far apart. As he swept in, a storm formed in his wake, blowing violently through the bush. Meanwhile, Ozidi and his orderlies—his servants—kept together.

They continued their march.
On that day, after they had walked on for some time . . .
(Laughter)

CALLER: O STORY!
GROUP: YES!

On that day, after they had walked on for some time . . . (hey! you people, I meant for some time, Ijo-people!)
(Laugher)
At a certain stage of their march, the hornblower, whose ears prickled at the slightest sound, heard it though they were still a long way off.
"Hey, Ozidi! Something is coming in in front.
Ahead there is something coming.
I hear a song at this very moment.
The song has a strong beat.
Now Oreame isn't with us.
Oh, I thought we could come out to play and return home without incidents, has it come to this! How awful!"
Said Ozidi: "What have you heard?
You drummer, what did you hear?

Say what you heard."
"Well, a song is coming in front.

Oh, Tebekawene, kill and be off, that's the song the person is singing on his march."
With this report given, Ozidi put one ear to the ground but he could hear nothing.
He listened with the other, but still could hear nothing.
At this point the hornblower added the weight of his horn, raucously he added it:
"Tron, ron, ron, diron, diron, diron.
Ozidi open your ears, open your ears, open your ears, open your ears!"
Raucously he continued: "Ozidi, trouble has come, in front there's trouble!
Trouble has come, something has come, something has come, something has come, something has come!"
Said Ozidi: "It's awful, I can't hear anything."
He trained his ear this way.
There was Tebekawene with his song . . . marching in with his song.
You should hear the noise of it.
The sky trembled with his every motion.

And the thunder of it tore the sky.
Thereupon the children warned him: "Ozidi, it looks as if rain is going to drench us thoroughly today, where shall we take shelter? There isn't a house nearby."
He replied: "There may be no house but the rain won't melt you. So move on, just push on."
"Oh, that thing is coming on even louder."
"Is it the true Ijo thing?" asked Ozidi.
"Oh, yes," they confirmed.
"All right then."
While they argued, Tebekawene came in vaunting:
"Oh, of the city of Ado, too, we have indeed heard a lot.
This very day, whoever is in this state of Orua, these Ozidi and Oreame about whom so much is spoken in a hush I shall creep upon them, and going into their house, I shall bind both together, and softly, softly again I shall go back to my house.
I've already put my cooking pots on the boil.
I've fired them all, all seven of them I've stoked with fire.
Then I shall cut them into small pieces, put them in there to cook, and for good seven days I don't have to cook again.
And I shall fall to directly."
SPECTATOR I: Quite a man of leisure!

CALLER: O STORY!
GROUP: YES!

"Such a feast to feed on!
Yes, how come such excellent meat has been around and I didn't know?

I am Tebekawene! I am Tebekawene! I am Tebekawene! I'm coming! I'm coming!
Right now, it's I on the march."
Thus he announced himself in.

By now, the children could hear nothing else.
"Hey, Ozidi, if we go on like this, it will not turn out well!
The ground is rumbling all over."

Ozidi looked out again: "Where is this noise coming from that you hear?"
He paused and pondered.
Closely, he listened all around.
And now the noise reached his ears faintly.
"Is it that faint sound you're hearing?"
"Oh yes.
But it's loud and strong.
How are your own ears made?"
And on trudged Te̱be̱kawe̱ne̱ with a storm for his wake.
"To kill Ozidi today, that's it . . . since they say he is a handsome boy, I shall cook him on the simmer, handle him with care before eating him up."

Spectator I: Much help that!

"How tasty today's meal will be!
Yes, my pot stands wide open."
Suddenly, he called to his wife.
He called out his wife: "Oh, Ekre̱kpo̱ oh, Ekre̱kpo̱!"

Te̱be̱kawe̱ne̱ now called in his wife: "Here, Ekre̱kpo̱!
Put fire to the pots before I come back. Put fire to the pots before I come back." If you saw this woman called Ekre̱kpo̱, like a thing made by white folk to scare people, she now appeared in the open
"I've already gathered so much firewood, the fire has been blazing for a long time."
"Is that so? Is that so? Is that so? Oh well then!" he said repeatedly.
"Then, look, this thing . . . the food, oh yes, let the pepper you add be hot."
Spectator II: What, to the meat still to slaughter!

Caller: O STORY!
Group: YES!
Caller: O STORY!
Group: YES!

Then the wife too said: "Yes, I've put pepper precisely to your taste."

"Is there salt as well?"
"The salt is also as you like it.
More can be added when you return."
"I don't want to come back to see things are just being put together.
I know it's when I'm back you'd start breaking the thing into bits to drop in, that's why I'm reminding you."
"Oh, yes, my husband, it can be quite hard.
So there, Te̱be̱kawe̱ne̱, my husband! He with a stump for his rump!"

(Laughter, appellation)

Yabuku: Agada akpa yen yen!
Okabou: It's fire!
"Yes, I see clearly what's to eat."
As for her own teeth, they were red all over.
If you saw her, her head was bald up to here, quite like a highway.
The teeth were like blocks.
Her head was one open field.
It was bald all round.
As we were saying, Tebekawene, in full passage, would hold down his hands like this, and springing, land each time almost where the beach market is.
Spectator: It's at the land market he would land.
Oh yes, today he went in the direction of the inland market.
And coming down there at the inland market, all of a sudden, there was Ozidi, and here he was facing him.
When Ozidi saw him in front, he had his head to the ground, his feet suspended in the air.
As for the height of that man, it was up to that electric pole there.
It rose right into the air.
And up there swayed his legs.
"Oh, hornblower, what thing is that?"

"It's that thing we spoke of has now got here.
We told you but you wouldn't listen.
Now the thing has come."
"O, Oh!
And I so rusty!
Here, here!
Hey, Oreame, my mother, my mother, my mother, my mother!
Oh, this unexpected battle is terrible, mother, mother, mother, mother, mother!
Hey, Oreame, my mother, my mother, my mother, my mother, my mother!
Oreame, bring me my sword, bring me my sword!
Hey, Oreame, my mother, my mother, my mother, my mother!
Tebekawene has arrived here, mother, mother, mother!"
As he wept, Tebekawene said to him: "Don't cry.
I'm taking you right away to grind pepper with.
My wife has in fact made fire already.
The pot too has since been boiling. Lightly, I shall pick you up, and take you off . . . Is your mother too here! Is she?
It's all of you I intend taking at once to cook together, I want no scanty dish. This time I'm out for a big meal."

Spectator: Help! all four persons together!
At this, Ozidi again burst out crying: "Hey, Oreame my mother!
Hey, Oreame, my mother, my mother, my mother!
Hey, Oreame, my mother, my mother, my mother!"
"Why are you crying?
Aren't you a war-monger . . . aren't you said to be a great hero? So why are you crying?
With you crying like this, how could they dub you weakling a hero!"
Tebekawene advanced directly upon him, but Ozidi's sword did not issue forth.

None of his battle equipment emerged from his body.
His bowels did not rage.
"Hey, O̱re̱ame̱, I'm dead, my mother, my mother, my mother, my mother, my my mother, my mother, my mother, my mother, my mother, my mother, my mother!
Hey, O̱re̱ame̱, my mother!
O̱re̱ame̱, where are you, mother, mother, mother, mother, mother!
Oh, O̱re̱ame̱, my mother, my mother, my mother!
Hey, O̱re̱ame̱, my mother, my mother, my mother!
Oh O̱re̱ame̱, come, come, come, come, come!"
"Don't cry, just be quiet where you are.
Does one who goes out to look for fights weep while fighting?
It's because I heard you've roved round the world doing battle that I've come to take you to roast.
I was coming to take you off to roast for food.
But now you've turned up here on your own. Even without your mother, if I take those two boys anon with you, when I've taken you all home, I can sit blissfully for two days."
Ozidi looked wildly around, shook himself strenuously, but sweat did not even break out of him.
However much he strained, he didn't as much as sweat.
Now Te̱be̱kawe̱ne̱ spun head over heels, coming to a rocking stance.
Then vaulting to his feet, out stretched his sword . . .

Caller: O STORY!
Group: YES!

SONG

(Te̱be̱kawe̱ne̱'s song)
(Repeated several times)

Caller: O CITY!
Group: YES!
Caller: HERE'S STORY!
Group: YES!

As we were saying, Te̱be̱kawe̱ne̱ advanced upon him, looking him over, and as soon as he stopped singing, he tore into Ozidi.
"Here, Ozidi, come on!
Come on.
Come on this way.
It won't be good for you if I come to drag you off where you are.
So come over here."
Instead Ozidi fell back.
Ozidi now drew back.
Still retreating and retreating, at last he halted.
"Hey, O̱re̱ame̱!
Oh, O̱re̱ame̱! Oh, O̱re̱ame̱! Oh O̱re̱ame̱! Oh, O̱re̱ame̱! Oh, O̱re̱ame̱, O̱re̱ame̱!
Oh, O̱re̱ame̱, my mother, my mother, my mother, my mother!
Oh O̱re̱ame̱, my mother, my mother, my mother!
This man with his anus open to the sky it is wants to kill me, how terrible. O̱re̱ame̱, my mother, my mother, my mother!"
As he wailed so an evil nerve began to pulsate and pulsate in O̱re̱ame̱.

"What's it?
Cool it!
There, make a stand!
What's happening again in this house."
She ran and looked at one shrine, then at another, all were quiet.
"Now, what has happened?"
Next, she took out her testing piece and tried it.
The test proved a failure.
Leaping up and looking from her vantage point, she leapt down again.
"Now, what's it?
Has Ozidi gone and fallen into some trap again?
The children have been out playing."
Up and down she paced, all restless was she.
She took a hop.
All on the alert, she snatched her medicine bag and slung it on.
Having slung on her bag of charms, she whipped out her magic fan . . .

SONG

(Oreame's flying song)

CALLER: O STORY!
GROUP: YES!

MASTER-DRUM: O Mother City!
OKABOU: It's a huge place, don't you see!
MASTER-DRUM: Tell it with ease! And it's with ease we must play.
Whether abroad in the bush we are forever a city.
All is well!
Bush is town, town is forever town.
That's how it is
The roots are in two places.

CALLER: O STORY!
GROUP: YES!

Believe me, in no time, Oreame had flown far away, and looking out in front, there stood Ozidi defenceless.
At the same time, Tebekawene . . . moving in upon him, was debating with himself: "Come, I won't butcher the boy here and now.
Boy, come here."
Lightly, he picked him up.
Ozidi stiffened up.
But with one hand he pinioned him; and kick as much as he could, Ozidi could not free himself.
Next . . .

SONG

(Tebekawene's theme song)

CALLER: O CITY!
GROUP: YES!

Believe me, he captured Ozidi's attendants in the same swoop.
"Oh, Ozidi, how is it!

Won't you bestir yourself?"
But though prodded, by now Ozidi was in no fit state to hear anybody.
Utterly lost he was.
And off, off Tebekawene bore him. And as he went, as he left . . .
SPECTATOR I: As he set off.

(Laughter)

CALLER: O STORY!
GROUP: YES!
CALLER: O STORY!
GROUP: YES!

As he set out . . .
MASTER-DRUM: Man, keep your ears to the ground!
It's a tough mission. No stuttering!
As we were saying, when Oreame looked out in front, there was Tebekawene with Ozidi pinioned under his arm, lapping him like a man his first daughter.
Though Ozidi struggled fiercely, he couldn't release himself.
He hadn't even the room to move, and already he was shivering as with cold. Said the old man: "Must first take him up to the pot before carving him up to throw in.
And though the people are many, I'm afraid, the food won't be enough to eat." They herded behind him, silent and subdued.
Oreame flying high in the sky, had in fact flown far out of sight, when she turned back suddenly, and reversed furiously.
And in a flash, wings beating and body swaying from side to side, she touched down.
There she stood.
Standing there, Tebekawene began stumping on his head towards her.
"Hey Tebekawene, Tebekawene!
When two fight a duel, is the engagement on the highway?
It's upon the public square they battle it out.
Have you moved this to your house?
If it's your house you are going to, then may your feet be rooted to the ground. May you never take another step!"
Now Tebekawene couldn't lift a foot; fastened down he was.
Then Tebekawene spoke: "Oreame, when two persons fight, after cutting each other round, one must emerge the killer.
Therefore let my feet be released.
Release them for me."
"May your feet remain stuck!
God herself will not accede to your prayer.
Your feet must remain rooted until I take you home."
Tebekawene swore aloud: "It can't happen!
As a matter of fact, I'm taking you along with me . . . my wife already has things on the boil, the pot is boiling there right now.
I'm taking all of you to cook . . . Tomorrow at dawn, I'll break my fast with you."

Said Oreame: "Hey, I Oreame! Oh, Ozidi, my boy, my boy, my boy, my boy, my boy, my boy, my boy, my boy!

Oh Ozidi, how unwise that you wouldn't take your walks with me, my son, my son! How this rank outsider could take you home pinioned to grind pepper with is absurd, my son, my son!
Hey, Ozidi! O Ozidi! Ozidi! Ozidi! O Ozidi! O Ozidi!
Now your sword has come! Here comes your sword!
Here, Ozidi! Here, Ozidi, Here, Ozidi!"
She flew off, snatched her magic fan, and slapped Tebekawene.
It sent Tebekawene tottering, tumbling, and rolling several times over, and before he could pick himself up, Ozidi was standing ready for him.
Standing out there, he invoked once more: "O Oreame, my mother, my mother, my mother, my mother, my mother!
Oh Oreame, my mother, my mother, my mother, my mother!
Oh, Oreame, my mother, my mother, my mother!
Has the sword come, mother, mother, mother!"
And then the stampede of those denizens, the screaming hornbill, the scrambling agama, all calling "Oh Ozidi the grove!"

SONG

SOLO: Come out now and take it!
CHORUS: Yes!
SOLO: Come out now and take it . . . !
SPECTATOR: One blow!
And then the cry: "Tebekawene is sacrifice! Tebekawene is sacrifice!"
And out there Tebekawene lay prostrate.
SPECTATOR I: Why, it wasn't much of a performance this time!
SPECTATOR II: Oh, yes, yes, yes, yes, yes, yes!
SPECTATOR III: Perform for the town.
SPECTATOR IV: Even to die for your fatherland Orua well befits you.
SPECTATOR V: We of Asema clan are all one.
SPECTATOR VI: The women folk of Orua carry no bald heads.

CALLER: O STORY!
GROUP: YES!
CALLER: O STORY!
GROUP: YES!

SPECTATOR: Oh yes, have you seen what you saw?
SPECTATOR: It's the grandchild of Ayakpo.
SPECTATOR: I am indeed of the same town with them: we are citizens of Orua.
SPECTATOR: It's the grandchild of Ayakpo who's goading me here.
SPECTATOR: Your name?
SPECTATOR: It's Owayei.

SPECTATOR: Owayei is her name.
SPECTATOR: She's the one goading me.

(Because it is the story of Orua that I'm telling, she appreciates it so much that she's forever at my back.)

(Laughter)

In case you don't hear that much, as I wasn't so sure, I had to tell you: I won't speak more, the matter is finished.

SPECTATOR: Hear! hear!
CALLER: And now the story!
GROUP: Yes!

As we were saying, yes, Oreame . . .

SONG

SOLO: Here, the woman who flies by spurts
Let none listen to her, Oreame
CHORUS: Here, the woman who flies by spurts
Let none listen to her, Oreame
(Repeated several times)

CALLER: O STORY!
GROUP: YES!

Taking all her brood by the hand, she flew away, she took all of them in tow and headed straight for home.
"Hey, Ozidi, this is too much!
Every time . . . wherever you go, is this how you go rolling on the ground?"

CALLER: O STORY!
GROUP: YES!

SPECTATOR I: On with it!

CALLER: O STORY!
GROUP: YES!
SPECTATOR II: You broke off at the name of Oreame.

For a long time, he stayed at home not knowing where to go.
Then one day, Ozidi expressed once more a desire to go out and play.
(The episode of Azemaroti which I once told you wasn't to this group, I had narrated it to you earlier.
Now, if I plunge into it, since you'll say I've already told it, I am reminding you of the fact.)

SPECTATOR I: Go on.
CALLER: O STORY!
GROUP: YES!

So one day, as we were saying, Ozidi again expressed a desire to go out and play.
Said Oreame: "Today you aren't going out alone.
If you must take a walk, your attendants must accompany you, indeed we'll all go out together.
If I stay at home, I shan't know what scrapes you'd be getting into, and there's no doubt you'd get into some before long.
Today we're all going out together.

You Orea, you stay at home and wait for us."

"Oh yes, mother.
You go and play and come back safely."
So, at dawn, at break of day, Oreame went out into the neighbourhood and began to bay, even though she was a woman.
Loud she bayed: "I am Oreame!
There's none in the state does not hear me.
Is there anybody in this state of Orua, in this city of Ado, that does not hear me, that has not heard of Oreame?
Yes, where were the bounds to this city?
Seven wards there were to this city.

Now I alone reign supreme."
Railing, she went on: "And at this very moment, if you call up even all of your people underground, there won't be any match for me among them.

All the champions that were said to be so strong before are now underground.
Today I'm going out again to play.

Of the state of Ado we have heard quite a bit, and now we're going out for a walk."
Having declared her intention, she gathered her kit straight into her bag.
Flying out, with all her things all encumbered she was, there was not an item that she didn't wear.
Ozidi with his figure showed to advantage.
His vest fitted him to perfection.
As for his calves, they were this big.
Flat was his belly, and his blackness was all sparkling and pure.
And so they all had a bath, dressed themselves, and combed out their hair.
There was not an item that Ozidi forgot.
In his hand was a handkerchief.
In this fashion, they went out to play.
They walked for quite a while, and at every village they arrived, at every remote hamlet they appeared, because Oreame had not disguised herself, all said: "That's the woman terror of Ado herself, therefore quicken your steps, quicken them at once," and straight into the bush they would run.

So it went on in every town they appeared "Oh, Oh! Oh! Look, she's reached here.

And is her strong son not with her today?
Such handsome youth!"
And tactfully, all would run past them.
They walked on, they walked on the walk now seemed endless.
So they went on, then came a time, a day, and listening ahead of the—(what a shame this tape won't run out before I lose myself!)

Caller: O STORY!
Group: YES!

Moving forward to listen better, they heard a cock calling "ko-ko-ro-ko-o."
Said Oreame: "There must be a town in front, it couldn't be more than that."
But whether it was a small hamlet she had no idea.
They were in fact close upon Azema and Oti, at the gates of Azema's town.
Before they walked further, the cock crowed again.
Turning round immediately, they caught sight of coco-nut trees.
"With those coco-nut palms, we must be near some settlement."
Then Oreame said: "It won't be good for me to arrive as I am.
So halt, halt for a while."
Accordingly, they all halted.
"Well, mother, what's it?"
"There, don't you know! I'm a woman with a well-known name.
If I appear like this, straight there will be alarm that warriors have come."
"Aha, but what are you going to do to yourself?"
"Just be quiet.
Stay here and wait for me."
"All right."
And withdrawing to one side, in the swiftest of shifts, when she emerged again, her bosom was full and rocking.
Indeed with those breasts . . .

Spectator I: She was like a young woman.
Spectator II: A young woman.

If you saw her Lagos blouse, or her headtie, you'd seen a spectacle.

Caller: O STORY!
Group: YES!

Or if it was the wrapper she tied about her waist you saw, it flowed right to the ground.
Indeed she looked like a young woman of Accra.

Spectator I: Most graceful.
Spectator II: And charming.

If you saw her figure, it really was graceful.
And if you looked from her to Ozidi, they made a perfect couple as of wife and husband.
"Now walk on" she said.
All her bags, all her kit, had quite melted into her body.

Spectator: Power!

(Laughter)

When at last they arrived at the town, there was no general scare since none recognized them.
"Greetings, visitors! Yes, greetings!"
"And greetings too!"
"What town are you from?"
"Er, we're coming from the next town."

They gave fictitious names of towns.
Thus they walked into the town where Aze̱maroti and Aze̱ma were leaders and rulers.
Now Azemaroti . . . this woman called Aze̱ma, her teeth were all scarlet with blood.
She fed only on men.
She didn't eat meat, she didn't eat fish.
She ate no meat, ate no fish, she ate only men.
If she touched meat at all, she took it raw.
On this occasion, she was sitting in front of her house.
She was seated there, when they all sauntered up and she greeted them:
"Hey, children, greetings!"
"Thanks, and greetings to you."
"Look, its I Aze̱ma living in this town.

Have you any business in town?"
"Well, yes.
We were just out touring and came this way by accident."
"Is that so?"

Caller: O STORY!
Group: YES!
Caller: O STORY!
Group: YES!

"Aze̱maroti, are you there?"
"Oh, yes mother, what's the matter?"
"Better go and look the house over.
Is there any meat left in the house?
Won't there be much hunger today?"
As she spoke, he ran into the house, and going into the kitchen, he found all the pots bare and empty: all seven of them were permanently on the boil and crackling on the fire.
In these seven pots they crammed and cooked themselves human beings.
He looked at them, and not one had a morsel in it.
"Oh, mother, it seems hunger is going to kill us today.
There isn't a thing in the house."
"Oh, then, we'll prepare those four persons . . ."
Spectator: What!

"They should fill up all seven pots!"
Spectator: Not even an exchange of words!
(Laughter)
"If we do this, we can throw them in.
These people who come from no-one-knows-where.
Why are we delaying? To spare them is out of the question."
"Oh yes, these fellows I don't even know.
But what a fetching party!
And oh, the girl is so beautiful and the youth so handsome!
Handsome too are the other boys."
"Oh, so because they are beautiful, should we stay hungry!
Oh yes!
And if they are so beautiful, aren't I also lovely?
Come and see my teeth,
Look at my teeth, aren't they lovely?"

Spectator: Quite a mask!
"Hey, mother, is there anybody as lovely as you!
Oh, yes, and what about my own figure?"
"There! aren't you king of youth!"
(Laughter)

Caller: O STORY!
Group: YES!

Then his mother added: "Young woman, call back your husband."
And O̱re̱ame̱ too played it up.

"What's it?"
"Come into the house, you are our guests, so come in.
Let's entertain you first and then you can resume your walk."
"That's fine," and she didn't call for long before he came along.
O̱re̱ame̱ had since recognized her.
(Laughter)
Oh yes, that this was the woman warrior of the town, the woman styled Aze̱ma, she knew already.
"You see, he was walking on because I hadn't called earlier.
As it is, we don't know anyone yet in town.
We are just tourists in town.
One has to have a good host to be a welcome guest."
"That's true, so enter."
Inside there was an earthen divan built into the wall, what we Ijo̱ call brimookpo, stretching from here to there; it was all very commodious.
It was there they sat people down before killing them off, so it spread as far as there. It had a beautiful mat spread over it. "Come right in."
As they acted on her invitation, she went on "Do sit down," and at her bidding they sat down.
Once all four of them were seated, she began: "Eh, eh! Hey, Aze̱maroti my son!
Aze̱maroti my son!"
"How is it?"
"It's time to eat.
Bring out the pots quick into the open for the boil."
O̱re̱ame̱ did not as much as open her mouth.

Caller: O STORY!
Group: YES!

Spectator I: Let nobody flag, you people.
O̱re̱ame̱ remained silent, not opening her mouth.
After a while, she had to advise Ozidi, "Let nobody stir yet."
Later, she quietened down the slaves.
She did so with the hornblower.

And she gave the same directives to the drummer.
They all kept their mouths shut, looking thoroughly innocent, and quiet.
As for O̱re̱ame̱, she thrust forward her bosom.
(Laughter)

CALLER: CHEERS!
GROUP: CHEERS!

She pushed those false breasts of hers forward, and they danced most seductively. And the moment Azemaroti saw those breasts, he gasped, "Why kill this one, why not marry her on the spot?"
So he thought to himself.
Later, he went and started the fires.

He set all the pots upon their hobs.
He poured water into each, all the seven pots, he put them on the boil.
"Mother, we can't put in the meat yet, I haven't anything to mix them with yet."
"Cut up those two bunches of plantain in the corner."
Bringing down both trees with three blows, he brought them in together.

As he deposited the bunches so he began splitting them from end to end; then with quick, sharp movement of hands, he sliced up all the plantain fingers, and filled all the seven pots with them.
"Here, mother, now I've them all on the boil."
"Yes, have you boiled them?
Now let me go and see.
You can be quite mingy and skimpy with your dishes.
This isn't enough.
Go and slice up another."
And immediately, the man ran off and cut down another tree.
After he'd cut it, again he set it down, pulled apart the various hands to the bunch, and before he got back he had already peeled the skin off each finger.
And again he piled the pots.
When she inspected them, she said: "Now it's good.
Add the meat, and it'll be perfect.
Add meat to this and it'll be right.
Add meat to this other one, and it'll be full."

SPECTATOR: All the seven pots?

Oh, yes, all the seven of them.
"Now we can feast, however filling, you can eat three, and I four.
That much you know, don't you?"
"Of course I do.
Er, well, what next?"
"Now the fires, are the pots boiling?
It's quick service we want.
As soon as the heat is on, in they go, they aren't sweet if first allowed to fall."
"That's right."
By now, he too paraded up and down in great excitement.
He got into quite a frenzy there.
But though he paced about wildly, the moment he caught sight of those breasts of Oreame, he gulped, ogled, and grew completely distracted.

(Laughter)

Caller: O STORY!
Group: YES!

Soon he called his mother: "Hey, mother!
Oh, Azema, my mother, come over first"
Azema now swept up to him.
"What's it?
What's happened?"
"Well, let's spare that young woman, I'd love to marry the girl.

The others, the three of them we can deal with, and shove in at once."
"Hey, Azemaroti! Is this girl more beautiful than all the belles in town?
Is she?
If we don't slaughter her the same time with the others, and there isn't enough to eat as it is, that means your share of the fare will be less."
"If it's a little that falls to my lot I'd be quite content to eat it.
The girl attracts me very much."
(Laughter)

Caller: O STORY!
Group: YES!
Caller: O STORY!
Group: YES!

After he spoke, Azema overruled: "Ha, ha! she won't be spared."
(Loud gasps)
"Oh yes," she said, "she won't be left.
We'll take all together.
When all four are caught and despatched, I can eat three and you one.
That would be best."
"In that case I won't eat.
Leave me the young woman.
You can eat all your three by yourself."
"Am I a mother who eats up everything in the house?
Am I? Even if I feed alone, won't you abuse me with that in the future?"
While they argued . . .

Caller: O STORY!
Group: YES!

While they argued, Azema already, with Azemaroti to one side,
Azema already had herself keyed up.
She was all set now to kill.
"I am Azema! I am Azema! All the four persons now in the house, they say they are my guests, now I am going to lick pepper with them.

I've in fact licked them up already this very moment.
Once I come out of my shrine house, I'm taking you all at one sweep."
Said Oreame: "What, but we are your guests, I thought!

Is it us you'll now kill to make pepper soup?
And all this time, we thought you were preparing things to entertain us.
Now is it us you're going to kill to lick your soup of pepper?"
"Woman, be quiet and shut up your mouth.
Even though my son was about to marry you, I'm going to eat you.
However pretty you are, I shall be licking you and your husband soon in my platter.
Your eyes should be most delectable, we'll carve up every part of you to eat."
SPECTATOR: Oh help!
"I shall eat all of you up."

CALLER: O STORY!
GROUP: YES!

At this point, the woman replied, O̲re̲ame̲ replied: "So be it.
It's nothing if you eat us.
Take us and eat."
Even as she spoke, both Aze̲ma and Aze̲maroti trooped into their shrine house.
There Aze̲maroti drew out his sword.
One pull and it was out of its sheath.
Then he proclaimed: "It's a girl! It's a girl!
Right now there are four persons in our house whom we shall make a feast of today.
If I don't announce this before cutting them up, it won't be fair.
That's why I've come out into the open to inform you . . . " Then after rousing up the neighbourhood, he turned round, sweat pouring down from him profusely.
From Aze̲mare, Aze̲maroti, too, by this time, sweat, although she was indoors, flowed down freely.
Then she too rushed outside.
"I am Aze̲maroti! I am Aze̲maroti! I am Aze̲maroti!"
As she raced past, how the sweat poured from her!
"Oh, my son, drop your sword!
Put down your sword, and let's first take a dip in the river."

CALLER: O STORY!
GROUP: YES!

"When we've had a swim and are cool and refreshed, having cut them up and stuffed them in, then we can start eating, and our bodies will be completely relaxed before we eat."
"Oh, yes! Oh, yes!"
And straightaway our man threw his sword to one side.
Tossing it aside, he called to his mother:
"Come on, mother!"
"Oh yes!"
Racing to the stream, they threw themselves in.
Both broke into free strokes, roaring through the waters for several laps.
These two, child and mother, played as if they were husband and wife.

They would roll into each other's arms and then plunge in, and then they would dive in again, one rolling over the other.
While they fell to dallying, rolling, and petting, Oreame had since transformed herself, and crying Orea, she emerged, all gaunt and taut.

CALLER: O STORY!
GROUP: YES!

SPECTATOR: Now for the fight!

All set for the fight, she aroused her son: "Hey, Ozidi, my son, my son, my son, my son, my son, my son, my son!
We've come into Azema's home for her to cook, how sad, my son, my son, my son, my son!"
Azema . . . Azema . . . now Azema exclaimed: "Woman, see what we have!
It is . . . it is this evil Oreame that has been in our house all the time, do you see!
Is it that woman about whom so much has been said has come herself?
Woman, sit in there quietly for the time being.
Immediately I come ashore, I shall take you directly.
Oh, today's pots, they really are special!

So it's Oreame's own head we're eating, oh, how delicious!"
"Hey, Ozidi, Oh, Ozidi! Oh, Ozidi! Ozidi! Oh Ozidi!
Ozidi, bestir yourself, one sits down to get up, Ozidi, rise, rise!"

Unknown to them Azemaroti had ordered his bottom to get stuck where he sat, so that when he tried to get up, he couldn't move.
Stuck he was.
But as soon as she called to him, they all rose, free and unfettered.
They all now sortied out, awake, alert, and aroused.
Thus when Azemaroti turned round, he called out in surprise:
"Oh, mother, they have all come out."
"Nonsense, go on quietly with your swim.
Where can they go . . . those prisoners standing chained?
I'm not coming."
"The fires are dying out."

"Those fires . . . run off then and collect some more firewood and come back.
Let's swim a bit more before going."
Out waded Azemaroti, dripping as he ran.
He ran past, cast a leering glance at Oreame, and having stoked the fires, back he went and again splashed into the stream.
They now stood looking at both swimmers, Ozidi too stood looking.
Oreame herself stood watching.
Still they swam and splashed about, then came a time, a . . .
Spectator I: Then came a certain time . . .

CALLER: O STORY!
GROUP: YES!

After some time, Azemaroti suggested: "We aren't enjoying this swimming to the fullest yet.
Look, come ashore and sit down, and I'll bring water to pour over your head, and then taking a leisurely run, you can dive back into the stream. That should be more interesting."

SPECTATOR II: Hear!

"O yes," the mother agreed.
And no sooner said than the mother waded ashore and sat herself in a regal manner.
Then he went and brought water in a bucket and poured it lingeringly over her head before both splashed back into the stream.
"Yes, it'll be a treat eating Oreame's head!"
Then she hobbled up, saying "Now, my son, install yourself on the seat!"
And she in turn took water and poured it over his head, and lovingly they raced back to the stream and plunged in.
"Hey, sweet is the head of Ozidi!"
And so the fire went out under all the pots they had put on the boil.

CALLER: O STORY!
GROUP: YES!

It was now Azema hobbled back to land and stood shouting:
"Hey, Oreame has broken my spell, has broken my spell, has broken my spell, has broken my spell!
Oreame is an evil woman, she's an evil woman, an evil woman, an evil woman, an evil woman!
Oh, come, Azema! Oh, come, Azema, come, come, come, come, come, come Azema, come, come, come, come, come, come!
Oh, Azema come, come, O come!
I am Azema!
Azemaroti, take your sword quick, our prisoners have escaped, so be quick, be quick!"
How Azemaroti broke loose from the stream, and as he leapt back on to the beach, pit formed where he landed.
Deep he cut into it.
So gigantic was the man.
Standing forcefully like that, and then rushing off into the house to snatch his sword, he tore straight into them.
Then Oreame said: "Hold it!
Stay your sword first!
Don't ever lift up your hand."
As stout as Azemaroti's hand was, to move his hand he couldn't, it stayed stuck in the air.
To drop it too was a burden, it couldn't come down again.
Believe me, how Oreame now took over the place, skipping from end to end, she screamed:
"Hey, Ozidi! Hey, Ozidi! Hey, Ozidi! Hey Ozidi! my son! my son! my son! my son! my son! Hey, Ozidi!"

SPECTATOR: Look at her!

"Oh, Ozidi! O Ozidi, O Ozidi! O Ozidi! O Ozidi! Karakarabiri, come and see what spectacle, O Ozidi, O Ozidi, O Ozidi, O Ozidi, O Ozidi, O Ozidi! Oh, Oh, Ozidi!
We escaped the sacrifice of Odogu himself, O Ozidi, O Ozidi, Oh, oh, Ozidi!
What shall we do to break out of here, O Ozidi, O Ozidi! O Ozidi!

Ozidi, rise, rise, rise, I say!"
The hornbill now began to shriek, the lizard to crawl, each calling "Ozidi to the grove!" And the monkey boomed forth "Go forth, go forth! Go forth, go forth!"
Then out hurtled the sword:

SONG

Solo: Come out now and take it!
Chorus: Yes!
Solo: Come out now and take it . . . !

Palpably hit, this Azemaroti we speak of ricochetted so far away he came down at a place where it was already night.

Caller: O STORY!
Group: YES!

Azemaroti shot off past his town.
Whether it was the town called Gbekebo, I don't quite remember.
Back on his feet, he looked here and there, and found it all forest.
He exclaimed: "I am Azemaroti! I am Azemaroti himself!
Now where is Ozidi?
Where is Oreame?"
So he railed on in the forest . . .
Meanwhile, Azemaroti had run amok on the field of battle.
Yelling "Help, where has my son gone?"
she charged, and she and Oreame gave it to each other.

SONG

Solo: Here's Azema, the forest Azema
Chorus: It's Azema, the forest Azema!
Solo: Here's Azema, the forest Azema
Chorus: It's Azema, the forest Aze
Solo: Here's Azema, the forest ma Azema
Chorus: It's Azema, the forest Azema . . .
(Repeated several times)

Caller: O CITY!
Group: YES!

As we were saying, after Azema had taken up her theme song, and charged in, she suddenly seized Oreame's head between her hands, biting off Oreame's hair and tangling it into wild knots.
(Ululation)

Caller: O STORY!
Group: YES!

All Oreame's hair, all her hair became torn and tugged in different directions. And Oreame pulled this way and that way, but couldn't free herself.
Frantic, she cried: "Never can another's herb kill me! never, never, never, never, never!"
With that cry, Azema shot away like a pellet, and where she eventually fell was nowhere near here.
She plummeted with a great thud.
But though floored, in a flash, she was up again and tearing in.
"I am Azema! I am Azema!"
Meanwhile, our other woman was nursing her head, her hair all scruffy and dishevelled.

(Laughter)

Spectator I: What fights!

Caller: O STORY!
Group: YES!

Only now was Azemaroti able to find his way through the forest, after beating about in circles to reach his town.
And Ozidi stood anchored like a tree, waiting for him.

Spectator II: Your mother has had her head all bitten.

Indeed, his mother's head was all ruffled up and bitten.

(Laughter)

Caller: O STORY!
Group: YES!

Said Oreame: "Yes, never again!
You Azemaroti, is it my hair you've torn apart like this and would want to tear up more?
Yes, never again!"
While pouring imprecations, she had already whipped out her fan, and was whisking about the place.
Then she flew off into the sky.

Spectator III: She's gone again to change.

Past the clouds she flew, then surfacing again, she perched as a fly upon Azema . . .
Azemaroti . . . upon Azema.
And Azema did not know a creature had come to roost on her head.
Next, Oreame took out needles and stuck them here, stuck them there, stuck them all over her head.

Spectator IV: What was it she planted in her?

It was a bundle of spikes that Oreame stuck into her.
Azema didn't feel a pinch.
"Oreame, come out into the open, and let me stuff you into my pot."

Still Oreame nestled there on her head, sticking more needles into it.
One after the other she spiked them in: sevenfold.
They all had poison to their tips.
Those special brews called kolokoloy i . . .
Spectator I: Those drugs . . .
Yes.
With all of them driven home, Azema began to feel the pangs:
"Oh, folks, how my head is knocking . . . why should my head ache so?
What's the matter?
If it's you, you Oreame, then come out here, quick.
This time when I bundle you up, I'm sure to throw you."
Said Oreame: "All right, I'm coming."
And Oreame whisked away once more.
Returning after a long flight, her hair was again back to normal, all flowing.
She looked thoroughly inhuman.
Her hair previously was in bits and pieces, her head half and half like a double-headed hatchet.
This time, still baiting her, she said: "Woman, come over quick, and I'll deal with you once and for all!" Azema tore in furiously, but when she grabbed Oreame's head and bit hard into it, she couldn't chew it.
Her teeth went blunt.
She tried here, tried there.
Oreame too pushed her one way, then pushed her up again, but she couldn't shake her.
And the other chewed away at her head, going through it in circles, and grinding her teeth so furiously that they sounded like a woodpecker at work.

(Laughter)

Caller: O STORY!
Group: YES!

So she snapped at her, until a time came, until came a time and the hapless woman, with the poison in the pins now spread from her head into her bloodstream, her body was no longer the same. She began to droop, droop, and droop.
"O Ozidi, my son! A woman cannot receive a scalp, a woman cannot receive a scalp, a woman cannot receive a scalp, a woman cannot receive a scalp!
Azema's dizzy and reeling here, be quick, come and take her, come and take her, come and take her!
Ozidi, hurry here, hurry, hurry!"

Eyes blazing, Ozidi turned round, and his bowels now would not leave him alone. They grew all hot:

SONG

Solo: Come out now and take it!
Chorus: Yes!
Solo: Come out now and take it . . .
Precisely here he chopped her.

And Azema dropped to one side.
Azemaroti was left standing.
The head lay in Ozidi's hand, eyes popping.
"Azemaroti is sacrifice! Azemaroti is sacrifice! Azema is sacrifice!"
So he bayed, storming up and down the place.
And streams of blood jetted into the air, streaking the skies.
Standing there swaying, suddenly he rose, and believe it or not, went and knocked Oreame down!
With that blow Oreame staggered and hit the ground.
As soon as she fell . . .

Spectator I: Was she standing too close?
(Laughter)

Caller: O Story!
Group: Yes!

The moment Oreame hit the ground Ozidi drew out his sword, and dealt Oreame one.
Thus struck, Oreame shot off in counter-shock like a bullet, and far into the sky she flew, screaming, panting with her customary bursts of speed.

SONG

Solo: She who flies by spurts
Let none listen to Oreame
Oreame, the woman who flies by spurts.
Let none listen to her!
Chorus: She who flies by spurts
Let none listen to Oreame
(Repeated several times)

Caller: O CITY!
Group: YES!

Believe me, when Oreame bounded back she was as she had always been, gaunt and petite.
By now Azema had fallen, Azemaroti had fallen, yes, Azema had long fallen.
Spectator I: Has the mother now fallen?

Oh, yes, his mother had since fallen.
With the fall of his mother, the man now took up her theme song:

SONG

Solo: Ah, Azema, the bush Azema
Azema the warrior
Ah, Azema the warrior
Chorus: Yes, Azema, the bush Azema!
(Repeated several times)

Caller: O CITY!
Group: YES!

As we were saying, both Oreame and Ozidi stood there crying "Azema.

Azemaroti . . . Azema is sacrifice."
Ozidi kept baying.
And when Azema turned up at the other end, lofty he was, the very image of manhood was Azemaroti when he emerged at last from the woods.
As he came into the open, came out there, my word, Ozidi who was baying all the time also surged forward, crying: "Oh, that's the man, that's him!"
And how they struck at each other, sparks flying about them.
With quick short steps they chased each other round, and Azemaroti all this time still hadn't known of his mother's death.
After they had grappled for a long time, Ozidi said, no, Oreame said, "You Ozidi, don't handle him as you did before lest he shoots off a second time.

This time try pulling him down.
Drag him down.
If he darts off again to some strange place we shall have a hard search of it.
To hunt for him would be tough work. So keep him down."
That one sword of Ozidi now resharpened and forged itself afresh upon its target. The grating sound of filing and flying flint filled the air with each blow.
Azema's head was now hurled to one side.
Then came more blows.
And with our man thrusting at him from all sides, the poison in which the sword tip had been boiled coursed gradually through Azema's body, through Azemaroti's body.

So the Azema battle raged on until came a time a day, a time . . .

Spectator I: Until a time came . . .
(Laughter)

Caller: O STORY!
Group: YES!
Caller: O STORY!
Group: YES!
(Laughter)
Caller: O STORY!
Group: YES!

At this point, Azema's mind turned to other matters.
When Azemaroti tried lifting his foot, it became a great burden, and when he tried lifting his hand, it was also very heavy.
"Hey, poor Azemaroti! Ah, Azema, my mother! Where have you gone?
My body's gone all heavy.
Azemaroti, how's it?
Do you believe Oreame really has more power than you?
These seven pots, brought out and filled to the brim with plantains, have since burnt themselves to ashes! Now what shall we do?"
To all his queries only tears flowed now from his mother.

Those teeth of hers continued gnashing inside Oreame's bag just as they had done on the ground.
Her decapitated head was still pulsating with life so that the teeth kept on grinding.

CALLER: O STORY!
GROUP: YES!

SPECTATOR I: Has the thing been changed?

SPECTATOR II: Go on!

OKABOU: If it's been changed say so for in truth I feel like stooling right now . . .

(Laughter)

SONG

SOLO: Oh, you Oreame, the shame!
Gaga gugo-o!
CHORUS: Hey, you can't take her.
SOLO: Hey, you Ozidi the challenge
Kill then before asking.
CHORUS: Oh, yes, he can't be taken!
(Repeated several times)

SONG

SOLO: The town is loud with ululation
What is it has happened?
The town is loud with ululation
What is it has happened?
I don't know what event Ozidi the strong man it is has come to kill me.
CHORUS: *(Ditto)*

CALLER: O IJO!
GROUP: YES!
CALLER: O IJO!
GROUP: YES!
CALLER: O IJO!
GROUP: YES!
CALLER: If you see a story will you listen?
GROUP: Of course, we will!
CALLER: If you see a fable, will you listen?
GROUP: Of course, we will!

YABUKU: Be strong of body.
There's no dispute.
This is how we are.
Today we have now told the story of Ozidi for seven days.

Now it looks as if we shall take the story right to the end today, at least so I think.
Indeed, we are Ijo people who are telling this story into that thing.

This story that we are now telling, we pray, let God lend a hand, so that we can present it to him who asked for it, that is, Egena.
Pepper, who asked us to come specially to have this story told to him so that he could record it into that radio set; that's why we've been telling this story.
Let his head be healthy, let his head remain strong, so that in future when he's searching for another fable, we shall again perform for him to listen.
What is it, is it dance?
That's a thing the Ijo have,
Is it song?
That's an Ijo thing.

Caller: O IJO!
Group: YES!
Caller: O IJO!
Group: YES!
Caller: If you see, will you act?
Group: Of course, we will!
Caller: If you see, will you act?
Group: Of course, we will!,
Caller: If it's play you see, will you play?
Group: Of course, we will!
Caller: If it's dancing you see, will you dance?
Group: Of course, we will!
Caller: O IJO!
Group: YES!

Spectator I: Now, on with it! You said you won't tell the story, that's what you said at first, now come on with it.

Spectator I: But first a song!

SONG

Solo: Death that does not touch God
Is what's come to kill me
Death that doesn't touch God
Is what's come to kill me
Tebesonoma, the injustice, my one and only child!
Chorus: Death that does not touch God
Is what's come to kill me
Death that doesn't touch God
Is what's come to kill me
Tebesonoma, the injustice, my one and only child!
(Repeated several times)

Caller: O STORY!
Group: YES!
Caller: O STORY!
Group: YES!
Caller: O CITY!
Group: YES!

By this time, by this time, as we were saying, Aze̱maroti could no longer bestir himself.
Though he strained in every direction, he just couldn't arouse himself.

SONG

(Horror strain sung partly in Ijo̱ and partly in some dialect of Igbo.)

Caller:	O IJO̱!
Group:	YES!
Caller:	O IJO̱!
Group:	YES!

Every time Ozidi slashed at him, he stood there undented, steadfast in his corner.

Once that number was sung, although now a veritable target for chopping, he proved impossible to fell down.
Pummelled from this side, he absorbed all the punishment, and pummelled from the far side, he still stood his ground.
"Oh," O̱re̱ame̱ exclaimed: "Hey, what's happening?
Are we going to get stuck here forever fighting this one battle?
What type of duel?
Is it so his head will not become scalp, will anyone pursue such a fight?"
To which Aze̱maroti retorted: "It's Oriri, Oriri is come I said.
Oriri has come!"
Declaring Oriri has come, by merely declaring this, chopped up though he was, Aze̱maroti remained there on his feet, stout and indefatigable.
They for their part grew quite tired.
Long they debated the matter, now what was it, what was it the man wanted to see?
Faced with this unexpected impasse, O̱re̱ame̱ said: "If this goes on like this, we shall stay here forever."
So off O̱re̱ame̱ flew.
Now where Aze̱ma lay fallen, lay slain and stretched out dead, had quite darkened into night.
The 'Oti said . . . And only now did Aze̱maroti realize his mother was dead.
In frenzy he charged about the place, and turning round, saw his mother had indeed fallen.
"Hey, Aze̱ma, my mother, my mother, my mother, my mother, my mother, my mother, my mother.
I didn't look back all along, my mother, my mother, my mother, my mother!
O̱re̱ame̱'s war is of the worst type, my mother, my mother, my mother, mother, mother!
I proposed earlier to marry the girl and let things pass but you wouldn't approve, my mother, my mother, my mother, my mother, my mother!
Ah, Aze̱ma, are you really dead, my mother, my mother, my mother, my mother, my mother?

Ah, Azema, wait for me, I'm coming!
My power now has no other repository, no other place, no other place of sway, Azema!
Hey, so Azema indeed is dead!
And, Azema, I don't know what to do to revive you, O pity, pity, pity, pity!
The plantains have shrivelled up in the pots, O the pity, pity, pity, pity, pity."
Thereupon, he leapt back to his feet, and how he shook himself, but since Ozidi himself was hot all over and waiting, wherever the man moved, he chopped away at him.
Yet though he struck again and again, the man stood his ground.
Bile now mounted in Oreame's bowels, and straight into the sky she flew.
There she vanished.

Caller: O STORY!
Group: YES!

All that time that Oreame flew away, Ozidi chopped and chopped at the man but in vain he battled.
With the sound of each blow . . .

Spectator I: Why not rest?
The blows!
How could he pause for breath, when he was in the field of battle?

Spectator II: Leave off when he hasn't killed!
However hard he hacked at him, he danced away.
At this point, the drummer took up his strain:
"Ozidi, be quick, be quick, be quick!
Keep it down, keep it down, keep it down, keep it down, keep it down!
Hey, Ozidi, hey, Ozidi, hey, Ozidi, hey, Ozidi, hey Ozidi!
Oreame is away, our woman is no longer here!
What shall we do now!"
And the hornblower joined in raucously.
"Go in, go in! Ranran rin! Ron rin ronron! Ronron rin!"
By now Ozidi had quite lost his head.

It was now like cutting up a dragonfly.
Some times, into three, four pieces he carved up the man, but Azema . . . Azemaroti always regrouped again whole "Hey, what shall I do now," he wondered.

Caller: O STORY
Group: YES!

At last, after a long flight, Oreame came back, levelling in from there to a screeching stop; and she brought with her a bunch of plantain, fresh unripe plantain, with the budding tail still dangling.
The young of a toad, she also brought with her a tadpole.
Next, (you give me your ears there)

That bird, what do we Ijo̱ call it now—this bird . . .

Spectator: Is it somewhat red?

Quite red.
That one too, she added to the lot.
And you should see her flying in with the egg of that bird.
Swooping in and then touching down, she called out: "Aze̱maroti!
Take, these are your gifts.
Now take them."
Though offered, Aze̱maroti refused to hear.
But when he tried to lift his sword to hit his opponent, he couldn't move, he just floundered.
So it went on.
He wouldn't turn round and look at them.
"Man, now take them!
These are things your mother asked to be given you as her legacy.
When you've taken your things, then you may fight on.
Hold them.
Your mother asked that these be given you first before killing you.
If it so happens that these things fail to reach you, you'll have a hard time of it defending yourself in court over there.
So grab them, grab them!"
Still Aze̱ma would not listen.
Aze̱maroti merely reeled around.
But imperceptibly, that poison at the sword-point began to hit him hard, and now his body felt like pulp.
All drooping, drooling, and drowsy was he.
Sometimes, Ozidi would take him by both legs and twist them till they broke apart.
But though halved, Aze̱ma would walk in there solid and whole.
So it went on until there came a time, yes, and . . .

Spectator: When two men fight, is there no running away?

And now, his turn had come at last.

The woman now flew around him like a dragon-fly, bobbing up here, bobbing up there!
So she now performed.
And since he could not but see what were taboo to his eyes, one more turn, and he stood defenceless.

Song

Solo: Come out now and take it!
Chorus: Yes!
Solo: Come out now and take it!
Chorus: Yes!

Then the chopping blow.

Spectator: HIP, HIP, HIP! HIP!
Spectator: HURRAH!

"Azemaroti is sacrifice! Azemaroti is sacrifice! Azemaroti is sacrifice!"
By this time, the entire town had fled.
Not a single person was left behind.
Meanwhile, Azemaroti, after staying immovable on his feet for some time, suddenly swayed over, and crashed down upon his mother.
As he crashed down on top of her, the mother immediately turned into a skeleton.
Pressing down on her like this, he went into throes.
Straightaway, Oreame leapt outside and took up her theme song:

SONG

SOLO: Oreame, fly in to the rescue
CHORUS: Fly in to the rescue
SOLO: Oreame, fly in to the rescue
CHORUS: Fly in to the rescue

And snatching all her children, she flew away.
With her brood in tow, off into the air she went, over tree tops, in powerful spurts, she sped without stop until she touched down in her own courtyard.
"I'm Oreame! I am Oreame! I'm Oreame!

One fights to come home.
I have brought my children safe home!
I've brought my children home and sound!"
And her daughter came out and welcomed them.
"O my mother! O my mother! O my mother! O my own!"
As soon as Ozidi got home and hurled down those two heads, up rose two temples.
How they roared . . . you couldn't count the shrines now sprouting the place.
Temples took over the whole place.
And out, out he flung those heads before him.
Where the grass grew uncut, once they were hurled there, the grass dried up to the ground and died.
The grass died to a blade.
And so they came to live peacefully finding no other battles to fight.
Ozidi, once he felt like play, now dressed, and went out to play.
Walking the area from end to end, he found nobody.
To find a girl to marry, there wasn't even one in view.
After some time, he asked: "Hey, Orea, can't one find fun outside; is this how we shall spend our days?"
"Be patient.
Just be patient.
Since we've taken care of all your father's assassins, there are no more adventures left to attract one outside.
If you like, we can go to my own town, and that should do it."
"Yes, but is it normal for me to remain without a wife?"
"Is it a wife you want?"
"Oh yes!"
"Then be patient."

She struck the ground with her fan, and a girl came walking in, like a goddess out of the stream.
Her bosom was full and large, all yearning and yielding.
The moment Ozidi saw her, he lost his head.
"Is that my woman!" he ejaculated and went directly into her.
Here at last was a companion for Ozidi to live peacefully with at home.
Now there were no more fights for Ozidi, though he searched here and there.
Some days, he grew quite beside himself.
And he would storm within his compound, and then slump into a seat.
By this time, Temugedege had grown dotty and besotted.
His eyes grew bleary and downcast with cataract.

CALLER: O STORY!
GROUP: YES!

One day, Ozidi told his mother: "Oh, mother, my father's brother, that man there, he has cursed me a lot.
Since he refuses to die, isn't it better to handle him at once and bundle him off to bury?
He can't even get on his feet."
SPECTATOR: He now wants to purify himself with him.
(Laughter)

CALLER: O STORY!
GROUP: YES!

"If he but gets up here he is a dead man, all his parts, his bones are wasted already in the sun.
Why not tap him with the butt of a cutlass and take him in at once, wouldn't that be better?"
(Laughter)
She said: "That's your father.
Once you kill him, whatever battle you take on afterwards, you shall lose.
Leave him alone, when God herself brings about his death, then you can take him away to bury.
All this time he has been cursing and wishing you dead, have you died?
Do leave him alone."
"I can't stand his sight," he persisted.

SPECTATOR I: What, is it because he couldn't find himself fights?

CALLER: O STORY!
GROUP: YES!

"The mere sight of him has been annoying me for a long time.
He denies I am his son, he wishes me dead, all his curses have been to kill me.
And now he is here wasted and useless.

As it is, I can see no other face in town.
It's his face, his senile face alone I see."
(Laughter)

CALLER: O STORY!
GROUP: YES!

"I hate the very sight of him."
"Yes, but forget it, don't touch him, don't touch him."
"Is that so!"
It was on this same day that Oreame herself decided to go into the bush and concoct a few things for them to eat, and so to the bush Oreame went.
The moment she left, he walked up to the old man: "Daddy, hey, my father!"
"Oh o," he mumbled and painfully lifting up his eyes, started.
"You said I should die, isn't that what you've always prayed for?"
"I didn't say so.
I said no such thing.
Yes, you being my son, why should I pray for you to die?
I didn't say so."
"You said it, man."
SPECTATOR: Don't press him, boy!

CALLER: O STORY!
GROUP: YES!

"Seize him by the jaws, didn't you say that?"
"Ay, I feel all funny in the head, please leave off, leave off."
(Laughter)
He regarded him closely for a while, then he took him by the head and pressed him down.
"Man, my head is singing with all sorts of bells, so hands off, hands off."
Fortunately, just at this point, the drummer saw what was happening and gave the peace formula "Ederigide-o-oo!"
So his hand went limp.
The old man was already choking and fainting when he took his hand off him.

CALLER: O STORY!
GROUP: YES!

Then his body calmed down.
And swiftly, he turned round and left.
After he left, by morning, Temugedege was already dead.
SPECTATOR II: Woe, woe!
SPECTATOR III: That's the fellow you wanted to slay.
Said Oreame: "Your father, do you go to see him regularly?"
"Oh yes, only yesterday I went over to see him.
I went to see him and he was there.
He isn't dead yet.
I took him food but he wouldn't eat.
Although I take him food, he refuses to eat."

Said Oreame: "Hey, Ozidi! Why did you go and dig your fingernails into him?
These hands of yours . . . don't you know all the shrines standing here are now in your hands?
Why did you go and dig your fingers into his head?"
"I didn't pierce him.
I just brushed his head."

(Laughter)

"Now go and see your father.
Is your father at present alive?
You go now and look at him."
When he got there, he found Temugedege spread out on the ground, eyes closed, he lay.
"Here, mother! Daddy is dead!"

SPECTATOR: Wasn't that what you wanted!

"Daddy is dead!"
"Well, didn't I tell you?
Don't you know he's dead because you stuck your fingernails into the middle of his head."
"Oh, I didn't even touch the crown of his head.
This is what I did.
I just stroked his head.
If that could kill him, then he should have died a long time ago."
"Now come and take your relation away to bury."
And so they dug a grave there, and they laid out Temugedege, lowered him into his grave and threw earth over him.
And that was the end of Temugedege.
Since Ozidi had nobody left to fight, night and day he passed the rounds quietly with his woman.
As he quietly laid her and lazed around, word reached Anglese.
"Oh, out there, there lives a man so powerful that he has executed everybody in town . . . completely laid waste what was once a proud capital city, and now it is said he lives there alone with his mother.
I can't but go and see him.
Let's go and visit him and see it we too are for him to murder.
So fit a boat immediately."
As for his boat, when fitted, one set of men paddled right, that was their order.

The set paddling to the left also were trained that way.
Each paddled right.
If the call went to the paddles at portside, all those on the left side paddled right.
Then those on the starboard also had to paddle the same way.
In other words, they disputed control of the craft.

CALLER: O STORY!
GROUP: YES!

YABUKU: One set pulled backwards, the other pulling forwards.
Yes, that's how they paddled.

As we were saying, having fitted the boat those for the stern took their stands and the man mounting the bow took his stance.
With all in position, the craft was fitted, complete with all manner of fearsome guns.
There were some primed with powder, there were others packed with pellets.
Believe me, if you saw the war boat, it was mighty.
Fully rigged, it stretched from here far out of sight.
(Yes, oh, yes, and now let the master-drum speak up.)

SONG

SOLO: Paddles to the right!
CHORUS: Oh yes!
SOLO: Paddles to the left!
CHORUS: O yes!
(Repeated several times)

CALLER: O STORY!
GROUP: YES!
CALLER: O STORY!
GROUP: YES!

After paddling for a long time, they came to the outskirt of the town.
When they reached the town outskirt, Ozidi and his mother were at home with their family.

SPECTATOR: All persons of the same type.

Slowing down, they had not berthed for long, when Ozidi came out for a stroll, and together with his wife stood stretching and yawning outside.

SPECTATOR: Ah, go in quickly!

Docking in style, the invaders found nobody.
For his part, Ozidi had no idea a warboat had come to dock at his waterside.
Having moored, the royal visitor caught sight of his victim, "Oh there he is!" he cried.
"He's out in the square.
Yes, yes, that's even better."
And from the moment they spotted Ozidi, the guns began to roar.

CALLER: O STORY!
GROUP: YES!

The guns mounted on the boat began to fire.
Salvoes followed upon salvoes: those with pellets found their target, so did the cannon.
All the marksmen hit Ozidi directly, riddling and pock-marking him all over.
And as soon as Ozidi walked back to his house, he cried: "Oh, Oreame, my head is aching terribly."

Now since his birth, Ozidi had never had a cold, had never been sick.
Such was his constitution.
"Here, here, mother, I'm cold too.
I can't bear the knocking in my head."
"Is that so, is it your head that's aching?"
She reached for this medicine, and reached for another.
Those for the eyes she dropped them in.
"Oh, I'm not cooled down.
I must lie down.
I must lie down and sleep."
And so he collapsed straight into a coma.
"Ozidi, get up and eat a little."
"I don't want any food."
His wife also urged him: "My husband, sit up for a moment,
you've been lying down for a long time.
Please get up so I can heat you water to bathe."
"To bathe is out of the question."
By dawn Ozidi's body had broken into rashes.
And in no time, pocks took over his body completely: eyes, nose, every part of his body.
You couldn't see his body for the spots.
The moment Oreame saw him, she wailed.
"You child, what manner of things are these?
Oh help!"
In panic she rushed straight for the forest, and going her rounds,
she collected first one thing, then she collected all that she knew,
but though she administered all on him, there was no relief.
By now, the boy had become weak and listless in bed.
Later, his body, when he turned over his body, maggots crawled out of his sides.

His body progressively rotted.
And pin-prick was now the last thing the warrior wanted, all poxed over was he.

Caller: O STORY!
Group: YES!

If you saw Ozidi, the pulse in him seemed all gone.
To open his eyes was impossible.
His face darkened.
And if you saw his wife, she did not know what to do.
"Oh, my husband, what shall we do?"
To hold his hand was torture, to hold his leg the same torture.
All became mouldy with decay.

On the second day, his body could no longer contain him.
Oreame herself grew distracted.
His mother too . . . yes, Orea, too ran up up and down distraught.
There was Orea agitated at one end, and at the other end was his grandmother, also agitated.
His grandmother couldn't sit anywhere in the house, but ran out,
first this way, then that way, each time unable to come up with any cure.

"Oh, is it this my only child!
After doing justice by his father, is it this wicked evil disease will come and kill my child!
Yes, I'm dead indeed!"
So they struggled on, and by break of day, Ozidi really was now completely out, down, and at his lowest ebb.
After dozing off for part of the day, his little mother, Orea, the woman who gave birth to Ozidi, after dozing off during the day from sheer exhaustion, she suddenly came to . . .
"Mother, mother!"
"Yes!"
"Look, since I had Ozidi he hasn't caught yaws.
Whether this is yaws . . . whether or not this is yaws we don't know.
Now your medicine for yaws used to be very effective."
"True, my daughter!
Yes, indeed!
Hey, Ozidi, my own, my own, my own!"
When she looked at him steadily, there he lay supine.
And low was his breath, faint his pulse.
Meanwhile, the crew in the boat became impatient: "Oh, how long we have been!
Hasn't he been taken yet? Or isn't it time we left?"

(Ululation)

"We've been moored here a long time.
What's happening?"
To this grumbling, their commander replied: "Only one night more.
At dawn we shall take him.
Just one night more is left.
We've spelt out the days."
"Yes, but one is beginning to famish.
In this whole town, we haven't found even a single person to welcome and entertain us."
Now, whenever Oreame wanted service from other people, because she was never asked to pay any fees, even if it was a shilling, she would use such money she saved for buying and stocking food in the house.
That was her practice.

Spectator I: Hmm!

And she always prescribed bush herbs and only medicines from the bush.

Spectator II: Hmm!

Now that she alone could find money to buy food, they went . . . the youths . . . the young paddlers went about the town starving.
Spectator III: Do you see!

Caller: O STORY!
Group: YES!

"Ah, Okrikpakpa! Oh, Engradon! we are dying of hunger.
Therefore, we are going."

Spectator I: Please go!
Then he spoke: "Stay on."
At dawn we'll pull out, tomorrow when I've taken him, we'll board, and set sail immediately."
"Yes, Sir! But is there food to eat today?"

"Yes, there's still some left.
Go and look in the boat.
Open the bags and look, and look also into the hold."
While the crew went off to open and inspect these things, Oreame and her daughter were each crying: "Ah, Oh, Ozidi, my child, my child,
Oh, Ozidi, my own, my own, my own!

Man to your finger-tips, son to your very feet, oh my child, my child, my child!

Hey, hero of the fight, my own, my own, my own child!
Oh pride of swords, my son, my son, my son!
You who the kilt fits, my son, my son, my son!
You who all belts match, my son, my son, my son!
What shall I do with you now?
Yes, I Oreame!"
So the old witch beat her breast until her daughter came up with her diagnosis, and she cried out in ecstasy: "Oho, Odumabe!"
Like Kabo people, she exclaimed rapturously: "Odumabe!"
And she no sooner said this than she vanished.
Away she flew at once.
After flying on for some time, as soon as she touched down in the bush, that medicine for yaws, her own brand of yaws medicine was indeed the rage.
Gathering this medicine, and returning home in the same dash, her daughter on her own brought out a fresh unfired pot, stood it up outside, and fell to boiling it.

Song

Solo: Word has fallen on the floor
In the city of the dead
Word has fallen on the floor
In the city that I too shall go
This city of the dead
Word has fallen on the floor.

Chorus: In the city of the dead
Word has fallen on the floor
In the city that I too shall go
Word has fallen on the floor
In the city of the dead
Word has fallen on the floor
In the city that I too shall go

(Song repeated several times)

Caller: O STORY!
Group: YES!
Caller: O STORY!
Group: YES!
Caller: O CITY!
Group: YES!

Spectator III: I am the child of Ase̲ne̲owei.
Ase̲ne̲owei gave me birth.
Oh, yes perform for the town to see!

Caller: O IJO̲!
Group: YES!
Caller: O IJO̲!
Group: YES!

As we were saying, O̲re̲ame̲ had hardly landed in her courtyard when she began squashing the herbs into the pot and the moment she finished squeezing them, she hailed on her son:
"Hey, Ozidi, my child, my child, my child!
Oh boy, my boy, since your birth you haven't fallen for yaws, my child, my child, my child!
It's time you had your yaws washed, my child, my child, my child!"
Believe me, O̲re̲ame̲ herself, then the hornblower, and last the drummer, together they now held Ozidi and led him outside to wash, all pock-marked as he was.
Some held his head, others held other parts.
Haggard and draggled, he lay in their arms.
Spectator I: Oh, my child!
They laid him out on a mat, his body festering with the pox.
And the maggots wriggled from all over him.
Hurriedly, O̲re̲ame̲ brought out that medicine of hers and began:
"Yaws expellant!
Yaws expellant!
Here's water!"
Spectator II: Didogban.
"Yaws expellant!
How's it, my child hadn't fallen with yaws before!
He's fallen at last with the yaws.
Here's water!
It's yaws!
It's only yaws!
It's a thing forbidden, a child of O̲re̲ame̲ cannot die of yaws!"
And she poured water over him; over his head.
So she performed.
Now all those festering maggots began to wriggle away, burrowing into the earth.
She would dash indoors only to turn back and skirt round him, stopping now and again to observe him closely.
Then, ducking, she would hurry in again.
This was the very day the Smallpox King was going to carry him off in his boat.
Said the Smallpox King: "This woman, what's she up to there, my people?

"Woman, will you keep back!" he ordered, and reaching out at the same time to grab his victim, the Smallpox King stretched out his hand, but it fell short of the target.
He reached farther out, but still his hand held air.

Caller: O STORY!
Group: YES!

Then the Smallpox King said: "This woman, what manner of woman is she?"
Even as he spoke, she was off again . . . and bringing back two more budding herbs, she stuffed them into the pot and squashed them in the water.
You should see the place frothing all over.
As the broth bubbled over so she bailed it out, splash, splash into his eyes, his nose, she gathered up the water between her palms and dashed it at him. And now his body which couldn't be seen before for its spots and scabs, by the time the soap was rinsed off him, his body began to glow and sparkle.
The doddering man now sprang up.
And his wife went for him: "Now that's my husband! That's my husband!"
While he stood there recovered, out surged the Smallpox King himself, his two guns slung over his shoulders and a kitbag at his either side . . .
Spectator: Hey, what guns!
. . . and the belt charms on him were scary to see.
"Will this woman withdraw and let me bear off my man?"
While he issued his decree, Oreame herself saw him in all his regalia and armoury.
Then Oreame turned back to her son watching him closely.
"Hey, Ozidi, my child, my child, my child, my child, my child!
What are you moping at still, my champion, my champion, my champion, my champion!
Don't you know who's come to kill you, you, my son, my son, my son, my son?
I am Oreame, my son, my son, my son!

Oh, my son, rise, rise, at once!
What are you dilly-dallying about, rise, rise, rise!" she aroused him and instantly his bowels broke into stampede, the hornbill screeching, the monitor lizard scrambling, and that call "Ozidi to the grove!" And "I am! I am! I am!" came the boom of the monkey.
Affronted, the Smallpox King commanded his men: "Quick, up at once!" And his forces broke ranks, boarded their boat, and pulled out.
"Quick, board quickly! Board at once!
What rude noise!"
And once Ozidi rose, with sword and battle kit all now out on the ready, before the invaders could scramble aboard . . .

SONG

Solo: Come out now and take it!
Chorus: Yes!
Solo: Come out now and take it!
Chorus: Yes . . . !

. . . he had taken all of them that were lined up on one side of the boat.
SPECTATOR: All in one sweep.
And only those lined up at the other gunnel were left standing.
As these stood in a file . . .
SPECTATOR: He caught sight of them.

CALLER: O STORY!
GROUP: YES!
CALLER: O STORY!
GROUP: YES!

At this stage, the master and owner of the boat gave his final orders: "Let half of you surviving go over to starboard, share up the boat between you, and let's push off directly.
I said be quick!"
While he issued his last orders, Ozidi shouted to him: "Here! Here! Here!
Oh, Engradon! Oh, Engradon! Hey Engradon!" and as he spoke so his scalp-collecting tune rose in the air:

SONG

SOLO: Come out now and take it!
CHORUS: Yes!

SOLO: Come out now and take it . . . !

Believe me, he chopped up Engradon himself along with his men, cutting up the boat into bits and pieces . . .

SPECTATOR: Hand has touched him this time.
And all fell overboard.

CALLER: O STORY!
GROUP: YES!

So the boat foundered and sank off the beach.
SPECTATOR: Indeed he wrecked it.

"I am Ozidi! I am Ozidi! I am Ozidi!
Orea gave me birth, oh, my mother!

It's Orea who bore me, oh my mother, my mother, my mother!
Oh Oreame, my mother, my mother, my mother, my mother!
It's I Ozidi, oh my mother, my mother, my mother!
I had not fallen for yaws before now, it was therefore with yaws I went down, oh, my mother, my mother!
Now you have scrubbed away my yaws, oh, mother, mother, mother!
Oh, Oreame, my mother, my mother, my mother, my mother!
Oh, you my mother, my mother, my mother! my mother, my mother, my mother! Help me!
It's been a terrible burden my mother, my mother!"

(Praise greetings)

Yabuku: Agadakpa!
Okabou: Dare touch it!
Yabuku: Agadakpa!
Master-drum: Take it ashore!

Having embraced his mother, he raced round the place in ecstasy.
He stormed this way, then he stormed that way.
"There's no unnatural death can kill me now!
There's no unnatural death can kill me now! Oh my mother, my mother!"
Next he gathered up his wife into his arms.
He surged up one end, he surged up the other.
Then he went up to his mother and deposited it in her hands.
Next, he stood back, and declared: "Hear, hear, hear! I am Ozidi, I am Ozidi, I am Ozidi, I am Ozidi!

Hey, Orea, my mother, my mother, my mother, my mother!
Those who killed my father I have now taken them all, my mother, mother, mother, mother!
It's the Smallpox King who almost knocked me down with a foul death, my mother, mother, mother!
Oh, Oreame, my mother, my mother, my mother!
Oreame, you the woman who knows everything, take my sword, take my sword, take my sword, take my sword!
Oh, Orea, my mother, my mother, my mother, my mother!
Hear me! hear me! hear me! hear me! hear me! hear me!
Master-drum: Where there's no love the bowels show no love.

Then bending forward and catching a handful of earth, he said:
"Yes, my mother, there's no other word left.
All the battles in the world I have fought them. I shall never seek another fight."
Okabou: This is as far as I know it.

Since I only know it as far as here, I have no knowledge of it to go any further.
I can't end the story here for you.
It is as much as I know of it that I have told, I myself was born by a citizen of Orua.

As for my father, Zobolo is the name of my father.
It's Zobolo who bore me.
And Deigbea is my mother's name.
She was a woman of Esama.
Now, (there, listen and be quiet!)
Yabuku did send for me.
"Atazi used to tell a story, now Atazi is dead.
If you know it, she said, "come and tell it."
Accordingly, I came, and I've told the story, right up to where I knew Atazi told it.
If I add some more, then I shall have told a false story.

It is Yabuku who sent for me to come and tell the story to the child of the grandson of Ambake̲de̲re̲mo̲.
The story will now end here.

I can't finish the story formally for you.
This is where it ends.
I won't tell more, I didn't start it, the matter is finished.

AUDIENCE: Hear! Hear! Hear! Hear! Hear!

SONG

SOLO: Oh new town, here's song to sally out.
Oh new town!

CHORUS: Oh new town, here's song to sally out
Oh new town . . . !

(Song repeated several times)

(END OF NIGHT SEVEN)

African Poetry and Proverbs

Once obscure or ignored because of African reliance on the oral tradition, upon which early African civilizations depended predominantly for the preservation of their tradition, African poetry and proverbs recently have become a source of great interest. Despite Africa's oral tradition, despite the diversity of languages within the continent, and later, the disruptive effects of colonialism, a sense of African literary continuity has been retained throughout the continent. As one would expect within the traditional African framework, African poetry and proverbs treat such topics as religion, happiness in the family and community, and life, death, love, and trust. Each tribe had a religious system of its own, and Africans were monotheistic in that they believed that a single Supreme Being was responsible for creation. Additionally, this omnipotent deity reigned supreme over lesser deities, spirits, and departed souls. African family life was based on a tribal society, the major subdivisions of which were clans. Families, a part of tribes and clans, included all ancestors, both living and dead. They also included all husbands, wives, children, grandparents, aunts, uncles, and cousins: all those who had common ancestors. In this social organization, the individual did not exist apart from the community.

Poetic expressions related to the life occurrences of this community were often recited by a griot. Rhythms and intonations were used dramatically to present poetic pieces which treated birth, joy, war, and death. Sometimes these recitations were intended for recreation and amusement. Valuing realism and resilience of spirit, some communities utilized professional verse makers who were responsible for songs of celebration or praise. These artists were classified as *nolodoto* (literally, "good-memory-say-person") and *ayisumo* ("heart-much-understand"). Though laments or prayers for a lifting of one's life burdens served as an acknowledgment of the acceptance of work, they revealed an appreciation of the cathartic quality of song. While the African poet did write about love, there is a tendency to diminish explicitness. Poetic protocol excludes sexual implications as an affront to good taste. Women also created poetic works. Many of their songs are lullabies, work songs, praise songs, dirges (or laments), and chants to gods and goddesses. In general, early oral traditional poetry examines the relationship between man and nature.

Ancient African literary tradition centered around oral communication, and ancient folktales, the basis for the proverbs, were recited by a tribal griot. This storyteller related the tales to educate, amuse, and entertain. These oral narratives also provided the basis for the history of the tribe, the prevailing value system, and the rituals that were practiced. Furthermore, explanations in the form of parables and tales justified events, such as death, sickness, and birth. Stories or tales also explained the reasons for and existence of natural occurrences, such as thunder, rain, famine, and drought. African poetry and proverbs in their written format are the results of an ancient oratory practice. This oral communication served as a vehicle to enrich, educate, and enable the African to be in harmony with self, family, community, and the Creator.

Selected Bibliography

Ngara, Emmanuel. *Ideology and Form in African Poetry.* Portsmouth: Heinemann, 1990.

Ollivier, John J. *The Wisdom of African Mythology*. Largo: Top of the Mountain, 1994.

Soyinka, Wole. *Myth, Literature and the African World*. Cambridge: Cambridge UP, 1976.

Vincent, K. E. Senanu T. *A Selection of African Poetry.* United Kingdom: Longman, 1976.

Akan People

The Creator

The path crosses the river;
the river crosses the path.
Which is the elder?
We made the path and found the river;
the river is from long ago,
from the creator of the universe.

Lament

Your death has taken me by surprise.
What were your wares
that they sold out so quickly?
When I meet my father, he will hardly recognize me:
He'll find me carrying all I have:
a torn old sleeping mat and a horde of flies.
The night is fast approaching.
The orphan is dying to see its mother.

Bushman

Prayer to the Moon

Take my face and give me yours!
Take my face, my unhappy face.
Give me your face,
with which you return
when you have died,
when you vanished from sight.
You lie down and return—
Let me reassemble you, because you have joy,
you return evermore alive,
after you vanished from sight.
Did you not promise us once
that we too should return
and be happy again after death?

Egyptian

Religious

God Is a Master Craftsman

God is a master craftsman;
          yet none can draw the lines of his Person.
Fair features first came into being
          in the hushed dark where he mused alone;
He forged his own figure there,
          hammered his likeness out of himself—
All powerful one (yet kindly,
          whose heart would lie open to men).

He mingled his heavenly god-seed
          with the inmost parts of his being.
Planting his image there
          in the unknown depths of his mystery.
He cared, and the sacred form
          took shape and contour, splendid at birth!
God, skilled in the intricate ways of the craftsman,
          first fashioned Himself to perfection.

How Splendid You Ferry the Skyways

How splendid you ferry the skyways,
Horus of Twin Horizons,
The needs of each new day
firm in your timeless pattern,
Who fashion the years,
weave months into order—
Days, nights, and the very hours
move to the gait of your striding.
Refreshed by your diurnal shining, you quicken,
bright above yesterday,
Making the zone of night sparkle
although you belong to the light,
Sole one awake there
—sleep is for mortals,
Who go to rest grateful:
your eyes oversee.
And theirs by the millions you open
when your face new-rises, beautiful;
Not a bypath escapes your affection
during your season on earth.
Stepping swift over stars,
riding the lightning flash,
You circle the earth in an instant,
with a god's ease crossing heaven,
Treading dark paths of the underworld,
yet, sun on each roadway,
You deign to walk daily with men.
The faces of all are upturned to you,
As mankind and gods
alike lift their morningsong:
"Lord of the daybreak,
Welcome!"

When Being Began Back in Days of the Genesis

When Being began back in days of the genesis,
it was Amun appeared first of all,
unknown his mode of inflowing;
There was no god come before him,
nor was other god with him there
when he uttered himself into visible form;
There was no mother to him, that she might have borne him his name,
there was no father to father the one
who first spoke the words, "I Am!"
Who fashioned the seed of him all on his own,
sacred first cause, whose birth lay in mystery,
who crafted and carved his own splendor—
He is God the Creator, self-created, the Holy;
all other gods came after;
with Himself he began the world.

All selections translated by John L. Foster.

Secular

Send Him Back Hard by Your Lady's Small Window

Send him back hard by your lady's small window
(she is alone now, there is no other);
Stuff yourself full in her banquet hall!
Then through bedrock be shaken sky high,
Though very heaven break down in the stormwind,
he shall not (lovely lady) be moved.

Lo where she comes to you, bright with her thousand pleasures!
Fragrance spreads like a floodtide
Drowning the eyes, and the head whirls.
Unable the poor fool before her.

Ah! this is the hand of Our Golden Lady!—
She gives the girl as your due
That you keep to your service in Her Holy Name,
able anon, old pecker, to say
You've had the world in your time.

Ho, What She's Done to Me—That Girl

Ho, what she's done to me—that girl!
And I'm to grin and just bear it?
Letting me stand there huge in her door
while she goes catfoot inside.
Not even a word: "Have a quiet walk home!"
(dear god give me relief)
Stopping her ears the whole damned night
and me only whispering, "Share!"

I Love a Girl, but She Lives Over There

I love a girl, but she lives over there
  on the too far side of the River.
A whole Nile at floodstage rages between,
  and a crocodile hunched on the sand
Keeps motionless guard at the crossing.
  Still I go down to the water,
Stride out into the waves—
  how is it
Desire can soar in the wrench of this current,
  rough water be tame as my fields?
Why she loves me! she loves me! hers is the love
  anchors the shifting toeholds;
My charming girl whispered water magic
  (crocodile sits spellbound)—O my love,
Where are you, whose hand
  is so small yet has mastered the River?
—There, over there! already waiting,
  right in the path of my burning eyes!
The only one dear to my heart,
  and she crowns the shore like a queen!

Whenever I Leave You, I Go Out of Breath

Whenever I leave you, I go out of breath
  (death must be lonely like I am);
I dream lying dreams of your love lost,
  and my heart stands still inside me.
I stare at my favorite datecakes—
  they would be salt to me now—
And pomegranate wine (once sweet to our lips)
  bitter, bitter as birdgall.

Touching noses with you, love, your kiss alone,
  and my stuttering heart speaks clear:
Breathe me more of your breath, let me live!
  Man meant for me,
God himself gave you as his holy gift,
  my love to outlast forever.

Ewe People

Lament for the Dead Mother

Mother dear,
Mother you freely give of what you have
fresh food and cooked meals alike.
Mother, listen to me:
the crying child will call after its mother.
Why don't you answer, Mother, when I call?
Are we quarrelling?

Longing for Death

I have been singing, singing,
I have cried bitterly
I'm on my way.
How large this world!
Let the ferryman bring his boat
on the day of the death.
I'll wave with my left hand,
I'm on my way.
I'm on my way,
the boat of death is rocking near,
I'm on my way,
I who have sung you many songs.

Sadness of Life

The beautiful playing field has fallen to ruins.
The beautiful pleasure ground has fallen to ruins.
Dense forest has reverted to savanna,
our beautiful town has become grassland,
our beautiful home is nothing but grassland.

May the gravedigger not bury me.
Let him bury my feet, let him leave bare my chest,
let my people come and see my face,
let them come and look at my eyes.

The drum does not beat for joy.
'Sadness of Life' 'Sadness of Life' sounds the drum.
The drum only sounds for sadness of life.

Loneliness

My wings are plucked—alas!
Must I climb the tree
with hands and feet?
A mother's son is a buttress:
if you have none
down falls the house.
A mother's daughter is
your everyday apparel:
if you have none
you're cold, exposed.
Relations on the father's side
Relations on the mother's side
I have none.
In whom shall I confide?
Oh brother!

Fang People

Hymn to the Sun

The fearful night sinks
trembling into the depth
before your lightning eye
and the rapid arrows
from your fiery quiver.
With sparking blows of light
you tear her cloak
the black cloak lined with fire
and studded with gleaming stars—
with sparking blows of light
you tear the black cloak.

Hottentot People

The Ancestors

The days have passed;
we are a wandering camp
brighter days before us
perhaps.

Light fades
night becomes darker.
Hunger tomorrow.

God is angry
the elders have gone
Their bones are far
their souls wander.
Where are their souls?

The passing wind
knows it perhaps.

Their bones are far
their souls wander.
Are they far away,
are they quite close?
Do they want sacrifice,
do they want blood?
Are they far,
are they near?
The passing wind
the spirit that whirls the leaf
knows it perhaps.

Song for the Sun that Disappeared behind the Rainclouds

The fire darkens, the wood turns black.
The flame extinguishes, misfortune upon us.
God sets out in search of the sun.
The rainbow sparkles in his hand,
the bow of the divine hunter.
He has heard the lamentations of his children.
He walks along the milky way, he collects the stars.
With quick arms he piles them into a basket
piles them up with quick arms
like a woman who collects lizards
and piles them into her pot, piles them up
until the pot overflows with lizards
until the basket overflows with light.

Prayer before the Dead Body

The gates of the underworld are closed.
Closed are the gates.

The spirits of the dead are thronging together
like swarming mosquitoes in the evening,
like swarming mosquitoes.

Like swarms of mosquitoes dancing in the evening,
When the night has turned black, entirely black,
when the sun has sunk, has sunk below,
when the night has turned black
the mosquitoes are swarming
like whirling leaves
dead leaves in the wind.

Dead leaves in the wind,
they wait for him who will come
for him who will come and will say:
'Come' to the one and 'Go' to the other.
He will say 'Come' to the one and 'Go' to the other
and God will be with his children.
And God will be with his children.

Ibo People

Funeral Song

Ojea noble Ojea
look around before you depart.
Ojea, behold the fight is over.
Fire has consumed the square,
fire has consumed the house,
Ojea, behold the fight is over.

Ojea, brother Ojea,
ponder and look.
Ojea, behold the fight is over.
If the rain soaks the body,
will the clothes be dry?
Ojea oh, the fight is over.

Kijoku People

Hymn to Lightning

In the West the clouds vegetate
in the East they are scattered.
Flowers unfold
white cloud unfolds
mistletoe branches ooze
lightning falls on mistletoe branches
ooze ilbaratree tuffed
killed
weeping
paralysed.
Cruched fire extending
fire having watched fire extending
wood for the fire
bends expands
lightning
beats breaks
water on the surface of clay
where the clouds were together
roaring
continuously
lightning
thundering with spite.

Kuba People

Death

There is no needle without piercing point.
There is no razor without trenchant blade.
Death comes to us in many forms.
With our feet we walk the goat's earth.
With our hands we touch God's sky.
Some future day in the heat of noon,
I shall be carried shoulder high
through the village of the dead.
When I die, don't bury me under forest trees,
I fear their thorns.
When I die, don't bury me under forest trees.
I fear the dripping water.
Bury me under the great shade trees in the market,
I want to hear the drums beating
I want to feel the dancers' feet.

Mahi People

Lament

Listen to my sorrow
listen to my lament.
The bat was struck by misfortune
its head is hanging low.
I too was struck by misfortune
my arms are hanging limp.
The monkey was struck by misfortune
his brothers cease their play.
The lake is full of water
the lake cannot move away.
The room where we are drinking
the room has become dark.
The forest has burst into flames
the hyena looks for its mother.
The antelope flees the forest
the antelope's life is sad.
Listen to my sorrow
listen to my lament.

Soussou People

The Moon

The moon lights the earth
it lights the earth but still
the night must remain the night.
The night cannot be like the day.
The moon cannot dry our washing.
Just like a woman cannot be a man
just like black can never be white

The Sweetest Thing

There is in this world something
that surpasses all other things
in sweetness.
It is sweeter than honey
it is sweeter than salt
it is sweeter than sugar
it is sweeter than all
existing things.
This thing is sleep.
When you are conquered by sleep
nothing can ever prevent you
nothing can stop you from sleeping.
When you are conquered by sleep
and numerous millions arrive
millions arrive to disturb you
millions will find you asleep.

Swahili People

The Poor Man

The poor man knows not how to eat with the rich man.
When they eat fish, he eats the head.

Invite a poor man and he rushes in
licking his lips and upsetting the plates.

The poor man has no manners, he comes along
with the blood of lice under his nails.

The face of the poor man is lined
from the hunger and thirst in his belly.

Poverty is no state for any mortal man.
It makes him a beast to be fed on grass.

Poverty is unjust. If it befalls a man,
though he is nobly born, he has no power with God.

Yoruba People

Invocation of the Creator

He is patient, he is not angry.
He sits in silence to pass judgement.
He sees you even when he is not looking.
He stays in a far place—but his eyes are on the town.

He stands by his children and lets them succeed.
He causes them to laugh—and they laugh.
Ohoho—the father of laughter.
His eye is full of joy.
He rests in the sky like a swarm of bees.

Obatala—who turns blood into children.

The Almighty

Young ones never hear the death of cloth
—Cloth only wears to shreds.
Old ones never hear the death of cloth
—Cloth only wears to shreds.
Young ones never hear the death of God
—Cloth only wears to shreds.
Old ones never hear the death of God
—Cloth only wears to shreds.

The Lazy Man

When the cock crows,
the lazy man smacks his lips and says:
So it is daylight again, is it?
And before he turns over heavily,
before he even stretches himself,
before he even yawns—
the farmer has reached the farm,
the water carriers arrived at the river,
the spinners are spinning their cotton,
the weaver works on his cloth,
and the fire blazes in the blacksmith's hut.

The lazy one knows where the soup is sweet
he goes from house to house.
If there is no sacrifice today,
his breastbone will stick out!
But when he sees the free yam,
he starts to unbutton his shirt,
he moves close to the celebrant.

Yet his troubles are not few.
When his wives reach puberty,
rich men will help him to marry them.

Three Friends

I had three friends.
One asked me to sleep on the mat.
One asked me to sleep on the ground.
One asked me to sleep on his breast.
I decided to sleep on his breast.
I saw myself carried on a river.
I saw the king of the river and the king of the sun.
There in that country I saw palm trees
so weighed down with fruit,
that the trees bent under the fruit,
and the fruit killed it.

Proverbs

Alta Jablow

I

On Ignorance and Knowledge

It is not only one mother who can cook a nice soup. *(Efik)*
If you have never drunk somebody else's mother's soup, you think only your mother's soup is good. *(Ga)*
A man is like a pepper; till you have chewed it, you do not know how hot it is. *(Hausa)*
A man who has not seen the new moon before, calls the stars the moon. *(Vai)*
If there were no elephant in the bush, the bush-cow would be a great animal. *(Kru)*
The stone in the water knows nothing of the hill which lies parched in the sun. *(Hausa)*

II

On Prudence

One is not sent up to have the ladder then drawn away from under him. *(Ga)*
Pull the child out of the water before you punish it. *(Vai)*
One does not set fire to the roof and then go to bed. *(Yoruba)*
One does not throw a stick after the snake is gone. *(Jabo)*
Should a man roof his house, without first building the walls? *(Efik)*

III

On Knowing One's Place

Even if you sit on the bottom of the sea, you cannot be a fish. *(Vai)*
An egg cannot fight with a stone. *(Bura)*
You are not the alligator's brother, though you swim well by his side. *(Mende)*
If a crocodile deserts the water, he will find himself on a spear. *(Bura)*
There is no man clever enough to lick his own back. *(Kru)*

IV

On Endurance

An elephant does not grow in one day. *(Gio)*
Bit by bit the fly ate the dog's ear. *(Ga)*
If a man live long enough, he shall have eaten a whole elephant. *(Vai)*
If there is a continual going to the well, one day there will be a smashing of the pitcher. *(Hausa)*

V

On Wealth

The pipe of the poor does not sound. *(Ga)*
An empty rice bag will not stand up. *(Loma)*
Wealth is the man; if you have nothing, no one loves you. *(Hausa)*
Being poor makes it hard to have friends but not impossible. *(Bura)*
The frog says, "I have nothing, but I have my hop." *(Vai)*

VI

On Being Content With Oneself

An elephant never gets tired of carrying his tusks. *(Vai)*
I have a pot, why then should I search for another? *(Kru)*
One who cannot pick up an ant and wants to pick up an elephant will someday see his folly. *(Jabo)*
Salt does not praise itself that it is sweet. *(Ga)*

VII

On Anger

Anger is a warmth which lights itself. *(Kru)*
One does not become so mad at his head that he wears his hat on his buttocks. *(Yoruba)*
If you are never angry, then you are unborn. *(Bassa)*
A frown is not a slap. *(Hausa)*
Sweetness walks with bitterness. *(Efik)*

VIII

On Consequences

The ashes are the children of the fire. *(Bura)*
Today is the elder brother of tomorrow, and a heavy dew is the elder brother of rain. *(Fan)*
The tail must follow the head. *(Kru)*
Beware of scattering ashes, the wind will blow them in your eye. *(Efik)*

IX

On Women

Regular work tires a woman, but totally wrecks a man. *(Fan)*
If you want peace, give ear to your wives' proposals. *(Fan)*
The old bachelor does his own cooking. *(Mande)*
Who marries a beautiful woman marries torment. *(Mande)*
A woman will find ninety-nine lies, but she will betray herself with the hundredth. *(Hausa)*
A mother who has twins doesn't lie on her side. *(Mano)*
Women take up their market baskets and also take up gossip. *(Efik)*

African Tales and Myths

Myths, traditional narratives common to members of a tribe, race, or nation; frequently include the supernatural and explain a natural phenomenon. Like classical myths, African myths were passed down orally from one generation to another. Although there are many different tribes and countries in Africa, scholars have identified common characteristics in the myths. All West African religions have a Supreme God, the name varying from one culture to another. There are basic questions, such as Who made the world? Who created man? Why does man have to die?

Unlike the anthropomorphic Greek and Roman gods and goddesses, the African Supreme God does not intervene in the lives of humans. The Supreme God is not worshiped directly; he is approached through lesser gods or orisha. In addition to the concept of polytheism, there is the concept of animism, the belief that everything in nature has a spirit.

Another part of the religion is ancestor worship which is vital to the well-being of the living. The prayer to a Christian saint can be compared, in some ways, to the invoking of the spirit of one's ancestors. There is the worship of the tribal ancestors, as well as ancestors of the family. Parrinder discusses African religion in terms of a triangle. As he explains, the worship of the Supreme God is at the top of the triangle; the belief in lesser gods and ancestor worship represents the sides of the triangle; at the base of the triangle, there are forces, such as animism, magic, and medicine. Man must place himself in the middle, by learning to live in harmony with the forces.

Obviously, there are many different versions of the myths in various African cultures. The myth "the Perverted Message" is just one example. The African creation myth "Life and Death," a Hausa Tale, and "the Origin of Death," a Hottentot Tale, are two other examples. In the Yoruba, one of the three major tribes in Nigeria, along with the Ibo and the Hausa/Fulani, the Chief god, Oludumare, or Olorun, has a different function from Obatala, the god of creation. Shango, the Yoruba god of thunder and lightning, is said to have been the third king of the Yoruba.

Myths are different from tales. There are two types of tales: *Tatsuniyoyi* are entertaining stories about animals and people; the aim of the tales is to teach lessons in social, moral, and personal behavior. *Labarai* are tales that are geared toward the male members of the tribe. These tales recount cultural, family, or tribal history. Parrinder explains that some animal fables have been exported, as well as imported. For example, there are versions of the stories from the Moslem world, stories from the *Arabian Nights,* especially from East Africa. Other stories can be traced from Africa to India in such collections as the *Hindu Panchatantra* or the Buddhist *Jataka* tales. Others, such as Grimm's *Fairy Tales,* are from Europe.

Selected Bibliography

Courlander, Harold. *A Treasury of African Folklore.* New York: Marlowe, 1996.

Parrinder, Geoffrey. *African Mythology.* London: Paul Hamlyn, 1967.

Thompson, Robert Farris. *Flash of the Spirit: African and Afro-American Art and Philosophy.* New York: Vintage, 1984.

Why the Earth Was Peopled

Efik

Abasi rose, sat there; made everything above and everything below, the water, the forest, the river, the springs, the beasts of the forest; he made every kind of thing in the whole world. He did not make man.

All the men lived up above, with Abasi. At that time there was no man living on the earth below, there were only the beasts of the forest, the fish in the waters, the birds which we see in the air, and many other beings which we have no need to mention. But man did not exist on the earth below. All the men were in exile, they dwelt with Abasi in his village. When Abasi sat down to eat they joined him and Altai.

At last Altai called Abasi; he answered, and she said to him: "Things are not right as they are now. You have the earth down there, you own heaven here in which they live, you have made a whole large place to dwell in and unless you make a place for the men too it is not right. Find some way of establishing them on the earth so they can live there and light a fire that will warm heaven a bit, for it gets very cold up here when there is no fire on earth."

The Story of Creation

Fan

Before anything at all was made, Mbere, the Creator, he made man out of clay. He took clay and he shaped it into a man. This was how man began, and he began as a lizard. This lizard, Mbere put it into a bowl of sea water. Five days, and this is what happened; five days passed with him in the bowl of water, and he had put him there, inside it. Seven days passed; he was in there for seven days. And the eighth day, Mbere took a look at him, and now the lizard came out; and now he was outside. But it was a man. And he said to the Creator: "Thank you!"

The Story of the Beginning of Things

Fan

This is what my father taught me, and he had it from his father, and so for a long, long time back, since the very beginning.

In the beginning of everything, in the very beginning, before anything was at all, neither man nor beast nor plant, nor sky nor earth, nothing, nothing, there was God, and he was called Nzame. And the three who are Nzame, we call them Nzame, Mbere and Nkwa. And first of all Nzame made the sky and the earth, and the sky he kept for himself. The earth, he breathed on it, and under his breath were born the land and the water, each in its place.

Nzame made everything; sky, sun, moon, stars, beasts and plants . . . everything. And when he had finished everything, just as we see it now, he called Mbere and Nkwa, and he showed them his work.

"Is it all right?" he asked them.

"Yes," they answered. "You have done well."

"Is there something more to make?"

And Mbere and Nkwa answered. "We see a great many beasts, but we do not see their chief; we see many plants, but we do not see their master."

So to give a master to everything, among all the creatures, they chose the elephant, because he was wise; the tiger, because he was strong; the monkey, because he was clever and quick.

But Nzame wanted to do better still, and so between the three of them they made a creature almost like themselves; one gave him strength, another power, the third, beauty. Then the three said:

"Take the earth," they said to him. "From now on you are master of everything that is. Like us, you have life; everything is subject to you; you are the master."

Nzame, Mbere and Nkwa returned to their dwelling in the sky; the new creature stayed alone, down here on earth, and everything obeyed him. But among the animals the elephant was still the first, the tiger the second in rank, and the monkey third, for so it was that Mbere and Nkwa had chosen first of all.

Nzame, Mbere and Nkwa named the first man Fam, which means strength.

Vain of his power, his strength and beauty, for in these three things he surpassed the elephant, the tiger and the monkey, vain of having conquered all the other animals, this first creature turned out badly; he became proud, would no longer adore the gods and began to despise them, singing:

> Yeye, oh, la, yeye!
> God above, man below,
> Yeye, oh, la, yeye!
> God is god,
> Man is man,
> To each his own place, let him keep to it.

God heard this song; he listened.

> "Who's singing down there?"
> "Find out!" replied Fam.
> "Who is singing?"

"Yeye, oh, la, yeye!"
"I want to know who is singing?"
"Eh?" cried Fam. "Well, it's me!"

In a rage, God called Nzalan, the thunder. "Nzalan, come here!"

And Nzalan came running, with a great noise: "Boo, boo, boo-oo!" And the fire from heaven swept the forest. Beside that fire, all forest fires since are only torches. Phew! Phew! Phew! . . . everything flared up. The earth was covered with woods, as it is now; the trees burned, the plants, the bananas and manioc, even the groundnuts, everything was scorched up, everything dead. But unluckily, in creating this first man, God had said to him: "You shall never die. What God has once given he does not take back." The first man was burned; what became of him after that I don't know. He is living somewhere, but where? My forefathers never told me what became of him, so I don't know. But wait a bit.

God looked at the earth, all black, with nothing at all on it, idle. He was ashamed, and wanted to make something better.

Nzame, Mbere and Nkwa made palaver together, in their council house, and this is what they did. Over the ground, all blackened and covered with cinders, they spread a new layer of earth; a tree sprouted, it grew . . . grew still more, and when one of its seeds fell to earth a new tree was born, and whenever a leaf fell off it grew and grew, and began to crawl, and it became an animal . . . an elephant, a tiger, an antelope, a tortoise . . . every kind of animal. And when a leaf fell into the water it began to swim, and there was a fish . . . a mullet, a crab, an oyster, a mussel . . . every kind of fish. The earth became once more that which it had been and which it still is today. And the proof, children, that my words are true, is that if you dig up the earth in certain places you will sometimes find, right underneath, a stone, black and hard, but which breaks easily; throw that stone into the fire and it will burn. For you know very well:

When the whistle sounds
The elephant comes.
Thanks, elephant.

This stone is what remains of the ancient forests, the forests that were burned up.

Nzame, Mbere and Nkwa, however, consulted again.

"We must have a chief to command all the animals," said Mbere.

"Certainly we must," said Nkwa.

"Yes," said Nzame, "we will make another man again, a man like Fam, with the same arms and legs, but we will give him a different head and he shall be death." And so it was done. That man, my friends, was like you and me.

The man who was the first man on earth, the father of us all, Nzame named him Sekume, but God did not want him to live alone. He said to him: "Make yourself a wife out of a tree." Sekume made himself a wife, and she walked about and he called her Mbonwe.

In making Sekume and Mbonwe, Nzame made them in two parts: the outside part, this which you call Gnoul, the body, and the other which lives inside the Gnoul and which we all call Nsissim.

Nsissim that makes the shadow; the shadow and Nsissim, they are both the same thing, it is this Nsissim which gives life to the Gnoul, it is Nsissim that wanders about in the night when one is asleep, but Nsissim never dies. While it is in the body, Gnoul, do you know where it dwells? In the eye. Yes, it dwells in the eye, and that little bright speck you see right in the middle, that is Nsissim.

The star above,
The fire below,
The embers on the hearth,
The soul in the eye.
Cloud, smoke, and death.

Sekume and Mbonwe lived happily on the earth, and they had three sons. They named them: the first Nkoure (the stupid, bad one); the second, Bekale (he who thinks of nothing); and this one bore on his back Mfere, the third (he who is good and clever). They also had daughters. How many? I don't know, but these three also had children, and these had children again. Mfere is the father of our tribe, and the others the fathers of other tribes.

Fam, however, the very first man, God shut him up in the earth, and then he took a very big stone and stopped up the hole. Ah, the wicked Fam! For a long, long time he dug away; one fine day he got out. Who had taken his place? Other man. And who is in a rage with them about it? Fam. Who is always trying to do harm to them? Fam. Who hides in the forest to kill them, and under the water to wreck their canoe? Fam, the famous Fam. Don't speak too loud; he may be there this minute listening to us.

Keep very still,
Fam is on the listen
To make trouble for men.
Keep very still!

Then God gave a commandment to the men he had made. Calling Sekume, Mbonwe and their sons, he called everyone, big and little, great and small.

"From now on," he said to them, "these are the laws which I give you, and which you must obey.

You shall steal nothing from your own tribe.
You shall not kill those who have done you no wrong.
You shall not go and eat other people in the night.

This is all that I ask; live peacefully in your villages. Those who give heed to my commandments shall be rewarded, I will give them their wages, but the others I shall punish. Thus."

This is how God punishes those who do not obey him.

After their death they go wandering in the night, suffering and wailing, and while the earth is in darkness, in the hours of fear, they enter the villages, killing and wounding all whom they meet, doing all the harm that they can.

In their honour we perform the funeral dance, the kedsam-kedsam; it does no good at all. We set out for them the most savoury dishes; they feast and laugh, but it does no good at all. And when all those whom they once knew are dead, then only do they hear Ngofio, Ngofio the bird of death; they become all at once thin, very thin, and they are dead! Where do they go to, my children? You know as well as I do, that before crossing the great river they stay for a long, long time on a big flat rock: they are cold, terribly cold. Br-r-r . . .

Cold and death, death and cold,
I would close my ears.
Cold and death, death and cold,
Misery, O my mother, misery.

And when all have passed over the sorrowful Bekun, then for a long time Nzame shuts them up in Ottolane, the bad place where they see only misery . . . misery.

As for the good ones, one knows that after death they return to the villages; but they are full of good feeling towards mankind, the funeral feast and the mourning dance rejoice their hearts. In the night-time they approach those whom they knew and loved, they bring them pleasant dreams, whisper to them what they must do in order to live long, to gain riches, to have faithful wives (just listen, now, you down there by the door!), to have plenty of children and kill lots of animals when they go hunting. The very last elephant I killed, it was thus, my friends, that I learned of his coming.

And when all those whom they knew are dead, then only do they hear Ngofio, Ngofio the bird of death; all at once they become fat, very fat—even too fat—and they are dead! Where do they go, my children? You know that as well as I do. God takes them up on high and sets them beside him in the evening star. From there they look down and see us, they are happy whenever we honour their memory, and it is the eyes of all the dead people that make this star shine so brightly.

This is what I have learned from my forefathers. I, Ndumemba, was taught it by my father, who had it from his father, and where the first learnt it from I don't know; I was not yet born. So.

The Origin of Death

Hottentot

The moon dies and comes back to life again. She said to the hare: "Go to man and say to him: 'Just as I die and return to life, so should you die and become alive again.'"

The hare came to man and said: "Just as I die and do not return to life, so must you die and not come back to life." When he returned the moon said: "What message did you give to man?" "I said to him: 'Just as I die and do not return to life so must you die and not come back to life.'"

"What!" cried the moon. "You told him that?" And she took a stick and hit him on his mouth, splitting it open.

Lie and Truth

Malinke

One day Lie and Truth went on a journey together.

Lie said politely to his companion: "You must do the talking everywhere we go, for if I am recognized no one will receive us."

At the first house they entered it was the master's wife who welcomed them; the master came home at nightfall and at once asked for something to eat. His wife said: "I have not prepared anything yet." Now at midday she had prepared dinner for two, and had hidden half of it away. Though her husband knew nothing of this he was very angry all the same, because he had come in very hungry from the fields. Turning to the strangers he said: "Do you think this is the way a good housewife should act?"

Lie wisely kept silence; but Truth, obliged to reply, answered with sincerity that a good housewife should have everything prepared for her husband's return. The wife of the host, very angry with these strangers who interfered in her household affairs, turned them out of doors.

At the second village they came to, Lie and Truth found some children busily dividing a sterile cow, very fat, which they had just killed.

When the travelers went to the chief's house they recognized the children, who had just brought the chief the head and other parts of the cow, saying: "Here is your share." Now everyone knows that it is always the chief who gives the shares in a distribution of this kind.

The chief, addressing the strangers who had watched all this, asked them: "Who do you think is in command here?"

"It seems," said Truth, "that the children command!" At these words the chief fell into a terrible fury and had the impertinent strangers driven away.

Then Lie said to Truth: "Really, I can't let you look after our affairs any longer, or we shall die of hunger. From now on I must provide myself."

At the next village, which they reached shortly after, they settled themselves under a tree near a well. Loud cries arose from the village, and they soon learned that the king's favourite was dead.

A servant, overcome with grief, came to draw some water. Lie said to her: "What disaster has happened, that you are weeping so and the whole village is plunged in grief?" She said: "It is because our good mistress, the king's favourite, is dead."

"What" said Lie. "All this fuss for a little thing like that? Go and tell the king to cease lamenting, for I can bring dead people back to life, even though they have been dead for several years."

The king sent a fine sheep to the strangers, to welcome them, and told Lie to wait a while, and he would call upon his talent at a suitable time.

The next day, and the day after that, the king again sent a fine sheep, with the same message to Lie. Lie pretended to lose patience, and sent word to the king that he was going to leave the next morning unless he were called upon. The king commanded Lie to appear before him next day.

At the hour set, Lie appeared before the king. The king began by asking the price of his services, and at last offered him a hundredth part of all he possessed. Lie refused, saying: "I want the half of your possessions." Before witnesses the king accepted.

Then Lie ordered a large hut to be built, just beside the spot where the favourite was buried. When the hut was built and roofed Lie entered it alone, with some tools for digging, and made sure that all the openings were well closed.

After a long spell of what seemed desperate work, they could hear Lie talking aloud, as though he were quarreling with several people; then he came out and said to the king: "Here's a pretty state of affairs! As soon as I had brought your wife to life again your father caught hold of her by the feet, saying, 'Let go of this woman! What use is she on the earth? What can she do for you? If, on the other hand, you bring me back to life, I will give you not one half but three quarters of my son's possessions, for I am far richer than he.' He had scarcely finished when his father appeared, pushed him aside, and in his turn offered me even the whole of your possessions; then he in turn was pushed aside by his father, who offered me still more. The truth is that all your ancestors are there now, and I don't know which one to listen to. But to cut matters short, tell me one thing only: which shall I bring back to life, your father or your wife?"

The king did not hesitate an instant. "My wife," he said. For he trembled at the mere thought of that terrible old man, who had kept him so long in tutelage, reappearing once more.

"Doubtless," said Lie. "But you see your father offers me a great deal more than you promise, and I really can't let such a chance go by . . . unless," he added, seeing how frightened the king was, "unless you will give me the same sum to be rid of him that you promised to give me for bringing your wife back to life."

"That would certainly be best!" cried all the marabouts, who had helped in the assassination of the late king.

"Oh, well!" said the king with a deep sigh. "Let my father stay where he is, and my wife with him."

So it was settled, and Lie received, for not having brought anyone back to life at all, one half the riches of the king, who promptly remarried in order to forget his loss.

The Human Race

Masai

Three men went one after another to Ouende, to tell him their needs. The first one said: "I want a horse." The other said: "I want some dogs to hunt with in the jungle." The third said: "I want to refresh myself."

And Ouende gave to each what he wanted: to the first, a horse; to the second, some dogs; to the third, a woman.

The three men went away. But the rain fell, so that they had to stay in the jungle for three days. Meantime the woman prepared food for them, for all three. The men said: "Let us return to Ouende." And they went.

All three of them then asked for wives. And Ouende willingly changed the horse into a woman, and the dogs into women.

The men went away. Now, the woman who came from the horse is greedy; the women who came from the dogs are spiteful; but the first wife, she whom Ouende gave to one of them, is good; she is the mother of the human race.

The Spider and the Mason-fly

Ngbandi People

The spider and the mason-fly went to the forest to hunt. The mason-fly discovered a dead elephant and told the spider. Spider said: 'Remember, I found it, not you, I want all that meat, not you!'

The mason-fly was sad and went to his uncle: 'Uncle, what shall I do to get some of that elephant's meat?' His uncle told him, and Mason-fly went back to the elephant, crept into the body through the hole the arrow had made, and waited.

Soon, Spider arrived and started carving up the elephant, wanting to carry all the meat home that day. Then the mason-fly started making noises from inside: 'Hooo, Hooo!' Spider was terrified, for he thought it was the spirit of the mighty elephant. So Spider shouted: 'All right, all right, Mason-fly found it, he may have it all.' And he went away.

Spider Tries His Wives

Spider had two wives, Dale and Kondo. He loved Dale more than Kondo. Dale always got what she wanted. One day Spider decided to try his wives to see who loved him most. He pretended to be terribly ill, thrashing his hands and feet like an animal in the throes of death. Then he lay quite still. As soon as Kondo realized that her husband was dead, she wept bitterly. Dale, however, did not cry at all, she only wailed a little, because it was the custom, but Spider could hear that she felt no grief. So, Spider got up, and Kondo was overjoyed: 'You are cured!' Dale was chased away for good. Spider now gave all his favours to Kondo.

The Dog and the Cock

Long ago, the dog and the cock lived together in the forest, for in those days they were still wild animals, and did not belong to Man.

One day they decided to go and steal Woman, so they went and abducted her. Man went to his uncle and asked him what to do. Uncle told him, for he was very wise. Man took four bags of maize and pounded them. Then he went near the village of the cock and scattered the maize on the road. Then he went to the village of the dog, took the bitch and all the puppies and put them in a bag.

The dog came back from hunting just at that moment, and tried to stop him, but Man wounded him with his spear. The dog howled with pain, and the cock, on hearing this, decided to go and help his ally. On the way from his village, however, he found the maize and could not resist the temptation. He ate it all up, and by the time he arrived at the dog's village, Man had gone with his bag.

Next day, Man went to the forest and shot a deer; then he went to the dog's village and put the dead animal down on the road. That done, he went to the village of the cock, took the hen and the chicks and put them all in his bag. The cock came flying home and attacked the man, but the spear wounded him. The dog in his village heard the cock crow and came running to help him, but on his path he found the carcass of the deer and he could not resist the temptation, so he ate it all. By the time he arrived at the cock's village, the man was gone with his bag. The cock and the dog then decided to go to the village of Man to beg for their families to be returned. They understood they had to bring Woman, so they took her out of the dog's house where they had hidden her, and went with her to the house of Man.

Having received his wife back, Man said: 'You may stay here, for I will keep your wives and children with me, just in case you deceive me again.'

This is how the dog and the cock became domesticated.

The Elephant and the *Dudu*-bird

The Elephant and the *Dudu*-bird decided to go on a hunting expedition together. When they had finished hunting they wanted their wives to know they would be coming home soon, so that their meals would be ready. The Elephant trumpeted so that the forest shook. 'Haaa, hooo!' Then the *Dudu*-bird called: *'dudu, dudu!'*

Some distance away there was another *dudu*-bird sitting in a tree, repeating the words, singing: *'Dudu, dudu!'* This was heard by a third dudu-bird farther away, who passed on the word, and so on, until the song reached the edge of the forest where the wife of the first *dudu*-bird lived.

When she heard *'dudu'*, she thought: 'My husband is calling me, he must be wanting his meal.' So she started cooking his dinner, a true *dudu*-dinner. When the Elephant and the Dudu arrived, the meal was ready.

The Dudu invited his friend, but Elephant declined politely, saying that there would of course be a real elephant-dinner waiting for him. But when he came home, there was not. His wife had never heard his trumpeting.

The Elephant and the Gazelle

The Gazelle was afraid that the elephant would trample on him, for Elephant was in an aggressive mood. So, Gazelle asked Locust to go and jump on Elephant's back and gnaw through the string of Elephant's loin-cloth, leaving only a thin thread. Locust took a big jump and did as he was asked.

As soon as Elephant saw Gazelle he jumped forward to trample on him, but at that moment the string of his loin-cloth broke on his back, so he had to hold it with his big hand lest his shame be uncovered. So, Gazelle had time to escape.

Kwan the Boa and Longo the Viper

Kwan suggested to Longo: 'Let us both cut off our tails!'

Longo agreed, but he said: 'How shall I know that you have done it?'

Kwan said: 'I will cut off my tail under water so that the coolness will relieve the pain. If the water is coloured red, that is the sign that I have cut off my tail.'

Longo said: 'All right, as soon as I see that, I will cut off my own tail too.'

Kwan, who is a very cunning animal, went and picked a zamba-fruit, the juice of which is blood-red. He squeezed it under water and pulled faces, as if he were feeling awful pains.

Longo, on seeing this, took his knife and cut off his own tail. Then Kwan came out of the water and showed his tail. Did he laugh!

Longo was furious and went for him, but without his tail he was too slow and could not overtake Kwan. There came a bushfire that advanced more rapidly through the dry grass than Longo, so the viper was burnt.

Still today, if someone is trying to cheat you, you say; 'Are you trying to do a Kwan on me?'

The Spider and the Crocodile

Spider went to visit Crocodile on the other bank of the river. Crocodile, as a good host, offered his house to Spider. Spider said: 'For firewood, I use only koso-wood.' This wood, contains much resin.

Crocodile obligingly went out, found some koso-wood, came back, built a fire for his guest in his own house, and left Spider alone for the night. Spider searched in all the corners until he found Crocodile's eggs under the bedstead. Crocodiles are very fertile. Spider took the eggs and fried them over the fire. They spluttered and crackled, but so did the resin in the koso-wood, so that Crocodile, who lay outside, was not perturbed by it. Spider ate all his host's eggs.

The next morning he demanded a canoe and two rowers to take him across the river. While the boat was being made ready, Spider locked the door of Crocodile's house with a well-tied string.

When they were in the middle of the river, Crocodile began to shout from the bank: 'Bring him back, he has stolen my e-e-e-e-eggs!'

The rowers asked Spider: 'What did he say?'

Spider answered: 'He says, row quickly, for a storm is gathering and this canoe capsizes easily.'

The rowers rowed as quickly as they could, and as soon as the boat hit the sand of the bank, Spider jumped ashore and said:

'What Crocodile really said was that I had stolen his eggs. That is quite true. I ate them all. It was a good meal. Good-bye!'

At that, Spider laughed heartily, and before the rowers could catch him, he had vanished into the forest.

Souls and Spirits

The importance of water is expressed thus in the Ngbandi language; the rain is called 'Water from Above', the river: 'Mother of Water'; ink is 'letter-water'; tears are 'face-water'; the sea is 'big water'; a stream is 'arm of the water'. Sap is 'tree-water'; and 'stem of the water' means 'salvation'. 'Body-water' is the word for semen. If the sky is clouded, people say: 'Water has taken away the face of the sun.' 'Water has conquered the land,' means a flood. A proverb says: 'Death does not thunder, it arrives imperceptibly like rain.'

A person has a soul that can be seen if you look in the mirror or in the water. This is why the older people do not wish to be photographed: it means trapping souls, and the soul-trapper will make you ill.

Another proof of the existence of the soul is dreaming. At night your soul may travel around and see strange places, while your body lies visibly on your bed. Or you may receive a visit from your husband who is far away in the army, or from your father who died years ago.

Once, in a dream, a man saw his brother, who was in the forest on a hunting expedition. Three days later his companions returned and told the dreamer that his brother had had an accident. That was what he had come to tell his brother in the dream.

Animals and plants too have their souls, some weak, some strong. Roots and fruits which kill or cure you if you eat them have in them a fragment of the powerful spirit of the tree to which they belong. The elements, too, have their spirits, for instance the fire, which is a voracious spirit. The water spirit makes you love it so much that you go and bathe in it; then you become drowsy—the water pulls you towards her bosom. If it has bewitched you, you feel a compulsion to go to it.

The Underworld

Nilotic Alur People

In the days of this story, Anguza was still a young man. One day he went out on the lake in his boat to catch fish. He rowed and rowed until he was far away from the shore, for he had been told that the fish were bigger there and more numerous. Suddenly he saw that the water-drops on his oar had changed into pearls. Each time he swung the blade out of the water there was a spray of shining pearls. He baled some of the lake water into his boat and pure pearls rattled over the bottom. He looked with attention at the water on the lake and saw big white fish swimming below the surface. He saw that the fish were as big as goats; in fact, they looked in every way like goats.

He jumped out of the boat and into the lake. Lower, lower, lower he sank. Then he stood on the bottom and saw lush green grass everywhere. And there were the goats—hundreds of them.

They belonged to the Lake God, Jokinam, who came forward to welcome the young earthling. He made him his shepherd, and so Anguza tended the goats of the lake-bottom and lived a good life, with plenty of meat to eat and milk to drink.

One day he said to the Lake God: 'I want to go home to my people.'

The Lake God said: 'As you wish, but on one condition: if you tell the people on earth what you have seen here you will die at once.'

Then the Lake God took him back to the surface, up, up, until he saw his boat. He was put down in it and rowed back to the shore. He hid the pearls in a cave and told nobody what he had seen. From time to time he travelled to the city to sell some of his pearls to the jewellers. He became a rich man with many cows. He married and had many children.

But one day, at a beer party, he forgot himself, and began to boast: 'I have lived on the bottom of the lake. I have been the herdsman of the Lake God's goats . . .' At once he fell down, as dead as a stone. The elders of the village consulted the diviner regarding Anguza's sudden death.

The Lake God spoke through the mouth of the diviner: 'Whoever divulges the secrets of the lake, will die. Anguza did not keep his promise, and he died.'

The Origin of the White People

Nkundo People

In this story we find the first mention of the great diviner Bongenge, who is to Lianja what Merlin was to King Arthur: a protector as well as a magician.

This notion of the origin of the white people is not uncommon in the region: i.e. that white men are the sons of spirits, and have learned their technical tricks from ghosts in the forest. White is the colour of apparitions. Obviously, whites are not normal people. Ordinary healthy children are born chocolate brown and grow up to be as black as bilberries.

Yendembe, one of Lianja's daughters, appeared to be pregnant without being married. The girl maintained and swore that she had known no man. Lianja consulted the famous diviner Bongenge, who pronounced:

'Lianja's daughter is pregnant of twins, a boy and a girl. Their father is a god; therefore they will be white-coloured children instead of black, as human babies ought to be. Because they are not the children of a man they will want to live separately as if they were superior beings, and they will make things we have never seen and engage in activities we have never heard of. They will be married together.'

When Lianja's daughter's time had come, she gave birth to a boy first, and then a girl, both quite white. The two kept apart from the black children and began to speak a different language. At fifteen, they asked to have a separate house built for them, a sign that they wished to sever the bonds with the clan. They began to write with pens on flat surfaces. To the amazement of the black people they started forging iron, saying they were building a boat. Who had ever heard of making a boat out of iron, which sinks like a stone? But the iron ship did not sink, and when they had added a propeller they could travel together along the rivers without engaging rowers. They built their own house downstream, with a roof made of iron, and also with keys made of iron instead of leather thongs to fasten the doors. The white woman became pregnant and gave birth to twins, a boy and a girl, who also married together.

The Origin of Jealousy

A wise husband leaves the choice of a second wife to his first wife. She will usually select a close relative, a younger sister or cousin, so that the two women may live in harmony, sharing one husband. The senior wife then has the feeling that it was really her idea that her husband should marry again.

The woodpecker is an important member of the bird family. He is a magician and a breaker of rocks.

Ilelangonda-Itonde reappears to his great-granddaughter as the spirit of death, but also as a saviour. The tortoise was the animal that caught him in its nets. It is the most intelligent of all animals.

Likinda's sister Botoma was married to a man named Bolonga. After some years, when it became appropriate for Bolonga to take a second wife, Botoma decided that the best candidate was Bolumbu, her niece, a daughter of Likinda. When Bolumbu entered Bolonga's household, it soon became clear that he loved her much more than his first wife, her aunt. She was an obedient wife and a good cook, so that her husband spent much more time in the hut of his second wife than with her aunt Botoma.

This was the origin of envy: Botoma began to hate her young niece, and to hatch a plan to get rid of her. The opportunity presented itself one day when they went out fishing together. Bolonga had dammed a stream and told his wives to collect all the fish in the dry bed. There were dozens of fish squirming in the mud. As soon as Aunt Botoma had her basket full, she told her niece and co-wife to carry on picking up the fish; she would go home to do the cooking, she said. Bolumbu stayed on working, stooping over the river bed under an intricate maze of tree roots. Aunt Botoma climbed out on to the bank, went to the dam, which was built of wooden poles, took one of the poles and used it as a lever to break the dam. The water rushed into the empty bed and Bolumbu was washed away.

When Botoma came home her husband asked her where Bolumbu was, but she only said: 'Oh, she went by another path.' When it was found that the river dam was broken, and Bolumbu did not come home, it was assumed that she was drowned. But she was not. God had decided that she should not yet die and had given her strength to survive the ordeal. The current carried her into a hollow rock where she could stand up. She could not get out, but she could breathe and so she lived.

It was at that place that the people of Likinda's village used to fetch their water; it was a waterfall in a rocky part of the land. One day, Lianja and Nsongo sent some children with earthenware jars to fetch water. As soon as the children arrived near the water they heard a voice singing:

Kelonge, kelonge,
Did you bring my father?
Did you bring my mother?
Do not bring the fool who broke the dam!

Terrified, the children dropped the jars so that they broke, ran home and stammered out a story about the frightening thing they had heard. The adults decided to go and see for themselves. When they came near the river they heard the voice singing inside the rock. They recognized it as Bolumbu's voice and concluded that her spirit lingered there in the rock. They went and consulted Bongenge, who was even more cautious than usual:

Do not say it was Bongenge, *ngelinge,*
When I speak my magic words, *ngelinge,*
I shall have to mention names, *ngelinge,*
You have called me for divining, *ngelinge,*
For you want to know who murdered, *ngelinge,*
Do not say it was Bongenge, *ngelinge,*
Blame the leopard, not the monkey, *ngelinge,*
Not the squirrel but the lion, *ngelinge,*
Do not kill me if I mention, *ngelinge,*
Names of men you want to honour, *ngelinge,*
Or of women leopardesses, *ngelinge.*

Lianja promised him and swore that he would go unhurt. Bongenge then revealed the treacherous murder exactly as it had happened, ending thus:

God decided her survival, *ngelinge,*
And concealed her in a boulder, *ngelinge,*
There she lives like normal mortals, *ngelinge,*
Not a spirit but a woman, *ngelinge,*
Singing all the time *kelenge, ngelinge,*
With her own voice of Bolumbu, *ngelinge,*
She is fed by the Creator, *ngelinge,*
Kept by Yemekonji's power, *ngelinge,*
She may now be liberated, *ngelinge,*
If we break the boulder open, *ngelinge,*
Let us take the song-birds' counsel, *ngelinge.*

With characteristic resolution, Lianja took his iron tools and began to hack away at the stone, but without success: no more than a few chips came away. Then the honey-bird began to sing from a tree:

Father Lianja, *tsen tsen tsen tsen,*
Listen to the song-bird's counsel, *tsen tsen tsen,*
Call the birds *tsen tsen tselenge,*
Don't forget the woodpecker *tsen, tselenge.*

The men ignored the honey-bird, so it flew away.

At last, when they were tired, they said to each other: 'Who said that about the birds? Wasn't it the honeybird? Call him back!'

Lianja asked the honey-bird to go and call all the birds. When they were all assembled, Lianja asked the honey-bird to break the rock, but it said: 'I break hives, not stones.' The crested starling tried, but broke its bill. So did all the other birds, one after the other. Finally, the eagle said haughtily that he of course should have been approached first about this problem. He was invited to test his strength; he hacked away at the rock, but he too broke his beautiful bill. At last they noticed that the woodpecker was not present at the roll-call. Lianja sent the honey-bird to look for him, and when at last he arrived, he sang this song:

Tsa tsa tsa, I am the woodpecker,
I am the father of magicians.

He pecked away at the stone so that an opening was formed, through which a face became visible. Lianja praised and encouraged him:

Bravo, Woodpecker,
Father of magicians,
Open the stone!

The woodpecker, Yondoko, tapped on and on until the opening was wide enough for Bolumbu to be pulled through. Lianja gave the woodpecker four baskets full of maize, and ten to all the other birds for having willingly tried and broken their bills.

Bolumbu was carried to her father's house, alive but unconscious. Lianja sent for Bongenge. The great diviner arrived and announced that he could only succeed this time if Bolumbu's Aunt Botoma was present. But no one could find her. At last her husband saw her in the fields and brought her to the meetingplace. There she was accused not only of attempted murder but also of witchcraft, because it was evident to an expert like Bongenge that a curse still weighed on the young woman. So he told her to remove the spell. She replied by admitting the attempted murder but denying the allegations of witchcraft.

Bongenge answered enigmatically: 'He who knows everything, does not know the tortoise yet. Take the plant of life, scrape it and put it on the young woman's head.'

Botoma, on his instructions, found the stalks of the bosaako and the bosaanga plants, chewed them, and so made the Water of Life. But it did not work, no matter how often Likinda called his daughter back to life. At last Lianja fetched his father's magic snuff and blew it into her nose. Bolumbu sneezed and woke up. Then she told her story, which she ended thus:

'The water found me on the bottom under the net of roots, and I knew I could not escape. I thought: shall I be going to grandfather Ilelangonda without reason? Suddenly I felt as if someone was with me, and I arrived in a place where the water stopped pushing me. At first I could not speak, but suddenly grandfather Ilelangonda ordered me to speak to the people so that they might hear me and know where I was. Will you now ask Aunt Botoma why I had to die?'

Bolonga went home with his first wife, and they kept Bolumbu with them for a while. Bolonga invited the elders of his father's village and told them the whole story. Their verdict was: 'If a rat has eaten the scam, it will soon eat the whole garment,' which meant in this case that it was too dangerous to keep a proven witch in the house, and that it would be safer to take her back to her powerful brothers. This he did, and in this way their marriage came to an end. Botoma stayed with her brothers, deeply ashamed. Bolumbu said she loved her husband Bolonga very deeply, but she feared her aunt. So she stayed with Bolonga. They lived together in peace.

The Maiden Nsia

Alta Jablow

There were once three friends, youths from Bontuku, and each of them had been given certain wonderful magic properties by their ancestors. One had a mirror in which he could see any person or place that he wished. Another of the young men possessed a fan of magic feathers. If the fan were held aloft it would transport him instantly anywhere he wished to go. The third youth had a wonderful cow-tail switch. He had only to wave it thrice over someone who had died, and it would cause him to be revived.

Now these young men all loved the beautiful maiden Nsia, daughter of the chief. They sought her in marriage, but she said to each of them, "No, I will not marry you. Though you have the outward aspect of a man, you are not yet a man. You have done nothing noteworthy. You have not proved yourself. And of the three of you, I know not who loves me best. When you can prove this, I will choose a husband."

Then the three set off from Bontuku to go to Cape Coast, where they might find work to do, and prove themselves. So the friends journeyed, and when they reached Cape Coast they dwelt together. Each evening, when they had finished their day's work, the youth would bring out his magic mirror, to see their village, Bontuku, and their beloved Nsia. He would tell his friends what he had seen.

One evening, as he looked thus in his mirror, he beheld Nsia, and she was dead. She lay in an open veranda room of her father's house, while about her, the people mourned. He cried out to his friends, "Oh, my brothers, our Nsia is dead! She lies in the veranda of the chief's house, and all mourn her. We must leave this place now, and return to Bontuku to join the mourning and to bury our maiden." And he wept and the others joined him in sorrow.

They prepared to make the journey home, but then the young man said, "We will arrive too late for the mourning and Nsia will be buried. If we wish to see her face again, hold you both fast to my cloak and do not let go." They grasped his clothing, and he held his feather fan above his head. At once they were in Bontuku, standing beside their beloved, and they mourned.

Then the youth drew out his cow-tail switch. He passed it three times over the body of the girl, saying, "Nsia, awake!", and the maiden rose up and was alive.

There was great rejoicing. Then the three youths urged Nsia to choose a husband from among them. They said, "We have proven ourselves, and shown our love. Nsia, you must decide who among us has done the greatest deed, and that which shows the greatest love, and him you will wed."

Neither Nsia, the youths, nor the people of Bontuku could decide. Can you?

Ashanti

The Jealous Husband

A story, a story! Let it go! Let it return! It is not possible to say in which town this occurred but, know you, it was not this town nor any other town near here, but it did occur and in a town like this one.

And in this town there dwelt a man named Afik, a man possessed of no great wealth, but overweeningly proud and jealous of his one possession—his wife, Emme. He guarded her day and night, alert always to the danger that some other man might take her from him, and even becoming angry and affronted when anyone bade her a good day. Indeed, his jealousy knew no bounds: he did not permit her to go about her daily tasks unaccompanied, following close behind as she drew water from the river or tended her garden.

The people of the town at first laughed at his behavior and then, as it persisted, grew annoyed. Finally Afik's jealous behavior came to the ears of the town chief, who said, "This man needs to be taught a lesson for he is without humility. Such jealousy can lead only to trouble."

The chief summoned the men of the town and spoke, "I will give a good horse, a fine cloak and 100,000 cowries, to any man who will shame Afik by lying with his wife before his eyes. Nor will this be a simple matter, for his jealousy is great and he may kill in anger." That is what the chief said.

Musa, a clever and resourceful man, agreed to carry out a plan to seduce the woman and so shame the jealous husband. He went off into the forest and sought some pods of the baobab tree. He opened them carefully, carefully, emptied them of seeds, and poured in small pieces of gold. Then he resealed them in such a manner that they seemed not to have been opened. Musa took the gold-filled baobab pods to Afik as a gift. When Afik broke them open one by one and saw the gold it aroused his greed.

"My friend, show me where this marvelous baobab tree is," he pleaded.

Musa replied, "Oh, that tree is very far from here, a day's journey, and so tall that it cannot be climbed except by a ladder. Only I know where it is, and I have no wish to tell anyone else."

Afik continued his entreaties until at last Musa appeared to be won over and agreed to take him to the forest and show him the baobab tree which bore seeds of gold.

So they set out and, just as Musa knew he would, Afik took his wife, for he did not allow his jealousy to dwindle even at the height of his greed. After a full day of walking they reached the forest and there Musa pointed to the tallest of the trees.

"There it is. That is the treasure-bearing tree."

Afik wanted to ascend immediately, but the trunk was tall and smooth, providing no footholds, so they must first construct a ladder. By then Afik could no longer contain himself and, without thought for Musa or Emme down below, climbed swiftly into the branches of the great tree.

Quickly then, the seducer moved the ladder out of Afik's reach, and while Afik raged and cursed above them, he seized Emme and threw her to the ground. He fornicated with her as her husband looked on, not able to descend from the tree. When Musa had finished, he rose and went back to the town to claim his reward.

Emme rose from the ground and with great difficulty lifted the ladder to replace it so that Afik might descend. It was heavy and so cumbersome that she was unable to place it correctly, and though she held on to the base, it overbalanced, and she and her husband fell to the ground.

Afik felt himself for bruises crying, "Aiye, aiye, shame and injury have overtaken me. And you, my wife, what of you? Are you injured?"

There was no answer from the woman. Afik saw the ladder had fallen on her. She was dead. And he wept bitterly at her loss. In anger and sorrow he went back to the town.

The woman was dead and who should be blamed? Was Musa at fault, since he had carried out the plan to seduce Emme? Was the chief at fault as his was the decision and his the offer of a reward for shaming Afik? Was Afik himself at fault because of his jealousy and his greed?

Who then was to blame?

Off with the rat's head!

Hausa

The Son-In-Law

An elderly man had but one daughter, Sangba, who was very beautiful and much desired by all men. But as each suitor came to ask for her, the father demanded that he who would have Sangba as a wife must first bring him a live deer. Some of the young men were discouraged immediately, and went away. Others, though they were good hunters and fleet of foot, tried to capture a live deer and failed. So they, too, withdrew their suits and left.

One day two young men came from a distant village, and they were friends. They said, "We have come to the old man who has a daughter, Sangba."

The old man came out of his house and greeted the two visitors, "I am the father of Sangba. What is it you wish?" Njila, one of the youths, spoke: "I have come to ask for your daughter, whom I want to marry." And the other young man, Sefu, said that he too had come for Sangba.

Then her father said, "There is but one Sangba. You are two who ask for her. I have but one daughter, and you are two. Which of you shall bring me a live deer, to him will I give my daughter."

The two young men then prepared themselves to capture a live deer. They went into the forest and quietly, quietly, sought about for traces and finally they came across a deer. They immediately gave chase, running swiftly to follow the animal.

Sefu, not as fleet as Njila, soon dropped behind and overcome with fatigue sat down beneath a tree, saying, "I have finished. No more will I run to catch a live deer for any woman. Why should I suffer such exhaustion and destroy myself for Sangba? There are other women who can be married more easily. Anyway, what sort of wooing is this, with a live deer? I have never heard of such a thing before. Here I will sit and wait for Njila, that we may return together." Then he slept.

When Sefu woke, he saw his friend approaching, carrying a bound, live deer upon his back. Njila exulted: "Here is the live deer for the old man. I have caught it because Sangba pleases me very much. Rather than lose her I would sleep in the forest and try again on the morrow until the deer is captured."

They went then together to the village of the girl and presented the deer to her father. He ordered the deer killed and cooked for the youths to eat, saying, "Keep the deer, friends. Eat it, please. Then we will discuss this matter of my daughter's marriage."

When they had done eating, the old man called a Council of Elders to assemble. He addressed them: "You all know I have but one child, Sangba, my daughter who is dearer to me than myself, and so I need a son-in-law that is a good man, gentle of heart. These youths came to me and asked for my daughter, and I said that he who wanted her must bring me a live deer. Now, they have done this, and again together have brought the deer. But of the two, only one caught a deer. Why did the other not return with a deer? Elders of my village, I leave the matter to you. It must be as if my daughter were yours. Choose, then, a son-in-law between these two men."

The Elders questioned the youths. "You came together, but both of you asked for Sangba. Now one has brought a deer. Why has not the other?"

Njila spoke first, saying, "We went into the forest and sought out a deer. We both gave chase and followed where the deer fled. Sefu, my companion, abandoned the chase, but I was so charmed by the beauty of Sangba that I pursued the deer till I had caught it. I bound it and carried it back, joining my friend at the place where he grew tired. He has come with me now only to accompany me."

Then Sefu spoke: "I have never heard of wooing a maiden with a live deer. Nevertheless I went with my friend to seek a deer and perhaps to catch it. But there was such running through the forest that I grew weary, and thought that there was not so great a need to run as to cost my life. Women are plentiful, and most of them easier to obtain than Sangba. So I sat down to await Njila, to return with him. I saw him return with the deer, and have come here only to accompany him. I have not come to ask again for your daughter."

The Council of Elders deliberated and finally they said, "You, Sefu, who abandoned the chase after the deer, you are our son-in-law. Njila caught the deer and is a man of great heart. If he wished to kill he would stop at nothing till he fulfilled his wish. He would not heed one who scolds or gives advice. If we gave him our daughter and she did wrong, he would beat her and not listen to one who pleads for her. We do not wish him for a son-in-law. But Sefu is our son-in-law because he would listen to us. If he were about to punish our daughter for any wrongdoing, he would heed us when we came to pacify him. Though his anger were great, it would then cease. He is our good and gentle son-in-law."

Bura

Affection or Wealth?

It happened that in a certain village there was a very wealthy man, and he died. There were no relatives to mourn him. Only Sparrow came and wept for his passing, and then Parrot of the beautiful plumage came from the bush to take his place at the mourning too.

After the man was buried came the question of who was to inherit his wealth. There were many who came from all over to establish a claim to the inheritance. "A man suddenly wealthy may as suddenly find he has many relatives." But the village chief and his councillors quickly dismissed all these claims.

They said, "There is no truth to your claims on this man's property. None of you stood at the mourning. None of you knew of his illness and his death. What kind of relatives are you, that do not know of these things and yet come flocking like hawks to pick at his wealth? Your claims to it are false. Go home!" And the people left in anger and in shame.

There were left only Sparrow and Parrot, and they presented their claims before the Council.

Sparrow said, "All our days the man and I lived close together in town. Wherever he moved, there also I moved. At whatever place he went to live, I lived by him. My song woke him in the morning, guided him home from his travels, and cheered him in sadness. I was his companion in the fields and by the river and was with him throughout his labors. Often I ate of his food and drank from his well. I knew these things were freely given me and in return I sang to please him. At his death, my sorrow was true and I alone stood at his mourning till Parrot came."

The Council listened to Sparrow and said his claim was well based. They turned then to Parrot and asked him to say on what ground he sought to inherit the man's property.

Parrot spoke: "I should inherit the man's wealth since I am the original cause of it. The man saw my beautiful tail feathers, and took me from the trees to live with him. He plucked my feathers and made of them a handsome cloak, which he sold. The proceeds of this sale enabled him to pay a good bride-price for a fine woman. She bore him many daughters who were given in marriage for much bride wealth. And their children also bore other children, and they all added to the man's wealth. But it was I who caused him to have a wife, and thus was the foundation of all this wealth. I did not live with him through love, but only so that he might use my plumage. Since in this way the man took me from my home in the trees only for gain, I should also receive some recompense. For these reasons I alone have rights of inheritance."

The Council pondered what Parrot had said, and decided that his claim was also well based. Then the chief said, "Sparrow's rights to the man's wealth are those of mutual trust and affection, and there is no question of gain. Parrot, though he and the man shared no affection, was the source of the man's wealth. These are both true claims to the inheritance. Which of them has the better right?"

The Council deliberated and could not decide. Can you?

Fan

Blind Man and Lame Man

This did not happen in my town, nor did it happen in your town, but it did happen in some other town.

There were two men who lived together in one hut; one was blind and the other was lame. It was a time of famine and all the people suffered hunger. These two were hungry also. As they sat in their hut, Lame Man saw a troupe of monkeys in their yard. He thought of monkey stew and smacked his lips. Then he groaned.

"What is it with you, friend? Are you not well?" asked Blind Man.

Lame Man answered, "Oh, I am well enough, but hungry. If I could only walk, I would shoot a monkey and cook a fine stew to eat."

Blind Man laughed. "I laugh so that I will not cry. My belly is empty, too. And the bush is empty of game. The hunters in our village go out each day and find nothing to shoot. Where would you find monkeys?"

"Right in the yard of our hut," said Lame Man. "Because you cannot see them there, don't think I am blind, too. There are monkeys outside!"

This convinced Blind Man and he said, "Climb onto my shoulders, and tell me where to walk and where to stop. I will carry you and the gun to shoot the game."

Lame Man got on Blind Man's shoulders and directed his steps. They came so outside, where the monkeys were in the pawpaw trees. Boom! Lame Man fires his gun and a monkey fell. The others fled speedily out of range.

They carried the game inside and Lame Man built the fire up and began to prepare the stew. As he stirred the pot, Blind Man asked, "Is it ready?"

"Not yet."

Lame Man added the palm oil and the pepper and continued stirring. And the other asked again, "Is it ready?"

"Not yet."

All the while he was cooking the stew, Lame Man kept tasting it for flavor, and because he was so hungry. And each time Blind Man asked, "Is it ready?" Lame Man had just taken a large mouthful of the hot stew and had to swallow it hastily to answer his companion. Before long there was nothing left in the pot but bones and a weak soup.

This time when Blind Man asked, "Is it ready?" the answer was, "Yes, it is ready," and he was given a bowlful of bones and soup.

"What is this? Bones? Ah, you wretched fellow! You have taken advantage of my blindness and eaten all the meat. Did I not share equally with you in its capture? Should I not then have equal share to eat? Without my legs you would not have shot anything at all."

Lame Man answered, "I saw the game. I shot it. I cooked it. This is the larger part of work, and hence I should get the larger portion of food. You used only your physical strength. I used my eyes, my skill as a hunter, and my talent as a cook. This is certainly more! If I had not first seen the monkeys there would be nothing in the pot at all."

Thus they disputed and grew very vexed with each other. Blind Man went from the house and stood on the road, stopping all the people to listen to his account and beseeching them to judge and punish Lame Man. From the hut, Lame Man shouted his arguments and besought the people to judge him right.

The people were not able to judge. Can you tell, of the two, who was right?

Gio

Ingratitude

A snake was seeking a hiding place to evade his pursuers. As he fled from them he came upon a man clearing his fields. He approached the man and said to him: "I come to you; hide me."

"All right," said the man. "Go to that tree. It has a hollow place. Get inside and hide yourself."

"In the tree?" cried the snake. "But I shall not be hidden there!"

"Then," said the man, "take refuge in that big ant hill."

But the snake said: "There again I shall not be hidden!"

"Then where can you go?" asked the man.

"Open your mouth," said the snake. "I will go inside it and there I will be well hidden."

"O, no!" cried the man "for the good I do you, you will return only evil."

"No, I will not do you the least harm," was the snake's promise.

"Then it will be as you wish," said the man. "Get inside my mouth and hide."

He opened his mouth and the snake crawled in. Just as it disappeared, those who were hunting it came up and searched everywhere. They could not see the snake and so returned home.

"Well," said the man then, "now you can come out, for they have gone away."

"I? Come out?" replied the snake. "Are you crazy? I must come out so that you may go on indulging yourself in eating couscous and drinking palm wine? Out of gratitude for the good turn you did for me I will agree not to touch your heart nor your liver, but I shall certainly eat the couscous that you swallow and drink the palm wine. That will be enough for me." And he added: "No, I shall certainly not come out."

When he heard that final statement, the man began to lament and weep, and his belly began to swell from the snake inside it. He made his way home; there his wives and daughters gathered around him and asked, "What has happened to you? Why do you weep so?"

He replied, "I have a snake in my belly; I did him good and he repays me with evil."

So then they all lamented and wept.

A heron flying by heard their cries and flew down to them. He asked, "Why do you weep?" The woman said, "We weep because our husband has a snake in his belly."

"Is that all?" said the heron. "That can be easily cured. But," he added, "gratitude is a heavy burden, and I can foresee that if I render you a service, you will repay me with ingratitude."

"No, no!" cried the man, "I shall be forever grateful. I shall never do you harm."

"Very well," said the heron. "Then open your mouth." The man opened his mouth and the heron put his claw down.

Now the snake, feeling something moving, thought, "Ah, that must be couscous!" And he opened his mouth in expectation, but it was the heron's claw and it took a firm hold on the snake. The heron pulled, rising in the air and pulling the snake out. When he was high enough he let the snake drop to the ground, and the snake was killed.

The heron flew down again and said to the man, "Now you should make me a present of two chickens, for the good I did you." The man then suddenly caught hold of the heron and said, "Here is one already. Now I have to find one more."

The heron said sadly, "This is just what I foresaw."

"What is that to me?" replied the man. And he opened his hen house and put the heron inside. He shut the door tightly, saying, "I am going out to look for another chicken, and when I have you both together, I shall cut your throats." The man went out.

Then the woman said, "This is ingratitude that I cannot allow!" She rose, opened the door of the hen house and released the heron, saying, "Fly away!"

The heron flew out of the hen house, but before he flew off, he swiped at the woman with his strong claws and killed her.

Which of the three was the most ungrateful? The snake, the man, and the heron—all three alike brought final death to the woman. All three repaid good with evil.

Off with the rat's head!

Hausa

The Narrative in Africa During the Middle Ages

Narrative is usually defined as an account in prose or verse of an historical or fictional event or a sequence of such events. The narrative might be simple in that it tells the events and is chronological in the arrangements of details, or the narrative might be more complicated in that it is less chronological and relies more on a plot which is usually arranged by a preconceived artistic principle determined by the plot itself. The African narrative of the Middle Ages follows the dictates of the narrative form; however, the narrative tradition in Africa is oral as well as written. The narrative in Africa, like the narrative in the West, embraces history, myth, legend, letters, travelogues, folk tales, prose, and songs.

What written narratives that exist of Africa during the Middle Ages are, for the most part, in Arabic. Scholars have been eager to point out, however, that we should not entertain the idea that written narratives did not exist in indigenous languages in Africa prior to Europeanization. Basil Davidson insists that a Swahili poem from the fourteenth century is extant, and other scholars suggest that indigenous written literature, perhaps narratives, did exist but that such literature was in the domain of priests and secret societies and that the common people did not use the written word.

Two written narratives that are reflective of Africa during the Middle Ages are the *Kilva Chronicles* and *Kano Chronicles*. The latter work was done in the seventeenth century, but this account is based on an earlier version written by the Arab geographer, al-Idrisi. The *Chronicle* discusses the emergence of the Hausa city states and especially the predominant state, Kano. According to the legend, there were seven original cities, with Kano, under the guidance of two strong leaders (Rumfa, 1463–1499 and Abdullah, 1499–1509) emerging together as a powerful kingdom with a strong government and a powerful center for trade and commerce from the caravan trade routes with North Africa. Perhaps Kano became a powerful center because its rulers adopted the Arabic alphabet for writing their own language or because the rulers developed a manual of government rules and statecraft to enable them to become better administrators.

Whereas the *Kano Chronicles* are concerned with developing kingdoms of West Africa, during the medieval period, the *Chronicle of Kilwa* is concerned with the developing cities of East Africa. Generally, the *Chronicle* refers to the development of cities along the east coast of Africa from Somalia to Tanganyika. Specifically, the *Chronicle* treats Kilwa Kasiwani, the island governed by a dynasty of powerful sultans from AD 957 to 1520. Because of the island's propitious location, all merchant vessels using the shipping lines of the Indian Ocean stopped at Kilwa. The port was ideal for refurbishing supplies. But if ships did not stop at Kilwa, the ruling sultan would send his fleet to intercept such vessels and force them to pay taxes. Kilwa became the major city state for trading in gold. This island kingdom also established trade with India, Portugal, China, and Siam.

The narratives of Kilwa and Kano are documents that were created for the ruling elite who could not be considered as disinterested individuals. However, there are two narratives that come out of medieval Africa that are considered to be objective. One of these works is the travelog of Abu Abdullah ibn Battuta. Born in 1301 in North Africa, ibn Battuta became one of the greatest world travelers of the fourteenth century. As a young man, he left home to make the hajj to Mecca, and he continued traveling for the next fifty years. Toward the end of his wanderings, Battuta made two excursions into sub-Sahara Africa. For six months during 1331 he traveled, by boat, down the east coast of Africa, stopping at Mogadisha, Mombassa, and Kilwa, supporting the facts of the *Kilwa Chronicle* by confirming the highly developed standard of living that had been achieved by the people of Kilwa.

Between 1352 and 1354, ibn Battuta made his second visit south of the Sahara. This time he traveled by caravan into West Africa. His timing was perfect. His visit occurred at a period when Mali was at the height of its glory under the leadership of Mansa Sulayman. Battuta states that Mali was a highly developed principality with extremely honest citizenry. He disapproved of the women's attire or lack of it and of the freedom with which they consorted with men who were not immediate relatives, but he praised the educational system which forced each child to learn the *Koran*, and he was intrigued with the procedure of the workings of Mansa Sulayman's court. He noted the various griots and their services to the Mansa.

The other narrative was written by Battuta's contemporary, ibn Fadl Allah al Omari. However, Omari's narrative is not from observation, but rather from the opinions of others who had traveled in sub-Sahara Africa or who had been in the presence of African rulers. Omari discusses the hajj of Mansa Musa and the kingdoms of West Africa. Although he was an arm-chair traveler, his contemporaries accepted his narrative as accurate and informative, and recent scholars, while noting that Omari's narrative is not based on observation, affirm its accuracy

As stated earlier, the written narratives that originate in sub-Sahara Africa during the Middle Ages were in Arabic or some other language such as Spanish, Latin, or Portuguese. The narratives, for the most part, were written by Africans, but they do not reflect the lives of the citizenry. The description of these lives in sub-Saharan Africa seems to fall into the domain of the oral tradition. Batutta, observing Mansa Sulayman's court, opines that on festival days when the people gather to celebrate the king, the Dugha, the chief poet or interpreter, recounts the king's ancestry and his greatness. Then, other poets (griots) praise the king in their traditional language. Here, the oral tradition is at work. Arabic might be the language of the church (mosque) and the university; it might even be the language of the court, but when the griots sing the king's praises to the people, these poets use the language and the tradition of the folk, the oral tradition.

Africa's oral tradition is rooted in antiquity and is centered in the people's way of life. This tradition embraces their myths, their symbols, their customs, their beliefs and their assumptions. It allows them to explain their unknown universe, to unravel the mysteries of existence, to understand themselves and their relationship to the universe. In short, the oral tradition is the African's way of recording life, visible and invisible. Western civilization relies on the written word (housed in libraries, museums, archives, or some other repository) to keep the records of the past. Africans rely on no such tradition. Racial history is stored in the heads of African historians, the griots who have been trained to record and to recite the people's story.

There are two kinds of oral narratives: *restrictive* and *nonrestrictive*. Restrictive narrative is reserved for royal dynasties and powerful families. The griot who records the history of royalty spends years preparing for the position. In many instances, the role of griot goes from father to son, from generation to generation. In some instances, there are schools which a griot may attend in order to prepare himself or herself. The nonrestrictive narrative, on the other hand, may be practiced by anyone with a minimum amount of training, and the griot who practices the nonrestrictive narrative is usually a free-lance artist who might only practice his/her art occasionally.

An important narrative form practiced or performed during the middle ages in Africa was the *epic*. This genre is eminent because it embraces many other literary traditions. The epic recounts the story of an historic or mythic hero who demonstrates superhuman power and therefore performs superhuman deeds. The most popular example of the medieval epic in Africa is *Sudiata*. This epic chronicles the deeds of Sundiata, a stalwart king, who with his martial skills and his supernatural powers, subdued other potentates and unified the kingdom of Mali during the thirteenth century. Another West African epic which predates *Sundiata* is the *Epic of Wagadu*. This epic concerns the founding of the Ghanian empire and its rise to power during the eleventh century.

For a long time, it was generally believed that the peoples of sub-Sahara Africa produced no epic literature. Eventually however, many epics were discovered. Two of these emerging texts from Central Africa that have gained popularity in the West are the *Ozidi Saga* (which is performed in an open space with the entire community involved) and the *Mwindo Epic*. When the *Mwindo Epic* was presented, the entire performance took twelve days.

Another narrative form that is usually subsumed by the epic tradition but is also an independent genre is the *praise song* or the *praise poem*. Inherent in the African world view is the fact that everything, animate and inanimate, is a praiseworthy subject and that the right words of praise could evoke in the person or even object being praised behavior that could be beneficial to the individual and/or the community. The praise song is as pervasive as the African people themselves and is as indigenous as these languages. Both royalty and commoner alike might be praised. On special occasions Mansa Sulayman had many griots to praise him; however, the soldier, the hunter, the precious child or anyone whom the community deemed worthy might be the subject of a praise song. These songs were also addressed to the gods, especially the minor gods that the individual and or the community might want to propitiate. Though there is some question as to whether the praise song actually originated in Africa, this form has been associated with the continent from the dawn of history. Though the Egyptians may have regarded them as praise songs or praise poems, a "Hymn to the Nile," which was written around 1600 BC and a "Hymn to Aten," written during the reign of Amenhotep IV (1370–1350 BC) are praise songs that reflect the African tradition.

The medieval African narrative has proven itself to be seminal in the reclamation of African culture in general and in African letters in particular. In the past, Africa was plundered of its most valuable assets: many of its strongest citizens and of its most valued artifacts. Others were then in a position to proclaim that Africa has made no valuable contributions to civilization; however, with the end of colonialism and the development of independent nations, African and Western scholars are now rediscovering Africa, and the narrative is aiding the discovery. Scholars are now turning to medieval narratives in order to examine and reaffirm the advanced cultures that existed prior to colonialism, and scholars and researchers are discovering that such ancient narratives, in many instances, are accurate. Anthropologists, historiographers, sociologists, linguists, and biologists are researching historical personages, dates, artifacts, and vegetation to clarify murky areas of the African past. In essence, the narrative, especially the oral narrative, helps scholars to ascertain and evaluate Africa's contributions to the world.

The African narrative of the Middle Ages has also proven itself to be fertile ground for contemporary writers. No reader can fully appreciate African writers such as Chinua Achebe, Camara Laye, and Aye Kwei Armah unless he/she knows something about the African oral tradition, the folktales, the proverbs, the praise songs, the myths, and the legends. The same is true of writers of the African diaspora such as Toni Morrison, Maryse Condé, Earl Lovelace, Charles Johnson, Paule Marshall, and Toni Cade Bambara. The African narrative, then, not only reconnects the reader to the past, but it is also informs him/her in the present and future as new discoveries emerge.

Selected Bibliography

Balandier, George, and Jacques Maquet. *Dictionary of Black African Civilization*. New York: Leon Amiel, 1974.

Courlander, Harold. *A Treasury of African Folklore*. New York: Crown, 1975.

Davidson, Basil. *African Civilization Revisited*. Trenton, NJ: African World, 1991.

Durosimi, Eldrid, et al., eds. *Orature in African Literature Today*. Trenton, NJ: African World, 1992.

Gleason, Judith, ed. *Leaf and Bone: African Praise Poems*. New York: Penguin, 1980.

Handum, Sied, and Noel King. *ibn Battuta in Black Africa*. Princeton: Markus Wiener, 1975.

Hansbury, Williams Leo. *Africa and Africans as Seen By Classical Writers*. Washington, DC: Howard UP, 1981.

Johnson, John William, and Thomas A. Hale. *Oral Epics from Africa: Vibrant Voices from a Vast Continent*. Bloomington: Indiana UP, 1997.

Josephy, Alvin M., Jr. *The Horizon History of Africa*. New York: American Heritage, 1971.

Okpewho, Isidore. *The Epic in Africa: Toward a Poetics of the Oral Performance*. New York: Columbia UP, 1975.

Owomoyela, Oyekan. *African Literatures: An Introduction*. Waltham, MA: African Studies, 1979.

Snowden, Frank M., Jr. *Blacks in Antiquity: Ethiopians in the Greco-Roman Experience*. Cambridge: Belknap Press of Harvard UP, 1970.

Sundiata: Background

Sundiata or *Sonjara* or *Sunjata* is an epic of the Mande-speaking people, the Mandingo of Old Mali. Since *Sundiata* is an epic, the story is part of the oral tradition of the people. The best-known written version of the epic is by D. T. Niane, who published the work in French in 1960. Niane translated the epic as he heard it from Djeli Marmudu Kuyate, a griot. *Sundiata* was translated into English by G. D. Pickett.

Sundiata has characteristics that are similar to those of the classical epics, such as the *Iliad*, the *Odyssey*, and the *Aeneid*. According to the legend, Sundiata Keita defeated Sumaguru, King of the Soso at the historic battle of Krina in 1235 and founded the Mandingo empire. He established civic, legal, and cultural institutions in Mali. Thus, *Sundiata* is an historical record, as well as an epic containing the values and customs of the people.

In the invocation or prayer, Sundiata is associated with Adam, whose story is in the Bible and the Koran. Also, he is believed to be the descendant of Bilal, a religious leader, who was a companion to Muhammad. Bilal's family migrated from the Near East and settled in the Manden area of Mali. The reference to Bilal, as well as other references to Islam in the epic, relates the hero to an established world religion. The interaction of Islamic practices with Manding beliefs and customs is depicted.

Selected Bibliography

Niane, D. T. *Sundiata: An Epic of Old Mali.* Trans. G.D. Picket. London: Longman, 1970.

Rosenberg, Donna, ed. *World Mythology: An Anthology of the Great Myths and Epics.* 2nd ed. Lincolnwood, IL: NTC, 1995.

Sundiata

The Words of the Griot Mamadou Kouyaté

I am a griot. It is I, Djeli Mamoudou Kouyaté, son of Bintou Kouyaté and Djeli Kendian Kouyaté, master in the art of eloquence. Since time immemorial the Kouyatés have been in the service of the Keita princes of Mali; we are vessels of speech, we are the repositories which harbour secrets many centuries old. The art of eloquence has no secrets for us; without us the names of kings would vanish into oblivion, we are the memory of mankind; by the spoken word we bring to life the deeds and exploits of kings for younger generations.

I derive my knowledge from my father Djeli Kedian, who also got it from his father; history holds no mystery for us; we teach to the vulgar just as much as we want to teach them, for it is we who keep the keys to the twelve doors of Mali.[1]

I know the list of all the sovereigns who succeeded to the throne of Mali. I know how the black people divided into tribes, for my father bequeathed to me all his learning; I know why such and such is called Kamara, another Keita, and yet another Sibibé or Traoré; every name has a meaning, a secret import.

I teach kings of history of their ancestors so that the lives of the ancients might serve them as an example, for the world is old, but the future springs from the past.

My word is pure and free of all untruth; it is the word of my father; it is the word of my father's father. I will give you my father's words just as I received them; royal griots do not know what lying is. When a quarrel breaks out between tribes it is we who settle the difference, for we are the depositaries of oaths which the ancestors swore.

Listen to my word, you who want to know; by my mouth you will learn the history of Mali.

By my mouth you will get to know the story of the ancestor of great Mali, the story of him who, by his exploits, surpassed even Alexander the Great; he who, from the East, shed his rays upon all the countries of the West.

Listen to the story of the son of the Buffalo, the son of the Lion.[2] I am going to tell you of Maghan Sundiata, of Mari-Djata, of Sogolon Djata, of Naré Maghan Djata; the man of many names against whom sorcery could avail nothing.

The First Kings of Mali

Listen then, sons of Mali, children of the black people, listen to my word, for I am going to tell you of Sundiata, the father of the Bright Country, of the savanna land, the ancestor of those who draw the bow, the master of a hundred vanquished kings.

I am going to talk of Sundiata, Manding Diara, Lion of Mali, Sogolon Djata, son of Sogolon, Naré Maghan Djata, son of Naré Maghan, Sogo Sogo Simbon Salaba, hero of many names.

I am going to tell you of Sundiata, he whose exploits will astonish men for a long time yet. He was great among kings, he was peerless among men; he was beloved of God because he was the last of the great conquerors.

Right at the beginning then, Mali was a province of the Bambara kings; those who are today called Mandingo,[3] inhabitants of Mali, are not indigenous; they come from the East. Bilali Bounama, ancestor of the Keitas, was the faithful servant of the Prophet Muhammad[4] (may the peace of God be upon him). Bilali Bounama had seven sons of whom the eldest, Lawalo, left the Holy City and came to settle in Mali; Lawalo had Latal Kalabi for a son, Latal Kalabi had Damul Kalabi who then had Lahilatoul Kalabi.

Lahilatoul Kalabi was the first black prince to make the Pilgrimage to Mecca. On his return he was robbed by brigands in the desert; his men were scattered and some died of thirst, but God saved Lahilatoul Kalabi, for he was a righteous man. He called upon the Almighty and jinn appeared and recognized him as king. After seven years' absence Lahilatoul was able to return, by the grace of Allah the Almighty, to Mali where none expected to see him any more.

Lahilatoul Kalabi had two sons, the elder being called Kalabi Bomba and the younger Kalabi Dauman; the elder chose royal power and reigned, while the younger preferred fortune and wealth and became the ancestor of those who go from country to country seeking their fortune.

Kalabi Bomba had Mamadi Kani for a son. Mamadi Kani was a hunter king like the first kings of Mali. It was he who invented the hunter's whistle;[5] he communicated with the jinn of the forest and bush. These spirits had no secrets from him and he was loved by Kondoln Ni Sané.[6] His followers were so numerous that he formed them into an army which became formidable; he often gathered them together in the bush and taught them the art of hunting. It was he who revealed to hunters the medicinal leaves which heal wounds and cure diseases. Thanks to the strength of his followers, he became king of a vast country; with them Mamadi Kani conquered all the lands which stretch from the Sankarani to the Bouré. Mamadi Kani had four sons—Kani Simbon, Kamignogo Simbon, Kabala Simbon and Simbon Tagnogokelin. They were all initiated into the art of hunting and deserved the title of Simbon. It was the lineage of Bamari Tagnogokelin which held on to the power; his son was M'Bali Nènè whose son was Bello. Bello's son was called Bello Bakon and he had a son called Maghan Kon Fatta, also called Frako Maghan Keigu, Maghan the handsome.

Maghan Kon Fatta was the father of the great Sundiata and had three wives and six children—three boys and three girls. His first wife was called Sassouma Bérété, daughter of a great divine; she was the mother of King Dankaran Touman and Princess Nana Triban. The second wife, Sogolon Kedjou, was the mother of Sundiata and the two princesses Sogolon Kolonkan and Sogolon Djamarou. The third wife was one of the Kamaras and was called Namandjé; she was the mother of Manding Bory (or Manding Bakary), who was the best friend of his half-brother Sundiata.

The Buffalo Woman

Maghan Kon Fatta, the father of Sundiata, was renowned for his beauty in every land; but he was also a good king loved by all the people. In his capital of Nianiba[7] he loved to sit often at the foot of the great silk-cotton tree[8] which dominated his palace of Canco. Maghan Kon Fatta had been reigning a long time and his eldest son Dankaran Touman was already eight years old and often came to sit on the ox-hide beside his father.

Well now, one day when the king had taken up his usual position under the silk-cotton tree surrounded by his kinsmen he saw a man dressed like a hunter coming towards him; he wore the tight-fitting trousers of the favourites of Kondolon Ni Sané, and his blouse oversewn with cowries showed that he was a master of the hunting art. All present turned towards the unknown man whose bow, polished with frequent usage, shone in the sun. The man walked up in front of the king, whom he recognized in the midst of his courtiers. He bowed and said, "I salute you, king of Mali, greetings all you of Mali. I am a hunter chasing game and come from Sangaran; a fearless doe has guided me to the walls of Nianiba. By the grace[9] of my master the great Simbon[10] my arrows have hit her and now she lies not far from your walls. As is fitting, oh king, I have come to bring you your portion'. He took a leg from his leather sack whereupon the king's griot, Gnankouman Doua, seized upon the leg and said, 'Stranger, whoever you may be you will be the king's guest because you respect custom; come and take your place on the mat beside us. The king is pleased because he loves righteous men.' The king nodded his approval and all the courtiers agreed. The griot continued in a more familiar tone, 'Oh you who come from the Sangaran, land of the favourites of Kondolon Ni Sané, you who have doubtless had an expert master, will you open your pouch of knowledge for us and instruct us with your conversation, for you have no doubt visited several lands.'

The king, still silent, gave a nod of approval and a courtier added, 'The hunters of Sangaran are the best soothsayers; if the stranger wishes we could learn a lot from him.'

The hunter came and sat down near Gnankouman Doua who vacated one end of the mat to him. Then he said, 'Griot of the king, I am not one of these hunters whose tongues are more dexterous than their arms; I am no spinner of adventure yarns, nor do I like playing upon the credulity of worthy folk; but, thanks to the lore which my master has imparted to me, I can boast of being a seer among seers.'

He took out of his hunter's bag[11] twelve cowries which he threw on the mat. The king and all his entourage now turned towards the stranger who was jumbling up the twelve shiny shells with his bare hand. Gnankouman Doua discreetly brought to the king's notice that the soothsayer was left-handed. The left hand is the hand of evil, but in the divining art it is said that left-handed people are the best. The hunter muttered some incomprehensible words in a low voice while he shuffled and jumbled the twelve cowries into different positions which he mused on at length. All of a sudden he looked up at the king and said, 'Oh king, the world is full of mystery, all is hidden and we know nothing but what we can see. The silk-cotton tree springs from a tiny seed—that which defies the tempest weighs in its germ no more than a grain of rice. Kingdoms are like trees; some will be silk-cotton trees, others will remain dwarf palms and the powerful silk-cotton tree will cover them with its shade. Oh, who can recognize in the little child the great king to come? The great comes from the small; truth and falsehood have both suckled at the same breast. Nothing is certain, but, sire, I can see two strangers over there coming towards your city.'

He fell silent and looked in the direction of the city gates for a short while. All present silently turned towards the gates. The soothsayer returned to his cowries. He shook them in his palm with a skilled hand and then threw them out.

'King of Mali, destiny marches with great strides, Mali is about to emerge from the night. Nianiba is lighting up, but what is this light that comes from the east?'

'Hunter,' said Gnankouman Doua, 'your words are obscure. Make your speech comprehensible to us, speak in the clear language of your savanna.'[12]

'I am coming to that now, griot. Listen to my message. Listen, sire. You have ruled over the kingdom which your ancestors bequeathed to you and you have no other ambition but to pass on this realm, intact if not increased, to your descendants; but, fine king, your successor is not yet born. I see two hunters coming to your city; they have come from afar and a woman accompanies them. Oh, that woman! She is ugly, she is hideous, she bears on her back a disfiguring hump. Her monstrous eyes seem to have been merely laid on her face, but, mystery of mysteries, this is the woman you must marry, sire, for she will be the mother of him who will make the name of Mali immortal for ever. The child will be the seventh star, the seventh conqueror of the earth. He will be more mighty than Alexander. But, oh king, for destiny to lead this woman to you a sacrifice is necessary; you must offer up a red bull, for the bull is powerful. When its blood soaks into the ground nothing more will hinder the arrival of your wife. There, I have said what I had to say, but everything is in the hands of the Almighty.'

The hunter picked up his cowries and put them away in his bag.

'I am only passing through, king of Mali, and now I return to Sangaran. Farewell.'

The hunter disappeared but neither the king, Naré Maghan, nor his griot, Gnankouman Doua, forgot his prophetic words; soothsayers see far ahead, their words are not always for the immediate present; man is in a hurry but time is tardy and everything has its season.

Now one day the king and his suite were again seated under the great silk-cotton tree of Nianiba, chatting as was their wont. Suddenly their gaze was drawn by some strangers who came into the city. The small entourage of the king watched in silent surprise.

Two young hunters, handsome and of fine carriage, were walking along preceded by a young maid. They turned towards the Court. The two men were carrying shining bows of silver on their shoulders. The one who seemed the elder of the two walked with the assurance of a master hunter. When the strangers were a few steps from the king they bowed and the elder spoke thus:

'We greet King Naré Maghan Kon Fatta and his entourage. We come from the land of Do,[13] but my brother and I belong to Mali and we are of the tribe of Traoré. Hunting and adventure led us as far as the distant land of Do where King Mansa Gnemo Diarra reigns. I am called Oulamba and my brother Oulani. The young girl is from Do and we bring her as a present to the king, for my brother and I deemed her worthy to be a king's wife.'

The king and his suite tried in vain to get a look at the young girl, for she stayed kneeling, her head lowered, and had deliberately let her kerchief hang in front of her face. If the young girl succeeded in hiding her face, she did not, however, manage to cover up the hump which deformed her shoulders and back. She was ugly in a sturdy sort of way. You could see her muscular arms, and her bulging breasts pushing stoutly against the strong pagne of cotton fabric which was knotted just under her armpit. The king considered her for a moment, then the handsome Maghan turned his head away. He stared a long time at Gnankouman Doua then he lowered his head. The griot understood all the sovereign's embarrassment.

'You are the guests of the king; hunters, we wish you peace in Nianiba, for all the sons of Mali are but one. Come and sit down, slake your thirst and relate to the king by what adventure you left Do with this maiden.'

The king nodded his approval. The two brothers looked at each other and, at a sign from the elder, the younger went up to the king and put down on the ground the calabash of cold water which a servant had brought him.

The hunter said: 'After the great harvest[14] my brother and I left our village to hunt. It was in this way that our pursuit of game led us as far as the approaches of the land of Do. We met two hunters, one of whom was wounded, and we learnt from them that an amazing buffalo was ravaging the countryside of Do. Every day it claimed some victims and nobody dared leave the village after sunset. The king, Do Mansa-Gnemo Diarra, had promised the finest rewards to the hunter who killed the buffalo. We decided to try our luck too and so we penetrated into the land of Do. We were advancing warily, our eyes well skinned, when we saw an old woman by the side of a river. She was weeping and lamenting, gnawed by hunger. Until then no passer-by had deigned to stop by her. She beseeched us, in the name of the Almighty, to give her something to eat. Touched by her tears I approached and took some pieces of dried meat from my hunter's bag. When she had eaten well she said, "Hunter, may God requite you with the charity you have given me." We were making ready to leave when she stopped me. "I know," she said, "that you are going to try your luck against the Buffalo of Do, but you should know that many others before you have met their death through their foolhardiness, for arrows are useless against the buffalo; but, young hunter, your heart is generous and it is you who will be the buffalo's vanquisher. I am the buffalo you are looking for, and your generosity has vanquished me. I am the buffalo that ravages Do. I have killed a hundred and seven hunters and wounded seventy-seven; every day I kill an inhabitant of Do and the king, Gnemo Diarra, is at his wit's end which jinn to sacrifice to. Here, young man, take this distaff and this egg and go to the plain of Ourantamba where I browse among the king's crops. Before using your bow you must take aim at me three times with this distaff; then draw your bow and I shall be vulnerable to your arrow. I shall fall but shall get up and pursue you into a dry plain. Then throw the egg behind you and a great mire will come into being where I shall be unable to advance and then you will kill me. As a proof of your victory you must cut off the buffalo's tail, which is of gold, and take it to the king, from whom you will exact your due reward. As for me, I have run my course and punished the king of Do, my brother, for depriving me of my part of the inheritance." Crazy with joy, I seized the distaff and the egg, but the old woman stopped me with a gesture and said, "There is one condition, hunter." "What condition?" I replied impatiently. "The king promises the hand of the most beautiful maiden of Do to the victor. When all the people of Do are gathered and you are told to choose her whom you want as a wife you must search in the crowd and you will find a very ugly maid—uglier than you can imagine—sitting apart on an observation platform; it is her you must choose. She is called Sogolon Kedjou, or Sogolon Kondouto, because she is a hunchback. You will choose her for she is my wraith.[15] She will be an extraordinary woman if you manage to possess her. Promise me you will choose her, hunter." I swore to, solemnly, between the hands of the old woman, and we continued on our way. The plain of Ourantamba was half a day's journey from there. On the way we saw hunters who were fleeing and who watched us quite dumbfounded. The buffalo was at the other end of the plain but when it saw us it charged with menacing horns. I did as the old woman had told me and killed the buffalo. I cut off its tail and we went back to the town of Do as night was falling, but we did not go before the king until morning came.[16] The king had the drums beaten and before midday all the inhabitants of the country were gathered in the main square. The mutilated carcass of the buffalo had been placed in the middle of the square and the delirious crowd abused it, while our names were sung in a thousand refrains. When the king appeared a deep silence settled on the crowd. "I promised the hand of the most beautiful maiden in Do to the brave hunter who saved us from the scourge which overwhelmed us. The buffalo of Do is dead and here is the hunter who has killed it. I am a man of my word. Hunter, here are all the daughters of Do; take your pick." And the crowd showed its approval by a great cheer. On that day all the daughters of Do wore their festive dress; gold shone in their hair and fragile wrists bent under the weight of heavy silver bracelets. Never did so much beauty come together in one place. Full of pride, my quiver on my back, I swaggered before the beautiful girls of Do who were smiling at me, with their teeth as white as the rice of Mali. But I remembered the words of the old woman. I went round the great circle many times until at last I saw Sogolon Kedjou sitting apart on a raised platform. I elbowed my way through the crowd, took Sogolon by the hand and drew her into the middle of the circle. Showing her to the king, I said, "Oh King Gnemo Diarra, here is the one I have chosen from among the young maids of Do; it is her I would like for a wife." The choice was so paradoxical that the king could not help laughing, and then general laughter broke out and the people split their sides with mirth. They took me for a fool, and I became a ludicrous hero. "You've got to belong to the tribe of Traoré to do things like that," said somebody in the crowd, and it was thus that my brother and I left Do the very same day pursued by the mockery of the Kondés.'[17]

The hunter ended his story and the noble king Naré Maghan determined to solemnize his marriage with all the customary formalities so that nobody could dispute the rights of the son to be born to him. The two hunters were considered as being relatives of Sogolon and it was to them that Gnankouman Doua bore the traditional cola nuts.[18] By agreement with the hunters the marriage was fixed for the first Wednesday of the new moon. The twelve villages of old Mali and all the peoples allied to them were acquainted with this and on the appointed day delegations flocked from all sides to Nianiba, the town of Maghan Kon Fatta.

Sogolon had been lodged with an old aunt of the king's. Since her arrival in Nianiba she had never once gone out and everyone longed to see the woman for whom Naré Maghan was preparing such a magnificent wedding. It was known that she was not beautiful, but the curiosity of everyone was aroused, and already a thousand anecdotes were circulating, most of them put about by Sassouma Bérété, the king's first wife.

The royal drums of Nianiba announced the festivity at crack of dawn. The town awoke to the sound of tam-tams which answered each other from one district to another; from the midst of the crowds arose the voices of griots singing the praises of Naré Maghan.

At the home of the king's old aunt, the hairdresser of Nianiba was plaiting Sogolon Kedjou's hair. As she lay on her mat, her head resting on the hairdresser's legs, she wept softly, while the king's sisters came to chaff her, as was the custom.

'This is your last day of freedom; from now onwards you will be our woman.'

'Say farewell to your youth', added another.

'You won't dance in the square any more and have yourself admired by the boys,' added a third.

Sogolon never uttered a word and from time to time the old hairdresser said, 'There, there, stop crying. It's a new life beginning, you know, more beautiful than you think. You will be a mother and you will know the joy of being a queen surrounded by your children. Come now, daughter, don't listen to the gibes of your sisters-in-law.' In front of the house the poetesses who belonged to the king's sisters chanted the name of the young bride.

During this time the festivity was reaching its height in front of the king's enclosure. Each village was represented by a troupe of dancers and musicians; in the middle of the courtyard the elders were sacrificing oxen which the servants carved up, while ungainly vultures, perched on the great silk-cotton tree, watched the hecatomb with their eyes.

Sitting in front of the palace, Naré Maghan listened to the grave music of the 'bolon'[19] in the midst of his courtiers. Doua, standing amid the eminent guests, held his great spear in his hand and sang the anthem of the Mandingo kings. Everywhere in the village people were dancing and singing and members of the royal family envinced their joy, as was fitting, by distributing grain, clothes, and even gold. Even the jealous Sassouma Bérété took part in this largesse and, among other things, bestowed fine loincloths on the poetesses.

But night was falling and the sun had hidden behind the mountain. It was time for the marriage procession to form up in front of the house of the king's aunt. The tam-tams had fallen silent. The old female relatives of the king had washed and perfumed Sogolon and now she was dressed completely in white with a large veil over her head.

Sogolon walked in front held by two old women. The king's relatives followed and, behind, the choir of young girls of Mali sang the bride's departure song, keeping time to the songs by clapping their hands. The villagers and guests were lined up along the stretch of ground which separated the aunt's house from the palace in order to see the procession go by. When Sogolon had reached the threshold of the king's antechamber one of his young brothers lifted her vigorously from the ground and ran off with her towards the palace while the crowd cheered.

The women danced in front of the palace of the king for a long while, then, after receiving money and presents from members of the royal family, the crowd dispersed and night darkened overhead.

'She will be an extraordinary woman if you manage to possess her.' Those were the words of the old woman of Do, but the conqueror of the buffalo had not been able to conquer the young girl. It was only as an afterthought that the two hunters, Oulani and Oulamba, had the idea of giving her to the king of Mali.

That evening, then, Naré Maghan tried to perform his duty as a husband but Sogolon repulsed his advances. He persisted, but his efforts were in vain and early the next morning Doua found the king exhausted, like a man who had suffered a great defeat.

'What is the matter, my king?' asked the griot.

'I have been unable to posses her—and besides, she frightens me, this young girl. I even doubt whether she is a human being; when I drew close to her during the night her body became covered with long hairs and that scared me very much. All night long I called upon my wraith but he was unable to master Sogolon's.'

All that day the king did not emerge and Doua was the only one to enter and leave the palace. All Nianiba seemed puzzled. The old women who had come early to seek the virginity pagne[20] had been discreetly turned away. And this went on for a week.

Naré Maghan had vainly sought advice from some great sorcerers but all their tricks were powerless in overcoming the wraith of Sogolon. But one night, when everyone was asleep, Naré Maghan got up. He unhooked his hunter's bag from the wall and, sitting in the middle of the house, he spread on the ground the sand which the bag contained. The king began tracing mysterious signs in the sand; he traced, effaced and began again. Sogolon woke up. She knew that sand talks,[21] but she was intrigued to see the king so absorbed at dead of night. Naré Maghan stopped drawing signs and with his hand under his chin he seemed to be brooding on the signs. All of a sudden he jumped up, bounded after his sword which hung above his bed, and said, 'Sogolon, Sogolon, wake up. A dream has awakened me out of my sleep and the protective spirit of the Mandingo kings has appeared to me. I was mistaken in the interpretation I put upon the words of the hunter who led you to me. The jinn has revealed to me their real meaning. Sogolon, I must sacrifice you to the greatness of my house. The blood of a virgin of the tribe of Kondé must be spilt, and you are the Kondé virgin whom fate has brought under my roof. Forgive me, but I must accomplish my mission. Forgive the hand which is going to shed your blood.'

'No, no—why me?—no, I don't want to die.'

'It is useless,' said the king. 'It is not me who has decided.'

He seized Sogolon by the hair with an iron grip, but so great had been her fright that she had already fainted. In this faint, she was congealed in her human body and her wraith was no longer in her, and when she woke up, she was already a wife. That very night, Sogolon conceived.[22]

The Lion Child

A wife quickly grows accustomed to her state. Sogolon now walked freely in the king's great enclosure and people also got used to her ugliness. But the first wife of the king, Sassouma Bérété, turned out to be unbearable. She was restless, and smarted to see the ugly Sogolon proudly flaunting her pregnancy about the palace. What would become of her, Sassouma Bérété, if her son, already eight years old, was disinherited in favour of the child that Sogolon was going to bring into the world? All the king's attentions went to the mother-to-be. On returning from the wars he would bring her the best portion of the booty—fine loin-cloths and rare jewels. Soon, dark schemes took form in the mind of Sassouma Bérété; she determined to kill Sogolon. In great secrecy she had the foremost sorcerers of Mali come to her, but they all declared themselves incapable of tackling Sogolon. In fact, from twilight onwards, three owls[23] came and perched on the roof of her house and watched over her. For the sake of peace and quiet Sassouma said to herself, 'Very well then, let him be born, this child, and then we'll see."

Sogolon's time came. The king commanded the nine greatest midwives of Mali to come to Niani, and they were now constantly in attendance on the damsel of Do. The king was in the midst of his courtiers one day when someone came to announce to him that Sogolon's labours were beginning. He sent all his courtiers away and only Gnankouman Doua stayed by his side. One would have thought that this was the first time that he had become a father, he was so worried and agitated. The whole palace kept complete silence. Doua tried to distract the sovereign with his one-stringed guitar but in vain. He even had to stop this music as it jarred on the king. Suddenly the sky darkened and great clouds coming from the east hid the sun, although it was still the dry season. Thunder began to rumble and swift lightning rent the clouds; a few large drops of rain began to fall while a strong wind blew up. A flash of lightning accompanied by a dull rattle of thunder burst out of the east and lit up the whole sky as far as the west. Then the rain stopped and the sun appeared and it was at this very moment that a midwife came out of Sogolon's house, ran to the antechamber and announced to Naré Maghan that he was the father of a boy.

The king showed no reaction at all. He was as though in a daze. Then Doua, realizing the king's emotion, got up and signalled to two slaves who were already standing near the royal 'tabala'.[24] The hasty beats of the royal drum announced to Mali the birth of a son; the village tam-tams took it up and thus all Mali got the good news the same day. Shouts of joy, tam-tams and 'balafons'[25] took the place of the recent silence and all the musicians of Niani made their way to the palace. His initial emotion being over, the king had got up and on leaving the antechamber he was greeted by the warm voice of Gnankouman Doua singing:

'I salute you, father; I salute you, king Naré Maghan; I salute you, Maghan Kon Fatta, Frako Maghan Keigu.[26] The child is born whom the world awaited. Maghan, oh happy father, I salute you. The lion child, the buffalo child is born, and to announce him the Almighty has made the thunder peal, the whole sky has lit up and the earth has trembled. All hail, father, hail king Naré Maghan!'

All the griots were there and had already composed a song in praise of the royal infant. The generosity of kings makes griots eloquent, and Maghan Kon Fatta distributed on this day alone six granaries of rice among the populace. Sassouma Bérété distinguished herself by her largesses, but that deceived nobody. She was suffering in her heart but did not want to betray anything.

The name was given the eighth day after his birth. It was a great feast day and people came from all the villages of Mali while each neighbouring people brought gifts to the king. First thing in the morning a great circle had formed in front of the palace. In the middle, serving women were pounding rice which was to serve as bread, and sacrificed oxen lay at the foot of the great silk-cotton tree.

In Sogolon's house the king's aunt cut off the baby's first crop of hair while the poetesses, equipped with large fans, cooled the mother who was nonchalantly stretched out on soft cushions.

The king was in his antechamber but he came out followed by Doua. The crowd fell silent and Doua cried, 'The child of Sogolon will be called Maghan after his father, and Mari Djata, a name which no Mandingo prince has ever borne. Sogolon's son will be the first of this name."

Straight away the griots shouted the name of the infant and the tam-tams sounded anew. The king's aunt, who had come out to hear the name of the child, went back into the house, and whispered the double name of Maghan and Mari Djata in the ear of the newly-born so that he would remember it.

The festivity ended with the distribution of meat to the heads of families and everyone dispersed joyfully. The near relatives one by one went to admire the newly-born.

Childhood

God has his mysteries which none can fathom. You, perhaps, will be a king. You can do nothing about it. You, on the other hand, will be unlucky, but you can do nothing about that either. Each man finds his way already marked out for him and he can change nothing of it.

Sogolon's son had a slow and difficult childhood. At the age of three he still crawled along on all-fours while children of the same age were already walking. He had nothing of the great beauty of his father Naré Maghan. He had a head so big that he seemed unable to support it; he also had large eyes which would open wide whenever anyone entered his mother's house. He was taciturn and used to spend the whole day just sitting in the middle of the house. Whenever his mother went out he would crawl on all fours to rummage about in the calabashes in search of food, for he was very greedy.[27]

Malicious tongues began to blab. What three-year-old has not yet taken his first steps? What three-year-old is not the despair of his parents through his whims and shifts of mood? What three-year-old is not the joy of his circle through his backwardness in talking? Sogolon Djata (for it was thus that they called him, prefixing his mother's name to his), Sogolon Djata, then, was very different from others of his own age. He spoke little and his severe face never relaxed into a smile. You would have thought that he was already thinking, and what amused children of his age bored him. Often Sogolon would make some of them come to him to keep him company. These children were already walking and she hoped that Djata, seeing his companions walking, would be tempted to do likewise. But nothing came of it. Besides, Sogolon Djata would brain the poor little things with his already strong arms and none of them would come near him any more.

The king's first wife was the first to rejoice at Sogolon Djata's infirmity. Her own son, Dankaran Touman, was already eleven. He was a fine and lively boy, who spent the day running about the village with those of his own age. He had even begun his initiation in the bush.[28] The king had had a bow made for him and he used to go behind the town to practise archery with his companions. Sassouma was quite happy and snapped her fingers at Sogolon, whose child was still crawling on the ground. Whenever the latter happened to pass by her house, she would say, 'Come, my son, walk, jump, leap about. The jinn didn't promise you anything out of the ordinary, but I prefer a son who walks on his two legs to a lion that crawls on the ground.' She spoke thus whenever Sogolon went by her door. The innuendo would go straight home and then she would burst into laughter, that diabolical laughter which a jealous woman knows how to use so well.

Her son's infirmity weighed heavily upon Sogolon Kedjou; she had resorted to all her talent as a sorceress to give strength to her son's legs, but the rarest herbs had been useless. The king himself lost hope.

How impatient man is! Naré Maghan became imperceptibly estranged but Gnankouman Doua never ceased reminding him of the hunter's words. Sogolon became pregnant again. The king hoped for a son, but it was a daughter called Kolonkan. She resembled her mother and had nothing of her father's beauty. The disheartened king debarred Sogolon from his house and she lived in semi-disgrace for a while. Naré Maghan married the daughter of one of his allies, the king of the Kamaras. She was called Namandjé and her beauty was legendary. A year later she brought a boy into the world. When the king consulted soothsayers on the destiny of this son he received the reply that Namandjé's child would be the right hand of some mighty king. The king gave the newly-born the name of Boukari. He was to be called Manding Boukari or Manding Bory later on.

Naré Maghan was very perplexed. Could it be that the stiff-jointed son of Sogolon was the one the hunter soothsayer has foretold?

'The Almighty has his mysteries,' Gnankouman Doua would say and, taking up the hunter's words, added, 'The silk-cotton tree emerges from a tiny seed.'

One day Naré Maghan came along to the house of Nounfaïri, the blacksmith seer of Niani. He was an old, blind man. He received the king in the anteroom which served as his workshop. To the king's question he replied, 'When the seed germinates growth is not always easy; great trees grow slowly but they plunge their roots deep into the ground.'

'But has the seed really germinated?' said the king.

'Of course,' replied the blind seer. 'Only the growth is not as quick as you would like it; how impatient man is.'

This interview and Doua's confidence gave the king some assurance. To the great displeasure of Sassouma Bérété the king restored Sogolon to favour and soon another daughter was born to her. She was given the name of Djamarou.

However, all Niani talked of nothing else but the stiff-legged son of Sogolon. He was now seven and he still crawled to get about. In spite of all the king's affection, Sogolon was in despair. Naré Maghan aged and he felt his time coming to an end. Dankaran Touman, the son of Sassouma Bérété, was now a fine youth.

One day Naré Maghan made Mari Djata come to him and he spoke to the child as one speaks to an adult. 'Mari Djata, I am growing old and soon I shall be no more among you, but before death takes me off I am going to give you a present each king gives his successor. In Mali every prince has his own griot. Doua's father was my father's griot, Doua is mine and the son of Doua, Balla Fasséké here, will be your griot. Be inseparable friends from this day forward. From his mouth you will hear the history of your ancestors, you will learn the art of governing Mali according to the principles which our ancestors have bequeathed to us. I have served my term and done my duty too. I have done everything which a king of Mali ought to do. I am handing an enlarged kingdom over to you and I leave you sure allies. May your destiny be accomplished, but never forget that Niani is your capital and Mali the cradle of your ancestors.'

The child, as if he had understood the whole meaning of the king's words, beckoned Balla Fasséké to approach. He made room for him on the hide he was sitting on and then said, 'Balla, you will be my griot.'

'Yes, son of Sogolon, if it pleases God,' replied Balla Fasséké.

The king and Doua exchanged glances that radiated confidence.

The Lion's Awakening

A short while after this interview between Naré Maghan and his son the king died. Sogolon's son was no more than seven years old. The council of elders met in the king's palace. It was no use Doua's defending the king's will which reserved the throne for Mari Djata, for the council took no account of Naré Maghan's wish. With the help of Sassouma Bérété's intrigues, Dankaran Touman was proclaimed king and a regency council was formed in which the queen mother was all-powerful. A short time after, Doua died.

As men have short memories, Sogolon's son was spoken of with nothing but irony and scorn. People had seen one-eyed kings, one-armed kings, and lame kings, but a stiff-legged king had never been heard tell of. No matter how great the destiny promised for Mari Djata might be, the throne could not be given to someone who had no power in his legs; if the jinn loved him, let them begin by giving him the use of his legs. Such were the remarks that Sogolon heard every day. The queen mother, Sassouma Bérété, was the source of all this gossip.

Having become all-powerful, Sassouma Bérété persecuted Sogolon because the late Naré Maghan had preferred her. She banished Sogolon and her son to a back yard of the palace. Mari Djata's mother now occupied an old hut which had served as a lumber-room of Sassouma's.

The wicked queen mother allowed free passage to all those inquisitive people who wanted to see the child that still crawled at the age of seven. Nearly all the inhabitants of Niani filed into the palace and the poor Sogolon wept to see herself thus given over to public ridicule. Mari Djata took on a ferocious look in front of the crowd of sightseers. Sogolon found a little consolation only in the love of her eldest daughter, Kolokan. She was four and she could walk. She seemed to understand all her mother's miseries and already she helped her with the housework. Sometimes, when Sogolon was attending to the chores, it was she who stayed beside her sister Djamarou, quite small as yet.

Sogolon Kedjou and her children lived on the queen mother's left-overs, but she kept a little garden in the open ground behind the village. It was there that she passed her brightest moments looking after her onions and gnougous.[29] One day she happened to be short of condiments and went to the queen mother to beg a little baobab leaf.[30]

'Look you,' said the malicious Sassouma, 'I have a calabash full. Help yourself, you poor woman. As for me, my son knew how to walk at seven and it was he who went and picked these baobab leaves. Take them then, since your son is unequal to mine.' Then she laughed derisively with that fierce laughter which cuts through your flesh and penetrates right to the bone.

Sogolon Kedjou was dumbfounded. She had never imagined that hate could be so strong in a human being. With a lump in her throat she left Sassouma's. Outside her hut Mari Djata, sitting on his useless legs, was blandly eating out of a calabash. Unable to contain herself any longer, Sogolon burst into sobs and seizing a piece of wood, hit her son.

'Oh son of misfortune, will you never walk? Through your fault I have just suffered the greatest affront of my life! What have I done, God, for you to punish me in this way?'

Mari Djata seized the piece of wood and, looking at his mother, said, 'Mother, what's the matter?'

'Shut up, nothing can ever wash me clean of this insult.'

'But what then?'

'Sassouma has just humiliated me over a matter of a baobab leaf. At your age her own son could walk and used to bring his mother baobab leaves.'

'Cheer up, Mother, cheer up.'

'No. It's too much. I can't.'

'Very well then, I am going to walk today,' said Mari Djata. 'Go and tell my father's smiths to make me the heaviest possible iron rod. Mother, do you want just the leaves of the baobab or would you rather I brought you the whole tree?'

'Ah, my son, to wipe out this insult I want the tree and its roots at my feet outside my hut.'

Balla Fasséké, who was present, ran to the master smith, Farakourou, to order an iron rod.

Sogolon had sat down in front of her hut. She was weeping softly and holding her head between her two hands. Mari Djata went calmly back to his calabash of rice and began eating again as if nothing had happened. From time to time he looked up discreetly at his mother who was murmuring in a low voice, 'I want the whole tree, in front of my hut, the whole tree.'

All of a sudden a voice burst into laughter behind the hut. It was the wicked Sassouma telling one of her serving women about the scene of humiliation and she was laughing loudly so that Sogolon could hear. Sogolon fled into the hut and hid her face under the blankets so as not to have before her eyes this heedless boy, who was more preoccupied with eating than with anything else. With her head buried in the bed-clothes Sogolon wept and her body shook violently. Her daughter, Sogolon Djamarou, had come and sat down beside her and she said, 'Mother, Mother, don't cry. Why are you crying?'

Mari Djata had finished eating and, dragging himself along on his legs, he came and sat under the wall of the hut for the sun was scorching. What was he thinking about? He alone knew.

The royal forges were situated outside the walls and over a hundred smiths worked there. The bows, spears, arrows and shields of Niani's warriors came from there. When Balla Fasséké came to order the iron rod, Farakourou said to him, 'The great day has arrived then?'

'Yes. Today is a day like any other, but it will see what no other day has seen.'

The master of the forges, Farakourou, was the son of the old Nounfaïri, and he was a soothsayer like his father. In his workshops there was an enormous iron bar wrought by his father Nounfaïri. Everybody wondered what this bar was destined to be used for. Farakourou called six of his apprentices and told them to carry the iron bar to Sogolon's house.

When the smiths put the gigantic iron bar down in front of the hut the noise was so frightening that Sogolon, who was lying down, jumped up with a start. Then Balla Fasséké, son of Gnankouman Doua, spoke.

'Here is the great day, Mari Djata. I am speaking to you, Maghan, son of Sogolon. The waters of the Niger can efface the stain from the body, but they cannot wipe out an insult. Arise, young lion, roar, and may the bush know that from henceforth it has a master.'

The apprentice smiths were still there, Sogolon had come out and everyone was watching Mari Djata. He crept on all-fours and came to the iron bar. Supporting himself on his knees and one hand, with the other hand he picked up the iron bar without any effort and stood it up vertically. Now he was resting on nothing but his knees and held the bar with both his hands. A deathly silence had gripped all those present. Sogolon Djata closed his eyes, held tight, the muscles in his arms tensed. With a violent jerk he threw his weight on to it and his knees left the ground. Sogolon Kedjou was all eyes and watched her son's legs which were trembling as though from an electric shock. Djata was sweating and the sweat ran from his brow. In a great effort he straightened up and was on his feet at one go—but the great bar of iron was twisted and had taken the form of a bow!

Then Balla Fasséké sang out the 'Hymn to the Bow', striking up with his powerful voice:

'Take your bow, Simbon,
Take your bow and let us go.
Take your bow, Sogolon Djata.'

When Sogolon saw her son standing she stood dumb for a moment, then suddenly she sang these words of thanks to God who had given her son the use of his legs:

'Oh day, what a beautiful day,
Oh day, day of joy;
Allah Almighty, you never created a finer day.
So my son is going to walk!'

Standing in the position of a soldier at ease, Sogolon Djata, supported by his enormous rod, was sweating great beads of sweat. Balla Fasséké's song had alerted the whole palace and people came running from all over to see what had happened, and each stood bewildered before Sogolon's son. The queen mother had rushed there and when she saw Mari Djata standing up she trembled from head to foot. After recovering his breath Sogolon's son dropped the bar and the crowd stood to one side. His first steps were those of a giant. Balla Fasséké fell into step and pointing his finger at Djata, he cried:

> 'Room, room, make room!
> The lion has walked;
> Hide antelopes,
> Get out of his way.'

Behind Niani there was a young baobab tree and it was there that the children of the town came to pick leaves for their mothers. With all his might the son of Sogolon tore up the tree and put it on his shoulders and went back to his mother. He threw the tree in front of the hut and said, 'Mother, here are some baobab leaves for you. From henceforth it will be outside your hut that the women of Niani will come to stock up.'

Sogolon Djata walked. From that day forward the queen mother had no more peace of mind. But what can one do against destiny? Nothing. Man, under the influence of certain illusions, thinks he can alter the course which God has mapped out, but everything he does falls into a higher order which he barely understands. That is why Sassouma's efforts were vain against Sogolon's son, everything she did lay in the child's destiny. Scorned the day before and the object of public ridicule, now Sogolon's son was as popular as he had been despised. The multitude loves and fears strength. All Niani talked of nothing but Djata; the mothers urged their sons to become hunting companions of Djata and to share his games, as if they wanted their offspring to profit from the nascent glory of the buffalo-woman's son. The words of Doua on the name-giving day came back to men's minds and Sogolon was now surrounded with much respect; in conversation people were fond of contrasting Sogolon's modesty with the pride and malice of Soussouma Bérété. It was because the former had been an exemplary wife and mother that God had granted strength to her son's legs for, it was said, the more a wife loves and respects her husband and the more she suffers for her child, the more valorous will the child be one day. Each is the child of his mother; the child is worth no more than the mother is worth. It was not astonishing that the king Dankaran Touman was so colourless, for his mother had never shown the slightest respect to her husband and never, in the presence of the late king, did she show that humility which every wife should show before her husband. People recalled her scenes of jealousy and the spiteful remarks she circulated about her co-wife and her child. And people would conclude gravely, 'Nobody knows God's mystery. The snake has no legs yet it is as swift as any other animal that has four.'

Sogolon Djata's popularity grew from day to day and he was surrounded by a gang of children of the same age as himself. These were Fran Kamara, son of the king of Tabon; Kamandjan, son of the king of Sibi; and other princes whose fathers had sent them to the court of Niani.[31] The son of Namandjé, Manding Bory, was already joining in their games. Balla Fasséké followed Sogolon Djata all the time. He was past twenty and it was he who gave the child education and instruction according to Mandingo rules of conduct. Whether in town or at the hunt, he missed no opportunity of instructing his pupil. Many young boys of Niani came to join in the games of the royal child.

He liked hunting best of all. Farakourou, master of the forges, had made Djata a fine bow, and he proved himself to be a good shot with the bow. He made frequent hunting trips with his troops, and in the evening all Niani would be in the square to be present at the entry of the young hunters. The crowd would sing the 'Hymn to the Bow' which Balla Fasséké had composed, and Sogolon Djata was quite young when he received the title of Simbon, or master hunter, which is only conferred on great hunters who have proved themselves.

Every evening Sogolon Kedjou would gather Djata and his companions outside her hut. She would tell them stories about the beasts of the bush, the dumb brothers of man. Sogolon Djata learnt to distinguish between the animals; he knew why the buffalo was his mother's wraith and also why the lion was the protector of his father's family. He also listened to the history of the kings which Balla Fasséké told him; enraptured by the story of Alexander the Great,[32] the mighty king of gold and silver, whose sun shone over quite half the world. Sogolon initiated her son into certain secrets and revealed to him the names of the medicinal plants which every hunter should know. Thus, between his mother and his griot, the child got to know all that needed to be known.

Sogolon's son was now ten. The name Sogolon Djata in the rapid Mandingo language became Sundiata or Sondjata. He was a lad full of strength; his arms had the strength of ten and his biceps inspired fear in his companions. He had already that authoritative way of speaking which belongs to those who are destined to command. His brother, Manding Bory, became his best friend, and whenever Djata was seen, Manding Bory appeared too. They were like a man and his shadow. Fran Kamara and Kamandjan were the closest friends of the young princes, while Balla Fasséké followed them all like a guardian angel.

But Sundiata's popularity was so great that the queen mother became apprehensive for her son's throne. Dankaran Touman was the most retiring of men. At the age of eighteen he was still under the influence of his mother and a handful of old schemers. It was Sassouma Bérété who really reigned in his name. The queen mother wanted to put an end to this popularity by killing Sundiata and it was thus that one night she received the nine great witches of Mali. They were all old women. The eldest, and the most dangerous too, was called Soumosso Konkomba. When the nine old hags had seated themselves in a semi-circle around her bed the queen mother said:

'You who rule supreme at night, nocturnal powers, oh you who hold the secret of life, you who can put an end to one life, can you help me?'

'The night is potent,' said Soumosso Konkomba, 'Oh queen, tell us what is to be done, on whim must we turn the fatal blade?'

'I want to kill Sundiata,' said Sassouma. 'His destiny runs counter to my son's and he must be killed while there is still time. If you succeed, I promise you the finest rewards. First of all I bestow on each of you a cow and her calf and from tomorrow go to the royal granaries and each of you will receive a hundred measures of rice and a hundred measures of hay on my authority.'

'Mother of the king,' rejoined Soumossa Konkomba, 'life hangs by nothing but a very fine thread, but all is interwoven here below. Life has a cause, and death as well. The one comes from the other. Your hate has a cause and your action must have a cause. Mother of the king, everything holds together, our action will have no effect unless we are ourselves implicated, but Mari Djata has done us no wrong. It is, then, difficult for us to compass his death.'

'But you are also concerned,' replied the queen mother, 'for the son of Sogolon will be a scourge to us all.'

'The snake seldom bites the foot that does not walk,' said one of the witches.

'Yes, but there are snakes that attack everybody. Allow Sundiata to grow up and we will all repent of it. Tomorrow go to Sogolon's vegetable patch and make a show of picking a few gnougou leaves. Mari Djata stands guard there and you will see how vicious the boy is. He won't have any respect for your age, he'll give you a good thrashing.'

'That's a clever idea,' said one of the old hags.

'But the cause of our discomfiture will be ourselves, for having touched something which did not belong to us.'

'We could repeat the offence,' said another, 'and then if he beats us again we would be able to reproach him with being unkind, heartless. In that case we would be concerned, I think.'

'The idea is ingenious,' said Soumosso Konkomba. 'Tomorrow we shall go to Sogolon's vegetable patch.'

'Now there's a happy thought,' concluded the queen mother, laughing for joy. 'Go to the vegetable patch tomorrow and you will see that Sogolon's son is mean. Beforehand, present yourselves at the royal granaries where you will receive the grain I promised you; the cows and calves are already yours.'

The old hags bowed and disappeared into the black night. The queen mother was now alone and gloated over her anticipated victory. But her daughter, Nana Triban, woke up.

'Mother, who were you talking to? I thought I heard voices.'

'Sleep, my daughter, it is nothing. You didn't hear anything.'

In the morning, as usual, Sundiata got his companions together in front of his mother's hut and said, 'What animal are we going to hunt today?'

Kamandjan said, 'I wouldn't mind if we attacked some elephants right now.'

'Yes, I am of this opinion too,' said Fran Kamara. 'That will allow us to go far into the bush.'

And the young band left after Sogolon had filled the hunting bags with eatables. Sundiata and his companions came back late to the village, but first Djata wanted to take a look at his mother's vegetable patch as was his custom. It was dusk. There he found the nine witches stealing gnougou leaves. They made a show of running away like thieves caught red-handed.

'Stop, stop, poor old women,' said Sundiata, 'what is the matter with you to run away like this. This garden belongs to all.'

Straight away his companions and he filled the gourds of the old hags with leaves, aubergines and onions.

'Each time that you run short of condiments come to stock up here without fear.'

'You disarm us,' said one of the old crones, and another added, 'And you confound us with your bounty.'

'Listen, Djata,' said Soumosso Konkomba, 'we had come here to test you. We have no need of condiments but your generosity disarms us. We were sent here by the queen mother to provoke you and draw the anger of the nocturnal powers upon you. But nothing can be done against a heart full of kindness. And to think that we have already drawn a hundred measures of rice and a hundred measures of millet[33]—and the queen promises us each a cow and her calf in addition. Forgive us, son of Sogolon.'

'I bear you no ill-will,' said Djata. 'Here, I am returning from the hunt with my companions and we have killed ten elephants, so I will give you an elephant each and there you have some meat!'

'Thank you, son of Sogolon.'

'Thank you, child of Justice.'

'Henceforth,' concluded Soumosso Konkomba, 'we will watch over you.' And the nine witches disappeared into the night. Sundiata and his companions continued on their way to Niani and got back after dark.

'You were really frightened; those nine witches really scared you, eh?' said Sogolon Kolonkan, Djata's young sister.

'How do you know,' retorted Sundiata, astonished.

'I saw them at night hatching their scheme, but I knew there was no danger for you.' Kolonkan was well versed in the art of witchcraft and watched over her brother without his suspecting it.

Exile

But Sogolon was a wise mother. She knew everything that Sassouma could do to hurt her family, and so, one evening, after the children had eaten, she called them together and said to Sundiata.

'Let us leave here, my son; Manding Bory and Djamarou are vulnerable. They are not yet initiated into the secrets of night, they are not sorcerers. Despairing of ever injuring you, Sassouma will aim her blows at your brother or sister. Let us go away from here. You will return to reign when you are a man, for it is in Mali that your destiny must be fulfilled.'

It was the wisest course. Manding Bory, the son of Naré Maghan's third wife, Namandjé, had no gift of sorcery. Sundiata loved him very much and since the death of Namandjé he had been welcomed by Sogolon. Sundiata had found a great friend in his half-brother. You cannot choose your relatives but you can choose your friends. Manding Bory and Sundiata were real friends and it was to save his brother that Djata accepted exile.

Balla Fasséké, Djata's griot, prepared the departure in detail. But Sassouma Bérété kept her eye on Sogolon and her family.

One morning the king, Dankaran Touman, called the council together. He announced his intention of sending an embassy to the powerful king of Sosso, Soumaoro Kanté. For such a delicate mission he had thought of Balla Fasséké, son of Doua, his father's griot. The council approved the royal decision, the embassy was formed and Balla Fasséké was at the head of it.

It was a very clever way of taking away from Sundiata the griot his father had given him. Djata was out hunting and when he came back in the evening, Sogolon Kedjou told him the news. The embassy had left that very morning. Sundiata flew into a frightful rage.

'What! take away the griot my father gave me! No, he will give me back my griot.'

'Stop!' said Sogolon. 'Let it go. It is Sassouma who is acting thus, but she does not know that she obeys a higher order.'

'Come with me,' said Sundiata to his brother Manding Bory, and the two princes went out. Djata bundled aside the guards on the house of Dankaran Touman, but he was so angry that he could not utter a word. It was Manding Bory who spoke.

'Brother Dankaran Touman, you have taken away our part of the inheritance. Every prince has had his griot, and you have taken away Balla Fasséké. He was not yours but wherever he may be, Balla will always be Djata's griot. And since you do not want to have us around you we shall leave Mali and go far away from here.'

'But I will return,' added the son of Sogolon, vehemently. 'I will return, do you hear?'

'You know that you are going away but you do not know if you will come back,' the king replied.

'I *will* return, do you hear me?' Djata went on and his tone was categorical. A shiver ran through the king's whole body. Dankaran Touman trembled in every limb. The two princes went out. The queen mother hurried in and found her son in a state of collapse.

'Mother, he is leaving but he says he will return. But why is he leaving? I intend to give him back his griot, for my part. Why is he leaving?'

'Of course, he will stay behind since you so desire it, but in that case you might as well give up your throne to him, you who tremble before the threats of a ten-year-old child. Give your seat up to him since you cannot rule. As for me, I am going to return to my parent's village for I will not be able to live under the tyranny of Sogolon's son. I will go and finish my days among my kinsfolk and I will say that I had a son who was afraid to rule.'

Sassouma bewailed her lot so much that Dankaran Touman suddenly revealed himself as a man of iron. Now he desired the death of his brothers—but he let them leave, it could not be helped, but if they should ever cross his path again—! He would reign, alone, for power could not be shared!

Thus Sogolon and her children tasted exile. We poor creatures! We think we are hurting our neighbour at the time when we are working in the very direction of destiny. Our action is not us for it is commanded of us.

Sassouma Bérété thought herself victorious because Sogolon and her children had fled from Mali. Their feet ploughed up the dust of the roads. They suffered the insults which those who leave their country know of. Doors were shut against them and kings chased them from their courts. But all that was part of the great destiny of Sundiata. Seven years passed, seven winters followed one another and forgetfulness crept into the souls of men, but time marched on at an even pace. Moons succeeded moons in the same sky and rivers in their beds continued their endless course.

Seven years passed and Sundiata grew up. His body became sturdy and his misfortunes made his mind wise. He became a man. Sogolon felt the weight of her years and of the growing hump on her back, while Djata, like a young tree, was shooting up to the sky.

After leaving Niani, Sogolon and her children had sojourned at Djedeba with the king, Mansa Konkon, the great sorcerer. Djedeba was a town on the Niger two days away from Niani. The king received them with a little mistrust, but everywhere the stranger enjoys the right to hospitality, so Sogolon and her children were lodged in the very enclosure of the king and for two months Sundiata and Manding Bory joined in the games of the king's children. One night, as the children were playing at knuckle-bones outside the palace in the moonlight, the king's daughter, who was no more than twelve, said to Manding Bory, 'You know that my father is a great sorcerer.'

'Really?' said the artless Manding Bory.

'Why yes, you mean you did not know? Well anyway, his power lies in the game of wori;[34] you can play wori.'

'My brother now, he is a great sorcerer.'

'No doubt he does not come up to my father.'

'But what did you say? Your father plays at wori?'

Just then Sogolon called the children because the moon had just waned.

'Mother is calling us,' said Sundiata, who was standing at one side. 'Come Manding Bory. If I am not mistaken, you are fond of that daughter of Mansa Konkon's.'

'Yes brother, but I would have you know that to drive a cow into the stable it is necessary to take the calf in.'

'Of course, the cow will follow the kidnapper. But take care, for if the cow is in a rage so much the worse for the kidnapper.'

The two brothers went in swopping proverbs. Men's wisdom is contained in proverbs and when children wield proverbs it is a sign that they have profited from adult company. That morning Sundiata and Manding Bory did not leave the royal enclosure but played with the king's children beneath the meeting tree.[35] At the beginning of the afternoon Mansa Konkon ordered the son of Sogolon into his palace.

The king lived in a veritable maze and after several twists and turns through dark corridors a servant left Djata in a badly-lit room. He looked about him but was not afraid. Fear enters the heart of him who does not know his destiny, whereas Sundiata knew that he was striding towards a great destiny. He did not know what fear was. When his eyes were accustomed to the semi-darkness, Sundiata saw the king sitting with his back to the light on a great ox-hide. He saw some splendid weapons hanging on the walls and exclaimed:

'What beautiful weapons you have, Mansa Konkon,'[36] and, seizing a sword, he began to fence on his own against an imaginary foe. The king, astonished, watched the extraordinary child.

'You had me sent for,' said the latter, 'and here I am.' He hung the sword back up.

'Sit down,' said the king. 'It is a habit with me to invite my guests to play, so we are going to play, we are going to play at wori. But I make rather unusual conditions; if I win—and I shall win—I kill you.'

'And if it is I who win,' said Djata without being put out.

'In that case I will give you all that you ask of me. But I would have you know that I always win.'

'If I win I ask for nothing more than that sword,' said Sundiata, pointing to the sword he had brandished.

'All right,' said the king, 'you are sure of yourself, eh?' He drew up the log in which the wori holes were dug and put four pebbles in each of the holes.

'I go first,' said the king, and taking the four pebbles from one hole he dealt them out, punctuating his actions with these words:

'I don don, don don Kokodji.
Wori is the invention of a hunter.
I don don, don don Kokodji.
I am unbeatable at this game.
I am called the "exterminator king".'

And Sundiata, taking the pebbles from another hole, continued:

'I don don, don don Kokodji.
Formerly guests were scared.
I don don, don don Kokodji.
But the gold came only yesterday.
Whereas I came before yesterday.'

'Someone has betrayed me,' roared the king Mansa Konkon, 'someone has betrayed me.'

'No, king, do not accuse anybody,' said the child.

'What then?'

'It is nearly three moons since I have been living with you and you have never up to now suggested a game of wori. God is the guest's tongue. My words express only the truth because I am your guest.'

The truth was that the queen mother of Niani had sent gold to Mansa Konkon so that he would get rid of Sundiata: 'the gold came only yesterday', and Sundiata was at the king's court prior to the gold. In fact, the king's daughter had revealed the secret to Manding Bory. Then the king, in confusion, said, 'You have won, but you will not have what you asked for, and I will turn you out of my town.'

'Thank you for two months' hospitality, but I will return, Mansa Konkon.'

Once again Sogolon and her children took to the path of exile. They went away from the river and headed west. They were going to seek hospitality from the king of Tabon in the country which is called the Fouta Djallon today. This region was at that time inhabited by the Kamara blacksmiths and the Djallonkés.[37] Tabon was an impregnable town firmly entrenched behind mountains, and the king had been for a long time an ally of the Niani court. His son, Fran Kamara, had been one of the companions of Sundiata. After Sogolon's departure from Niani the companion princes of Sundiata had been sent back to their respective families.

But the king of Tabon was already old and did not want to fall out with whoever ruled at Niani. He welcomed Sogolon with kindness and advised her to go away as far as possible. He suggested that court of Ghana,[38] whose king he knew. A caravan of merchants was shortly leaving for Ghana. The old king commended Sogolon and her children to the merchants and even delayed the departure for a few days to allow the mother to recover a little from her fatigues.

It was with joy that Sundiata and Manding Bory met Fran Kamara again. The latter, not without pride, showed them round the fortresses of Tabon and had them admire the huge iron gates and the king's arsenals. Fran Kamara was very glad to receive Sundiata at his home but was very grieved when the fatal day arrived, the day of departure. The night before he had given a hunting party to the princes of Mali and the youngsters had talked in the bush like men.

'When I go back to Mali,' Sundiata had said, 'I will pass through Tabon to pick you up and we will go to Mali together.'

'Between now and then we will have grown up,' Manding Bory had added.

'I will have all the army of Tabon for my own,' Fran Kamara had said, 'The blacksmiths and the Djallonkés are excellent warriors. I already attend the gathering of armed men which my father holds once a year.'

'I will make you a great general, we will travel through many countries and emerge the strongest of all. Kings will tremble before us as a woman trembles before a man.' The son of Sogolon had spoken thus.

The exiles took to the road again. Tabon was very far from Ghana,[39] but the merchants were good to Sogolon and her children. The king had provided the mounts and the caravan headed to the north, leaving the land of Kita on the right. On the way the merchants told the princes a great deal about events of the past. Mari Djata was particularly interested in the stories bearing on the great king of the day, Soumaoro Kanté. It was to him at Sosso that Balla Fasséké had gone as envoy. Djata learnt that Saumaoro was the richest and most powerful king and even the king of Ghana paid him tribute. He was also a man of great cruelty.

The country of Ghana is a dry region where water is short. Formerly the Cissés of Ghana were the most powerful of princes. They were descended from Alexander the Great, the king of gold and silver, but ever since the Cissés had broken the ancestral taboo[40] their power had kept on declining. At the time of Sundiata the descendants of Alexander were paying tribute to the king of Sosso. After several days of travelling the caravan arrived outside Wagadou. The merchants showed Sogolon and her children the great forest of Wagadou, where the great serpent-god used to live.[41] The town was surrounded with enormous walls, very badly maintained. The travellers noticed that there were a lot of white traders at Wagadou[42] and many encampments were to be seen all around the town. Tethered camels were everywhere.

Ghana was the land of the Soninke,[43] and the people there did not speak Mandingo any more, but nevertheless there were many people who understood it, for the Soninke travel a lot. They are great traders. Their donkey caravans came heavily laden to Niani every dry season. They would set themselves up behind the town and the inhabitants would come out to barter.

The merchants made their way towards the colossal city gate. The head of the caravan spoke to the guards and one of them beckoned to Sundiata and his family to follow him, and they entered the city of the Cissés. The terraced houses did not have straw roofs in complete contrast to the towns of Mali. There were also a lot of mosques in this city, but that did not astonish Sundiata in the least, for he knew that the Cissés were very religious;[44] at Niani there was only one mosque. The travellers noticed that the anterooms were incorporated in the houses whereas in Mali the anteroom or 'bollon' was a separate building. As it was evening everybody was making his way to the mosque. The travellers could understand nothing of the prattle which the passers-by exchanged when they saw them on their way to the palace.

The palace of the king of Ghana was an imposing building. The walls were very high and you would have thought it was a dwelling-place for jinn not for men. Sogolon and her children were received by the king's brother, who understood Mandingo. The king was at prayer, so his brother made them comfortable in an enormous room and water was brought for them to quench their thirst. After the prayer the king came back into his palace and received the strangers. His brother acted as interpreter.

'The king greets the strangers.'

'We greet the king of Ghana,' said Sogolon.

'The strangers have entered Wagadou in peace, may peace be upon them in our city.'

'So be it.'

'The king gives the strangers permission to speak.'

'We are from Mali,' began Sogolon. 'The father of my children was the king Naré Maghan, who, a few years ago sent a goodwill embassy to Ghana. My husband is dead but the council has not respected his wishes and my eldest son,' (she pointed to Sundiata) 'has been excluded from the throne. The son of my co-wife was preferred before him. I have known exile. The hate of my co-wife has hounded me out of every town and I have trudged along every road with my children. Today I have come to ask for asylum with the Cissés of Wagadou.'

There was silence for a few moments; during Sogolon's speech the king and his brother had not taken their eyes off Sundiata for an instant. Any other child of eleven would have been disconcerted by the eyes of adults, but Sundiata kept cool and calmly looked at the rich decorations of the king's reception hall—the rich carpets, the fine scimitars hanging on the wall—and the splendid garments of the courtiers.

To the great astonishment of Sogolon and her children the king also spoke in the very same Mandingo language.

'No stranger has ever found our hospitality wanting. My court is your court and my palace is yours. Make yourself at home. Consider that in coming from Niani to Wagadou you have done no more than change rooms. The friendship which unites Mali and Ghana goes back to a very distant age, as the elders and griots know. The people of Mali are our cousins.'

And, speaking to Sundiata, the king said in a familiar tone of voice, 'Approach, cousin, what is your name?'

'My name is Mari-Djata and I am also called Maghan, but most commonly people call me Sundiata. As for my brother, he is called Manding Boukary, my youngest sister is called Djamarou and the other Sogolon-Kolonkan.'

'There's one that will make a great king. He forgets nobody,'

Seeing that Sogolon was very tired, the king said, 'Brother, look after our guests. Let Sogolon and her children be royally treated and from tomorrow let the princes of Mali sit among our children.'

Sogolon recovered fairly quickly from her exertions. She was treated like a queen at the court of king Soumaba Cissé. The children were clothed in the same fashion as those of Wagadou. Sundiata and Manding Bory had long smocks splendidly embroidered. They were showered with so many attentions that Manding Bory was embarrassed by them, but Sundiata found it quite natural to be treated like this. Modesty is the portion of the average man, but superior men are ignorant of humility. Sundiata even became exacting, and the more exacting he became the more the servants trembled before him. He was held in high esteem by the king, who said to his brother one day, 'If he has a kingdom one day everything will obey him because he knows how to command.'

However, Sogolon found no more lasting peace at Wagadou than she had found at the courts of Djedeba or Tabon; she fell ill after a year.

King Soumaba Cissé decided to send Sogolon and her people to Mema to the court of his cousin, Tounkara. Mema was the capital of a great kingdom on the Niger beyond the land of Do. The king reassured Sogolon of the welcome she would be given there. Doubtless the air which blew from the river would be able to restore Sogolon's health.

The children were sorry to leave Wagadou for they had made many friends, but their destiny lay elsewhere and they had to go away.

King Soumaba Cissé entrusted the travellers to some merchants who were going to Mema. It was a large caravan and the journey was done by camel. The children had for a long time accustomed themselves to these animals which were unknown in Mali. The king had introduced Sogolon and her children as members of his family and they were thus treated with much consideration by the merchants. Always keen to learn, Sundiata asked the caravaneers many questions. They were very well-informed people and told Sundiata a lot of things. He was told about the countries beyond Ghana; the land of the Arabs; the Hejaz, cradle of Islam, and of Djata's ancestors (for Bibali Bounama, the faithful servant of the Prophet, came from Hejaz). He learnt many things about Alexander the Great, too, but it was with terror that the merchants spoke of Soumaoro, the sorcerer-king, the plunderer who would rob the merchants of everything when he was in a bad mood.

A courier, despatched earlier from Wagadou, had heralded the arrival of Sogolon at Mema; a great escort was sent to meet the travellers and a proper reception was held before Mema. Archers and spearmen formed up in a double line and the merchants showed even more respect to their travelling companions. Surprisingly enough, the king was absent. It was his sister who had organized this great reception. The whole of Mema was at the city gate and you would have thought it was the king's homecoming. Here many people could speak Mandingo and Sogolon and her children could understand the amazement of the people, who were saying to each other, 'Where do they come from? Who are they?'

The king's sister received Sogolon and her children in the palace. She spoke Maninkakan[45] very well and talked to Sogolon as if she had known her for a long time. She lodged Sogolon in a wing of the palace.

As usual, Sundiata very soon made his presence felt among the young princes of Mema and in a few days he knew every corner of the royal enclosure.

The air of Mema, the air of the river, did Sogolon's health a lot of good, but she was even more affected by the friendliness of the king's sister, who was called Massiran. Massiran disclosed to Sogolon that the king had no children and that the new companions of Sundiata were only the sons of Mema's vassal kings. The king had gone on a campaign against the mountain tribes who lived on the other side of the river. It was like this every year, because as soon as these tribes were left in peace they came down from the mountains to pillage the country.

Sundiata and Manding Bory again took up their favourite pastime, hunting, and went out with the young vassals of Mema.

At the approach of the rainy season the king's return was announced. The city of Mema gave a triumphal welcome to its king. Moussa Tounkara, richly dressed, was riding on a magnificent horse while his formidable cavalry made an impressive escort. The infantry marched in ranks carrying on their heads the booty taken from the enemy. The war drums rolled while the captives, heads lowered and hands tied behind their backs, moved forward mournfully to the accompaniment of the crowd's derisive laughter.

When the king was in his palace, Massiran, his sister, introduced Sogolon and her children and handed him the letter from the king of Ghana. Moussa Tounkara was very affable and said to Sogolon, 'My cousin Soumaba recommends you and that is enough. You are at home. Stay here as long as you wish.'

It was at the court of Mema that Sundiata and Manding Bory went on their first campaign. Moussa Tounkara was a great warrior and therefore he admired strength. When Sundiata was fifteen the king took him with him on campaign. Sundiata astonished the whole army with his strength and with his dash in the charge. In the course of a skirmish against the mountaineers he hurled himself on the enemy with such vehemence that the king feared for his life, but Mansa Tounkara admired bravery too much to stop the son of Sogolon. He followed him closely to protect him and he saw with rapture how the youth sowed panic among the enemy. He had remarkable presence of mind, struck right and left and opened up for himself a glorious path. When the enemy had fled the old 'sofas'[46] said, 'There's one that'll make a good king.' Moussa Tounkara took the son of Sologon in his arms and said, 'It is destiny that has sent you to Mema. I will make a great warrior out of you.'

From that day Sundiata did not leave the king any more. He eclipsed all the young princes and was the friend of the whole army. They spoke about nothing but him in the camp. Men were even more surprised by the lucidity of his mind. In the camp he had an answer to everything and the most puzzling situations resolved themselves in his presence.

Soon it was in Mema itself that people began to talk about Sundiata. Was it not Providence which had sent this boy at a time when Mema had no heir? People already averred that Sundiata would extend his dominion from Mema to Mali. He went on all the campaigns. The enemy's incursions became rarer and rarer and the reputation of Sogolon's son spread beyond the river.

After three years the king appointed Sundiata Kan-Koro-Sigui, his Viceroy, and in the king's absence it was he who governed. Djata had now seen eighteen winters and at that time he was a tall young man with a fat neck and a powerful chest. Nobody else could bend his bow. Everyone bowed before him and he was greatly loved. Those who did not love him feared him and his voice carried authority.

The king's choice was approved of both by the army and the people; the people love all who assert themselves over them. The soothsayers of Mema revealed the extraordinary destiny of Djata. It was said that he was the successor of Alexander the Great and that he would be even greater; the soldiers already had a thousand dreams of conquest. What was impossible with such a gallant chief? Sundiata inspired confidence in the sofas by his example, for the sofa loves to see his chief share the hardship of battle.

Djata was now a man, for time had marched on since the exodus from Niani and his destiny was now to be fulfilled. Sogolon knew that the time had arrived and she had performed her task. She had nurtured the son for whom the world was waiting and she knew that now her mission was accomplished, while that of Djata was about to begin. One day she said to her son, 'Do not deceive yourself. Your destiny lies not here but in Mali. The moment has come. I have finished my task and it is yours that is going to begin, my son. But you must be able to wait. Everything in its own good time.'

Soumaoro Kanté, the Sorcerer King

While Sogolon's son was fighting his first campaign far from his native land, Mali had fallen under the domination of a new master, Soumaoro Kanté, king of Sosso.

When the embassy sent by Dankaran Touman arrived at Sosso, Suomaoro demanded that Mali should acknowledge itself tributary to Sosso. Balla Fasséké found delegates from several other kingdoms at Soumaoro's court. With his powerful army of smiths the king of Sosso had quickly imposed his power on everybody. After the defeat of Ghana and Diaghan[47] no one dared oppose him any more. Soumaoro was descended from the line of smiths called Diarisso who first harnessed fire and taught men how to work iron, but for a long time Sosso had remained a little village of no significance. The powerful king of Ghana was the master of the country. Little by little the kingdom of Sosso had grown at the expense of Ghana and now the Kantés dominated their old masters. Like all masters of fire, Soumaoro Kanté was a great sorcerer. His fetishes[48] had a terrible power and it was because of them that all kings trembled before him, for he could deal a swift death to whoever he pleased. He had fortified Sosso with a triple curtain wall and in the middle of the town loomed his palace, towering over the thatched huts of the villages.[49] He had had an immense seven-storey tower built for himself and he lived on the seventh floor in the midst of his fetishes. This is why he was called 'The Untouchable King'.

Soumaoro let the rest of the Mandingo embassy return but he kept Balla Fasséké back and threatened to destroy Niani if Dankaran Touman did not make his submission. Frightened, the son of Sassouma immediately made his submission, and he even sent his sister, Nana Triban, to the king of Sosso.

One day when the king was away, Balla Fasséké managed to get right into the most secret chamber of the palace where Soumaoro safeguarded his fetishes. When he had pushed the door open he was transfixed with amazement at what he saw. The walls of the chamber were tapestried with human skins and there was one in the middle of the room on which the king sat; around an earthenware jar nine heads formed a circle; when Balla had opened the door the water had become disturbed and a monstrous snake had raised its head. Balla Fasséké, who was also well versed in sorcery, recited some formulas and everything in the room fell quiet, so he continued his inspection. He saw on a perch above the bed three owls which seemed to be asleep; on the far wall hung strangely-shaped weapons, curved swords and knives with three cutting edges. He looked at the skulls attentively and recognized the nine kings killed by Soumaoro. To the right of the door he discovered a great balafon, bigger than he had ever seen in Mali. Instinctively he pounced upon it and sat down to play. The griot always has a weakness for music, for music is the griot's soul.

He began to play. He had never heard such a melodious balafon. Though scarcely touched by the hammer, the resonant wood gave out sounds of an infinite sweetness, notes clear and as pure as gold dust; under the skilful hand of Balla the instrument had found its master. He played with all his soul and the whole room was filled with wonderment. The drowsy owls, eyes half closed, began to move their heads as though with satisfaction. Everything seemed to come to life upon the strains of this magic music. The nine skulls resumed their earthly forms and blinked at hearing the solemn 'Vulture Tune';[50] with its head resting on the rim, the snake seemed to listen from the jar. Balla Fasséké was pleased at the effect his music had had on the strange inhabitants of this ghoulish chamber, but he quite understood that this balafon was not at all like any other. It was that of a great sorcerer. Soumaoro was the only one to play this instrument. After each victory he would come and sing his own praises. No griot had ever touched it. Not all ears were made to hear that music. Soumaoro was constantly in touch with this xylophone and no matter how far away he was, one only had to touch it for him to know that someone had got into his secret chamber.

The king was not far from the town and he rushed back to his palace and climbed up to the seventh storey. Balla Fasséké heard hurried steps in the corridor and Soumaoro bounded into the room, sword in hand.

'Who is there?' he roared. 'It is you, Balla Fasséké!'

The king was foaming with anger and his eyes burnt fiercely like hot embers. Yet without losing his composure the son of Doua changed key and improvised a song in honour of the king:

There he is, Soumaoro Kanté.
All hail, you who sit on the skins of kings.
All hail, Simbon of the deadly arrow.
I salute you, you who wear clothes of human skin.

This improvised tune greatly pleased Soumaoro and he had never heard such fine words. Kings are only men, and whatever iron cannot achieve against them, words can. Kings, too, are susceptible to flattery, so Soumaoro's anger abated, his heart filled with joy as he listened attentively to this sweet music:

All hail, you who wear clothes of human skin.
I salute you, you who sit on the skins of kings.

Balla sang and his voice, which was beautiful, delighted the king of Sosso.

'How sweet it is to hear one's praises sung by someone else; Balla Fasséké, you will nevermore return to Mali for from today you are my griot.'

Thus Balla Fasséké, whom king Naré Maghan had given to his son Sundiata, was stolen from the latter by Dankaran Touman; now it was the king of Sosso, Soumaoro Kanté, who, in turn, stole the precious griot from the son of Sassouma Bérété. In this way war between Sundiata and Soumaoro became inevitable.

History

We are now coming to the great moments in the life of Sundiata. The exile will end and another sun will arise. It is the sun of Sundiata. Griots know the history of kings and kingdoms and that is why they are the best counsellors of kings. Every king wants to have a singer to perpetuate his memory, for it is the griot who rescues the memories of kings from oblivion, as men have short memories.

Kings have prescribed destinies just like men, and seers who probe the future know it. They have knowledge of the future, whereas we griots are depositories of the knowledge of the past. But whoever knows the history of a country can read its future.

Other peoples use writing to record the past, but this invention has killed the faculty of memory among them. They do not feel the past any more, for writing lacks the warmth of the human voice. With them everybody thinks he knows, whereas learning should be a secret.[51] The prophets did not write and their words have been all the more vivid as a result. What paltry learning is that which is congealed in dumb books!

I, Djeli Mamoudou Kouyaté, am the result of a long tradition. For generations we have passed on the history of kings from father to son. The narrative was passed on to me without alteration and I deliver it without alteration, for I received it free from all untruth.

Listen now to the story of Sundiata, the Na'Kamma, the man who had a mission to accomplish.

At the time when Sundiata was preparing to assert his claim over the kingdom of his fathers, Soumaoro was the king of kings, the most powerful king in all the lands of the setting sun. The fortified town of Sosso was the bulwark of fetishism against the word of Allah. For a long time Soumaoro defied the whole world. Since his accession to the throne of Sosso he had defeated nine kings whose heads served him as fetishes in his macabre chamber. Their skins served as seats and he cut his footwear from human skin. Soumaoro was not like other men, for the jinn had revealed themselves to him and his power was beyond measure. So his countless sofas were very brave since they believed their king to be invincible. But Soumaoro was an evil demon and his reign had produced nothing but bloodshed. Nothing was taboo for him. His greatest pleasure was publicly to flog venerable old men. He had defiled every family and everywhere in his vast empire there were villages populated by girls whom he had forcibly abducted from their families without marrying them.

The tree that the tempest will throw down does not see the storm building up on the horizon. Its proud head braves the winds even when it is near its end. Soumaoro had come to despise everyone. Oh! how power can pervert a man. If man had but a mithkal[52] of divine power at his disposal the world would have been annihilated long ago. Soumaoro arrived at a point where he would stop at nothing. His chief general was his nephew the smith, Fakoli Koroma. He was the son of Soumaoro's sister, Kassia.

Fakoli had a wonderful wife, Keleya, who was a great magician like her husband. She could cook better than the three hundred wives of Soumaoro put together.[53] Soumaoro abducted Keleya and locked her up in his palace. Fakoli fell into a dreadful rage and went to his uncle and said, 'Since you are not ashamed to commit incest by taking my wife, I am freed from all my ties with you from this day forward. Henceforth I shall be on the side of your enemies. I shall combine insurgent Mandingoes with my own troops and wage war against you.' And he left Sosso with the smiths of the Koroma tribe.

It was like a signal. All those long-repressed hates and rancours burst out and everywhere men answered the call of Fakoli. Straight away Dankaran Touman, the king of Mali, mobilized and marched to join Fakoli. But Soumaoro, casting his nephew's threat aside, swooped down on Dankaran Touman, who gave up the struggle and fled to the land of the cola; and in those forested regions he founded the town of Kissidougou.[54] During this period Soumaoro, in his anger, punished all the Mandingo towns which had revolted. He destroyed the town of Niani and reduced it to ashes. The inhabitants cursed the king who had fled.

It is in the midst of calamity that man questions himself about his destiny. After the flight of Dankaran Touman, Soumaoro proclaimed himself king of Mali by right of conquest, but he was not recognized by the populace and resistance was organized in the bush. Soothsayers were consulted as to the fate of the country. The soothsayers were unanimous in saying that it would be the rightful heir to the throne who would save Mali. This heir was 'The Man with Two Names'. The elders of the court of Niani then remembered the son of Sogolon. The man with two names was no other than Maghan Sundiata.

But where could he be found? No one knew where Sogolon and her children lived. For seven years nobody had had any news of them. Now the problem was to find them. Nevertheless a search party was formed to seek him out. Among the people included must be mentioned Kountoun Manian, an old griot from the court of Naré Maghan; Mandjan Bérété, a brother of Sassouma's, who did not want to follow Dankaran Touman in flight; Singbin Mara Cissé, a divine of the court, Siriman Touré, another divine; and, finally, a woman, Magnouma. According to the clues of the soothsayers they had to search towards the riverine lands, that is, towards the east. The searchers left Mali while war raged between Sosso Soumaoro and his nephew Fakoli Koroma.

The Baobab Leaves

At Mema Sundiata learnt that Soumaoro had invaded Mali and that his own brother, Dankaran Touman, had fled. He learnt also that Fakoli was holding his own against the king of Sosso. That year the kingdom of Mema was at peace and the king's viceroy had a lot of leisure time. As always, he went out hunting, but since the news about Mali had arrived Sundiata had become very gloomy. The aged Sogolon was ill. Manding Bory was fifteen and was now a lively youth like his brother and friend Sundiata. Djata's sisters had grown up and Kolonkan was now a tall maiden of marriageable age. Now that Sogolon had grown old it was she who did the cooking and she often went to the town market with her serving women.

Well, one day when she was at the market she noticed a woman who was offering for sale nafiola[55] and gnougou, condiments unknown to the people of Mema, who looked in astonishment at the woman who was selling them. Kolonkan approached. She recognized baobab leaves and many other vegetables which her mother used to grow in her garden at Niani.

'Baobab leaves,' she muttered, 'and gnougou, I know these,' she said, taking some.

'How do you know them princess?' said the woman. 'I have been offering them for sale here in the market of Mema for days but nobody wants any here.'

'But I am from Mali. At home my mother used to have a vegetable garden and my brother would go to seek baobab leaves for us.'

'What is your brother's name princess?'

'He is called Sogolon Djata, and the other one is called Manding Bory. I also have a sister called Sogolon Djamarou.'

Meanwhile a man had drawn near and he spoke thus to Sogolin Kolonkan, 'Princess, we are also from Mali. We are merchants and are going from town to town. I am selling colas myself. Here, I give you one. Princess, could your mother receive us today?'

'Of course, she will be happy to talk to people who come from Mali. Don't budge from here and I'll go and talk to her about it.'

Kolonkan, without caring about the scandal of the viceroy's sister being seen running across the market-place, had knotted her long dress about her middle and was running at full speed towards the royal enclosure.

'N'na,[56] she said, out of breath and addressing her mother, 'I have found baobab leaves, gnougou and many other things at the market, look. Some merchants from Mali are selling them. They would like to see you.'

Sogolon took the baobab leaves and gnougou in her hand and put her nose to them as though to inhale all the scent. She opened her eyes wide and looked at her daughter.

'They come from Mali, you say? Then run to the market and tell them that I am waiting for them, run, my daughter.'

Sogolon remained alone. She was turning the precious condiments over and over in her hands when she heard Sundiata and Manding Bory returning from the hunt.

'Hail, mother. We have returned,' said Manding Bory.

'Hail, mother,' said Sundiata, 'we have brought you some game.'

'Come in and sit down,' she said, and held out of them what she had in her hand.

'Why, it's gnougou,' said Sundiata, 'where did you find it? The people here grow it very little.'

'Yes, some merchants from Mali are offering it for sale in the market. Kolonkan has gone to fetch them for they want to see me. We are going to have some news of Mali.'

Kolonkan soon appeared followed by four men and a woman; straight away Sogolon recognized the eminent members of her husband's court. The salutations began and greetings were exchanged with all the refinement demanded by Mandingo courtesy. At last Sogolon said, 'Here are my children; they have grown up far from their native country. Now let us talk of Mali.'

The travellers quickly exchanged meaningful glances, then Mandjan Bérété, Sassouma's brother, began to speak in these words:

'I give thanks to God the Almighty that we are here in the presence of Sogolon and her children. I give thanks to God that our journey will not have been in vain. It is two months since we left Mali. We went from one royal town to another posing as merchants and Magnouma offered vegetables of Mali for sale. In these eastern lands people are unacquainted with these vegetables. But at Mema our plan worked out perfectly. The person who bought some gnougou was able to tell us of your fate and that person, by a crowning stroke of fortune, turned out to be Sogolon Kolonkan.'

'Alas! I bring you sad tidings. That is my mission. Soumaoro Kanté, the powerful king of Sosso, has heaped death and desolation upon Mali. The king, Dankaran Touman, has fled and Mali is without a master, but the war is not finished yet. Courageous men have taken to the bush and are waging tireless war against the enemy. Fakoli Koroma, the nephew of the king of Sosso, is fighting pitilessly against his incestuous uncle who robbed him of his wife. We have consulted the jinn and they have replied that only the son of Sogolon can deliver Mali. Mali is saved because we have found you, Sundiata.'

'Maghan Sundiata, I salute you; king of Mali, the throne of your fathers awaits you. Whatever rank you may hold here, leave all these honours and come and deliver your fatherland. The brave await you, come and restore rightful authority to Mali. Weeping mothers pray only in your name, the assembled kings await you, for your name alone inspires confidence in them. Son of Sogolon, your hour has come, the words of the old Gnankouman Doua are about to come to pass, for you are the giant who will crush the giant Soumaoro.'

After these words a profound silence reigned over the room of Sogolon. She, her eyes cast down, remained silent; Kolonkan and Manding Bory had their eyes fixed on Sundiata.

'Very well,' he said, 'it is no longer the time for words. I am going to ask the king's leave and we will return immediately. Manding Bory, take charge of the envoys from Mali. The king will return this evening and we will set out first thing tomorrow.'

Sundiata got up and all the envoys stood up while Djata went out. He was already king.

The king returned to Mema at nightfall. He had gone to spend the day in one of his neighbouring residences. The viceroy was not at the king's reception and nobody knew where he was. He returned at night and before going to bed he went and saw Sogolon. She had a fever and was trembling under the blankets. With a feeble voice she wished her son good night. When Sundiata was in his chamber alone he turned to the east and spoke thus:

'Almighty God, the time for action has come. If I must succeed in the reconquest of Mali, Almighty, grant that I may bury my mother in peace here.' Then he lay down.

In the morning, Sogolon Kedjou, the buffalo woman, passed away, and all the court of Mema went into mourning, for the viceroy's mother was dead. Sundiata went to see the king, who offered his condolences. He said to the king, 'King, you gave me hospitality at your court when I was without shelter. Under your orders I went on my first campaign. I shall never be able to thank you for so much kindness. However, my mother is dead; but I am now a man and I must return to Mali to claim the kingdom of my fathers. Oh king, I give you back the powers you conferred upon me, and I ask leave to depart. In any case, allow me to bury my mother before I go.'

These words displeased the king. Never did he think that the son of Sogolon could leave him. What was he going to seek in Mali? Did he not live happy and respected by all at Mema? Was he not already the heir to the throne of Mema? How ungrateful, thought the king, the son of another is always the son of another.

'Ungrateful creature,' said the king, 'since this is how it is, go away, leave my kingdom, but take your mother's remains with you; you will not bury her at Mema.'

But after a pause he went on, 'Very well then, since you insist on burying your mother, you will pay me the price of the earth where she will lie.'

'I will pay later,' replied Sundiata. 'I will pay when I reach Mali.'

'No, now, or you will have to take your mother's corpse with you.'

Then Sundiata got up and went out. He came back after a short while and brought the king a basket full of bits of pottery, guinea fowl feathers, feathers of young partridges and wisps of straw. He said, 'Very well king, here is the price of the land.'

'You are mocking, Sundiata, take your basket of rubbish away. That is not the price of the land. What do you mean by it?'

Then the old Arab who was the king's adviser said, 'Oh king, give this young man the land where his mother must rest. What he has brought you has a meaning. If you refuse him the land he will make war on you. These broken pots and wisps of straw indicate that he will destroy the town. It will only be recognized by the fragments of broken pots. He will make such a ruin of it that guinea-fowl and young partridges will come to take their dust baths there. Give him the land for if he reconquers his kingdom he will deal gently with you, your family, and his will be forever allied.'

The king understood. He gave him the land and Sogolon received her funeral honours with all the regal obsequies.

The Return

Every man to his own land! If it is foretold that your destiny should be fulfilled in such and such a land, men can do nothing against it. Mansa Tounkara could not keep Sundiata back because the destiny of Sogolon's son was bound up with that of Mali. Neither the jealousy of a cruel stepmother, nor her wickedness, could alter for a moment the course of great destiny.

The snake, man's enemy, is not long-lived, yet the serpent that lives hidden will surely die old. Djata was strong enough now to face his enemies. At the age of eighteen he had the stateliness of the lion and the strength of the buffalo. His voice carried authority, his eyes were live coals, his arm was iron, he was the husband of power.

Moussa Tounkara, king of Mema, gave Sundiata half of his army. The most valiant came forward of their own free will to follow Sundiata in the great adventure. The cavalry of Mema, which he had fashioned himself, formed his iron squadron. Sundiata, dressed in the Muslim fashion of Mema, left the town at the head of his small but redoubtable army. The whole population sent their best wishes with him. He was surrounded by five messengers from Mali and Manding Bory rode proudly at the side of his brother. The horsemen of Mema formed behind Djata a bristling iron squadron. The troop took the direction of Wagadou, for Djata did not have enough troops to confront Soumaoro directly, and so the king of Mema advised him to go to Wagadou and take half of the men of the king, Soumaba Cissé. A swift messenger had been sent there and so the king of Wagadou came out in person to meet Sundiata and his troops. He gave Sundiata half of his cavalry and blessed the weapons. Then Manding Bory said to his brother, 'Djata, do you think yourself able to face Soumaoro now?'

'No matter how small a forest may be, you can always find there sufficient fibres to tie up a man. Numbers mean nothing; it is worth that counts. With my cavalry I shall clear myself a path to Mali.'

Djata gave out his orders. They would head south, skirting Soumaoro's kingdom. The first objective to be reached was Tabon, the iron-gated town in the midst of the mountains, for Sundiata had promised Fran Kamara that he would pass by Tabon before returning to Mali. He hoped to find that his childhood companion had become king. It was a forced march and during the halts the divines, Singbin Mara Cissé and Mandjan Bérété, related to Sundiata the history of Alexander the Great and several other heroes, but of all of them Sundiata preferred Alexander, the king of gold and silver, who crossed the world from west to east. He wanted to outdo his prototype both in the extent of his territory and the wealth of his treasury.

However, Soumaoro Kanté, being a great sorcerer, knew that the son of Sogolon had set out and that he was coming to lay claim to Mali. The soothsayers told him to forestall this calamity by attacking Sundiata, but good fortune makes men blind. Soumaoro was busy fighting Fakoli, the insurgent nephew who was holding out against him. Even before he had given battle the name of Sundiata was already well known throughout the kingdom. Those of the western frontier who had seen his army marching southwards spread extraordinary reports. Having just ascended the throne that year, Fran Kamara, the friend of Sundiata, had revolted in his turn against Soumaoro. In place of the policy of prudence followed by the old king of Tabon, Fran Kamara pursued a policy of war. Proud of his troops and above all spurred on by the imminent arrival of Sundiata, Fran Kamara, now called Tabon Wana (the Dread One of Tabon), had called to arms all the smiths and the mountain-dwelling Djallonkés.

Soumaoro sent a detachment under his son Sosso Balla to block Sundiata's route to Tabon. Sosso Balla was about the same age as Sundiata. He promptly deployed his troops at the entrance to the mountains to oppose Sundiata's advance to Tabon.

In the evening, after a long day's march, Sundiata arrived at the head of the great valley which led to Tabon. The valley was quite black with men, for Sosso Balla had deployed his men everywhere in the valley, and some were positioned on the heights which dominated the way through. When Djata saw the layout of Sosso Balla's men he turned to his generals laughing.

'Why are you laughing, brother, you can see that the road is blocked.'

'Yes, but no mere infantrymen can halt my course towards Mali,' replied Sundiata.

The troops stopped. All the war chiefs were of the opinion that they should wait until the next day to give battle because, they said, the men were tired.

'The battle will not last long,' said Sundiata, 'and the men will have time to rest. We must not allow Soumaoro the time to attack Tabon.'

Sundiata was immovable, so the orders were given and the war drums began to beat. On his proud horse Sundiata turned to right and left in front of his troops. He entrusted the rearguard, composed of a part of the Wagadou cavalry, to his younger brother Manding Bory. Having drawn his sword, Sundiata led the charge, shouting his war cry.

The Sossos were surprised by this sudden attack for they all thought that the battle would be joined the next day. The lightning that flashes across the sky is slower, the thunderbolts less frightening and floodwaters less surprising than Sundiata swooping down on Sosso Balla and his smiths. In a trice, Sundiata was in the middle of the Sossos like a lion in the sheepfold. The Sossos, trampled under the hooves of his fiery charger, cried out. When he turned to the right the smiths of Soumaoro fell in their tens, and when he turned to the left his sword made heads fall as when someone shakes a tree of ripe fruit. The horsemen of Mema wrought a frightful slaughter and their long lances pierced flesh like a knife sunk into a paw-paw. Charging ever forwards, Sundiata looked for Sosso Balla; he caught sight of him and like a lion bounded towards the son of Soumaoro, his sword held aloft. His arm came sweeping down but at that moment a Sosso warrior came between Djata and Sosso Balla and was sliced like a calabash. Sosso Balla did not wait and disappeared from amidst his smiths. Seeing their chief in flight, the Sossos gave way and fell into a terrible rout. Before the sun disappeared behind the mountains there were only Djata and his men left in the valley. Manding Bory, who was keeping an eye on the men perched on the heights, seeing that his brother had got the upper hand, dispatched some horsemen across the mountains to dislodge the Sossos. The Sossos were pursued until nightfall and several of them were taken prisoner.

Tabon Wana arrived too late, for the victory had already fallen to the son of Sogolon. The meeting of the two armies occasioned an all-night celebration in the very valley where the Sossos had been defeated. Tabon Wana Fran Kamara had a lot of food brought to the army of Sundiata and dancing went on all night, then at break of day the victors entered impregnable Tabon to the cheering of women standing on the ramparts.

The news of the battle of Tabon spread like wildfire in the plains of Mali. It was known that Soumaoro was not present at the battle, but the mere fact that his troops had retreated before Sundiata sufficed to give hope to all the peoples of Mali. Soumaoro realized that from now on he would have to reckon with this young man. He got to know of the prophecies of Mali, yet he was still too confident. When Sosso Balla returned with the remnant he had managed to save at Tabon, he said to his father, 'Father, he is worse than a lion; nothing can withstand him.'

'Be quiet, you ill-starred son,' Soumaoro had said, 'what, you tremble before a lad of your own age!' Nonetheless, these words of Balla made a deep impression on Soumaoro and he decided to march on Tabon with the largest of his forces.

The son of Sogolon had already decided on his plan of campaign—to beat Soumaoro, destroy Sosso and return triumphantly to Niani. He now had five army corps at his disposal, namely, the cavalry and infantry of Mema, those of Wagadon and the three tribes forming the army of Tabon Wana Fran Kamara. He must assume the offensive as soon as possible.

Soumaoro marched out to meet Sundiata. The meeting took place at Neguéboria in the Bouré country.[57] As usual, the son of Sogolon wanted to join battle straight away. Soumaoro thought to draw Sundiata into the plain, but Sundiata did not allow him the time to do it. Compelled to give battle, the king of Sosso drew up his men across the narrow valley of Neguéboria, the wings of his army occupying the slopes. Sundiata adopted a very original form of deployment. He formed a tight square with all his cavalry in the front line. The archers of Wagadou and Tabon were stationed at the back. Soumaoro was on one of the hills dominating the valley and he could be distinguished by his height and his helmet bristling with horns. Under an overpowering sun the trumpets sounded, on both sides the drums and bolons echoed and courage entered the hearts of the Sofas. Sundiata charged at the gallop and the valley soon disappeared in a cloud of red dust kicked up by thousands of feet and hooves. Without giving an inch, the smiths of Soumaoro stopped the wave.

As though detached from the battle, Soumaoro Kanté watched from the top of his hill. Sundiata and the king of Tabon were laying about them with mighty blows. Sundiata could be distinguished by his white turban and Soumaoro could see the breach he was opening up in the middle of his troops. The centre was about to cave in under the crushing pressure of Djata.

Soumaoro made a sign and from the hills came smiths swooping down into the bottom of the valley to encircle Sundiata. Then, without the slightest order from Sundiata, who was in the thick of the struggle, his square stretched and elongated itself into a great rectangle. Everything had been foreseen. The change was so quick that Soumaoro's men, halted in their mad career, could not use their weapons. In Djata's rear the archers of Wagadou and those of Tabon, on one knee, shot arrows into the sky, which fell thickly, like a rain of iron, on the ranks of Soumaoro. Like a stretching piece of elastic, Djata's line ascended to attack the hills. Djata caught sight of Sosso Balla and bore down on him, but the latter slipped away and the warriors of the buffalo woman's son raised a huzza of triumph. Soumaoro rushed up and his presence in the centre revived the courage of the Sossos. Sundiata caught sight of him and tried to cut a passage through to him. He struck to the right and struck to the left and trampled underfoot. The murderous hooves of his 'Daffeké'[58] dug into the chests of the Sossos. Soumaoro was now within spear range and Sundiata reared up his horse and hurled his weapon. It whistled away and bounced off Soumaoro's chest as off a rock and fell to the ground. Sogolon's son bent his bow but with a motion of the hand Soumaoro caught the arrow in flight and showed it to Sundiata as if to say 'Look, I am invulnerable.'

Furious, Sundiata snatched up his spear and with his head bent charged at Soumaoro, but as he raised his arm to strike his enemy he noticed that Soumaoro had disappeared. Manding Bory riding at his side pointed to the hill and said, 'Look, brother.'

Sundiata saw Soumaoro on the hill, sitting on his black-coated horse. How could he have done it, he who was only two paces from Sundiata? But what power had he spirited himself away on to the hill? The son of Sogolon stopped fighting to watch the king of Sosso. The sun was already very low and Soumaoro's smiths gave way but Sundiata did not give the order to pursue the enemy. Suddenly, Soumaoro disappeared!

How can I vanquish a man capable of disappearing and reappearing where and when he likes? How can I affect a man invulnerable to iron? Such were the questions which Sogolon's son asked himself. He had been told many things about Sosso-Soumaoro but he had given little credence to so much gossip. Didn't people say that Soumaoro could assume sixty-nine different shapes to escape his enemies? According to some, he could transform himself into a fly in the middle of the battle and come and torment his opponent; he could melt into the wind when his enemies encircled him too closely—and many other things.

The battle of Neguéboria showed Djata, if he needed to be shown, that to beat the king of Sosso other weapons were necessary.

The evening of Neguéboria, Sundiata was master of the field, but he was in a gloomy mood. He went away from the field of battle with its agonized cries of the wounded, and Manding Bory and Tabon Wana watched him go. He headed for the hill where he had seen Soumaoro after his miraculous disappearance from the midst of his troops. From the top of the hill he watched the compact mass of Soumaoro's smiths withdrawing in a cloud of dust.

'How was he able to escape me? Why did neither my spear nor my arrow wound him?' he wondered. 'What is the jinn that protects Soumaoro? What is the mystery of his power?'

He dismounted from his horse and picked up a piece of the earth which Soumaoro's horse had trampled on. Complete darkness had already fallen, the village of Neguéboria was not far away and the Djallonkés came out in a crowd to greet Sundiata and his men. The fires were already lit in the camp and the soldiers were beginning to prepare a meal, but what was their joy when they saw a long procession of girls from Neguéboria carrying on their heads enormous gourds of rice. All the sofas took up the girls' song in chorus. The chief of the village and its notables followed behind. Djata came down from the hill and received the Djallonké chief of Neguéboria, who was a vassal of Tabon Wana. For the sofas the day had been a victory because Soumaoro had fled, so the drums of war became drums of joy and Djata let his men celebrate what they called a victory. He stayed in his tent. In the life of every man there comes a moment when doubt settles in and the man questions himself on his own destiny, but on this evening it was not yet doubt which assailed Djata, for he was thinking rather of what powers he could employ to injure Sosso-Soumaoro. He did not sleep that night. At daybreak they struck camp. Peasants on their line of march told Sundiata that Soumaoro and his men were making a forced march without stopping so only in the evening did Sundiata halt the army to take a little food and rest. This was near the village of Kankigné. The men set up camp in the middle of the plain whilst guards were stationed on the heights. As usual, the men grouped themselves by tribes and busied themselves cooking their food. The tent of Sundiata stood in the middle of the camp surrounded by makeshift huts hastily built by the Mema horsemen.

But all of a sudden the sound of warning horns was heard. The men hardly had time to snatch their weapons before the camp was surrounded by enemies looming out of the darkness. The men of Mema were used to these surprise attacks on their camp and therefore unsaddled their horses. As the camp did not constitute a single unit, each kin group had to defend itself individually. Having escaped encirclement, Djata and the horsemen of Mema went to the help of Tabon Wana who seemed to be overwhelmed by numbers. In the pitch dark, no one knows how the men acquitted themselves. All that can be said is that the son of Sogolon broke the vice that was squeezing the breath out of Tabon Wana. The archers of Wagadou had quickly pulled themselves together and fired into the air torches and flaming arrows which fell among the enemy. Suddenly there was a panic. The burning brands crashed on to the bare backs of Soumaoro's sofas, cries of pain filled the sky and the Sossos began a headlong retreat while the cavalry cut them to pieces. The overwhelmed Sossos took to flight, again leaving many captives in the hands of Sundiata's men. Leaving to Tabon Wana the task of regrouping the men, Sundiata pursued the enemy with his cavalry to beyond the village of Kankigné. When he returned the struggle was over. The Sossos' night attack had caused more fright than real damage. On the ground near Tabon Wana's tent were found several split skulls. The king of Tabon never hit a man twice! The battle of Kankigné was not a great victory but it demoralized the Sossos. However, there had been great fear in Djata's ranks and that is why the griots sing:

'Kankigné Tabe bara djougonya.'[59]

The Names of the Heroes

The surprise attack at Kankigné had turned out badly for Soumaoro and succeeded only in increasing the wrath of Sundiata, who decimated the whole of the Sosso rearguard.

Soumaoro got back to Sosso to recover his strength while on all sides villages opened their gates to Sundiata. In all these villages Sundiata recruited soldiers. In the same way as light precedes the sun, so the glory of Sundiata, overleaping the mountains, shed itself on all the Niger plain.

All the rebellious kings of the savanna country had gathered at Sibi under the command of Kamandjan, the very same childhood friend of Sundiata and now himself the king of Sibi. Kamandjan and Tabon Wana were cousins, the former being the king of the Dalikimbon group of Kamaras, the latter being king of the iron-working Kamaras who were called Sinikimbon. Thus the Niani trio were going to meet again. Fakoli, the nephew of Soumaoro, had gone right to the south to recruit troops. He was bent on having his revenge on his uncle and recovering his wife, Keleya, she who was called 'the woman of the three hundred and thirty-three gourds of rice.'

Sundiata had now entered the region of the plains, the land of the powerful Niger. The trees that he saw were those of Mali, everything indicated that old Mali was near.

All the allies had arranged to meet up in the great plain of Sibi, and all the children of the savanna were there about their kings. There they were, the valorous sons of Mali, awaiting what destiny had promised them. Pennants[60] of all colours fluttered above the sofas divided up by tribes.

With whom should I begin; with whom end?

I shall begin with Siara Kouman Konaté. Siara Kouman Konaté, the cousin of Sundiata was there. He was the ancestor of those who live in the land of Toron. His spear-armed troops formed a thick hedge around him.

I will also mention Faony Kondé, Faony Diarra, the king of the land of Do whence came Sogolon. Thus the uncle had come to meet his nephew. Faony, king of Do and Kri, was surrounded by sofas armed with deadly arrows. They formed a solid wall around his standard.

You also will I cite, Mansa Traoré, king of the Traoré tribe; Mansa Traoré, the double-sighted king, was at Sibi. Mansa Traoré could see what was going on behind him just as other men can see in front of them. His sofas, formidable archers with quivers on their shoulders, thronged around him.

As for you, Kamandjan, I cannot forget you among those whom I extol, for you are the father of the Dalikimbon Kamaras. The Kamaras, armed with long spears, raised their menacing pikes around Kamandjan.

In short, all the sons of Mali were there, all those who say 'N'ko',[61] all who speak the clear language of Mali were represented at Sibi.

When the son of the buffalo woman and his army appeared, the trumpets, drums and tam-tams blended with the voices of the griots. The son of Sogolon was surrounded by his swift horsemen and his horse pranced along. All eyes were fixed on the child of Mali, who shone with glory and splendour. When he was within call, Kamandjan made a gesture and the drums, tam-tams and voices fell silent. Leaving the ranks, the king of Sibi went towards Sundiata and cried, 'Maghan Sundiata, son of Sogolon, son of Naré Maghan, assembled Mali awaits you. Hail to you, I am Kamandjan, king of Sibi.'

Raising his hand, Maghan Sundiata spoke thus: 'I salute you all, sons of Mali, and I salute you, Kamandjan. I have come back, and as long as I breathe Mali will never be in thrall—rather death than slavery. We will live free because our ancestors lived free. I am going to avenge the indignity that Mali has undergone.'

A shout of joy issuing from thousands of throats filled the whole heaven. The drums and tam-tams rumbled while the griots struck up Balla Fasséké's 'Hymn to the Bow'. It was thus that Sundiata met the sons of Mali gathered at Sibi.

Nana Triban and Balla Fasséké

Sundiata and his mighty army stopped at Sibi for a few days. The road into Mali lay open, but Soumaoro was not yet vanquished. The king of Sosso had mustered a powerful army and his sofas were numbered by the thousand. He had raised contingents in all the lands over which he held sway and got ready to pounce again on Mali.

With scrupulous care, Sundiata had made his preparations at Sibi. Now he had sufficient sofas to meet Soumaoro in the open field, but it was not a question of having a lot of troops. In order to defeat Soumaoro it was necessary first of all to destroy his magical power. At Sibi, Sundiata decided to consult the soothsayers, of whom the most famous in Mali were there.

On their advice Djata had to sacrifice a hundred white bulls, a hundred white rams and a hundred white cocks. It was in the middle of this slaughter that it was announced to Sundiata that his sister Nana Triban and Balla Fasséké, having been able to escape from Sosso, had now arrived. Then Sundiata said to Tabon Wana, 'If my sister and Balla have been able to escape from Sosso, Soumaoro has lost the battle.'

Leaving the site of the sacrifices, Sundiata returned to Sibi and met his sister and his griot.

'Hail, my brother,' said Nana Triban.

'Greetings, sister.'

'Hail Sundiata,' said Balla Fasséké.

'Greetings, my griot.'

After numerous salutations, Sundiata asked the fugitives to relate how they had been able to elude the vigilance of a king such as Soumaoro. But Triban was weeping for joy. Since the time of their childhood she had shown much sympathy towards the crippled child that Sundiata had been. Never had she shared the hate of her mother, Sassouma Bérété.

'You know, Djata,' she said, weeping, 'for my part I did not want you to leave the country. It was my mother who did all that. Now Niani is destroyed, its inhabitants scattered, and there are many whom Soumaoro has carried off into captivity in Sosso.'

She cried worse than ever. Djata was sympathetic to all this, but he was in a hurry to know something about Sosso. Balla Fasséké understood and said, 'Triban, wipe away your tears and tell your story, speak to your brother. You know that he has never thought ill of you, and besides, all that was in his destiny.'

Nana Triban wiped her tears away and spoke.

'When you left Mali, my brother sent me by force to Sosso to be the wife of Soumaoro, whom he greatly feared. I wept a great deal at the beginning but when I saw that perhaps all was not lost I resigned myself for the time being. I was nice to Soumaoro and was the chosen one among his numerous wives. I had my chamber in the great tower where he himself lived. I knew how to flatter him and make him jealous. Soon I became his confidante and I pretended to hate you, to share the hate which my mother bore you. It was said that you would come back one day, but I swore to him that you would never have the presumption to claim a kingdom you had never possessed, and that you had left never to see Mali again. However, I was in constant touch with Balla Fasséké, each of us wanting to pierce the mystery of Soumaoro's magic power. One night I took the bull by the horns and said to Soumaoro: "Tell me, oh you whom kings mention with trembling, tell me Soumaoro, are you a man like others or are you the same as the jinn who protects humans? No one can bear the glare of your eyes, your arm has the strength of ten arms. Tell me, king of kings, tell me what jinn protects you so that I can worship him also." These words filled him with pride and he himself boasted to me of the might of his Tana.[62] That very night he took me into his magic chamber and told me all.

'Then I redoubled my zeal to show myself faithful to his cause, I seemed more overwhelmed than him. It was even he who went to the extent of telling me to take courage, that nothing was yet lost. During all this time, in complicity with Balla Fasséké, I was preparing for the inevitable flight. Nobody watched over me any more in the royal enclosure, of which I knew the smallest twists and turns. And one night when Soumoro was away, I left that fearsome tower. Balla Fasséké was waiting for me at the gate to which I had the key. It was thus, brother, that we left Sosso.'

Balla Fasséké took up the story.

'We hastened to you. The news of the victory of Tabon made me realize that the lion had burst his chains. Oh son of Sogolon, I am the word and you are the deed, now your destiny begins.'

Sundiata was very happy to recover his sister and his griot. He now had the singer who would perpetuate his memory by his words. There would not be any heroes if deeds were condemned to man's forgetfulness, for we ply our trade to excite the admiration of the living, and to evoke the veneration of those who are to come.

Djata was informed that Soumaoro was advancing along the river and was trying to block his route to Mali. The preparations were complete, but before leaving Sibi, Sundiata arranged a great military review in the camp so that Balla Fasséké, by his words, should strengthen the hearts of his sofas. In the middle of a great circle formed by the sofas, Balla Fasséké extolled the heroes of Mali. To the king of Tabon he said: 'You whose iron arm can split ten skulls at a time, you, Tabon Wana, king of the Sinikimbon and the Djallonké, can you show me what you are capable of before the great battle is joined?'

The griot's words made Fran Kamara leap up. Sword in hand and mounted on his swift steed he came and stood before Sundiata and said, 'Maghan Sundiata, I renew my oath to you in the sight of all the Mandingoes gathered together. I pledge myself to conquer or to die by your side. Mali will be free or the smiths of Tabon will be dead.'

The tribes of Tabon shouted their approval, brandishing their weapons, and Fran Kamara, stirred by the shouts of the sofas, spurred his charger and charged forward. The warriors opened their ranks and he bore down on a great mahogany tree. With one stroke of his sword he split the giant tree just as one splits a paw-paw. The flabbergasted army shouted, 'Wassa Wassa . . . Ayé . . .'[63]

Then, coming back to Sundiata, his sword held aloft, the king of Tabon said, 'Thus on the Niger plain will the smiths of Tabon cleave those of Sosso in twain.' And the hero came and fell in beside Sundiata.

Turning towards Kamandjan, the king of Sibi and cousin of the king of Tabon, Balla Fasséké said, 'Where are you, Kamandjan, where is Fama Djan?[64] Where is the king of the Dalikimbon Kamaras. Kamandjan of Sibi, I salute you. But what will I have to relate of you to future generations?'

Before Balla had finished speaking, the king of Sibi, shouting his war-cry, started his fiery charger off at full gallop. The sofas, stupefied, watched the extraordinary horseman head for the mountain that dominates Sibi. . . . Suddenly a tremendous din filled the sky, the earth trembled under the feet of the sofas and a cloud of red dust covered the mountain. Was this the end of the world? . . . But slowly the dust cleared and the sofas saw Kamandjan coming back holding a fragment of a sword. The mountain of Sibi, pierced through and through, disclosed a wide tunnel!

Admiration was at its highest pitch. The army stood speechless and the king of Sibi, without saying a word, came and fell in beside Sundiata.

Balla Fasséké mentioned all the chiefs by name and they all performed great feats; then the army, confident in its leadership, left Sibi.

Krina

Sundiata went and pitched camp at Dayala in the valley of the Niger. Now it was he who was blocking Soumaoro's road to the south. Up till that time, Sundiata and Soumaoro had fought each other without a declaration of war. One does not wage war without saying why it is being waged. Those fighting should make a declaration of their grievances to begin with. Just as a sorcerer ought not to attack someone without taking him to task for some evil deed, so a king should not wage war without saying why he is taking up arms.

Soumaoro advanced as far as Krina, near the village of Dayala on the Niger and decided to assert his rights before joining battle. Soumaoro knew that Sundiata also was a sorcerer, so, instead of sending an embassy, he committed his words to one of his owls. The night bird came and perched on the roof of Djata's tent and spoke. The son of Sogolon in his turn sent his own to Soumaoro. Here is the dialogue of the sorcerer kings:

'Stop, young man. Henceforth I am the king of Mali. If you want peace, return to where you came from,' said Soumaoro.

'I am coming back, Soumaoro, to recapture my kingdom. If you want peace you will make amends to my allies and return to Sosso where you are the king.'

'I am king of Mali by force of arms. My rights have been established by conquest.'

'Then I will take Mali from you by force of arms and chase you from my kingdom.'

'Know, then, that I am the wild yam of the rocks; nothing will make me leave Mali.'

'Know, also that I have in my camp seven master smiths who will shatter the rocks. Then, yam, I will eat you.'

'I am the poisonous mushroom that makes the fearless vomit.'

'As for me, I am the ravenous cock, the poison does not matter to me.'

'Behave yourself, little boy, or you will burn your foot, for I am the red-hot cinder.'

'But me, I am the rain that extinguishes the cinder; I am the boisterous torrent that will carry you off.'

'I am the mighty silk-cotton tree that looks from on high on the tops of other trees.'

'And I, I am the strangling creeper that climbs to the top of the forest giant.'

'Enough of this argument. You shall not have Mali.'

'Know that there is not room for two kings on the same skin, Soumaoro; you will let me have your place.'

'Very well, since you want war I will wage war against you, but I would have you know that I have killed nine kings whose heads adorn my room. What a pity, indeed, that your head should take its place beside those of your fellow madcaps.'

'Prepare yourself, Soumaoro, for it will be long before the calamity that is going to crash down upon you and yours comes to an end.'

Thus Sundiata and Soumaoro spoke together. After the war of mouths, swords had to decide the issue. Sogolon's son was in his tent when someone came to announce to him the arrival of Fakoli, Soumaoro's insurgent nephew. All the men stood to arms and the war chiefs drew up their men. When everything was in order in the camp, Djata and the Mandingo leaders received Fakoli followed by his warriors. Fakoli halted before Sundiata and spoke thus:

'I salute you, Sundiata. I am Fakoli Koroma, king of the tribe of Koroma smiths. Soumaoro is the brother of my mother Kassia. I have taken up arms against my uncle because he has outraged me. Without fearing incest he has pushed his effrontery to the lengths of robbing me of my wife Keleya. As for you, you are coming to reconquer the kingdom of your fathers, you are fighting Soumaoro. We have the same goal and therefore I come to place myself under your orders. I bring you my strong-armed smiths, I bring you sofas who do not know what fear is. Sundiata, I and my men are yours.'

Balla, Sundiata's griot, said, 'Fakoli, come and sit among your brothers whom Soumaoro's injustice has smitten, the judge folds you to his bosom. You could not do better than entrust your cause to the son of Sogolon.'

Sundiata made a sign indicating that the griot had spoken well, but he added, 'I defend the weak, I defend the innocent, Fakoli. You have suffered an injustice so I will render you justice, but I have my lieutenants about me and I would like to know their opinions.'

All the war chiefs agreed. Fakoli's cause became Sundiata's cause. Justice had to be granted to the man who came to implore justice. Thus Sundiata accepted Fakoli Da-Ba, Large-Mouthed Fakoli, among his war chiefs.

Sundiata wanted to have done with Soumaoro before the rainy season, so he struck camp and marched on Krina where Soumaoro was encamped. The latter realized that the decisive battle had come. Sundiata deployed his men on the little hill that dominates the plain. The great battle was for the next day.

In the evening, to raise the men's spirits, Djata gave a great feast, for he was anxious that his men should wake up happy in the morning. Several oxen were slaughtered and that evening Balla Fasséké, in front of the whole army, called to mind the history of old Mali. He praised Sundiata, seated amidst his lieutenants, in this manner:

'Now I address myself to you, Maghan Sundiata, I speak to you king of Mali, to whom dethroned monarchs flock. The time foretold to you by the jinn is now coming. Sundiata, kingdoms and empires are in the likeness of man; like him they are born, they grow and disappear. Each sovereign embodies one moment of that life. Formerly, the kings of Ghana extended their kingdom over all the lands inhabited by the black man, but the circle has closed and the Cissés of Wagadou are nothing more than petty princes in a desolate land. Today, another kingdom looms up, powerful, the kingdom of Sosso. Humbled kings have borne their tribute to Sosso, Soumaoro's arrogance knows no more bounds and his cruelty is equal to his ambition. But will Soumaoro dominate the world? Are we, the griots of Mali, condemned to pass on to future generations the humiliations which the king of Sosso cares to inflict on our country? No, you may be glad, children of the "Bright Country", for the kingship of Sosso is but the growth of yesterday, whereas that of Mali dates from the time of Bilali. Each kingdom has its childhood, but Soumaoro wants to force the pace, and so Sosso will collapse under him like a horse worn out beneath its rider.

'You, Maghan, you are Mali. It has had a long and difficult childhood like you. Sixteen kings have preceded you on the throne of Niani, sixteen kings have reigned with varying fortunes, but from being village chiefs the Keitas have become tribal chiefs and then kings. Sixteen generations have consolidated their power. You are the outgrowth of Mali just as the silk-cotton tree is the growth of the earth, born of deep and mighty roots. To face the tempest the tree must have long roots and gnarled branches. Maghan Sundiata, has not the tree grown?

'I would have you know, son of Sogolon, that there is not room for two kings around the same calabash of rice. When a new cock comes to the poultry run the old cock picks a quarrel with him and the docile hens wait to see if the new arrival asserts himself or yields. You have come to Mali. Very well, then, assert yourself. Strength makes a law of its own self and power allows no division.

'But listen to what your ancestors did, so that you will know what you have to do.

'Balali, the second of the name, conquered old Mali. Latal Kalabi conquered the country between the Niger and the Sankarani. By going to Mecca, Lahibatoul Kalabi, of illustrious memory, brought divine blessing upon Mali. Mamadi Kani made warriors out of hunters and bestowed armed strength upon Mali. His son Bamari Tagnokelin, the vindictive king, terrorized Mali with this army, but Maghan Kon Fatta, also called Naré Maghan, to whom you owe your being, made peace prevail and happy mothers yielded Mali a populous youth.

'You are the son of Naré Maghan, but you are also the son of your mother Sogolon, the buffalo-woman, before whom powerless sorcerers shrank in fear. You have the strength and majesty of the lion, you have the might of the buffalo.

'I have told you what future generations will learn about your ancestors, but what will we be able to relate to our sons so that your memory will stay alive, what will we have to teach our sons about you? What unprecedented exploits, what unheard-of feats? By what distinguished actions will our sons be brought to regret not having lived in the time of Sundiata?

'Griots are men of the spoken word, and by the spoken word we give life to the gestures of kings. But words are nothing but words; power lies in deeds. Be a man of action; do not answer me any more with your mouth, but tomorrow, on the plain of Krina, show me what you would have me recount to coming generations. Tomorrow allow me to sing the "Song of the Vultures" over the bodies of the thousands of Sossos whom your sword will have laid low before evening.'

It was on the eve of Krina. In this way Balla Fasséké reminded Sundiata of the history of Mali so that, in the morning, he would show himself worthy of his ancestors.

At break of day, Fakoli came and woke up Sundiata to tell him that Soumaoro had begun to move his sofas out of Krina. The son of Sogolon appeared dressed like a hunter king. He wore tight-fitting, ochre-coloured trousers. He gave the order to draw up the sofas across the plain, and while his chiefs bustled about, Manding Bory and Nana Triban came into Djata's tent.

'Brother,' said Manding Bory, 'have you got the bow ready?'

'Yes,' replied Sundiata. 'Look.'

He unhooked his bow from the wall, along with the deadly arrow. It was not an iron arrow at all, but was made of wood and pointed with the spur of a white cock. The cock's spur was the Tana of Soumaoro, the secret which Nana Triban had managed to draw out of the king of Sosso.

'Brother,' said Nana Triban, 'Soumaoro now knows that I have fled from Sosso. Try to get near him for he will avoid you the whole battle long.'

These words of Nana Triban left Djata worried, but Balla Fasséké, who had just come into the tent, said to Sundiata that the soothsayer had seen the end of soumaoro in a dream.

The sun had risen on the other side of the river and already lit the whole plain. Sundiata's troops deployed from the edge of the river across the plain, but Soumaoro's army was so big that other sofas remaining in Krina had ascended the ramparts to see the battle. Soumaoro was already distinguishable in the distance by his tall headdress, and the wings of his enormous army brushed the river on one side and the hills on the other. As at Neguéboria, Sundiata did not deploy all his forces. The bowmen of Wagadou and the Djallonkés stood at the rear ready to spill out on the left towards the hills as the battle spread. Fakoli Koroma and Kamandjan were in the front line with Sundiata and his cavalry.

With his powerful voice Sundiata cried 'An gnewa.'[65] The order was repeated from tribe to tribe and the army started off. Soumaoro stood on the right with his cavalry.

Djata and his cavalry charged with great dash but they were stopped by the horsemen of Diaghan and a struggle to the death began. Tabon Wana and the archers of Wagadou stretched out their lines towards the hills and the battle spread over the entire plain, while an unrelenting sun climbed in the sky. The horses of Mema were extremely agile, and they reared forward with their fore hooves raised and swooped down on the horsemen of Diaghan, who rolled on the ground trampled under the horses' hooves. Presently the men of Diaghan gave ground and fell back towards the rear. The enemy centre was broken.

It was then that Manding Bory galloped up to announce to Sundiata that Soumaoro, having thrown in all his reserve, had swept down on Fakoli and his smiths. Obviously Soumaoro was bent on punishing his nephew. Already overwhelmed by the numbers, Fakoli's men were beginning to give ground. The battle was not yet won.

His eyes red with anger, Sundiata pulled his cavalry over to the left in the direction of the hills where Fakoli was valiantly enduring his uncle's blows. But wherever the son of the buffalo passed, death rejoiced. Sundiata's presence restored the balance momentarily, but Soumaoro's sofas were too numerous all the same. Sogolon's son looked for Soumaoro and caught sight of him in the middle of the fray. Sundiata struck out right and left and the Sossos scrambled out of his way. The king of Sosso, who did not want Sundiata to get near him, retreated far behind his men, but Sundiata followed him with his eyes. He stopped and bent his bow. The arrow flew and grazed Soumaoro on the shoulder. The cock's spur no more than scratched him, but the effect was immediate and Soumaoro felt his powers leave him. His eyes met Sundiata's. Now trembling like a man in the grip of a fever, the vanquished Soumaoro looked up towards the sun. A great black bird flew over above the fray and he understood. It was a bird of misfortune.

'The bird of Krina,' he muttered.

The king of Sosso let out a great cry and, turning his horse's head, he took to flight. The Sossos saw the king and fled in their turn. It was a rout. Death hovered over the great plain and blood poured out of a thousand wounds. Who can tell how many Sossos perished at Krina? The rout was complete and Sundiata then dashed off in pursuit of Soumaoro. The sun was at the middle of its course. Fakoli had caught up with Sundiata and they both rode in pursuit of the fugitives. Soumaoro had a good start. Leaving the plain, the king of Sosso had dashed across the open bush followed by his son Balla and a few Sosso chiefs. When night fell Sundiata and Fakoli stopped at a hamlet. There they took a little food and rest. None of the inhabitants had seen Soumaoro. Sundiata and Fakoli started off in pursuit again as soon as they were joined by some horsemen of Mema. They galloped all night and at daybreak Djata learnt from some peasants that some horsemen had passed that way when it was still dark. The king of Sosso shunned all centres of population for he knew that the inhabitants, seeing him on the run, would no longer hesitate to lay hands on him in order to get into favour with the new master. Soumaoro was followed by none but his son Balla. After having changed his mount at daybreak, the king of Sosso was still galloping to the north.

With difficulty Sundiata found the trail of the fugitives. Fakoli was as resolute as Djata and he knew this country better. It was difficult to tell which of these two men harboured the greatest hatred towards Soumaoro. The one was avenging his humiliated country while the other was prompted by the love of a wife. At noon the horses of Sundiata and Fakoli were out of breath and the pursuers halted at Bankoumana. They took a little food and Djata learnt that Soumaoro was heading for Koulikoro. He had only given himself enough time to change horses. Sundiata and Fakoli set off again straight away. Fakoli said, 'I know a short cut to Koulikoro, but it is a difficult track and our horses will be tired.'

'Come on,' said Djata.

They tackled a difficult path scooped out by the rain in a gully. Cutting across country they now crossed the bush until, pointing a finger in front of him, Fakoli said, 'Look at the hills over there which herald Koulikoro. We have made up some time.'

'Good,' replied Djata simply.

However, the horses were fatigued, they went more slowly and painfully lifted their hooves from the ground. As there was no village in sight, Djata and Fakoli dismounted to let their mounts get their wind back. Fakoli, who had a small bag of millet in his saddle, fed them. The two men rested under a tree. Fakoli even said that Soumaoro, who had taken an easy but lengthy route, would not arrive at Koulikoro until nightfall. He was speaking like a man who had ridden over the whole country.

They continued on their way and soon climbed the hills. Arrived at the top, they saw two horsemen at the bottom of the valley going towards the mountain.

'There they are,' cried Djata.

Evening was coming on and the sun's rays were already kissing the summit of Koulikoro mountain. When Soumaoro and his son saw the two riders behind them, they broke off and began to climb the mountain. The king of Sosso and his son Balla seemed to have fresher horses. Djata and Fakoli redoubled their efforts.

The fugitives were within spear range when Djata shouted to them, 'Stop, stop.'

Like Djata, Fakoli wanted to take Soumaoro alive. Keleya's husband sheered off and outflanked Soumaoro on the right, making his horse jump. He was going to lay hands on his uncle but the latter escaped him by a sudden turn. Through his impetus Fakoli bumped into Balla and they both rolled on the ground. Fakoli got up and seized his cousin while Sundiata, throwing his spear with all his might, brought Soumaoro's horse tumbling down. The old king got up and the foot race began. Soumaoro was a sturdy old man and he climbed the mountain with great agility. Djata did not want either to wound him or kill him. He wanted to take him alive.

The sun had just disappeared completely. For a second time the king of Sosso escaped from Djata. Having reached the summit of Koulikoro, Soumaoro hurried down the slope followed by Djata. To the right he saw the gaping cave of Koulikoro and without hesitation he entered the black cavern. Sundiata stopped in front of the cave. At this moment arrived Fakoli who had just tied the hands of Sosso Balla, his cousin.

'There,' said Sundiata, 'he has gone into the cave.'

'But it is connected to the river,' said Fakoli.

The noise of horses' hooves was heard and it turned out to be a detachment of Mema horsemen. Straight away the son of Sogolon sent some of them towards the river and had all the mountain guarded. The darkness was complete. Sundiata went into the village of Koulikoro and waited there for the rest of his army.[66]

The victory of Krina was dazzling. The remains of Soumaoro's army went to shut themselves up in Sosso. But the empire of Sosso was done for. From everywhere around kings sent their submission to Sundiata. The king of Guidimakhan sent a richly furnished embassy to Djata and at the same time gave his daughter in marriage to the victor. Embassies flocked to Koulikoro, but when Djata had been joined by all the army he marched on Sosso. Soumaoro's city, Sosso, the impregnable city, the city of smiths skilled in wielding the spear.

In the absence of the king and his son, Noumounkeba, a tribal chief, directed the defence of the city. He had quickly amassed all that he could find in the way of provisions from the surrounding countryside.

Sosso was a magnificent city. In the open plain her triple rampart with awe-inspiring towers reached into the sky. The city comprised a hundred and eighty-eight fortresses and the palace of Soumaoro loomed above the whole city like a gigantic tower. Sosso had but one gate; colossal and made of iron, the work of the sons of fire. Noumounkeba hoped to tie Sundiata down outside of Sosso, for he had enough provisions to hold out for a year.

The sun was beginning to set when Sogolon-Djata appeared before Sosso the Magnificent. From the top of a hill, Djata and his general staff gazed upon the fearsome city of the sorcerer-king. The army encamped in the plain opposite the great gate of the city and fires were lit in the camp. Djata resolved to take Sosso in the course of a morning. He fed his men a double ration and the tam-tams beat all night to stir up the victors of Krina.

At daybreak the towers of the ramparts were black with sofas. Others were positioned on the ramparts themselves. They were the archers. The Mandingoes were masters in the art of storming a town. In the front line Sundiata placed the sofas of Mali, while those who held the ladders were in the second line protected by the shields of the spearmen. The main body of the army was to attack the city gate. When all was ready, Djata gave the order to attack. The drums resounded, the horns blared and like a tide the Mandingo front line moved off, giving mighty shouts. With their shields raised above their heads the Mandingoes advanced up to the foot of the wall, then the Sossos began to rain large stones down on the assailants. From the rear, the bowmen of Wagadou shot arrows at the ramparts. The attack spread and the town was assaulted at all points. Sundiata had a murderous reserve; they were the bowmen whom the king of the Bobos had sent shortly before Krina. The archers of Bobo are the best in the world. On one knee the archers fired flaming arrows over the ramparts. Within the walls the thatched huts took fire and the smoke swirled up. The ladders stood against the curtain wall and the first Mandingo sofas were already at the top. Seized by panic through seeing the town on fire, the Sossos hesitated a moment. The huge tower surmounting the gate surrendered, for Fakoli's smiths had made themselves masters of it. They got into the city where the screams of women and children brought the Sossos' panic to a head. They opened the gates to the main body of the army.

Then began the massacre. Women and children in the midst of fleeing Sossos implored mercy of the victors. Djata and his cavalry were now in front of the awesome tower palace of Soumaoro. Noumounkeba, conscious that he was lost, came out to fight. With his sword held aloft he bore down on Djata, but the latter dodged him and, catching hold of the Sosso's braced arm, forced him to his knees whilst the sword dropped to the ground. He did not kill him but delivered him into the hands of Manding Bory.

Soumaoro's palace was now at Sundiata's mercy. While everywhere the Sossos were begging for quarter, Sundiata, preceded by Balla Fasséké, entered Soumaoro's tower. The griot knew every nook and cranny of the palace from his captivity and he led Sundiata to Soumaoro's magic chamber.

When Balla Fasséké opened the door to the room it was found to have changed its appearance since Soumaoro had been touched by the fatal arrow. The inmates of the chamber had lost their power. The snake in the pitcher was in the throes of death, the owls from the perch were flapping pitifully about on the ground. Everything was dying in the sorcerer's abode. It was all up with the power of Soumaoro. Sundiata had all Soumaoro's fetishes taken down and before the palace were gathered together all Soumaoro's wives, all princesses taken from their families by force. The prisoners, their hands tied behind their backs, were already herded together. Just as he had wished, Sundiata had taken Sosso in the course of a morning. When everything was outside of the town and all that there was to take had been taken out, Sundiata gave the order to complete its destruction. The last houses were set fire to and prisoners were employed in the razing of the walls. Thus, as Djata intended, Sosso was destroyed to its very foundations.

Yes, Sosso was razed to the ground. It has disappeared, the proud city of Soumaoro. A ghastly wilderness extends over the places where kings came and humbled themselves before the sorcerer king. All traces of the houses have vanished and of Soumaoro's seven-storey palace there remains nothing more. A field of desolation, Sosso is now a spot where guinea fowl and young partridges come to take their dust baths.

Many years have rolled by and many times the moon has traversed the heaven since these places lost their inhabitants. The bourein,[67] the tree of desolation, spreads out its thorny undergrowth and insolently grows in Soumaoro's capital. Sosso the Proud is nothing but a memory in the mouths of griots. The hyenas come to wail there at night, the hare and the hind come and feed on the site of the palace of Soumaoro, the king who wore robes of human skin.

Sosso vanished from the earth and it was Sundiata, the son of the buffalo, who gave these places over to solitude. After the destruction of Soumaoro's capital the world knew no other master but Sundiata.

The Empire

While Sosso succumbed to the mattocks of its own sons, Sundiata marched on Diaghan. The king of Diaghan had been Soumaoro's most formidable ally and after Krina he still remained faithful to Soumaoro's cause. He had shut himself up in his city, which was proud of its cavalry, but like a hurricane Sundiata beat upon Diaghan, the city of divines.[68] Like Sosso, Diaghan was taken in one morning. Sundiata had the heads of all the young men shaved and made sofas of them.

Sundiata had divided his army into three bodies; the first, under the command of Fakoli Koroma, waged war in Bambougou; the second, under the command of Fran Kamara, fought in the mountains of the Fouta; Sundiata and the main body of the army marched on the great city of Kita.

Kita Mansa was a powerful king and was under the protection of the jinn of the great mountain which dominates the town of Kita, Kita Kourou. In the middle of the mountain was a little pool of magic water. Whoever got as far as this pool and drank its waters became powerful, but the jinn of the pool were very evil and only the king of Kita had access to the mysterious pool.

Sundiata camped to the east of Kita and demanded submission of the king. Vainglorious in the protection of the mountain jinn, Kita Mansa answered Djata with arrogance. Sogolon's son had in his army some infallible soothsayers. On their advice, Sundiata invoked the jinn of Kita Kourou and sacrificed to them a hundred white oxen, a hundred white rams and a hundred white cocks. All the cocks died on their backs, facing upwards; the jinn had replied favourably. Then Sundiata did not hesitate any longer and first thing in the morning he gave the signal to attack. The assaulting sofas sang the 'Hymn to the Bow'. Balla Fesséké, dressed as a great griot, rode at Djata's side. At the first assault the east gate surrendered, but there was no massacre at all. Men, women and children all were spared, but Kita Mansa had been killed outside his palace. Sundiata accorded him royal obsequies. Sundiata did not take one prisoner at Kita and the inhabitants, who were Kamaras, became his allies.

First thing next morning Sundiata determined to go into the mountain to sacrifice to the jinn and thank them for his victory over Kita. The whole army followed him. The mountain of Kita is as steep as a wall and Sundiata resolved to go all round it to receive the submission of the numerous villages lying at the foot of Kita Kourou. At Boudofou, a Kamara village, there was a great celebration between Kamandjan's tribes and the inhabitants. There was dancing and eating around the sacred stone of Boudofou. Today the Kamaras still sacrifice at this stone, but only those Kamaras who have known how to respect the Dio of their ancestors. In the evening the army camped at Kourou-Koto on the slope of the mountain opposite. Kita Djata was well received by the king Mansa Kourou and several tribes fraternized there.

At break of day Sundiata, followed by Balla Fasséké and a few members of the royal tribe of Mali,[69] went to the foot of a large rock. He sacrificed a hundred cocks to the jinn of the mountain, then, accompanied by Balla Fasséké alone, Sundiata went off in search of the pool. He found it in the midst of the mountain. He knelt down at the water's edge and said,

'Oh jinn of the water, Master of the Moghoya-Dji, master of the magic water, I sacrificed to you a hundred bulls, I sacrificed to you a hundred rams, and I sacrificed to you a hundred cocks. You gave me the victory but I have not destroyed Kita. I, the successor to Kita Mansa, come to drink the magic water, the moghoya dji.'

He scooped up some water in his two hands and drank. He found the water good and drank three times of it, then he washed his face.

When Djata rejoined his men his eyes had an unbearable brilliance. He radiated like a star. The moghoya dji had transfigured him.

From Kourou-Koto Sundiata returned to Kita, the trip round the mountain having lasted two days. At Kita he found delegations from the kingdoms conquered by Fakoli and Tabon Wana. The king of Mali stayed at Kita for some time and often went hunting with his brother Manding Bory and Sibi Kamandjan. The people of Kita never hunted the mountain game for fear of the jinn. As for Sundiata, he hunted on the mountain for he had become the chosen one of the jinn. A Simbon from his early years, he was well enough versed in the art of Sané ni Kondolon. He and his companions used to bathe in one of the mountain springs and the people of Kita still distinguish this spring and surround it with great veneration.[70]

Leaving Kita, Sundiata and his large army headed for Do, the country of his mother Sogolon. At Do Sundiata was received as the uncle receives the nephew. Djata and Balla Fasséké betook themselves to the famous plain of Ourantamba and a member of the Traoré tribe accompanied them. The inhabitants of Do had raised a great mound on the spot where the buffalo had expired. Sundiata sacrificed a white cock on the mound. When the cock had died on its back a big whirlwind swirled up and blew towards the west.

'Look,' said Balla Fasséké,' 'the whirlwind is going towards Mali.'

'Yes, it is time to go back there.'

From Do, Sundiata sent a richly furnished embassy to Mema loaded with costly gifts. Thus he paid off his contracted debt and the embassy made it known to the king that the Cissé-Tounkaras and the Keitas would be allies for ever.

It was from Do, also, that Sundiata ordered all his generals to meet him at Ka-ba on the Niger in the land of the king of Sibi. Fakoli had completed his conquests and the king of Tabon had subjugated the mountaineers of the Fouta. The arms of Sundiata had subdued all the countries of the savanna. From Ghana in the north to Mali in the south and from Mema in the east to the Fouta in the west, all the lands had recognized Sundiata's authority.

Djata's army followed the Niger valley to make its way to Ka-ba.

Kouroukan Fougan or The Division of the World

Leaving Do, the land of ten thousand guns, Sundiata wended his way to Ka-ba, keeping to the river valley. All his armies converged on Ka-ba and Fakoli and Tabon Wana entered it laden with booty. Sibi Kamandjan had gone ahead of Sundiata to prepare the great assembly which was to gather at Ka-ba, a town situated on the territory belonging to the country of Sibi.

Ka-ba was a small town founded by Niagalin M'Bali Faly, a hunter of Sibi, and by Sounoumba Traore, a fisherman. Ka-ba belonged to the king of Sibi and nowadays you can also find Keitas at Ka-ba, but the Keitas did not come there until after Sundiata's time.[71] Ka-ba stands on the left bank of the Niger and it is through Ka-ba that the road to old Mali passes.

To the north of the town stretches a spacious clearing and it is there that the great assembly was to foregather. King Kamandjan had the whole clearing cleaned up and a great dais was got ready. Even before Djata's arrival the delegations from all the conquered peoples had made their way to Ka-ba. Huts were hastily built to house all these people. When all the armies had reunited, camps had to be set up in the big plain lying between the river and the town. On the appointed day the troops were drawn up on the vast square that had been prepared. As at Sibi, each people was gathered round its king's pennant. Sundiata had put on robes such as are worn by a great Muslim king.[72] Balla Fasséké, the high master of ceremonies, set the allies around Djata's great throne. Everything was in position. The sofas, forming a vast semicircle bristling with spears, stood motionless. The delegations of the various peoples had been planted at the foot of the dais. A complete silence reigned. On Sundiata's right, Balla Fasséké, holding his mighty spear, addressed the throng in this manner:

'Peace reigns today in the whole country; may it always be thus. . . .'

'Amen,' replied the crowd, then the herald continued:

'I speak to you, assembled peoples. To those of Mali I convey Maghan Sundiata's greeting; greetings to those of Do, greetings to those of Ghana, to those from Mema greetings, and to those of Fakoli's tribe. Greetings to the Bobo warriors and, finally, greetings to those of Sibi and Ka-ba. To all the peoples assembled, Djata gives greetings.

'May I be humbly forgiven if I have made any omission. I am nervous before so many people gathered together.

'Peoples, here we are, after years of hard trials, gathered around our saviour, the restorer of peace and order. From the east to the west, from the north to the south, everywhere his victorious arms have established peace. I convey to you the greetings of Soumaoro's vanquisher, Maghan Sundiata, king of Mali.

'But in order to respect tradition, I must first of all address myself to the host of us all, Kamandjan, king of Sibi; Djata greets you and gives you the floor.'

Kamandjan, who was sitting close by Sundiata, stood up and stepped down from the dais. He mounted his horse and brandished his sword, crying 'I salute you all, warriors of Mali, of Do, of Tabon, of Mema, of Wagadou, of Bobo, of Fakoki . . .; warriors, peace has returned to our homes, may God long preserve it.'

'Amen,' replied the warriors and the crowd. The king of Sibi continued.

'In the world man suffers for a season, but never eternally. Here we are at the end of our trials. We are at peace. May God be praised. But we owe this peace to one man who, by his courage and his valiance, was able to lead our troops to victory.

'Which one of us, alone, would have dared face Soumaoro? Ay, we were all cowards. How many times did we pay him tribute? The insolent rogue thought that everything was permitted him. What family was not dishonoured by Soumaoro? He took our daughters and wives from us and we were more craven than women. He carried his insolence to the point of stealing the wife of his nephew Fakoli! We were prostrated and humiliated in front of our children. But it was in the midst of so many calamities that our destiny suddenly changed. A new sun arose in the east. After the battle of Tabon we felt ourselves to be men, we realized that Soumaoro was a human being and not an incarnation of the devil, for he was no longer invincible. A man came to us. He had heard our groans and came to our aid, like a father when he sees his son in tears. Here is that man. Maghan Sundiata, the man with two names foretold by the soothsayers.

'It is to you that I now address myself, son of Sogolon, you, the nephew of the valorous warriors of Do. Henceforth it is from you that I derive my kingdom for I acknowledge you my sovereign. My tribe and I place ourselves in your hands. I salute you, supreme chief, I salute you, Fama of Famas.[73] I salute you, Mansa!"[74]

The huzza that greeted these words was so loud that you could hear the echo repeat the tremendous clamour twelve times over. With a strong hand Kamandjan stuck his spear in the ground in front of the dais and said, 'Sundiata, here is my spear, it is yours.'

Then he climbed up to sit in his place. Thereafter, one by one, the twelve kings of the bright savanna country got up and proclaimed Sundiata 'Mansa' in their turn. Twelve royal spears were stuck in the ground in front of the dais. Sundiata had become emperor. The old tabala of Niani announced to the world that the lands of the savanna had provided themselves with one single king. When the imperial tabala had stopped reverberating, Balla Fasséké, the grand master of ceremonies, took the floor again following the crowd's ovation.

'Sundiata, Maghan Sundiata, king of Mali, in the name of the twelve kings of the "Bright Country", I salute you as "Mansa".'

The crowd shouted 'Wassa, Wassa. . . . Ayé.'

It was amid such joy that Balla Fasséké composed the great hymn 'Niama' which the griots still sing:

Niama, Niama, Niama,
You, you serve as a shelter for all,
All come to seek refuge under you.
And as for you, Niama,
Nothing serves you for shelter,
God alone protects you.[75]

The festival began. The musicians of all the countries were there. Each people in turn came forward to the dais under Sundiata's impassive gaze. Then the war dances began. The sofas of all the countries had lined themselves up in six ranks amid a great clatter of bows and spears knocking together. The war chiefs were on horseback. The warriors faced the enormous dais and at a signal from Balla Fasséké, the musicians, massed on the right of the dais, struck up. The heavy war drums thundered, the bolons gave off muted notes while the griot's voice gave the throng the pitch for the 'Hymn to the Bow'. The spearmen, advancing like hyenas in the night, held their spears above their heads; the archers of Wagadou and Tabon, walking with a noiseless tread, seemed to be lying in ambush behind bushes. They rose suddenly to their feet and let fly their arrows at imaginary enemies. In front of the great dais the Kéké-Tigui, or war chiefs, made their horses perform dance steps under the eyes of the Mansa. The horses whinnied and reared, then, overmastered by the spurs, knelt, got up and cut little capers, or else scraped the ground with their hooves.

The rapturous people shouted the 'Hymn to the Bow' and clapped their hands. The sweating bodies of the warriors glistened in the sun while the exhausting rhythm of the tam-tams wrenched from them shrill cries. But presently they made way for the cavalry, beloved by Djata. The horsemen of Mema threw their swords in the air and caught them in flight, uttering mighty shouts. A smile of contentment took shape on Sundiata's lips, for he was happy to see his cavalry manoeuvre with so much skill.

In the afternoon the festivity took a new aspect. It began with the procession of prisoners and booty. Their hands tied behind their backs and in triple file, the Sosso prisoners made their entry into the giant circle. All their heads had been shaved. Inside the circle they turned and passed by the foot of the dais. Their eyes lowered, the poor prisoners walked in silence, abuse heaped upon them by the frenzied crowd. Behind came the kings who had remained faithful to Soumaoro and who had not intended to make their submission. They also had their heads shorn, but they were on horseback so that everyone could see them. At last, right at the back, came Sosso Balla, who had been placed in the midst of his father's fetishes. The fetishes had been loaded onto donkeys. The crowd gave loud cries of horror on seeing the inmates of Soumaoro's grisly chamber. People pointed with terror at the snake's pitcher, the magic balafon, and the king of Sosso's owls. Soumaoro's son Balla, his hands bound, was on a horse but did not dare look up at this throne, which formerly used to tremble with fear at mere talk of his father. In the crowd could be heard:

'Each in his turn, Sosso Balla; lift up your head a bit, impudent little creature!' Or else: 'Did you have any idea that one day you would be a slave, you vile fellow!'

'Look at your useless fetishes. Call on them then, son of a sorcerer!'

When Sosso Balla was in front of the dais, Djata made a gesture. He had just remembered the mysterious disappearance of Soumaoro inside the mountain. He became morose, but his griot Balla Fasséké noticed it and so he spoke thus:

'The son will pay for the father, Soumaoro can thank God that he is already dead.'

When the procession had finished Balla Fasséké silenced everyone. The sofas got into line and the tam-tams stopped.

Sundiata got up and a graveyard silence settled on the whole place. The Mansa moved forward to the edge of the dais. Then Sundiata spoke as Mansa. Only Balla Fasséké could hear him, for a Mansa does not speak like a town-crier.

'I greet all the peoples gathered here.' And Djata mentioned them all. Pulling the spear of Kamandjan, king of Sibi, out of the ground, he said:

'I give you back your kingdom, king of Sibi, for you have deserved it by your bravery; I have known you since childhood and your speech is as frank as your heart is straightforward.

'Today I ratify for ever the alliance between the Kamaras of Sibi and the Keitas of Mali. May these two people be brothers henceforth. In future, the land of the Keitas shall be the land of the Kamaras, and the property of the Kamaras shall be henceforth the property of the Keitas.

'May there nevermore be falsehood between a Kamara and a Keita, and may the Kamaras feel at home in the whole extent of my empire.'

He returned the spear to Kamandjan and the king of Sibi prostrated himself before Djata, as is done when honoured by a Fama.

Sundiata took Tabon Wana's spear and said, 'Fran Kamara, my friend, I return your kingdom to you. May the Djallonkés and Mandingoes be forever allies. You received me in your own domain, so may the Djallonkés be received as friends throughout Mali. I leave you the lands you have conquered, and henceforth your children and your children's children will grow up at the court of Niani where they will be treated like the princes of Mali.'

One by one all the kings received their kingdoms from the very hands of Sundiata, and each one bowed before him as one bows before a Mansa.

Sundiata pronounced all the prohibitions which still obtain in relations between the tribes. To each he assigned its land, he established the rights of each people and ratified their friendships. The Kondés of the land of Do became henceforth the uncles of the imperial family of Keita, for the latter, in memory of the fruitful marriage between Naré Maghan and Sogolon, had to take a wife in Do. The Tounkaras and the Cissés became 'banter-brothers' of the Keitas. While the Cissés, Bérétés and Tourés were proclaimed great divines of the empire. No kin group was forgotten at Kouroukan Fougan; each had its share in the division. To Fakoli Koroma, Sundiata gave the kingdom of Sosso, the majority of whose inhabitants were enslaved. Fakoli's tribe, the Koromas, which others call Doumbouya or Sissoko, had the monopoly of the forge, that is, of iron working. Fakoli also received from Sundiata part of the lands situated between the Bafing and Bagbé rivers. Wagadou and Mema kept their kings who continued to bear the title of Mansa, but these two kingdoms acknowledged the suzerainty of the supreme Mansa. The Konaté of Toron became the cadets of the Keitas so that on reaching maturity a Konaté could call himself Keita.

When Sogolon's son had finished distributing lands and power he turned to Balla Fasséké, his griot, and said: 'As for you, Balla Fasséké, my griot, I make you grand master of ceremonies. Henceforth the Keitas will choose their griot from your tribe, from among the Kouyatés. I give the Kouyatés the right to make jokes about all the tribes, and in particular about the royal tribe of Keita.'

Thus spoke the son of Sogolon at Kouroukan Fougan. Since that time his respected word has become law, the rule of conduct for all the peoples who were represented at Ka-ba.

So, Sundiata had divided the world at Kouroukan Fougan. He kept for this tribe the blessed country of Kita, but the Kamaras inhabiting the region remained masters of the soil.

If you go to Ka-ba, go and see the glade of Kouroukan Fougan and you will see a linké tree planted there, perpetuating the memory of the great gathering which witnessed the division of the world.

Niani

After this great assembly Sundiata stayed a few more days at Ka-ba. For the people these were days of festivity. For them Djata caused hundreds of oxen, taken from Soumaoro's immense exchequer, to be slaughtered every day. In the main square of Ka-ba the girls of the town came and laid big calabashes of rice and meat at the foot of the observation platforms. Anybody could come and eat his fill and go away. Soon Ka-ba was full of people who had come from all directions attracted by the opulence. A year of war had emptied all the granaries so each came to take his share of the king of Sosso's reserves. It is even said that certain people had set up their household gods on that very spot during Djata's stay at Ka-ba. These were the summer months so these people slept on the observation platforms during the night and on awakening found calabashes of rice at their feet. That was the time when people sang the 'Hymn to Abundance' in Sundiata's honour:

He has come
And happiness has come
Sundiata is here
And happiness is here.

But it was time to return to his native Mali. Sundiata assembled his army in the plain and each people provided a contingent to accompany the Mansa to Niani. At Ka-ba all the peoples separated in friendship and in joy at their new-found peace.

Sundiata and his men had to cross the Niger in order to enter old Mali. One might have thought that all the dug-out canoes in the world had arranged to meet at the port of Ka-ba. It was the dry season and there was not much water in the river. The fishing tribe of Somono, to whom Djata had given the monopoly of the water, were bent on expressing their thanks to the son of Sogolon. They put all their dug-outs side by side across the Niger so that Sundiata's sofas could cross without wetting their feet.

When the whole army was on the other side of the river, Sundiata ordered great sacrifices. A hundred oxen and a hundred rams were sacrificed. It was thus that Sundiata thanked God on returning to Mali.

The villages of Mali gave Maghan Sundiata an unprecedented welcome. At normal times a traveller on foot can cover the distance from Ka-ba to Niani with only two halts, but Sogolon's son with his army took three days. The road to Mali from the river was flanked by a double human hedge. Flocking from every corner of Mali, all the inhabitants were resolved to see their saviour from close up. The women of Mali tried to create a sensation and they did not fail. At the entrance to each village they had carpeted the road with their multi-coloured pagnes so that Sundiata's horse would not so much as dirty its feet on entering their village. At the village exits the children, holding leafy branches in their hands, greeted Djata with cries of 'Wassa, Wassa, Ayé'.

Sundiata was leading the van. He had donned his costume of a hunter king—a plain smock, skin-tight trousers and his bow slung across his back. At his side Balla Fasséké was still wearing his festive garments gleaming with gold. Between Djata's general staff and the army Sosso Balla had been placed, amid his father's fetishes. But his hands were no longer tied. As at Ka-ba, abuse was everywhere heaped upon him and the prisoner did not dare look up at the hostile crowd. Some people, always ready to feel sympathy, were saying among themselves:

'How few things good fortune prizes!'

'Yes, the day you are fortunate is also the day when you are the most unfortunate, for in good fortune you cannot imagine what suffering is.'

The troops were marching along singing the 'Hymn to the Bow', which the crowd took up. New songs flew from mouth to mouth. Young women offered the soldiers cool water and cola nuts. And so the triumphal march across Mali ended outside Niani, Sundiata's city.

It was a ruined town which was beginning to be rebuilt by its inhabitants. A part of the ramparts had been destroyed and the charred walls still bore the marks of the fire. From the top of the hill Djata looked on Niani, which looked like a dead city. He saw the plain of Sounkarani, and he also saw the site of the young baobab tree. The survivors of the catastrophe were standing in rows on the Mali road. The children were waving branches, a few young women were singing, but the adults were mute.

'Rejoice,' said Balla Fasséké to Sundiata, 'for your part you will have the bliss of rebuilding Niani, the city of your fathers, but nevermore will anyone rebuild Sosso out of its ruins. Men will lose recollection of the very site of Soumaoro's city.'

With Sundiata peace and happiness entered Niani. Lovingly Sogolon's son had his native city rebuilt. He restored in the ancient style his father's old enclosure where he had grown up. People came from all the villages of Mali to settle in Niani. The walls had to be destroyed to enlarge the town, and new quarters were built for each kin group in the enormous army.

Sundiata had left his brother Manding Bory at Bagadou-Djeliba on the river. He was Sundiata's Kankoro Sigui, that is to say, viceroy. Manding Bory had looked after all the conquered countries. When reconstruction of the capital was finished he went to wage war in the south in order to frighten the forest peoples. He received an embassy from the country of Sangaran where a few Kondé clans had settled, and although these latter had not been represented at Kouroukan Fougan, Sundiata granted his alliance and they were placed on the same footing as the Kondés of the land of Do.

After a year Sundiata held a new assembly at Niani, but this one was the assembly of dignitaries and kings of the empire. The kings and notables of all the tribes came to Niani. The kings spoke of their administration and the dignitaries talked of their kings. Fakoli, the nephew of Soumaoro, having proved himself too independent, had to flee to evade the Mansa's anger. His lands were confiscated and the taxes of Sosso were payed directly into the granaries of Niani. In this way, every year, Sundiata gathered about him all the kings and notables; so justice prevailed everywhere, for the kings were afraid of being denounced at Niani.

Djata's justice spared nobody. He followed the very word of God. He protected the weak against the strong and people would make journeys lasting several days to come and demand justice of him. Under his sun the upright man was rewarded and the wicked one punished.

In their new-found peace the villages knew prosperity again, for with Sundiata happiness had come into everyone's home. Vast fields of millet, rice, cotton, indigo and fonio surrounded the villages. Whoever worked always had something to live on. Each year long caravans carried the taxes in kind[76] to Niani. You could go from village to village without fearing brigands. A thief would have his right hand chopped off and if he stole again he would be put to the sword.

New villages and new towns sprang up in Mali and elsewhere. 'Dyulas', or traders, became numerous and during the reign of Sundiata the world knew happiness.

There are some kings who are powerful through their military strength. Everybody trembles before them, but when they die nothing but ill is spoken of them. Others do neither good nor ill and when they die they are forgotten. Others are feared because they have power, but they know how to use it and they are loved because they love justice. Sundiata belonged to this group. He was feared, but loved as well. He was the father of Mali and gave the world peace. After him the world has not seen a greater conqueror, for he was the seventh and last conqueror. He had made the capital of an empire out of his father's village, and Niani became the navel of the earth. In the most distant lands Niani was talked of and foreigners said, 'Travellers from Mali can tell lies with impunity', for Mali was a remote country for many peoples.

The griots, fine talkers that they were, used to boast of Niani and Mali saying: 'If you want salt, go to Niani, for Niani is the camping place of the Sahel[77] caravans. If you want gold, go to Niani, for Bouré, Bambougou and Wagadou work for Niani. If you want fine cloth, go to Niani, for the Mecca road passes by Niani. If you want fish, go to Niani, for it is there that the fishermen of Maouti and Djenné come to sell their catches. If you want meat, go to Niani, the country of the great hunters, and the land of the ox and the sheep. If you want to see an army, go to Niani, for it there that the united forces of Mali are to be found. If you want to see a great king, go to Niani, for it is there that the son of Sogolon lives, the man with two names.'

This is what the masters of the spoken word used to sing.

I must mention Kita among the great cities of the empire, the city of holy water which became the second capital of the Keitas. I shall mention vanished Tabon, the iron-gated city. I shall not forget Do, nor Kri, the motherland of Sogolon, the buffalo woman. I shall also cite Koukouba, Batamba and Kambasiga, towns of the sofas. I shall mention the town of Diaghan, Mema, the town of hospitality, and Wagadou, where the descendants of Alexander the Great used to reign. How many heaped-up ruins, how many vanished cities! How many wildernesses peopled by the spirits of great kings! The silk-cotton trees and baobabs that you see in Mali are the only traces of extinct cities.

Eternal Mali

How many piled-up ruins, how much buried splendour! But all the deeds I have spoken of took place long ago and they all had Mali as their background. Kings have succeeded kings, but Mali has always remained the same.

Mali keeps its secrets jealously. There are things which the uninitiated will never know, for the griots, their depositaries, will never betray them. Maghan Sundiata, the last conqueror on earth, lies not far from Niani-Niani at Balandougou, the weir town.[78]

After him many kings and many Mansas reigned over Mali and other towns sprang up and disappeared. Hajji Mansa Moussa, of illustrious memory, beloved of God, built houses at Mecca for pilgrims coming from Mali, but the towns which he founded have all disappeared, Karanina, Bouroun-Kouna—nothing more remains of these towns. Other kings carried Mali far beyond Djata's frontiers, for example Mansa Samanka and Fadima Moussa, but none of them came near Djata.[79]

Maghan Sundiata was unique. In his own time no one equalled him and after him no one had the ambition to surpass him. He left his mark on Mali for all time and his taboos still guide men in their conduct.

Mali is eternal. To convince yourself of what I have said go to Mali. At Tigan you will find the forest dear to Sundiata. There you will see Fakoli Koroma's plastron. Go to Kirikoroni near Niassola and you will see a tree which commemorates Sundiata's passing through these parts. Go to Bankoumana on the Niger and you will see Soumaoro's balafon, the balafon which is called Balguintiri. Go to Ka-ba and you will see the clearing of Kouroukan. Fougan, where the great assembly took place which gave Sundiata's empire its constitution. Go to Krina near Ka-ba and you will see the bird that foretold the end to Soumaoro. At Keyla, near Ka-ba, you will find the royal drums belonging to Djolofin Mansa, king of Senegal, whom Djata defeated. But never try, wretch, to pierce the mystery which Mali hides from you. Do not go and disturb the spirits in their eternal rest. Do not ever go into the dead cities to question the past, for the spirits never forgive. Do not seek to know what is not to be known.

* * *

Men of today, how small you are beside your ancestors, and small in mind too, for you have trouble in grasping the meaning of my words. Sundiata rests near Niani-Niani, but his spirit lives on and today the Keitas still come and bow before the stone under which lies the father of Mali.

To acquire my knowledge I have journeyed all round Mali. At Kita I saw the mountain where the lake of holy water sleeps; at Segou, I learnt the history of the kings of Do and Kri; at Fadama, in Hamana, I heard the Kondé griots relate how the Keitas, Kondés and Kamaras conquered Wouroula.[80] At Keyla, the village of the great masters, I learnt the origins of Mali and the art of speaking. Everywhere I was able to see and understand what my masters were teaching me, but between their hands I took an oath to teach only what is to be taught and to conceal what is to be kept concealed.

Notes

1. The twelve doors of Mali refer to the twelve provinces of which Mali was originally composed. After Sundiata's conquests the number of conquests increased considerably. Early Mali seems to have been a confederation of the chief Mandingo tribes: Keita, Kondé, Traoré, Kamara and Koroma. D. T. N.
2. According to tradition Sundiata's mother had a buffalo for a totem, namely the fabulous buffalo which, it is said, ravaged the land of Do. The lion is the totem and ancestor of the Keitas. Thus, through his father Sundiata is the son of the lion, and, through his mother, the son of the buffalo. D. T. N.
3. I have used this word 'Mandingo' to mean the people who inhabited Mali and their language, and as an adjective to mean anything pertaining to these people, though the adjective 'Mandingan' exists too. Old Mali, where much of the action of this story takes place, is a vaguely defined area between the Niger and Sankarani rivers and should not be confused with the modern Republic of Mali of which it is only a fraction. G. D. P.

   The inhabitants of Mali call themselves Maninka or Mandinka. Malli and Malinke are the Fulani deformations of the words Manding and Mandinka respectively. 'Mali' in the Mandingo language means 'a hippopotamus' and it is not impossible that Mali was the name given to one of the capitals of the emperors. One tradition tells us that Sundiata changed himself into a hippopotamus in the Sankarani river. So it is not astonishing to find villages in old Mali which have 'Mali' for a name. This name could have formerly been that of a city. In old Mali there is one village called Malikoma, i.e. New Mali. D. T. N.
4. Bilali Bounama was the first muezzin and the Companion of the Prophet Muhammad. Like most medieval Muslim dynasties, the Mali emperors were careful to link themselves with the Prophet's family, or at least with someone near to him. In the fourteenth century we will see Mansa Moussa return to Mali after his pilgrimage with some representatives of the Arab tribe of Qureish (Muhammad's tribe) in order to bring down the Prophet of God's blessing on his empire. After Kankan Moussa, several princes of Mali were to imitate him, notably Askia Muhammad in the sixteenth century. D. T. N.

   This Askia Muhammad (1493–1528) ruled the Songhay Empire which overran that of Mali, but Muhammad's surname—Touré—indicates his Mandingo origin and in this sense he can be styled a 'prince of Mali'. G. D. P.

5. The Mandingo word is 'Simbon' and it literally means 'a hunter's whistle', but it is also used as an honorific title to denote a great hunter, a title which Sundiata later bore. The funeral wake which the hunters of a district organize in honour of a dead colleague is called 'Simbon-si'. D. T. N.
6. Kondolon Ni Sané is a dual hunting deity. Kondolon is a god of the chase and has Sané as an inseparable companion. These two deities are always linked and they are invoked as a pair. This dual deity has the property of being everywhere at once and when it reveals itself to the hunter the latter frequently comes across game. The guardianship of the bush and forest devolves on this deity and it is also the symbol of union and friendship. One must never invoke them separately at the risk of incurring very severe punishments. The two deities sometimes rival each other in skill but never fall out. In Hamana (Kouroussa) Mamadi Kani is accredited with the oath which the hunter takes before being received as a Simbon. Here is the oath:
   (a) Will you resolve to satisfy Kondolon Ni Sané before your own father? (i.e. one should opt for the Master Hunter when confronted with an order from him and a conflicting order from one's own father.)
   (b) Will you learn that respect does not mean slavery and give respect and submission at all times to your Master Hunter?
   (c) Will you learn that cola is good, tobacco is good, honey is sweet, etc.—and give them over to your Master?

   If the answer is 'yes' the apprentice hunter is accepted. In certain provinces of Siguiri, this oath is attributed to a certain Allah Mamadi who was not a king. D. T. N.
7. All the traditions acknowledge that the little village of Niani was the first capital of Mali and the residence of the first kings. It is said that Sundiata made it into a great city and thus it was called 'Niani-ba'—Niani the Great. Today it is a little village of a few hundred inhabitants on the Sankarani river and one kilometre from the frontier of the republics of Guinea and Mali. In the songs to Sundiata the town also bears the name of Niani-Niani, which is an emphatic title. D. T. N.
8. The silk-cotton tree of Malabar is the tree referred to here. It was brought to West Africa by the Portuguese in the fourteenth to fifteenth centuries so their frequent mention here is anachronistic, for the action described in this book took place between about 1217 and 1237. G. D. P.
9. The word M. Niane uses is 'Baraka' and it means blessing or the gift of divine power, to which our word 'grace' approximates. The word is fully discussed by Trimingham in his *Islam in West Africa*, pp. 111–12. G. D. P.
10. See note 5.
11. A hunter's bag is called 'sassa' in the original. It is a sort of goatskin but there are several different kinds. Usually hunters have a little sassa for their personal fetishes. D. T. N.
12. The clear language *par excellence* is Mandingo. For the Mandingoes their language is clear like their country of open savannas, which they often contrast with the dark forest—hence references to Mali as the 'Bright Country'. D. T. N.
13. The land of Do seems to be the present-day region of Segou. Tradition speaks of Do as a powerful country. In modern times Do has been associated with the land of Kri and hence one speaks of 'Do ni Kri'. It is the land of ten thousand guns according to tradition and here is a poem which extols the land of Do:

    Land of ten cities
    Where Mansa Oumalé Kondé reigns,
    Do and Kri
    Land of the guns, Diarra
    Do and Kri. D. T. N.

14. In Mali the great harvest takes place in November and December. The young men, freed after these great labours, leave the villages, perhaps to seek a little fortune, or perhaps for the mere love of travel. They generally return a little before the great rains in May and June. D. T. N.
15. Most West African tribes believe in wraiths or doubles, but beliefs vary and are often difficult to determine even for one tribe. The Mandingoes believe that there are two spiritual principles in man; the life principle (ni) which returns to God at death, and the wraith or double (dya) which can leave the body during sleep, and after death stays in the house of mourning until the performance of ritual sacrifices releases it to wander among the places frequented by the dead person until, after fifty years, it rejoins

the ni. Much of the activity of the double in this book, however, seems better explained by references to the Hausa concepts of 'kurwa' and 'iska'. For a full discussion of all these ideas see Trimingham, op. cit., pp. 58 - 60. G. D. P.

16. According to tradition, it was at the death of the buffalo that the distinction between Traoré and Dioubaté arose. The two brothers Oulani and Oulamba were both Traorés. When the younger had killed the buffalo, Oulamba, the elder, composed off the cuff a song to the victor which said: 'Brother, if you were a griot, nobody would resist you,' in Mandingo: 'Koro toun Bake Djeli a Dian-Bagate.' The expression 'Dian-Baga-te' became 'Diabate' and by corruption 'Dioubaté'. Thus the Dioubaté griots are related to the Traorés. D. T. N.
17. From this ludicrous choice the Traorés and Kondés became 'sanakhou' which might be expressed by the coined word 'banter-brothers'. It means that as a token of some historical relationship two tribes or clans acquired the right to poke fun at one another with impunity. 'Banter-brotherhood' exists among many tribes of the savanna zone to this day. I once heard my servant allow himself to be called a bastard by a member of a tribe related to his only by this curious bond, and he merely laughed at this very grave insult. G. D. P.
18. The giving of cola nuts marks the opening of any sort of negotiation among the Mandingoes, and in this case the negotiation of a marriage. G. D. P.
19. The 'bolon' is a three-stringed instrument similar to the 'kora' which, however, has twenty-seven strings. The music of the bolon is war music whereas the kora is for domestic music. D. T. N.
20. A bloodstained cloth which showed publicly that the marriage had been consummated and that the bride had been a virgin. G. D. P.
21. Sand was used in divination and could give messages to the initiated. G. D. P.
22. The blood is the vehicle of the spiritual principles in man, of which the wraith is one. Shedding blood releases these principles, congealing paralyses them. G. D. P.
23. Owls are birds of ill-omen in West Africa, supposed to contain the spirits of the dead. G. D. P.
24. The 'tabala' was the royal ceremonial drum, one of the insignia of Muslim kingship. G. D. P.
25. The 'balafon' is an instrument like a xylophone made of blocks of wood set on gourds. G. D. P.
26. Maghan the Handsome. G. D. P.
27. Sundiata's gluttony was also legendary and some connect his surname with this: Soun (thief)—Djata (lion). It is said that he went marauding from house to house. According to another tradition (the one I have adopted), the name of Sundiata came from a contraction of his mother's name, Sogolon, placed before the name of the son, Djata, a very frequent practice among the Mandingoes. This gives Sogolon Djata—So-on Djata. The exact pronounciation in Mandingo lands is 'Sondjata'. D. T. N.
28. It is customary for West African boys to go for a few months to 'bush school' where they learn tribal lore in preparation for circumcision at the age of about twelve, when they become fully initiated members of the tribe. G. D. P.
29. I have been unable to find out the botanical name for this plant so I have used the word as it appears in the original. G. D. P.
30. The baobab is sometimes known as the monkey bread tree; its leaves are used for flavouring. G. D. P.
31. It was the custom to send princes of one court to be brought up in another. The political motive was twofold. The princes would probably preserve their boyhood friendships on coming to the throne, and while they were at the foreign court they could serve as hostages guaranteeing their fathers' loyalty. G. D. P.
32. M. Niane uses throughout the Mandingo name for Alexander, 'Djoulou Kara Niani', which is a corruption of the Arabic 'Dhu'l Qarnein'. G. D. P. In all the Mandingo traditions they like to compare Sundiata to Alexander. It is said that Alexander was the second last great conqueror of the world and Sundiata the seventh and last. D. T. N.
33. This oversight is in the original French. Sassouma Bérété offered the witches hay, not millet. Millet, however, seems a more likely thing for her to offer. G. D. P.
34. Wori is a very popular game in the western Sudan. It is like draughts, but the pieces are small stones laid out in holes bored in a tree-trunk. D. T. N.
35. Meetings and consultations were, and still are, held under a prominent tree. G. D. P.

36. Sundiata here addresses Mansa Konkon in the familiar second person singular. G. D. P.
37. The Mandingoes are part of a racial group including Bambaras, Sosso (pron. Soosoos) and Diallonkés, all speaking closely related languages and occupying adjacent territory; these we can refer to as tribes. Within these tribes there are clans such as the Traorés, Keitas, Kondés and Kamaras, who speak the same language but claim different ancestors and totems. Among these clans there are castes of craftsmen, endogamous groups with their own rituals, protective deities, etc. One of the most important castes was that of the smiths who, in an iron age society, had the power to make the best weapons and use them to their own advantage. After Islamization these castes held on to many of their pagan practices and became feared for their occult powers, though they occupied an inferior social position and kept to their own villages. Hence in this book smiths are often mentioned as being great sorcerers or soothsayers. G. D. P.
38. Wagadou is the Mandingo name for the land of old Ghana reigned over by the Tounkara-Cissé princes. D. T. N.

    In translating I have made a distinction which does not appear in the original since M. Niane uses the word Wagadou throughout. I have used Wagadou to mean the city where the Cissé kings reigned and Ghana, a more familiar word to English readers, to mean the empire as a whole. In fact, in Sundiata's day Ghana had been reduced to the area of the city of Wagadou and its environs. G. D. P.
39. The distance was approximately 550 km. G. D. P.
40. I have used the word 'taboo' to translate the French *pacte*. M. Niane explains that the original word is 'dio', a prohibition pronounced by an ancestor and which the descendants must respect. Here the taboo relates to the well-known legend of the snake of Wagadou. This city had as a protective jinn a gigantic snake to which a young woman was sacrificed every year. The choice having fallen on the beautiful Sia, her betrothed, Mamadou Lamine (called 'Amadou the Silent' by other traditions), cut off the snake's head and saved his beloved. Ever after, calamities kept falling on the city, whose inhabitants fled following a drought which struck the whole country. It is in any case difficult to fix the date of the disappearance of Wagadou. According to Delafosse the city was annihilated by Sundiata himself in 1240, but Ibn Khaldun still mentions an interpreter from Ghana at the end of the fourteenth century. D. T. N.
41. The original gives 'serpent-Bida'. G. D. P.
42. The white traders referred to were probably Moors from the Sahara. G. D. P.
43. The Soninke are a tribe related to the Mandingos but interpenetrated by Berbers and Fulanis. They were Islamized earlier than other West African tribes and thus gained the reputation of being very religious. They are also great traders and travellers. See Trimingham, op. cit., pp. 13 - 14. G. D. P.
44. The French word is *marabout*, but it is used in West Africa to mean a Muslim cleric or divine, or even someone who is merely very religious, as the distinction between clergy and laity is not marked. G. D. P.
45. Mandingo. G. D. P.
46. 'Sofas' are Sundanese infantrymen, or soldiers, warriors generally. D. T. N.
47. Diaghan lay on either side of the Falémé river, a tributary of the Senegal. The Diarisso dynasty was founded by a certain Kambine in the eleventh century and was formed from Soninke refugees who had escaped the attacks of the Almoravids by fleeing south from Ghana. Soumaoro (sometimes spelt Soumangourou) was the son of a Soninke warrior, Djara of the Kanté clan. Some scholars think that the present-day Sossos who inhabit the coastal region of Guinea had nothing to do with Soumaoro's city of Sosso. M. Niane, however, maintains that they are the descendants of Soumaoro's followers who fled to the Fouta Djallon after their leader's defeat at Krina. G. D. P.
48. The material symbol which is the abode of some supernatural power, e.g. a statuette, altar, mask, etc. See Trimingham, op. cit., p. 104. G. D. P.
49. Like many other African cities, Sosso seems to have been an agglomeration of villages belonging to distinct clans or castes. G. D. P.
50. The 'Vulture Tune', with the 'Hymn to the Bow', is frequently mentioned in the text. They are traditional songs still current among the Mandingoes. D. T. N.
51. Here is one of the dicta that often recurs in the mouths of the traditional griots. This explains the parsimony with which these vessels of historical traditions give their knowledge away. According to them, the Whites have vulgarized knowledge. When a White knows something everybody knows it. One

would have to be able to change this state of mind if one wanted to know some day all that the griots decline to give away. D. T. N.

52. The mithkal was an Arab measurement of weight equal to 4.25 grammes. In Mandingo this term is used to denote the smallest fraction of something. D. T. N.

53. Some traditions say that Fakoli's wife, Keleya, managed on her own to regale the whole army with her cooking, while the three hundred wives of Soumaoro never managed to feed the troops to their satisfaction. Jealous, Soumaoro abducted Keleya. This was the origin of Fakoli's defection. He rallied to Sundiata. D. T. N.

54. It is known that in the forest region of Guinea, south of Kankan, many Mansaré/Keitas are to be found. It is said that they are the descendants of Dankaran Touman, who colonized (Mandingized) the whole region of Kissidougou. These Keitas are called Farmaya Keita. It is said that when Dankaran Touman arrived on the site of Kissidougou he cried, 'An bara kissi' (We are saved), whence the name given to the town. Kissidougou is thus, etymologically, the city of safety. D. T. N.

    A bit dubious, I feel. The dominant tribe in that area is the Kissi tribe and 'dougou' is a common ending for place names in this region. G. D. P.

55. I have been unable to find the botanical name for this so I use the original. G. D. P.

56. Mother. G. D. P.

57. Bouré is the region to the north-west of Siguiri in Guinea. G. D. P.

58. 'Daffeké' is an emphatic word for 'a fine charger'. D. T. N.

59. The tradition of Dioma represents the battle of Kankigne as a semi-defeat for Sundiata:

    Kankigne Tabe bara djougouya
    Djan ja bara bogna mayadi.

    'The battle of Kankigne was terrible; men were less dignified than slaves there.' D. T. N.

60. The word I have translated as 'pennant' is 'bandari' which comes from the Arabic and means a banner, standard, flag, pennant. Another word also borrowed from Arabic is 'raya' which denotes a banner formerly carried by great clerics on the move. Even now regional chiefs still raise their 'bandari' above their house. D. T. N.

61. 'N'Ko' means 'I say' in Mandingo. The Mandingoes like to distinguish themselves from other peoples by their language. For them, Mandingo is the 'Kan gbe' (clear language *par excellence*). All those who say 'N'Ko' are, in theory, Mandingoes. D. T. N.

62. A 'tana' is a hereditary taboo, and can also mean a totem, i.e. the object of the taboo. In this case Soumaoro was forbidden to touch ergot, of which a cock's spur is composed, and as long as he observed this he could concentrate in himself the power of his ancestors. On his touching ergot and thus breaking the taboo his ancestors withdrew their power and his downfall followed. Power and life-force are regarded as communal possessions in Africa and when a man cuts himself off from the group by breaking a taboo he is as good as dead unless he performs a sacrifice in expiation. G. D. P.

63. This is an expression of joy in Mandingo. D. T. N.

64. 'Fama-Djan' means 'the tall chief'. Later, particularly under Kankan Moussa, 'Fama' was to be the title of provincial governors, the word 'Farin' being reserved for military governors. 'Ke-Farin' means 'valorous warrior'. D. T. N.

65. Forward. D. T. N.

66. There are numerous versions of Soumaoro's end. Here it is the Hamana version. That of Dioma says that Soumaoro, pursued by Sundiata, invoked his protective jinn for the last time, asking them not to let him fall into Sundiata's hands. So he was transformed into stone on the mountain of Koulikoro. Other traditions say that Soumaoro, hit by the cock's spur at Krina, disappeared right on the battlefield. The fact remains that after Krina the king of Sosso is never heard of again. His son Balla, captured by Fakoli, was taken in captivity to Mali. D. T. N.

67. The bourein is a dwarf shrub which grows in poor ground. It is a savanna variety of gardenia. Its use in the kitchen is forbidden and it is a shrub of ill-omen. D. T. N.

68. Diaghan was the town of Dia, which, according to the traditions, was a town of great divines. The Diawara reigned at Dia; the name means 'Wild Beast of Dia'. D. T. N.

69. The Keitas. G. D. P.

70. On the emperor's stay at Kita it is the Dioma version that I have followed. The Keitas of Dioma claim that their ancestor, a grandson of Sundiata, left Kita to come and settle in Dioma. Kiat was one of the big towns of the empire. D. T. N.

71. It is generally believed that Ka-ba (the present-day Kangaba) was one of the earliest residences of the Keitas. Local tradition states that the Keitas did not settle there until after Sundiata. Kangaba is a foundation of the Sibi Kamaras and the Traorés. The Keitas who settled there came from Mali in this way. There were two brothers of whom the younger, Bemba Kanda, left his brother at the halting-place of Figuera-Koro, came and settled at Ka-ba and allied himself to the Kamaras. In consequence several Keita families came and settled there. D. T. N.

72. The dynasty Sundiata founded is always treated as a Muslim dynasty through outside of the royal tribe Islam was weak and, as the text shows, mixed with a lot of pagan survivals. G. D. P.

73. King of kings. D. T. N.

74. 'Mansa' is a title equivalent to emperor or paramount king. The French version often has 'roi' before Mansa as if Mansa were a name. I have followed this in translating, but it is not strictly correct. G. D. P.

75. This song is one of the most famous which Balla Fasséké composed to Sundiata. It expresses the idea that Sogolon's son was the rampart behind which everyone found refuge. In other songs also attributed to Balla Fasséké Sundiata is constantly compared to Alexander (cf. recording number L.D.M. 30.081 'Vogue' made by Keita Fodeba). For my part I am inclined to attribute these songs to griots of the time of Kankan Moussa (1307 - 1332). In fact at that time the griots knew general history much better, at least through Arabic writings and especially the Koran. D. T. N.

76. The original has 'moude', a Mandingo deformation of Arabic 'mudd', which is a cereal measure, in fact, the legal measure fixed by the Prophet. As the taxes were paid in kind they were calculated by the mudd and finally the word came to mean simply a tax. A mudd of rice weighed 10 - 15 kilos, i.e. the contents of a basket of rice. D. T. N.

77. The Sahel is the region of the Sudan bordering on the Sahara. G. D. P.

78. Here Djeli Mamadou Kouyaté declined to go any further. However, there are many accounts of Sundiata's end. The first says that Sundiata was killed by an arrow in the course of public demonstration in Niani. The second, very popular in Mali, is rendered feasible by the presence of Sundiata's tomb near the Sankarani. According to the second account Sundiata was drowned in the Sankarani and was buried near the very place where he was drowned. I have heard this version from the mouths of several traditionists, but following what events did Sundiata meet his death in the waters? That is the question to which a reply must be found. D. T. N.

79. Here Djeli Mamadou Kouyaté mentions several kings of Mali. Hajji Mansa Moussa is no other than the famous Kankan Moussa (1307 - 1332) made for ever illustrious by his celebrated pilgrimage in 1325. The Dioma tradition attributes to Kankan Moussa the foundation of many towns which have now disappeared. D. T. N.

80. Griot traditionists travel a great deal before being 'Belen-Tigui'—Master of Speech in Mandingo. This expression is formed from 'belen', which is the name for the tree-trunk planted in the middle of the public square and on which the orator rests when he is addressing the crowd. 'Tigui' means 'master of'. There are several famous centres for the study of history, e.g. Fadama in Hamana (Kouroussa), situated on the right bank of the Niandan opposite Baro; but more especially Keyla, the town of traditionists; and Diabaté near Kangaba (Ka-ba), Republic of Mali. Mamadou Kouyaté is from the village of Djeliba Koro in Dioma (south of Siguiri), a province inhabited by the Keitas who came from Kita at the end of the fourteenth century and the beginning of the fifteenth century (see my *Diplôme d'Etudes Superieures*). D. T. N.

African Art

As late as 1985, Weiner Gillon laments the facts that African art has been miserably understudied and that the examination of its history trails a century behind the study of comparable arts, owing in part to the under-funding of sub-Saharan archaeological activity and to the perishable materials with which much of the art was constructed. For this reason, understanding of much traditional African art is limited to surviving and more durable bronze, iron, stone, and terra cotta objects. Despite this limitation, it is possible to identify general characteristics of African art and the relatively overlapping traits of sub-Saharan and Egyptian art culture.

Historically speaking, African art is ancient, rooted in 6,000 years of Tassili and Ennedi carvings, engravings, and rock paintings; monumental Egyptian and Sudanese architecture and sculpture; bronze works of Igbo Ukwu; lovely terra-cotta sculptures; remarkable Benin pieces; sculpted figures and masks; royal, religious, burial, and domestic dwellings; and decorative or functional objects such as furniture, textiles, pottery, and jewelry. Not only do these arts enjoy an ancient tradition and stunning variety of form and material such as wood, bronze, iron, gold, ivory, clay, and stone, but also they are extremely diverse in style, ranging from the highly naturalistic Nok bronzes (Figure 1), wrongly believed to have been influenced by Greek sculpture because of perceived stylistic similarities, to the highly abstract figures much imitated by modern European artists like Pablo Picasso, Georges Braque, and Paul Cezanne. Particularly in achieving abstract stylistic effects, artists consciously distort bodily proportions; emphasize the vertical rather than horizontal axis of human forms, as a way of linking the human to the divine; and employ *ephebism* (depiction of idealized, youthful figures) and *hypermimesis* (mere resemblance to a subject, instead of photographic accuracy in representing it). Not infrequently, the horrific or asymmetrical features of some African sculpture were used consciously to depict evil or unworthy behavior, whereas more pleasing or symmetrical features represented those beings who were deemed good or beneficial to the community.

Figure 1. Head. Nok Culture. Terracotta. Characteristic perforated facial features, with tiers of symmetrically arranged hair. Found in 1943 in tin mine near Jamaica. Courtesy National Commission for Museums and Monuments, Lagos, Photo: André Held.

The age, form, and style of art aside, African societies tend to be particularly protective of their artistic traditions, and artists are esteemed specialists, some of them trained by masters or within sophisticated art guilds, and in nearly all cases, executing their art with stunning technical expertise. Invariably, the profession of the artist is hereditary, as well as linked to religious custom, even falling under religious prescription and control. In Nigeria, Ghana, the

Figure 2. Seated Figure from Kerma. Black Granite; H. 65 cm. Th. 22 cm. Th. 28.5 cm. Turn. K III, Comp. 4/1 (Status No. 49) Harvard University-MFA Boston Expedition. February 1914, Field No. 14-2-1. Middle Kingdom, Thirteenth Dynasty, c. 1700 BC.
Source: The Metropolitan Museum of Art, NY.

Cameroons, and Zaire, the royal court patronized artists, who were in turn to develop their art according to royal dictates. Organized clubs or associations of women and men, who commissioned works for community or religious cult purposes, also were patrons of the arts.

The purposes of African art are also quite diverse. At times, figures were constructed to commemorate events or personages or to preserve the myths and history of a people. At times, too, community officials such as judges, policemen, or court representatives were provided with skillfully carved masks, which these officials wore professionally, to emphasize their status and ceremonial responsibility. When not educational or ceremonial, African art preserved community behavioral standards by reinforcing gender distinctions—often depicting women as nurturers and men as hunters, warriors, or community leaders. As an enforcer of standards of conduct, African art not infrequently held up to public ridicule the anti-social behaviors of greed, gossip, incompetence, and vice. Finally, African art had a protective and divinatory role. Sculptures were produced with the aim of embodying spirits which could protect the community from harm. Other objects became vehicles of *divination* (the art of foretelling the future), with the aim of answering specific public or private questions or of finding ways of resolving conflicts or responding to disaster.

From the northern to the southern most points of Africa, one finds tens of thousands of neolithic paintings and engravings on the walls of mountainous rock shelters, surpassing in artistic skill, variety, and number all other world art of the time. Achieving a dynamic quality because of their use of compelling reds, yellows, blues, and greens, these highly symbolic and usually abstract or non-photographic rock pictorials are doubtless the forerunners of traditional African art. Many of these symbolic or abstract designs probably depicted rituals and dramatized myths required in the socio-religious life of the community. Besides the Sudan and other northern locales, these paintings and engravings were discovered in Malawi, Zambia, Zimbabwe, the Transvaal, the Cape, and Drakensberg in Lesotho. There is doubtless a significant connection between these ancient rock paintings and the later paintings and engravings of Nubia (Color Figure 1) and Egypt, which are thought to have appeared during the Egyptian Pre-Dynastic Era, from 4000–3000 BC.

Nubian culture itself had developed as early as 6000–5000 BC. Because of the Nile River, Nubians early established links with Egyptians, and even, it seems, with Asian and Mediterranean peoples. Hence, because of the age of its civilization, Nubia is thought to be the cradle of much African art after the age of rock paintings. In fact, Nubian art had already passed its zenith when Egypt reached the end of the Early Dynastic Period (c. 2955 BC). In AD 1907–1908, finely crafted clay vessels and statuary dating as far back as 3000 BC were unearthed, all reflecting a distinctly Nubian style. The next wave of Nubian art, that of Kerma, began around 2200 BC, ending about 1500 BC when the Egyptian New Kingdom conquered large parts of Nubia. Figure 2 depicts a seated figure from Kerma. During the eighth century BC under the Kushite-dominated 25th Dynasty of Egypt, the Kushite conquerors retained many features of their indigenous artistic expression, as can be seen in the facial features, the close-fitting cap, and the position of the arms of the figure of King Shabago (Figure 3), whose purpose was likely that of housing the soul of the king. According to Timothy Kendall, the highly devout Kushite kings of Egypt's 25th Dynasty regarded themselves, not as foreigners, but descendants of an ancient god who had first brought civilization to the Nile Valley, which Kushites treated as one and the same culture. Dietrich Wildung also suggests that Egypt owes some cultural debt to the early Sudanese civilizations. Perhaps because of this early link between the Sudan and Egypt, the Kushite pharaohs revived the art and traditions of the Old Kingdom, believing themselves descendants of the original pharaohs. The 25th Dynasty having collapsed before Assyrian invaders in AD seventh century, these Kushite kings retired to the south, continuing to pursue a distinctly Kushite art in Napata and Meroë, while preserving the traditions of Egypt in the Sudan for the next 1000 years.

Figure 3. King Shabago in Offering Gesture. From area of Kush. Solid cast bronze, dark brown. 15.6 cm (6 ins).
National Museum, Athens, 632. Photo: courtesy National Museum.

Sharing predominantly the artistic values and attitudes of sub-Saharan African cultures, then, ancient Egyptian art was preoccupied with the royal family, as well as with the concept of royal immortality. While this art seems to celebrate the temporal power of the pharaoh, it makes clear that his power emanated from the gods. Because Egyptian art covers a period before the dawn of written history to the first century Roman era, historical demarcations vary among scholars, but a typical division might include eight periods, three of which can be regarded as intermediate or transitional—(1) the pre-dynastic era, (2) the old kingdom, (3) the first intermediate period, (4) the middle kingdom, (5) the second intermediate era, (6) the new kingdom, (7) the third intermediate period, and (8) the late period.

The Pre-Dynastic, Old Kingdom, and First Intermediate Periods stretch from 5500–2040 BC. The Pre-Dynastic, covering the time from c. 5500–3100 BC, produced the early Nile settlements and the earliest form of hieroglyphs. Art of this era is often *funereal* (related to rites and practices of burial), emphasizing household or daily implements supposed to be needed by the dead after they reach the underworld. Dynasties I–II (3100–2688 BC) witnessed the unification of Upper and Lower Egypt under a single leader, with Memphis in Lower Egypt as the capital. During the Old Kingdom (2686–2181 BC, Dynasties III–IV) the pharaoh came to be regarded as the incarnation of the god Horus on earth, offspring of the great sun god Re or Ra. The art of the Old Kingdom was a system of structures, statuary, and other objects which glorified the monarchs. Though many structures were royal tombs built on a colossal scale, often reminiscent of palaces, the human form, frequently the image of the pharaoh, was not neglected. But the anatomical features of these forms, rather than being naturalistic, tended to be idealized—possibly because the king was himself considered a demigod, thereby requiring a reverent representation. Wall paintings and carvings were also common, and these either reverenced the king or depicted the underworld.

Figure 4. Step Pyramid of King Zoser at Saqqara. Sandstone. Old Kingdom, Third Dynasty, c. 230 BC.
Photo courtesy of Steven Beikirch.

Striking monuments of the Old Kingdom were the Step Pyramid at Saqqara, the Pyramids at Giza, and the Sphinx of Giza. The interior of Figure 4, the Step Pyramid at Saqqara, is associated with a huge, largely unexcavated necropolis or cemetery found near Cairo and ancient Memphis, and the Pyramid is considered the oldest stone structure in the world, probably built around the Third Dynasty (c. 2630 BC) for King Zoser. The Great Pyramid at Giza, the only standing structure among the so-called Seven Wonders of the World, was constructed to commemorate Khufu or Cheops (c. 2638–2613 BC). For over 4 millennia, it was the largest structure in the world, its sides oriented to the four points of the compass, suggesting for it some type of astronomical or astrological role. In Figure 5, the left most pyramid is that of Khufu; the center pyramid, that of Khufu's son, Khafre (2613–2578 BC); and the right most structure, that of Khafre's son, Menkaure (2578–2553 BC). The Sphinx at Giza (Figure 6) is thought to be one of the oldest monuments on earth, dating back over 4,500 years. The face probably is the likeness of King Khafre, whereas the body is that of a lion. Some speculate that these two features of the Giza Sphinx may be related to the astrological signs Aquarius (the head of a man) and Leo (the lion). Figure 7 shows the full view of the statue, in front of which stands the Sphinx Temple (Figure 8). Following the Old Kingdom, the First Intermediate Period (2181–2040, Dynasties VII–X), was characterized by the collapse of central government, the rise of defiant, purely provincial leaders, and wide-spread famine.

The Middle Kingdom and the Second Intermediate Period extend from 2040–1567 BC. The art of the Middle Kingdom (from 2040–1797 BC, Dynasties XI–XII) witnessed a distinct shift towards a more realistic presentation of royal figures and a virtual renaissance of Egyptian literature and art. Mentuhotep II (2007–1986 BC), who was first to rule the united Middle Kingdom during the 11th Dynasty, created a style of tomb architecture which incorporated temple structures in a valley and on a hillside, connected by an extended, raised road or causeway. Color Figure 2 is a limestone from his mortuary temple. The Second Intermediate Period of foreign invaders from Asia known as the Hyksos, saw the establishment of Dynasties XIII–XVII (1786–1567 BC), which were relatively short-lived. Though the history of this period is obscure, it is known that the Hyksos introduced into Egypt the horse-drawn chariot, the composite bow, and bronze weapons; and that during this period, the term pharaoh was first used to mean "king."

Figure 5. Pyramids on the Giza Plateau. Pyramids of Khufu (Cheops), Khafre, and Menkaure. Old Kingdom, c. 2638–2553 BC.
Photo courtesy of Steven Beikirch.

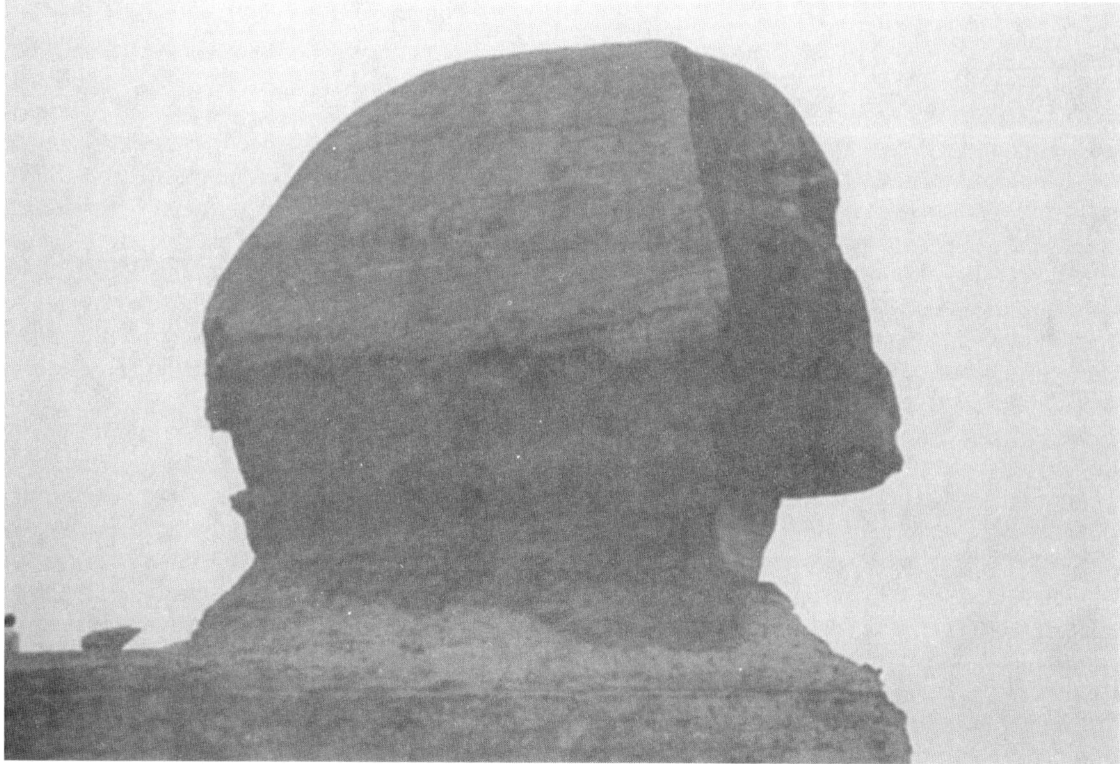

Figure 6. Sphinx at Giza (head or close-up view). Egyptian, Old Kingdom, c. 2500 BC.
Photo courtesy of Steven Beikirch.

Figure 7. Sphinx at Giza (full view). Egyptian, Old Kingdom c. 2500 BC.
Photo courtesy of Steven Beikirch.

Figure 8. Interior, Sphinx Valley Temple. Egyptian, Old Kingdom.
Photo courtesy of Steven Beikirch.

The New Kingdom and the Third Intermediate Period stretch from 1567–525 BC. The art of the New Kingdom (1567–1070 BC, Dynasties XVIII–XX) was characterized by magnificent religious architecture, including elaborate structures built by Queen Hatshepsut, Amenhotep III, Seti I, and Ramses II. Under the leadership of Queen Hatshepsut (c. 1504–1483 BC), who served as regent for her young son, Tuthmosis III, and later under the direction of Tuthmosis III himself (1483–1450 BC), the Egyptian empire expanded from Nubia to the Near East. Built by the Queen's architect lover and courtier Senmut, the Temple of Hatshepsut (Figures 9–12) is a three-tiered structure dedicated to the gods Amon and Hathor. The vertical colonnades of Hatshepsut's temple, echoing the cliff backdrop, suggest architectural harmony between man and nature. Now largely in ruins, the Temple of Khnum or Khnemu (Figure 13) at Elephantine Island in the Aswan region of Egypt is also thought to have been built by the Queen and dedicated to the god Khnum, believed to have created mankind from a potter's wheel. This temple was later partially restored by the Greeks and Romans. In addition to the structures built by Hatshepsut, the New Kingdom saw the construction of the famous Valley of the Kings, which a number of successive rulers expanded by building tombs, among them the stunning temple complex at Karnak. These temples were buried deep inside of rock tombs cut from cliff sides in the desert. The statues of Memnon (Figure 14) were constructed in the Valley during the Eighteenth Dynasty by Amenhotep III (1383–1349 BC). Only these two statues survive from the mortuary temple built between 1391–1353 BC.

Though during the fourteenth century BC the worship of the official god Amun-Re had reached its height under an influential clergy, the unorthodox pharaoh Akhenaten or Amenhotep IV (1350–1346 BC) established for the sun god Aten a monotheistic religion greatly at odds with the primarily polytheistic vision of the Egyptians. The reign of Akhenaton brought with it a pronounced realism which to some suggested dazzlingly beautiful caricature. However, Akhenaten's son, Tutankhaten (later Tutankhamun), who began his short reign while only nine years old (1334–1325 BC), reversed his father's religious innovation by restoring the state gods. During this period of stylish court art, many of the objects, such as those in the tomb of Tutankhamen, were exquisite, made of ebony, gold, ivory, and other semiprecious materials (Color Figures 3–10). Discovered in 1922 in the Valley of the Kings at Luxor by British archaeologists Lord Carnarvon and Howard Carter, the boy king's tomb had escaped meaningful plundering. Now displayed at the Cairo Museum are contents of the tomb, which included many treasures, together with the king's solid-gold coffin (Color Figure 11), which is one of two of the innermost sarcophagi. The outermost coffin, still holding Tutankhamun's remains, can be found in the Valley of the Kings. Following the conservative religious policies of Tutankhamen, Seti I (1291–1279 BC) constructed the original Temple of Osiris (Figures 15–17 and Color Figure 12) both as a personal act of reverence and as a public attempt to restore faith in the traditional gods destroyed by Akhenaten. The front of the temple is covered with images which are said to welcome the major Egyptian trinity—Osiris, Isis, and Horus.

The 19th and 20th Dynasties saw the rise of Ramses I and his grandson Ramses II (1278–1212 BC), who became one of the greatest builders of Egypt. Figures 18–20 show portions of his Karnak Temple located in Luxor, a monumental structure honoring three main gods: Montu, a regional warrior god; Amun, main god of Thebes; and Mut, wife of Amun. Begun during the Middle Kingdom and finished by Ramses, this over-five-acre structure took 1,600 years to complete. The design of the first temple at Karnak was said to have been given by the gods, allowing them to channel divine energy onto the earth plane. Because of this divine intent, the successive temples carefully copy the design of the first. Leading to the entrance of the first pylon or wall gate is a magnificent avenue of sphinxes, whose heads are those of curly-horned rams. These figures are supposed to stand for the great sun god Amun-Re, between whose paws is the small statue of Ramses II, who defeated the Syrian Hittites in the 1274 BC at the Battle of Qadesh. One of the major structures in the Luxor complex is the Ramesseum, a magnificent mortuary temple also built by Ramses II, whose statue is seen in Figure 21. Figures 22–24 give additional views of the structure. Likewise constructed by Ramses II was the great rock-carved Temple of Abu Simbel (Figures 25–28), built to commemorate himself and three gods: Amon-Ra, Ptah, and Ra-Harakhte. He also dedicated a temple to Hathor (goddess of love and beauty) and Nefertari (his favorite wife). This structure is the smaller of the two Abu Simbel temples which he built near the border between Egypt and Sudan in 1278 BC. The façade of Nefertari's Temple is adorned with six statues, two of the queen and four of Ramses (Figure 29). In Color Figure 13 is found a painted bas-relief from the tomb of Nefertari. From AD 1966–67, these temples were moved in sections before the site was flooded by Lake Nasser upon the completion of the Aswan High Dam. The mummy of Ramses II now resides in the Egyptian Museum at Cairo. Unfortunately, the Third Intermediate Period of Egyptian history (from 1070–525 BC, Dynasties XXI–XXVI) saw a dramatic

Figure 9. Temple of Hatshepsut, Upper Colonnade. Façade, showing harmonious columns. New Kingdom, eighteenth dynasty, c. 1470 BC.
Photo courtesy of Steven Beikirch.

Figure 10. Temple of Hatshepsut Lower Colonnade. Temple entrance. New Kingdom, eighteenth dynasty, c. 1470 BC.
Photo courtesy of Steven Beikirch.

Figure 11. Temple of Hatshepsut. Anubis Chapel. New Kingdom, eighteenth dynasty, c. 1470 BC.
Photo courtesy of Steven Beikirch.

Figure 12. Temple of Hatshepsut. Wall Painting. New Kingdom, eighteenth dynasty, c. 1470 BC.
Photo courtesy of Steven Beikirch.

Figure 13. Ceiling Detail, Temple of Khnum of Khnemu. Elephantine Island structure, thought to have been built by Queen Hatshepsut. New Kingdom, eighteenth dynasty, c. 1504 BC. Partially restored by the Greeks and Romans up to about AD 100.
Photo courtesy of Steven Beikirch.

Figure 14. Seated statues of Amenhotep III. Known as the Colossi of Memnon. New Kingdom, eighteenth dynasty, c. 1391–1353BC.
Photo courtesy of Steven Beikirch.

Figure 15. Steps leading to the entrance of the Temple of Osiris at Abydos. New Kingdom, constructed by Seti I, c. 1300 BC.
Photo courtesy of Steven Beikirch.

Figure 16. Columns in the Hypostyle Hall of the Temple of Osiris located at Abydos. New Kingdom, constructed by Seti I, c. 1300 BC.
Photo courtesy of Steven Beikirch.

Figure 17. Wall carving depicting Seti I with the Gods, in the Temple of Osiris located at Abydos. New Kingdom, constructed by Seti I, c. 1300 BC.
Photo courtesy of Steven Beikirch.

Figure 18. Hypostyle Hall, Karnak Temple complex. New Kingdom.
Photo courtesy of Steven Beikirch.

Figure 19. Entrance to the Temple of Ramses II. New Kingdom.
Photo courtesy of Steven Beikirch.

Figure 20. Temple of Ramses II, Karnak temple complex. New Kingdom.
Photo courtesy of Steven Beikirch.

Figure 21. Seated Colossus of Ramses II Temple of Luxor. New Kingdom, nineteenth dynasty, c. 1278–1212 BC.
Photo courtesy of Steven Beikirch.

Figure 22. Avenue of the Sphinxes. The Avenue leads to the complex entrance. New Kingdom, nineteenth dynasty, c. 1278–1212 BC.
Photo courtesy of Steven Beikirch.

Figure 23. Striding Colossus. Temple of Luxor. New Kingdom, nineteenth dynasty, c. 1278–1212 BC.
Photo courtesy of Steven Beikirch.

Figure 24. Hypostyle Hall. Temple of Luxor. New Kingdom, nineteenth dynasty, c. 1278–1212 BC.
Photo courtesy of Steven Beikirch.

Figure 25. Façade, Temple of Ramses II at Abu Simbel in southern Egypt. Seated statues of Ramses II, New Kingdom nineteenth dynasty, c. 1278–1212 bc.
Photo courtesy of Steven Beikirch.

Figure 26. Temple of Ramses II at Abu Simbel in southern Egypt. Exterior View. New Kingdom, nineteenth dynasty, c. 1250 BC.
Photo courtesy of Steven Beikirch.

Figure 27. Temple of Ramses II at Abu Simbel. Carved ceremonial scenes in the Hypostyle Hall, c. 1250 BC.
Photo courtesy of Steven Beikirch.

Figure 28. Temple of Ramses II at Abu Simbel in southern Egypt. Carved ceremonial scenes in the Hypostyle Hall, c. 1250 BC.
Photo courtesy of Steven Beikirch.

Figure 29. Façade, Temple of Nefertari located at Abu Simbel in southern Egypt. Two statues of Nefertari and four of Ramses II, c. 1330 BC.
Photo courtesy of Steven Beikirch.

Figure 30. Entrance, Temple of Horus at Edfu. Egyptian, late period, c. 50 BC.
Photo courtesy of Steven Beikirch.

Figure 31. Great Court, Temple of Horus at Edfu. Egyptian, late period, c. 50 BC.
Photo courtesy of Steven Beikirch.

depletion of Egyptian wealth, although the style of the pharaohs continued to be lavish. For instance, Ramses III (20th Dynasty), considered the last of the powerful rulers in Egypt, built a majestic burial temple around 1198–1167 BC. As Egyptian power declined, the Third Intermediate Period of Egyptian history (1070–525 BC, Dynasties XXI–XXVI) was marked by a number of new invasions and challenges. Pharaohs of Libyan descent rose to power by the 22nd Dynasty; and by the 8th century BC or the 25th Dynasty, those of Nubian descent. These Kushites conducted many restorations of the monumental architectural styles of the Old Kingdom and preserved many Egyptian traditions, as did the Assyrians, who, by AD 671, initiated a 26th Dynasty at Sais, Egypt.

Not surprisingly, the Late Period (from 525–332 BC , Dynasties XXVII–XXXI) is marked by continued conflict and war to defend Egypt, first from the Persians (525 BC) and later the Greeks (333 BC) and Romans (30 BC). Following the conquering of Egypt by Alexander the Great in 332 BC, Egypt fell under Greek control, and by 305 BC the Macedonian general Ptolemy had begun the long line of Ptolemaic rulers. This rule continued until the death of Cleopatra VII in 30 BC. After AD 395, Egypt became part of the Christianized Byzantine Empire until the beginnings of Islam in AD 641. Of note during this period was the founding of the city of Alexandria (after Alexander the Great) and the splendid library there. One of the monuments of this Late Period is the Temple of Horus at Edfu (Figures 30–31), on one of whose *pylons* or building gateways are images of the pharaoh Ptolemy XII. Doubtless, because of its late construction, this structure is the best preserved Egyptian temple of the ancient world, exceeded in size only by Karnak. Symbolically, the temple is associated with the Temple of Hathor at the Dendera complex, since Hathor is the wife of Horus, who is represented in Color Figure 14 as the falcon headed god.

Clearly, African art, the oldest aesthetic tradition in the world, offers enormous subtlety and scope. The African artist was a highly skilled, inventive craftsman whose work was always aimed at the social or spiritual enrichment of the community. The art of sub-Saharan Africa is linked to that of Egypt by similarity of attitude and technique, governed by a profoundly complex notion of a divinity to which humans are not only subordinate but also before whom they are profoundly awed. Communicated either by the miniature, abstract figure delicately carved from wood and meant to house the soul of the deceased or by a colossal temple from which stylized faces gaze towards eternity, African art depicts a perpetual state of worship and meditation.

Selected Bibliography

Eyo, Ekpo, and Frank Willett. *Treasures of Ancient Nigeria.* New York: Knopf, 1988.

Gillon, Werner. *A Short History of African Art.* New York: Penguin, 1991.

Janson, H. W. *History of Art.* 5th ed. New York: Abrams, 1995.

Kendall, Timothy. *Kerma and the Kingdom of Kush: 2500–1500 B.C.—The Archaeological Discovery of an Ancient Nubian Empire.* Washington, DC: National Museum of African Art, Smithsonian Institution, 1997.

Silverman, David P., ed. *Searching for Ancient Egypt: Art, Architecture, and Artifacts from the University of Pennsylvania Museum of Archaeology and Anthropology.* Ithaca, NY: Cornel UP, 1997.

Smith, William Stevenson. *The Art and Architecture of Ancient Egypt.* 3rd ed. New Haven: Yale UP, 1998.

Wildung, Dietrich, ed. *Sudan: Ancient Kingdoms of the Nile.* Trans. Peter Der Manuelian and Kathleen Guillaume. New York: Flammarion, 1997.

African Music

The music of the vast continent of Africa is characterized by great variety and complexity. The most important observation that can be made about African music is that it developed as an integral part of the community, thus functioning as an important part of everyday life. Enjoyment of leisure, recreational activities, and performances of ceremonies are all occasions where music plays an integral role. The indigenous music of Africa shares certain common characteristics. These include repetition, improvisation, antiphony, polyphony and syncopation, and rhythm. Repetition and improvisation are closely related. As musicians repeat lines or phrases, they also make changes or additions, including cries, trills, and yodels, serving to enrich the texture of the music. Antiphony occurs whenever a musical phrase, sung or played by a soloist, is repeated or answered by an instrumental or vocal group. Hence, another term for antiphony is call and response. Singing or playing two or more independent musical phrases constitute polyphony, resulting in what is called linear harmony. Rhythm and syncopation (stressing usually unstressed beats) stimulate body movement and involves the audience in the performance. The rhythm in combination with tone also makes it possible to imitate the speech patterns of African dialects.

Finally, while most people think of the drum when they think of African music, Africans make wide use of musical instruments from all four major classifications: idiophones, membranophones, aerophones, and chordophones. Idiophones, the most common and the simplest form of African instruments, can be defined as instruments whose sounds are produced without a stretched membrane, vibrating string or reed. They include stamping sticks, rattles, and xylophones. Membranophones are drums with parchment heads. Drums can be as simple as those made from skin aprons stretched over pots or as complicated as those that are intricately carved out of wood and elaborately decorated and considered to be objects of art. Drums also come in various shapes and sizes and may be played singly, in pairs or in larger ensembles.

Aerophones are wind instruments, instruments that are blown and include flutes, reed pipes, horns, and trumpets. Many flutes are made from natural materials, such as bamboo, the husk of cane, or the tip of a gourd. The reed pipes are not considered as important or as widespread as the flutes. Some reed pipes use a single reed while others use double reeds. These instruments are also made from natural materials, such as the stalk of millet or a similar plant. Horns and trumpets are made of animal horns and elephants' tusks as well as gourd, bamboo, or wood. Trumpets may be as long as six feet and may be played singly or with one or more additional trumpets.

The final class of instruments are the chordophones or string instruments. The musical bow, considered to be unique to Africa, is believed to be the most common chordophone. The simplest form is the earth bow, made from a flexible stick stuck in the ground. A piece of string is attached to its upper end and is buried in the earth. The string is held in position by a stone placed on top of the earth. Other examples of chordophones are various forms of zithers, lutes, harps, and lyres. Again, these instruments are made of natural materials, such as bark, sticks, wood, and goats' skin. Chordophones are considered ideal for accompanying solo singers, such as the praise singer or the griot.

It is clear that there is variety in African music. The music of Africa has been central to the development of African-American music, which in turn has a far-reaching impact on American music. African music will continue to be of interest.

Selected Bibliography

Floyd, Samuel A., Jr. *The Power of Black Music: Interpreting Its History From Africa to the United States.* New York: Oxford UP, 1995.

Nketia, J. H., Jr. *The Music of Africa.* New York: Norton, 1974.

W. E. B. Du Bois' *The World and Africa*: An Early Attempt at Redefining Africa

Armed with his wit and pen, W.E.B. DuBois rereads history and gives us a new historiography in the *World and Africa* (1946). He seeks to remind readers of the necessity of understanding the critical role of Africa in the history of mankind. Engaged in a trans-Atlantic conversation, DuBois seeks to change the exegesis or practice of interpretation based on a Eurocentric model (or a model of the universe with Europe at the center). DuBois changes the understanding not only of *Europe* but also of *Africa* as text or as sites of interpretation. In this binary relationship, *Europe* has come to represent a zone of positives: law, order, civilization, religion, and beauty, whereas *Africa* has come to signify a zone of negatives: chaos, disorder, the lack of civilization, superstition, and ugliness. (One sees this binary relationship at work, for instance, in Joseph Conrad's *Heart of Darkness*.)

In his poem "Heritage," the African-American poet Countee Cullen attempted to convey to a 1920's audience the spiritual and socio-political meanings of the term *Africa*, thereby pursuing a poetic redefinition. DuBois, however, is engaged in more than an exercise of the imagination. Rather, he refutes the prevailing orthodoxy that Africans are on the bottom rung of the great chain of being and that blackness is a badge of shame. He illuminates the nexus between color and economics in the global economy. Along with a few others, he advanced the then radical notion that the world would not be free until Africa was free. DuBois sees the continent of Africa as the center of a global conversation that has been muted or delayed as a result of the modern European slave trade. This delay has led to the devaluation of things African and a discrediting of the history of Africans. Most pronounced is the cultural hijacking of Egypt by Europeans in the nineteenth century. Through these and other observations, DuBois struggles to restore blacks to their former standing on the textual meeting ground of culture and aesthetics.

In the *World and Africa*, DuBois makes the following points about Egypt: that Egyptian history is an integral part of African history, that Egypt was the first great human experiment, and that Egyptian culture has made enormous contributions to the advancement of civilization. DuBois not only introduces a paradigm shift in how we view aesthetics, but he also calls into question (in fact, lifts the veil from) the footnotes of Plato and Aristotle. Like Alain Locke, he saw "truth and beauty" as the supreme values of culture that are invariably inseparable from our notions of humanity. A community's aesthetics is invariably integrated with its morality. DuBois wages the battle to restore blacks to their former standing on the world stage by seeking to break the chain imposed by imperialist aesthetics, which promote the insistent misreading of the text called the continent of Africa—a misreading seen, for example, in the work of Rudyard Kipling and Joseph Conrad. DuBois understood that the children of the Diaspora could no longer see their faces as made in the image of God—the end point of a community's aesthetic pyramid.

Ultimately, then, in the *World and Africa*, DuBois sets in motion an oppositional discourse that led to the dismantling of European hegemony and the colonial enterprise. This discourse rejected the notion of *culture* as an ideologically-charged semantic field used to justify Anglo-European supremacy while systematically devaluing the contributions of Asians and Africans to world thought. Carby believes that culture is a necessarily uneven terrain of a struggle between groups and that there is no whole, authentic, autonomous black culture that lives outside of these relations of cultural power and domination. Elevating what Africa has to offer, DuBois presents blackness as the locus of creativity and vitality. He, therefore, lays the intellectual groundwork, by which one can resist the distorted image of Africa as a backward and unregenerate jungle—a picture of Africa without history. He thus would admonish that Countee Cullen not "call the forest that shelters you a jungle" (Ashanti Proverb).

DuBois re-imagines Africa. In the *World and Africa*, he presents a challenging, comprehensive look at the significance of Africa for world thought. The *World and Africa* provides the post 1960s Africanist with an intellectual framework for studying Africa, especially in relation to culture, religion, aesthetics, and political economy. In his discussion of Egypt, DuBois pays particular attention to issues of cultural pluralism at this crossroads of the world where continental and sub-Saharan Africa and East and West meet. In the final analysis, W.E.B. DuBois, the intellectual baobob tree of twentieth century Africanist discourse, promotes an aesthetic of reconciliation. He wants people to engage freely in a global conversation with the knowledge that their respective communities have contributed affirmatively to world thought and the advancement of humanity. Concerned with how Africa relates to the human family, he re-imagines the text called *Africa*, offers a greater racial balance and correction to European hermeneutics, and challenges Eurocentric historiographic assumptions.

Selected Bibliography

Carby, Hazel V. "The Canon: Civil War and Reconstruction." *Michigan Quarterly Review* 28 (1989): 35–43.

Hubbard, Dolan. "Writing Culture: Alain Locke, Paris, and the Pan-African World." *MAWA Review* 7.1 (June 1992): 50–59.

Randall, Dudley, ed. *The Black Poets.* New York: Bantham, 1971.

Vaillant, Janet G. *Leopold Sedar Senghor.* Cambridge: Harvard UP, 1990.

Martin Bernal's *Black Athena*

Were the ancient Egyptians black? Were the origins of classical western civilization, the celebrated Greek achievements in the sciences, philosophy, religion, and the arts, heavily indebted to Afroasiatic sources? Has the racist legacy of slavery and European hegemony denied these connections and substituted a one-way model of Aryan Supremacy? Such claims are not new. Until recently, however, such discussions were well outside the province of scholarship. Then came Martin Bernal, whose 1987 book, *Black Athena: The Afroasiatic Roots of Classical Civilization*, rocked the staid, professional world of classical studies. Half historiography and half a sociology of knowledge, Bernal's work (a second volume appeared in 1991) laboriously documents what he sees as the shift from an "Ancient" model, which understood Greek civilization in terms of Levantine interconnectedness, to an "Aryan" model of perceived European cultural uniqueness, superiority, and domination. A decade later, Bernal's work remains highly controversial. Yet, while archaeological evidence is inconclusive, scholars find they can no longer ignore his plea for a sustained re-evaluation of multi-cultural approaches to classical historiography. Nor can they ignore his documentation of how the cultural assumptions of our academic institutions shape professional practice.

Bernal's starting point is his characterization of the "Ancient" model of Greek origins, patterned on what the Greeks believed about their own beginnings: that Greece was colonized somewhere around 1500 BC by Afroasiatic peoples, largely Egyptians and Phoenicians, who civilized the local inhabitants, spread their own cultures, and laid the foundation for later Greek achievements. This paradigm is actually quite explicit throughout Herodotus' *Histories*, written about 450 BC. Writing in Book VI, for example, Herodotus not only indicates his own belief in past foreign colonization but assumes it as common knowledge. In the *Histories* he is even more specific, mentioning the daughters of Danaos, who, fleeing the sons of Aigyptos, brought Egypt's gods and religions to Greece. For Herodotus it was clear that the gods of Greece originated from Egypt. The *Histories* also credits the Phoenicians, a Semitic people from what is now Syria, for introducing the alphabet into Greece. Greek writers in succeeding generations continued to give credit to Egypt as the source of major aspects of classical culture. Isocrates, the teacher of Socrates, praised the Egyptians for their governing caste of philosopher-priests. Indeed, his use of the term "philosopher" in his *Bousiris* is one of its earliest extant uses. His account of a "rule by the wisest" has clear resemblances to Plato's civic model in the *Republic*. Bernal notes, also, that Aristotle studied under Egyptian-trained scholars and called that country the "cradle of mathematics" exactly because of this priestly caste.

Black Athena next traces the esoteric history of Egyptian Hermetic wisdom and its influence on western thought. This tradition is identified with the figure of Hermes Trismegistos, a late Hellenic version of Thoth, Egyptian god of wisdom. Throughout the middle ages and Renaissance, the Greeks (especially those of the Platonic and Neo-Platonic traditions) were seen as the transmitters of this wisdom by scholars like Copernicus, Giordano Bruno, and Isaac Newton. Newton himself declared in his *Principia Mathematica* that the priests of Egypt knew of gravity, atomic theory and heliocentrism. From them, he wrote, the Greeks acquired their most fundamental philosophical concepts—concepts which the Egyptians had otherwise kept hidden from the uninitiated through an elaborate symbology. For almost two thousand years then, in Bernal's view, the West had little difficulty in ascribing its origins to non-white, Afroasiatic sources. As late as 1784, in his *History of Greece*, the then standard work on the subject in English, Edward Gibbon's friend, William Mitford, could credit the advance of Greek civilization to its contact with the East, particularly with Egyptians who had established colonies in Greece. Thus, the Ancient model, so many centuries after Herodotus and Plato, was still alive and well even at the end of the eighteenth century.

In the nineteenth century, however, a major paradigm shift occurs, a shift to what Bernal calls the "Aryan" model. Based largely on linguistic evidence, the Aryan model replaced the previous ancient view of Levantine interconnectedness with a more Eurocentric one. This model rationalized the substitution by holding up as evidence of Aryan superiority the fact of the previous Indo-European conquest of militarily weaker Mediterranean peoples. These conquerors, originally from the Caucasus Mountains (and hence the term "Caucasian"), then spread their presumably advanced culture throughout the region. This new paradigm effectively separated Greek culture from the non-white cultures of the South and East and preserved Europe as both independent and dominant. In Bernal's view, this new configuration is not due to new evidence so much as to social and political factors generated by later colonialism, anti-semitism, and racism—thereby making the ancient model increasingly unacceptable to the dominant Eurocentric bias.

In order to understand the academic triumph of the Aryan model, Bernal examines the relationship between scholarly activities and major components of nineteenth century ideology. For most Victorians, history was a Darwinian struggle among cultures and races. As bearers of civilization, Europeans were to take on the "white man's burden" and modernize supposedly "inferior" people. This notion of progress went directly against the evidence that non-whites had long ago developed highly advanced civilizations. It became important, then, to denigrate the achievements of Egypt, China, Islam, India, Phoenicia and to emphasize Aryan conquests as catalysts of growth and cultural change (as happened supposedly in India) or to downplay a culture's blackness (as happened with Egypt). Thus, Bernal notes that in 1904 the English Egyptologist Wallis Budge could ridicule the notion that a God posited by what he regarded as "a half-civilized African people" was in any way comparable to the concept of God presented by a presumably more "cultivated" Greco-Roman civilization. It was common, in fact, to assert the mental inferiority of non-white peoples. For instance, Bernal points to the claim of James Henry Breasted, in his the *Development of Religion and Thought in Ancient Egypt*, that Egyptians lacked both the terminology and mental capacity for abstract thought.

As Greek art came to be more and more accepted as the classical standard, Egyptian art was denigrated. In fact, Bernal observes that Winckelmann, the celebrated German art critic of early Romanticism, dismisses the art of Egypt exactly because it accentuated African features, skin color, and physique. Here, nineteenth century race biology and art criticism meet. To thinkers like Winckelmann, the "European" proportions of a Venus de Milo or Perseus are models of perfection in both nature and art, and the Caucasian physique is both evolutionarily and aesthetically advanced. On the other hand, according to such writers, the African physical features are inferior. Bernal also connects romantic views of Greek culture to the general academic acceptance of the Aryan model. He identifies this fusion as "Romantic Hellenism." Culturally, Romantic Hellenism drew upon the celebration of the "Volk" to create a myth of a common past for all Europeans. The Greeks became the childhood of Europe and were regarded by the proponents of Romantic Hellenism as a pure Aryan stock stronger than their neighbors and destined for greatness. Both the Germans and the British looked on the Greeks as more than cultural ancestors: a racial connection was seen between the Indo-European Dorian invaders from the North, the "true" Greeks, and the Teutonic peoples of Northern Europe.

Since 1987 scholars have hotly debated all of Bernal's major points. Does he take too seriously old Greek myths that, too, might have had their own political agendas? Are the etymological connections he finds between Greek and Egyptian words sound or wild speculations? Are the quotations he uses to document his charge of nineteenth century racism distortions and out of context snippets? All of these charges can be made with some justification. Nevertheless, *Black Athena* has opened up the world of classical scholarship by raising salient issues.

Part II: The European Perspective

European Backgrounds: History and Culture

European literature is still believed by some individuals to have begun with the major influences which the Greeks, and later, the Romans had on Western thought and literature. However, the Bible of the ancient Hebrews has exerted a formidable influence in style, subject matter, religion, and philosophy, not only on the early Greeks and Romans, and later, on virtually all European culture and literature, not just during the Middle Ages but to this day.

The written history and literature of the Hebrew people began approximately from 1000–300 B.C., with the ancient Palestinians who were of Semitic, Arab and Assyrian stock. The historical and literary records of these Palestinians start with the Talmud, a body of Jewish civil and religious law consisting of the Mishnah (rabbinical rules), the Gemara (commentaries on the Mishnah), the Halakah (detailed regulations and rites), the Haggadah (tales, parables, anecdotes and legends), and the Bible, a collection of sixty-six (or eighty) books that were written in their present form from c. 750 B.C., to c. A.D. 100. The Bible is divided into three major divisions: the Old Testament (containing history, prophecy, lyric poetry, drama, wisdom literature and tales); the New Testament (consisting of the four gospels, church history, and epistles); and the Apocrypha (comprised of history, tales and more wisdom literature). Some stories in the Bible, the most read and translated book in the world, recount the legendary origin of the Hebrews, initially an animistic[1] and polytheistic people. This and other stories, like God's creation of the world and of humans, Adam and Eve's fate, Cain's murder of Abel, Noah's flood, and the tower of Babel, are recorded in Genesis, the Bible's first book. The first leader of the Hebrews was Abraham, the progenitor of the Hebrew people, whose life began in Chaldea. The Hebrew language thus began initially as Chaldaic mixed with some Phoenician. After the Hebrews were invaded, captured and defeated, more and more foreign words crept into their vocabulary. This altered language was called Aramaic.[2]

The forms of writing already in use (from 3300–2900 B.C.) were Egyptian hieroglyphics (which was later modified into hieratic and demotic cursive characters to make writing easier and faster) and cuneiform (which was used by Akkadians, Babylonians, Hittites and Assyrians for more than two thousand years). However, another unidentified writing system was developed by the Phoenicians (of Semitic origin) who owned trading seaports on the coast of Tyre and Sidon. The Hebrews used this system to record their history. These records became known later, by the Christians as the Old Testament.

The remaining chapters of the Bible provide legendary information about Abraham's sons, Isaac, Jacob and Joseph. Other stories include Lot and his wife, whom God turned into a pillar of salt; Abraham's near sacrifice of his son, Isaac; Jacob's marriage to Leah and Rachel; Jacob's ladder; and Joseph's brothers' ruthless sale of Joseph into slavery in Egypt. The Hebrews resided in ancient Palestine for several generations until drought and famine forced the Palestinians to relocate to Egypt where they lived for many years until Moses helped them to escape and eventually return to Palestine.[3]

After their return to Palestine, the Hebrews were governed first by "judges" or religious and military men. After many petty wars, kings replaced the judges. The two most renowned of these kings were David (c. 1060?–970 B.C.), a shepherd boy who later became king after he killed Goliath, and David's son, wise king Solomon (c. 974?–937 B.C.) Under the able leadership of David and Solomon, the Hebrews rose in political importance. When Solomon's reign ended, however, the kingdom was divided into two parts: Israel in the north and Judah in the south. As the petty wars that the Hebrews fought with their neighbors escalated, the Hebrews were captured, first by the Assyrians (in 721 B.C.), then by the Babylonians (in 586 B.C.). The warfare ended when the Hebrews were deported to Babylon in 586 B.C. When the Edict of Cyrus was issued by Persian Emperor Cyrus in 539 B.C., the exile of the Hebrews ended, they returned to Palestine, they became prosperous, they were able to rebuild their cities, and they codified the Pentateuch (the first five books of the Bible) for themselves and for posterity. By 300 B.C., however, after Alexander the Great's successors annexed the Palestinian state, the Hebrews' homeland became part of the Greek-speaking world. The Greeks modified the Phoenician script and adopted it as their own. When the Romans conquered the Greeks, the Hebrew people were annexed to the Roman empire. After the second of two revolts by the Hebrews against Emperor Hadrian in A.D. 131–34, the Hebrews, now a stateless people, were scattered throughout the ancient world's cities and did not regroup as a nation until the middle of the twentieth century.

Unlike the Greeks and Romans, however, the Hebrews did not bequeath to future generations any visual arts like painting or sculpture, nor did they leave epic poems or dramas. However, they did leave a religious literature and, in an area populated by believers of polytheism, the revolutionary belief in one God. This concept of an omniscient, omnipotent and omnipresent God began initially as a blood-thirsty, jealous, and vengeful being. As centuries passed, however, God's attributes and qualities became ennobled. He became a just, merciful, holy, moral and universal God, accessible to Jew and Gentile alike.

Overlapping the period of Hebraic development, Gilgamesh became king in Uruk (2700 B.C.); the Hebrews' migration from Mesopotamia began (c. 1900 B.C.); Hammurabi's Code of Law was written in Babylon (1800 B.C.); the epic of Gilgamesh was being formed (1600 B.C.); the Egyptian *Book of the Dead* was written (1500 B.C.); Akhenaten dedicated his capital to Aten, the sun god and composed his *"Hymn to the Sun"* (1375–1354 B.C.); the Epic of Gilgamesh was recorded (1300 B.C.); The *Leiden Hymns* were written down (1238 B.C.); Moses led the Jews from Egypt to Palestine (1200 B.C.); the text of the Torah was assembled along with the Psalms (1000 B.C.); and first David, then Solomon became kings in Israel (1000–927 B.C.).

Unlike the ancient Hebrews, certain Greeks of antiquity, notably the Dorians and the Northern Indo-Europeans, overran their neighbors. These people, who inhabited the southern area of Hellas (the Balkan peninsula), part of Asia Minor, Italy and the Mediterranean islands, including Sicily and Crete, were mixed with three different strains: (1) the Pelasgians or Heladics (3000–1800 B.C.), who were the earliest known non Indo-Europeans. The corresponding historical period was the Pelasgian or Helladic era (same dates as above), which was probably a Stone or Bronze age culture; (2) the Aegeo-Cretans (c. 1800–1400 B.C.), whose corresponding historical period was called the Cretan-Minoan era (same dates as above), and whose culture contained Egyptian traces; and (3) the Northern Indo-Europeans (2000–1000 B.C.), also called Achaeans, Danaans and Hellenes. Two other historical periods overlap with and extend beyond the 2000–1000 year period. The first period is the Mycenean (c. 1400–900 B.C.), in which Northern Indo-Europeans overran Creto-Minoan culture, and the Dorian era (c. 1100–900 B.C.), which was characterized by great wars and migrations. During this time, also, the Indo-Europeans split up into all three strains (the Dorian, Ionian and Aeolian) and the Aegean culture was nearly destroyed. In approximately 1150 B.C., three different racial groups inhabited the area: (1) the combative, reserved, and pious Dorians with their rugged, cacophonous dialect; (2) the imaginative, impressionable Aeolians, with their soft, melodious speech, who gave passionate poetry to posterity; and (3) the energetic, versatile Ionians, whose language, soft, graceful and flowing, became the principal language of Greece.

Greek government was not centralized during the ninth and eighth centuries but was comprised of city-states that, much like large tribes, engaged in petty wars. Each *basileus* or ruler inherited his position, and was also a priest, a judge and a military chief who enjoyed absolute power. The council of nobles who advised him was called a *boule*. In addition, there was the assembly, a group of freemen who had little political power. However, they could vote "yes" or "no" on certain issues.

A polytheistic people, the Greeks had a rich body of religious literature which consisted of various creation myths involving a plethora of gods and demi-gods, all of whom, in many ways, thought and acted no better than humans. Moreover, Grecian myths of creation are confusing and contradictory. In the first myth, Homer tells readers that the river Ocean encircled land and sea. In a second, Night and Darkness bore Light. In a third, Chaos sprang from Time, and from Chaos came Night, Mist, and Ether (fiery air). The comic poet Aristophanes states that Time caused mist to swirl around Ether until the mass became an egg, from whose center Love was born. The egg broke into two halves: Heaven and Earth. In a fourth, from Chaos, which was comprised of Darkness, Mass and Void, emerged Ge (Gaea) Love, and Night, and from Gaea were born Uranus (Heaven) and Earth. The past repeats itself in each of the three mythical dynasties, for in each, one of the sons of the ruling king usurped and overturned his father's kingdom, then assumed the throne.

The second and most prominent of these dynasties begins with Cronus, who had learned that one of his children would dethrone him. Motivated by the fear of losing his kingdom, he thought to alter fate by swallowing his children as soon as they were born. When Rhea, his sister-wife, gave birth to Zeus, she had someone carry the baby away secretly. She then gave Cronus a large stone wrapped in swaddling clothes, which he thought was the baby Zeus, and swallowed it. Later, when Zeus became grown, he overthrew Cronus with the help of his grandmother, Earth, and made his father regurgitate the stone and the other children. A war then broke out between Cronus and the other Titans against Zeus. Zeus won the war, partly with the help of the hundred-handed monsters whom Zeus freed to help him, and partly because Prometheus, a child of the Titan, Iapetus, aligned himself with Zeus. After Zeus' seizure of power, his brothers and sisters—Demeter, Hades, Hera, Hestia, and Poseidon—ruled with him secondarily. These five formed the beginning of what later became known as the twelve great Olympians. The rest of the anthropomorphic Olympians—Aphrodite, Apollo, Ares, Artemis, Athena, Hephaestus, and Hermes—consisted of Zeus's children with various women.

Grecian gods made mistakes, they felt human emotions, and they could be tricked by each other and by humans. Some were vindictive, manipulative, jealous, angry, promiscuous, amoral and immoral. For example, the chief god, Zeus, was a womanizer, and his wife and sister, Hera, nagged him much of the time. Aphrodite, Athena and Hera were vain, and Hephaestus was lame. These gods communicated with humans not directly, on a one-to-one basis, but through such intermediaries as oracles (priestesses), dreams, and fortune-tellers.

Prior to the appearance of humans on earth, the Greeks tell of mysterious beings, the Cimmerians, who lived on the farthest side of Ocean, in a misty, cloudy land, though the actual direction, north, south, east or west, is not known. The origin of the second group of beings is equally mysterious. These blissful Hyperboreans, for whom sickness, old age and death did not exist, lived behind the North Wind, not far from the Muses. A third group of beings who are held in such high esteem by the gods that the latter often feasted with them in their banquet rooms were the Ethiopians.

Most of the nearly perfect people in these seemingly utopic settings were still not human. The origin of man (the word *man* is used because a man was the first human created) is told in three different myths. In the first, man sprang from Mother Earth, and could, quite possibly, be as old as the gods. In the second, the gods gave the task of man's creation to two brothers: Prometheus (whose name means forethought), was wiser than the gods; Epimetheus (whose name signifies afterthought), acted on impulse and later regretted his actions. Before creating men, Epimetheus gave so many gifts (courage, swiftness, and strength; feathers, wings and fur) to the lower animals, that there were none left for man. Since man had no qualities or body covering that would protect him from the elements or the beasts, he would not have been the strongest, would have been no match for these animals, and therefore, could not have survived in the wild. Epimetheus, who later realized his mistake, went to his brother, Prometheus, for help. Prometheus gave man the advantage by first ennobling his form by constructing it in an upright fashion, then increased man's superiority by giving humans the gift of fire which Prometheus got from the sun. In yet a third, the gods themselves were experimenting with metals in the making of man. Each man that they made, like the metals themselves, declined in worth, from excellent, to good to poor. The first men were made of gold and were superior to any that came after them. They are described as perfect, pure, beneficent human guardians whose spirits lived on after they died. The second race, made of silver, was inferior to the golden race. Lacking in intelligence, they could not avoid harming each other. When they died, their spirits did not live on after them. The third race, that of men of brass, were strong, powerful, vicious men who loved war and violence so much that they ended by annihilating their entire race by their own hands. The fourth race, that of the god-like heroes, was a great improvement over the third; they were adventurers and great warriors, whose heroic exploits have been sung and talked about throughout the ages. After death, they, like the golden race, went to the blessed isles where they lived in eternal bliss. The fifth race is the wicked iron race, which now inhabits the earth. Their characters are filled with evil and their children are inferior to them. These men, who worship power, to whom might is right, will have to toil in sorrow as long as they live. When the time comes when they are no longer incensed at wrong-doing, or ashamed when they see another human being in misery, the iron race will be destroyed also. However, this doomsday prophesy could be avoided if they mend their ways.

The creation of woman is told in two different myths about Pandora. In the first, Zeus created woman as a punishment for Prometheus who not only gave fire to men but who gave the best part of any animal sacrificed to men. Prometheus accomplished this by cutting up an ox, putting the best parts in one pile and disguising it by placing parts of the intestine on top. He then made a second pile consisting of bones and entrails covered up with fat and asked Zeus to choose one of the heaps. Zeus chose the latter and was angry when he saw the bones underneath. He never forgot this trickery by Prometheus. He got revenge by creating a beautiful, stunning woman in whom both men and gods were enchanted when they beheld her. Past, present and future generations of women were believed to have all come from Pandora, whose name means "the gift of all." In a second story, the gods gave Pandora a box which contained things that were harmful to humans; then, they instructed her not to ever open it. It was not her evil nature or her propensity to do evil that made her the source of human misfortune, but her curiosity that introduced evil to humankind. Pandora's curiosity finally got the best of her, and when she opened the box, plagues and sorrows of all kinds sprang forth. This myth ends on a positive note, however, for the last quality to come out of the box was Hope.

During the eighth and ninth centuries, B.C., in order to establish a literary tradition, Greek tribal chiefs consulted bards[4] who told tales called lays, from centuries long gone, of the glorified exploits of gods and demigods from the Heroic Age. This large body of orally transmitted literature constituted the foundation for the heroic poems of Homer and for other epic literature. This divine heritage entitled these men to enjoy certain advantages and privileges. For example, Thetis attempted to immortalize her son, Achilles, by dipping his body in the river Styx and she created a protective golden halo around his head and torso when he fought with the Trojans.

The earliest and greatest classical writer of western literature is the epic poem writer, Homer (c. 850 B.C.), who probably lived in an Ionian district of Asia Minor. The debate still rages regarding whether or not Homer wrote most of the *Iliad* and the *Odyssey*.[5] These two poems form the basis for eight epic conventions, each of which asks that the poem fulfill the following requirements in order to qualify as epic poetry: one, that the poem have as the play's theme, the adventures of a national hero; two, that the poet invoke the aid of the muse (of epic poetry), Calliope; three, that the story begins in the middle (*in medias res);*[6] four, that the poem contain stereotyped epithets;[7] five, that the text of the poem contain epic similes[8]; six, that the poem incorporate extensive monologues;[9] seven, that the poet show the gods intervening in human affairs; and eight, that the poem be written in classical dactylic hexameter.

In addition to Homer's *Iliad* and *Odyssey,* and Hesiod's *Works and Days* and his *Theogony,* other kinds of epics, called cyclical, independent, and mock remain extant. Only fragments of the two kinds of cyclical epics, the Theban Cycle and the Trojan Cycle, are extant. The main epics of the former are the *Theogonia* (which tells of the origin of heaven and earth), the *Thebais,* the *Oedipodeia,* and the *Epigoni,* each of which recounts the Oedipus story. The primary epics in the latter are *Cypria, Aethiopis, The Little Iliad, The Sack of Troy, The Return of the Atridae,* and *Telegonia,* all of which provide the background of the Trojan War story.

During the age of lyric poetry,[10] extending from approximately 700–450 B.C., the monarch's power weakened, and that of other nobility strengthened. Citizenship was greatly valued in what had now become autonomous political units or city-states. At the beginning of the sixth century, tyrants overthrew the nobles; at its end, the tyrants themselves were overthrown, and the city-states, which became either democratic or oligarchic,[11] focused less on centralization of power and more on the self-realizing capacities of the individual.

The Attic Age (500–333 B.C.) in Greece begins in the fourth and third centuries B.C., when Greece was at its political, cultural and aesthetic zenith. Because of the reforms of Cleisthenes, Athenian male citizens enjoyed the first democratic government, although that same democracy excluded women, foreigners and slaves. After 490 B.C., when Persia invaded Greece on three different occasions, Athenians formed the Delian League, a confederacy of nations which banded together for military advantage against Persia. During the Age of Pericles (461–429 B.C.), Pericles, the chief general and popular assembly leader, was, unofficially, the ruler of Athens. During his tenure, Athens experienced cultural development, prosperity, and pervasive influence that was unparalleled in its history. Nearly all citizens received a basic education in science, math, writing, literature, music and sports.

In 431 B.C., however, both Athens and Sparta entered into the Peloponnesian War, and after fighting for nearly ten years, the two city-states declared a short-lived truce. Though Athens seized Syracuse in 415–413 B.C., the victory depleted Athenian resources to such a degree that Sparta, in 404 B.C., was able to conquer Athens. From 404–359 B.C., disillusionment, internal strife, and class struggle were the norm, though Sparta maintained power until 371 B.C., when Thebes defeated the city-state. Thebes maintained power until defeated by Athens and Sparta in the battle of Mantinea. After a chaotic period (from 354–338 B.C.), Philip of Macedon conquered Greece, died two years afterward and was replaced by his son, Alexander the Great, who had, by 331 B.C., conquered Greece, Asia Minor, South Central Asia, Persia, and Egypt.

The Attic Age was one in which the most renowned Greek authors lived and worked in such disciplines as history, oratory, literature and philosophy. Three such personalities that made their marks were Herodotus of Halicarnassus (c. 484–425 B.C.), Thucycides of Athens (c. 470–398 B.C.), and Xenophon (c. 434–355 B.C.), also from Athens. Unlike Herodotus, Thucydides, one of ten Athenian generals, was known as the world's first critical historian. He was an admirer of Herodotus, whom he had read when he was an adolescent. Having a close-up, inside view of the Peloponnesian War enabled him to examine the war's underlying causes and eventually to write his *History of the Peloponnesian War,* a survey of a fifty-year span of Greek history. Unlike both Herodotus and Thucydides, Zenophon of Athens, a soldier and an acquaintance of Socrates, wrote several works. The *Dialogues* is a record of his memories of Socrates. His other three historical texts are as follows: *Hellenica, Anaasis,* and *The Education of Cyrus (The Cyropaedia).*

In addition to these historical texts and authors, Greek literature (tragedy , comedy, rhetoric, oratory and philosophy), flourished during the sixth and fifth centuries. Like English drama, Greek tragedy, which developed from religious ceremonies, began as a chorus which, at its height, consisted of all men, who, to honor Dionysus, the "party-hearty" god of wine and vegetation, masqueraded as goats (satyrs) as they sang and danced. In the mid-sixth century B.C., the "father of drama," Thespis of Athens, introduced an "answerer" *(hypocrites)* who spoke a few words, intermittently, to the chorus. Aeschylus, the first of three great Greek tragedians, added a second answerer (actor), Sophocles added a third, and Euripides (and many who came after him), kept the chorus at three for some time. Under Sophocles, the spoken parts were in iambic pentameter or trochaic tetrameter. The chorus' number eventually reached as many as fifty members.[12] As time passed, new mythological material was added, the number of answerers increased and spoke more, and the importance and number of the chorus decreased.

Greek tragedy, taken from stories about the gods or about great men of the Heroic Age, consisted of five parts: the *prologue,* which introduces and explains the drama; (2) the *parados,* which is the chorus' entrance song; (3) the *episodes,* which are three or four sections of the plot which the main characters enact; (4) the *stasima* (the singular form is *stasimon*), which are choral songs following each episode); and (5) the *exodus,* which is the action occurring after the last *episode.* The unities of time and place were sometimes adhered to, but the unity of action was nearly always observed. Usually, Greek lovers of drama were knowledgeable about the stories before they attended the performances. They came to see the dramas as critics, to assess how the plays were produced and to examine the ways in which the actors interpreted their roles.

In terms of staging and production, each dramatist submitted four plays, called a tetralogy, which consisted of one trilogy and a satyr play. Property, scenery and costumes were extravagant. A *choragus* (producer and director) bore the brunt of the expenses incurred to equip both the chorus and the actors. During Aeschylus' time, two actors were assigned to each choragus. The characters themselves, who were mainly created as types though some were individualized, wore masks, wigs, and high-heeled shoes. This form of dress helped to identify their genders and roles. The tragedy contained very little plot development, and precious little on-stage action. The theater itself, an open-air structure whose seats were made first of wood, then of stone, formed nearly a complete circle around the *orchestra* (stage). The front wall of the *skene* (dressing room), located behind the orchestra, was called a *proscenium* which formed a backdrop for the *orchestra.*

Aeschylus of Athens (c. 525–456 B.C.) dealt, in his plays, with some of the most complex moral and religious concerns of his time. He believed that the gods are supreme and just, that humans should obey the gods' decrees, that each person has personal responsibility for his or her thoughts and actions, and that certain sins, which can only be expiated through suffering, bring the sufferer wisdom. Aeschylus wrote, during his lifetime, ninety tragedies and satyr plays of which only seven are extant. They are *The Suppliants,* (c. 490 B.C.), *The Persians* (472 B.C.), *The Seven Against Thebes* (c. 466 B.C.), *Prometheus Bound* (c. 466 B.C.), and *The Oresteia* (458 B.C.).[13]

Sophocles of Athens (495–406 B.C.), believed that the gods were just but that they did not intervene much in human affairs. Like Aeschylus, he also believed that guilt can be passed down from father to son, but that character flaws are, more often than not, the cause of human downfall. He also believed, again like Aeschylus, that suffering will eventually bring wisdom and create, in the individual, a strong character. Sophocles wrote approximately 123 plays of which these seven have survived: *Ajax* (445 B.C.),

Antigone (c. 441 B.C.), *Oedipus the King* (c. 430 B.C.), *Manders of Trachis* (413 B.C.), *Electra* (c. 410 B.C.), *Philoctetes* (409 B.C.), and *Oedipus at Colonus* (401 B.C.).

Euripides of Athens (c. 480–408 B.C.) was a visionary who criticized traditionally held views of the gods, altered divine legends at will, attacked prevalent beliefs in oracles, and satirized orthodox heroes. For him, Athenian democracy was debauched, and controlled by the rich. A misogynist and a pessimist, Euripides yearned for a democracy based on reason, merit and sincerity. He wrote ninety plays, of which eighteen are extant. Some of his most popular dramas are *Alcestis* (438 B.C.), *Medea* (431 B.C.), *Hippolytus* (428 B.C.), *Mad Hercules* (c. 422 B.C.), *The Trojan Women* (415 B.C.), *Electra* (c. 413 B.C.), *Ion* (c. 417 B.C.), *Iphigenia in Tauris* (c. 414–412 B.C.), *Helen* (412 B.C.), *The Phoenician Women* (c. 409 B.C.), *Orestes* (408 B.C.), *The Devotees of Dionysus* (c. 405 B.C.), *Iphigenia at Aulis* (c. 405 B.C.), and *The Cyclops* (c. 423 B.C.).

Unlike Greek tragedy, the obscure origins of Grecian comedy can be traced to two sources: to Sicilian mime or farce, which was comprised of coarse, rude, familiar references to persons in the audience; and to the Athenian *comos* (Dionysian songs or revelry), which were sung mainly at the *Lenaea* festival in January, and the *City Dionysia* festival in March. Revelers who dressed outlandishly and carried phallic symbols, were later divided into two antiphonal groups. Both the *comos* and the mime together form comedy, though how the two combined in this way is unknown.

The structure, staging, production of Greek comedy resembled that of Greek tragedy. The structure of Old Comedy is nearly the same as that for tragedy, except for two differences: the *agon* (a debate between the winner of the debate, who introduces the happy idea, and the opponent), came after the *prologue* and the *parados*; and the *parabasis*, an opinionated choral interlude was spoken directly to the audience. The *parabasis* follows the *agon* and precedes the rest of the comedy, with *episodes*, *stasima* and the *exodos* following suit in that respective order. At these festivals, five comedies were presented after the tragedies, by five different authors, and a prize was offered for the best comedy. Like tragic actors, comic actors wore masks but donned low rather than high-heeled shoes. The chorus consisted of twenty-four costumed men.

The greatest writer of Old Comedy was Aristophanes of Athens (c. 448–380 B.C.), who, unlike Sophocles, was a great believer in orthodoxy. His two-part comedies containing a happy idea that is debated, and the putting of that idea into practice, usually expresses a yearning for "the good old days," and protestations against the frivolity and decadence of his age, whether they be in the area of etiquette, customs, religion, politics or philosophy. Aristophanes wrote approximately forty comedies, of which eleven still survive. They are *The Acharnians* (425 B.C.), *The Knights* (424 B.C.), *The Clouds* (423 B.C.), *The Wasps* (422 B.C.), *Peace* (421 B.C.), *The Birds* (414 B.C.), *The Thesmophoriazusae* (411 B.C.), *Lysistrata* (411 B.C.), *The Frogs* (405 B.C.), *The Assembly-Women*, also known as *The Ecclesiazusae* (c. 393 B.C.), and *Plutus* (388 B.C.). Middle Comedy (380–336 B.C.), about which little is known, was a transitional genre, a hybrid drama with characteristics of both Old and New Comedy. New Comedy (336–262 B.C.), consisting of five-act plays, evolved naturally from Middle Comedy.

After rhetoric and oratory, philosophy is the last major category of knowledge in Greece. A rhetorician is one who is showy or artificially eloquent in literary style. Inventors of early rhetoric were Corax and Tisias, his student, both of whom were well known for their subtlety, quick repartees and usage of the "bon mot." The Sophists, paid professional Athenian teachers (rhetoricians), taught in all branches of knowledge. Ostentatious in dress and manner, they are known for their arguments which, in Plato's view, made the worse appear to be the better cause. The most visible Sophist was Protagoras of Adera (b. 480 B.C.), recognized as a great humanist and founder of grammar.

Oratory originated with the early rhetoricians. An orator, a person who can give an eloquent and forceful speech, was very highly esteemed in Greece. Early leaders sought to become not only good soldiers but well-trained orators as well. One such person was Demosthenes, who used rich figures of speech (taken from natural forces), proverbs, sentence variety, rhetorical questions, amplification, antithesis, puns and varied rhythms to create carefully polished speech. His most famous orations are *For the Rhodians* (353 B.C.) defending democracy, *Three Philippics*, criticizing Philip of Macedon, and *On the Crown*, justifying his political conduct.

However, Socrates of Athens, considered by some to be the father of ethics, wrote nothing, though he profoundly influenced Greek thought. Socrates believed that his divinely ordained mission was to awaken individuals to their ignorance and to inspire in them a desire for truth. He taught Zenophon, Plato and others without pay, using his question-answer method of dialectical inquiry. Rejecting materialism, he sought to establish absolute standards of conduct after which human beings should model their own. Not abandoning his polytheistic ideas, he believed, nonetheless, in personal immortality and in a Supreme God who would guide others in matters of morality.

Unlike Plato, who was Socrates' student, Aristotle (Plato's student) believed in a teleological creator God (the final universal cause). He also thinks that happiness, the highest good, can be attained through material goods, moderation, moral virtue and wisdom. He rejects Plato's theory of Forms and contends that intellectual concepts can only exist in things. Thus, form can neither exist without matter nor matter without form. Likewise, the soul can neither exist on earth without the body, nor the body without the soul. After Plato died, Aristotle left Athens. From 342 to 335 B.C., at the request of Philip of Macedon, he became tutor to Alexander. In 335 B.C., he founded *The Lyceum*. Though many of his writings are lost to posterity, thirty-two are still extant, the most significant of which are *The Instrument (Organon)*, (treatises on deductive and inductive logic along with Sophistic refutations), and *The Poetics*, an early example of literary criticism which contains discussions on character motivation and flaws, the three unities, probability, pity, fear, and catharsis. When Aristotle died in 322 B.C., the age of Greek literature ended and most of the literary activity moved to Alexandria. When Alexander the Great died in 323 B.C., his empire was divided among his generals. Egypt was given to Ptolemy Soter, who made Alexandria his capital.

The Roman conquest of Corinth marked the fall of Greece and the beginning of recorded Roman history (146 B.C.–A.D. 529). During this period, no poetry of note was written, and only a handful of writers actually produced prose. One was Plutarch of Chaeronea (c. A.D. 46–120), who studied in Athens and visited Rome. He is known for his *Parallel Lives*, fifty biographies of great men in public service. In history, Polybius of Megalopolis (c. 205–125 B.C.), who was taken as a hostage to Rome in 167 B.C., and who became a friend to Scipio Africanus (a literary patron and Roman general), wrote *Universal History*, a forty-book collection. In philosophy, Marcus Aurelius Antonius (A.D. 121–180), a Roman emperor and the last great Stoic, exhibited his opposition to Christianity by persecuting Christians. He wrote *To Himself*, twelve books called *Meditations* in which he admonishes himself. He believed that people should avoid vanity, regard other human beings as brothers, practice forgiveness, consider their souls their inner guides, and suffer and die bravely. In satire, Lucien of Samosata (c. A.D. 125–200) criticizes hypocrisy in society, literature, and religion. His principal works are *Dialogues of the Gods, Dialogues of the Dead, How to Write History*, and *The True Story*. In these texts, he ridicules belief in the gods, philosophers, the exaggerated enthusiasm of historians, and Greek mythology and history. In literary criticism, Longinus (c. A.D. 90), about whose life nothing is known, wrote a critical essay entitled *On the Sublime*. In it, he defines what the sublime in literature means: it must be written by great souls; it must have distinctive and striking diction; and it must please everyone, everywhere.

Latin or Roman literature began, according to Horace, during the Republic, in 240 B.C., with Lucius Livius Andronicus (c. 272–207 B.C.), the first Roman dramatist after the first Punic War. For two hundred years after this war, Rome was busy conquering one Mediterranean power after another: Greece, Macedonia, Syria, Carthage and Spain. When Julius Caesar conquered Gaul (France) in 50 B.C., Rome became ruler of the known world. Though in name a republic, in reality, aristocratic classes ruled Rome.

Roman literature can be subdivided into three periods: the Republic (240–27 B.C.), the Augustan Age (27 B.C.–A.D. 14), and the Empire (A.D. 14–476). During the Republic, some indigenous literature had been written, e.g., songs for festive celebrations, litanies, half dramatic verses and farces, but not much Latin poetry or prose existed before 27 B.C. However, most Roman literature was patterned after the texts of Greek giants like Homer, Sappho, Demosthenes and Thucycides. In 272 B.C., Lucius Livius Andronicus (c. 272–207 B.C.) was brought from Greece to Rome as a prisoner of war, and was made a slave. He adopted his master's name, Livius, and in 240 B.C., after he was freed, he rewrote the *Odyssey* in Latin using rough, archaic Saturnian verse. Fragments of this text still survive.

Another dramatist, Titus Marcus Plautus (c. 254–184 B.C.) also moved to Rome and worked odd jobs in a theater. His financial status improved when he began writing plays. He is purported to have written over one hundred and thirty New Comedy plays, though he authored probably no more than forty-five. The twenty that still exist, which fall into four categories—plays of mistaken identity, of intrigue, of character, and of recognition—contain a mixture of both Greek and Roman elements. The Greek scenes usually refer to Roman places and customs. Though his plays have closely-knit plots and stock characters, some themes and character types are repeated from one play to the next.

A comedy writer, Publius Terentius Terrence (c. 185–159 B.C.), born in Carthage, was brought to Rome by Terentius Lucanus as a slave. Lucanus educated Terrence and later liberated him. Allegedly Terrence became intimate with Scipio Africanus, the Younger. At any rate, he wrote and produced six plays. All are extant, though four are adaptations from Menander, and two are adapted from Apollodorus. Critics say that his well constructed plots are stereotypical and repetitive and his writing is too serious.

Satire was the only clearly Roman literary invention during the Republic. The originator of satire as a separate genre was Gaius Lucilius (180–102 B.C.), who produced thirty books of satire which he calls "readings" (sermones), of which only 1300 fragments survive. In most of these, he attacks, in coarse, graphic, unorthodox language, persons or public faults or foibles.

In philosophy, Titus Lucretius Carus (99 or 95–55 or 51 B.C.) a poet and philosopher himself, was also a patron to Catullus as well as a friend of Cicero and Menander.[14] His unfinished poem *On the Nature of Things* is written in six books. Its text, which provides a materialistic view of the universe, attempts to free people from their fear of the gods and death. Lucretius was heavily influenced by Homer, Democritus and Epicurus but greatly influenced Catullus, Hobbes, Rousseau and Voltaire.

Three of the four other artists who were principally influenced by Greek writers were Gaius Valerius Catullus[15] (84–54 B.C.), Marcus Tullius Cicero (106–43 B.C.), and Gaius Sallustius Crispus (86–c. 34 B.C.). Still extant are one hundred and sixteen "long" and "short"poems by Catullus, who was influenced by Sappho, Alcaeus, Callimachus and some Alexandrian poets. These poems are characterized by subjectivity, sincerity, tenderness, pathos, and passion. The second, Cicero, who had a good education at Arpinum, served in the military, then moved to Rome where he studied law, rhetoric and philosophy. His principal works are rhetorical, political, moral, and theological treatises and orations on public and private matters. He insisted on straightforward speech, a pure vocabulary (which meant no usage of foreign words) and accurate idioms. The name of one of his orations, *The Philippics (Philippicae)* was borrowed from Demosthenes. The third, Sallust, wrote an account of the Jugurthine War and the Catalinian Conspiracy as well as a text entitled *History*, a ten-year account. Sallust, an imitator of Thucycides, was honest and objective but sometimes provided inaccurate chronology in his work. The fourth, Gaius Julius Caesar (c. 100–44 B.C.), a general, statesman, dramatist, poet and historian, wrote *Commentaries on the Gallic War* (seven books which defend his military policy in Gaul), and *Commentaries on the Civil War,* three books describing the conflict between Caesar and Pompey.

The Augustan Age (27 B.C.–A.D. 14), an era of peace and security, began when Octavian Caesar Augustus announced the re-establishment of the Roman Republic while paradoxically governing the Republic as an emperor. During this time, citizens began to extol Rome's past, present and future glory. This nationalism brought with it the rich and famous patronage of writers of literature. The reduction of political controversy diminished the need for oratory and redirected the focus to poetry and technical expertise. It was in such an atmosphere that men of letters like the following lived and wrote: Publius Virgilius Maro or Virgil (70–19 B.C.) in literature; Quintus Horatius Flaccus or Horace (65–8 B.C.) in literary criticism, satire and philosophy; Publius Ovidius Naso or Ovid (43 B.C.–A.D. 17) in drama and epic poetry; and Titus Livius Patavius or Livy (59 B.C.–A.D. 17) in history. The epic, lyric and elegy were their chosen media.

Virgil, who studied grammar, rhetoric, Greek and philosophy, was influenced, early in life by Homer, Pisander, Euripides, Catullus and Lucretius. Initially attracted to Epicurianism, he became more orthodox in view later in life. Although he wrote minor poetry and is recognized and appreciated for his *Bucolics*, and *Georgics,* he is especially renowned for his masterpiece, *The Aeneid.* He was influenced by Homer (whose epic conventions he incorporated into *The Aeneid*). Virgil wrote *The Aeneid* to personify Roman virtues and to create for Rome a glorious history. Like the Greeks, *The Aeneid* had as its main character, a half-god who was also a dutiful, compassionate, virtuous, and pious, national hero. *The Aeneid* is not as repetitious as *The Iliad:* it is more subjective, intimate, morally earnest, and meticulously constructed. Initially, Virgil reputedly wanted to destroy this text, but the epic poem was allegedly saved by Augustus himself.

Horace, who wrote satire, epodes, odes, epistles and literary criticism *(The Art of Poetry),* did not believe in the Roman gods or in personal immortality. Rather, he leaned more toward a mixture of Stoicism and Epicureanism, moderated by Aristotle's Golden Mean.[16] He thought that excess of any kind often resulted in misery. Posterity has remembered Horace primarily for his lyrics and literary criticism. He is excellent in technique, relies heavily on common sense, and is good-natured as a satirist. However, he has been criticized for being too spontaneous and emotional.

Ovid, born in central Italy in the town of Sulmo, was educated in Rome, in rhetoric and law. However, he soon abandoned law to write poetry. Ovid wrote many love poems and letters, but his name has gone down in history for his masterpiece, *Metamorphoses,* a long, narrative poem which describes the ways in which humans and objects become transformed from the time of their creation to 43 B.C. The work consists of 246 stories, each of which ends in some kind of transformation. His works contain some religious or ethical content: he complains about the injustices of traditional Roman gods in whom he seems to have had little faith or belief, and he vaguely includes the theme of monotheism in his narratives. Because of his psychological depth, his metrical skill, his versatility, and creative imagination, he is ranked as one of the most prolific and widely-read erotic poets.

Livy, a historian, was born in Padua, but moved to Rome when he and Octavian became friends. Livy, who was especially interested in portraying the personalities and actions of Roman people, wrote *The Annals (Histories),* in 142 books of which Books I–X and XXI–XLV survive as long fragments. The first few books of *The Annals* cover a period of 460 years and borrow from other sources, often carelessly failing to acknowledge or provide accurate historical dates.

The Empire (A.D. 14–180), became increasingly disruptive, moving from the suppression of individual freedoms, (from Caligula (A.D. 37–41) to Nero (A.D. 54–68), to the enjoyment of prosperity and happiness (from Nerva to Marcus Aurelius 96–180). These latter days of the Empire were an age of prose, letters, histories, biographies, tales and religious treatises. However, some poetry—like Seneca's dramas in verse, Martial's epigrams, and Statius' epic—was written and reached its zenith during the Empire. After Marcus Aurelius, economic, political and social conditions worsened, then plummeted during and after barbaric invasions , in spite of the temporary stability that Diocletian brought with his rule. Other important dates during the Empire were Christ's crucifixion (A.D. 30), Rome's burning (A.D. 64), Jerusalem's destruction (A.D. 70), Vesuvius' eruption and Pompeii's and Herculaneum's burning (A.D. 79), The Goth's first invasion (A.D. 251), the Empire's division (A.D. 364), the Goth's sack of Rome (A.D. 410), the Vandals' conquest of Rome (A.D. 455), and the fall of the Roman Empire (A.D. 476).

Like literature in Greece, Roman literature during the Silver Age was inferior to that of the Golden Age which preceded it. Emperors encouraged literary productions, severely restricted the writer's freedom of literary expression, and discouraged philosophic writing. Five "Empire" writers made specific contributions: Seneca, Petronius, Martial, Lucanus and Juvenal. Lucius Anneaus Seneca (c. 3 B.C.–A.D. 65) bequeathed to posterity the innovative use of the prologue, the drama's division into five acts, and philosophic fatalism (as opposed to Aeschylus' and Sophocles' religious fatalism). Petronius' prose work, *The Satyricon,* contains an impoverished plot, and his satire is said to be not only sensually depraved but also lacking in decorum. His work has become noteworthy for a verisimilitude found in his choice of vocabulary, which illustrates a specific vernacular spoken by the half-educated Roman. Martial's short, bold epigrams were written on humorous, sardonic, complimentary, congratulatory, supplicatory or eulogistic subjects. Marcus Annaeus Lucanus (A.D. 39–65), one of the Empire's two great epic poets, is known primarily for having written an unfinished historical epic entitled *Pharsalia.* The second epic poet, Publius Papinus Statius (c. A.D. 40–96), borrowed extensively from Virgil's *The Aeneid* when he wrote *The Thebaid,* an epic poem in twelve books. Juvenal's sixteen satires are full of powerful vitriol and invective, along with a high moral tone of righteous indignation at the baseness of his society. A voracious reader, Pliny the Elder wrote several histories, including a thirty-one-book history of Rome and a thirty-seven volume *Natural History,* which he compiled from source books. Although this multivolume text was accepted as an accurate authority during his time, his data was later found to be unreliable: the text contains few original observations or source verifications. Pliny the Younger wrote *Letters* (containing nine books that were modeled on Cicero's letters). Though less significant, it gives readers a slice of life of the manners and customs from A.D. 75–112. He also wrote *The Panegyric Oration,* an overly elaborate speech which was a poor example of oration but which contained valuable historical information.

During the Empire, because Christianity was initially thought of as a religion of the illiterate lower classes, there was little Christian literature. Christian literature was taken more seriously during the second century, A.D. Early Christian writers included Minucius Felix, Tertulian, St. Cyprian and Lactantius. Important later writers were St. Jerome, St. Augustine and Boethius. St. Jerome, (Eusebius Hieronymus, c. 340–420), wrote the *Vulgate,* a Latin translation of the Bible, as well as commentaries on the prophets, homilies, biographies of saints, letters and brief histories. St. Augustine, (Aurelius Augustinus, 354–430), Bishop of Hippo, was born of a devout, Christian mother and pagan father in Algeria. As a young man, he was a promiscuous, fun-loving Manichaean.[17] After listening to the sermons of St. Ambrose in Milan, he converted to Christianity and became a zealous theologian and writer of voluminous literature including moral treatises, philosophy, sermons and polemics. Two of his important works are the *Confessions,* an autobiography of his early life and conversion, and *The City of God,* which deals with the final conflict, leading to judgment day, between good and evil. Ancius Manlius Severinus Boethius (c. A.D. 475–525) was the counsel and a favorite of Theodoric the Ostrogoth. In A.D. 525, he was accused of conspiracy against the emperor and was imprisoned, then executed. During his incarceration, he wrote his most famous work, *The Consolation of Philosophy,* an allegorical handbook in five books. He also translated Aristotle's *Categories,* and wrote *On Interpretations* (commentaries on Aristotle, Cicero and Porphyry), as well as texts on logic, astronomy, mathematics, geometry and music.

Rome fell in A.D. 476 after the Barbarians dethroned the last Roman emperor. However, the country remained unstable principally because of the turmoil created by the Ostrogoths, Visigoths and Byzantines. In A.D. 568, Italy was invaded by the Langobards (Lombards), who dominated the country for two hundred years. In A.D. 774, Charlemagne, the legendary king of France, overthrew the Langobards, and was later crowned Emperor of the Holy Roman Empire. Charlemagne's dynasty remained in power for approximately 100 years, from A.D. 774 to 888. After his rule ended, the country was plagued with anarchy until Otto the Great, the Saxon, became emperor in A.D. 962. Then the Normans infiltrated southern Italy and by A.D. 1137, had become rulers of Sicily, Naples, Capua and Apulia. During the twelfth and thirteenth centuries, city-states developed, and the Pope struggled for political power.

When the seven-hundred-year period which we now call the Middle Ages (also called the Dark Ages) occurred, the people of that time knew neither that they characterized an age, nor did they call themselves medieval. When contemporary readers reflect on the Middle Ages, images are evoked of grim and foreboding castles or cathedrals high on mountaintops, of the coexistence of both superstition and religious faith, of knights in shining armor, of beautiful damsels in distress wearing long dresses and sporting cone-shaped hats, and of a strange mixture of court jesters, robber barons and wretched serfs. Though these mental pictures of the darkness and gloom hovering over the Middle Ages are not inaccurate, the Middle Ages as a period in history, encompassed much more than a dark, unproductive period that divides ancient from modern times. It is true that the first half of the Middle Ages, before A.D. 800, was an age of regression in the sense that the Roman Empire fell, commerce ceased to flow, and men seemed to forget how to construct buildings, to paint pictures and to write literature. However, after A.D. 800, this process of decay and forgetfulness ended, and people gradually remembered, began to recapture clumsily, the old classical wisdom, to rebuild their world, and to find their own new wisdom.

Several characteristics define the Middle Ages not just in Italy, but in other European countries as well. First, this period of retrogression was caused in large part by The Black Death, a plague that annihilated half of Europe's population during the fourteenth and fifteenth centuries, and, in France, The Hundred Years War brought almost as much misery and death. Second, in Europe in general, society was arranged on the coherent system of organized obligation, called feudalism, in which each participant was obligated to his superior and inferior. Each was both master and vassal, until the bottom of this hierarchical pyramid was reached. In this system, a man "commended" himself, i.e., offered to serve and be loyal to his "master," and, in return, he would receive protection and a sense of security from his "lord." At the pyramid's top, a noble might pledge fidelity to the king, or he might believe that he is the king's equal, making him the king's enemy. At the bottom of the feudal pyramid were the wretched serfs, each of whom pledged loyalty to someone higher than he, but who had no one lower who would serve him. However, all humans, regardless of rank, had to subject themselves to the Church, which had complete control over the fate of the soul, and the Church had to submit to God. Third, the Church introduced a Christian ideal that pervaded all aspects of society; thus it determined, to a large degree, the culture of the citizens. It preserved ancient learning, inspired a great deal of the literature by providing subject matter for artists, and was the patron of art and architecture. It is therefore not surprising that mysticism flourished during the Middle Ages, which began in Italy.

During the thirteenth century, no medieval literature written in Italian was produced initially by Italian writers. Writers like St. Francis of Assisi, Guido Cavalcante (who wrote lyrics), and Brunetto Lantini (who compiled an encyclopedia) preferred to write in Latin rather than Italian, a new language which gradually grew out of classical Latin. In fact, Italian was considered by the learned to be a vulgar dialect until A.D. 915, when it was officially recognized. The first Italian to write in Italian was Dante Aligieri. Though Dante wrote other works such as *The New Life, The Banquet, On the Vulgar Tongue,* and *On Monarchy,* he is best known for having written *The Divine Comedy,* a literary epic based not on orally transmitted legends as was the case with the classical Greek epic writer, Homer, but on an ingenious fictional creation formed largely in the mind of Dante himself. *The Divine Comedy,* an allegorical tale about a human soul's journey through hell, purgatory and eventually heaven, is not an epic poem in the classical sense, for it does not depict the exploits of a national hero. Rather, it mirrors the disruptions so typical in society during Dante's time.

Unlike that of Italy, the history of France prior to the earliest known inhabitants, the Galli, remains obscure: nothing is known about the Galli before the Romans conquered Gaul. The area now known as Brittany was first populated by the Brythonic Celts who were driven into the northwestern peninsula of France by the Anglo-Saxons who invaded England. Most of France's history consists of battles by Germanic tribes for supremacy during the sixth to the eleventh centuries. In A.D. 507, Clovis became king of the Franks and made Christianity the religion of the country. In A.D. 702, the Moors, who had conquered France and Spain, were defeated by Charles Martel. By A.D. 800, Charlemagne had consolidated much of France and Germany and was crowned emperor. In A.D. 842, grandsons of Charlemagne, Charles the Bald and Louis the German, took the famous *Serments de Strasbourg,* against their brother Lothair. Each of them took an oath of mutual fidelity in the language of the other's territory. In the tenth century, the northeast area now known as Normandy was appropriated by Norsemen. There were two main dialects spoken from the tenth to the fourteenth centuries: the *langue d'oc* (south of the Loire river), and the *langue d'oïl* (north of the Loire). After the fourteenth century, the northern dialect, now predominant, became the ancestor of modern French. During the eleventh century, feudalism and chivalry were practiced and reached their peak and decline in the twelfth century. The Hundred Years War reversed the gains made during the preceding hundred years, and commercial activity as well as cultural progress stopped. The Middle Ages in France came to an end with the death of Joan of Arc in A.D. 1431.

The French language is the result of the effort of the people of Gaul to speak the classical Latin which the Roman officials and colonists had declared the official language of the government, of the schools and of the Church. Roman soldiers and the less educated classes spoke Low or Vulgar Latin. By the fifth century, Low Latin, which had undergone more changes, became Gallo-Latin. When the Barbarians invaded France, they helped to make this popular speech the national tongue. Eventually the Church, in order to communicate more easily with the people, began to conduct its business in Gallo-Latin, which later became French. The first document written in French was the *Serments de Strasbourg.*

The three types of literature produced during the twelfth century, saints' lives, neo-Latin religious works, and *chansons de geste,* illustrate the importance of the Church and feudalism. The thirteenth century is known for its prose romances (of adventure, of antiquity, of Breton [Brittany]), along with chronicles and lyric poetry. By the middle of the thirteenth century, a large body of bourgeois literature circulated, which lacked heroism and the romanticism of courtly writings. Instead, it contained the *esprit gaulois,* an attitude of mocking and jovial, yet realistic and rationalistic criticism. The fabliaux, tales in verse written in octosyllabic couplets, were an effective representative of this spirit. Along with beast fables and satires, people of the Middle Ages were also fond of didactic or allegorical poetry (usually intended to teach a moral lesson) in which people or things symbolized abstract ideas.

Though the origin of serious drama in France grew out of religious rites as was the case in Greece, Germany and England, the genesis of comic drama is obscure. Liturgical drama, which began with the reading of the gospel in dialogue interrupted by hymns, was the ancestor to the mystery play, which represented some historical or Biblical event. Two other types of drama were the miracle play, which depicted the intervention of a saint, often the Virgin Mary, into human affairs, and the morality play, a dramatization in the human soul, of the conflict between good and evil. In the comic domain, the first known writer of French comedy was Adam de la Halle, who wrote *Le Jeu de la Feuilée,* and *Robin and Marion.* However, the greatest French poet of the Middle Ages was François Villon, who is best known for his *Le Petit Testament* and his *Le Grand Testament.* By the fifteenth century, two types of poetry existed: the *sotie,* a burlesque in which inferior churchmen satirized their superiors, and the *farce,* a short, dramatized fabliau or comic skit in the mystery plays.

English history is replete with accounts of multiple invaders and missionaries from foreign nations and cultures, each of whose beliefs, culture, language, and government left permanent imprints on British life. Both the history and literature of England begins with the branch of Indo-Europeans known as the Celts who settled in western Europe possibly from the seventh century B.C., to A.D. 82. The Goidels, or Gaels, occupied, at one time, much of the region now called England. Around 400 B.C., the Goidels were driven north and west by another group of Celts, the Brythons or Britons. The Goidels then made their home in Scotland and Ireland, and the Brythons appropriated the southern part of England. In 55 or 54 B.C., Julius Caesar invaded Britain. During the Roman-Celtic period in Britain, which occurred from 43 B.C. to A.D. 410, Rome's military colonized ancient Britain. As a result, the government was Roman, but the population was largely Celtic. No literature was preserved from this period. In A.D. 82, Roman power was firmly established in Britain. In 98 B.C., Tacitus, in his *Germania,* traces the Teutonic ancestry of the

English. In the fifth century A.D., after the Angles, Saxons and Jutes invaded Britain, which had already been inhabited by Celtic Britons and Picts, some of the Brythons migrated to Brittany on the continent, while others retreated to Wales and Cornwall. By A.D. 410, Rome had been sacked by Alaric, and Roman legions left Britain.

The Old English (Anglo-Saxon), also known as the Teutonic period in Britain, or "Dark Ages," occurred from A.D. 428–1066. Saxon monarchies were established during the fifth and sixth centuries; Anglian monarchies reigned during the sixth and seventh centuries. At this time also, Christianity was introduced and gradually replaced pagan culture. In A.D. 563, an Irish monk named St. Columba prepared the way for the spread of Celtic Christianity in Scotland and Northern England when he established a monastery at Iona. During the ninth century, after their intertribal conflicts and struggles with the Danes, the various Teutonic groups became unified. Although cultural development was at a low ebb, learning did flourish in the monasteries.

The earliest Old English pagan literature reflecting Teutonic life, was initially written in the Anglian dialect in Northumbria, and later in Mercian and West Saxon dialects. Because hostile relations continued between the Celts and the invading Teutonics, the Celtic language exerted no influence on the Teutonic dialect. During the sixth and seventh centuries (A.D. 450–700), chiefly pagan epic and lyric poems like *Beowulf, Waldere* (a fragmentary epic of the Theororic saga), *Finnsburg* (also a fragment), *Widsith* (a lyric), *Deor's Lament* (a lyric account of a poet's troubles), and *The Husband's Message* (love poems) were written, but these were later replaced by Christian literature. In A.D. 597, Roman Christianity was placed on a solid foundation by Saint Augustine, a missionary, and for a century thereafter, powerful Anglo-Saxon kingdoms were formed. By A.D. 700, Christian monks began to write in the vernacular. In the north of England, Whitby was the center of English poetry, and in the south, prose flourished in Winchester. In the seventh, eighth and ninth centuries, Christian poems, Biblical paraphrases, legends, and lyrics were written. *Beowulf,* which celebrates the exploits of a pagan hero, was the main poem preserved from this era. From the ninth to the eleventh century, most prose creations (laws, chronicles, sermons, and Christian legends), consisted of Latin translations. Around A.D. 670, Caedmon, the first English poet known by name, wrote *Hymns* and c. 690, Adamnan wrote *Life of St. Columba,* the first authentic attempt to write a biography in England. In approximately A.D. 700, *Beowulf* was composed in its present form, and by A.D. 731, Bede, the Venerable, had written, in Latin, his *Ecclesiastical History,* a source book of great import and the first history of the English people. Other important dates are as follows: in A.D. 787, the first Danish invasion occurred, and Charlemagne gave the order to establish schools in the abbeys; in c. A.D. 800, Nennius, a Welshman, had written *History of the Britons,* the first text that mentions King Arthur; from A.D. 800–814, during Charlemagne's reign, learning and literature were reborn; from A.D. 827–1017, several Anglo-Saxon kings, from Egbert to Edmund Ironside, reigned; in c. A.D. 850, the Danes conquered England, but from 871–901, during the reign of Alfred the Great, author and patron of literature, the Danes were repulsed.

The Middle Ages, as a period in English history, probably began c. A.D. 875–900 with the medieval dramatization of liturgy. The first known text was an Easter trope (a figure of speech), *Quem Quaritis.* In A.D. 878, the Danish were partially evacuated. During the later Old English period, from A.D. 901–1066, poetry, sermons, Biblical translations and paraphrases, as well as saints' lives and lyrics, continued to be written. The years from A.D. 979–1016 mark the second Danish invasion, and around A.D. 991, the *Battle of Maldon,* a heroic poem was written. During the transition from English to Norman French, from A.D. 1000–1200, English literary activity lessened, though the germ of medieval English lyrics and romances existed in ballads and tales.

During the Anglo-Norman and Early Middle English period, from A.D.1066–1350, Latin was used for learned works, and French for courtly literature, but English, which was transitioning from the old to the modern period, was reserved for popular works. A type of cultural internationalism was taking place. As the use of English increased during the thirteenth and fourteenth centuries, some inflections were lost and a progressively more dominant French influence added—along with French words incorporated into the English language—grace, humor and chivalric ideals to English culture and literature. Parliament was formed, and Oxford and Cambridge universities were constructed. For critics, *allegoresis,* a trope in oratory, was the preferred method and literary device. Functioning as a literary tool, allegoresis explains and controls the dissemination of meanings in sacred scriptures. Introduced in the fourth century, allegorisis, an entire system of sin, repentance, death, reward and punishment cohering as one mammoth system of meaning, had become standardized by the twelfth century. The System of Fourfold Allegory, the most widespread system of Biblical exegesis, creates four levels of Biblical textual interpretation:

1. The Historical (Literal) level (the scriptural text is read on this level first as a record of an event that actually took place): The story of Jesus' raising of Lazarus from the dead at Lazarus' sister's request as this resurrection is accepted as a literal truth.
2. The Allegorical (Spiritual) level: the story of Lazarus as it prefigures Christ's death, descent into hell and resurrection.
3. The Tropological (Moral) level: the story of Lazarus as it represents the sacrament of penance whereby the individual soul is raised from the death of sin.
4. The Anagogical (Mystical) level: the raising of Lazarus as it prefigures the resurrection of the body after the last judgment.

By the fourteenth century, this allegorical system was being applied to secular texts. However, the system was not as precise as it claimed to be. Four levels may not be present in every Biblical passage, and not every interpreter conceives of the four levels in an identical way.

At any rate, along with religious drama, English poetry (lyrics, plays, romances and religious verse) and prose were both still being produced in the form of mystery and miracle plays supervised first by the clergy, then later by towns and trade guilds. The Crusades (the first lasting from 1096–1099) greatly influenced Western European literature by stimulating creative pursuits, extending mental boundaries and introducing Oriental culture to the people. By A.D. 1200, not only had French literature dominated Western Europe, but French poets like Chrétien de Troyes, Marie de France and Benoit de Ste. More were flourishing. In A.D. 1200 English metrical romances began to use English themes. In c. A.D. 1225, St. Thomas Aquinas, a great scholar, teacher, writer, and founder of the "Thomists" was born, and in 1258, Henry III used English and French in his proclamation. The English language grew progressively in subtlety and in power from A.D. 1300–1400, and writers began to use it increasingly in learned works. Soon thereafter, the East Midland dialect (originating with Mercian) became standard literary English, and shortly thereafter, English replaced French in schools and in law pleadings as the preferred language of the upper classes.

During the Late Middle English period, from A.D. 1350–1500, a wave of humanism,[18] especially in literature, flourished in England. There was, in addition to some intellectual unrest and religious dissatisfaction, a growing nationalistic spirit following England's military successes against France, as well as a reduction in the usage of Latin and French by writers of literature. By A.D. 1362, the English language was used to open Parliament. Chaucer, who was born c. A.D. 1340, nearly a decade before the Black Death ravaged Europe, was at his most intense creative peak and was publishing courtly poetry under the influence of Italian and French authors. Printing was introduced from A.D. 1400–1500, America was "discovered" by Christopher Columbus, and the simultaneous occurrence of the Wars of the Roses, which checked the democratic movement, also signaled, along with a comparative dearth of literature, the end of the Middle Ages in England.

Like England, Spain experienced a fusion of different languages and cultures during its development. Several hundred years before Christ, two groups, the Iberians (origin unknown) and the Berbers (from North Africa) inhabited the region now divided into Spain and Portugal. People from Phoenicia, Greece and Carthage (the dominant power) had also settled along the coast. The races of these settlers fused in the fifth century B.C., after the Celts invaded the peninsula. Carthage was destroyed in 206 B.C. by the Romans who began to occupy and latinize Spain. The Roman power remained present until A.D. 409, when Barbarians Suevi, Alani and Vandals overran the country. Five years later, the Visigoths, who adopted Roman civilization after their arrival, made a few legal and social changes. The Moslem invasion began in A.D. 711, and by A.D. 758, these invaders had conquered nearly all of the region. Instead of abandoning their country, the Spanish Christians not only lived in peace with the Moslems for several centuries, but they also absorbed a great deal of Moslem culture and knowledge. The reconquest of Spain is marked by the taking back of Toledo from the Moors in A.D. 1085, followed by the recapturing of Cordoba in A.D. 1236 and of Seville in A.D. 1248. In A.D. 1469, national unity became a reality when Ferdinand d'Aragon married Isabella of Castille. The last Mohammedan stronghold, Granada, fell in A.D. 1492.

After the Romans moved into Carthage, the residue of the Celtic presence was obliterated, and Latin became Spain's official language. As in France, Vulgar Latin, the popular language, gradually evolved into the national language. Medieval Spanish literature, which began in the twelfth century and lasted until the beginning of the Renaissance, lacked originality and excellence of style since most tales, apologues, exempla, law, satire, allegory, and religious and didactic poetry were either translated from the French or imitated French authors. As developed in France, also, drama originated with Church ritual. The most significant literature that medieval Spain produced was in the area of the epic, the chronicle, the lyric and the ballad.

The Spanish *cantares,* or folk epics, which began as oral literature in the tenth century, were stylistically and artistically inferior to their French counterparts, the *chansons de geste*. Only fragments of the six principal *cantares,* which were developed around the heroic exploits of such legendary Spanish figures as Rodrigo the Goth, Barnardo del Carpio, and Rodrigo Diaz *(El Cantar de Mio Cid),* are extant.

A great many churches recorded sketchy and dull chronicles in Latin from the fifth century onward. Two writers, Rodrigo Jimenez de Rada (A.D. 1170–1247) and Lucan de Tuy (d. A.D. 1249), wrote, in Latin, real history in the form of national and world events, but the first vernacular chronicle was compiled in Castilian by King Alphonso the Wise (1226–1284). His *General Chronicle* was considered by many to be the most important historical work of the Middle Ages, though its author made little attempt to distinguish between fact and fantasy.

It is generally believed that lyrics like watchmen's songs, Christmas songs, love songs and serranillas (songs like the French *pastourelle,* in which a maiden accepts or rejects a lover) were written during the Middle Ages in Spain, but few lyrics were preserved for posterity. The greatest Spanish lyricist is, without a doubt, Juan Ruiz (c. A.D. 1283–1351), archpriest of Hita, whose fame stems from his one work, *The Book of Good Love.* Ruiz' alleged purpose was to emphasize moral principles by contrasting love for righteousness with sensual love. However, if readers are to judge by the text's content, Ruiz seems to prefer sensual love to the love for God and goodness.

The type of medieval Spanish literature popular at the time was the ballad, a short epic-lyric poem. Most scholars still debate the issue of whether or not the ballad originated in or is the residue of the epic. Most traditional ballads, which were preserved over hundreds of years, and which were written in their present form after 1400, contain humorous incidents, depict love stories, record historical events, tell of the courageous deeds of epic heros, or recount the bitterness and bravery of Christians when they struggled against the Saracens. Some of the best known ballads are "The Lamentation of Don Roderick," "Lady Alda's Dream," "Abenamar, Abenamar," "The Cid's Courtship," "Count Arnaldos," and "The Lamentation for Celin."

These European countries—Italy, France, England and Spain—developed under many influences until they became the dynamic modern entities that continue to move and act in the twenty-first century. Clearly, then, the Middle Ages, consisting of both a period of dearth and, later, one of historical, cultural and literary plenitude, deserves to be remembered and accorded full recognition for the various cultural and historical forms which its expression assumed, and not lumped together as an amorphous whole existing between ancient and modern times.

Notes

1. Animism is any of various beliefs whereby natural phenomena and things animate and inanimate are said to possess an innate soul.
2. Aramaic, the language of Jesus, had, by 300 B.C., nearly replaced the Hebrew spoken earlier. Writers preferred to write in Greek after A.D. 25 because they believed it to be a higher, more literary form of expression.
3. The story of Moses is recounted in "Exodus" a book in the Bible.
4. Historically, the term "bard"refers to poets who recited verses that glorified the deeds of national heros or leaders. Usually the harp accompanied the recitation of these verses.
5. The Separatists Xenon and Hillanicus base their arguments against Homer's authorship on inconsistencies in tone, diction, erudition and artistry of the poems. Those who object to the Separatist theory claim that some time had elapsed between Homer's writing of the *Odyssey* and that of the *Iliad.* In 1795, Friedrich Wolfe based his multiple authorship on several solid ideas:
    1. that Greek was not written prior to 700 A.D.;
    2. that the poems are too complex to have been written in an early literary past;

3. that they would not have been transmitted orally because they are too long;
4. that multiple authorship would help to explain the irregularities and contradictions in the works.

6. The *Iliad* begins when the war is in its tenth year; the *Odyssey* begins with a summary of earlier events. The plot begins when Odysseus asks to leave Calypso.
7. An epithet, in the strictest sense of the term, is an adjective or adjective phrase (or sometimes a noun phrase) used to point out a characteristic of a person or thing. A stereotyped epithet takes one characteristic of a fictional person and uses it to define the whole character. Examples are: "fleet-footed" Achilles, "blue-eyed" Athena, and "all-seeing" Jove.
8. Epic similes are long comparisons of processes or actions usually derived from nature.
9. A monologue is an oral or written composition given by one speaker.
10. The term lyric was originally employed to designate a poem that was either sung or accompanied by the lyre. In Greek poetry, it signifies any poem expressing the author's or poet's personal feelings or emotions.
11. An oligarchy is a form of government in which a few persons rule.
12. These numbers are in stark contrast to the current role of the chorus, which has been reduced to music only, while the roles of the actors form a major part of the play.
13. *The Oresteia* consists of *The Agamemnon, The Choephoroi,* and *The Eumenides.*
14. It is rumored that Lucretius wrote *On the Nature of Things* in lucid moments between bouts of insanity caused by a love potion, that Cicero revised it, and that Lucretius committed suicide when he was only forty-nine years old.
15. Catullus is discussed at length elsewhere in this anthology.
16. The Golden Mean means moderation.
17. A member of a gnostic sect arising in Persia in the A.D. 200's, composed of Christian, Buddhistic, Zoroastrian, and other beliefs, and maintaining a theological dualism in which the body and matter were identified with darkness and evil, and the soul, striving to liberate itself, was identified with light and goodness.
18. Humanism can be defined narrowly as a distinctive habit of thought that pervaded Renaissance art and philosophy. Broadly, it is any view of the world that places humankind at the center of attention.

Ancient Poetry

Of the great, ancient civilizations—of the Mesopotamian, Hebrew, Egyptian, Greek, and Roman cultures—so few poetic works survive in relation to the total number that once existed that it is difficult to discuss the surviving corpus in terms of absolutes. The human impulses to tell stories long preceded the creation of any standard system of writing, so many creative efforts first preserved only through oral tradition have been lost. In addition, that which was written down has faded or been destroyed over time; fragments of clay tablets and papyrus only suggest how vast and varied the complete body of literature must have been. Nonetheless, readers can discern the evolution of two distinct poetic traditions in the extant works of those civilizations: the epic tradition and the lyric tradition.

In 2700 BC, a tyrant-king named Gilgamesh, who lived in the Babylonian city of Uruk, was immortalized in a series of stories. Evidence suggests that these tales—part history, part myth—were originally transmitted orally in varying versions but were eventually collected into a coherent narrative and a single "fixed" text: *Gilgamesh*. The composite text marked the beginning of epic poetry: the presentation of the hero as a flawed representative of humankind, the definition of a heroic quest, the necessity of divine intervention in mortal affairs.

The Greeks continued the epic tradition with two epics attributed to the poet Homer (eighth century BC?): the *Iliad*, a detailed and sometimes disturbing account of the Trojan War; and the *Odyssey*, the fantastic tale of the Achaean war hero Odysseus' decade-long journey home. Like *Gilgamesh*, Homer's work offers evidence that it was originally transmitted orally. Complex, yet repetitious metrical formulae, the prevalence of mnemonic devices, among which are the repetition of descriptive phrases and themes; and the use of various stock scenes, all suggest that the poems were structured so that a bard could recite them from memory.

The literary revolution in epic tradition took place at Rome, in the first century BC. There Virgil composed his mythological epic, the *Aeneid*, which centers around the wanderings of Aeneas after the Trojan War. While the theme of the *Aeneid* is derived from the Homeric epic, the poem contains new epic themes. Virgil's intentions were not to rework or embellish a mythical national history, which was at the heart of the *Iliad*, for example, or to enshrine a reflection of national consciousness; instead, at the request of the emperor Augustus, the poet wished to glorify Rome by celebrating the triumphs of its supposed ancestors as well as the present achievements of its people. For the first time, an epic was not adapted to a specific occasion but was created for a specific reason, to reflect a precise moment in Roman cultural history. Virgil's *Aeneid* also reflected an evolution in the technical form of the epic. He created the work as a literary piece and not as a written "capture" of a work which was to be memorized and recited. Adapting the dactylic hexameter as used by the poet Quintus Ennius, Virgil made subtle changes to the form, developing the style with such flair that his verse is still considered the model of literary perfection in Latin verse.

Occasionally, an author adapted elements of the epic for his own use, composing a work unique to surviving literature. The Roman poet Ovid did just that when he composed the *Metamorphoses*, using Greek and Roman mythology as material for a soaring fifteen-book narrative which functions as storybook, cultural history, and philosophical treatise. Beginning with the creation of the world, Ovid explored the theme of metamorphosis through Greek mythological cycles and then through legends of early Rome. In every book, he included another variation on his theme: by turn, the narrative moves from the creation of the world and that original transfiguration of matter by the gods, to tales involving the creation of natural phenomena through divine transformation of humans into trees or animals, to the transformation of human and divine minds through love or jealousy. In the final book, Ovid provides the philosophical foundations of all the transformations to be found in human lives and in nature; he has the philosopher Pythagoras explain the constancy of change to Remus, the legendary founder of Rome. Ovid's *Metamorphoses* stands alongside the *Aeneid* and the *Iliad* as a masterwork so influential that later giants of Western literature, Chaucer and Dante among them, adapted their themes and devices for their own works.

If the epic reflected the national or collective consciousness of the culture which had produced it, the lyric tradition reflected the individual impulse to express intimate emotions sparked by interpersonal relationships. There were two types of lyrics: the private lyric, a personal expression of friendship, romantic love, regret, or sorrow which is written in conversational language, usually in the first person singular, and usually has an intimate tone; and the public lyric, a song of praise or adoration, which is written in formal diction and has a regal tone.

The earliest examples of the private lyric to survive come from Egypt where they were composed during the reign of the Pharaohs Ramses (1300–1100 BC). The *Love Poems*, as referred to the collection, includes any number of vignettes which might have been written today: a young man feigns sickness in hopes that his beloved will visit his sickbed; a young woman invites her beloved to the pond for a swim, seduction, perhaps, at the back of her mind; a teenage girl wilts with embarrassment as an older boy on whom she has a crush passes by with his friends. Class considerations notwithstanding, these poems reflect the timeless nature of romantic love and courtship rituals.

The tradition of the private lyric is marked not so much by further development as by a consistency of theme, if not form. For each of the great civilizations, a representative body of private lyrics has been preserved. In the Old Testament, are found the Songs of Songs (also known as Songs of Solomon), a highly erotic series of poems of desire and lament. In Greek literature, the poets Sappho (born ca. 630 BC) and Anakreon (575–490?) wrote of being rejected by the beloved; in Latin, Catullus (first century BC) in a single series of poems describes being passionately enamored and then just as passionately disillusioned with the adulteress with whom he was having an affair. Later poets known for their private lyrics, Donne and Byron among others, acknowledged their influence by this first, millennium-long wave of private lyrics.

The public lyric differs from the private lyric in that it usually expresses religious devotion or political affinities. In the earliest examples of the private lyric, however, those two ideas were usually interconnected. Conveniently, kings often considered themselves divine by nature, by birth or by sanctification, and hymns of praise raised by citizens to their god or gods were also addressed to the king. In the Egyptian "Akhenaten's Hymn to the Sun," for example, the pharaoh praises his father, the Sun-god Aten, and conflates the concepts of serving one's god and king. In contrast, the public lyric found in other cultures was used strictly to draw the populace together in their worship of a divine and immortal being. The Old Testament Psalms, for example, offer hymns of praise to the Creator and thanks for His creation, as well as songs of comfort to those whose trials threaten to overwhelm; and as a whole they reflect the commitment of the community to worship according to a communally understood concept of the divine. The public lyric linked members of the community in a way that the private lyric did not; it might be said that the public lyric tradition bridged the concept of a collective consciousness as represented in the epic tradition and the concept of personal experience as represented in the tradition of the private lyric.

Selected Bibliography

Bloom, Harold, ed. *Vergil's Aeneid.* New York: Chelsea, 1996.

Hexter, Ralph J. *A Guide to the Odyssey: A Commentary on the English Translation of Robert Fitzgerald.* New York: Vintage, 1993.

Levi, Peter. *A History of Greek Literature.* New York: Viking, 1985.

Ogilvie, R.M. *Roman Literature and Society.* New York: Penguin, 1980.

Schein, Seth L. *The Mortal Hero: An Introduction to Homer's Iliad.* Berkeley: U of California P, 1984.

Hebraic, Greco-Roman and Medieval Narrative

Narratives involve the telling of stories or the accounts of daily life. In almost all societies, individuals resort to narratives as a means to communicate with each other. As a result, these forms of communication serve to illustrate a point, to answer a question, or to entertain. It is important to point out that narratives are better presented orally than when they are written. The oral method of presentation captures elements of a story that are missing when compared to the written form. Unlike the written word, an oral presentation allows listeners to detect the sounds of words, elements of syntax, rate of speech, tone of voice, mimicry involved, and gestures that accompany speech.

In addition, narratives appear in various forms: folk, romance, adventure story. There are specific structural features of narratives that make them a distinct literary genre. Among these features are an opening formula, sequence of events, character traits, dialogue among characters, significant details, and closing point to the story . The narratives are better examined if they are studied within the philosophical and material elements of the cultures that produce them. In short, readers must have some background, however brief, about the thoughts of the narrator and the events in society that shape the narrator's work. Whether they are accounts of the Creation or the life of Frederick Douglass, narratives, as forms of communication, reflect events in specific societies, and these events must be taken into account if readers are to grasp the content, meaning, and purpose of narratives.

In *Humanities in the Ancient and Pre-Modern World*, the reader is given a general overview of narratives from three periods: Hebraic, Greco-Roman and Medieval. The term Hebraic narrative is used to denote those accounts of Jewish life that date back to the earliest recordings of such events. As mentioned above, an understanding of narratives must be carried out within a larger understanding of a society's belief system. This approach to Hebraic narratives is relevant if readers are to obtain some sense of this genre. First, the Hebrews were cognizant of man's inadequacy and God's omnipotence. Thus, they were absorbed with such issues as the Creation, evil, and man's free will. To that extent, it can be argued that Hebraic narratives began with the Book of Genesis and the subsequent four Books. The collection of these five Books are referred to as the Pentateuch. Second, the Hebrews were involved in a constant struggle for freedom against the Babylonians, Greeks, and Romans. Consequently, the content of narratives revealed the need for redress of these grievances. Third, issues of suffering, redemption, salvation, and redemption also marked Hebraic narratives. Regarding suffering, for example, Hebraic narratives explore the suffering of individuals and the result of such suffering. The stories of Joseph and Job are two examples of this phenomenon.

Like Hebraic narratives, Greco-Roman narratives were shaped by events in the larger society and the thinking that governed that society. One such event that marked Greco-Roman narratives was the occupation of war. Subsequently, narratives at this time reflected the larger society's occupation with men in battle. The *Iliad* and the *Odyssey* are the most salient narratives that come to mind in a discussion of this Greco-Roman literary genre. Written by Homer about 2700 years ago, the *Iliad* conveys the story of the siege of Troy (present-day north east Turkey) in which the Greeks defeated the Trojans. The *Odyssey*, in a similar manner, continues the story with emphasis on Odysseus' delay to return to the kingdom of Ithaca. These stories began in oral form prior to their being recorded in written form which portray elements of war, of men in battle, and of excruciating details and emotions. With respect to narrative structure, the

Iliad, for instance, has an opening statement, many details of war, and evokes emotions from readers. These are some of the features of narratives mentioned earlier that make narratives what they are.

Medieval, refers to the Middle Ages, a period that is dated approximately from AD 500–1500. As humans moved from the Golden Age Greco-Roman to the Middle Ages, narratives did not lose their place in literary forms. Issues that were dominant at this time were sought as valor, loyalty, glory, power, and wealth. Societal events helped to produce the content of narratives during the Middle Ages. The Christian faith was one such event that shaped Medieval narratives. Christianity under a series of events, called the Crusades, had as its mission the conversion of nonbelievers, primarily Muhammadans, to its faith.

With the fall of the Roman Empire, individuals turned their attention to a society in which issues as glory, loyalty, and valor were valued. To pursue these ideals, a king had to be present to maintain a sense of order. Coupled with order are wealth, glory, valor, and loyalty.

Moreover, these concepts would cut across the nations of Western Europe, for example, France, Germany, Ireland, and Scandinavia. Of the narratives noted during the Medieval Age, those that are most often connected with this period are Dante's the *Divine Comedy*, Chaucer's the *Canterbury Tales*, the *Song of Roland*, and *Aucassin and Nicolette*. What is central to these narratives is a system of human values. This feature of human values is demonstrated in the *Divine Comedy*. Considered by some to be the greatest literary work of the Middle Ages, Dante examines the stages of evil and various types of individuals who occupy certain places in Hell. These individuals do not submit to the will of God and are thus punished for their failure to follow the laws of God. In the *Canterbury Tales*, Chaucer presents a varied audience of pilgrims on their way to thank St. Thomas á Becket of Canterbury for his assistance in keeping them attuned to a positive way of life. In Dante's case, Chaucer, too, examines the good and bad traits of humanity.

A work of unknown author and date, the *Song of Roland* gives the reader many details of the First Crusade. This narrative, in keeping with the values of right and wrong, shows feudal civility with exquisite details of expeditions to capture the Holy Land for Christendom. A final example of a narrative within the Medieval Ages is *Aucassin and Nicolette*. Although its author is unknown, this love story, written in the northern part of France in the twelfth century, provides readers with themes central to those narratives at this time. In keeping with the broader structure of Medieval society, the themes observed in this story are a reflection of the Medieval Era. These themes include love of prince and pauper, the child of royalty in disguise, and the conversion of the heathen. For the narrative form, much dialogue exists in the work, and it is replete with repetition of statements, a feature observed in many narratives.

Narratives are literary tools for examining cultures and the individuals who live in them. As literary genre, they provide the reader with specific structural properties that make narratives what they are; they are avenues for presenting the inner and outer expressions of society.

Hebraic Literature (Poetry)
King David (1060?–970 BC)

David, the youngest son of Jesse, a descendant of the tribe of Judah was destined to rule over Israel by divine order. As a boy, shepherding his father's sheep, God sent Samuel to anoint him as king. Twenty-two years passed, however, before David ascended the throne and ruled Israel. Within that time frame, David killed Goliath, soothed King Saul with his music, married Saul's daughter, developed a unique relationship with Saul's son, became a fugitive, and feigned insanity.

It was not until the deaths of King Saul and Prince Jonathan that David was anointed as king over the tribe of Judah. Meanwhile, Abner had proclaimed Ishboseth, a surviving son of Saul, as Israel's king over the other eleven tribes. As a result, a civil war broke out, and David's Southern Kingdom proved its military might against the northern tribes. Fearing for their own lives in the face of David's sure victory, two of Ishboseth's soldiers beheaded him and went to David to receive their reward, but David had them executed for their treacherous deed against Saul's son. Their act of treason caused the complete breakdown of the rival kingdom, and David finally ascended the throne to rule over the entire twelve tribes of Israel (II Samuel 5:4, 5).

As the first theocratic King of the Jews, David did three things to establish his theocentricity. He captured Jerusalem and identified it as the capitol of his kingdom and the center of worship. Second, David went to war against the Philistines and successfully defeated them; and third, he restored the holy Ark of the Covenant, the symbol of God's throne. His fourth plan was to build a house for God, but Jehovah denied the privilege and made a covenant with him known as the "Davidic Covenant." God promised David an eternal seed, (realized in the person of Jesus Christ); eternal kingdom, (to be re-established when Jesus comes back to earth); and eternal throne, (upon which Christ, Himself will sit).

Although David continued to be a great warrior/king, he suffered a tragic downfall. At the pinnacle of power, he committed adultery with Uriah's wife, Bathsheba; and after learning of her pregnancy, he had Uriah killed and married Bathsheba. His actions displeased God and subjugated David to divine discipline and judgment that affected him and his family for the rest of his life. David lived to see his daughter raped by her half-brother, Ammon, who was later murdered by his son Absalom. His heart was broken by Absalom's outright attempt to oust him from the throne by poisoning the people's minds against David. This son's betrayal led to David's flight once again and forced him into warfare against his own son, resulting in Absalom's death. Brokenhearted at the loss of his son, David returned to the kingdom and continued to reign over the united kingdom until his death. Prior to his death, Adonijah conspired to thwart Solomon's accession to the throne, but Nathan (the prophet) and Bathsheba intervened and stopped his devious plan, and David identified Solomon as the next heir to the throne.

Book of Psalms

While the authorship of the Book of Psalms has been debated, it is commonly agreed that David's is the dominant voice of the text. Seventy-three of the one hundred and fifty Psalms are attributed to him, twelve to Asaph, eleven to the sons of Korah, two to Solomon, one to Moses, one to Ethan, and fifty to anonymous authors. The composite work is presented in highly emotional language which gives an intense portrayal of the interaction between God and His chosen people during the times of crisis, affliction, war, disappointments, anger, hope, and celebration. As literature, these psalms are viewed as an anthology of lyrical poetry, revealing the historico-religious experience of the Hebrew people and pointing to the coming Messiah, who will carry on the lineage of David. Written within the context of a culture that is identified by its theocentricity, the text establishes a peculiar connection between the Old and New Testaments which cannot be ignored. Its correspondence to the Five Books of the Law, its Messianic Psalms, and its unique artistic form distinguish the Book of Psalms from other books of the Bible.

One feature of the text appealing to scholars is the artistic form of the work (pattern, design, unity, theme, balance, harmony, contrast, recurrence, and variation). As a literary work, the Psalms are considered one of the most important contributions to lyrical poetry in literature. And each poem, indeed, recalls the lyric spirit often associated with the musical, by displaying emotions which invite the reader to become poetically engaged in thought, praise, anger, vengeance, or hope. The intensity of this poetry is vividly portrayed by the varied use of parallelism, which is the most essential characteristic of Hebrew poetry. This parallelism includes such techniques as *synonymous parallelism*, in which the poet makes a statement in one line that is restated in a second line; *emblematic symbolism*, in which the poet makes a point, evokes a picture, and then reiterates the point; and *antithetic parallelism*, in which in the first line the poet makes a statement and in the second line gives a reason for making it.

Another significant contribution to literature appears in the Alphabet or Acrostic Psalms. These are psalms in which successive units (half verses, verses, or groups of verses) begin with the successive letter of the Hebrew Alphabet. For instance in Psalms 9, 10, 25, 34, and 145, the verses begin with words whose first letter repeats the corresponding, consecutive letter of the Hebrew Alphabet. Scholars believe that the orderliness of this poem reflects the Law of God and celebrates on an artistic level the beauty of order that God has established on a moral or spiritual level.

Just as the Book of Psalms reaches back to the Law of the Old Testament, it reaches forward to the Messiah of the New Testament in its presentation of the Messianic Psalms. Of the several groupings of the poems (the Imprecatory Psalms, the Shepherd Psalms, the Hallelujah Psalms, and the Historical Psalms), none are considered so important as the Messianic Psalms. These contain statements about the coming Messiah and His millennial reign, in continuation of David's dynasty. The Messiah emerges as a suffering servant (Psalms 22, 31, 34, 69, 129) and as a descendant of David. The Messiah is destined to become the Redeemer and Ruler, having universal dominion (Psalm 72). These remarkable prophecies have no point of reference in the historical context in which they were written. It was not until the appearance of Christ (the one to whom the prophecies pointed) that the prophecy of the Psalms was fulfilled. In Luke 24:44, Jesus identifies Himself as the one who is spoken of "in the law of Moses, in the prophets and in the psalms." He identifies himself as the long-awaited Redeemer Who will suffer; and in so doing, He speaks the very words of the psalter, "My God, My God, why hast thou forsaken me?" (Psalm 22:1; Matthew 27:46) Because of their literary and philosophical value, these poems, that portray the emotion of a people in their historico-religious encounters with God, have claimed the attention of scholars and theologians all over the world.

Psalm 8

1. O Lord our Lord, how excellent is thy name in all the earth! who has set thy glory above the heavens.
2. Out of the mouth of babes and sucklings hast thou ordained strength because of thine enemies, that thou mightest still the enemy and the avenger.
3. When I consider thy heavens, the work of thy fingers, the moon and the stars, which thou hast ordained;
4. What is man, that thou art mindful of him? and the son of man, that thou visitest him?
5. For thou hast made him a little lower than the angels, and hast crowned him with glory and honour.
6. Thou madest him to have dominion over the works of thy hands; thou hast put all things under his feet:
7. All sheep and oxen, yea, and the beasts of the field;
8. The fowl of the air, and the fish of the sea, and whatsoever passeth through the paths of the seas.
9. O Lord our Lord, how excellent is thy name in all the earth!

Psalm 19

1. The heavens declare the glory of God; and the firmament sheweth his handywork.
2. Day unto day uttereth speech, and night unto night sheweth knowledge.
3. There is no speech nor language, where their voice is not heard.
4. Their line is gone out through all the earth, and their words to the end of the world. In them hath he set a tabernacle for the sun,
5. Which is as a bridegroom coming out of his chamber, and rejoiceth as a strong man to run a race.
6. His going forth is from the end of the heaven, and his circuit unto the ends of it: and there is nothing hid from the heat thereof.
7. The law of the Lord is perfect, converting the soul: the testimony of the Lord is sure, making wise the simple.
8. The statutes of the Lord are right, rejoicing the heart: the commandment of the Lord is pure, enlightening the eyes.
9. The fear of the Lord is clean, enduring for ever: the judgments of the Lord are true and righteous altogether.
10. More to be desired are they than gold, yea, than much fine gold: sweeter also than honey and the honeycomb.
11. Moreover by them is thy servant warned: and in keeping of them there is great reward.
12. Who can understand his errors? cleanse thou me from secret faults.
13. Keep back thy servant also from presumptuous sins; let them not have dominion over me: then shall I be upright, and I shall be innocent from the great transgression.
14. Let the words of my mouth, and the meditation of my heart, be acceptable in thy sight, O Lord, my strength, and my redeemer.

Psalm 23

1. The Lord is my shepherd; I shall not want.
2. He maketh me to lie down in green pastures: he leadeth me beside the still waters.
3. He restoreth my soul: he leadeth me in the paths of righteousness for his name's sake.
4. Yea, though I walk through the valley of the shadow of death, I will fear no evil: for thou art with me; thy rod and thy staff they comfort me.
5. Thou preparest a table before me in the presence of mine enemies: thou anointest my head with oil; my cup runneth over.
6. Surely goodness and mercy shall follow me all the days of my life: and I will dwell in the house of the Lord for ever.

Psalm 137

1. By the rivers of Babylon, there we sat down, yea, we wept, when we remembered Zion.
2. We hanged our harps upon the willows in the midst thereof.
3. For there they that carried us away captive required of us a song; and they that wasted us required of us mirth, saying, Sing us one of the songs of Zion.
4. How shall we sing the Lord's song in a strange land?
5. If I forget thee, O Jerusalem, let my right hand forget her cunning.
6. If I do not remember thee, let my tongue cleave to the roof of my mouth; if I prefer not Jerusalem above my chief joy.
7. Remember, O Lord, the children of Edom in the day of Jerusalem; who said, Rase it, rase it, even to the foundation thereof.
8. O daughter of Babylon, who art to be destroyed; happy shall he be, that rewardeth thee as thou hast served us.
9. Happy shall he be, that taketh and dasheth thy little ones against the stones.

King Solomon (974?–937? BC)

Solomon, the second son born to David and Bathsheba, became the successor of his father's throne, the third king to rule over Israel. He ascended the throne at the time of the nation's greatest period of prosperity and peace. His responsibility, for the most part, was to build the temple of God, for which David had made previous preparations. Early in his reign, God appeared to Solomon in a dream and asked him, "What shall I give thee?" (I Kings 3:5), and Solomon asked for "an understanding to judge [God's] people" and the ability to discern between good and bad." God was so pleased with Solomon that he not only granted his plea, but he included "both riches and honor; so that there [would] not be any among the kings like [Solomon] all [his] days" (3:13). In this first appearance to Solomon, God established the "if-then" principle that governed the relationship between the two of them (3:14).

Shortly after his encounter with God, the young king's wisdom was tested, and he settled a dispute between two harlots as to who was the mother of a child. His decision identified the true mother, saved the life of the child, and caused his subjects to believe that "the wisdom of God was in him" (3:28). The wisdom of this ruler spread rapidly, attracting the grand monarch, the Queen of Sheba (1 Kings 10:1–13; II Chronicles 9:1–12; Matthew 12:42). The Bible narrative indicates that Sheba's visit with him resulted in the development of an admirable relationship between the two monarchs (1 Kings 10:1–13).

Despite Solomon's wisdom and wealth, most commentators reflect upon the wasted life of a virtuous yet flawed king. He was a lavish spender and oriental despot, who practiced polygamy. He performed sacrilegious worship in the sight of the temple of God, divided the kingdom, and brought the wrath of God against Israel. God repeated the "if-then" principle to Solomon, "If thou wilt walk with me, as David thy father walked . . . then I will establish the throne of thy kingdom upon Israel forever . . . But if ye shall at all turn away from following me . . . then I will cut off Israel out of the land which I have given them; and this house . . . will I cast out of my sight . . ." (I Kings 9:3–4; 9:6–8). Apparently Solomon ignored God's warnings because he sank deeper into the mire of apostasy and began to worship the false gods of his foreign wives: "His wives turned away his heart after other gods: and his heart was not perfect with the Lord his God, as was the heart of David, his father" (I Kings 11:4). And upon God's third meeting with Solomon, He pronounced judgment against him (I Kings 11:9–13), promising that He would take the kingdom from Solomon and give it to his servant (I Kings 11:11). After that meeting, Solomon was vexed by the enemies which God caused to rise up against him until his death.

The Song of Songs: Background

When the Song of Songs, also known as the Song of Solomon, is studied without preconceived notions, it emerges as superb lyrical variety, containing songs of love and nature, of courtship and marriage, all which revel in the physical aspects of love and reveal its spiritual character. The two Greek terms *Eros*, "carnal love," and *Agape Caritas*, "spiritual love," reflect a dichotomy that has entered into classical Christian theology. The classical Hebrew outlook, on the contrary, finds it entirely proper to apply the same root *ahabah*, to all aspects of love. The ideal relationship of man to God, "Thy shalt love the Lord thy God" (Deuteronomy 6:5); the love of one's fellow man, "Thy shalt love thy neighbor as thyself" (Leviticus 19:18), "they shalt love him [the stranger] as thyself" (Leviticus 19:34); and the love of man for woman, "How fair and how pleasant you are, O love with its delights!" (the Song of Songs 7:7) are all expressed in the Bible by the same word.

Studying the Song of Solomon without preconceived notions is quite impossible considering the controversial nature and varied interpretations of the book. The conflict which surrounded its admission to the biblical canon had to do with the sexual nature of the Song. While opponents viewed it as pure erotica, Jews and Christians understood it as a spiritual allegory. For the Jews it symbolizes the union between Yahweh and His wife, Israel; and for Christians, it represents the relationship between Jesus Christ and His bride, the Church. The Song of Solomon has been viewed as drama, erotic literature, and literal interpretation. The rationalists of the eighteenth and nineteenth centuries understood the song as a poem of human love.

The book, written by Solomon, was placed in the third division of the Hebrew canon, and it has a long history of liturgical use by the Jews on the eight day of Passover celebration. In fact they will use it at the conclusion of the Passover, if it begins on the Sabbath. They believe that it pictures their intimate relationship with Jehovah. Old Testament scriptures support the allegory of Israel as a wayward wife who has committed adultery against Jehovah, her husband. In like manner, the Christian view of the Church, as the Bride of Christ, is depicted in the New Testament. In both cases, the metaphors and symbols of the lyrical poem are easily identifiable. Although the Song of Solomon contains beautiful and sensuous lyric poetry, it lacks an introduction, formal structure, plot, and conclusion.

The Song of Songs

Solomon

Let Him Kiss Me with the Kisses of His Mouth

The Song of Songs, which is Solomon's.

Let him kiss me with the kisses of his mouth.
Your love is more delightful than wine;
delicate is the fragrance of your perfume,
your name is an oil poured out,
and that is why the maidens love you.
Draw me in your footsteps, let us run.
The King has brought me into his rooms;
you will be our joy and our gladness.
We shall praise your love above wine;
how right it is to love yo.

I am Black but Lovely, Daughters of Jerusalem

I am black but lovely, daughters of Jerusalem,
like the tents of Kedar,
like the pavilions of Salmah.
Take no notice of my swarthiness,
it is the sun that has burnt me.
My mother's sons turned their anger on me,
they made me look after the vineyards.
Had I only looked after my own!

—How beautiful you are, my love,
how beautiful you are!
Your eyes are doves.
—How beautiful you are, my Beloved,
and how delightful!
All green is our bed.
—The beams of our house are of cedar,
the panelling of cypress.
—I am the rose of Sharon,
the lily of the valleys.
—As a lily among the thistles,
so is my love among the maidens.
—As an apple tree among the trees of the orchard,
so is my Beloved among the young men.
In his longed-for shade I am seated
and his fruit is sweet to my taste.

He has taken me to his banquet hall,
and the banner he raises over me is love.
Feed me with raisin cakes,
restore me with apples,
for I am sick with love.
His left arm is under my head,
his right embraces me.
—I charge you,
daughters of Jerusalem,
by the gazelles, by the hinds of the field,
not to stir my love, nor rouse it,
until it please to awake.

See Where He Stands

See where he stands
behind our wall.
He looks in at the window,
he peers through the lattice.
My Beloved lifts up his voice,
he says to me,
'Come then, my love,
my lovely one, come.
For see, winter is past,
the rains are over and gone.
The flowers appear on the earth.
The season of glad songs has come,
the cooling of the turtledove is heard in our land.
The fig tree is forming its first figs
and the blossoming vines give out their fragrance.
Come then, my love,
my lovely one, come.
My dove, hiding in the clefts of the rock,
in the coverts of the cliff,
show me your face,
let me hear your voice;
for your voice is sweet
and your face is beautiful.

. . .

On my bed, at night, I sought him
whom my heart loves.
I sought but did not find him.
So I will rise and go through the City;
in the streets and the squares
I will seek him whom my heart loves.
The watchmen came upon me
on their rounds in the City:
'Have you seen him whom my heart loves?'
Scarcely had I passed them
than I found him whom my heart loves.
I held him fast, nor would I let him go
till I had brought him
into my mother's house,
into the room of her who conceived me.

How Beautiful You Are, My Love

How beautiful you are, my love,
how beautiful you are!
Your eyes, behind your veil,
are doves;
your hair is like a flock of goats
frisking down the slopes of Gilead.
Your teeth are like a flock of shorn ewes
as they come up from the washing.
Each one has its twin,
not one unpaired with another.
Your lips are a scarlet thread
and your words enchanting.
Your cheeks, behind your veil,
are halves of pomegranate.
Your neck is the tower of David
built as a fortress,
hung round with a thousand bucklers,
and each the shield of a hero.
Your two breasts are two fawns,
twins of a gazelle,
that feed among the lilies.
Before the dawn-wind rises,
before the shadows flee,
I will go to the mountain of myrrh,
to the hill of frankincense.
You are wholly beautiful, my love,
and without a blemish.
Come from Lebanon, my promised bride,
come from Lebanon, come on your way.
Lower your gaze, from the heights of Amana,
from the crests of Senir and Hermon,
the haunt of lions,
the mountains of leopards.
You ravish my heart,
my sister, my promised bride,
you ravish my heart
with a single one of your glances,
with one single pearl of your necklace.
What spells lie in your love,
my sister, my promised bride!

I Sleep, but My Heart Is Awake

I sleep, but my heart is awake.
I hear my Beloved knocking.
'Open to me, my sister, my love,
my dove, my perfect one,
for my head is covered with dew,
my locks with the drops of night.'
—'I have taken off my tunic,
am I to put it on again?

I have washed my feet,
am I to dirty them again?'
My Beloved thrust his hand
through the hole in the door;
I trembled to the core of my being.
Then I rose to open to my Beloved,
myrrh ran off my hands,
pure myrrh off my fingers,
on to the handle of the bolt.
I opened to my Beloved,
but he had turned his back and gone!
My soul failed at his flight.
I sought him but I did not find him,
I called to him but he did not answer.
The watchmen came upon me
as they made their rounds in the City.
They beat me, they wounded me,
they took away my cloak,
they who guard the ramparts.
I charge you, daughters of Jerusalem,
if you should find my Beloved,
what must you tell him?
That I am sick with love.
What makes your Beloved better than other lovers,
O loveliest of women?
What makes your Beloved better than other lovers,
to give us a charge like this?
My Beloved is fresh and ruddy,
to be known among ten thousand.
His head is golden, purest gold,
his locks are palm fronds
and black as the raven.
His eyes are doves
at the pool of water,
bathed in milk,
at rest on a pool.
His cheeks are beds of spices,
banks sweetly scented.
His lips are lilies,
distilling pure myrrh.
His hands are golden, rounded,
set with jewels of Tarshish.
His belly a block of ivory
covered with sapphires.
His legs are alabaster columns
set in sockets of pure gold.
His appearance is that of Lebanon,
unrivalled as the cedars.
His conversation is sweetness itself,
he is altogether lovable.
Such is my Beloved, such is my friend,
O daughters of Jerusalem.

You Are Beautiful as Tirzah, My Love

You are beautiful as Tirzah, my love,
fair as Jerusalem.
Turn your eyes away,
for they hold me captive.

. . .

The maidens saw her, and proclaimed her blessed,
queens and concubines sang her praises:
'Who is this arising like the dawn,
fair as the moon,
resplendent as the sun,
terrible as an army with banners?'

. . .

How beautiful are your feet in their sandals,
O prince's daughter!
The curve of your thighs is like the curve of a necklace,
work of a master hand.
Your navel is a bowl well rounded
with no lack of wine,
your belly a heap of wheat
surrounded with lilies.
Your two breasts are two fawns,
twins of a gazelle.
Your neck is an ivory tower.
Your eyes, the pools of Heshbon,
by the gate of Bath-rabbim.
Your nose, the Tower of Lebanon,
sentinel facing Damascus.
Your head is held high like Carmel,
and its plaits are as dark as purple;
a king is held captive in your tresses.
How beautiful you are, how charming,
my love, my delight!
In stature like the palm tree,
its fruit-clusters your breasts.
'I will climb the palm tree,' I resolved,
'I will seize its clusters of dates.'
May your breasts be clusters of grapes,
your breath sweet-scented as apples,
your speaking, superlative wine.

. . .

Wine flowing straight to my Beloved,
as it runs on the lips of those who sleep.
I am my Beloved's, and his desire is for me.
Come, my Beloved, let us go to the fields.
We will spend the night in the villages,
and in the morning we will go to the vineyards.
We will see if the vines are budding,
if their blossoms are opening,
if the pomegranate trees are in flower.
Then I shall give you the gift of my love.
The mandrakes yield their fragrance,
the rarest fruits are at our doors;

the new as well as the old,
I have stored them for you, my Beloved.
Ah, why are you not my brother,
nursed at my mother's breast!
Then if I met you out of doors, I could kiss you
without people thinking ill of me.
I should lead you, I should take you
into my mother's house, and you would teach me!
I should give you spiced wine to drink,
juice of my pomegranates.
His left arm is under my head
and his right embraces me.
I charge you,
daughters of Jerusalem,
not to stir my love, nor rouse it,
until it please to awake.

Who Is This Coming Up from the Desert/ Leaning on Her Beloved?

Who is this coming up from the desert
leaning on her Beloved?
I awakened you under the apple tree,
there where your mother conceived you,
there where she who gave birth to you conceived you.
Set me like a seal on your heart,
like a seal on your arm.
For love is strong as Death,
jealousy relentless as Sheol.
The flash of it is a flash of fire,
a flame of Yahweh himself.
Love no flood can quench,
no torrents drown.

Narrative

The Bible: The Old Testament

Genesis 1–3

[The Creation—The Fall]

1. In the beginning God created the heaven and the earth. And the earth was without form, and void; and darkness was upon the face of the deep. And the Spirit of God moved upon the face of the waters.

And God said, Let there be light: and there was light. And God saw the light, that it was good: and God divided the light from the darkness. And God called the light Day, and the darkness he called Night. And the evening and the morning were the first day.

And God said, Let there be a firmament in the midst of the waters, and let it divide the waters from the waters. And God made the firmament, and divided the waters which were under the firmament from the waters which were above the firmament: and it was so. And God called the firmament Heaven. And the evening and the morning were the second day.

And God said, Let the waters under the heaven be gathered together unto one place, and let the dry land appear: and it was so. And God called the dry land Earth; and the gathering together of the waters called he Seas: and God saw that it was good. And God said, Let the earth bring forth grass, the herb yielding seed, and the fruit tree yielding fruit after his kind, whose seed is in itself, upon the earth: and it was so. And the earth brought forth grass, and herb yielding seed after his kind, and the tree yielding fruit, whose seed was in itself, after his kind: and God saw that it was good. And the evening and the morning were the third day.

And God said, Let there be lights in the firmament of the heaven to divide the day from the night; and let them be for signs, and for seasons, and for days, and years: and let them be for lights in the firmament of the heaven to give light upon the earth: and it was so. And God made two great lights; the greater light to rule the day, and the lesser light to rule the night: he made the stars also. And God set them in the firmament of the heaven to give light upon the earth, and to rule over the day and over the night, and to divide the light from the darkness: and God saw that it was good. And the evening and the morning were the fourth day. And God said, Let the waters bring forth abundantly the moving creature that hath life, and fowl that may fly above the earth in the open firmament of heaven. And God created great whales, and every living creature that moveth, which the waters brought forth abundantly, after their kind, and every winged fowl after his kind: and God saw that it was good. And God blessed them, saying, Be fruitful, and multiply, and fill the waters in the seas, and let fowl multiply in the earth. And the evening and the morning were the fifth day.

And God said, Let the earth bring forth the living creature after his kind, cattle, and creeping thing, and beast of the earth after his kind: and it was so. And God made the beast of the earth after his kind, and cattle after their kind, and everything that creepeth upon the earth after his kind: and God saw that it was good.

And God said, Let us make man in our image, after our likeness: and let them have dominion over the fish of the sea, and over the fowl of the air, and over the cattle, and over all the earth, and over every creeping thing that creepeth upon the earth. So God created man in his own image, in the image of God created he him; male and female created he them. And God blessed them, and God said unto them, Be fruitful, and multiply, and replenish the earth, and subdue it: and have dominion over the fish of the sea, and over the fowl of the air, and over every living thing that moveth upon the earth.

And God said, Behold, I have given you every herb bearing seed, which is upon the face of all the earth, and every tree, in which is the fruit of a tree yielding seed; to you it shall be for meat. And to every beast of the earth, and to every fowl of the air, and to every thing that creepeth upon the earth, wherein there is life, I have given every green herb for meat: and it was so. And God saw every thing that he had made, and, behold, it was very good. And the evening and the morning were the sixth day.

2. Thus the heavens and the earth were finished, and all the host of them. And on the seventh day God ended his work which he had made; and he rested on the seventh day from all his work which he had made. And God blessed the seventh day, and sanctified it: because that in it he had rested from all his work which God created and made.

These are the generations of the heavens and of the earth when they were created, in the day that the Lord God made the earth and the heavens, and every plant of the field before it was in the earth, and every herb of the field before it grew: for the Lord God had not caused it to rain upon the earth, and there was not a man to till the ground. But there went up a mist from the earth, and watered the whole face of the ground. And the Lord God formed man of the dust of the ground, and breathed into his nostrils the breath of life; and man became a living soul.

And the Lord God planted a garden eastward in Eden; and there he put the man whom he had formed. And out of the ground made the Lord God to grow every tree that is pleasant to the sight, and good for food; the tree of life also in the midst of the garden, and the tree of knowledge of good and evil. And a river went out of Eden to water the garden; and from thence it was parted, and became into four heads. The name of the first is Pison: that is it which compasseth the whole land of Havilah, where there is gold; and the gold of that land is good: there is bdellium and the onyx stone. And the name of the second river is Gihon: the same is it that compasseth the whole land of Ethiopia. And the name of the third river is Kiddekel: that is it which goeth toward the east of Assyria. And the fourth river is Euphrates. And the Lord God took the man, and put him into the garden of Eden to dress it and to keep it. And the Lord God commanded the man, saying, Of every tree of the garden thou mayest freely eat: but of the tree of the knowledge of good and evil, thou shalt not eat of it: for in the day that thou eatest thereof thou shalt surely die.

And the Lord God said, It is not good that the man should be alone; I will make him an help meet for him. And out of the ground the Lord God formed every beast of the field, and every fowl of the air; and brought them unto Adam to see what he would call them: and whatsoever Adam called every living creature, that was the name thereof. And Adam gave names to all cattle, and to the fowl of the air, and to every beast of the field; but for Adam there was not found an help meet for him. And the Lord God caused a deep sleep to fall upon Adam, and he slept: and he took one of his ribs, and closed up the flesh instead thereof; and the rib, which the Lord God had taken from man, made he a woman, and brought her unto the man. And Adam said, This is now bone of my bones, and flesh of my flesh: she shall be called Woman, because she was taken out of Man. Therefore shall a man leave his father and his mother, and shall cleave unto his wife: and they shall be one flesh. And they were both naked, the man and his wife, and were not ashamed.

3. Now the serpent was more subtil than any beast of the field which the Lord God had made. And he said unto the woman, Yea, hath God said, Ye shall not eat of every tree of the garden? And the woman said unto the serpent, We may eat of the fruit of the trees of the garden: but of the fruit of the tree which is in the midst of the garden, God hath said, Ye shall not eat of it, neither shall ye touch it, lest ye die. And the serpent said unto the woman, Ye shall not surely die: for God doth know that in the day ye eat thereof, then your eyes shall be opened, and ye shall be as gods, knowing good and evil. And when the woman saw the tree was good for food, and that it was pleasant to the eyes, and a tree to be desired to make one

wise, she took of the fruit thereof, and did eat, and gave also unto her husband with her; and he did eat. And the eyes of them both were opened, and they knew that they were naked; and they sewed fig leaves together, and made themselves aprons. And they heard the voice of the Lord God walking in the garden in the cool of the day: and Adam and his wife hid themselves from the presence of the Lord God amongst the trees of the garden. And the Lord God called unto Adam, and said unto him, Where art thou? And he said, I heard thy voice in the garden, and I was afraid, because I was naked; and I hid myself. And he said, Who told thee that thou wast naked? Hast thou eaten of the tree, whereof I commanded thee that thou shouldest not eat? And the man said, The woman whom thou gavest to be with me, she gave me of the tree, and I did eat. And the Lord God said unto the woman, What is this that thou has done? And the woman said, The serpent beguiled me, and I did eat. And the Lord God said unto the serpent, Because thou hast done this, thou art cursed above all cattle, and above every beast of the field; upon thy belly shalt thou go, and dust shall thou eat all the days of they life: and I will put enmity between thee and the woman, and between thy seed and her seed; it shall bruise thy head, and thou shalt bruise his heel. Unto the woman he said, I will greatly multiply thy sorrow and they conception; in sorrow thou shalt bring forth children; and thy desire shall be to thy husband, and he shall rule over thee. And unto Adam he said, Because thou hast hearkened unto the voice of thy wife, and hast eaten of the tree, of which I commanded thee, saying, Thou shalt not eat of it: cursed is the ground for thy sake; in sorrow shalt thou eat of it all the days of thy life; thorns also and thistles shall it bring forth to thee; and thou shalt eat the herb of the field; in the sweat of thy face shalt thou eat bread, till thou return unto the ground; for out of it wast thou taken: for dust thou art, and unto dust shalt thou return. And Adam called his wife's name Eve; because she was the mother of all living. Unto Adam also and to his wife did the Lord God make coats of skins, and clothed them.

And the Lord God said, Behold, the man is become as one of us, to know good and evil: and now, lest he put forth his hand, and take also of the tree of life, and eat, and live forever: therefore the Lord God sent him forth from the garden of Eden, to till the ground from whence he was taken. So he drove out the man; and he placed at the east of the garden of Eden Cherubims, and a flaming sword which turned every way, to keep the way of the tree of life.

Genesis 4

[The First Murder]

4. And Adam knew Eve his wife; and she conceived, and bare Cain, and said, I have gotten a man from the Lord. And she again bare his brother Abel. And Abel was a keeper of sheep, but Cain was a tiller of the ground. And in process of time it came to pass, that Cain brought of the fruit of the ground an offering unto the Lord. And Abel, he also brought of the firstlings of his flock and of the fat thereof. And the Lord had respect unto Abel and to his offering: but unto Cain and to his offering he had not respect. And Cain was very wroth, and his countenance fell. And the Lord said unto Cain, Why art thou wroth? and why is thy countenance fallen? If thou doest well, shalt thou not be accepted? and if thou doest not well, sin lieth at the door. And unto thee shall be his desire, and thou shall rule over him. And Cain talked with Abel his brother: and it came to pass, when they were in the field, that Cain rose up against Abel his brother, and slew him.

And the Lord said unto Cain, Where is Abel thy brother? And he said, I know not: am I my brother's keeper? And he said, What hast thou done? the voice of thy brother's blood crieth unto me from the ground. And now art thou cursed from the earth, which hath opened her mouth to receive thy brother's blood from thy hand; when thou tillest the ground, it shall not henceforth yield unto thee her strength, a fugitive and a vagabond shalt thou be in the earth. And Cain said unto the Lord, My punishment is greater than I can bear. Behold, thou hast driven me out this day from the face of the earth; and from thy face shall I be hid; and I shall be a fugitive and a vagabond in the earth; and it shall come to pass, that every one that findeth me shall slay me. And the Lord said unto him, Therefore whosoever slayeth Cain, vengeance shall be taken on him sevenfold. And the Lord set a mark upon Cain, lest any finding him should kill him.

Genesis 6–9

[The Flood]

6. * * * And God saw that the wickedness of man was great in the earth, and that every imagination of the thoughts of his heart was only evil continually. And it repented the Lord that he had made man on the earth, and it grieved him at his heart. And the Lord said, I will destroy man whom I have created from the face of the earth; both man, and beast, and the creeping thing, and the fowls of the air; for it repenteth me that I have made them. But Noah found grace in the eyes of the Lord.

These are the generations of Noah: Noah was a just man and perfect in his generations, and Noah walked with God. And Noah begat three sons, Shem, Ham, and Japheth.

The earth also was corrupt before God, and the earth was filled with violence. And God looked upon the earth, and, behold, it was corrupt; for all flesh had corrupted his way upon the earth. And God said unto Noah, The end of all flesh is come before me; for the earth is filled with violence through them; and, behold, I will destroy them with the earth. Make thee an ark of gopher wood; rooms shalt thou make in the ark, and shalt pitch it within and without with pitch. And this is the fashion which thou shalt make it of: The length of the ark shall be three hundred cubits, the breadth of it fifty cubits, and the height of it thirty cubits. A window shalt thou make to the ark, and in a cubit shall thou finish it above; and the door of the ark shalt thou set in the side thereof; with lower, second, and third stories shalt thou make it. And, behold, I, even I, do bring a flood of waters upon the earth, to destroy all flesh, wherein is the breath of life, from under heaven; and every thing that is in the earth shall die. But with thee will I establish my covenant; and thou shalt come into the ark, thou, and thy sons, and thy wife, and thy sons' wives with thee. And of every living thing of all flesh, two of every sort shalt thou bring into the ark, to keep them alive with thee; they shall be male and female. Of fowls after their kind, and of cattle after their kind, of every creeping thing of the earth after his kind, two of every sort shall come unto thee, to keep them alive. And take thou unto thee of all food that is eaten, and thou shalt gather it to thee; and it shall be for food for thee, and for them. Thus did Noah; according to all that God commanded him, so did he.

7. * * * And Noah was six hundred years old when the flood of waters was upon the earth. And Noah went in, and his sons, and his wife, and his sons' wives with him, into the ark, because of the waters of the flood. Of clean beasts, and of beasts that are not clean, and of fowls, and of every thing that creepeth upon the earth, There went in two and two unto Noah into the ark, the male and the female, as God had commanded Noah. And it came to pass after seven days, that the waters of the flood were upon the earth. In the six hundredth year of Noah's life, in the second month, the seventeenth day of the month, the same day were all the fountains of the great deep broken up, and the windows of heaven were opened. And the rain was upon the earth forty days and forty nights. In the selfsame day entered Noah, and Shem, and Ham, and Japheth, the sons of Noah, and Noah's wife, and the three wives of his sons with them, into the ark; they, and every beast after his kind, and all the cattle after their kind, and every creeping thing that creepeth upon the earth after his kind, and every fowl after his kind, every bird of every sort. And they went in unto Noah into the ark, two and two of all flesh, wherein is the breath of life. And they that went in, went in male and female of all flesh, as God had commanded him: and the Lord shut him in. And the flood was forty days upon the earth; and the waters increased, and bare up the ark, and it was lift up

above the earth. And the waters prevailed, and were increased greatly upon the earth; and the ark went upon the face of the waters. And the waters prevailed exceedingly upon the earth; and all the high hills, that were under the whole heaven, were covered. Fifteen cubits upward did the waters prevail; and the mountains were covered. And all flesh died that moved upon the earth, both of fowl, and of cattle, and of beast, and of every creeping thing that creepeth upon the earth, and every man: all in whose nostrils was the breath of life, of all that was in the dry land, died. And every living substance was destroyed which was upon the face of the ground, both man, and cattle, and the creeping things, and the fowl of the heaven; and they were destroyed from the earth: and Noah only remained alive, and they that were with him in the ark. And the waters prevailed upon the earth an hundred and fifty days.

8. And God remembered Noah, and every living thing, and all the cattle that was with him in the ark: and God made a wind to pass over the earth, and the waters assuaged; The fountains also of the deep and the windows of heaven were stopped, and the rain from heaven was restrained; And the waters returned from off the earth continually: and after the end of the hundred and fifty days the waters were abated. And the ark rested in the seventh month, on the seventeenth day of the month, upon the mountains of Ararat. And the waters decreased continually until the tenth month: in the tenth month, on the first day of the month, were the tops of the mountains seen.

And it came to pass at the end of forty days, that Noah opened the window of the ark which he had made: and he sent forth a raven, which went forth to and fro, until the waters were dried up from off the earth. Also he sent forth a dove from him, to see if the waters were abated from off the face of the ground; but the dove found no rest for the sole of her foot, and she returned unto him into the ark, for the waters were on the face of the whole earth: then he put forth his hand, and took her, and pulled her in unto him into the ark. And he stayed yet another seven days; and again he sent forth the dove out of the ark; and the dove came in to him in the evening; and, lo, in her mouth was an olive leaf plucked off: so Noah knew that the waters were abated from off the earth. And he stayed yet other seven days; and sent forth the dove; which returned not again unto him any more.

And it came to pass in the six hundredth and first year, in the first month, the first day of the month, the waters were dried up from off the earth: and Noah removed the covering of the ark, and looked, and, behold, the face of the ground was dry. And in the second month, on the seven and twentieth day of the month, was the earth dried.

And God spake unto Noah, saying, Go forth of the ark, thou, and thy wife, and thy sons, and thy sons' wives with thee. Bring forth with thee every living thing that is with thee, of all flesh, both of fowl, and of cattle, and of every creeping thing that creepeth upon the earth; that they may breed abundantly in the earth, and be fruitful, and multiply upon the earth. And Noah went forth, and his sons, and his wife, and his sons' wives with him: every beast, every creeping thing, and every fowl, and whatsoever creepeth upon the earth, after their kinds, went forth out of the ark. And Noah builded an altar unto the Lord; and took of every clean beast, and of every clean fowl, and offered burnt offerings on the altar. And the Lord smelled a sweet savour; and the Lord said in his heart, I will not again curse the ground any more for man's sake; for the imagination of man's heart is evil from his youth; neither will I again smite any more every thing living, as I have done. While the earth remaineth, seedtime and harvest, and cold and heat, and summer and winter, and day and night shall not cease.

9. And God blessed Noah and his sons, and said unto them, Be fruitful, and multiply, and replenish the earth. And the fear of you and the dread of you shall be upon every beast of the earth, and upon every fowl of the air, upon all that moveth upon the earth, and upon all the fishes of the sea; into your hand are they delivered. Every moving thing that liveth shall be meat for you; even as the green herb have I given you all things. But flesh with the life thereof, which is the blood thereof, shall ye not eat. And surely your blood of your lives will I require; at the hand of every beast will I require it, and at the hand of man; at the hand of every man's brother will I require the life of man. Whoso sheddeth man's blood, by man shall his blood be shed, for in the image of God made he man. And you, be ye fruitful, and multiply; bring forth abundantly in the earth, and multiply therein.

And God spake unto Noah, and to his sons with him, saying, And I, behold, I establish my covenant with you, and with your seed after you; And with every living creature that is with you, of the fowl, of the cattle, and of every beast of the earth with you; from all that go out of the ark, to every beast of the earth. And I will establish my covenant with you; neither shall all flesh be cut off any more by the waters of a flood; neither shall there any more be a flood to destroy the earth. And God said, This is the token of the covenant which I make between me and you and every living creature that is with you, for perpetual generations: I do set my bow in the cloud, and it shall be for a token of a covenant between me and the earth. And it shall come to pass, when I bring a cloud over the earth, that the bow shall be seen in the cloud: and I will remember my covenant, which is between me and you and every living creature of all flesh; and the waters shall no more become a flood to destroy all flesh. And the bow shall be in the cloud; and I will look upon it, that I may remember the everlasting covenant between God and every living creature of all flesh that is upon the earth. And God said unto Noah, This is the token of the covenant, which I have established between me and all flesh that is upon the earth.

Genesis 11

[The Origin of Languages]

11. And the whole earth was of one language, and of one speech. And it came to pass, as they journeyed from the east, that they found a plain in the land of Shinar; and they dwelt there. And they said one to another, Go to, let us make brick, and burn them throughly. And they had brick for stone, and slime had they for mortar. And they said, Go to, let us build us a city and a tower, whose top may reach unto heaven; and let us make us a name, lest we be scattered abroad upon the face of the whole earth. And the Lord came down to see the city and the tower, which the children of men builded. And the Lord said, Behold, the people is one, and they have all one language; and this they begin to do: and now nothing will be restrained from them, which they have imagined to do. Go to, let us go down, and there confound their language, that they may not understand one another's speech. So the Lord scattered them abroad from thence upon the face of all the earth: and they left off to build the city. Therefore is the name of it called Babel; because the Lord did there confound the language of all the earth: and from thence did the Lord scatter them abroad upon the face of all the earth.

Genesis 37, 39–46

[The Story of Joseph]

37. * * * Joseph, being seventeen years old, was feeding the flock with his brethren; and the lad was with the sons of Bilhah, and with the sons of Zilpah, his father's wives: and Joseph brought unto his father their evil report. Now Israel loved Joseph more than all his children, because he was the son of his old age: and he made him a coat of many colours. And when his brethren saw that their father loved him more than all his brethren, they hated him, and could not speak peaceably unto him.

And Joseph dreamed a dream, and he told it his brethren: and they hated him yet the more. And he said unto them, Hear, I pray you, this dream which I have dreamed: for, behold, we were binding sheaves in the field, and, lo, my sheaf arose, and also stood upright; and, behold, your sheaves stood round about, and made obeisance to my sheaf. And his brethren said to him, Shalt thou indeed reign over us? or shalt thou indeed have dominion over us? And they hated him yet the more for his dreams, and for his words.

And he dreamed yet another dream, and told it his brethren, and said, Behold, I have dreamed a dream more; and, behold, the sun and the moon and the eleven stars made obeisance to me. And he told it to his father, and to his brethren: and his father rebuked him, and said unto him, What is this dream that thou hast dreamed? Shall I and thy mother and thy brethren indeed come to bow down ourselves to thee to the earth? And his brethren envied him; but his father observed the saying.

And his brethren went to feed their father's flock in Shechem. And Israel said unto Joseph, Do not thy brethren feed the flock in Shechem? come, and I will send thee unto them. And he said to him, Here am I. And he said to him, Go, I pray thee, see whether it be well with thy brethren, and well with the flocks; and bring me word again. So he sent him out of the vale of Hebron, and he came to Shechem.

And a certain man found him, and, behold, he was wandering in the field: and the man asked him, saying, What seekest thou? And he said, I seek my brethren: tell me, I pray thee, where they feed their flocks. And the man said, They are departed hence; for I heard them say, Let us go to Dothan. And Joseph went after his brethren, and found them in Dothan. And when they saw him afar off, even before he came near unto them, they conspired against him to slay him. And they said one to another, Behold, this dreamer cometh. Come now therefore, and let us slay him, and cast him into some pit, and we will say, Some evil beast hath devoured him: and we shall see what will become of his dreams. And Reuben heard it, and he delivered him out of their hands; and said, Let us not kill him. And Reuben said unto them, Shed no blood, but cast him into this pit that is in the wilderness, and lay no hand upon him; that he might rid him out of their hands, to deliver him to his father again.

And it came to pass, when Joseph was come unto his brethren, that they stripped Joseph out of his coat, his coat of many colours that was on him; and they took him, and cast him into a pit; and the pit was empty, there was no water in it. And they sat down to eat bread: and they lifted up their eyes and looked, and, behold, a company of Ishmeelites came from Gilead with their camels bearing spicery and balm and myrrh, going to carry it down to Egypt. And Judah said unto his brethren, What profit is it if we slay our brother, and conceal his blood? Come, and let us sell him to the Ishmeelites, and let not our hand be upon him; for he is our brother and our flesh. And his brethren were content. Then there passed by Midianites merchantmen; and they drew and lifted up Joseph out of the pit, and sold Joseph to the Ishmeelites for twenty pieces of silver: and they brought Joseph into Egypt.

And Reuben returned unto the pit; and, behold, Joseph was not in the pit; and he rent his clothes. And he returned unto his brethren, and said, The child is not; and I, whither shall I go? And they took Joseph's coat, and killed a kid of the goats, and dipped the coat in the blood; and they sent the coat of many colours, and they brought it to their father; and said, This have we found: know now whether it be thy son's coat or no. And he knew it, and said, It is my son's coat; an evil beast hath devoured him; Joseph is without doubt rent in pieces. And Jacob rent his clothes, and put sackcloth upon his loins, and mourned for his son many days. And all his sons and all his daughters rose up to comfort him; but he refused to be comforted; and he said, For I will go down into the grave unto my son mourning. Thus his father wept for him. * * *

39. And Joseph was brought down to Egypt; and Potiphar, an officer of Pharaoh, captain of the guard, an Egyptian, bought him of the hands of the Ishmeelites, which had brought him down thither. And the Lord was with Joseph, and he was a prosperous man; and he was in the house of his master the Egyptian. And his master saw that the Lord was with him, and that the Lord made all he did to prosper in his hand. And Joseph found grace in his sight, and he served him: and he made him overseer over his house, and all that he had he put into his hand. And it came to pass from the time that he had made him overseer in his house, and over all that he had, that the Lord blessed the Egyptian's house for Joseph's sake; and the blessing of the Lord was upon all that he had in the house, and in the field. And he left all that he had in Joseph's hand; and he knew not ought he had, save the bread which he did eat. And Joseph was a goodly person, and well favoured.

And it came to pass after these things, that his master's wife cast her eyes upon Joseph; and she said, Lie with me. But he refused, and said unto his master's wife, Behold, my master wotteth not what is with me in the house, and he hath committed all that he hath to my hand; there is none greater in this house than I; neither hath he kept back any thing from me but thee, because thou art his wife: how then can I do this great wickedness, and sin against God? And it came to pass, as she spake to Joseph day by day, that he hearkened not unto her, to lie by her, or to be with her. And it came to pass about this time, that Joseph went into the house to do his business; and there was none of the men of the house there within. And she caught him by his garment, saying, Lie with me: and he left his garment in her hand, and fled, and got him out. And it came to pass, when she saw that he had left his garment in her hand, and was fled forth, that she called unto the men of her house, and spoke unto them, saying, See, he hath brought in an Hebrew unto us to mock us; he came in unto me to lie with me, and I cried with a loud voice: and it came to pass, when he heard that I lifted up my voice and cried, that he left his garment with me, and fled, and got him out. And she laid up his garment by her, until his lord came home. And she spake unto him according to these words, saying, The Hebrew servant, which thou hast brought unto us, came in unto me to mock me: and it came to pass, as I lifted up my voice and cried, that he left his garment with me, and fled out. And it came to pass, when his master heard the words of his wife, which she spake unto him, saying, After this manner did thy servant to me; that his wrath was kindled. And Joseph's master took him, and put him into the prison, a place where the king's prisoners were bound: and he was there in the prison.

But the Lord was with Joseph, and showed him mercy, and gave him favour in the sight of the keeper of the prison. And the keeper of the prison committed to Joseph's hand all the prisoners that were in the prison; and whatsoever they did there, he was the doer of it. The keeper of the prison looked not to any thing that was under his hand; because the Lord was with him, and that which he did, the Lord made it to prosper.

40. And it came to pass after these things that the butler of the king of Egypt and his baker had offended their lord the king of Egypt. And Pharaoh was wroth against two of his officers, against the chief of the butlers, and against the chief of the bakers. And he put them in ward in the house of the captain of the guard, into the prison, the place where Joseph was bound. And the captain of the guard charged Joseph with them, and he served them: and they continued a season in ward.

And they dreamed a dream both of them, each man his dream in one night, each man according to the interpretation of his dream, the butler and the baker of the king of Egypt, which were bound in the prison. And Joseph came in unto them in the morning, and looked upon them, and, behold, they were sad. And he asked Pharaoh's officers that were with him in the ward of his lord's house, saying, Wherefore look ye so sadly to day? And they said unto him, We have dreamed a dream, and there is no interpreter of it. And Joseph said unto them, Do not interpretations belong to God? tell me them, I pray you. And the chief butler told his dream to Joseph, and said to him, In my dream, behold, a vine was before me; and in the vine were three branches: and it was as though it budded, and her blossoms shot forth; and the clusters thereof brought forth ripe grapes: and Pharaoh's cup was in my hand: and I took the grapes, and pressed them into Pharaoh's cup, and I gave the cup into Pharaoh's hand. And Joseph said unto him, This is the interpretation of it: the three branches are three days: yet within three days shall Pharaoh lift up thine head, and restore thee unto thy place: and thou shalt deliver Pharaoh's cup into his hand, after the former manner when thou wast his butler. But think on me when it shall be well with thee, and shew kindness, I pray thee, unto me, and make mention of me unto Pharaoh, and bring me out of this house: for indeed I was stolen away out of the land of the Hebrews: and here also have I done nothing that they should put me into the dungeon. When the chief baker saw that the interpretation was good, he said unto Joseph, I also was in my dream, and, behold, I had three white baskets on my head: and in the uppermost basket there was of all manner of bakemeats for Pharaoh; and the birds did eat them out of the basket upon my head. And Joseph answered and said, This is the interpretation thereof: the three baskets are three days: yet within three days shall Pharaoh lift up thy head from off thee, and shall hang thee on a tree; and the birds shall eat thy flesh from off thee.

And it came to pass the third day, which was Pharaoh's birthday, that he made a feast unto all his servants: and he lifted up the head of the chief butler and of the chief baker among his servants. And he restored the chief butler unto his butlership again; and he gave the cup into Pharaoh's hand. But he hanged the chief baker: as Joseph had interpreted to them. Yet did not the chief butler remember Joseph, but forgat him.

41. And it came to pass at the end of two full years, that Pharaoh dreamed: and, behold, he stood by the river. And, behold, there came up out of the river seven well favoured kine and fatfleshed; and they fed in a meadow. And, behold, seven other kine came up after them out of the river, ill favoured and leanfleshed; and stood by the other kine upon the brink of the river. And the ill favoured and leanfleshed kine did eat up the seven well favoured and fat kine. So Pharaoh awoke. And he slept and dreamed the second time: and, behold, seven ears of corn came up upon one stalk, rank and good. And, behold, seven thin ears and blasted with the east wind sprung up after them. And the seven thin ears devoured the seven rank and full ears. And Pharaoh awoke, and, behold, it was a dream. And it came to pass in the

morning that his spirit was troubled; and he sent and called for all the magicians of Egypt, and all the wise men thereof: and Pharaoh told them his dream; but there was none that could interpret them unto Pharaoh.

Then spake the chief butler unto Pharaoh, saying, I do remember my faults this day: Pharaoh was wroth with his servants, and put me in ward in the captain of the guard's house, both me and the chief baker: and we dreamed a dream in one night, I and he; we dreamed each man according to the interpretation of his dream. And there was there with us a young man, an Hebrew, servant to the captain of the guard; and we told him, and he interpreted to us our dreams; to each man according to his dream he did interpret. And it came to pass, as he interpreted to us, so it was; me he restored unto mine office, and him he hanged.

Then Pharaoh sent and called Joseph, and they brought him hastily out of the dungeon: and he shaved himself, and changed his raiment, and came in unto Pharaoh. And Pharaoh said unto Joseph, I have dreamed a dream, and there is none that can interpret it: and I have heard say of thee that thou canst understand a dream to interpret it. And Joseph answered Pharaoh, saying, It is not in me: God shall give Pharaoh an answer of peace. And Pharaoh said unto Joseph, In my dream, behold, I stood upon the bank of the river; and, behold, there came up out of the river seven kine, fatfleshed and well favoured; and they fed in a meadow: and, behold, seven other kine came up after them, poor and very ill favoured and leanfleshed, such as I never saw in all the land of Egypt for badness: and the lean and the ill favoured kine did eat up the first seven fat kine: and when they had eaten them up, it could not be known that they had eaten them; but they were still ill favoured, as at the beginning. So I awoke. And I saw in my dream, and, behold, seven ears came up in one stalk, full and good: and, behold, seven ears, withered, thin, and blasted with the east wind, sprung up after them: and the thin ears devoured the seven good ears: and I told this unto the magicians; but there was none that could declare it to me.

And Joseph said unto Pharaoh, The dream of Pharaoh is one: God hath shewed Pharaoh what he is about to do. The seven good kine are seven years; and the seven good ears are seven years: the dream is one. And the seven thin and ill favoured kine that came up after them are seven years; and the seven empty ears blasted with the east wind shall be seven years of famine. This is the thing which I have spoken unto Pharaoh: what God is about to do he sheweth unto Pharaoh. Behold, there come seven years of great plenty throughout all the land of Egypt: and there shall arise after them seven years of famine; and all the plenty shall be forgotten in the land of Egypt; and the famine shall consume the land; and the plenty shall not be known in the land by reason of that famine following; for it shall be very grievous. And for that the dream was doubled unto Pharaoh twice; it is because the thing is established by God, and God will shortly bring it to pass. Now therefore let Pharaoh look out a man discreet and wise, and set him over the land of Egypt. Let Pharaoh do this, and let him appoint officers over the land, and take up the fifth part of the land of Egypt in the seven plenteous years. And let them gather all the food of those good years that come, and lay up corn under the hand of Pharaoh, and let them keep food in the cities. And that food shall be for store to the land against the seven years of famine, which shall be in the land of Egypt; that the land perish not through the famine.

And the thing was good in the eyes of Pharaoh, and in the eyes of all his servants. And Pharaoh said unto his servants, Can we find such a one as this is, a man in whom the Spirit of God is? And Pharaoh said unto Joseph, Forasmuch as God hath shewed thee all this, there is none so discreet and wise as thou art: thou shalt be over my house, and according unto thy word shall all my people be ruled: only in the throne will I be greater than thou. And Pharaoh said unto Joseph, See, I have set thee over all the land of Egypt. And Pharaoh took off his ring from his hand, and put it upon Joseph's hand, and arrayed him in vestures of fine linen, and put a gold chain about his neck; and he made him to ride in the second chariot which he had; and they cried before him, Bow the knee: and he made him ruler over all the land of Egypt. And Pharaoh said unto Joseph, I am Pharaoh, and without thee shall no man lift up his hand or foot in all the land of Egypt. And Pharaoh called Joseph's name Zaphnathpaaneah; and he gave him to wife Asenath, the daughter of Poti-pherah priest of On. And Joseph went out over all the land of Egypt.

And Joseph was thirty years old when he stood before Pharaoh king of Egypt. And Joseph went out from the presence of Pharaoh, and went throughout all the land of Egypt. And in the seven plenteous years the earth brought forth by handfuls. And he gathered up all the food of the seven years, which were in the land of Egypt, and laid up the food in the cities: the food of the field, which was round about every city, laid he up in the same. And Joseph gathered corn as the sand of the sea, very much, until he left numbering; for it was without number. And unto Joseph were born two sons before the years of famine came, which Asenath, the daughter of Poti-pherah priest of On, bare unto him. And Joseph called the name of the first born Manasseh: For God, said he, hath made me forget all my toil, and all my father's house. And the name of the second called he Ephraim: For God hath caused me to be fruitful in the land of my affliction.

And the seven years of plenteousness, that was in the land of Egypt, were ended. And the seven years of dearth began to come, according as Joseph had said: and the dearth was in all lands; but in all the land of Egypt there was bread. And when all the land of Egypt was famished, the people cried to Pharaoh for bread: and Pharaoh said unto all the Egyptians, Go unto Joseph; what he saith to you, do. And the famine was over all the face of the earth. And Joseph opened all the storehouses, and sold unto the Egyptians; and the famine waxed sore in the land of Egypt. And all countries came into Egypt to Joseph for to buy corn; because that the famine was so sore in all lands.

42. Now when Jacob saw that there was corn in Egypt, Jacob said unto his sons, Why do ye look one upon another? And he said, Behold, I have heard that there is corn in Egypt: get you down thither, and buy for us from thence; that we may live, and not die.

And Joseph's ten brethren went down to buy corn in Egypt. But Benjamin, Joseph's brother, Jacob sent not with his brethren; for he said, Lest peradventure mischief befall him. And the sons of Israel came to buy corn among those that came: for the famine was in the land of Canaan. And Joseph was the governor over the land, and he it was that sold to all the people of the land: and Joseph's brethren came, and bowed down themselves before him with their faces to the earth. And Joseph saw his brethren, and he knew them, but made himself strange unto them, and spake roughly unto them; and he said unto them, Whence come ye? And they said, From the land of Canaan to buy food. And Joseph knew his brethren, but they knew not him. And Joseph remembered the dreams which he dreamed of them, and said unto them, Ye are spies; to see the nakedness of the land ye are come. And they said unto him, Nay, my lord, but to buy food are thy servants come. We are all one man's sons; we are true men, thy servants are no spies. And he said unto them, Nay, but to see the nakedness of the land ye are come. And they said, Thy servants are twelve brethren, the sons of one man in the land of Canaan; and, behold, the youngest is this day with our father, and one is not. And Joseph said unto them, That is it that I spake unto you, saying, Ye are spies: Hereby ye shall be proved: By the life of Pharaoh ye shall not go forth hence, except your youngest brother come hither. Send one of you, and let him fetch your brother, and ye shall be kept in prison, that your words may be proved, whether there be any truth in you: or else by the life of Pharaoh surely ye are spies. And he put them all together into ward three days. And Joseph said unto them the third day, This do, and live; for I fear God: if ye be true men, let one of your brethren be bound in the house of your prison: go ye, carry corn for the famine of your houses: but bring your youngest brother unto me; so shall your words be verified, and ye shall not die. And they did so.

And they said one to another, We are verily guilty concerning our brother, in that we saw the anguish of his soul, when he besought us, and we would not hear; therefore is this distress come upon us. And Reuben answered them, saying, Spake I not unto you, saying, Do not sin against the child; and ye would not hear? therefore, behold, also his blood is required. And they knew not that Joseph understood them; for he spake unto them by an interpreter. And he turned himself about from them, and wept; and returned to them again, and communed with them, and took from them Simeon, and bound him before their eyes.

Then Joseph commanded to fill their sacks with corn, and to restore every man's money into his sack, and to give them provision for the way: and thus did he unto them. And they laded their asses with the corn, and departed thence. And as one of them opened his sack to give his ass provender in the inn, he espied his money; for, behold, it was in his sack's mouth. And he said unto his brethren, My money is restored; and, lo, it is even in my sack: and their heart failed them, and they were afraid, saying one to another, What is this that God hath done unto us?

And they came unto Jacob their father unto the land of Canaan, and told him all that befell unto them; saying, The man, who is lord of the land, spake roughly to us, and took us for spies of the country. And we said unto him, We are true men; we are no spies: we be twelve brethren, sons of our father; one is not, and the youngest is this day with our father in the land of Canaan. And the man, the lord of the country, said unto us, Hereby shall I know that ye are true men; leave one of your brethren here with me, and take the food for the famine of your households, and be gone: and bring your youngest brother unto me: then shall I know that ye are no spies, but that ye are true men: so will I deliver you your brother, and ye shall traffick in the land.

And it came to pass as they emptied their sacks, that, behold, every man's bundle of money was in his sack: and when both they and their father saw the bundles of money, they were afraid. And Jacob their father said unto them, Me have ye bereaved of my children: Joseph is not, and Simeon is not, and ye will take Benjamin away: all these things are against me.

And Reuben spake unto his father, saying, Slay my two sons, if I bring him not to thee: deliver him into my hand, and I will bring him to thee again. And he said, My son shall not go down with you; for his brother is dead, and he is left alone: if mischief befall him by the way in the which ye go, then shall ye bring down my gray hairs with sorrow to the grave.

43. And the famine was sore in the land. And it came to pass, when they had eaten up the corn which they had brought out of Egypt, their father said unto them, Go again, buy us a little food. And Judah spake unto him, saying, The man did solemnly protest unto us, saying, Ye shall not see my face, except your brother be with you. If thou wilt send our brother with us, we will go down and buy thee food: but if thou wilt not send him, we will not go down: for the man said unto us, Ye shall not see my face, except your brother be with you. And Israel said, Wherefore dealt ye so ill with me, as to tell the man whether ye had yet a brother? And they said, The man asked us straitly of our state, and of our kindred, saying, Is your father yet alive? have ye another brother? and we told him according to the tenor of these words: could we certainly know that he would say, Bring your brother down? And Judah said unto Israel his father, Send the lad with me, and we will arise and go; that we may live, and not die, both we, and thou, and also our little ones. I will be surety for him; of my hand shalt thou require him: if I bring him not unto thee, and set him before thee, then let me bear the blame for ever: for except we had lingered, surely now we had returned this second time. And their father Israel said unto them, If it must be so now, do this; take of the best fruits in the land in your vessels, and carry down the man a present, a little balm, and a little honey, spices, and myrh, nuts and almonds: and take double money in your hand: and the money that was brought again in the mouth of your sacks, carry it again in your hand; peradventure it was an oversight: take also your brother, and arise, go again unto the man: and God Almighty give you mercy before the man, that he may send away your other brother, and Benjamin. If I be bereaved of my children, I am bereaved.

And the men took that present, and they took double money in their hand, and Benjamin; and rose up, and went down to Egypt, and stood before Joseph. And when Joseph saw Benjamin with them, he said to the ruler of his house, Bring these men home, and slay, and make ready; for these men shall dine with me at noon. And the man did as Joseph bade; and the man brought the men into Joseph's house. And the men were afraid, because they were brought into Joseph's house; and they said, Because of the money that was returned in our sacks at the first time are we brought in; that he may seek occasion against us, and fall upon us, and take us for bondmen, and our asses. And they came near to the steward of Joseph's house, and they communed with him at the door of the house, and said, O sir, we came indeed down at the first time to buy food; and it came to pass, when we came to the inn, that we opened our sacks, and behold, every man's money was in the mouth of his sack, our money in full weight: and we have brought it again in our hand. And other money have we brought down in our hands to buy food: we cannot tell who put our money in our sacks. And he said, Peace be to you, fear not: your God, and the God of your father, hath given you treasure in your sacks: I had your money. And he brought Simeon out unto them. And the man brought the men into Joseph's house, and gave them water, and they washed their feet; and he gave their asses provender. And they made ready the present against Joseph came at noon: for they heard that they should eat bread there.

And when Joseph came home, they brought him the present which was in their hand into the house, and bowed themselves to him to the earth. And he asked them of their welfare, and said, Is your father well, the old man of whom ye spake? Is he yet alive? And they answered, Thy servant our father is in good health, he is yet alive. And they bowed down their heads, and made obeisance. And he lifted up his eyes, and saw his brother Benjamin, his mother's son, and said, Is this your younger brother, of whom ye spake unto me? And he said, God be gracious unto thee, my son. And Joseph made haste; for his bowels did yearn upon his brother: and he sought where to weep; and he entered into his chamber, and wept there. And he washed his face, and went out, and refrained himself, and said, Set on bread. And they set on for him by himself, and for them by themselves, and for the Egyptians, which did eat with him, by themselves: because the Egyptians might not eat bread with the Hebrews; for that is an abomination unto the Egyptians. And they sat before him, the firstborn according to his birthright, and the youngest according to his youth: and the men marvelled one at another. And he took and sent messes unto them from before him: but Benjamin's mess was five times so much as any of theirs. And they drank, and were merry with him.

44. And he commanded the steward of his house, saying, Fill the men's sacks with food, as much as they can carry, and put every man's money in his sack's mouth. And put my cup, the silver cup, in the sack's mouth of the youngest, and his corn money. And he did according to the word that Joseph had spoken. As soon as the morning was light, the men were sent away, they and their asses. And when they were gone out of the city, and not yet far off, Joseph said unto his steward, Up, follow after the men; and when thou dost overtake them, say unto them, Wherefore have ye rewarded evil for good? Is not this it in which my lord drinketh, and whereby indeed he divineth? ye have done evil in so doing.

And he overtook them, and he spake unto them these same words. And they said unto him, Wherefore saith my lord these words? God forbid that thy servants should do according to this thing: behold, the money, which we found in our sacks' mouths, we brought again unto thee out of the land of Canaan: how then should we steal out of thy lord's house silver or gold? With whomsoever of thy servants it be found, both let him die, and we also will be my lord's bondmen. And he said, Now also let it be according unto your words: he with whom it is found shall be my servant; and ye shall be blameless. Then they speedily took down every man his sack to the ground, and opened every man his sack. And he searched, and began at the eldest, and left at the youngest: and the cup was found in Benjamin's sack. Then they rent their clothes, and laded every man his ass, and returned to the city.

And Judah and his brethren came to Joseph's house; for he was yet there: and they fell before him on the ground. And Joseph said unto them, What deed is this that ye have done? wot ye not that such a man as I can certainly divine? And Judah said, What shall we say unto my lord? what shall we speak? or how shall we clear ourselves? God hath found out the iniquity of thy servants: behold, we are my lord's servants, both we, and he also with whom the cup is found. And he said, God forbid that I should do so: but the man in whose hand the cup is found, he shall be my servant; and as for you, get you up in peace unto your father.

Then Judah came near unto him, and said, Oh my lord, let thy servant, I pray thee, speak a word in my lord's ears, and let not thine anger burn against thy servant: for thou art even as Pharaoh. My lord asked his servants, saying, Have ye a father, or a brother? And we said unto my lord, We have a father, an old man, and a child of his old age, a little one; and his brother is dead, and he alone is left of his mother, and his father loveth him. And thou saidst unto thy servants, Bring him down unto me, that I may set mine eyes upon him. And we said unto my lord, The lad cannot leave his father: for if he should leave his father, his father would die. And thou saidst unto thy servants, Except your youngest brother come down with you, ye shall see my face no more. And it came to pass when we came up unto thy servant my father, we told him the words of my lord. And our father said, Go again, and buy us a little food. And we said, We cannot go down: if our youngest brother be with us, then will we go down: for we may not see the man's face, except our youngest brother be with us. And thy servant my father said unto us, Ye know that my wife bare me two sons: and the one went out from me, and I said, Surely he is torn in pieces; and I saw him not since: and if ye take this also from me, and mischief befall him, ye shall bring down my gray hairs with sorrow to the grave. Now therefore when I come to thy servant my father, and the lad be not with us; seeing that his life is bound up in the lad's life; it shall come to pass, when he seeth that the lad is not with us, that he will die: and thy servants shall bring down the gray hairs of thy servant our father with sorrow to the grave. For thy servant became surety for the lad unto my father, saying, If I bring him not unto thee, then I shall bear the blame to my father for ever. Now therefore, I pray thee, let thy servant abide instead of the lad a bondman to my lord; and let the lad go up with his brethren. For how shall I go up to my father, and the lad be not with me? lest peradventure I see the evil that shall come on my father.

45. Then Joseph could not refrain himself before all them that stood by him; and he cried, Cause every man to go out from me. And there stood no man with him, while Joseph made himself known unto his brethren. And he wept aloud: and the Egyptians and the house of Pharaoh heard. And Joseph said unto his brethren, I am Joseph; doth my father yet live? And his brethren could not answer him; for they were troubled at his presence. And Joseph said unto his brethren, Come near to me, I pray you. And they came near. And he said, I am Joseph your brother, whom ye sold into Egypt. Now therefore be not grieved, nor angry with yourselves, that ye sold me hither: for God did send me before you to preserve life. For these two years hath the famine been in the land: and yet there are five years, in the which there shall neither be earing nor harvest. And God sent me before you to preserve you a posterity in the earth, and

to save your lives by a great deliverance. So now it was not you that sent me hither, but God: and he hath made me a father to Pharaoh, and lord of all his house, and a ruler throughout all the land of Egypt. Haste ye, and go up to my father, and say unto him, Thus saith thy son Joseph, God hath made me lord of all Egypt: come down unto me, tarry not: and thou shalt dwell in the land of Goshen, and thou shalt be near unto me, thou, and thy children, and thy children's children, and thy flocks, and thy herds, and all that thou hast: and there will I nourish thee; for yet there are five years of famine; lest thou, and thy household, and all that thou hast, come to poverty. And, behold, your eyes see, and the eyes of my brother Benjamin, that it is my mouth that speaketh unto you. And ye shall tell my father of all my glory in Egypt, and of all that ye have seen; and ye shall haste and bring down my father hither. And he fell upon his brother Benjamin's neck, and wept; and Benjamin wept upon his neck. Moreover he kissed all his brethren, and wept upon them: and after that his brethren talked with him.

And the fame thereof was heard in Pharaoh's house, saying, Joseph's brethren are come: and it pleased Pharaoh well, and his servants. And Pharaoh said unto Joseph, Say unto thy brethren, This do ye; lade your beasts, and go, get you unto the land of Canaan; and take your father and your households, and come unto me: and I will give you the good of the land of Egypt, and ye shall eat the fat of the land. Now thou art commanded, this do ye; take you wagons out of the land of Egypt for your little ones, and for your wives, and bring your father, and come. Also regard not your stuff; for the good of all the land of Egypt is yours. And the children of Israel did so: and Joseph gave them wagons, according to the commandment of Pharaoh, and gave them provision for the way. To all of them he gave each man changes of raiment; but to Benjamin he gave three hundred pieces of silver, and five changes of raiment. And to his father he sent after this manner; ten asses laden with the good things of Egypt, and ten she-asses laden with corn and bread and meat for his father by the way. So he sent his brethren away, and they departed: and he said unto them, See that ye fall not out by the way.

And they went up out of Egypt, and came into the land of Canaan unto Jacob their father, and told him, saying, Joseph is yet alive, and he is governor over all the land of Egypt. And Jacob's heart fainted, for he believed them not. And they told him all the words of Joseph, which he had said unto them: and when he saw the wagons which Joseph had sent to carry him, the spirit of Jacob their father revived. And Israel said, It is enough; Joseph my son is yet alive: I will go and see him before I die.

46. And Israel took his journey with all that he had, and came to Beer-sheba, and offered sacrifices unto the God of his father Isaac. And God spake unto Israel in the visions of the night, and said, Jacob, Jacob. And he said, Here am I. And he said, I am God, the God of thy father: fear not to go down into Egypt; for I will there make of thee a great nation: I will go down with thee into Egypt; and I will also surely bring thee up again: and Joseph shall put his hand upon thine eyes. And Jacob rose up from Beer-sheba: and the sons of Israel carried Jacob their father, and their little ones, and their wives, in the wagons which Pharaoh had sent to carry him. And they took their cattle, and their goods, which they had gotten in the land of Canaan, and came into Egypt, Jacob, and all his seed with him: his sons, and his sons' sons with him, his daughters, and his sons' daughters, and all his seed brought he with them into Egypt.

The Book of Job: Background

The Book of Job, typically assessed by literary critics and Bible scholars as a work of literary art without peer, presents the dilemma of unjustified suffering. The British essayist Thomas Carlyle regarded the story as one of the finest statements concerning a human's destiny and God's role in that destiny, and the French novelist Victor Hugo considered it to be a lofty, magnificent tale.

There is good reason for such high praise of this book of the Bible. First, it is distinguished by its unique content consisting of poetry and prose, of monologue and dialogue. Between the prose of the Prologue (Job 1:1–42: 7–17), there is a lengthy section of poetry (3:1–46:6) consisting of a monologue by Job, three cycles of a dialogue between Job and his friends, four speeches by another friend, a response to Job by God, and a portrayal of the repentant Job in the face of an omnipotent God. Second, this book claims such high critical praise because of the richness of its vocabulary. It contains as many as 110 Old Testament words unique to this text and reveals influences besides the Hebrew, including Akkadian, Arabic, Aramaic, Sumerian, and Ugartic. Third, with respect to literary technique, metaphors, similes, and parallelism abound throughout the book.

Naturally, many questions have arisen about the text's uniqueness. The mystery of its authorship is intriguing to literary critics and Bible scholars. The name of both the book and its hero appears in extrabiblical texts as early as 2000 BC. But the author is still unknown, and speculations about authorship range from a single author to several authors and editors. Another debate surrounds the question of genre. While many are content to classify Job as "Wisdom Literature," others regard it as tragedy. Some argue that it is a drama, whereas others call it a narrative. Such claims are based on evidence of Job's elements that allow the book to fit into the category of choice. However, most modern critics are satisfied to discuss the text, rather than determine the genre: they agree that it reflects wisdom, tragedy, drama, narrative, and philosophy. While these debates continue, there is no controversy about the message of the Book of Job. The problem of innocent suffering, unmerited agony, and evil aggression against the undeserving is explored from every possible angle, and in the end, God alone is seen to have the solution.

From Job

1. There was a man in the land of Uz whose name was Job, and that man was perfect and upright, and one that feared God, and eschewed evil. And there were burn unto him seven sons and three daughters. His substance also was seven thousand sheep, and three thousand camels, and five hundred yoke of oxen, and five hundred she asses, and a very great household; so that this man was the greatest of all the men of the east. And his sons went and feasted in their houses, every one his day; and sent and called for their three sisters to eat and to drink with them. And it was so, when the days of their feasting were gone about, that Job sent and sanctified them, and rose up early in the morning, and offered burnt offerings according to the number of them all: for Job said, It may be that my sons have sinned, and cursed God in their hearts. Thus did Job continually.

Now there was a day when the sons of God came to present themselves before the Lord, and Satan came also among them. And the Lord said unto Satan, whence comest thou? Then Satan answered the Lord, and said, From going to and fro in the earth, and from walking up and down in it. And the Lord said unto Satan, Hast thou considered my servant Job, that there is none like him in the earth, a perfect and an upright man, one that feareth God, and escheweth evil? Then Satan answered the Lord, and said, Doth Job fear God for nought? Hast not thou made an hedge about him, and about his house, and about all that he hath on every side? thou hast blessed the work of his hands, and his substance is increased in the land. But put forth thine hand now, and touch all that he hath, and he will curse thee to thy face. And the Lord said unto Satan, Behold, all that he hath is in thy power; only upon himself put not forth thine hand. So Satan went forth from the presence of the Lord.

And there was a day when his sons and his daughters were eating and drinking wine in their eldest brother's house: and there came a messenger unto Job, and said, The oxen were plowing, and the asses feeding beside them: and the Sabeans fell upon them, and took them away; yea, they have slain the servants with the edge of the sword; and I only am escaped alone to tell thee. While he was yet speaking, there came also another, and said, The fire of God is fallen from heaven, and hath burned up the sheep, and the servants, and consumed them; and I only am escaped alone to tell thee. While he was yet speaking, there came also another, and said, The Chaldeans made out three bands, and fell upon the camels, and have carried them away, yea, and slain the servants with the edge of the sword; and I only am escaped alone to tell thee. While he was yet speaking, there came also another, and said, Thy sons and thy daughters were eating and drinking wine in their eldest brother's house: and, behold, there came a great wind from the wilderness, and smote the four corners of the house, and it fell upon the young men, and they are dead; and I only am escaped alone to tell thee.

Then Job arose and rent his mantle, and shaved his head, and fell down upon the ground, and worshipped, and said, Naked came I out of my mother's womb, and naked shall I return thither: the Lord gave, and the Lord hath taken away; blessed be the name of the Lord. In all this Job sinned not, nor charged God foolishly.

2. Again there was a day when the sons of God came to present themselves before the Lord, and Satan came also among them to present himself before the Lord. And the Lord said unto Satan, From whence comest thou? And Satan answered the Lord, and said, From going to and fro in the earth, and from walking up and down in it. And the Lord said unto Satan, Hast thou considered my servant Job, that there is none like him in the earth, a perfect and an upright man, one that feareth God, and escheweth evil? and still he holdeth fast his integrity, although thou movedst me against him, to destroy him without cause. And Satan answered the Lord, and said, Skin for skin, yea, all that a man hath will he give for his life. But put forth thine hand now, and touch his bone and his flesh, and he will curse thee to thy face. And the Lord said unto Satan, Behold, he is in thine hand; but save his life.

So went Satan forth from the presence of the Lord, and smote Job with sore boils from the sole of his foot unto his crown. And he took him a potsherd to scrape himself withal; and he sat down among the ashes.

Then said his wife unto him, Dost thou still retain thine integrity? curse God, and die. But he said unto her, Thou speakest as one of the foolish women speaketh. What? shall we receive good at the hand of God, and shall we not receive evil? In all this did not Job sin with his lips.* * *

3. After this opened Job his mouth, and cursed his day. And Job spake, and said, Let the day perish wherein I was born, and the night in which it was said, There is a man child conceived. Let that day be darkness; let not God regard it from above, neither let the light shine upon it. Let darkness and the shadow of death stain it; let a cloud dwell upon it; let the blackness of the day terrify it. As for that night, let darkness seize upon it; let it not be joined unto the days of the year, let it not come into the number of the months. Lo, let that night be solitary, let no joyful voice come therein. Let them curse it that curse the day, who are ready to raise up their mourning. Let the stars of the twilight thereof be dark; let it look for light, but have none; neither let it see the dawning of the day: because it shut not up the doors of my mother's womb, nor hid sorrow from mine eyes. Why died I not from the womb? Why did I not give up the ghost when I came out of the belly? Why did the knees prevent me? or why the breasts that I should suck? For now should I have lain still and been quiet, I should have slept: then had I been at rest, with kings and counsellors of the earth, which built desolate places for themselves; or with princes that had gold, who filled their houses with silver: or as an hidden untimely birth I had not been; as infants which never saw light. There the wicked cease from troubling; and there the weary be at rest. There the prisoners rest together; they hear not the voice of the oppressor. The small and great are there; and the servant is free from his master. Wherefore is light given to him that is in misery, and life unto the bitter in soul; which long for death, but it cometh not; and dig for it more than for hid treasures; which rejoice exceedingly, and are glad, when they can find the grave? Why is light given to a man whose way is hid, and whom God hath hedged in? For my sighing cometh before I eat, and my roarings are poured out like the waters. For the thing which I greatly feared is come upon me, and that which I was afraid of is come unto me. I was not in safety, neither had I rest, neither was I quiet; yet trouble came.

Summary At this point three friends of Job come to comfort him. Their approach is to tell him that since God has punished him he must in some way have offended God; he must admit his guilt and ask forgiveness. But he refuses to do so.

12. And Job answered and said, No doubt but ye are the people, and wisdom shall die with you. But I have understanding as well as you; I am not inferior to you: yea, who knoweth not such things as these? I am as one mocked of his neighbour, who calleth upon God, and he answered him: the just upright man is laughed to scorn. He that is ready to slip with his feet is as a lamp despised in the thought of him that is at ease. The tabernacles of robbers prosper, and they that provoke God are secure, into whose hand God bringeth abundantly. But ask now the beasts, and they shall teach thee; and the fowls of the air, and they shall tell thee: or speak to the earth, and it shall teach thee: and the fishes of the sea shall declare unto thee. Who knoweth not in all these that the hand of the Lord hath wrought this? In whose hand is the soul of every living thing, and the breath of all mankind. Doth not the ear try words? and the mouth taste his meat? With the ancient is wisdom; and in length of days understanding. With him is wisdom and strength, he hath counsel and understanding. Behold, he breaketh down, and it cannot be built again: he shutteth up a man, and there can be no opening. Behold, he withholdeth the waters, and they dry up: also he sendeth them out, and they overturn the earth. With him is strength and wisdom: the deceived and the deceiver are his. He leadeth counsellors away spoiled, and maketh the judges fools. He looseth the bond of kings, and girdeth their loins with a girdle. He leadeth princes away spoiled, and overthroweth the mighty. He removeth away the speech of the trusty, and taketh away the understanding of the aged. He poureth contempt upon princes, and weakeneth the strength of the mighty. He discovereth deep things out of darkness, and bringeth out to light the shadow of death. He increaseth the nations, and destroyeth them: he enlargeth the nations, and straiteneth them again. He taketh away the heart of the chief of the people of the earth, and causeth them to wander in a wilderness where there is no way. They grope in the dark without light, and he maketh them to stagger like a drunken man.

13. Lo, mine eye hath seen all this, mine ear hath heard and understood it. What ye know, the same do I know also: I am not inferior unto you. Surely I would speak to the Almighty, and I desire to reason with God. But ye are forgers of lies, ye are all physicians of no value. O that ye would altogether hold

your peace! and it should be your wisdom. Hear now my reasoning, and hearken to the pleadings of my lips. Will ye speak wickedly for God? and talk deceitfully for him? Will ye accept his person? Will ye contend for God? Is it good that he should search you out? or as one man mocketh another, do ye so mock him? He will surely reprove you, if ye do secretly accept persons. Shall not his excellency make you afraid? and his dread fall upon you? Your remembrances are like unto ashes, your bodies to bodies of clay. Hold your peace, let me alone, that I may speak, and let come on me what will. Wherefore do I take my flesh in my teeth, and put my life in mine hand? Though he slay me, yet will I trust in him: but I will maintain mine own ways before him. He also shall be my salvation; for an hypocrite shall not come before him. Hear diligently my speech. and my declaration with your ears. Behold now, I have ordered my cause; I know that I shall be justified. Who is he that will plead with me? for now, if I hold my tongue, I shall give up the ghost. Only do not two things unto me: then will I not hide myself from thee. Withdraw thine hand far from me: and let not thy dread make me afraid. Then call thou, and I will answer: or let me speak, and answer thou me. How many are mine iniquities and sins? Make me to know my transgression and my sin. Wherefore hidest thou thy face, and holdest me for thine enemy? Wilt thou break a leaf driven to and fro? and wilt thou pursue the dry stubble? For thou writest bitter things against me, and makest me to possess the iniquities of my youth. Thou puttest my feet also in the stocks, and lookest narrowly unto all my paths; thou settest a print upon the heels of my feet. And he, as a rotten thing, consumeth, as a garment that is moth eaten.

14. Man that is born of a woman is of few days, and full of trouble. He cometh forth like a flower, and is cut down: he fleeth also as a shadow, and continueth not. And dost thou open thine eyes upon such an one, and bringest me into judgment with thee? Who can bring a clean thing out of an unclean? not one. Seeing his days are determined, the number of his months are with thee, thou hast appointed his bounds that he cannot pass; turn from him, that he may rest, till he shall accomplish, as an hireling, his day. For there is hope of a tree, if it be cut down, that it will sprout again, and that the tender branch thereof will not cease. Though the root thereof wax old in the earth, and the stock thereof die in the ground; yet through the scent of water it will bud, and bring forth boughs like a plant. But man dieth, and wasteth away: yea, man giveth up the ghost, and where is he? As the waters fail from the sea, and the flood decayeth and drieth up: so man dieth down, and riseth not: till the heavens be no more, they shall not awake, nor be raised out of their sleep. O that thou wouldest hide me in the grave, that thou wouldest keep me secret, until thy wrath be past, that thou wouldest appoint me a set time, and remember me! If a man die, shall he live again? All the days of my appointed time will I wait, till my change come. Thou shalt call, and I will answer thee: thou wilt have a desire to the work of thine hands. For now thou numberest my steps: dost thou not watch over my sin? My transgression is sealed up in a bag, and thou sewest up mine iniquity. And surely the mountain falling cometh to nought, and the rock is removed out of his place. The waters wear the stones: thou washest away the things which grow out of the dust of the earth; and thou destroyest the hope of man. Thou prevailest for ever against him, and he passeth; thou changest his countenance, and sendest him away. His sons come to honour, and he knoweth it not; and they are brought low, but he perceiveth it not of them. But his flesh upon him shall have pain, and his soul within him shall mourn.

29. Moreover Job continued his parable, and said, Oh that I were as in months past, as in the days when God preserved me; when his candle shined upon my head, and when by his light I walked through darkness; as I was in the days of my youth, when the secret of God was upon my tabernacle; when the Almighty was yet with me, when my children were about me; when I washed my steps with butter and the rock poured me out rivers of oil; when I went out to the gate through the city, when I prepared my seat in the street! The young men saw me, and hid themselves: and the aged arose, and stood up. The princes refrained talking, and laid their hand on their mouth. The nobles held their peace, and their tongue cleaved to the roof of their mouth. When the ear heard me, then it blessed me; and when the eye saw me, it gave witness to me: because I delivered the poor that cried, and the fatherless, and him that had none to help him. The blessing of him that was ready to perish came upon me: and I caused the widow's heart to sing for joy. I put on righteousness, and it clothed me: my judgment was as a robe and a diadem. I was eyes to the blind, and feet was I to the lame. I was a father to the poor; and the cause which I knew not I searched out. And I brake the jaws of the wicked, and plucked the spoil out of his teeth. Then I said, I shall die in my nest, and I shall multiply my days as the sand. My root was spread

out by the waters, and the dew lay all night upon my branch. My glory was fresh in me, and my bow was renewed in my hand. Unto me men gave ear, and waited, and kept silence at my counsel. After my words they spake not again; and my speech dropped upon them. And they waited for me as for the rain; and they opened their mouth wide as for the latter rain. If I laughed on them, they believed it not; and the light of my countenance they cast not down. I chose out their way, and sat chief, and dwelt as a king in the army, as one that comforteth the mourners.

30. But now they that are younger than I have me in derision, whose fathers I would have disdained to have set with the dogs of my flock. Yea, whereto might the strength of their hands profit me, in whom old age was perished? For want and famine they were solitary; fleeing into the wilderness in former time desolate and waste. Who cut up mallows by the bushes, and juniper roots for their meat. They were driven forth from among men, (they cried after them as after a thief;) to dwell in the cliffs of the valleys, in caves of the earth, and in the rocks. Among the bushes they brayed; under the nettles they were gathered together. They were children of fools, yea, children of base men: they were viler than the earth. And now am I their song, yea, I am their byword. They abhor me, they flee far from me, and spare not to spit in my face. Because he hath loosed my cord, and afflicted me, they have also let loose the bridle before me. Upon my right hand rise the youth; they push away my feet, and they raise up against me the ways of their destruction. They mar my path, they set forward my calamity, they have no helper. They came upon me as a wide breaking in of waters: in the desolation they rolled themselves upon me. Terrors are turned upon me: they pursue my soul as the wind; and my welfare passeth away as a cloud. And now my soul is poured out upon me; the days of affliction have taken hold upon me. My bones are pierced in me in the night season: and my sinews take no rest. By the great force of my disease is my garment changed: it bindeth me about as the collar of my coat. He hath cast me into the mire, and I am become like dust and ashes. I cry unto thee, and thou dost not hear me; I stand up, and thou regardest me not. Thou art become cruel to me: with thy strong hand thou opposest thyself against me. Thou liftest me up to the wind; thou causest me to ride upon it, and dissolvest my substance. For I know that thou wilt bring me to death, and to the house appointed for all living. Howbeit he will not stretch out his hand to the grave, though they cry in his destruction. Did not I weep for him that was in trouble? Was not my soul grieved for the poor? When I looked for good, then evil came unto me: and when I waited for light, there came darkness. My bowels boiled, and rested not: the days of affliction prevented me. I went mourning without the sun: I stood up, and I cried in the congregation. I am a brother to dragons, and a companion to owls. My skin is black upon me, and my bones are burned with heat. My harp also is turned to mourning, and my organ into the voice of them that weep.

31. I made a covenant with mine eyes; why then should I think upon a maid? For what portion of God is there from above? and what inheritance of the Almighty from on high? Is not destruction to the wicked? and a strange punishment to the workers of iniquity? Doth not he see my ways, and count all my steps? If I have walked with vanity, or if my foot hath hasted to deceit; let me be weighed in an even balance, that God may know mine integrity. If my step hath turned out of the way, and mine heart walked after mine eyes, and if any blot hath cleaved to mine hands; then let me sow, and let another eat; yea, let my offspring be rooted out. If mine heart have been deceived by a woman, or if I have laid wait at my neighbour's door; then let my wife grind unto another, and let others bow down upon her. For this is an heinous crime; yea, it is an iniquity to be punished by the judges. For it is a fire that consumeth to destruction, and would root out all mine increase.

If I did despise the cause of my manservant or of my maidservant, when they contended with me; what then shall I do when God riseth up and when he visiteth, what shall I answer him? Did not he that made me in the womb make him? and did not one fashion us in the womb? If I have withheld the poor from their desire, or have caused the eyes of the widow to fail; or have eaten my morsel myself alone, and the fatherless hath not eaten thereof; (For from my youth he was brought up with me, as with a father, and I have guided her from my mother's womb;) if I have seen any perish for want of clothing, or any poor without covering; if his loins have not blessed me, and if he were not warmed with the fleece of my sheep; if I have lifted up my hand against the fatherless, when I saw my help in the gate: then let mine arm fall from my shoulder blade, and mine arm be broken from the bone. For destruction from God was a terror to me, and by reason of his highness I could not endure. If I have made gold my hope, or have said to the fine gold, Thou are my confidence; if I rejoiced because my wealth was great, and because mine hand had gotten much: if I beheld the sun when it shined, or the moon walking in brightness; and my heart hath been secretly enticed, or my mouth hath kissed my hand: this also were an iniquity to be punished by the judge: for I should have denied the God that is above.

If I rejoiced at the destruction of him that hated me, or lifted up myself when evil found him: neither have I suffered my mouth to sin by wishing a curse to his soul. If the men of my tabernacle said not, Oh that we had of his flesh! We cannot be satisfied. The stranger did not lodge in the street: but I opened my doors to the traveller. If I covered my transgressions as Adam, by hiding mine iniquity in my bosom: did I fear a great multitude, or did the contempt of families terrify me, that I kept silence, and went not out of the door? Oh that one would hear me! Behold, my desire is, that the Almighty would answer me, and that mine adversary had written a book. Surely I would take it upon my shoulder, and bind it as a crown to me. I would declare unto him the number of my steps; as a prince would I go near unto him. If my land cry against me, or that the furrows likewise thereof complain; if I have eaten the fruits thereof without money, or have caused the owners thereof to lose their life; let thistles grow instead of wheat, and cockle instead of barley. The words of Job are ended.

38. Then the Lord answered Job out of the whirlwind, and said, Who is this that darkeneth counsel by words without knowledge? Gird up now thy loins like a man; for I will demand of thee, and answer thou me. Where wast thou when I laid the foundations of the earth? Declare, if thou hast understanding. Who hath laid the measures thereof, if thou knowest? or who hath stretched the line upon it? Whereupon are the foundations thereof fastened? or who laid the corner stone thereof; when the morning stars sang together, and all the sons of God shouted for joy? Or who shut up the sea with doors, when it brake forth, as if it had issued out of the womb? When I made the cloud the garment thereof, and thick darkness a swaddlingband for it, and brake up for it my decreed place, and set bars and doors, and said, Hitherto shalt thou come, but no further; and here shall thy proud waves be stayed? Hast thou commanded the morning since thy days; and caused the dayspring to know his place; that it might take hold of the ends of the earth, that the wicked might be shaken out of it? It is turned as clay to the seal; and they stand as a garment. And from the wicked their light is withholden, and the high arm shall be broken. Hast thou entered into the springs of the sea? or hast thou walked in the search of the depth? Have the gates of death been opened unto thee? or hast thou seen the doors of the shadow of death? Hast thou perceived the breadth of the earth? Declare if thou knowest it all. Where is the way where light dwelleth? And as for darkness, where is the place thereof, and that thou shouldest take it to the bound thereof, and that thou shouldest know the paths to the house thereof? Knowest thou it, because thou wast then born? or because the number of thy days is great? Hast thou entered into the treasures of the snow? or hast thou seen the treasures of the hail, which I have reserved against the time of trouble, against the day of battle and war? By what way is the light parted, which scattereth the east wind upon the earth? Who hath divided a watercourse for the overflowing of waters, or a way for the lightning of thunder; to cause it to rain on the earth, where no man is; on the wilderness, wherein there is no man; to satisfy the desolate and waste ground; and to cause the bud of the tender herb to spring forth? Hath the rain a father? or who hath begotten the drops of dew? Out of whose womb came the ice? And the hoary frost of heaven, who hath gendered it? The waters are hid as with a stone, and the face of the deep is frozen. Canst thou bind the sweet influences of Pleiades, or loose the bands of Orion? Canst thou bring forth Mazzaroth in his season? or canst thou guide Arcturus with his sons? Knowest thou the ordinances of heaven? Canst thou set the dominion thereof in the earth? Canst thou lift up thy voice to the clouds, that abundance of waters may cover thee? Canst thou send lightnings, that they may go, and say unto thee, Here we are? Who hath put wisdom in the inward parts? or who hath given understanding to the heart? Who can number the clouds in wisdom? or who can stay the bottles of heaven, when the dust groweth into hardness, and the clods cleave fast together? Wilt thou hunt the prey for the lion? or fill the appetite of the young lions, when they couch in their dens, and abide in the covert to lie in wait? Who provideth for the raven his food? when his young ones cry unto God, they wander for lack of meat.

39. Knowest thou the time when the wild goats of the rock bring forth? or canst thou mark when the hinds do calve? Canst thou number the months that they fulfil? or knowest thou the time when they bring forth? They bow themselves, they bring forth their young ones, they cast out their sorrows. Their young ones are in good liking, they grow up with corn; they go forth, and return not unto them. Who hath sent out the wild ass free? or, who hath loosed the bands of the wild ass? Whose house I have made the wilder-

ness, and the barren land his dwellings. He scorneth the multitude of the city, neither regardeth he the crying of the driver. The range of the mountains is his pasture, and he searcheth after every green thing. Will the unicorn be willing to serve thee, or abide by thy crib? Canst thou bind the unicorn with his band in the furrow? or will he harrow the valleys after thee? Wilt thou trust him, because his strength is great? or wilt thou leave thy labour to him? Wilt thou believe him, that he will bring home thy seed, and gather it into thy barn? Gavest thou the goodly wings unto the peacocks? or wings and feathers unto the ostrich? Which leaveth her eggs in the earth, and warmeth them in dust, and forgetteth that the foot may crush them, or that the wild beast may break them. She is hardened against her young ones, as though they were not here: her labour is in vain without fear; because God hath deprived her of wisdom, neither hath he imparted to her understanding. What time she lifteth up herself on high, she scorneth the horse and his rider. Hast thou given the horse strength? Hast thou clothed his neck with thunder? Canst thou make him afraid as a grasshopper? The glory of his nostrils is terrible. He paweth in the valley, and rejoiceth in his strength: he goeth on to meet the armed men. He mocketh at fear, and is not affrighted; neither turneth he back from the sword. The quiver rattleth against him, the glittering spear and the shield. He swalloweth the ground with fierceness and rage: neither believeth he that it is the sound of the trumpet. He saith among the trumpets, Ha, ha; and he smelleth the battle afar off, the thunder of the captains, and the shouting. Doth the hawk fly by thy wisdom, and stretch her wings toward the south? Doth the eagle mount up at thy command, and make her nest on high? She dwelleth and abideth on the rock, upon the crag of the rock, and the strong place. From thence she seeketh the prey, and her eyes behold afar off. Her young ones also suck up blood: and where the slain are, there is she.

40. Moreover the Lord answered Job, and said, Shall he that contendeth with the Almighty instruct him? He that reproveth God, let him answer it.

Then Job answered the Lord, and said, Behold, I am vile; what shall I answer thee? I will lay mine hand upon my mouth. Once have I spoken; but I will not answer: yea, twice; but I will proceed no further.

Then answered the Lord unto Job out of the whirlwind, and said, Gird up thy loins now like a man: I will demand of thee, and declare thou unto me. Wilt thou also disannul my judgment? Wilt thou condemn me, that thou mayest be righteous? Hast thou an arm like God: or canst thou thunder with a voice like him? Deck thyself now with majesty and excellency; and array thyself with glory and beauty. Cast abroad the rage of thy wrath: and behold every one that is proud, and abase him. Look on every one that is proud, and bring him low; and tread down the wicked in their place. Hide them in the dust together; and bind their faces in secret. Then will I also confess unto thee that thine own right hand can save thee.

Behold now behemoth, which I made with thee; he eateth grass as an ox. Lo now, his strength is in his loins, and his force is in the navel of his belly. He moveth his tail like a cedar: the sinews of his stones are wrapped together. His bones are as strong pieces of brass; his bones are like bars of iron. He is the chief of the ways of God: he that made him can make his sword to approach unto him. Surely the mountains bring him forth food, where all the beasts of the field play. He lieth under the shady trees, in the covert of the reed, and fens. The shady trees cover him with their shadow; the willows of the brook compass him about. Behold, he drinketh up a river, and hasteth not: he trusteth that he can draw up Jordan into his mouth. He taketh it with his eyes: his nose pierceth through snares.

41. Canst thou draw out leviathan with an hook? or his tongue with a cord which thou lettest down? Canst thou put an hoot into his nose? or bore his jaw through with a thorn? Will he make many supplications unto thee? wilt thou take him for a servant for ever? Wilt thou play with him as with a bird? or wilt thou bind him for thy maidens? Shall the companions make a banquet of him? Shall they part him among the merchants? Canst thou fill his skin with barbed irons? or his head with fish spears? Lay thine hand upon him, remember the battle, do no more. Behold, the hope of him is in vain: shall not one be cast down even at the sight of him? None is so fierce that dare stir him up: who then is able to stand before me? Who hath prevented me, that I should repay him? Whatsoever is under the whole heaven is mine. I will not conceal his parts, nor his power, nor his comely proportion. Who can discover the face of his garment? or who can come to him with his double bridle? Who can open the doors of his face? His teeth are terrible round about. His scales are his pride, shut up together as with a close seal. One is so near to another, that no air can come between them. They are joined one to another, they stick together, that they cannot be sundered. By his neesings a light doth shine, and his eyes are like the eyelids of the morning. Out of his mouth go burning lamps, and sparks of fire leap out. Out of his nostrils goeth smoke, as out of a

seething pot or caldron. His breath kindleth coals, and a flame goeth out of his mouth. In his neck remaineth strength, and sorrow is turned into joy before him. The flakes of his flesh are joined together: they are firm in themselves; they cannot be moved. His heart is as firm as a stone; yea, as hard as a piece of the nether millstone. When he raiseth up himself, the mighty are afraid: by reason of breakings they purify themselves. The sword of him that layeth at him cannot hold: the spear, the dart, nor the habergeon. He esteemeth iron as straw, and brass as rotten wood. The arrow cannot make him flee: slingstones are turned with him into stubble. Darts are counted as stubble: he laugheth at the shaking of a spear. Sharp stones are under him: he spreadeth sharp pointed things upon the mire. He maketh the deep to boil like a pot: he maketh the sea like a pot of ointment. He maketh a path to shine after him; one would think the deep to be hoary. Upon earth there is not his like, who is made without fear. He beholdeth all high things: he is a king over all the children of pride.

42. Then Job answered the Lord, and said, I know that thou canst do every thing, and that no thought can be withholden from thee. Who is he that hideth counsel without knowledge? Therefore have I uttered that I understood not; things too wonderful for me, which I knew not. Hear, I beseech thee, and I will speak: I will demand of thee, and declare thou unto me. I have heard of thee by the hearing of the ear; but now mine eye seeth thee. Wherefore I abhor myself, and repent in dust and ashes.

And it was so, that after the Lord had spoken these words unto Job, the Lord said to Eliphaz the Temanite, My wrath is kindled against thee, and against they two friends: for ye have not spoken to me the thing that is right, as my servant Job hath. Therefore take unto you now seven bullocks and seven rams, and go to my servant Job, and offer up for yourselves a burnt offering; and my servant Job shall pray for you: for him will I accept: let I deal with you after your folly, in that ye have not spoken to me the thing which is right, like my servant Job. So Eliphaz the Temanite and Bildad the Shuhite and Zophar the Naamathite went, and did according as the Lord commanded them: the Lord also accepted Job. And the Lord turned the captivity of Job, when he prayed for his friends: also the Lord gave Job twice as much as he had before. Then came there unto him all his brethren, and all his sisters, and all they that had been of his acquaintance before, and did eat bread with him in his house: and they bemoaned him, and comforted him over all the evil that the Lord had brought upon him: every man also gave him a piece of money, and every one an earring of gold. So the Lord blessed the latter end of Job more than his beginning: for he had fourteen thousand sheep, and six thousand camels, and a thousand yoke of oxen, and a thousand she asses. He had also seven sons and three daughters. And he called the name of the first, Jemima; and the name of the second, Kezia; and the name of the third, Kerenhappuch. And in all the land were no women found so fair as the daughters of Job: and their father gave them inheritance among their brethren. After this lived Job an hundred and forty years, and saw his sons, and his sons' sons, even four generations. So Job died, being old and full of days.

Greek Theater

Of the distinctive genres for which Greek literature is responsible for creating, the drama is surely one of the most significant. It gave birth to Western drama. Inexplicably, form and philosophical inquiry came together to produce a model known for aesthetic achievements as much as for a consistent profundity in exploring human consciousness, the position of man and his relation with the gods. Clearly, the classics still have much to reveal. The passions, dreams, and hates have not changed. Melville's Ahab and his quest for the white whale, for example, is the same fateful necessity that confronts Oedipus.

Early Greek theater dates from about the fifth century BCE with the religious festivals held in honor of and on ground sacred to the god Dionysus. The subjects were limited to well-known legends and myths of the time. The actors, all men, usually held high positions or were the priests of Dionysus. The actors all wore masks and elaborate costumes in a performance that was idealized and stylized, not realistic. There were no acts of violence; any act of violence took place offstage or was communicated in a messenger's speech. The audience's interest was heightened because these early dramas were often contests for prizes. Thespis, for example, won the prize at the first official presentation of tragedy in Athens in 534 BCE. Thus, the term *thespian* refers to drama.

The structure of the theater was composed of three elements: the orchestra, the auditorium, and the *skene*. The chorus and actors performed in the orchestra. The auditorium was constructed so that the audience sat and viewed the presentation in a round rather than frontally. The skene was comparable to backstage where the actors could retire to change masks. It was also the place from which the gods appeared in a play to make things right, a kind of forced invention. The Latin term for this "god from the machine" is known as *deus ex machina*.

Aristotle's "Poetics" provides useful information about Greek theater. According to Aristotle, the basic elements of tragedy are plot, character, diction, thought, scenery, and song. Together these elements imitate real actions. The two chief parts of the tragedy are choric songs and dialogue, where the chorus represents a popular view of life or comments on individual actions. Aristotle also insisted upon the three unities. The three unities involve limitations of time (one day), place (one locale), and action (the exclusion of irrelevant episodes or subplots).

Aristotle's definition of a tragedy focuses on a *catharsis*, a purging, of the two emotions of pity and fear. He believes that the best plot line of a tragedy should show a generally good man who has some fatal flaw moving from prosperity and good fortune to misfortune and ruin. In such a plot, he maintains that the audience pities such a hero because it recognizes undeserved misfortune. The tragic hero comes from an illustrious, aristocratic family class. Such a social standing does not mitigate his relation to the audience. In fact, it enhances it because his high standing suggests a universality. Aristotle believes that *Oedipus Rex* is a model tragedy.

The major tragedians of the Greek theater are Aeschylus (525–456 BCE), Sophocles (497–406 BCE), and Euripides (481–406 BCE). During his lifetime, Aeschylus wrote between eighty and ninety plays, winning first prize fifty-two times. Seven of his plays have survived. Today he is known primarily for his *Orestia*, his only surviving trilogy that includes, among many actions, sacrifice of a daughter, a wife's revenge for that sacrifice and matricide. Sophocles wrote more than 123 plays. He won first prize for seventy-two plays, more than any of his rivals. He survives today through his *Oedipus* trilogy and *Antigone*. Euripides wrote approximately eighty-eight plays, many of them have survived because of his popularity. *Medea, Electra*, and the *Trojan Women* are surviving testaments to Euripides' reputation as the ancient tragedian most closely identified with the modern world.

Each tragedian in his distinctive way shows extreme states of mental suffering. King Agamemnon sacrifices his daughter Iphigenia, and his son Creon kills his mother, who along with her lover Aegisthus, has murdered Agamemnon. Oedipus blinds himself, choosing to live out his days in guilt and pain. Medea kills her children to avenge herself against the husband who has cast her aside for another woman. For each of these writers, suffering leads to learning. The stark hopelessness of individual characters' struggle against fate is necessary even if it is hopeless. Whereas the Greek epics present the physical pain of war and death in battle, the tragedies depict the internal sufferings of pain, despair, and guilt.

Aristotle (384–322 BC)

Aristotle, Greek philosopher, teacher, critic, and scientist, was born at Stagira, in the Greek region known as Chalcidice, in 384 BC and died at Chalcis on the island of Euboea in 322 BC. He was the son of Nicomachus, the court physician of Amnytas III, the Macedonian king. Since Aristotle's parents died when he was young, Aristotle was raised by Proxenus, probably a relative or a friend of his family.

When Aristotle was about eighteen, he became a member of Plato's Academy at Athens, where he later was regarded as the most distinguished member of the school. During this time, he expanded his knowledge in many disciplines, especially Platonic philosophy, which he defended in a number of written treatises. Aristotle was not only a pupil but also a teacher in the Academy, where he remained for twenty years until Plato died in 347 BC. Then he left Athens and went to northwest Asia Minor. There he married Pythias, the adopted daughter of Hermias, a Greek ruler. Subsequently, Aristotle became the father of a daughter, Pythias (named after her mother) and a son, Nicomachus (named after his grandfather). Meanwhile, in 342 BC, King Philip invited Aristotle to tutor his thirteen-year-old son, Alexander, who became known as Alexander the Great. Aristotle tutored him approximately three years.

In 334 BC Aristotle returned to Athens and founded the Lyceum, also known as the Peripatetic School of philosophy; the school's name, Peripatetic, was derived from the Greek word *peripatetikos*, meaning to "walk about." Presumably Aristotle, together with the members of his audience, usually walked to-and-fro while he lectured. Aristotle taught at the Lyceum, where the emphasis was on teaching, research, and independent investigation, until a year before he died.

Aristotle's writings cover a wide variety of topics, including logic, politics, rhetoric, metaphysics, ethics, poetry, zoology, biology, psychology, and physics. Many of his surviving works consist of lecture notes, which most likely were not meant to be published. Among Aristotle's most significant works are *Politics*, composed of eight books; *Rhetoric*, composed of three books; *Organon*, concerning logic; *Nicomachean Ethics*, his principal work on ethics, composed of ten books, dedicated to Nicomachus, his son; and the "Poetics," a treatise which is considered a very significant piece of literary criticism. Other important works include *Metaphysics*, *Psychology*, *Physics*, and the *History of Animals*. Aristotle was a very prolific writer, but only a small number of his works have survived. Nevertheless, his writings have had a powerful impact on the world's thought.

Selected Bibliography

Magnusson, Magnus, ed. *Cambridge Biographical Dictionary*. Cambridge, NY: Press Syndicate of U of Cambridge, 1990.

McKeon, Richard. *Introduction to Aristotle*. New York: Modern Library, 1992.

Poetics

103. Let us proceed now to the discussion of Tragedy; before doing so, however, we must gather up the definition resulting from what has been said. A tragedy, then, is the imitation of an action that is serious and also, as having magnitude, complete in itself; in language with pleasurable accessories, each kind brought in separately in the parts of the work; in a dramatic, not in a narrative form; with incidents arousing pity and fear, wherewith to accomplish its catharsis of such emotions. Here by 'language with pleasurable accessories' I mean that with rhythm and harmony or song superadded; and by 'the kinds separately' I mean that some portions are worked out with verse only, and others in turn with song.

I. As they act the stories, it follows that in the first place the Spectacle (or stage-appearance of the actors) must be some part of the whole; and in the second Melody and Diction, these two being the means of their imitation. Here by 'Diction' I mean merely this, the composition of the verses; and by 'Melody', what is too completely understood to require explanation. But further: the subject represented also is an action; and the action involves agents, who must necessarily have their distinctive qualities both of character and thought, since it is from these that we ascribe certain qualities to their actions. There are in the natural order of things, therefore, two causes, Thought and Character, of their actions, and consequently of their success or failure in their lives. Now the action (that which was done) is represented in the play by the Fable or Plot. The Fable, in our present sense of the term, is simply this, the combination of the incidents, or things done in the story; whereas Character is what makes us ascribe certain moral qualities to the agents; and Thought is shown in all they say when proving a particular point or, it may be, enunciating a general truth. There are six parts consequently of every tragedy, as a whole (that is) of such or such quality, viz. a Fable or Plot, Characters, Diction, Thought, Spectacle, and Melody; two of them arising from the means, one from the manner, and three from the objects of the dramatic imitation; and there is nothing else besides these six. Of these, its formative elements, then, not a few of the dramatists have made due use, as every play, one may say, admits of Spectacle, Character, Fable, Diction, Melody, and Thought.

II. The most important of the six is the combination of the incidents of the story. Tragedy is essentially an imitation not of persons but of action and life, of happiness and misery. All human happiness or misery takes the form of action; the end for which we live is a certain kind of activity, not a quality. Character gives us qualities, but it is in our actions—what we do—that we are happy or the reverse. In a play accordingly they do not act in order to portray the Characters; they include the Characters for the sake of the action. So that it is the action in it, i.e. its Fable or Plot, that is the end and purpose of the tragedy; and the end is everywhere the chief thing. Besides this, a tragedy is impossible without action, but there may be one without Character. The tragedies of most of the moderns are characterless—a defect common among poets of all kinds, and with its counterpart in painting in Zeuxis as compared with Polygnotus; for whereas the latter is strong in character, the work of Zeuxis is devoid of it. And again: one may string together a series of characteristic speeches of the utmost finish as regards Diction and Thought, and yet fail to produce the true tragic effect; but one will have much better success with a tragedy which, however inferior in these respects, has a Plot, a combination of incidents, in it. And again: the most powerful elements of attraction in Tragedy, the Peripeties and Discoveries, are parts of the Plot. A further proof is in the fact that beginners succeed earlier with the Diction and Characters than with the construction of a story; and the same may be said of nearly all the early dramatists. We maintain, therefore, that the first essential, the life and soul, so to speak, of Tragedy is the Plot; and that the Characters come second—compare the parallel in painting, where the most beautiful colours laid on without order will not give one the same pleasure as a simple black-and-white sketch of a portrait. We maintain the Tragedy is primarily an imitation of action, and that it is mainly for the sake of the action that it imitates the personal agents. Third comes the element of Thought, i.e. the power of saying whatever can be said, or what is appropriate to the occasion. This is what, in the speeches in Tragedy, falls under the arts of Politics and Rhetoric; for the older poets make their personages discourse like statesmen, and the moderns like rhetoricians. One must no confuse it with Character. Character in a play is that which reveals the moral purpose of the agents, i.e. the sort of thing they seek or avoid, where that is not obvious—hence there is no room for Character in a speech on a purely indifferent subject. Thought, on the other hand, is shown in all they say when proving or disproving some particular point, or enunciating some universal proposition. Fourth among the literary elements is the Diction of the personages, i.e., as before explained, the expression of their thoughts in works, which is practically the same thing with verse as with prose. As for the two remaining parts, the Melody is the greatest of the pleasurable accessories of Tragedy. The Spectacle, though an attraction, is the least artistic of all the parts, and has least to do with the art of poetry. The tragic effect is quite possible without a public performance and actors; and besides, the getting-up of the Spectacle is more a matter for the costumier than the poet.

Having thus distinguished the parts, let us now consider the proper construction of the Fable or Plot, as that is at once the first and the most important thing in Tragedy. We have laid it down that a tragedy is an imitation of an action that is complete in itself, as a whole of some magnitude; for a whole may be of no magnitude to speak of. Now a whole is that which has beginning, middle, and end. A beginning is that which is not itself necessarily after anything else, and which has naturally something else after it; an end is that which is naturally after something itself, either as its necessary or usual consequent, and with nothing else after it; and a middle, that which is by nature after one thing and has also another after it. A well-constructed Plot, therefore, cannot either begin or end at any point one likes; beginning and end in it must be of the forms just described. Again: to be beautiful, a living creature, and every whole made up of parts, must not only present a certain order in its arrangement of parts, but also be of certain definite magnitude. Beauty is a matter of size and order, and therefore impossible either (1) in a very minute creature, since our perception becomes indistinct as it approaches instantaneity; or (2) in a creature of vast size—one, say, 1,000 miles long—as in that case, instead of the object being seen all at once, the unity and wholeness of it is lost to the beholder. Just in the same way, then, as a beautiful whole made up of parts, or a beautiful living creature, must be of some size, but a size to be taken in by the eye, so a story or Plot must be of some length, but of a length to be taken in by the memory. As for the limit of its length, so far as that is relative to public performances and spectators, it does not fall within the theory of poetry. If they had to perform a hundred tragedies, they would be timed by water-clocks, as they are said to have been at one period. The limit, however, set by the actual nature of the things is this; the longer the story, consistently with its being comprehensible as a whole, the finer it is by reason of its magnitude. As a rough general formula, 'a length which allows of the hero passing by a series of probable or necessary stages from misfortune to happiness, or from happiness to misfortune', may suffice as a limit for the magnitude of the story.

The Unity of a Plot does not consist, as some suppose, in its having one man as its subject. An infinity of things befall that one man, some of which it is impossible to reduce to unity; and in like manner there are many actions of one man which cannot be made to form one action. One sees, therefore, the mistake of all the poets who have written a *Heracleid*, a *Theseid*, or similar poems; they suppose that, because Heracles was one man, the story also of Heracles must be one story. Homer, however, evidently understood this point quite well, whether by art or instinct, just in the same way as he excels the rest in every other respect. In writing an *Odyssey*, he did not make the poem cover all that ever befell his hero—it befell him, for instance, to get wounded on Parnassus and also to feign madness at the time of the call to arms, but the two incidents had no necessary or probable connexion with one another—instead of doing that, he took as the subject of the *Odyssey*, as also of the *Iliad*, an action with a Unity of the kind we are describing. The truth is that, just as in the other imitative arts one imitation is always of one thing, so in poetry the story, as an imitation of action, must represent one action, a complete whole, with its several incidents so closely connected that the transposal or withdrawal of any one of them will disjoin and dislocate the whole. For that which makes no perceptible difference by its presence or absence is no real part of the whole.

From what we have said it will be seen that the poet's function is to describe, not the thing that has happened, but a kind of thing that might happen, i.e. what is possible as being probable or necessary. The distinction between historian and poet is not in the one writing prose and the other verse—you might put the work of Herodotus into verse, and it would still be a species of history; it consists really in this, that the one describes the thing that has been, and the other a kind of thing that might be. Hence poetry is something more philosophic and of graver import than history, since its statements are of the nature rather of universals, whereas those of history are singulars. By a universal statement I mean one as to what such or such a kind of man will probably or necessarily say or do—which is the aim of poetry, though it affixes proper names to the characters; by a singular statement, one as to what, say, Alcibiades did or had done to him. In Comedy this has become clear by this time; it is only when their plot is already made up of probable incidents that they give it a basis of proper names, choosing for the purpose any names that may occur to them, instead of writing like the old iambic poets about particular persons. In Tragedy, however, they still adhere to the historic names; and for this reason: what convinces is the possible; now whereas we are not yet sure as to the possibility of that which has not happened, that which has happened is manifestly possible, else it would not have come to pass. Nevertheless even in Tragedy there are some plays with but one or two known names in them, the rest being inventions; and there are some without a single known name, e.g. Agathon's *Antheus,* in which both incidents and names are of the poet's invention; and it is no less delightful on that account. So that one must not aim at a rigid adherence to the traditional stories on which tragedies are based. It would be absurd, in fact, to do so, as even the known stories are only known to a few, though they are a delight none the less to all.

It is evident from the above that the poet must be more the poet of his stories or Plots than of his verses, inasmuch as he is a poet by virtue of the imitative element in his work, and it is actions that he imitates. And if he should come to take a subject from actual history, he is none the less a poet for that; since some historic occurrences may very well be in the probable and possible order of things; and it is in that aspect of them that he is their poet.

Of simple Plots and actions the episodic are the worst. I call a Plot episodic when there is neither probability nor necessity in the sequence of its episodes. Actions of this sort bad poets construct through their own fault, and good ones on account of the players. His work being for public performance, a good poet often stretches out a Plot beyond its capabilities, and is thus obliged to twist the sequence of incident.

Tragedy, however, is an imitation not only of a complete action, but also of incidents arousing pity and fear. Such incidents have the very greatest effect on the mind when they occur unexpectedly and at the same time in consequence of one another; there is more of the marvellous in them then than if they happened of themselves or by mere chance. Even matters of chance seem most marvellous if there is an appearance of design as it were in them; as for instance the statue of Mitys at Argos killed the author of Mitys' death by falling down on him when a looker-on at a public spectacle; for incidents like that we think to be not without a meaning. A plot, therefore, of this sort is necessarily finer than others.

Plots are either simple or complex, since the actions they represent are naturally of this two-fold description. The action, proceeding in the way defined, as one continuous whole, I call simple, when the change in the hero's fortunes takes place without Peripety or Discovery; and complex, when it involves one or the other, or both. These should each of them arise out of the structure of the Plot itself, so as to be the consequence, necessary or probable, of the antecedents. There is a great difference between a thing happening *propter hoc* and *post hoc*.

A Peripety is the change of the kind described from one state of things within the play to its opposite, and that too in the way we are saying, in the probable or necessary sequence of events; as it is for instance in *Oedipus*: here the opposite state of things is produced by the Messenger, who, coming to gladden Oedipus and to remove his fears as to his mother, reveals the secret of this birth. And in *Lynceus*: just as he is being led off for execution, with Danaus at his side to put him to death, the incidents preceding this bring it about that he is saved and Danaus put to death. A Discovery is, as the very word implies, a change from ignorance to knowledge, and thus to either love or hate, in the personages marked for good or evil fortune. The finest form of Discovery is one attended by Peripeties, like that which goes with the Discovery in *Oedipus*. There are no doubt other forms of it; what we have said may happen in a way in reference to inanimate things, even things of a very casual kind; and it is also possible to discover whether some one has done or not done something. But the form most directly connected with the Plot and the action of the piece is the first-mentioned. This, with a Peripety, will arouse either pity or fear—actions of that nature being what Tragedy is assumed to represent; and it will also serve to bring about the happy or unhappy ending. The Discovery, then, being of persons, it may be that of one party only to the other, the latter being already known; or both the parties may have to discover themselves. Iphigenia, for instance, was discovered to Orestes by sending the letter; and another Discovery was required to reveal him to Iphigenia.

Two parts of the Plot, then, Peripety and Discovery, are on matters of this sort. A third part is Suffering; which we may define as an action of a destructive or painful nature, such as murders on the stage, tortures, woundings, and the like. The other two have been already explained. . . .

The next points after what we have said above will be these: (1) What is the poet to aim at, and what is he to avoid, in constructing his Plots? and (2) What are the conditions on which the tragic effect depends?

We assume that, for the finest form of Tragedy, the Plot must be not simple but complex; and further, that it must imitate actions arousing fear and pity, since that is the distinctive function of this kind of imitation. It follows, therefore, that there are three forms of Plot to be avoided. (1) A good man must not be seen passing from happiness to misery, or (2) a bad man from misery to happiness. The first situation is not fear-inspiring or piteous, but simply odious to us. The second is the most untragic that can be; it has no one of the requisites of Tragedy; it does not appeal either to the human feeling in us, or to our pity, or to our fears. Nor, on the other hand, should (3) an extremely bad man be seen falling from happiness into misery. Such a story may arouse the human feeling in us, but it will not move us to either pity or fear; pity is occasioned by undeserved misfortune, and fear by that of one like ourselves; so that there will be nothing either piteous or fear-inspiring in the situation. There remains, then, the intermediate kind of personage, a man not pre-eminently virtuous and just, whose misfortune, however, is brought upon him not by vice and depravity but by some error of judgment, of the number of those in the enjoyment of great reputation and prosperity; e.g. Oedipus, Thyestes, and the men of note of similar families. The perfect Plot, accordingly, must have a single, and not (as some tell us) a double issue; the change in the hero's fortunes must be not from misery to happiness, but on the contrary from happiness to misery; and the cause of it must lie not in any depravity, but in some great error on his part; the man himself being either such as we have described, or better, not worse, than that.

Fact also confirms our theory. Though the poets began by accepting any tragic story that came to hand, in these days the finest tragedies are always on the story of some few houses, on that of Alemeon, Oedipus, Orestes, Meleager, Thyestes, Telephus, or any others that may have been involved, as either agents or sufferers, in some deed of horror. The theoretically best tragedy, then, has a Plot of this description. The critics, therefore, are wrong who blame Euripides for taking this line in his tragedies, and giving many of them an unhappy ending. It is, as we have said, the right line to take. The best proof is this: on the stage, and in the public performances, such plays, properly worked out, are seen to be the most truly tragic; and Euripides, even if his execution be faulty in every other point, is seen to be nevertheless the most tragic certainly of the dramatists. After this comes the construction of Plot which some rank first, one with a double story (like the *Odyssey*) and an opposite issue for the good and the bad personages. It is ranked as first only through the weakness of the audiences; the poets merely follow their public, writing as its wishes dictates. But the pleasure here is not that of Tragedy. It belongs rather to Comedy, where the bitterest enemies in the piece (e.g. Orestes and Aegisthus) walk off good friends at the end, with no slaying of any one by any one.

The tragic fear and pity may be aroused by the Spectacle; but they may also be aroused by the very structure and incidents of the play—which is the better way and shows the better poet. The Plot in fact should be so framed that, even without seeing the things take place, he who simply hears the account of them shall be filled with horror and pity at the incidents; which is just the effect that the mere recital of the story in *Oedipus* would have on one. . . .

The Dénouement should arise out of the plot itself, and not depend on a stage-artifice, as in *Medea*, or in the story of the (arrested) departure of the Greeks in the *Iliad*. The artifice must be reserved for matters outside the play—for past events beyond human knowledge, or events yet to come, which require to be foretold or announced; since it is the privilege of the Gods to know everything. There should be nothing improbable among the actual incidents. If it be unavoidable, however, it should be outside the tragedy, like the improbability in the *Oedipus* of Sophocles. But to return to the Characters. As Tragedy is an imitation of personages better than the ordinary man, we in our way should follow the example of good portrait-painters, who reproduce the distinctive features of a man, and at the same time, without losing the likeness, make him handsomer than he is. The poet in like manner, in portraying men quick or slow to anger, or with similar infirmities of character, must know how to represent them as such, and at the same time as good men, as Agathon and Homer have represented Achilles.

Sophocles (496?–406? BC)

Sophocles, along with Aeschylus and Euripides, played a major role in the development of Greek tragic drama. Considered the most successful tragedian, Sophocles was born about 496 BC at Colonus, near Athens, where he remained until his death in 406? BC His father, Sophillus, was probably a wealthy manufacturer. Sophocles is said to have married twice, and he had two sons, one of whom became a tragedian. Respected and admired by many, Sophocles wrote approximately 123 plays. In addition to his role as a dramatist, he was a general, a poet, a priest and a public administrator.

In 468 BC Sophocles entered his first competition in tragedy at the annual Great Dionysia festival in which Aeschylus, a veteran, was a participant. Sophocles defeated him and won first prize. Although Sophocles was defeated by Euripides in 441 BC, he came in second, but he never came in third in any of the competitions. During his many years of creative productivity, he won more than twenty first prizes.

Sophocles made several technical innovations regarding the performance of tragedy. He introduced a third actor (Aeschylus being responsible for adding the second), abolished the practice of using one unified theme for a trilogy (in preference to producing three distinct tragedies based on unrelated subjects), changed the membership of the chorus from twelve to fifteen, and initiated scenery which consisted of painted backdrops.

The following seven complete plays are extant: *Ajax*, circa 445 BC; *Antigone*, circa 440 BC; *Trachinian Women*, circa 431 BC; *Oedipus Rex*, circa 430 BC, his masterpiece, which Aristotle considered the perfect Greek tragedy; *Electra*, circa 411 BC; *Philoctetes*, 409 BC; and *Oedipus at Colonus*, 401 BC Sophocles was almost 90 when he wrote this play; it was produced posthumously. Also, in 1907 a fragment of *Ichneutae*, a satirical play, was recovered.

Selected Bibliography

Hadas, Moses, ed. *Greek Drama*. New York: Bantam, 1982.

Scodel, Ruth. *Sophocles*. Boston: Twayne, 1984.

Oedipus Rex: Background

Oedipus Rex is the first in a trilogy by Sophocles about the classic myth of Oedipus ("swollen foot"). It portrays in the most Sophoclean way the elemental struggle between man and his destiny. Everyone making his way to the theater to see Sophocles' tragedy, which was first presented sometime between 439 and 412 BCE, knew the awful story of the son of Laius, King of Thebes, and Jocasta, his wife. Today, the student is probably acquainted with the work merely in terms of a character whose fate is fixed. Such is a misreading of Sophocles' tragedy, for Sophocles, in all of his dramas, emphasizes that free will is an essential component of the tragic hero's character. Thus free will must be considered when assessing Oedipus' tragedy. Oedipus explores the idea of undeserved suffering much in the same way as Job does.

Oedipus' character must also be examined for the Greeks believed that character is fate. If this is true, then the reader's assessment of Oedipus must be re-evaluated. Is there something in his character that would lead him to his fate? If as Aristotle posits the tragic hero possesses some harmatia, some tragic flaw such as hubris, and *Oedipus Rex* is the model tragedy, then readers need to examine Oedipus closely for those clues to his tragic end.

Oedipus Rex is filled with dramatic irony; one of the most obvious is Oedipus' frustrated and impatient momentary outburst against Teiresias' blindness; that is Oedipus is mentally blind. But these lapses in judgment or flaws in character should not blind readers to what makes Oedipus so heroic, despite his tragedy. In the final act of the tragedy, Oedipus blinds himself with Jocasta's broaches. He, too, could have easily made the choice that she makes, which is suicide. But Oedipus chooses to blind himself, which is nothing to the psychological pain that he has already experienced. This act is consistent with Oedipus' previous actions and sets him apart from his fellowmen. Ironically, Oedipus' blinding himself shows his free will and heroism.

Œdipus Tyrannus

DRAMATIS PERSONÆ

Œdipus, *King of Thebes*
Jocasta, *Wife of Œdipus*
Creon, *Brother of Jocasta*
Tiresias, *a Blind Prophet of Thebes*
A Shepherd, *from Corinth*
An Old Shepherd, *formerly belonging to Laius*
High Priest of Jupiter
Chorus, composed of Priests and Ancient Men of Thebes,
Theban Youths, Children of Œdipus, Attendants, &c.

SCENE—Thebes, *before the Palace of* Œdipus.

ACT I.

Scene I.

Œdipus, High Priest of Jupiter.

Œdipus. O my loved sons! the youthful progeny
Of ancient Cadmus, wherefore sit you here
And suppliant thus, with sacred boughs adorned,
Crowd to our altars? Frequent sacrifice
And prayers and sighs and sorrows fill the land.
I could have sent to learn the fatal cause;
But see, your anxious sovereign comes himself
To know it all from you; behold your king,
Renowned Œdipus; do thou, old man,
For best that office suits thy years, inform me,
Why you are come; is it the present ill
That calls you here, or dread of future woe?
Hard were indeed the heart that did not feel
For grief like yours, and pity such distress:
If there be aught that Œdipus can do
To serve his people, know me for your friend.

Priest. O king! thou seest what numbers throng thy altars;
Here, bending sad beneath the weight of years,
The hoary priests, here crowd the chosen youth
Of Thebes, with these a weak and suppliant train
Of helpless infants, last in me behold
The minister of Jove: far off thou seest
Assembled multitudes, with laurel crowned,
To where Minerva's hallowed temples rise
Frequent repair, or where Ismenus laves
Apollo's sacred shrine: too well thou knowst
Thy wretched Thebes, with dreadful storms oppressed,
Scarce lifts her head above the whelming flood;
The teeming earth her blasted harvest mourns,
And on the barren plain the flocks and herds
Unnumbered perish; dire abortion thwarts
The mother's hopes, and painful she brings forth

The half-formed infant; baleful pestilence
Hath laid our city waste, the fiery god
Stalks o'er deserted Thebes; whilst with our groans
Enriched, the gloomy god of Erebus
Triumphant smiles. O Œdipus! to thee
We bend; behold these youths, with me they kneel,
And suppliant at thy altars sue for aid,
To thee the first of men, and only less
Than them whose favour thou alone canst gain,
The gods above; thy wisdom yet may heal
The deep-felt wounds, and make the powers divine
Propitious to us. Thebes long since to thee
Her safety owed, when from the Sphynx delivered
Thy grateful people saw thee, not by man
But by the gods instructed, save the land:
Now then, thou best of kings, assist us now,
Oh! by some mortal or immortal aid
Now succour the distress; On wisdom oft,
And prudent counsels in the hour of ill,
Success awaits. O dearest prince! support,
Relieve thy Thebes; on thee, its saviour once,
Again its calls. Now, if thou wouldst not see
The mem'ry perish of thy former deeds,
Let it not call in vain, but rise, and save!
With happiest omens once and fair success
We saw thee crowned: oh! be thyself again,
And may thy will and fortune be the same!
If thou art yet to reign, O king! remember
A sovereign's riches is a peopled realm;
For what will ships or lofty towers avail
Unarmed with men to guard and to defend them?

ŒDI. O my unhappy sons! too well I know
Your sad estate. I know the woes of Thebes;
And yet amongst you lives not such a wretch
As Œdipus; for oh! on me, my children,
Your sorrows press. Alas! I feel for you
My people, for myself, for Thebes, for all!
Think not I slept regardless of your ills;
Oh no! with many a tear I wept your fate,
And oft in meditation deep revolved
How best your peace and safety to restore:
The only medicine that my thoughts could find
I have administered: Menæceus' son,
The noble Creon, went by my command
To Delphos from Apollo's shrine, to know
What must be done to save this wretched land:
'Tis time he were returned: I wonder much
At his delay. If, when he comes, your king
Perform not all the god enjoins, then say
He is the worst of men.

PRIEST. O king! thy words
Are gracious, and if right these youths inform me,
Creon is here.

ŒDI. O Phœbus! grant he come
With tidings cheerful as the smile he wears!

PRIEST. He is the messenger of good; for see,
His brows are crowned with laurel.
ŒDI. We shall soon
Be satisfied: he comes.

SCENE II.

CREON, ŒDIPUS, PRIEST, CHORUS.

ŒDI. My dearest Creon,
Oh! say, what answer bearst thou from the god;
Or good, or ill?
CREON. Good, very good; for know,
The worst of ills, if rightly used, may prove
The means of happiness.
ŒDI. What says my friend?
This answer gives me nought to hope or fear.
CREON. Shall we retire, or would you that I speak
In public here?
ŒDI. Before them all declare it;
Their woes sit heavier on me than my own.
CREON. Then mark what I have heard: the god commands
That instant we drive forth the fatal cause
Of this dire pestilence, nor nourish here
The accursed monster.
ŒDI. Who? What monster? How
Remove it?
CREON. Or by banishment, or death.
Life must be given for life; for yet his blood
Rests on the city.
ŒDI. Whose? What means the god?
CREON. O king! before thee Laius ruled o'er Thebes.
ŒDI. I know he did, though I did ne'er behold him.
CREON. Laius was slain, and on his murderers,
So Phœbus says, we must have vengeance.
ŒDI. Where,
Where are the murderers? Who shall trace the guilt
Buried so long in silence?
CREON. Here, he said,
E'en in this land, what's sought for may be found,
But truth unsearched for seldom comes to light.
ŒDI. How did he fall, and where?—at home, abroad?
Died he at Thebes, or in a foreign land?
CREON. He left his palace, fame reports, to seek
Some oracle; since that, we ne'er beheld him.
ŒDI. But did no messenger return? Not one
Of all his train, of whom we might inquire
Touching this murder?
CREON. One, and one alone,
Came back, who, flying, 'scaped the general slaughter.
But nothing save one little circumstance
Or knew, or e'er related.
ŒDI. What was that?
Much may be learned from that. A little dawn
Of light appearing may discover all.

CREON. Laius, attacked by robbers, and oppressed
By numbers, fell. Such is his tale.

ŒDI. Would they—
Would robbers do so desperate a deed,
Unbribed and unassisted?

CREON. So, indeed,
Suspicion whispered then. But—Laius dead—
No friend was found to vindicate the wrong.

ŒDI. But what strange cause could stop inquiry thus
Into the murder of a king?

CREON. The Sphynx.
Her dire enigma kept our thoughts intent
On present ills, nor gave us time to search
The past mysterious deed.

ŒDI. Myself will try
Soon to unveil it. Thou, Apollo, well,
And well hast thou, my Creon, lent thy aid,
Your Œdipus shall now perform his part.
Yes, I will fight for Phœbus and my country.
And so I ought. For not to friends alone,
Or kindred, owe I this, but to myself.
Who murdered him, perchance would murder me!
His cause is mine. Wherefore, my children, rise;
Take hence your suppliant boughs, and summon here
The race of Cadmus—my assembled people.
Nought shall he left untried. Apollo leads,
And we shall rise to joy, or sink for ever.

PRIEST. Haste, then, my sons, for this we hither came:
About it quick, and may the god who sent
This oracle, protect, defend, and save us! [*Exeunt.*

CHORUS.

Strophe I.

O thou great oracle divine!
Who didst to happy Thebes remove
From Delphi's golden shrine,
And in sweet sounds declare the will of Jove.
Daughter of hope, oh! soothe my soul to rest,
And calm the rising tumult in my breast.
Look down, O Phœbus! on thy loved abode.
Speak, for thou knowst the dark decrees of fate,
Our present and our future state.
O Delian! be thou still our healing god?

Antistrophe I.

Minerva, first on thee I call,
Daughter of Jove, immortal maid,
Low beneath thy feet we fall:
Oh! bring thy sister Dian to our aid.
Goddess of Thebes, from thy imperial throne
Look with an eye of gentle pity down;
And thou, far-shooting Phœbus, once the friend

Of this unhappy, this devoted land,
Oh! now, if ever, let thy hand
Once more be stretched to save and to defend!

Strophe 2.

Great Thebes, my sons, is now no more;
She falls and ne'er again shall rise,
Nought can her health or strength restore,
The mighty nation sinks, she droops, she dies.
Stripped of her fruits, behold the barren earth—
The half-formed infant struggles for a birth.
The mother sinks unequal to her pain:
Whilst quick as birds in airy circles fly,
Or lightnings from an angry sky,
Crowds press on crowds to Pluto's dark domain.

Antistrophe 2.

Behold what heaps of wretches slain,
Unburied, unlamented lie,
Nor parents now nor friends remain
To grace their deaths with pious obsequy.
The aged matron and the blooming wife,
Cling to the altars—sue for added life.
With sighs and groans united Pæans rise;
Re-echoed, still doth great Apollo's name
Their sorrows and their wants proclaim.
Frequent to him ascends the sacrifice.

Strophe 3.

Haste then, Minerva, beauteous maid,
Descend in this afflictive hour,
Haste to thy dying people's aid,
Drive hence this baneful, this destructive power!
Who comes not armed with hostile sword or shield,
Yet strews with many a corse th' ensanguined field;
To Amphitrite's wide extending bed
Oh! drive him, goddess, from thy favourite land,
Or let him, by thy dread command,
Bury in Thracian waves his ignominious head.

Antistrophe 3.

Father of all, immortal Jove!
Oh! now thy fiery terrors send;
From thy dreadful stores above
Let lightnings blast him and let thunders rend;
And thou, O Lydian king! thy aid impart;
Send from thy golden bow, th' unerring dart;
Smile, chaste Diana, on this loved abode,
Whilst Theban Bacchus joins the maddening throng,
O god of wine and mirth and song!
Now with thy torch destroy the base inglorious god.
[*Exeunt.*

ACT II.

Scene I.

ŒDIPUS, CHORUS. *The People assembled.*

ŒDI. Your prayers are heard: and if you will obey
Your king, and hearken to his words, you soon
Shall find relief; myself will heal your woes.
I was a stranger to the dreadful deed,
A stranger e'en to the report till now;
And yet without some traces of the crime
I should not urge this matter; therefore hear me.
I speak to all the citizens of Thebes,
Myself a citizen—observe me well:
If any know the murderer of Laius,
Let him reveal it; I command you all.
But if restrained by dread of punishment
He hide the secret, let him fear no more;
For nought but exile shall attend the crime
Whene'er confessed; if by a foreign hand
The horrid deed was done, who points him out
Commands our thanks, and meets a sure reward;
But if there be who knows the murderer,
And yet conceals him from us, mark his fate,
Which here I do pronounce: Let none receive
Throughout my kingdom, none hold converse with him,
Nor offer prayer, nor sprinkle o'er his head
The sacred cup; let him be driven from all,
By all abandoned, and by all accursed,
For so the Delphic oracle declared;
And therefore to the gods I pay this duty
And to the dead. Oh! may the guilty wretch,
Whether alone, or by his impious friends
Assisted, be performed the horrid deed,
Denied the common benefits of nature,
Wear out a painful life! And oh! if here,
Within my palace, I conceal the traitor,
On me and mine alight the vengeful curse!
To you, my people, I commit the care
Of this important business; 'tis my cause,
The cause of Heaven, and your expiring country.
E'en if the god had nought declared, to leave
This crime unexpiated were most ungrateful.
He was the best of kings, the best of men;
That sceptre now is mine which Laius bore;
His wife is mine; so would his children be
Did any live; and therefore am I bound,
E'en as he were my father, to revenge him.
Yes, I will try to find this murderer,
I owe it to the son of Labdacus,
To Polydorus, Cadmus, and the race
If great Agenor. Oh! if yet there are,
Who will not join me in the pious deed,
From such may earth withhold her annual store,

And barren be their bed, their life most wretched,
And their death cruel as the pestilence
That wastes our city! But on you, my Thebans,
Who wish us fair success, may justice smile
Propitious, and the gods for ever bless!

CHOR. O king! thy imprecations unappalled
I hear, and join thee, guiltless of the crime,
Nor knowing who committed it. The god
Alone, who gave the oracle, must clear
Its doubtful sense, and point out the offender.

ŒDI. 'Tis true. But who shall force the powers divine
To speak their hidden purpose?

CHOR. One thing more,
If I might speak.

ŒDI. Say on, Whate'er thy mind
Shall dictate to thee.

CHOR. As amongst the gods
All-knowing Phœbus, so to mortal men
Doth sage Tiresias in foreknowledge sure
Shine forth pre-eminent. Perchance his aid
Might much avail us.

ŒDI. Creon did suggest
The same expedient, and by his advice
Twice have I sent for this Tiresias; much
I wonder that he comes not.

CHOR. 'Tis most fitting
We do consult him; for the idle tales
Which rumour spreads are not to be regarded.

ŒDI. What are those tales? for nought should we despise.

CHOR. 'Tis said some travellers did attack the king.

ŒDI. It is; but still no proof appears.

CHOR. And yet,
If it be so, thy dreadful execration
Will force the guilty to confess.

ŒDI. Oh no!
Who fears not to commit the crime will ne'er
Be frightened at the curse that follows it.

CHOR. Behold he comes, who will discover all,
The holy prophet. See! they lead him hither;
He knows the truth and will reveal it to us.

SCENE II.

TIRESIAS, ŒDIPUS, CHORUS.

ŒDI. O sage Tiresias, thou who knowest all
That can be known, the things of Heaven above
And earth below, whose mental eye beholds,
Blind as thou are, the state of dying Thebes,
And weeps her fate, to thee we look for aid,
On thee alone for safety we depend.
This answer, which perchance thou has not heard,
Apollo gave: the plague, he said, should cease
When those who murdered Laius were discovered
And paid the forfeit of their crime by death

Or banishment. Oh! do not then conceal
Aught that thy art prophetic from the flight
Of birds or other omens may disclose,
Oh! save thyself, save this afflicted city,
Save Œdipus, avenge the guiltless dead
From this pollution! Thou art all our hope;
Remember, 'tis the privilege of man,
His noblest function, to assist the wretched.

TIR. Alas! what misery it is to know
When knowledge is thus fatal! O Tiresias!
Thou art undone! Would I had never come!

ŒDI. What sayst thou? Whence this strange dejection? Speak.

TIR. Let me be gone; 'twere better for us both
That I retire in silence: be advised.

ŒDI. It is ingratitude to Thebes, who bore
And cherished thee—it is unjust to all,
To hide the will of heaven.

TIR. 'Tis rash in thee
To ask, and rash I fear will prove my answer.

CHOR. Oh! do not, by the gods, conceal it from us,
Suppliant we all request, we all conjure thee.

TIR. You know not what you ask; I'll not unveil
Your miseries to you.

ŒDI. Knowst thou then our fate,
And wilt not tell it? Meanst thou to betray
Thy country and thy king?

TIR. I would not make
Myself and thee unhappy; why thus blame
My tender care, nor listen to my caution?

ŒDI. Wretch as thou art, thou wouldst provoke a stone—
Inflexible and cruel—still implored
And still refusing.

TIR. Thou condemn'st my warmth,
Forgetful of thy own.

ŒDI. Who would not rage
To see an injured people treated thus
With vile contempt?

TIR. What is decreed by heaven
Must come to pass, though I reveal it not.

ŒDI. Still, 'tis thy duty to inform us of it.

TIR. I'll speak no more, not though thine anger swell
E'en to its utmost.

ŒDI. Nor will I be silent.
I tell thee once for all thou wert thyself
Accomplice in this deed. Nay, more, I think,
But for thy blindness, wouldst with thy own hand
Have done it too.

TIR. 'Tis well. Now hear, Tiresias.
The sentence, which thou didst thyself proclaim,
Falls on thyself. Henceforth shall never man
Hold converse with thee, for then art accursed—
The guilty cause of all this city's woes.

ŒDI. Audacious traitor! thinkst thou to escape
The hand of vengeance?

TIR. Yes, I fear thee not;
For truth is stronger than a tyrant's arm.
ŒDI. Whence didst thou learn this? Was it from thy art?
TIR. I learned it from thyself. Thou didst compel me
To speak, unwilling as I was.
ŒDI. Once more
Repeat it then, that I may know my fate
More plainly still.
TIR. Is it not plain already?
Or meanst thou but to tempt me?
ŒDI. No, but say,
Speak it again.
TIR. Again then I declare
Thou art thyself the murderer whom thou seekst.
ŒDI. A second time thou shalt not pass unpunished.
TIR. What wouldst thou say, if I should tell thee all?
ŒDI. Say what thou wilt. For all is false.
TIR. Know then,
That Œdipus, in shameful bonds united
With those he loves, unconscious of his guilt,
Is yet most guilty.
ŒDI. Dar'st thou utter more,
And hope for pardon?
TIR. Yes, if there be strength
In sacred truth.
ŒDI. But truth dwells not in thee:
Thy body and thy mind are dark alike,
For both are blind. Thy ev'ry sense is lost.
TIR. Thou dost upbraid me with the loss of that
For which thyself ere long shall meet reproach
From every tongue.
ŒDI. Thou blind and impious traitor!
Thy darkness is thy safeguard, or this hour
Had been thy last.
TIR. It is not in my fate
To fall by thee. Apollo guards his priest.
ŒDI. Was this the tale of Creon, or thy own?
TIR. Creon is guiltless, and the crime is thine.
ŒDI. O riches, power, dominion! and thou far
Above them all, the best of human blessings,
Excelling wisdom, how doth envy love
To follow and oppress you! This fair kingdom,
Which by the nation's choice, and not my own,
I here possess, Creon, my faithful friend,
For such I thought him once, would now wrest from me,
And hath suborned this vile impostor here,
This wandering hypocrite, of sharpest sight
When interest prompts, but ignorant and blind
When fools consult him. Tell me, prophet, where
Was all thy art when the abhorred Sphynx
Alarmed our city? Wherefore did not then
Thy wisdom save us? Then the man divine
Was wanting. But thy birds refused their omens,
Thy god was silent. Then came Œdipus,
This poor, unlearned, uninstructed sage;

Who not from birds uncertain omens drew,
But by his own sagacious mind explored
The hidden mystery. And now thou com'st
To cast me from the throne my wisdom gained,
And share with Creon my divided empire.
But you should both lament your ill-got power,
You and your bold compeer. For thee, this moment,
But that I bear respect unto thy age,
I'd make thee rue thy execrable purpose.

CHOR. You both are angry, therefore both to blame;
Much rather should you join, with friendly zeal
And mutual ardour, to explore the will
Of all-deciding Heaven.

TIR. What though thou rul'st
O'er Thebes despotic, we are equal here:
I am Apollo's subject, and not thine,
Nor want I Creon to protect me. No;
I tell thee, king, this blind Tiresias tells thee,
Seeing thou seest not, knowst not where thou art,
What, or with whom. Canst thou inform me who
Thy parents are, and what thy horrid crimes
'Gainst thy own race, the living and the dead?
A father's and a mother's curse attend thee;
Soon shall their furies drive thee from the land,
And leave thee dark like me. What mountain then,
Or conscious shore, shall not return the groans
Of Œdipus, and echo to his woes?
When thou shalt look on the detested bed,
And in that haven where thou hop'st to rest,
Shalt meet with storm and tempest, then what ills
Shall fall on thee and thine! Now vent thy rage
On old Tiresias and the guiltless Creon;
We shall be soon avenged, for ne'er did Heaven
Cut off a wretch so base, so vile as thou art.

ŒDI. Must I bear this from thee? Away, begone!
Home, villain, home!

TIR. I did not come to thee
Unsent for.

ŒDI. Had I thought thou wouldst have thus
Insulted me, I had not called thee hither.

TIR. Perhaps thou holdst Tiresias as a fool
And madman; but thy parents thought me wise.

ŒDI. My parents, saidst thou? Speak, who were my parents?

TIR. This day, that gives thee life, shall give thee death.

ŒDI. Still dark, and still perplexing are the words
Thou utter'st.

TIR. 'Tis thy business to unriddle,
And therefore thou canst best interpret them.

ŒDI. Thou dost reproach me for my virtues.

TIR. They,
And thy good fortune, have undone thee.

ŒDI. Since I saved the city, I'm content.

TIR. Farewell.
Boy, lead me hence.

ŒDI. Away with him, for here
His presence but disturbs us; being gone,
We shall be happier.

TIR. Œdipus, I go,
But first inform me, for I fear thee not,
Wherefore I came. Know then, I came to tell thee.
The man thou seekst, the man on whom thou pouredst
Thy execrations, e'en the murderer
Of Laius, now is here—a seeming stranger
And yet a Theban. He shall suffer soon
For all his crimes: from light and affluence driven
To penury and darkness, poor and blind,
Propped on his staff, and from his native land
Expelled, I see him in a foreign clime
A helpless wanderer; to his sons at once
A father and a brother; child and husband
Of her from whom he sprang. Adulterous,
Incestuous parricide, now fare thee well
I Go, learn the truth, and if it be not so,
Say I have ne'er deserved the name of prophet.

CHORUS.

Strophe 1.

When will the guilty wretch appear,
Whom Delphi's sacred oracle demands;
Author of crimes too black for mortal ear,
Dipping in royal blood his sacrilegious hands?
Swift as the storm by rapid whirlwinds driven;
Quick let him fly th' impending wrath of Heaven;
For lo! the angry son of Jove,
Armed with red lightnings from above,
Pursues the murderer with immortal hate,
And round him spreads the snares of unrelenting fate.

Antistrophe 1.

From steep Parnassus' rocky cave,
Covered with snow, came forth the dread command;
Apollo thence his sacred mandate gave,
To search the man of blood through every land:
Silent and sad, the weary wanderer roves
O'er pathless rocks and solitary groves,
Hoping to 'scape the wrath divine,
Denounced from great Apollo's shrine;
Vain hopes to 'scape the fate by Heaven decreed,
For vengeance hovers still o'er his devoted head.

Strophe 2.

Tiresias, famed for wisdom's lore,
Hath dreadful ills to Œdipus divined;
And as his words mysterious I explore,
Unnumbered doubts perplex my anxious mind.

Now raised by hope, and now with fears oppressed,
Sorrow and joy alternate fill my breast:
How should these hapless kings be foes,
When never strife between them rose?
Or why should Laius, slain by hands unknown,
Bring foul disgrace on Polybus' unhappy son?

Antistrophe 2.

From Phœbus and all-seeing Jove
Nought can be hid of actions here below;
But earthly prophets may deceitful prove,
And little more than other mortals know:
Though much in wisdom man doth man excel,
In all that's human error still must dwell:
Could he commit the bloody deed,
Who from the Sphinx our city freed?
Oh no! he never shed the guiltless blood;
The Sphynx declares him wise, and innocent, and good.
[*Exeunt.*

ACT III.

SCENE I.

CREON, CHORUS

CREON. O citizens! with grief I hear your king
Hath blasted the fair fame of guiltless Creon!
And most unjustly brands me with a crime
My soul abhors: whilst desolation spreads
On every, side, and universal ruin
Hangs o'er the land, if I in word or deed
Could join to swell the woes of hapless Thebes,
I were unworthy—nay, I would not wish—
To live another day: alas! my friends,
Thus to be deemed a traitor to my country,
To you my fellow-citizens, to all
That hear me, 'tis infamy and shame;
I cannot, will not bear it.

CHOR. 'Twas th' effect
Of sudden anger only—what he said
But could not think.

CREON. Who told him I suborned
The prophet to speak falsely? What could raise
This vile suspicion?

CHOR. Such he had, but whence
I know not.

CREON. Talked he thus with firm composure
And confidence of mind?

CHOR. I cannot say;
'Tis not for me to know the thoughts of kings,
Or judge their actions! But behold! he comes.

Scene II.

Œdipus, Creon, Chorus.

Œdi. Ha! Creon here? And dar'st thou thus approach
My palace, thou who wouldst have murdered me,
And ta'en my kingdom? By the gods I ask thee;
Answer me, traitor, didst thou think me fool,
Or coward, that I could not see thy arts,
Or had not strength to vanquish them? What madness,
What strange infatuation led thee on,
Without or force or friends, to grasp at empire,
Which only their united force can give?
What wert thou doing?

Creon. Hear what I shall answer,
Then judge impartial.

Œdi. Thou canst talk it well,
But I shall ne'er attend to thee; thy guilt
Is plain; thou art my deadliest foe.

Creon. But hear
What I shall urge.

Œdi. Say not thou art innocent.

Creon. If self-opinion void of reason seem
Conviction to thee, know, thou err'st most grossly.

Œdi. And thou more grossly, if thou thinkst to pass
Unpunished for this injury to thy friend.

Creon. I should not, were I guilty; but what crime
Have I committed? Tell me.

Œdi. Wert not thou
The man who urged me to require the aid
Of your all-knowing prophet?

Creon. True, I was;
I did persuade you; so I would again.

Œdi. How long is it since Laius—

Creon. Laius! What?

Œdi. Since Laius fell by hands unknown?

Creon. A long,
Long tract of years.

Œdi. Was this Tiresias then
A prophet?

Creon. Ay; in wisdom and in fame
As now excelling.

Œdi. Did he then say aught
Concerning me?

Creon. I never heard he did.

Œdi. Touching this murder, did you ne'er inquire
Who were the authors?

Creon. Doubtless; but in vain.

Œdi. Why did not this same prophet then inform you?

Creon. I know not that, and when I'm ignorant
I'm always silent.

Œdi. What concerns thyself
At least thou knowst, and therefore shouldst declare it.

Creon. What is it? Speak; and if 'tis in my power,
I'll answer thee.

ŒDI. Thou knowst, if this Tiresias
Had not combined with thee, he would not thus
Accuse me as the murderer of Laius.

CREON. What he declares, thou best canst tell: of me,
What thou requirest, myself am yet to learn.

ŒDI. Go, learn it then; but ne'er shalt thou discover,
That Œdipus is guilty.

CREON. Art not thou
My sister's husband?

ŒDI. Granted.

CREON. Joined with her,
Thou rul'st o'er Thebes.

ŒDI. 'Tis true, and all she asks
Most freely do I give her.

CREON. Is not Creon
In honour next to you?

ŒDI. Thou art; and therefore
The more ungrateful.

CREON. Hear what I shall plead
And thou wilt never think so. Tell me, prince,
Is there a man who would prefer a throne,
With all its dangers, to an equal rank
In peace and safety? I am not of those
Who choose the name of king before the power;
Fools only make such wishes: I have all
From thee, and fearless I enjoy it all:
Had I the sceptre, often must I act
Against my will. Know then, I am not yet
So void of sense and reason as to quit
A real 'vantage for a seeming good.
Am I not happy, am I not revered,
Embraced, and loved by all? To me they come
Who want thy favour, and by me acquire it:
What then should Creon wish for; shall he leave
All this for empire? Bad desires corrupt
The fairest mind. I never entertained
A thought so vile, nor would I lend my aid
To forward such base purposes. But go
To Delphos, ask the sacred oracle
If I have spoke the truth; if there you find
That with the prophet I conspired, destroy
The guilty Creon; not thy voice alone
Shall then condemn me, for myself will join
In the just sentence. But accuse me not
On weak suspicion's most uncertain test.
Justice would never call the wicked good,
Or brand fair virtue with the name of vice,
Unmerited: to cast away a friend,
Faithful and just, is to deprive ourselves
Of life and being, which we hold most dear:
But time and time alone revealeth all;
That only shows the good man's excellence:
A day sufficeth to unmask the wicked.

CHOR. O king! his caution merits your regard;
Who judge in haste do seldom judge aright.

ŒDI. When they are quick who plot against my life,
'Tis fit I should be quick in my defence;
If I am tame and silent, all they wish
Will soon be done, and Œdipus must fall.

CREON. What wouldst thou have? my banishment?

ŒDI. Thy death,

CREON. But first inform me wherefore I should die.

ŒDI. Dost thou rebel then? Wilt thou not submit?

CREON. Not when I see thee thus deceived.

ŒDI. 'Tis fit I should defend my own.

CREON. And so should I.

ŒDI. Thou art a traitor.

CREON. What if it should prove I am not so.

ŒDI. A king must be obeyed.

CREON. Not if his orders are unjust.

ŒDI. O Thebes! O citizens!

CREON. I too can call on Thebes;
She is my country.

CHOR. Oh! no more, my lords;
For see Jocasta comes in happiest hour
To end your contest.

SCENE III.

JOCASTA, CREON, ŒDIPUS, CHORUS.

JOC. Whence this sudden tumult?
O princes! Is this well, at such a time
With idle broils to multiply the woes
Of wretched Thebes? Home, home, for shame! nor thus
With private quarrels swell the public ruin.

CREON. Sister, thy husband hath most basely used me;
He threatens me with banishment or death.

ŒDI. I do confess it; for he did conspire
With vile and wicked arts against my life.

CREON. Oh I may I never prosper, but accursed,
Unpitied, perish if I ever did.

JOC. Believe him, Œdipus; revere the gods
Whom he contests, if thou dost love Jocasta;
Thy subjects beg it of thee.

CHOR. Hear, O king!
Consider, we entreat thee.

ŒDI. What wouldst have?
Think you I'll e'er submit to him?

CHOR. Revere
His character, his oath, both pleading for him.

ŒDI. But know you what you ask?

CHOR. We do.

ŒDI. What is it?

CHOR. We ask thee to believe a guiltless friend,
Nor cast him forth dishonoured thus, on slight
Suspicion's weak surmise.

ŒDI. Requesting this,
You do request my banishment, or death.

CHOR. No; by yon leader of the heavenly host,
Th' immortal sun, I had not such a thought;
I only felt for Thebes' distressful state,
And would not have it by domestic strife
Embittered thus.
ŒDI. Why, let him then depart:
If Œdipus must die, or leave his country
For shameful exile, be it so; I yield
To thy request, not his; for hateful still
Shall Creon ever be.
CREON. Thy stubborn soul
Bends with reluctance, and when anger fires it
Is terrible; but natures formed like thine
Are their own punishment.
ŒDI. Wilt thou not hence?
Wilt not begone?
CREON. I go; thou knowst me not;
But these will do me justice. [*Exit* CREON.

SCENE IV.

JOCASTA, ŒDIPUS, CHORUS.

CHOR. Princess, now
Persuade him to retire.
JOC. First, let me know
The cause of this dissension.
CHOR. From reports
Uncertain, and suspicions most injurious,
The quarrel rose.
JOC. Was th' accusation mutual?
CHOR. It was.
JOC. What followed then?
CHOR. Ask me no more;
Enough's already known; we'll not repeat
The woes of helpless Thebes.
ŒDI. You are all blind,
Insensible, unjust; you love me not,
Yet boast your piety.
CHOR. I said before,
Again I say, that not to love my king
E'en as myself, would mark me for the worst
Of men. For thou didst save expiring Thebes.
Oh! rise once more, protect, preserve thy country!
JOC. O king! inform me, whence this strange dissension?
ŒDI. I'll tell thee, my Jocasta, for thou knowst
The love I bear thee, what this wicked Creon
Did artfully devise against me.
JOC. Speak it,
If he indeed be guilty.
ŒDI. Creon says
That I did murder Laius.
JOC. Spake he this
As knowing it himself, or from another?

ŒDI. He had suborned that evil-working priest,
And sharpens every tongue against his king.

JOC. Let not a fear perplex thee, Œdipus;
Mortals know nothing of futurity,
And these prophetic seers are all impostors;
I'll prove it to thee. Know then, Laius once,
Not from Apollo, but his priests, received
An oracle, which said it was decreed
He should be slain by his own son, the offspring
Of Laius and Jocasta. Yet he fell
By strangers, murdered, for so fame reports,
By robbers, in the place where three ways meet,
A son was born, but ere three days had passed
The infant's feet were bored. A servant took
And left him on the pathless mountain's top,
To perish there. Thus Phœbus ne'er decreed
That he should kill his father, or that Laius,
Which much he feared, should by his son be slain
Such is the truth of oracles. Henceforth
Regard them not. What heaven would have us know,
It can with ease unfold, and will reveal it.

ŒDI. What thou hast said, Jocasta, much disturbs me;
I tremble at it.

JOC. Wherefore shouldest thou fear?

ŒDI. Methought I heard thee say, Laius was slain
Where three ways meet.

JOC. 'Twas so reported then,
And is so still.

ŒDI. Where happened the misfortune?

JOC. In Phocis, where the roads unite that lead
To Delphi and to Daulia.

ŒDI. How long since?

JOC. A little time ere you began to reign
O'er Thebes, we heard it.

ŒDI. O almighty Jove!
What wilt thou do with me?

JOC. Why talkst thou thus?

ŒDI. Ask me no more; but tell me of this Laius:
What was his age and stature?

JOC. He was tall;
His hairs just turning to the silver hue;
His form not much unlike thy own.

ŒDI. O me!
Sure I have called down curses on myself
Unknowing.

JOC. Ha! what sayst thou, Œdipus?
I tremble whilst I look on thee.

ŒDI. Oh! much
I fear the prophet saw too well; but say,
One thing will make it clear.

JOC. I dread to hear it;
Yet speak, and I will tell thee.

ŒDI. Went he forth
With few attendants, or a numerous train,
In kingly pomp?

JOC. They were but five in all,
The herald with them; but one chariot there,
Which carried Laius.
ŒDI. Oh ! 'tis but too plain.
Who brought the news?
JOC. A servant, who alone
Escaped with life.
ŒDI. That servant, is he here?
JOC. Oh no! His master slain, when he returned
And saw thee on the throne of Thebes, with prayer
Most earnest he beseeched me to dismiss him,
That he might leave this city, where he wished
No longer to be seen, but to retire,
And feed my flocks; I granted his request,
For that and more his honest services
Had merited.
ŒDI. I beg he may be sent for
Immediately.
JOC. He shall; but wherefore is it?
ŒDI. I fear thou'st said too much, and therefore wish
To see him.
JOC. He shall come; but, O my lord!
Am I not worthy to be told the cause
Of this distress ?
ŒDI. Thou art, and I will tell thee;
Thou art my hope—to whom should I impart
My sorrows, but to thee? Know then, Jocasta,
I am the son of Polybus, who reigns
At Corinth, and the Dorian Merope
His queen; there long I held the foremost rank,
Honoured and happy, when a strange event
(For strange it was, though little meriting
The deep concern I felt) alarmed me much
A drunken reveller at a feast proclaimed
That I was only the supposed son
Of Corinth's king. Scarce could I bear that day
The vile reproach. The next, I sought my parents
And asked of them the truth; they too, enraged,
Resented much the base indignity.
I liked their tender warmth, but still I felt
A secret anguish, and, unknown to them,
Sought out the Pythian oracle. In vain.
Touching my parents nothing could I learn:
But dreadful were the miseries it denounced
Against me. 'Twas my fate, Apollo said,
To wed my mother, to produce a race
Accursed and abhorred; and last, to slay
My father who begat me. Sad decree!
Lest I should e'er fulfil the dire prediction,
Instant I fled from Corinth, by the stars
Guiding my hapless journey to the place
Where thou report'st this wretched king was slain.
But I will tell thee the whole truth. At length
I came to where the three ways meet, when, lo!
A herald, with another man like him

Whom thou describst, and in a chariot, met me.
Both strove with violence to drive me back;
Enraged, I struck the charioteer, when straight,
As I advanced, the old man saw, and twice
Smote me o' th' head, but dearly soon repaid
The insult on me; from his chariot rolled
Prone on the earth, beneath my staff he fell,
And instantly expired! Th' attendant train
All shared his fate. If this unhappy stranger
And Laius be the same, lives there a wretch
So cursed, so hateful to the gods as I am?
Nor citizen nor alien must receive,
Or converse, or communion hold with me,
But drive me forth with infamy and shame.
The dreadful curse pronounced with my own lips
Shall soon o'ertake me. I have stained the bed
Of him whom I had murdered; am I then
Aught but pollution? If I fly from hence,
The bed of incest meets me, and I go
To slay my father Polybus, the best,
The tenderest parent. This must be the work
Of some malignant power. Ye righteous gods!
Let me not see that day, but rest in death,
Rather than suffer such calamity.

CHOR. O king! we pity thy distress; but wait
With patience his arrival, and despair not.

ŒDI. That shepherd is my only hope: Jocasta,
Would he were here!

JOC. Suppose he were; what then?
What wouldst thou do?

ŒDI. I'll tell thee: if he says
The same as thou dost, I am safe and guiltless.

JOC. What said I, then?

ŒDI. Thou saidst he did report
Laius was slain by robbers; if 'tis true
He fell by numbers, I am innocent,
For I was unattended; if but one
Attacked and slew him, doubtless I am he.

JOC. Be satisfied it must be as he first
Reported it; he cannot change the tale:
Not I alone, but the whole city heard it.
Or grant he should, the oracle was ne'er
Fulfilled; for Phœbus said, Jocasta's son
Should slay his father. That could never be;
For oh! Jocasta's son long since is dead.
He could not murder Laius; therefore never
Will I attend to prophecies again.

ŒDI. Right, my Jocasta; but, I beg thee, send
And fetch this shepherd; do not fail.

JOC. I will
This moment; come, my lord, let us go in;
I will do nothing but what pleases thee. [*Exeunt.*

SCENE V.

CHORUS.

Strophe 1.

Grant me henceforth, ye powers divine,
In virtue's purest paths to tread
In every word, in every deed,
May sanctity of manners ever shine!
Obedient to the laws of Jove,
The laws descended from above,
Which, not like those by feeble mortals given,
Buried in dark oblivion lie,
Or worn by time decay, and die,
But bloom eternal like their native heaven!

Antistrophe 1.

Pride first gave birth to tyranny:
That hateful vice, insulting pride,
When, every human power defied,
She lifts to glory's height her votary;
Soon stumbling, from her tottering throne
She throws the wretched victim down.
But may the god indulgent hear my prayer,
That god whom humbly I adore,
Oh! may he smile on Thebes once more,
And take its wretched monarch to his care!

Strophe 2.

Perish the impious and profane,
Who, void of reverential fear,
Nor justice nor the laws revere,
Who leave their god for pleasure or for gain!
Who swell by fraud their ill-got store,
Who rob the wretched and the poor!
If vice unpunished virtue's meed obtain,
Who shall refrain the impetuous soul,
The rebel passions who control,
Or wherefore do I lead this choral train?

Antistrophe 2.

No more to Delphi's sacred shrine
Need we with incense now repair,
No more shall Phocis hear our prayer;
Nor fair Olympia see her rites divine;
If oracles no longer prove
The power of Phœbus and of Jove.
Great lord of all, from thy eternal throne
Behold, how impious men defame
Thy loved Apollo's honoured name;
Oh! guard his rights, and vindicate thy own. [*Exeunt.*

ACT IV.

SCENE I.

JOCASTA, CHORUS.

JOC. Sages and rulers of the land, I come
To seek the altars of the gods, and there
With incense and oblations to appease
Offended Heaven. My Œdipus, alas!
No longer wise and prudent, as you all
Remember once he was, with present things
Compares the past, nor judges like himself;
Unnumbered cares perplex his anxious mind,
And ever'y tale awakes new terrors in him;
Vain is my counsel, for he hears me not.
First, then, to thee, O Phœbus! for thou still
Art near to help the wretched, we appeal,
And suppliant beg thee now to grant thy aid
Propitious; deep is our distress; for, oh!
We see our pilot sinking at the helm,
And much already fear the vessel lost.

SCENE II.

SHEPHERD FROM CORINTH, JOCASTA, CHORUS.

SHEP. Can you instruct me, strangers, which way lies
The palace of king Œdipus; himself
I would most gladly see. Can you inform me?

CHOR. This is the palace; he is now within;
Thou seest his queen before thee.

SHEP. Ever blest
And happy with the happy mayst thou live!

JOC. Stranger, the same good wish to thee, for well
Thy words deserve it; but say, wherefore com'st thou,
And what's thy news?

SHEP. To thee, and to thy husband,
Pleasure and joy.

JOC. What pleasure? And whence art thou?

SHEP. From Corinth. To be brief, I bring thee tidings
Of good and evil.

JOC. Ha! what mean thy words
Ambiguous?

SHEP. Know then, if report say true,
The Isthmian people will choose Œdipus
Their sovereign.

JOC. Is not Polybus their king?

SHEP. No; Polybus is dead.

JOC. What sayst thou? Dead?

SHEP. If I speak falsely, may death seize on me!

JOC. [*to one of her* ATTENDANTS]. Why fliest thou not to tell thy master? Hence!
What are you now, you oracles divine?
Where is your truth? The fearful Œdipus
From Corinth fled, lest he should slay the king,
This Polybus, who perished, not by him,
But by the hand of Heaven.

Scene III.

Œdipus, Jocasta, Shepherd, Chorus.

Œdi. My dear Jocasta,
Why hast thou called me hither?
Joc. Hear this man,
And when thou hearst him, mark what faith is due
To your revered oracles.
Œdi. Who is he?
And what doth he report?
Joc. He comes from Corinth,
And says thy father Polybus is dead.
Œdi. What sayst thou, stranger? Speak to me—oh! speak!
Shep. If touching this thou first desir'st my answer;
Know, he is dead.
Œdi. How died he? Say, by treason,
Or some disease?
Shep. Alas ! a little force
Will lay to rest the weary limbs of age.
Œdi. Distemper then did kill him?
Shep. That in part,
And part a length of years that wore him down.
Œdi. Now, my Jocasta, who shall henceforth trust
To prophecies, and seers, and clamorous birds
With their vain omens—they who had decreed
That I should kill my father. He thou seest
Beneath the earth lies buried, whilst I live
In safety here and guiltless of his blood:
Unless perhaps sorrow for loss of me
Shortened his days, thus only could I kill
My father. But he's gone, and to the shades
Hath carried with him those vain oracles
Of fancied ills, no longer worth my care.
Joc. Did I not say it would be thus?
Œdi. Thou didst;
But I was full of fears.
Joc. Henceforth, no more
Indulge them.
Œdi. But my mother's bed—that still
Must be avoided. I must fly from that.
Joc. Why should man fear, whom chance, and chance alone,
Doth ever rule? Foreknowledge, all is vain,
And can determine nothing. Therefore best
It is to live as fancy leads, at large,
Uncurbed, and only subject to our will.
Fear not thy mother's bed. Oftimes in dreams
Have men committed incest. But his life
Will ever be most happy who contemns
Such idle phantoms.
Œdi. Thou wert right, Jocasta,
Did not my mother live. But as it is,
Spite of thy words, I must be anxious still.
Joc. Think on thy father's death; it is a light
To guide thee here.

ŒDI. It is so. Yet I fear
Whilst she survives him.
SHEP. Who is it you mean?
What woman fear you?
ŒDI. Merope, the wife
Of Polybus.
SHEP. And wherefore fear you her?
ŒDI. Know, stranger, a most dreadful oracle
Concerning her affrights me.
SHEP. May I know it,
Or must it be revealed to none but thee?
ŒDI. Oh no! I'll tell thee. Phœbus hath declared
That Œdipus should stain his mother's bed,
And dip his hands in his own father's blood;
Wherefore I fled from Corinth, and lived here,
In happiness indeed. But still thou knowst
It is a blessing to behold our parents,
And that I had not.
SHEP. Was it for this cause
Thou wert an exile then?
ŒDI. It was. I feared
That I might one day prove my father's murderer.
SHEP. What if I come, O king! to banish hence
Thy terrors, and restore thy peace?
ŒDI. Oh stranger!
Couldst thou do this, I would reward thee nobly.
SHEP. Know then, for this I came. I came to serve,
And make thee happy.
ŒDI. But I will not go
Back to my parents.
SHEP. Son, I see thou knowst not
What thou art doing.
ŒDI. Wherefore thinkst thou so?
By heaven I beg thee then do thou instruct me.
SHEP. If thou didst fly from Corinth for this cause—
ŒDI. Apollo's dire predictions still affright me.
SHEP. Fearst thou pollution from thy parents?
ŒDI. That,
And that alone I dread.
SHEP. Thy fears are vain.
ŒDI. Not if they are my parents.
SHEP. Polybus
Was not akin to thee.
ŒDI. What sayst thou? Speak
Say, was not Polybus my father?
SHEP. No;
No more than he is mine.
ŒDI. Why call me then
His son?
SHEP. Because long since I gave thee to him
He did receive thee from these hands.
ŒDI. Indeed!
And could he love another's child so well?
SHEP. He had no children; that persuaded him
To take and keep thee.

ŒDI. Didst thou buy me, then,
Or am I thine, and must I call thee father?
SHEP. I found thee in Cithæron's woody vale.
ŒDI. What brought thee there?
SHEP. I came to feed my flocks
On the green mountain's side.
ŒDI. It seems thou wert
A wandering shepherd.
SHEP. Thy deliverer;
I saved thee from destruction.
ŒDI. How? What then
Had happened to me?
SHEP. Thy own feet will best
Inform thee of that circumstance.
ŒDI. Alas!
Why callst thou to remembrance a misfortune
Of so long date?
SHEP. 'Twas I who loosed the tendons
Of thy bored feet.
ŒDI. It seems in infancy
I suffered much, then.
SHEP. To this incident
Thou ow'st thy name.
ŒDI. My father, or my mother,
Who did it? Knowst thou?
SHEP. He who gave thee to me
Must tell thee that.
ŒDI. Then from another's hand
Thou didst receive me.
SHEP. Ay; another shepherd.
ŒDI. Who was he? Canst thou recollect?
SHEP. 'Twas one,
At least so called, of Laius' family.
ŒDI. Laius, who ruled at Thebes?
SHEP. The same; this man
Was shepherd to King Laius.
ŒDI. Lives he still?
And could I see him?
SHEP. [*pointing to the* CHORUS]. Some of these perhaps,
His countrymen, may give you information.
ŒDI. [*to the* CHORUS]. Oh! speak, my friends, if any of you know
This Shepherd; whether still he lives at Thebes,
Or in some neighbouring country. Tell me quick,
For it concerns us near.
CHOR. It must be he
Whom thou didst lately send for; but the queen
Can best inform thee.
ŒDI. Knowst thou, my Jocasta,
Whether the man whom thou didst order hither,
And whom the shepherd speaks of, be the same?
JOC. Whom meant he? for I know not. Œdipus,
Think not so deeply of this thing.

ŒDI. Good heaven!
Forbid, Jocasta, I should now neglect
To clear my birth, when thus the path is marked
And open to me.

JOC. Do not, by the gods
I beg thee, do not, if thy life be dear,
Make further search, for I have felt enough
Already from it.

ŒDI. Rest thou satisfied;
Were I descended from a race of slaves,
'Twould not dishonour thee.

JOC. Yet hear me; do not,
Once more I beg thee, do not search this matter.

ŒDI. I will not be persuaded. I must search
And find it too.

JOC. I know it best, and best
Advise thee.

ŒDI. That advice perplexes more.

JOC. Oh! would to heaven that thou mayst never know
Or who, or whence thou art!

ŒDI. [*to the* ATTENDANTS]. Let some one fetch
That Shepherd quick, and leave this woman here
To glory in her high descent.

JOC. Alas!
Unhappy Œdipus! that word alone
I now can speak: remember 'tis my last.

[*Exit* JOCASTA.

SCENE IV.

ŒDIPUS, CHORUS.

CHOR. Why fled the queen in such disorder hence?
Sorely distressed she seemed, and much I fear
Her silence bodes some sad event.

ŒDI. Whate'er
May come of that, I am resolved to know
The secret of my birth, how mean soever
It chance to prove. Perhaps her sex's pride
May make her blush to find I was not born
Of noble parents; but I call myself
The son of fortune, my indulgent mother,
Whom I shall never be ashamed to own.
The kindred months that are like me, her children,
The years that roll obedient to her will,
Have raised me from the lowest state to power
And splendour. Wherefore, being what I am,
I need not fear the knowledge of my birth.

SCENE V.

CHORUS.

Strophe.

If my prophetic soul doth well divine,
Ere on thy brow to-morrow's sun shall shine,
Cithæron, thou the mystery shalt unfold;
The doubtful Œdipus, no longer blind,
Shall soon his country and his father find,
And all the story of his birth be told.
Then shall we in grateful lays
Celebrate our monarch's praise,
And in the sprightly dance our songs triumphant raise.

Antistrophe.

What heavenly power gave birth to thee, O king!
From Pan, the god of mountains, didst thou spring,
With some fair daughter of Apollo joined;
Art thou from him who o'er Cyllene reigns,
Swift Hermes, sporting in Arcadia's plains?
Some nymph of Helicon did Bacchus find—
Bacchus, who delights to rove
Through the forest, hill and grove—
And art thou, prince, the offspring of their love?

SCENE VI.

ŒDIPUS, CHORUS, SHEPHERD FROM CORINTH.

ŒDI. If I may judge of one whom yet I ne'er
Had converse with, yon old man, whom I see
This way advancing, must be that same shepherd
We lately sent for, by his age and mien,
E'en as this stranger did describe him to us;
My servants too are with him. But you best
Can say, for you must know him well.
CHOR. 'Tis he,
My lord; the faithful shepherd of King Laius.
ŒDI. [*to the* SHEPHERD *from Corinth*]. What sayst thou, stranger?—is it he?
SHEP. It is.

SCENE VII.

OLD SHEPHERD, ŒDIPUS, SHEPHERD FROM CORINTH, CHORUS.

ŒDI. Now answer me, old man; look this way—speak:
Didst thou belong to Laius?
OLD SHEP. Sir, I did;
No hireling slave, but in his palace bred,
I served him long.
ŒDI. What was thy business there?
OLD SHEP. For my life's better part I tended sheep.
ŒDI. And whither didst thou lead them?

OLD SHEP. To Cithæron,
And to the neighbouring plains.
ŒDI. Behold this man:
[*Pointing to the* SHEPHERD *of Corinth*
Dost thou remember to have seen him?
OLD SHEP. Whom?
What hath he done?
ŒDI. Him, who now stands before thee,
Callst thou to mind, or converse or connection
Between you in times past?
OLD SHEP. I cannot say
I recollect it now.
SHEP. *of Corinth.* I do not wonder
He should forget me, but I will recall
Some facts of ancient date. He must remember
When on Cithæron we together fed
Our several flocks, in daily converse joined
From spring to autumn, and when winter bleak
Approached, retired. I to my little cot
Conveyed my sheep; he to the palace led
His fleecy care. Canst thou remember this?
OLD SHEP. I do; but that is long, long since
SHEP. *of Corinth.* It is;
But say, good shepherd, canst thou call to mind
An infant whom thou didst deliver to me,
Requesting me to breed him as my own?
OLD SHEP. Ha! wherefore askst thou this?
SHEP. *of Corinth.* [*pointing to* ŒDIPUS]. Behold him here,
That very child.
OLD SHEP. Oh! say it not: away!
Perdition on thee!
ŒDI. Why reprove him thus?
Thou art thyself to blame, old man.
OLD SHEP. In what
Am I to blame, my lord?
ŒDI. Thou wilt not speak
Touching this boy.
OLD SHEP. Alas! poor man, he knows not
What be hath said.
ŒDI. If not by softer means
To be persuaded, force shall wring it from thee.
OLD SHEP. Treat not an old man harshly.
ŒDI. [*to the* ATTENDANTS]. Bind his hands.
OLD SHEP. Wherefore, my lord? What wouldst thou have me do?
ŒDI. That child he talks of, didst thou give it to him?
OLD SHEP. I did; and would to heaven I then had died!
ŒDI. Die soon thou shalt, unless thou tellst it all.
OLD SHEP. Say, rather if I do.
ŒDI. This fellow means
To trifle with us, by his dull delay.
OLD SHEP. I do not; said I not I gave the child?
ŒDI. Whence came the boy? Was he thy own, or who
Did give him to thee?
OLD SHEP. From another hand
I had received him.

ŒDI. Say, what hand? From whom?
Whence came he?

OLD SHEP. Do not—by the gods I beg thee,
Do not inquire.

ŒDI. Force me to ask again,
And thou shalt die.

OLD SHEP. In Laius' palace born—

ŒDI. Son of a slave, or of the king?

OLD SHEP. Alas!
'Tis death for me to speak.

ŒDI. And me to hear;
Yet say it.

OLD SHEP. He was called the son of Laius;
But ask the queen, for she can best inform thee.

ŒDI. Did she then give the child to thee?

OLD SHEP. She did.

ŒDI. For what?

OLD SHEP. To kill him.

ŒDI. Kill her child! Inhuman
And barbarous mother!

OLD SHEP. A dire oracle
Affrighted, and constrained her to it.

ŒDI. Ha!
What oracle?

OLD SHEP. Which said, her son should slay
His parents.

ŒDI. Wherefore gav'st thou then the infant
To this old Shepherd?

OLD SHEP. Pity moved me to it:
I hoped he would have soon conveyed his charge
To some far distant country; he, alas!
Preserved him but for misery and woe;
For, O my lord! if thou indeed art he,
Thou art of all mankind the most unhappy.

ŒDI. O me! at length the mystery's unravelled;
'Tis plain, 'tis clear; my fate is all determined,
Those are my parents who should not have been
Allied to me; she is my wife, e'en she
Whom Nature had forbidden me to wed;
I have slain him who gave me life; and now
Of thee, O light! I take my last farewell,
For Œdipus shall ne'er behold thee more. [*Exeunt*.

SCENE VIII.

CHORUS.

Strophe 1.

O hapless state of human race!
How quick the fleeting shadows pass
Of transitory bliss below,
Where all is vanity and woe!
By thy example taught, O prince! we see
Man was not made for true felicity.

Antistrophe 1.

Thou, Œdipus, beyond the rest
Of mortals wert supremely blest;
Whom every hand conspired to raise,
Whom every tongue rejoiced to praise,
When from the Sphinx thy all-preserving hand
Stretched forth its aid to save a sinking land.

Strophe 2.

Thy virtues raised thee to a throne,
And grateful Thebes was all thy own;
Alas! how changed that glorious name!
Lost are thy virtues and thy fame;
How couldst thou thus pollute thy father's bed?
How couldst thou thus thy hapless mother wed?

Antistrophe 2.

How could that bed unconscious bear
So long the vile incestuous pair?
But time, of quick and piercing sight,
Hath brought the horrid deed to light;
At length Jocasta owns her guilty flame,
And finds a husband and a child the same.

Epode.

Wretched son of Laius, thee
Henceforth may I never see,
But absent shed the pious tear,
And weep thy fate with grief sincere!
For thou didst raise our eyes to life and light,
To close them now in everlasting night.

ACT V.

SCENE I.

MESSENGER, CHORUS.

MESSENGER. Sages of Thebes, most honoured and revered,
If o'er the house of Labdacus was dear
And precious to you, what will be your grief
When I shall tell the most disastrous tale
You ever heard, and to your eyes present
A spectacle more dreadful than they yet
Did e'er behold: not the wide Danube's waves
Nor Phasis' streams can wash away the stains
Of this polluted palace; and dire crimes
Long time concealed at length are brought to light;
But those which spring from voluntary guilt
Are still more dreadful.

CHOR. Nothing can be worse
Than that we know already; bringst thou more
Misfortunes to us?

MES. To be brief, the queen,
Divine Jocasta's dead.
CHOR. Jocasta dead! Say, by what hand?
MES. Her own;
And what's more dreadful, no one saw the deed.
What I myself beheld you all shall hear.
Inflamed with rage, soon as she reached the palace,
Instant retiring to the nuptial bed,
She shut the door, then raved and tore her hair,
Called out on Laius dead, and bade him think
On that unhappy son who murdered him
And stained his bed; then turning her sad eyes
Upon the guilty couch, she cursed the place
Where she had borne a husband from her husband,
And children from her child; what followed then
I know not, by the cries of Œdipus
Prevented, for on him our eyes were fixed
Attentive; forth he came, beseeching us
To lend him some sharp weapon, and inform him
Where he might find his mother and his wife,
His children's wretched mother and his own.
Some ill-designing Power did then direct him
(For we were silent) to the queen's apartment;
Forcing the bolt, he rushed into the bed,
And found Jocasta, where we all beheld her,
Entangled in the fatal noose, which soon
As he perceived, loosing the pendant rope,
Deeply he groaned, and casting on the ground
His wretched body, showed a piteous sight
To the beholders; on a sudden, thence
Starting, be plucked from off the robe she wore
A golden buckle that adorned her side,
And buried in his eyes the sharpened point,
Crying, he ne'er again would look on her,
Never would see his crimes or miseries more,
Or those whom guiltless he could ne'er behold,
Or those to whom he now must sue for aid.
His lifted eyelids then, repeating still
These dreadful plaints, he tore; whilst down his cheek
Fell showers of blood! Such fate the wretched pair
Sustained, partakers in calamity,
Fallen from a state of happiness (for none
Were happier once than they) to groans and death,
Reproach and shame, and every human woe.
CHOR. And where is now the poor unhappy man?
MES. Open the doors, he cries, and let all Thebes
Behold his parents' murderer, adding words
Not to be uttered; banished now, he says,
He must be, nor, devoted as he is
By his own curse, remain in this sad place.
He wants a kind conductor and a friend
To help him now, for 'tis too much to bear.
But you will see him soon, for lo! the door's
Are opened, and you will behold a sight
That would to pity move his deadliest foe.

SCENE II.

ŒDIPUS, MESSENGER, CHORUS.

CHOR. Oh! horrid sight! more dreadful spectacle
Than e'er these eyes beheld! what madness urged thee
To this sad deed? What power malignant heaped
On thy poor head such complicated woe?
Unhappy man, alas! I would have held
Some converse with thee, but thy looks affright me;
I cannot bear to speak to thee.

ŒDI. O me!
Where am I ? and whence comes the voice I hear?
Where art thou fortune?

CHOR. Changed to misery,
Dreadful to hear, and dreadful to behold.

ŒDI. O cruel darkness! endless, hopeless night,
Shame, terrors, and unutterable woe!
Mere pain is the memory of my crimes
Than all the wounds my wild distraction made.

CHOR. Thus doubly cursed, O prince! I wonder not
At thy affliction.

ŒDI. Art thou here, my friend?
I know thy voice; thou wouldst not leave the wretched;
Thou art my faithful, kind assistant still.

CHOR. How couldst thou thus deprive thyself of sight?
What madness drove thee to the desperate deed?
What god inspired?

ŒDI. Apollo was the cause;
He was, my friends, the cause of all my woes;
But for these eyes—myself did quench their light—
I want not them; what use were they to me,
But to discover scenes of endless woe;

CHOR. 'Tis but too true.

ŒDI. What pleasure now remains
For Œdipus? He cannot joy in aught
To sight or ear delightful. Curse on him,
Whoe'er he was, that loosened my bound feet,
And saved me, in Cithæron's vale, from death!
I owe him nothing: had I perished then,
Much happier had it been for you, my friends,
And for myself.

CHOR. I too could wish thou hadst.

ŒDI. I should not then have murdered Laius; then
I had not ta'en Jocasta to my bed;
But now I am a guilty wretch, the son
Of a polluted mother, father now
To my own brothers, all that's horrible
To nature is the lot of Œdipus.

CHOR. Yet must I blame this cruel act, for sure
The loss of sight is worse than death itself.

ŒDI. I care not for thy counsel or thy praise;
For with what eyes could I have e'er beheld
My honoured father in the shades below,
Or my unhappy mother, both destroyed
By me? This punishment is worse than death,
And so it should be. Sweet had been the sight
Of my dear children—them I could have wished
To gaze upon; but I must never see
Or them, or this fair city, or the palace
Where I was born. Deprived of every bliss
By my own lips, which doomed to banishment
The murderer of Laius, and expelled
The impious wretch, by gods and men accursed:
Could I behold them after this? Oh no!
Would I could now with equal ease remove
My hearing too, be deaf as well as blind,
And from another entrance shut out woe!
To want our senses, in the hour of ill,
Is comfort to the wretched. O Cithæron!
Why didst thou e'er receive me, or received,
Why not destroy, that men might never know
Who gave me birth? O Polybus! O Corinth!
And thou, long time believed my father's palace,
Oh! what a foul disgrace to human nature
Didst thou receive beneath a prince's form!
Impious myself and from an impious race.
Where is my splendour now? O Daulian path!
The shady forest, and the narrow pass
Where three ways meet, who drank a father's blood
Shed by these hands, do you not still remember
The horrid deed, and what, when here I came,
Followed more dreadful? Fatal nuptials, you
Produced me, you returned me to the womb
That bare me; thence relations horrible
Of fathers, sons, and brothers came; of wives,
Sisters, and mothers, sad alliance! all
That man holds impious and detestable.
But what in act is vile the modest tongue
Should never name. Bury me, hide me, friends,
From every eye; destroy me, cast me forth
To the wide ocean—let me perish there
Do anything to shake off hated life.
Seize me; approach, my friends—you need not fear,
Polluted though I am, to touch me; none
Shall suffer for my crimes but I alone.

CHOR. In most fit time, my lord, the noble Creon
This way advances; he can best determine
And best advise; sole guardian now of Thebes,
To him thy power devolves.

ŒDI. What shall I say?
Can I apply to him for aid whom late
I deeply injured by unjust suspicion?

SCENE III.

CREON, ŒDIPUS, CHORUS.

CREON. I come not, prince, to triumph o'er thy woes
With vile reproach; I pity thy misfortunes.
But, O my Thebans! if you do not fear
The censure of your fellow-citizens,
At least respect the all-creating eye
Of Phœbus, who beholds you thus exposing
To public view a wretch accursed, polluted,
Whom neither earth can bear, nor sun behold,
Nor holy shower besprinkle. Take him hence
Within the palace; those who are by blood
United should alone be witnesses
Of such calamity.

ŒDI. O Creon! thou,
The best of men, and I the worst, how kind
Thou art to visit me! Oh! by the gods
Let me entreat thee, since beyond my hopes
Thou art so good, now hear me; what I ask,
Concerns thee most.

CREON. What is it thou desirest
Thus ardently?

ŒDI. I beg thee, banish me
From Thebes this moment, to some land remote,
Where I may ne'er converse with man again.

CREON. Myself long since had done it, but the gods
Must be consulted first.

ŒDI. Their will is known
Already, and their oracle declared
The guilty parricide should die.

CREON. It hath;
But, as it is, 'twere better to inquire
What must be done.

ŒDI. For such a wretch as me
Wouldst thou again explore the will of Heaven?

CREON. Thy hapless fate should teach us to believe,
And reverence the gods.

ŒDI. Now, Creon, list;
I beg thee, I conjure thee, let a tomb
Be raised, and all due honours paid to her
Who lies within: she was thy sister, Creon;
It is a duty which thou ow'st: for me,
I cannot hope this city now will deign
To keep me here. O Creon! let me go,
And seek the solitary mountain's top,
My own Cithæron, by my parents doomed
Long since to be the grave of Œdipus;
Where would I die, as they decreed I should.
Alas! I cannot, must not perish yet,
Till I have suffered evils worse than death,
For I was only saved to be unhappy;
But I must meet my fate, whate'er it be.
My sons are men, and wheresoever fortune

May place them, cannot want the means of life;
They shall not burthen thee; but, O my friend!
What will become of my unhappy daughters,
With tenderest love, beneath a father's hand,
Cherished so long? Oh! take them to thy care,
Thou best of men! Oh! might I but embrace them,
But shed a tear o'er their disastrous fate,
Might I be suffered but to touch them here,
I should rejoice, and think I saw them still.
But hark! methinks e'en now I hear the voice
Of my dear daughters; hath the gracious Creon,
In pity to my woes, already brought
My children to me?—is it so?

CREON. It is:
Thy wishes are prevented; they are here.

SCENE IV.

DAUGHTERS OF ŒDIPUS, ŒDIPUS, CREON, CHORUS.

ŒDI. May Heaven reward thee for this goodness to me,
And give thee much more bliss than I have known!
Now, my dear children, come towards me, come
Towards your father and your—brother; see
These sightless eyes, pierced by my own mad hands;
Behold that wretched father who begat you
Unknowingly on her who gave me birth;
I cannot see you now—I can but weep
Your fate, to think what hours of wretchedness
You have to know hereafter. Whither now
Must my poor children fly? From every feast
Joyless with grief and shame, shall you return;
And when the time shall come when riper years
Should give you to the nuptial bed, who then,
Careless of fame, will let his child partake
The infamy of my abhorred race,
Sprung from a wretch accursed, who killed his father,
And from the womb that bare him did beget
You my unhappy daughters? Such reproach
Must still be yours, to virgin solitude
Devoted ever, and a barren bed.
Son of Menæceus, thou alone art left
Their father now, for, oh! Jocasta's dead,
And I am—nothing. Do not then forsake
Thy kindred; nor, deserted and forlorn,
Suffer them still in penury and woe
To wander helpless, in their tender age:
Remember they have no support but thee.
O generous prince! have pity on them; give me
Thy friendly hand in promise of thy aid.
To you, my daughters, had your early years
Permitted, I had given my last advice:
Too young for counsel, all I ask of you
Is but to pray the gods that my sad life
May not be long; but yours, my children, crowned
With many days, and happier far than mine.

CREON. It is enough; go in—thy grief transports thee
Beyond all bounds.
ŒDI. 'Tis hard; but I submit.
CREON. The time demands it; therefore go.
ŒDI. Oh Creon!
Knowst thou what now I wish?
CREON. What is it? Speak.
ŒDI. That I may quit this fatal place.
CREON. Thou ask'st
What Heaven alone can grant.
ŒDI. Alas! to Heaven
I am most hateful.
CREON. Yet shalt thou obtain
What thou desirest.
ŒDI. Shall I indeed?
CREON. Thou shalt;
I never say aught that I do not mean.
ŒDI. Then let me go: may I depart?
CREON. Thou mayst
But leave thy children.
ŒDI. Do not take them from me.
CREON. Thou must not always have thy will. Already
Thou'st suffered for it.
CHOR. Thebans, now behold
The great, the mighty Œdipus, who once
The Sphinx's dark enigma could unfold,
Who less to fortune than to wisdom owed,
In virtue as in rank to all superior,
Yet fallen at last to deepest misery.
Let mortals hence be taught to look beyond
The present time, nor dare to say, a man
Is happy till the last decisive hour
Shall close his life without the taste of woe.

Antigone: Background

Antigone completes Sophocles' trilogy, along with *Oedipus Rex* and *Oedipus at Colonus*. Of this trilogy, *Antigone* remains the most controversial: the debate still rages regarding the identity of the true tragic hero of this work. Was it Antigone or Creon? As the luckless daughter of Oedipus, Antigone possesses many of her father's character strengths and flaws. Like him, she is a stubborn and overly proud woman whose character hints at a yearning for martyrdom. Some argue that because her tragedy is foreseeable at the beginning, Antigone is less worthy as a tragic heroine. Others see Creon as the hero, for he has many more crosses to bear than does Antigone. Creon suffers the loss of his son, Haemon, his wife, Eurydice, and the state itself because of his own misjudgments. However, readers cannot escape the idea that Sophocles offers a far more tragic and less heroic view of man.

The stark hopelessness of Sophocles' characters derives in some way from the play's timeless, irreconcilable tensions: man and woman, divine law and man's law, living and dead, old and young. Creon pleads with his son never to be "unmanned" by a woman. His inflexibility is matched only by Antigone's. Both are caught in each other's commitment to the law.

Antigone

DRAMATIS PERSONÆ

CREON, *King of Thebes*
EURYDICE, *Wife of Creon*
HÆMON, *Son of Creon*
ANTIGONE, *Daughter of Œdipus*
ISMENE, *Sister of Antigone*
TIRESIAS, *a Prophet*
A MESSENGER, GUARD, SERVANT, *and* ATTENDANTS
CHORUS, composed of Ancient Men of Thebes

ACT I.

SCENE I.

ANTIGONE, ISMENE

ANTIGONE. O my dear sister, by best-beloved Ismene!
Is there an evil, by the wrath of Jove
Reserved for Œdipus' unhappy race,
We have not felt already? Sorrow and shame,
And bitterness and anguish, all that's sad,
All that's distressful, hath been ours, and now
This dreadful edict from the tyrants comes
To double our misfortunes. Hast thou heard
What harsh commands he hath imposed on all,
Or art thou still to know what future ills
Our foes have yet in store to make us wretched?

ISM. Since that unhappy day, Antigone,
When by each other's hand our brothers fell,
And Greece dismissed her armies, I have heard
Naught that could give or joy or grief to me.

ANT. I thought thou wert a stranger to the tidings,
I might impart them to thee.

ISM. Oh! what are they?
For something dreadful labours in thy breast.

ANT. Know the, from Creon, our indulgent lord,
Our hapless brothers met a different fate:
To honour one, and one to infamy
He hath consigned. With funeral rights he graced
The body of our dear Eteocles,
Whilst Polynices' wretched carcase lies
Unburied, unlamented, left exposed
A feast for hungry vultures on the plain.
No pitying friend will dare to violate
The tyrant's harsh command, for public death
Awaits th' offender. Creon comes himself
To tell use of it—such is our condition.
This is the crisis, this the hour, Ismene,
That must declare thee worthy of they birth,
Or show thee mean, base, and degenerate.

ISM. What wouldst thou have me do?—defy his power?
Contemn the laws?

ANT. To act with me, or not:
Consider and resolve.

ISM. What daring deed
Wouldst thou attempt? What is it? Speak!

ANT. To join
And take the body, my Ismene.

ISM. Ha!
And wouldst thou dare to bury it, when thus
We are forbidden?

ANT. Aye, to bury *him*!
He is my brother, and thine too, Ismene;
Therefore, consent or not, I have determined
I'll not disgrace my birth.

ISM. Hath not the king
Pronounced it death to all?

ANT. He hath no right,
No power to keep me from my own.

ISM. Alas!
Remember our unhappy father's fate:
His eyes torn out by his own fatal hand,
Oppressed with shame and infamy he died;
Fruit of his crimes! a mother, and a wife—
Dreadful alliance!—self-devoted, fell;
And last, in one sad day, Eteocles
And Polynices by each other slain.
Left as we are, deserted and forlorn,
What from our disobedience can we hope
But misery and ruin? Poor weak women,
Helpless, not formed by nature to contemn
With powerful man. We are his subjects too.
Therefore to this, and worse than this, my sister,
We must submit. For me, in humblest prayer
Will I address me to th' infernal powers
For pardon of that crime which well they know
Sprang from necessity, and they obey;
Since to attempt what we can never hope
To execute, is folly and madness.

ANT. Wert thou to proffer what I do not ask—
Thy poor assistance—I would scorn it now.
Act as thou wilt; I'll bury him myself;
Let me perform but that, and death is welcome:
I'll do the pious deed, and lay me down
By my dear brother. Loving and beloved
We'll rest together; to the powers below
'Tis fit we pay obedience; longer there
We must remain than we can breathe on earth.
There I shall dwell for ever; thou, meantime,
What the gods hold most precious mayst despise.

ISM. I reverence the gods; but, in defiance
Of laws, and unassisted to do this,
It were most dangerous.

ANT. That be thy excuse,
Whilst I prepare the funeral pile.

ISM. Alas!
I tremble for thee.
ANT. Tremble for thyself,
And not for me.
ISM. Oh! do not tell they purpose,
I beg thee, do not. I shall ne'er betray thee.
ANT. I'd have it known; and I shall hate thee more
For thy concealment, than, if loud to all,
Thou wouldst proclaim the deed.
ISM. Thou hast a heart
Too daring, and ill-suited to they fate.
ANT. I know my duty, and I'll pay it there
Where 'twill be best accepted.
ISM. Couldst thou do it!
But 'tis not in they power.
ANT. When I know that
It will be time enough to quit my purpose.
ISM. It cannot be; 'tis folly to attempt it.
ANT. Go on, and I shall hate thee! Our dead brother,
He too shall hate thee as his bitterest foe;
Go, leave me here to suffer for my rashness;
Whate'er befalls, it cannot be so dreadful
As not to die with honour.
ISM. Then farewell,
Since thou wilt have it so; and know, Ismene
Pities thy weakness, but admires they virtue.
[*Exeunt.*

SCENE II.

CHORUS.

Strophe 1.

By Dirce's sweetly-flowing stream,
Ne'er did the golden eye of day
On Thebes with fairer lustre beam,
Or shine with more auspicious ray.
See the proud Argive, with his silver shield
And glittering armour, quits the hostile plain;
No longer dares maintain the luckless field,
But vanquished flies, nor checks the loosened rein.
With dreadful clangour, like the bird of Jove,
On snowy wings descending from above,
His vaunted powers to this devoted land,
In bitterest wrath did Polynices lead,
With crested helmets, and a numerous band
He came, and fondly hoped that Thebes should bleed.

Antistrophe 1.

High on the lofty tower he stood,
And viewed th' encircled gates below,
With spears that thirsted for our blood,
And seemed to scorn th' unequal foe;

But, fraught with vengeance, ere the rising flame
  Could waste our bulwarks, or our walls surround,
Mars to assist the fiery serpent came,
  And brought the towering eagle to the ground.
That god who hates the boastings of the proud
Saw the rude violence of th' exulting crowd;
  Already now the triumph was prepared,
    The wreath of victory and the festal song,
  When Jove the clash of golden armour heard,
    And hurled his thunder on the guilty throng.

Strophe 2.

Then Capaneus, elate with pride,
  Fierce as the rapid whirlwind came,
Eager he seemed on every side
  To spread the all-devouring flame;
But soon he felt the wing'ed lightning's blast,
  By angry heaven with speedy vengeance sent—
Down from the lofty turrets headlong cast,
  For his foul crimes he met the punishment.
Each at his gate, long time the leaders strove,
Then fled, and left their arms to conquering Jove;
  Save the unhappy death-devoted pair,
    The wretched brethren, who unconquered stood,
  With rancorous hate inspired, and fell despair,
    They reeked their vengeance in each other's blood.

Antistrophe 2.

And lo! with smiles propitious see
  To Thebes, for numerous cars renowned,
The goddess comes, fair Victory,
  With fame and endless glory crowned!
Henceforth, no longer vexed by war's alarms,
  Let all our sorrows, all our labours cease;
Come, let us quit the din of rattling arms,
  And fill our temples with the songs of peace.
The god of Thebes shall guide our steps aright,
And crown with many a lay the festive night.
  But see, still anxious for his native land,
    Our kind, Menaeceus' valiant son, appear:
  With some fair omen by the gods' command
    He comes to met his aged council here. [Exeunt.

ACT II.

SCENE I.

CREON, CHORUS.

CREON. At length our empire, shook by civil broils,
The gods to peace and safety have restored;
Wherefore, my friends, you had our late request
That you should meet us here; for well I know
Your firm allegiance to great Laius, next

To Œdipus, and his unhappy sons;
These by each other's hand untimely slain,
To me the sceptre doth of right descend,
As next in blood. Never can man be know,
His mind, his will, his passions ne'er appear
Till power and office call them forth; to me,
'Tis my firm thought, and I have held it ever,
That he who rules and doth not follow that
Which wisdom counsels, but, restrained by fear,
Shuts up his lips, must be the worst of men;
Nor do I deem him worthy who prefers
A friend, how dear soever, to his country
Should I behold—witness all-seeing Jove!—
This city wronged, I never would be silent,
Never would make the foe of Thebes my friend,
For on her safety must depend our own;
And if she flourish we can never want
Assistance or support. Thus would I net,
And therefore have I sent my edict forth
Touching the sons of Œdipus, commanding
That they should bury him who nobly fought
And died for Thebes, the good Eteocles,
Gracing his memory with each honour due
To the illustrious dead. For Polynices,
Abandoned exile, for a brother's blood
Thirsting insatiate—he who would in flames
Have wasted all, his country and his gods,
And made you slaves—I have decreed he lie
Unburied, his vile carcase to the birds
And hungry dogs a prey. There let him rot
Inglorious—'tis my will; for ne'er from me
Shall vice inherit virtue's due reward,
But him alone who is a friend of Thebes.
Living or dead shall Creon reverence still.

CHOR. Son of Menaeceus, 'twas thy great behest
Thus to reward them both; thine is the power
O'er all supreme, the living and the dead.

CREON. Be careful then my orders are obeyed.

CHOR. O sir! to younger hands commit the task.

CREON. I have appointed some to watch the body.

CHOR. What then remains for us?

CREON. To see that none
By your connivance violate the law.

CHOR. Scarce will the man be found so fond of death
As to attempt it.

CREON. Death is the reward
Of him who dares it; but oftimes by hope
Of sordid gain are men betrayed to ruin.

SCENE II.

MESSENGER, CREON, CHORUS.

MES. O king! I cannot boast that hither sent
I came with speed, for oft my troubled thoughts
Have driven me back; oft to myself I said,

Why dost thou seek destruction? Yet again
If thou report it not, from other tongues
Creon must hear the tale, and thou wilt suffer.
With doubts like these oppressed, slowly I came,
And the short way seemed like a tedious journey;
At length I come, resolved to tell thee all:
Whate'er the event, I must submit to fate.

CREON. Whence are they fears, and why this hesitation?

MES. First for myself; I merit not they wrath;
It is not I, nor have I seen the man
Who did the guilty deed.

CREON. Something of weight
Thou hast t'impart, by this unusual care
To guard thee from our anger.

MES. Fear will come
Where danger is.

CREON. Speak, and thou hast they pardon.

MES. The body of Polynices some rash hand
Hath buried, scattered o'er his corpse the dust,
And funeral rites performed.

CREON. Who dared do this?

MES. 'Tis yet unknown; no mark of instrument
Is left behind: the earth still level all,
Nor worn by track of chariot wheel. The guard,
Who watched that day, call it a miracle;
No tomb was raised; light lay the scattered earth,
As only meant to avoid the imputed curse;
Nor could we trace the steps of dog or beast
Passing that way. Instant a tumult rose;
The guards accused each other; nought was proved,
But each suspected each, and all denied,
Offering, in proof of innocence, to grasp
The burning steel, to walk through fire, and take
Their solemn oath they knew not of the deed;
At length, one mightier than the rest, proposed—
Nor could we think of better means—that all
Should be to thee discovered; 'twas my lot
To bring th' unwelcome tidings, and I come
To pour my news unwilling into ears
Unwilling to receive it, for I know
None ever loved the messenger of ill.

CHOR. To me it seems as if the hand of heaven
Were in this deed.

CREON. Be silent, ere my rage,
Thou rash old man, pronounce thee fool and
dotard;
Horrid suggestion! Think'st thou, then, the gods
Take care of men like these? Would they preserve
Or honour him who came to burn their altars,
Profane their rites, and trample on their laws?
Will they reward the bad? It cannot be.
But well I know the murmuring citizens
Brooked not our mandate, shook their heads in
secret,
And, ill-affected to me, would not stoop

Their haughty crests, or bend beneath my yoke.
By hire corrupted, some of these have dared
The venturous deed. Gold is the worst of ills
That ever plagued mankind: this wastes our cities,
Drives forth their natives to a foreign soil,
Taints the pure heart, and turns the virtuous mind
To basest deeds; artificer of fraud
Supreme, and source of every wickedness.
The wretch corrupted for this hateful purpose
Must one day suffer; for, observe me well,
As I revere that power by whom I swear,
Almighty Jove, if you conceal him from me,
If to my eyes you do not bring the traitor,
Know, death alone shall not suffice to glut
My vengeance; living shall you hang in torments
Till you confess, till you have learned from me
There is a profit not to be desired,
And own dishonest gains have ruined more
Than they have saved.

MES. O king! may I depart,
Or wait thy further orders?

CREON. Knowst thou not
Thy speech is hateful? Hence!

MES. Wherefore, my lord?

CREON. Know you not why?

MES. I but offend your ear,
They who have done the deed afflict your soul.

CREON. Away! They talk but makes thy guilt appear.

MES. My lord, I did not do it.

CREON. Thou hast sold
Thy life for gain.

MES. 'Tis cruel to suspect me.

CREON. Thou talkst it bravely; but remember all,
Unless you do produce him, you shall find
The miseries which on ill-got wealth await. [*Exit.*

MES. Would he were found. That we must leave to fate;
Be it as it may, I never will return:
Thus safe beyond my hopes, 'tis fit I pay
My thanks to the kind gods who have preserved me.
[*Exit.*

SCENE III.

CHORUS.

Strophe 1.

Since first this active world began,
Nature is busy all in every part;
But passing all in wisdom and in art,
Superior shines inventive man:
Fearless of wintry winds and circling waves,
He rides the ocean and the tempest braves;
On him unwearied earth with lavish hand,
Immortal goddess, all her bounty pours,
Patient beneath the rigid plough's command,
Year after year she yields her plenteous stores.

Antistrophe 1.

To drive the native of the wood
From their rude haunts, or in the cruel snare,
To catch the winged inhabitants of air,
Or trap the scaly brood;
To tame the fiery courser yet unbroke
With the hard rein, or to the untried yoke
To bend the mountain bull, who wildly free
O'er the steep rocks had wandered unconfined—
These are the arts of mortal industry,
And such the subtle power of humankind.

Strophe 2.

By learning, and fair science crowned,
Behold him now, full-fraught with wisdom's lore,
The laws of nature anxious to explore,
With depth of thought profound,
But naught, alas! can human wisdom see
In the dark bosom of futurity.
The power of wisdom may awhile prevail,
Awhile suspend a mortal's fleeting breath,
But never can her fruitless arts avail
To conquer fate, or stop the hand of death.

Antistrophe 2.

Man's ever-active changeful will
Sometimes to good shall bend his virtuous mind,
Sometimes, behold him to foul deeds inclined,
And prone to every ill.
Who guiltless keeps the laws is still approved
By every tongue, and by his country loved;
But he who doth now, from his native land
A wretched exile, far, oh! far from me
May he be driven, by angry Heaven's command,
And live devote to shame and infamy!

CHOR. Amazement! Can it be Antigone?
Or do my eyes deceive me? No, she comes.
O! wretched daughter of a wretched father!
Hast thou transgressed the laws, and art thou ta'en
In this adventurous deed, unhappy maid?

SCENE IV.

ANTIGONE, GUARD, CREON.

GUARD. Behold the woman who hath done the deed!
I' th' very act of burial we surprised her.
Where is the king?
CHOR. Returned, as we could wish;
E'en now he comes this way.

Scene V.

Creon, Antigone, Guard, Chorus

Creon. Whom have we here?
Doth justice smile upon us?

Guard. O my lord!
Never should man too confident assert,
Much less by oath should bind himself to aught,
For soon our judgments change, and one opinion
Destroys another. By thy threats alarmed
But now, I vowed I never would return;
Yet thus preserved beyond my hope, I come,
Bound by that duty which I owe to thee
And to my country, to bring here this virgin,
Whom, as she sprinkled o'er her brother's dust
The varied wreath, we seized. The willing task
Was mine, nor as of late by lot determined.
Receive her then, O king! Judge and condemn
The guilty as it best becomes thy wisdom;
Henceforth I stand acquitted.

Creon. But say how,
Where didst thou find her?

Guard. To say all, 'twas she
Who buried Polynices.

Creon. Art thou sure?

Guard. These eyes beheld her.

Creon. But say, how discovered?

Guard. Thus then it was. No sooner had I left thee
Than, mindful of thy wrath, with careful hands
From off the putrid carcase we removed
The scattered dust; then, to avoid the stench,
Exhaling noisome, to a hill retired;
There watched at distance, till the mid-day sun
Scorched o'er our heads. Sudden a storm arose,
Shook every leaf, and rattled through the grove,
Filling the troubled element. We closed
Our eyes, and patient bore the wrath of heaven.
At length the tempest ceased, when we beheld
This virgin issuing forth, and heard her cries
Distressful, like the plaintive bird who views
The plundered nest, and mourns her ravished young.
E'en thus the maid, when on the naked corse
She cast her eyes, loud shrieked, and cursed the hand
That did the impious deed, then sprinkled o'er
The crumbled earth, and from a brazen urn,
Of richest work, to the loved relics thrice
Her due libations poured. We saw, and straight
Pursued her. Unappalled she seemed, and still
As we did ourselves released from woe is bliss
Supreme, but thus to see our friends unhappy
Embitters all. I must be thankful still
For my own safety, which I hold most dear.

Creon. Speak thou, who bendst to earth thy drooping head;
Dost thou deny the fact?

ANT. Deny it? No!
'Twas I.
CREON. [*to the* GUARD]. Retire, for thou art free; and now
[*turning to* ANTIGONE
Be brief, and tell me; heardst thou our decree?
ANT. I did' 'twas public. How could I avoid it?
CREON. And dar'st thou then to disobey the law?
ANT. I had it not from Jove, nor the just gods
Who rule below; nor could I ever think
A mortal's law of power or strength sufficient
To abrogate th' unwritten law divine,
Immutable, eternal, not like these
Of yesterday, but made ere time began.
Shall men persuade me then to violate
Heaven's great commands, and make the gods my foes?
Without thy mandate, death had one day come;
For who shall 'scape it? and if not I fall
A little sooner, 'tis the thing I wish.
To those who live in misery like me,
Believe me, king, 'tis happiness to die;
Without remorse I shall embrace my fate;
But to my brother had I left the rites
Of sepulture unpaid, I then indeed
Had been most wretched. This to thee may seem
Madness and folly. If it be, 'tis fit
I should act thus—it but resembles thee.
CREON. Sprung from a sire perverse and obstinate,
Like him she cannot bend beneath misfortune;
But know, the proudest hearts may be subdued;
Hast thou marked the hardest steel by fire
Made soft and flexible? Myself have seen
By a slight rein the fiery courser held.
'Tis not for slaves to be so haughty; yet
This proud offender, not content, it seems
To violate my laws, adds crime to crime,
Smiles at my threats, and glories in her guilt;
If I should suffer her to 'scape my vengeance,
She were the man, not I; but though she sprang
E'en from my sister, were I bound to her
By ties more dear than in Hercaean Jove,
She should not 'scape. Her sister too I find
Accomplice in the deed—go, call her forth!
[*to one of the Attendants*
She is within, I saw her raving there,
Her senses lost, the common fate of those
Who practise dark and deadly wickedness.
[*Turning to* ANTIGONE
I cannot bear to see the guilty stand
Convicted of their crimes, and yet pretend
To gloss them o'er with specious names of virtue.
ANT. I am thy captive; thou wouldst have my life;
Will that content thee?
CREON. Yes; tis all I wish.
ANT. Why this delay then, when thou knowst my words
To thee as hateful are as thine to me?

Therefore dispatch; I cannot live to do
A deed more glorious; and so these would all
[*pointing to the* CHORUS
Confess, were not their tongues restrained by fear;
It is the tyrant's privilege, we know,
To speak and act whate'er he please, uncensured.

CREON. Lives there another in the land of Thebes
Who thinks as thou dost?

ANT. Yes, a thousand; these—
These think so too, but dare not utter it.

CREON. Dost thou not blush?

ANT. For what? Why blush to pay
A sister's duty?

CREON. But, Eteocles!
Say, was not he thy brother too?

ANT. He was.

CREON. Why then thus reverence him who least deserved it?

ANT. Perhaps that brother thinks not so.

CREON. He must,
If thou payst equal honour to them both.

ANT. He was a brother, not a slave.

CREON. One fought
Against that country which the other saved.

ANT. But equal death with rites of sepulture
Decrees to both.

CREON. What! Reverence alike
The guilty and the innocent!

ANT. Perhaps
The gods below esteem it just.

CREON. A foe,
Though dead, should as a foe be treated still.

ANT. My love shall go with thine, but not my hate.

CREON. Go then, and love them in the tomb! But know,
No woman rules in Thebes whilst Creon lives.

CHOR. Lo! At the portal stands the fair Ismene,
Tears in her lovely eyes, a cloud of grief
Sits on her brow, wetting her beauteous cheek
With pious sorrow for a sister's fate.

SCENE VI.

ISMENE, ANTIGONE, CREON, CHORUS.

CREON. Come forth, thou serpent! Little did I think
That I had nourished two such deadly foes
To suck my blood, and cast me from my throne.
What sayst thou? Wert thou accomplice in the deed,
Or wilt thou swear that thou art innocent?

ISM. I do acknowledge it, if she permit me;
I was accomplice, and the crime was mine.

ANT. 'Tis false; thou didst refuse, nor would I hold
Communion with thee.

ISM. But in thy misfortunes
Let me partake, my sister; let me be
A fellow-sufferer with thee.

ANT. Witness, death,
And ye infernal gods, to which belongs
The great, the glorious deed! I do not love
These friends in word alone.
ISM. Antigone,
Do not despise me; I but ask to die
With thee, and pay due honour to the dead.
ANT. Pretend not to a merit which thou has not.
Live thou; it is enough for me to perish.
ISM. But what is life without thee?
ANT. Ask they friend
And patron there. [*Pointing to* Creon.
ISM. Why that unkind reproach,
When thou shouldst rather comfort me?
ANT. Alas!
It gives me pain when I am forced to speak
So bitterly against thee.
ISM. Is there aught
That I can do to save thee?
ANT. Save thyself,
I shall not envy thee.
ISM. And will you not
Permit me then to share your fate?
ANT. Thy choice
Was life. 'Tis mine to die.
ISM. I told thee oft
It would be so.
ANT. Thou didst, and was't not well
Thus to fulfil thy prophecy?
ISM. The crime
Was mutual; mutual be the punishment.
ANT. Fear not. Thy life is safe, but mine long since
Devoted to the dead.
CREON. Both seem deprived
Of reason. One indeed was ever thus.
ISM. O king! The mind doth seldom keep her seat
When sunk beneath misfortunes.
CREON. Sunk indeed
Thou wert in wretchedness to join with her.
ISM. But what is life without Antigone?
CREON. Then think not of it. For she is no more.
ISM. Wouldst thou destroy thy son's long-destined wife?
CREON. Oh! we shall find a fitter bride.
ISM. Alas!
He will not think so.
CREON. I'll not wed my son
To a base woman.
ANT. O my dearest Haemon!
And is it thus thy father doth disgrace thee?
CREON. Such an alliance were as hateful to me
As is thyself.
ISM. Wilt thou then take her from him?
CREON. Their nuptials shall be finished by death.
ISM. She then must perish?

CREON. So must you and I;
Therefore no more delay. Go, take them hence;
Confine them both. Henceforth they shall not stir;
When death is near at hand the bravest fly.

CHORUS.

Strophe 1.

Thrice happy they, whose days in pleasure flow,
Who never taste the bitter cup of woe;
For when the wrath of heaven descends
On some devoted house, there foul disgrace,
With grief and all her train attends,
And shame and sorrow o'erwhelm the wretched race,
E'en as the Thracian sea, when vexed with storms,
Whilst darkness hangs incumbent o'er the deep,
When the black north the troubled scene deforms,
And the black sands in rapid whirlwinds sweep,
The groaning waves beat on the trembling shore,
And echoing hills rebellow to the roar.

Antistrophe 1.

O Labdacus! thy house must perish all—
E'en now I see the stately ruin fall;
Shame heaped on shame, and ill on ill,
Disgrace and never-ending woes;
Some angry god pursues thee still,
Nor grants or safety or repose.
One fair and lovely branch unwithered stood
And braved th' inclement skies;
But Pluto comes, inexorable god—
She sinks, she raves, she dies.

Strophe 2.

Shall man below control the gods above,
Whose eyes by all-subduing sleep
Are never closed as feeble mortals' are,
But still their watchful vigils keep
Through the large circle of th' eternal year!
Great lord of all, who neither time nor age
With envious stroke can weaken or decay;
He who alone the future can presage,
Who knows alike to-morrow as to-day;
Whilst wretched man is doomed, by Heaven's decree,
To toil and pain, to sin and misery.

Antistrophe 2.

Oftimes the flatterer Hope, that joy inspires,
Fills the proud heart of man with fond desires;
He, careless traveller, wanders sill
Through life, unmindful of deceit,

Nor dreads the danger, till he feel
The burning sands beneath his feet.
When heaven impels to guilt the maddening mind,
Then good like ill appears,
And vice, for universal hate designed,
The face of virtue wears. [*Exeunt.*

ACT III.

SCENE I.

CREON, HÆMON, CHORUS.

CHOR. Behold, O king! thy youngest hope appear—
The noble Haemon. Lost in grief he seems,
Weeping the fate of poor Antigone.

CREON. He comes, and better than a prophet, soon
Shall we divine his inmost thoughts. My son,
Com'st thou, well knowing our decree to mourn
Thy promised bride, and angry to dispute
A father's will; or, whatsoe'er we do
Still to hold best, and pay obedience to us?

HÆ. My father, I am thine. Do thou command,
And I in all things shall obey. 'Tis fit
My promised nuptial rites give place to thee.

CREON. It will become thee with obedience thus
To bear thee ever, and in every act
To yield submissive to a father's will:
'Tis therefore, O my son! that men do pray
For children who with kind officious duty
May guard their helpless age, resist their foes,
And like their parents love their parents' friend;
But he who gets a disobedient child,
What doth he get but misery and woe?
His enemies will laugh the wretch to scorn.
Take heed, my son, thou yield not up thy reason,
In hopes of pleasure from a worthless woman;
For cold is the embrace of impious love,
And deep the wounds of false dissembled friendship.
Hate then thy bitterest foe, despise her arts,
And leave her to be wedded to the tomb.
Of all the city her alone I found
Rebellious; but I have her, nor shall Thebes
Say I'm a liar: I pronounce her fate,
And she must perish. Let her call on Jove,
Who guards the rights of kindred and the ties
Of nature; for if those by blood united
Transgress the laws, I hold myself more near
E'en to a stranger. Who is private life
Is just and good, will to his country too
Be faithful ever; but the man who, proud
And fierce of soul, contemns authority,
Despiseth justice, and o'er those who rule
Would have dominion, such shall never gain
Th' applauding voice of Creon. He alone,
Whom the consenting citizens approve

Th' acknowledged sovereign, should in all command,
Just or unjust his laws, in things of great
Or little import, whatsoe'er he bids:
A subject is not to dispute his will;
He knows alike to rule and to obey;
And in the day of battle will maintain
The foremost rank, his country's best defence.
Rebellion is the worst of human ills;
This ruins kingdoms, this destroys the peace
Of noblest families, this wages war,
And puts the brave to flight; whilst fair obedience
Keeps all in safety. To preserve it ever
Should be a king's first care. We will not yield
To a weak woman; if we must submit,
At least we will be conquered by a man,
Nor by a female arm tush fall inglorious.

HÆ. Wisdom, my father, is the noblest gift
The gods bestow on man, and better far
Than all his treasures. Why thy judgment deems
Most fit, I cannot, would not reprehend.
Others perhaps might call it wrong. For me,
My duty only bids me to inform you
If aught be done or said that casts reproach
Or blame on you. Such terror would thy looks
Strike on the low plebeian, that he dare not
Say aught unpleasing to thee; be it mine
To tell thee then what I of late have heard
In secret whispered. Your afflicted people
United mourn th' unhappy virgin's fate
Unmerited, most wretched of her sex,
To die for deeds of such distinguished virtue,
For that she would not let a brother lie
Unburied, to the dogs and birds a prey;
Was it not rather, say the murmuring crowd,
Worthy of golden honours and fair praise?
Such are their dark and secret discontents.
Thy welfare and thy happiness alone
Are all my wish; what can a child desire
More than a father's honour, or a father
More than his child's? Oh! do not then retain
Thy will, and still believe no sense but thine
Can judge aright! The man who proudly thinks
None but himself or eloquent, or wise,
By time betrayed, is branded for an idiot;
True wisdom will be ever glad to learn,
And not too fond of power. Observe the trees
That mend to wintery torrents, how their boughs
Unhurt remain, whilst those that brave the storm,
Uprooted torn, shall wither and decay;
The pilot, whose unslackened sail defies
Contending winds, with shattered bark pursues
His dangerous course. Then mitigate thy wrath
My father, and give way to sweet repentance.
If to my youth be aught to judgment given,
He, who by knowledge and true wisdom's rules

Guides every action, is the first of men;
But since to few that happiness is given,
The next is he, who, not too proud to learn,
Follows the counsels of the wise and good,

CHOR. O king! if right the youth advise, 'tis fit
That thou shouldst listen to him; so to thee
Should he attend, as best may profit both.

CREON. And have we lived so long then to be taught
At last our duty by a boy like thee?

HÆ. Young though I am, I still may judge aright;
Wisdom in action lies, and not in years,

CREON. Call you it wisdom then to honour those
Who disobey the laws?

HÆ. I would not have thee
Protect the wicked.

CREON. Is she not most guilty

HÆ. Thebes doth not think her so.

CREON. Shall Thebes prescribe
To Creon's will?

HÆ. How weakly dost thou talk!

CREON. Am I king here, or shall another reign?

HÆ. 'Tis not a city where but one man rules.

CREON. The city is the king's.

HÆ. Go by thyself then,
And rule henceforth o'er a deserted land.

CREON. [*to the* Chorus]. He pleads the woman's cause.

HÆ. If thou art she,
I do; for, oh! I speak but for thy sake—
My care is all for thee.

CREON. Abandoned wretch!
Dispute a father's will!

HÆ. I see thee err,
And therefore do it.

CREON. Is it then a crime
To guard my throne and rights from violation?

HÆ. He cannot guard them who contemns the gods
And violates their laws.

CREON. Oh! thou are worse,
More impious e'en than her thou hast defended.

HÆ. Naught have I done to merit this reproof.

CREON. Hast thou not pleaded for her?

HÆ. No, for thee,
And for myself—for the infernal gods.

CREON. But know, she shall not live to be thy wife.

HÆ. Then she must die; another too may fall.

CREON. Ha! dost thou threaten me, audacious traitor?

HÆ. What are my threats? Alas! thou heedst them not.

CREON. That thou shalt see; thy insolent instruction
Shall cost thee dear.

HÆ. But for thou art my father
Now would I say thy senses were impaired.

CREON. Think not to make me thus thy scorn and laughter,
Thou woman's slave.

HÆ. Still wouldst thou speak thyself,

And never listen to the voice of truth;
Such is they will.

CREON. Now, by Olympus here!
I swear thy vile reproaches shall not pass
Unpunished. Call her forth!
[*To one of the Attendants.*
Before her bridegroom
She shall be brought, and perish in his sight.

HÆ. These eyes shall never see it. Let the slaves
Who fear thy rage submit to it; but know,
'Tis the last time thou shalt behold thy son.
[*Exit* HÆMON.

SCENE II.

CREON, CHORUS.

CHOR. Sudden in anger fled the youth. O king!
A mind oppressed like his is desperate.

CREON. Why, let him go! and henceforth better learn
Than to oppose me. Be it as it may,
Death is their portion, and he shall not save them.

CHOR. Must they both die then?

CREON. No; 'tis well advised,
Ismene lives; but for Antigone—

CHOR. O king! what death is she decreed to suffer?

CREON. Far from the haunts of men I'll have her led,
And in a rocky cave, beneath the earth,
Buried alive; with her a little food,
Enough to save the city from pollution.
There let her pray the only god she worships
To save her from this death; perhaps he will,
Or, if he doth not, let her learn how vain
It is to reverence the powers below. [*Exit* CREON.

SCENE III.

CHORUS.

Strophe 1.

Mighty power, all powers above,
Great unconquerable love!
Thou, who liest in dimple sleek
On the tender virgin's cheek,
Thee the rich and great obey,
Every creature owns thy sway.
O'er the wide earth and o'er the main
Extends thy universal reign;
All thy maddening influence know,
Gods above and men below;
All thy powers resistless prove,
Great unconquerable love!

Antistrophe 1.

Thou canst lead the just astray
From wisdom and from virtue's way;
The ties of nature cease to bind,
When thou disturbst the captive mind
Behold, enslaved by fond desire,
The youth condemns his aged sire
Enamoured of his beauteous maid,
Nor laws nor parents are obeyed;
Thus Venus wills it from above,
And great unconquerable love.

CHOR. E'en I beyond the common bounds of grief
Indulge my sorrows, and from these sad eyes
Fountains of tears will flow, when I behold
Antigone, unhappy maid, approach
The bed of death, and hasten to the tomb.

SCENE IV.

ANTIGONE, CHORUS.

ANT. Farewell, my friends, my countrymen, farewell!
Here on her last sad journey you behold
The poor Antigone; for never more
Shall I return, or view the light of day:
The hand of death conducts me to the shore
Of dreary Acheron; no nuptial song
Reserved for me—the wretched bride alone
Of Pluto now, and wedded to the tomb.

CHOR. Be it thy glory still, that by the sword
Thou fallst not, nor the slow-consuming hand
Of foul distemperature, but far distinguished
Above thy sex, and to thyself a law,
Doomst thy own death: so shall thy honour live,
And future ages venerate thy name.

ANT. Thus Tantalus' unhappy daughter fell,
The Phrygian Niobe. High on the top
Of towering Sipylus the rock enfolds her,
E'en as the ivy twines her tendrils round
The lofty oak; there still (as fame reports)
To melting showers and everlasting snow
Obvious she stands, her beauteous bosom wet
With tears, that from her ever-streaming eyes
Incessant flow. Her fate resembles mine.

CHOR. A goddess she, and from a goddess sprung;
We are but mortal, and from mortals born:
To meet the fate of gods thus in thy life,
And in thy death, oh! 'tis a glorious doom!

ANT. Alas! thou mockst me! Why, whilst yet I live,
Wouldst thou afflict me with reproach like this?
O my dear country! and my dearer friends
Its blest inhabitants, renowned Thebes!
And ye Dircaean fountains! you I call
To witness that I die by laws unjust,
To my deep prison unlamented go,

To my sad tomb—to fellow-sufferer there
To soothe my woes, the living, or the dead.

CHOR. Rashness like thine must meet with such reward;
A father's crimes, I fear, lie heavy on thee.

ANT. Oh! thou has touched my worst of miseries,
My father's fate, the woes of all our house,
The wretched race of Labdacus, renowned
For its misfortunes! Oh! the guilty bed
Of those from whom I sprang—unhappy offspring
Of parents most unhappy! Lo! to them
I go accursed—a virgin and a slave.
O my poor brother! most unfortunate
Were they sad nuptials—they have slain thy sister.

CHOR. Thy piety demands our praise; but know,
Authority is not to be despised;
'Twas thy own rashness brought destruction on thee.

ANT. Thus friendless, unlamented, I must tread
The destined path, no longer to behold
Yon sacred light, and none shall mourn my fate.

SCENE V.

CREON, ANTIGONE, CHORUS.

CREON. Know ye not, slaves like her, to death devoted,
Would never cease their wailings? Wherefore is it
You thus delay to execute my orders?
Let her be carried instant to the cave,
And leave her there alone, to live, or die;
Her blood rests not on us; but she no longer
Shall breathe on earth. [*Exit* CREON.

SCENE VI.

ANTIGONE, CHORUS.

ANT. O dreadful marriage bed!
O my deep dungeon! My eternal home,
Whither I go to join my kindred dead!
For now a few hath fell Persephone
Already ta'en; to her I go, the last
And most unhappy, ere my time was come;
But still I have sweet hope I shall not go
Unwelcome to my father, nor to thee,
My mother. Dear to thee, Eteocles,
Still shall I ever be. These pious hands
Washed your pale bodies, and adorned you both
With rites sepulchral, and libations due!
And thus, my Polynices, for my care
Of thee I am rewarded, and the good
Alone shall praise me. For a husband dead,
Nor, had I been a mother, for my children
Would I have dared to violate the laws:
Another husband and another child
Might soothe affliction. But, my parents dead,
A brother's loss could never be repaired,

And therefore did I dare the venturous deed,
And therefore die by Creon's dread command.
Ne'er shall I taste of Hymen's joys, or know
A mother's pleasures in her infant race;
But, friendless and forlorn, alive descend
Into the dreary mansions of the dead.
And how have I offended the just gods!
But wherefore call on them? Will they protect me,
When thus I meet with the reward of ill
For doing good? If this be just, ye gods,
If I am guilty, let me suffer for it.
But if the crime be theirs, oh! let them feel
That weight of misery they have laid on me!

CHOR. The storm continues, and her angry soul
Still pours its sorrows forth.

SCENE VII.

CREON, ANTIGONE, CHORUS.

CREON. The slaves shall suffer
For this delay.

ANT. Alas! death cannot be
Far from that voice.

CREON. I would not have thee hope
A moment's respite.

ANT. O my country's gods!
And thou, my native Thebes! I leave you now.
Look on me, princes—see the last of all
My royal race—see what I suffer, see
From whom I bear it, from the worst of men,
Only because I did delight in virtue. [*Exit* CREON.

SCENE VIII.

ANTIGONE, CHORUS.

CHORUS.

Strophe 1.

Remember what fair Danae endured,
Condemned to change heaven's cheerful light
For scenes of horror and of night,
Within a brazen tower long time immured;
Yet was the maid of noblest race,
And honoured e'en with Jove's embrace;
But, oh! when fate decrees a mortal's woe
Naught can reverse the doom or stop the blow—
Nor heaven above, nor earth and seas below.

Antistrophe 1.

The Thracian monarch, Dryas' hapless son,
Chained to a rock in torment lay,
And breathed his angry soul away,
By wrath misguided, and by pride undone;

Taught by the offended god to know
From foul reproach what evils flow;
For he the rites profaned with slanderous tongue,
The holy flame he quenched, disturbed the song,
And waked to wrath the Muses' tuneful throng.

Strophe 2.

His turbid waves where Salmydessus rolled,
And proud Cyanea's rocks divide the flood,
There from thy temple, Mars, didst thou behold
The sons of Phineus weltering in their blood;
A mother did the cruel deed,
A mother bade her children bleed;
Both by her impious hand, deprived of light,
In vain lamented long their ravished sight,
And closed their eyes in never-ending night.

Antistrophe 2.

Long time they wept a better mother's fate,
Unhappy offspring of a luckless bed?
Yet nobly born, and eminently great
Was she, and midst sequestered caverns bred—
Her father's angry storms among,
Daughter of gods, from Boreas sprung—
Equal in swiftness to the bounding steed,
She skimmed the mountains with a courser's speed,
Yet was the nymph to death and misery decreed.
[*Exeunt.*

ACT IV.

SCENE I.

TIRESIAS, GUIDE, CREON, CHORUS.

TIR. Princes of Thebes, behold, conducted hither
By my kind guide—such is the blind man's fate—
Tiresias comes!
CREON. O venerable prophet!
What hast thou to impart?
TIR. I will inform thee;
Observe, and be obedient.
CREON. Have I not been ever so?
TIR. Thou hast; and therefore Thebes
Hath flourished still—
CREON. By thy protecting hand.
TIR. Therefore be wise. For know, this very hour
Is the important crisis of thy fate.
CREON. Speak then! What is it? How I dread words!
TIR. When thou has heard the portents which my art
But now discovered, thou wilt see it all.
Know then that, sitting on my ancient throne
Augurial, whence each divination comes,
Sudden a strange unusual noise was heard

Of birds, whose loud and barbarous dissonance
I knew not how to interpret. By the sound
Of clashing wings I could discover well
That with their bloody claws they tore each other;
Amazed and fearful, instantly I tried
On burning altars holy sacrifice—
When, from the victim, lo! the sullen flame
Aspired not. Smothered in the ashes still
Laid the moist flesh, and, rolled in smoke, repelled
The rising fire, whilst from their fat the thighs
Were separate. All these signs of deadly omen,
Boding dark vengeance, did I learn from him;
[*Pointing to the* Guide.
He is my leader, king, and I am thine.
Then mark me well. From thee these evils flow,
From thy unjust decree. Our altars all
Have been polluted by th' unhallowed food
Of birds and dogs, that preyed upon the corse
Of wretched Œdipus's unhappy son;
Nor will the gods accept our offered prayers,
Or from our hands receive the sacrifice;
No longer will the birds send forth their sounds
Auspicious, fattened thus with human blood.
Consider this, my son. And, oh! remember,
To err is human—'tis the common lot
Of frail mortality; and he alone
Is wise and happy, who, when ills are done,
Persists not, but would heal the wound he made;
But self-sufficient obstinacy ever
Is folly's utmost height. Where is the glory
To slay the slain or persecute the dead?
I wish thee well, and therefore have spoke thus;
When those who love advise 'tis sweet to learn.

CREON. I know, old man, I am the general mark,
The butt of all, and you all aim at me.
For me I know your prophecies were made,
And I am sold to this detested race—
Betrayed to them. But make your gains! Go, purchase
Your Sardian amber, and your Indian gold;
They shall not buy a tomb for Polynices.
No, should the eagle seek him for his food,
And towering bear him to the throne of Jove,
I would not bury him. For well I know
The gods by mortals cannot be polluted;
But the best men, by sordid gain corrupt,
Say all that's ill, and fall beneath the lowest.

TIR. Who knows this, or who dare accuse us of it?

CREON. What meanst thou by that question? Askst thou who?

TIR. How far is wisdom beyond every good!

CREON. As far as folly beyond every ill.

TIR. That's a distemper thou 'rt afflicted with.

CREON. I'll not revile a prophet.

TIR. But thou dost;
Thou'lt not believe me.

CREON. Your prophetic race

Are lovers all of gold.
TIR. Tyrants are so,
Howe'er ill-gotten.
CREON. Knowst thou 'tis a king
Thou'rt talking thus to?
TIR. Yes, I know it well;
A king who owes to me his country's safety.
CREON. Thou'rt a wise prophet, but thou art unjust.
TIR. Thou will oblige me then to utter that
Which I had purposed to conceal.
CREON. Speak out,
Say what thou wilt, but say it not for hire.
TIR. Thus may it seem to thee.
CREON. But know, old man,
I am not to be sold.
TIR. Remember this:
Not many days shall the bright sun perform
His stated course, ere, sprung from thy own loins,
Thyself shall yield a victim. In thy turn
Thou too shalt weep, for that thy cruel sentence
Decreed a guiltless virgin to the tomb,
And kept on earth, unmindful of the gods,
Ungraced, unburied, and unhallowed corse,
Which not to thee, nor to the gods above
Of right belonged. 'Twas arbitrary power:
But the avenging furies lie concealed,
The ministers of death have spread the snare,
And with like woes await to punish thee.
Do I say this from hopes of promised gold?
Pass but a little time, and thou shalt hear
The shrieks of men, the women's loud laments
O'er all thy palace; see th' offended people
Together rage; thy cities all by dogs
And beasts and birds polluted, and the stench
Of filth, obscene on ever altar laid.
Thus from my angry soul have I sent forth
Its keenest arrows—for thou hast provoked me—
Nor shall they fly in vain, or thou escape
The destined blow. Now, boy, conduct me home.
On younger heads the tempest of his rage
Shall fall; but, henceforth let him learn to speak
In humbler terms, and bear a better mind.
[*Exit* TIRESIAS.

SCENE II.

CREON, CHORUS.

CHOR. He's gone, and dreadful were his prophecies;
Since these grey hairs were o'er my temples spread
Nought from those lips hath flowed but sacred truth.
CREON. I know there hath not, and am troubled much.
For the event; 'tis grating to submit.
And yet the mind spite of itself must yield
In such distress.
CHOR. Son of Menaeceus, now

	Thou needst most counsel.
CREON.	What wouldst thou advise? I will obey thee.
CHOR.	Set the virgin free, And let a tomb be raised for Polynices.
CREON.	And dost thou counsel thus?—and must I yield?
CHOR.	Immediately, O king! for vengeance falls With hasty footsteps on the guilty head.
CREON.	I cannot—yet I must reverse the sentence; There is no struggling with necessity.
CHOR.	Do it thyself, nor trust another hand.
CREON.	I will; and you my servants, be prepared; Each with his axe quick hasten to the place; Myself-for thus I have resolved—will go, And the same hand that bound shall set her free; For, oh! I fear 'tis wisest still through life To keep our ancient laws, and follow virtue.

SCENE III.

CHORUS.

Strophe 1.

Bacchus, by various names to mortals known,
Fair Semele's illustrious son,
Offspring of thunder-bearing Jove,
Who honourst famed Italia with thy love!
Who dwellst where erst the dragon's teeth were strewed,
Or where Ismenus pours his gentle flood;
Who dost o'er Ceres' hallowed rites preside,
And at thy native Thebes propitious still reside.

Antistrophe 1.

Where famed Parnassus' forked hills uprise,
To thee ascends the sacrifice;
Corycia's nymphs attend below,
Whilst from Castalia's fount fresh waters flow:
O'er Nysa's mountains wreaths of ivy twine,
And mix their tendrils with the clustering vine:
Around their master crowd the virgin throng,
And praise the god of Thebes in never-dying song.

Strophe 2.

Happiest of cities, Thebes! above the rest
By Semele and Bacchus blest!
Oh! visit now thy once beloved abode,
Oh! heal our woes, thou kind protecting god!
From steep Parnassus, or th' Eubaean sea,
With smiles auspicious come, and bring with thee
Health, joy, and peace, and fair prosperity.

Antistrophe 2.

Immortal leader of the maddening choir,
Whose torches blaze with unextinguished fire,
Great son of Jove, who guidst the tuneful throng,
Thou, who presidest o'er the nightly song,
Come with thy Naxian maids, a festive train,
Who, wild with joy, and raging o'er the plain,
For thee the dance prepare, to thee devote the strain.

[*Exeunt.*

ACT V.

SCENE I.

MESSENGER, CHORUS.

MESSENGER. Ye race to Cadmus, sons of ancient Thebes,
Henceforth no state of human life to me
Shall be or valued or despised: for all
Depends on fortune; she exalts the low,
And casts the mighty down. The fate of men
Can never be foretold. There was a time
When Creon lived in envied happiness,
Ruled o'er renowned Thebes, which from her foes
He had delivered, with successful power;
Blest in his kingdom, in his children blest,
He stretched o'er all his universal sway.
Now all is gone: when pleasure is no more,
Man is but an animated corse,
Nor can be said to live; he may be rich,
Or decked with regal honours, but if joy
Be absent from him, if he tastes them not,
'Tis useless grandeur all, and empty shade.

CHOR. Touching our royal master, bringst thou news
Of sorrow to us?

MES. They are dead; and those
Who lived with dreadful cause.

CHOR. Quick, tell us who—
The slayer and the slain!

MES. Haemon is dead.

CHOR. Dead! by what hand, his father's or his own?

MES. Enraged and grieving for his murdered love,
He slew himself.

CHOR. O prophet! thy predictions
Were but too true!

MES. Since thus it be, 'tis fit
We should consult; our present state demands it,

CHOR. But see! Eurydice, the wretched wife
Of Creon, comes this way; or chance hath brought her,
Or Haemon's hapless fate hath reached her ear.

SCENE II.

EURYDICE, MESSENGER, CHORUS.

EUR. O citizens! as to Minerva's fane
E'en now I went to pay my vows, the doors
I burst, and heard imperfectly the sound
Of most disastrous news which touched me near.
Breathless I fell amidst the virgin throng;
And now I come to know the dreadful truth:
Whate'er it be, I'll hear it now; for, oh!
I am no stranger to calamity.

MES. The mark, my mistress, I will tell thee all,
Nor will I pass a circumstance unmentioned.
Should I deceive thee with an idle tale
'Twere soon discovered. Truth is always best.
Know then, I followed Creon to the field,
Where, torn by dogs, the wretched carcase lay
Of Polynices. First to Proserpine
And angry Pluto, to appease their wrath,
Our humble prayers addressing, there we laved
In the pure stream the body; then, with leaves
Fresh gathered covering, burnt his poor remains,
And on the neighbouring turf a tomb upraised.
Then, towards the virgin's rocky cave advanced,
When from the dreadful chamber a sad cry
As from afar was heard, a servant ran
To tell the king, and still as we approached
The sound of sorrow from a voice unknown
And undistinguished issued forth. Alas!
Said Creon: "Am I then a faithful prophet?
And do I tread a more unhappy path
Than e'er I went before? It is my son—
I know his voice! But get ye to the door,
My servants, close, look through the stony heap;
Mark if it be so. Is it Haemon's voice?"
Again he cried: "Or have the gods deceived me?"
Thus spoke the king. We, to our mournful lord
Obedient, looked, and saw Antigone
Down in the deepest hollow of the cave,
By her own vestments hung. Close by her side
The wretched youth, embracing in his arms
Her lifeless corse, weeping his father's crime,
His ravished bride, and horrid nuptial bed,
Creon beheld, and loud reproaching cried:
"What art thou doing? What's thy dreadful purpose?
What means my son? Come forth, my Haemon, come!
Thy father begs thee." With indignant eye
The youth looked up, nor scornful deigned an answer,
But silent drew his sword, and with fell rage
Struck at his father, who by flight escaped
The blow; then on himself bent all his wrath,
Full in his side the weapon fixed; but still,
Whilst life remained, on the soft bosom hung
Of the dear maid, and his lost spirit breathed

O'er her pale cheek discoloured with his blood.
Thus lay the wretched pair in death united,
And celebrate their nuptials in the tomb—
To future times a terrible example
Of the sad woes which rashness ever brings.
[*Exit* EURYDICE.

SCENE III.

MESSENGER, CHORUS.

CHOR. What can this mean? She's gone, without a word.
MES. 'Tis strange, and yet I trust she will not loud
Proclaim her griefs to all, but—for I know
She's ever prudent—with her virgin train
In secret weep her murdered Haemon's fate.
CHOR. Clamour indeed were vain; but such deep silence
Doth ever threaten horrid consequence.
MES. Within we soon shall know if aught she hide
Of deadly purport in her angry soul;
For well thou sayst her silence is most dreadful.
[*Exit* MESSENGER.
CHOR. But lo! the king himself: and in his arms
See his dead son, the monument accursed
Of his sad fate, which, may we say unblamed,
Sprang not from others' guilt, but from his own.

SCENE IV.

CREON, MESSENGER, CHORUS.

CREON *enters, bearing the body of* HÆMON

CREON. Ah me! What deadly woes from the bad mind
Perpetual flow. Thus in one wretched house
Have you beheld the slayer and the slain!
O fatal counsels! O unhappy son!
Thus with thy youthful bride to sink to death;
Thou diest, my child, and I alone have killed thee!
CHOR. Oh king! thy justice comes too late.
CREON. It doth,
I know it well, unhappy as I am;
For oh! the god this heavy weight of woe
Hast cast upon me, and his fiercest wrath
Torments me now, changing my joyful state
To keenest anguish. Oh! the fruitless toils
Of wretched mortals!

SCENE V.

MESSENGER, CREON, CHORUS.

MES. Thus oppressed, my lord,
With bitterest misfortune, more affliction
Awaits thee still, which thou wilt find within.

CREON. And can there be more woes? Is aught to come
More horrible than this?

MES. The queen is dead;
Her wounds yet fresh. Eager, alas! to show
A mother's love, she followed her lost child.

CREON. O death insatiate! how dost thou afflict me!
What cruel news, thou messenger of ill,
Hast thou brought now?

CHOR. A wretch, already dead
With grief, thy horrid tale once more hath slain.

CREON. Didst thou not say a fresh calamity
Had fallen upon me? Didst thou not say my wife
Was dead, alas! for grief of Haemon's fate?
[*Scene opens and discovers the body of* EURYDICE.

MES. Behold her there!

CREON. O me! another blow!
What now remains? What can I suffer more,
Thus bearing in these arms my breathless son?
My wife too dead! O most unhappy mother!
And oh! thou wretched child!

MES. Close by the altar
She drew the sword, and closed her eyes in death,
Lamenting first her lost Megareus' fate
And Haemon's death, with imprecations dire
Still poured on thee, the murderer of thy son.

CREON. I shudder at it? Will no friendly hand
Destroy me quickly? For oh! I am most wretched—
Beset with miseries!

MES. She accused thee oft,
And said the guilt of both their deaths was thine.

CREON. Alas! I only am to blame. 'Twas I
Who killed thee, Haemon; I confess my crime.
Bear me, my servants, bear me far from hence,
For I am—nothing.

CHOR. If in ills like these
Aught can be well, thou has determined right:
When least we see our woes, we feel them least.

CREON. Quick let my last, my happiest hour appear!
Would it were come, the period of my woes!
Oh! that I might not see another day!

CHOR. Time must determine that: the present hour
Demands our care; the rest be left to heaven.

CREON. But I have wished and prayed for't.

CHOR. Pray for nothing;
There's no reversing the decrees of fate.

CREON. Take hence this useless load, this guilty wretch
Who slew his child, who slew e'en thee, my wife;
I know not whither to betake me, where
To turn my eyes, for all is dreadful round me,
And fate hath weighed me down on every side.

CHOR. Wisdom alone is man's true happiness;
We are not to dispute the will of heaven;
For ever are the boastings of the proud
By the just gods repaid, and man at last
Is taught to fear their anger, and be wise.

Poetry: Sappho (615?–? BC)

Sappho, a Greek lyric poet, was born on the island of Lesbos off the coast of Asia Minor and spent most of her life there. Sappho married Cercolas, a wealthy member of the island nobility. She was devoted to her daughter, Cleis, whose name survives in a poetic fragment. Little beyond these facts is known about Sappho. Sappho gathered around her a group of girls interested in poetry and organized perhaps as a cult in honor of Aphrodite, and in their honor, she composed many of her poems. These poems reveal Sappho's profound affection for girls and women in her circle of friends: how they delight and disappoint her and how they bring her sorrow and happiness. Sappho also invokes Aphrodite to help her when her affection for these women is not reciprocated. Though these homoerotic affections for friends are thematic, they do not necessarily imply active lesbianism. Rather they may be considered in the context of a world in which domineering male nobility was often absent, at war; consequently, close associations among women were natural, honorable, and acceptable.

The Poetry of Sappho: Background

Of the early Greek lyricists, Sappho is easily the most important. Her accomplishment as an artist was virtually unrivaled, and the ancient world referred to her as the "Tenth Muse," a distinction not to be taken lightly. Living in a time when women did not write, Sappho proved that a woman could equal—even surpass—the male poets of her day. As headmistress of a school devoted to the education of bright young women, Sappho composed some nine books of poetry, only a fragment of which is extant, that acquired a commanding position in the world of poetry.

Sappho's poems are *monodies*, songs for a single voice. As lyrics, her poems were intended to be performed with the accompaniment of a lyre. She personally invented a twenty-one string lyre, which she used when reciting her poems. Love is the predominant theme of her poems. Sappho's style is marked by intense emotion, eroticism, sensuality, controlled meter, simplicity of form, and beauty of diction, with powerful expressions of love, introspection, and yearning. While her themes are sensuous, her expression of them is exalted and refined.

The Sapphic stanza derived its name from the Greek poet. The pattern consists of a four-lined stanza, three lines of eleven syllables (two trochees, a dactyl, and two more trochees) and a fourth and shorter line of five syllables (a dactyl and a trochee). Her characteristic metrical form can be imitated though not exactly reproduced in English. However, her form greatly influenced later poets such as Catullus and Horace. As evidenced by her careful attention to verse patterns, Sappho by no means was given to artificial embellishment. Her seemingly simple style embodied a keen sensitivity to graceful, polished art forms.

The fragmentary remains of her poems include wedding songs (written for the girls who left the group to marry), elegies, hymns, and odes. Because her students were frequently the objects of her affection in these very sensual poems of love, Sappho's name has been associated with lesbianism. Without doubt however, Sappho was a poetic genius and a lone female voice in a literary world dominated by men. Her painstaking craftsmanship and bold expression helped her rise to her place as preeminent Greek lyricist.

Selected Bibliography

Snyder, Jane McIntosh. *The Woman and the Lyre: Women Writers in Classical Greece and Rome*. Carbondale: Southern Illinois UP, 1989.

Throned in Splendor, Deathless, O Aphrodite

Throned in splendor, deathless, O Aphrodite,
child of Zeus, charm-fashioner, I entreat you
not with griefs and bitternesses to break my spirit,
O goddess:

standing by me rather, if once before now
far away you heard, when I called upon you,
left your father's dwelling place and descended,
yoking the golden

chariot to sparrows, who fairly drew you
down in speed aslant the black world, the bright air
trembling at the heart to the pulse of countless
fluttering wingbeats.

Swiftly then they came, and you, blessed lady,
smiling on me out of immortal beauty,
asked me what affliction was on me, why I
called thus upon you,

what beyond all else I would have befall
my tortured heart: "Whom then would you have Persuasion
force to serve desire in your heart? Who is it,
Sappho, that hurt you?

Though she now escape, she soon will follow;
though she take not gifts from you, she will give them:
though she love not, yet she will surely love you
even unwilling."

In such guise come even again and set me
free from doubt and sorrow; accomplish all those
things my heart desires to be done; appear and
stand at my shoulder.

Like the Very Gods in My Sight Is He

Like the very gods in my sight is he who
sits where he can look in your eyes, who listens
close to you, to hear the soft voice, its sweetness
murmur in love and

laughter, all for him. But it breaks my spirit;
underneath my breast all the heart is shaken.
Let me only glance where you are, the voice dies,
I can say nothing,

but my lips are stricken to silence, underneath my skin the tenuous flame suffuses;
nothing shows in front of my eyes, my ears are
muted in thunder.

And the sweat breaks running upon me, fever
shakes my body, paler I turn than grass is;
I can feel that I have been changed, I feel that
death has come near me.

Some There Are Who Say That the Fairest Thing Seen

Some there are who say that the fairest thing seen
on the black earth is an array of horsemen;
some, men marching; some would say ships; but I say
she whom one loves best

is the loveliest. Light were the work to make this
plain to all, since she, who surpassed in beauty
all mortality. Helen once forsaking
her lordly husband,

fled away to Troy—land across the water.
Not the thought of child nor beloved parents
was remembered, after the Queen of Cyprus[1]
won her at first sight.

Since young brides have hearts that can be persuaded
easily, light things, palpitant to passion
as am I, remembering Anaktória
who has gone from me

and whose lovely walk and the shining pallor
of her face I would rather see before my
eyes than Lydia's chariots in all their glory
armored for battle.

1. Aphrodite.

Narrative
Hesiod (8th Century BC)

Little is known of the life of Hesiod, a Greek peasant and epic poet who probably lived during the 700's B.C. He was born in Ascra, a village in Boeotia, a district in ancient Greece. His father, who was from Aeolia, had settled in Ascra, near Mount Helicon. Hesiod lived in Ascra as a farmer for most of his life. Though such works have been ascribed to him as *The Shield, Catalogue of Women, The Precepts of Chiron,* and the epic *Aegimus* (all extinct), Hesiod is known to have written only two very different poems: *Works and Days,* a long, four-part poem written in dactylic hexameter; and the *Theogony.* Among other themes, in *Works and Days,* Hesiod describes his life and his tribulations. Readers are given accounts of everyday reality, e.g., of a man of humble status who speaks of topics ranging from summer feasts, winter clothing, and harvest times to Hesiod's origins, his differences with his brother, and his trip to Chalcis, which he took to further his career. In Part I of *Works and Days* Hesiod gives moral advice to Perses, his brother, who, with the help of judges, defrauded him of his inheritance. Part II deals with farm operations and information about navigation. Part III contains general precepts and practical, though philosophical proverbs. Part IV consists of a collection of superstitions. Written in dactylic hexameter, the *Theogony,* said to be one of the earliest sources of Greek religion, is a systematized mythology that provides pedigrees of the divinities as well as their genealogy. It also recounts stories of the war between the Titans, particularly Sky, whom Cronus dethrones, and Cronus' son Zeus, who, with the other Olympians, usurps Cronus' throne.

Theogony: Background

The overall design of the *Theogony* is based on the genealogy of Grecian divinities as well as their violent succession to the throne, i.e., the handing of power from one god to another younger, more powerful one through a means most brutal. This pattern begins with the evolution of the gods from Chaos (the Void), Eros, and Earth, whose offspring are Sky and Sea. The older gods, the Titans (Ocean, Tethys, Cronus, Rhea, and their siblings) are also children of earth. Cronus overthrew Sky, and later his son, Zeus, overthrew Cronus, to usher in a new regime.

In the prologue to the *Theogony,* Hesiod introduces several innovative, personal, realistic and surprisingly modern themes like morality, justice, force, and work, along with a few original syntactical devices like depictions of his personal life. Hesiod begins the *Theogony* by praising Zeus' victory, and, in so doing, implying that Zeus' new and different reign is more morally right than that of his predecessors. He continues this moral theme by providing genealogies for "gods" who are, in fact, moral concepts. For example, he says that nominal abstractions like Strife or Eris, painful Sorrow, Oblivion, Hunger, tearful Griefs, though personified, are, in fact, moral concepts. He shows his craving for morality and justice when he asserts at the beginning of the *Theogony* that the gifts of the muses are to insure that kings administer justice with fairness and objectivity. He even has Justice appear as one of Zeus' kin in the form of Themis, one of Zeus' lovers. Later, he portrays Zeus as the guarantor of justice. The tale of the nightingale and the hawk shows the conflict between justice and force when the hawk remarks satirically to the nightingale that the latter should not cry out because the nightingale was caught in the grip of someone much stronger than he. Hesiod links justice to work. He believes that human beings must live honest lives and that no good will result from advantages or benefits accrued by corrupt means. He contrasts hard work with dishonesty and believes work brings human beings closer to the gods.[1]

The *Theogony* contains several accounts of personal experiences in which Hesiod mentions a specific place and an individual man, himself. He invokes the aid of the nine muses who inspire him when they appear to him on Mount Helicon. In fact, he names himself in the third person when he says that the muses taught Hesiod a beautiful song. They also offered him a laurel and breathed into him divine speech so that he could sing of both the past and the future. The direct link between the muses and the poet implies a higher, more exalted level of poetic expression than that of his forbears.

The *Theogony* also traces the myths of Prometheus and of Pandora as well as delineates the devolving races of man: the golden, silver, bronze, heroic and iron. Each race is heavier in material composition and inferior in word and deed than the preceding one. The iron race not only still exists on the earth but is the one most filled with violence, corruption and human suffering.

Note

1. The Greeks have never valued work nor does it figure prominently as a theme in their literary productions.

Theogony

Verily at the first Chaos came to be, but next wide-bosomed Earth, the ever-sure foundation of all the deathless ones who hold the peaks of snowy Olympus, and dim Tartarus in the depth of the wide-pathed Earth, and Eros (Love), fairest among the deathless gods, who unnerves the limbs' and overcomes the mind and wise counsels of all gods and all men within them. From Chaos came forth Erebus and black Night; but of Night were born Aether and Day, whom she conceived and bare from union in love with Erebus. And Earth first bare starry Heaven, equal to herself, to cover her on every side, and to be an ever-sure abiding-place for the blessed gods. And she brought forth long Hills, graceful haunts of the goddess-Nymphs who dwell amongst the glens of the hills. She bare also the fruitless deep with his raging swell, Pontus, without sweet union of love. But afterwards she lay with Heaven and bare deep-swirling Oceanus, Coeus and Crius and Hyperion and Iapetus, Theia and Rhea, Themis and Mnemosyne and gold-crowned Phoebe and lovely Tethys. After them was born Cronos the wily, youngest and most terrible of her children, and he hated his lusty sire.

And again, she bare the Cyclopes, overbearing in spirit, Brontes, and Steropes and stubborn-hearted Arges, who gave Zeus the thunder and made the thunderbolt: in all else they were like the gods, but one eye only was set in the midst of their foreheads. And they were surnamed Cyclopes (Orb-eyed) because one orbed eye was set in their foreheads. Strength and might and craft were in their works.

And again, three other sons were born of Earth and Heaven, great and doughty beyond telling, Cottus and Briareos and Gyes, presumptuous children. From their shoulders sprang an hundred arms, not to be approached, and each had fifty heads upon his shoulders on their strong limbs, and irresistible was the stubborn strength that was in their great forms. For of all the children that were born of Earth and Heaven, these were the most terrible, and they were hated by their own father from the first. And he used to hide them all away in a secret place of Earth so soon as each was born, and would not suffer them to come up into the light: and Heaven rejoiced in his evil doing. But vast Earth groaned within, being straitened, and she thought a crafty and an evil wile. Forthwith she made the element of grey flint and shaped a great sickle, and told her plan to her dear sons. And she spoke, cheering them, while she was vexed in her dear heart:

"My children, gotten of a sinful father, if you will obey me, we should punish the vile outrage of your father; for he first thought of doing shameful things."

So she said; but fear seized them all, and none of them uttered a word. But great Cronos the wily took courage and answered his dear mother:

"Mother, I will undertake to do this deed, for I reverence not our father of evil name, for he first thought of doing shameful things."

So he said: and vast Earth rejoiced greatly in spirit, and set and hid him in an ambush, and put in his hands a jagged sickle, and revealed to him the whole plot.

And Heaven came, bringing on night and longing for love, and he lay about Earth spreading himself full upon her. Then the son from his ambush stretched forth his left hand and in his right took the great long sickle with jagged teeth, and swiftly lopped off his own father's members and cast them away to fall behind him. And not vainly did they fall from his hand; for all the bloody drops that gushed forth Earth received, and as the seasons moved round she bare the strong Erinyes and the great Giants with gleaming armour, holding long spears in their hands, and the Nymphs whom they call Meliae all over the boundless earth. And so soon as he had cut off the members with flint and cast them from the land into the surging sea, they were swept away over the main a long time: and a white foam spread around them from the immortal flesh, and in it there grew a maiden. First she drew near holy Cythera, and from there, afterwards, she came to sea-girt Cyprus, and came forth an awful and lovely goddess, and grass grew up about her beneath her shapely feet. Her gods and men call Aphrodite, and the foam-born goddess and rich-crowned Cytherea, because she grew amid the foam, and Cytherea because she reached Cythera, and Cyprogenes because she was born in billowy Cyprus, and Philommedes because she sprang from the members. And with her went Eros, and comely Desire followed her at her birth at the first and as she went into the assembly of the gods. This honour she has from the beginning, and this is the portion allotted to her amongst men and undying gods,—the whisperings of maidens and smiles and deceits with sweet delight and love and graciousness.

But these sons whom he begot himself great Heaven used to call Titans (Strainers) in reproach, for he said that they strained and did presumptuously a fearful deed, and that vengeance for it would come afterwards.

And Night bare hateful Doom and black Fate and Death, and she bare Sleep and the tribe of Dreams. And again the goddess murky Night, though she lay with none, bare Blame and painful Woe, and the Hesperides who guard the rich, golden apples and the trees bearing fruit beyond glorious Ocean. Also she bare the Destinies and ruthless avenging Fates, Clotho and Lachesis and Atropos, who give men at their birth both evil and good to have, and they pursue the transgressions of men and of gods; and these goddesses never cease from their dread anger until they punish the sinner with a sore penalty. Also deadly Night bare Nemesis (Indignation) to afflict mortal men, and after her, Deceit and Friendship and hateful Age and hard-hearted Strife.

But abhorred Strife bare painful Toil and Forgetfulness and Famine and tearful Sorrows, Fightings also, Battles, Murders, Manslaughters, Quarrels, Lying Words, Disputes, Lawlessness and Ruin, all of one nature, and Oath who most troubles men upon earth when anyone wilfully swears a false oath.

And Sea begat Nereus, the eldest of his children, who is true and lies not: and men call him the Old Man because he is trusty and gentle and does not forget the laws of righteousness, but thinks just and kindly thoughts. And yet again he got great Thaumas and proud Phoreys, being mated with Earth, and fair-cheekèd Ceto and Eurybia who has a heart of flint within her.

And of Nereus and rich-haired Doris, daughter of Ocean the perfect river, were born children, passing lovely amongst goddesses, Ploto, Eucrante, Sao, and Amphitrite, and Eudora, and Thetis, Galene and Glauce, Cymothoë, Speo, Thoë and lovely Halie, and Pasithea, and Erato, and rosy-armed Eunice, and gracious Melite, and Eulimene, and Agaue, Doto, Proto, Pherusa, and Dynamene, and Nisaea, and Actaea, and Protomedea, Doris, Panopea, and comely Galatea, and lovely Hippothoë, and rosy-armed Hipponoë, and Cymodoce who with Cymatolege and Amphitrite easily calms the waves upon the misty sea and the blasts of raging winds, and Cymo, and Eïone, and rich-crowned Alimede, and Glauconome, fond of laughter, and Pontoporea, Leagore, Euagore, and Laomedea, and Polynoë, and Autonoë, and Lysianassa, and Euarne, lovely of shape and without blemish of form, and Psamathe of charming figure and divine Menippe, Neso, Eupompe, Themisto, Pronoë, and Nemertes who has the nature of her deathless father. These fifty daughters sprang from blameless Nereus, skilled in excellent crafts.

And Thaumas wedded Electra the daughter of deep-flowing Ocean, and she bare him swift Iris and the long-haired Harpies, Aëllo (Storm-swift) and Ocypetes (Swift-flier) who on their swift wings keep pace with the blasts of the winds and the birds; for quick as time they dart along.

And again, Ceto bare to Phoreys the fair-cheeked Graiae, sisters grey from their birth: and both deathless gods and men who walk on earth call them Graiae, Pemphredo well-clad, and saffron-robed Enyo, and the Gorgons who dwell beyond glorious Ocean in the frontier land towards Night where are the clear-voiced Hesperides, Sthenno, and Euryale, and Medusa who suffered a woeful fate: she was mortal, but the two were undying and grew not old. With her lay the Dark-haired One in a soft meadow amid spring flowers. And when Perseus cut off her head, there sprang forth great Chrysaor and the horse Pegasus who is so called because he was born near the springs (*pegae*) of Ocean; and that other, because he held a golden blade (*aor*) in his hands. Now Pegasus flew away and left the earth, the mother of flocks, and came to the deathless gods: and he dwells in the house of Zeus and brings to wise Zeus the thunder and lightning. But Chrysaor was joined in love to Callirrhoë, the daughter of glorious Ocean, and begot three-headed Geryones. Him mighty Heracles slew in sea-girt Erythea by his shambling oxen on that day when he drove the wide-browed oxen to holy Tiryns, and had crossed the ford of Ocean and killed Orthus and Eurytion the herdsman in the dim stead out beyond glorious Ocean.

And in a hollow cave she bare another monster, irresistible, in no wise like either to mortal men or to the undying gods, even the goddess fierce Echidna who is half a nymph with glancing eyes and fair cheeks, and half again a huge snake, great and awful, with speckled skin, eating raw flesh beneath the secret parts of the holy earth. And there she has a cave deep down under a hollow rock far from the deathless gods and mortal men. There, then, did the gods appoint her a glorious house to dwell in: and she keeps guard in Arima beneath the earth, grim Echidna, a nymph who dies not nor grows old all her days.

Men say that Typhaon the terrible, outrageous and lawless, was joined in love to her, the maid with glancing eyes. So she conceived and brought forth fierce offspring; first she bare Orthus the hound of Geryones, and then again she bare a second, a monster not to be overcome and that may not be described,

Cerberus who eats raw flesh, the brazen-voiced hound of Hades, fifty-headed, relentless and strong. And again she bore a third, the evil-minded Hydra of Lerna, whom the goddess, white-armed Hera nourished, being angry beyond measure with the mighty Heracles. And her Heracles, the son of Zeus, of the house of Amphitryon, together with warlike Iolaus, destroyed with the unpitying sword through the plans of Athene the spoil-driver. She was the mother of Chimaera who breathed raging fire, a creature fearful, great, swift-footed and strong, who had three heads, one of a grim-eyed lion, another of a goat, and another of a snake, a fierce dragon; in her forepart she was a lion; in her hinderpart, a dragon; and in her middle, a goat, breathing forth a fearful blast of blazing fire. Her did Pegasus and noble Bellerophon slay; but Echidna was subject in love to Orthus and brought forth the deadly Sphinx which destroyed the Cadmeans, and the Nemean lion, which Hera, the good wife of Zeus, brought up and made to haunt the hills of Nemea, a plague to men. There he preyed upon the bribes of her own people and had power over Tretus of Nemea and Apesas: yet the strength of stout Heracles overcame him.

And Ceto was joined in love to Phoreys and bare her youngest, the awful snake who guards the apples all of gold in the secret places of the dark earth at its great bounds. This is the offspring of Ceto and Phoreys.

And Tethys bare to Ocean eddying river, Nilus, and Alpheus, and deep-swirling Eridanus, Strymon, and Meander, and the fair stream of Ister, and Phasis, and Rhesus, and the silver eddies of Achelous, Nessus, and Rhodius, Haliaemon, and Heptaporus, Granicus, and Aesepus, and holy Simoïs, and Peneüs, and Hermus, and Caieus' fair stream, and great Sangarius, Ladon, Parthenius, Euenus, Ardescus, and divine Scamander.

Also she brought forth a holy company of daughters who with the lord Apollo and the Rivers have youths in their keeping—to this charge Zeus appointed them—Peitho, and Admete, and Ianthe, and Electra, and Doris, and Prymno, and Urania divine in form, Hippo, Clymene, Rhodea, and Callirrhoë, Zeuxo and Clytie, and Idyia, and Pasithoë, Plexaura, and Galaxaura, and lovely Dione, Melobosis and Thoë and handsome Polydora, Cerceïs lovely of form, and soft eyed Pluto, Perseïs, Ianeira, Acaste, Xanthe, Petraea the fair, Menestho, and Europa, Metis, and Eurynome, and Telesto saffron-clad, Chryseis and Asia and charming Calypso, Eudora, and Tyche, Amphirho, and Oeyrrhoë, and Styx who is the chiefest of them all. These are the eldest daughters that sprang from Ocean and Tethys; but there are many besides. For there are three thousand neat-ankled daughters of Ocean who are dispersed far and wide, and in every place alike serve the earth and the deep waters, children who are glorious among goddesses. And as many other rivers are there, babbling as they flow, sons of Ocean, whom queenly Tethys bare, but their names it is hard for a mortal man to tell, but people know those by which they severally dwell.

And Theia was subject in love to Hyperion and bare great Helius (Sun) and clear Selene (Moon) and Eos (Dawn) who shines upon all that are on earth and upon the deathless Gods who live in the wide heaven.

And Eurybia, bright goddess, was joined in love to Crius and bare great Astraeus, and Pallas, and Perses who also was eminent among all men in wisdom.

And Eos bare to Astraeus the strong-hearted winds, brightening Zephyrus, and Boreas, headlong in his course, and Notus,—a goddess mating in love with a god. And after these Erigeneia bare the star Eosphorus (Dawn-bringer), and the gleaming stars with which heaven is crowned.

And Styx the daughter of Ocean was joined to Pallas and bare Zelus (Emulation) and trim-ankled Nike (Victory) in the house. Also she brought forth Cratos (Strength) and Bia (Force), wonderful children. These have no house apart from Zeus, nor any dwelling nor path except that wherein God leads them, but they dwell always with Zeus the loud-thunderer. For so did Styx the deathless daughter of Ocean plan on that day when the Olympian Lightener called all the deathless gods to great Olympus, and said that whosoever of the gods would fight with him against the Titans, he would not cast him out from his rights, but each should have the office which he had before amongst the deathless gods. And he declared that he who was without office or right under Cronos, should be raised to both office and rights as is just. So deathless Styx came first to Olympus with her children through the wit of her dear father. And Zeus honoured her, and gave her very great gifts, for her he appointed to be the great oath of the gods, and her children to live with him always. And as he promised, so he performed fully unto them all. But he himself mightily reigns and rules.

Again, Phoebe came to the desired embrace of Coeus. Then the goddess through the love of the god conceived and brought forth dark-gowned Leto, always mild, kind to men and to the deathless gods, mild from the beginning, gentlest in all Olympus. Also she bare Asteria of happy name, whom Perses once led to his great house to be called his dear wife. And she conceived and bare Hecate whom Zeus the son of Cronos honoured above all. He gave her splendid gifts, to have a share of the earth and the unfruitful sea. She received honour also in starry heaven, and is honoured exceedingly by the deathless gods.

For to this day, whenever any one of men on earth offers rich sacrifices and prays for favour according to custom, he calls upon Hecate. Great honour comes full easily to him whose prayers the goddess receives favourably, and she bestows wealth upon him; for the power surely is with her. For as many as were born of Earth and Ocean amongst all these she has her due portion. The son of Cronos did her no wrong nor took anything away of all that was her portion among the former Titan gods: but she holds, as the division was at the first from beginning, privilege both in earth, and in heaven, and in sea. Also, because she is an only child, the goddess receives not less honour, but much more still, for Zeus honours her. Whom she will she greatly aids and advances: she sits by worshipful kings in judgment, and in the assembly whom she will is distinguished among the people. And when men arm themselves for the battle that destroys men, then the goddess is at hand to give victory and grant glory readily to whom she will. Good is she also when men contend at the games, for there too the goddess is with them and profits them: and he who by might and strength gets the victory wins the rich prize easily with joy, and brings glory to his parents. And she is good to stand by horsemen, whom she will: and to those whose business is in the grey discomfortable sea, and who pray to Hecate and the loud-crashing Earth-Shaker, easily the glorious goddess gives great catch, and easily she takes it away as soon as seen, if so she will. She is good in the byre with Hermes to increase the stock. The droves of kine and wide herds of goats and flocks of fleecy sheep, if she will, she increases from a few, or makes many to be less. So, then, albeit her mother's only child, she is honoured amongst all the deathless gods. And the son of Cronos made her a nurse of the young who after that day saw with their eyes the light of all-seeing Dawn. So from the beginning she is a nurse of the young, and these are her honours.

But Rhea was subject in love to Cronos and bare splendid children, Hestia, Demeter, and gold-shod Hera and strong Hades, pitiless in heart, who dwells under the earth, and the loud-crashing Earth-Shaker, and wise Zeus, father of gods and men, by whose thunder the wide earth is shaken. These great Cronos swallowed as each came forth from the womb to his mother's knees with this intent, that no other of the proud sons of Heaven should hold the kingly office amongst the deathless gods. For he learned from Earth and starry Heaven that he was destined to be overcome by his own son, strong though he was through the contriving of great Zeus. Therefore he kept no blind outlook, but watched and swallowed down his children: and unceasing grief seized Rhea. But when she was about to bear Zeus, the father of gods and men, then she besought her own dear parents, Earth and starry Heaven, to devise some plan with her that the birth of her dear child might be concealed, and that retribution might overtake great, crafty Cronos for his own father and also for the children whom he had swallowed down. And they readily heard and obeyed their dear daughter, and told her all that was destined to happen touching Cronos the king and his stout-hearted son. So they sent her to Lyctus, to the rich land of Crete, when she was ready to bear great Zeus, the youngest of her children. Him did vast Earth receive from Rhea in wide Crete to nourish and to bring up. Thither came Earth carrying him swiftly through the black night to Lyctus first, and took him in her arms and hid him in a remote cave beneath the secret places of the holy earth on thick-wooded Mount Aegeum; but to the mightily ruling son of Heaven, the earlier king of the gods, she gave a great stone wrapped in swaddling clothes. Then he took it in his hands and thrust it down into his belly: wretch! he knew not in his heart that in place of the stone his son was left behind, unconquered and untroubled, and that he was soon to overcome him by force and might and drive him from his honours, himself to reign over the deathless gods.

After that, the strength and glorious limbs of the prince increased quickly, and as the years rolled on, great Cronos the wily was beguiled by the deep suggestions of Earth, and brought up again his offspring, vanquished by the arts and might of his own son, and he vomited up first the stone which he had swallowed last. And Zeus set it fast in the wide-pathed earth at goodly Pytho under the glens of Parnassus, to be a sign thenceforth and a marvel to mortal men. And he set free from their deadly bonds the brothers of his father, sons of Heaven whom his father in his foolishness had bound. And they remembered to be grateful to him for his kindness, and gave him thunder and the glowing thunderbolt and lightning: for before that, huge Earth had hidden these. In them he trusts and rules over mortals and immortals.

Homer (8th Century BC)

Few details are known about Homer's life. Yet for centuries knowledge of Homer has been considered necessary for the student who seeks a liberal education. Although it is a cliché to say that Western literature began with Homer, this notion is based upon just two of the Western world's greatest epics, Homer's the *Iliad* and the *Odyssey*. Aristotle's elevation of poetic truth, above historical truth, may explain why Homer's towering position has remained intact in the liberal education canon. Alexander the Great, Aristotle's student, was rumored to have carried the *Iliad* with him in a jewel casket as he conquered the known world.

The *Iliad* and the *Odyssey* are a repository of secular knowledge of Greek culture; they are the Bible of Greek culture. Both epics, along with the major tragedies, offer readers a pattern for civilized behavior and an outline of the heroic ideal. For example, the first four books of the *Odyssey* are concerned with the education of Telemachus, Odysseus' son, and the responsibilities of his aristocratic birth. The heroic ideal is also individualistic and anthropocentric, along with the immediancy of experience. Homer's works reveal aspects of humanity: mortality, limited power, wisdom, and divine assistance.

The *Iliad:* Background

Homer's the *Iliad* is seminal in the European epic tradition, for he sets the standard by which later epics have been measured. Although the *Iliad* and the *Odyssey* are the products of a long oral tradition, Homer is primarily noted as the one responsible for the form in which these works are found today. The *Iliad* tells primarily two stories: the passion of Achilles and the Tale of Troy. Homer tells his story through a series of adventures relating to Achilles and the Trojan War; the story is told in episodes that are specific to the Greek culture. Homer's epic is objective and never intrudes or manipulates the central characters. Achilles is the prototype of Greek culture. He embodies the physical prowess and beauty emblematic of the culture. Exemplifying legendary significance and sharing an affinity with the gods are epic characteristics which are evidenced in the Homeric hero Achilles.

The brutal passion and wrath of Achilles begin the *Iliad*, for he withdraws from the war as a protest against Agamemnon's slight of his worth. With the death of his best friend, Patroclus, who had won Achilles' armor in battle, Achilles rejoins the Greek army to wreck harsh penalties on the Trojans, especially Hector who has slain Patroclus believing Patroclus was Achilles.

Book XXIV of the *Iliad* embodies much of what has made Homer's work so important that it has survived for so many centuries: glory, honor, birth, wealth, and physical prowess. In this book, which is near the end of the epic, Hector's father, Priam, upon the advice of the gods, carefully makes his way to Achilles to retrieve the body of his son. Achilles has been unmerciful in his defilement of Hector's body. Understandably, such hatred, passion, and wrath make Priam fearful. This meeting between Achilles and Priam is also important because both, no matter how immense their grief, must give themselves to the living. They meet as conqueror and the fallen, as son and as father, and finally as victims of war. Previous books have shown the overwhelming devastation of this long war, but here the consequences are seen in its most famous warrior and in the father of his most famous victim. Both men grow, but Achilles sees beyond his personal misfortune and achieves a measure of maturity. Both realize that too much reliance on grief denies an affirmation of life.

The Iliad

Book I

ACHILLES sing, O Goddess! Peleus' son;
His wrath pernicious, who ten thousand woes
Caused to Achaia's host, sent many a soul
Illustrious into Ades premature,
And Heroes gave (so stood the will of Jove)
To dogs and to all ravening fowls a prey,
When fierce dispute had separated once
The noble chief Achilles from the son
Of Atreus, Agamemnon, King of men.
Who them to strife impell'd? What power divine?
Latona's son and Jove's.[1] For he, incensed
Against the King, a foul contagion raised
In all the host, and multitudes, destroy'd,
For that the son of Atreus had his priest
Dishonored, Chryses. To the fleet he came
Bearing rich ransom glorious to redeem
His daughter, and his hands charged with the wreath
And golden sceptre[2] of the God shaft-arm'd.
His supplication was at large to all
The host of Greece, but most of all to two,
The sons of Atreus, highest in command.
Ye gallant Chiefs, and ye their gallant host,
(So may the Gods who in Olympus dwell
Give Priam's treasures to you for a spoil
And ye return in safety,) take my gifts
And loose my child, in honor of the son
Of Jove, Apollo, archer of the skies.[3]
At once the voice of all was to respect
The priest, and to accept the bounteous price;
But so it pleased not Atreus' mighty son,
Who with rude threatenings stern him thence dismiss'd.
Beware, old man! that at these hollow barks
I find thee not now lingering, or henceforth
Returning, lest the garland of thy God
And his bright sceptre should avail thee nought
I will not loose thy daughter, till old age
Steal on her. From her native country far.
In Argos, in my palace, she shall ply
The loom, and shall be partner of my bed.
Move me no more. Begone; hence while thou may'st.
He spake, the old priest trembled and obey'd.
Forlorn he roamed the ocean's sounding shore,
And, solitary, with much prayer his King
Bright-hair'd Latona's son, Phoebus, implored.[4]
God of the silver bow, who with thy power
Encirclest Chrysa, and who reign'st supreme

In Tenedos and Cilli the divine,
Sminthian[5] Apollo![6] If I e'er adorned
Thy beauteous fane, or on the altar burn'd
The fat acceptable of bulls or goats, so
Grant my petition. With thy shafts avenge
On the Achaian host thy servant's tears.
Such prayer he made, and it was heard.[7] The God,
Down from Olympus with his radiant bow
And his full quiver o'er his shoulder slung,
Marched in his anger; shaken as he moved
His rattling arrows told of his approach.
Gloomy he came as night; sat from the ships
Apart, and sent an arrow. Clang'd the cord[8]
Dread-sounding, bounding on the silver bow.[9]
Mules first and dogs lie struck,[10] but at themselves
Dispatching soon his bitter arrows keen,
Smote them. Death-piles on all sides always blazed.
Nine days throughout the camp his arrows flew;
The tenth, Achilles from all parts convened
The host in council. Juno the white-armed
Moved at the sight of Grecians all around
Dying, imparted to his mind the thought.[11]
The full assembly, therefore, now convened,
Uprose Achilles ardent, and began.
Atrides! Now, it seems, no course remains
For us, but that the seas roaming again,
We hence return; at least if we survive;
But Haste, consult we quick some prophet here
Or priest, or even interpreter of dreams,
(For dreams are also of Jove,) that we may learn
By what crime we have thus incensed Apollo,
What broken vow, what hecatomb unpaid
He charges on us, and if soothed with steam
Of lambs or goats unblemish'd, he may yet
Be won to spare us, and avert the plague.
He spake and sat, when Thestor's son arose
Calchas, an augur foremost in his art,
Who all things, present, past, and future knew,
And whom his skill in prophecy, a gift
Conferr'd by Phoebus on him, had advanced
To be conductor of the fleet to Troy;
He, prudent, them admonishing, replied.[12]
Jove-loved Achilles! Wouldst thou learn from me
What cause hath moved Apollo to this wrath,
The shaft-arm'd King? I shall divulge the cause.
But thou, swear first and covenant on thy part
That speaking, acting, thou wilt stand prepared
To give me succor; for I judge amiss,
Or he who rules the Argives, the supreme
O'er all Achaia's host, will be incensed.
Woe to the man who shall provoke the King
For if, to-day, he smother close his wrath,
He harbors still the vengeance, and in time
Performs it. Answer, therefore, wilt thou save me?

To whom Achilles, swiftest of the swift.
What thou hast learn'd in secret from the God
That speak, and boldly. By the son of Jove,
Apollo, whom thou, Calchas, seek'st in prayer
Made for the Danai, and who thy soul
Fills with futurity, in all the host
The Grecian lives not, who while I shall breathe,
And see the light of day, shall in this camp
Oppress thee; no, not even if thou name
Him, Agamemnon, sovereign o'er us all.
Then was the seer embolden'd, and he spake.
Nor vow nor hecatomb unpaid on us
He charges, but the wrong done to his priest
Whom Agamemnon slighted when he sought
His daughter's freedom, and his gifts refused.
He is the cause. Apollo for his sake
Afflicts and will afflict us, neither end
Nor intermission of his heavy scourge
Granting, 'till unredeem'd, no price required,
The black-eyed maid be to her father sent,
And a whole hecatomb in Chrysa bleed.
Then, not before, the God may be appeased.
He spake and sat; when Atreus' son arose,
The Hero Agamemnon, throned supreme.
Tempests of black resentment overcharged
His heart, and indignation fired his eyes.
On Calchas lowering, him he first address'd.
Prophet of mischief! from whose tongue no note
Of grateful sound to me, was ever heard
Ill tidings are thy joy, and tidings glad
Thou tell'st not, or thy words come not to pass.
And now among the Danai thy dreams
Divulging, thou pretend'st the Archer-God
For his priest's sake, our enemy, because
I scorn'd his offer'd ransom of the maid
Chryseïs, more desirous far to bear
Her to my home, for that she charms me more
Than Clytemnestra, my own first espoused,
With whom, in disposition, feature, form,
Accomplishments, she may be well compared.
Yet, being such, I will return her hence
If that she go be best. Perish myself—
But let the people of my charge be saved
Prepare ye, therefore, a reward for me,
And seek it instant. It were much unmeet
That I alone of all the Argive host
Should want due recompense, whose former prize
Is elsewhere destined, as ye all perceive.
To whom Achilles, matchless in the race.
Atrides, glorious above all in rank,
And as intent on gain as thou art great,
Whence shall the Grecians give a prize to thee?
The general stock is poor; the spoil of towns
Which we have taken, hath already passed
In distribution, and it were unjust

To gather it from all the Greeks again.
But send thou back this Virgin to her God,
And when Jove's favor shall have given us Troy,
A threefold, fourfold share shall then be thine.
  To whom the Sovereign of the host replied.
Godlike Achilles, valiant as thou art,
Wouldst thou be subtle too? But me no fraud
Shall overreach, or art persuade, of thine.
Wouldst thou, that thou be recompensed, and I
Sit meekly down, defrauded of my due?
And didst thou bid me yield her? Let the bold
Achaians give me competent amends,
Such as may please me, and it shall be well.
Else, if they give me none, I will command
Thy prize, the prize of Ajax, or the prize
It may be of Ulysses to my tent,
And let the loser chafe. But this concern
Shall be adjusted at convenient time.
Come—launch we now into the sacred deep
A bark with lusty rowers well supplied;
Then put on board Chryseïs, and with her
The sacrifice required. Go also one
High in authority, some counsellor,
Idomeneus, or Ajax, or thyself,
Thou most untractable of all mankind
And seek by rites of sacrifice and prayer
To appease Apollo on our host's behalf.
  Achilles eyed him with a frown, and spake.
Ah! clothed with impudence as with a cloak,
And full of subtlety, who, thinkest thou—
What Grecian here will serve thee, or for thee
Wage covert war, or open? Me thou know'st,
Troy never wronged; I came not to avenge
Harm done to me; no Trojan ever drove
My pastures, steeds or oxen took of mine,
Or plunder'd of their fruits the golden fields
Of Phthia[13] the deep-soil'd. She lies remote,
And obstacles are numerous interposed,
Vale-darkening mountains, and the dashing sea,
No,[14] Shameless Wolf! For thy good pleasure's sake
We came, and,[15] Face of flint! to avenge the wrongs
By Menelaus and thyself sustain'd,
On the offending Trojan—service kind,
But lost on thee, regardless of it all.
And now—What now? Thy threatening is to seize
Thyself, the just requital of my toils,
My prize hard-earn'd, by common suffrage mine.
I never gain, what Trojan town soe'er
We ransack, half thy booty. The swift march
And furious onset—these I largely reap,
But, distribution made, thy lot exceeds
Mine far; while I, with any pittance pleased,
Bear to my ships the little that I win
After long battle, and account it much.
But I am gone, I and my sable barks

(My wiser course) to Phthia, and I judge,
Scorn'd as I am, that thou shalt hardly glean
Without me, more than thou shalt soon consume.[16]
He ceased, and Agamemnon thus replied
Fly, and fly now; if in thy soul thou feel
Such ardor of desire to go—begone!
I woo thee not to stay; stay not an hour
On my behalf, for I have others here
Who will respect me more, and above all
All-judging Jove. There is not in the host
King or commander whom I hate as thee,
For all thy pleasure is in strife and blood,
And at all times; yet valor is no ground
Whereon to boast, it is the gift of Heaven,
Go, get ye back to Phthia, thou and thine!
There rule thy Myrmidons.[17] I need not thee,
Nor heed thy wrath a jot. But this I say,
Sure as Apollo takes my lovely prize
Chrysëis, and I shall return her home
In mine own bark, and with my proper crew,
So sure the fair Brisëis shall be mine.
I shall demand her even at thy tent.
So shalt thou well be taught, how high in power
I soar above thy pitch, and none shall dare
Attempt, thenceforth, comparison with me.
He ended, and the big, disdainful heart
Throbbed of Achilles; racking doubt ensued
And sore perplex'd him, whether forcing wide
A passage through them, with his blade unsheathed
To lay Atrides breathless at his foot,
Or to command his stormy spirit down.
So doubted he, and undecided yet
Stood drawing forth his falchion huge; when lo!
Down sent by Juno, to whom both alike
Were dear, and who alike watched over both,
Pallas descended. At his back she stood
To none apparent, save himself alone,
And seized his golden locks. Startled, be turned,
And instant knew Minerva. Flashed her eyes
Terrific;[18] whom with accents on the wing
Of haste, incontinent be questioned thus.
Daughter of Jove, why comest thou? that thyself
May'st witness these affronts which I endure
From Agamemnon? Surely as I speak,
This moment, for his arrogance, he dies.
To whom the blue-eyed Deity. From heaven
Mine errand is, to sooth, if thou wilt hear,
Thine anger. Juno the white-arm'd alike
To him and thee propitious, bade me down:
Restrain thy wrath. Draw not thy falchion forth.
Retort, and sharply, and let that suffice.
For I foretell thee true. Then short receive,
Some future day, thrice told, thy present loss
For this day's wrong. Cease, therefore, and be still.

To whom Achilles. Goddess, although much
Exasperate, I dare not disregard
Thy word, which to obey is always best.[19]
Who hears the Gods, the Gods hear also him.
He said; and on his silver hilt the force
Of his broad band impressing, sent the blade
Home to its rest, nor would the counsel scorn
Of Pallas. She to heaven well-pleased return'd,
And in the mansion of Jove Aegis[20]-armed
Arriving, mingled with her kindred Gods.
But though from violence, yet not from words
Abstained Achilles, but with bitter taunt
Opprobrious, his antagonist reproached.
Oh charged with wine, in steadfastness of face
Dog unabashed, and yet at heart a deer!
Thou never, when the troops have taken arms,
Hast dared to take thine also; never thou
Associate with Achaia's Chiefs, to form
The secret ambush.[21] No. The sound of war
Is as the voice of destiny to thee.
Doubtless the course is safer far, to range
Our numerous host, and if a man have dared
Dispute thy will, to rob him of his prize.
King! over whom? Women and spiritless—
Whom therefore thou devourest; else themselves
Would stop that mouth that it should scoff no more.
But hearken. I shall swear a solemn oath.
By this same sceptre,[22] which shall never bud,
Nor boughs bring forth as once, which having left
Its stock on the high mountains, at what time
The woodman's axe lopped off its foliage green,
And stript its bark, shall never grow again;
Which now the judges of Achaia bear,
Who under Jove, stand guardians of the laws,
By this I swear (mark thou the sacred oath)
Time shall be, when Achilles shall be missed;
When all shall want him, and thyself the power
To help the Achaians, whatsoe'er thy will;
When Hector at your heels shall mow you down;
The Hero-slaughtering Hector! Then thy soul,
Vexation-stung, shall tear thee with remorse,
That thou hast scorn'd, as he were nothing worth,
A Chief, the soul and bulwark of your cause.
So saying, he cast his sceptre on the ground
Studded with gold, and sat. On the other side
The son of Atreus all impassion'd stood,
When the harmonious orator arose
Nestor, the Pylian oracle, whose lips
Dropped eloquence—the honey not so sweet.
Two generations past of mortals born
In Pylus, coëtaneous with himself,
He govern'd now the third—amid them all
He stood, and thus, benevolent, began.
Ah! what calamity hath fall'n on Greece!
Now Priam and his song may well exult,

Now all in Ilium shall have joy of heart
Abundant, hearing of this broil, the prime
Of Greece between, in council and in arms.
But be persuaded; ye are younger both
Than I, and I was conversant of old
With Princes your superiors, yet from them
No disrespect at any time received.
Their equals saw I never; never shall
Exadius, Cœneus, and the Godlike son
Of Ægeus, mighty Theseus; men renown'd
For force superior to the race of man.
Brave Chiefs they were, and with brave foes they fought,
With the rude dwellers on the mountain-heights
The Centaurs,[23] whom with havoc such as fame
Shall never cease to celebrate, they slew.
With these men I consorted erst, what time
From Pylus, though a land from theirs remote,
They called me forth, and such as was my strength,
With all that strength I served them. Who is he?
What Prince or Chief of the degenerate race
Now seen on earth who might with these compare?
Yet even these would listen and conform
To my advice in consultation given,
Which bear ye also; for compliance proves
Oft times the safer and the manlier course.
Thou, Agamemnon! valiant as thou art,
Seize not the maid, his portion from the Greeks,
But leave her his; nor thou, Achilles, strive
With our imperial Chief; for never King
Had equal honor at the hands of Jove
With Agamemnon, or was throned so high.
Say thou art stronger, and art Goddess-born,
How then? His territory passes thine,
And he is Lord of thousands more than thou.
Cease, therefore, Agamemnon; calm thy wrath;
And it shall be mine office to entreat
Achilles also to a calm, whose might
The chief munition is of all our host.
To whom the sovereign of the Greeks replied,
The son of Atreus. Thou hast spoken well,
Old Chief, and wisely. But this wrangler here—
Nought will suffice him but the highest place;
He must control us all, reign over all,
Dictate to all; but he shall find at least
One here, disposed to question his commands.
If the eternal Gods have made him brave,
Derives he thence a privilege to rail?
Whom thus Achilles interrupted fierce.
Could I be found so abject as to take
The measure of my doings at thy lips,
Well might they call me coward through the camp,
A vassal, and a fellow of no worth.
Give law to others. Think not to control
Me, subject to thy proud commands no more.
Hear yet again! And weigh what thou shalt hear.

I will not strive with thee in such a cause,
Nor yet with any man; I scorn to fight
For her, whom having given, ye take away.
But I have other precious things on board;
Of those take none away without my leave.
Or if it please thee, put me to the proof
Before this whole assembly, and my spear
Shall stream that moment, purpled with thy blood.
Thus they long time in opposition fierce
Maintained the war of words; and now, at length,
(The grand consult dissolved,) Achilles walked
(Patroclus and the Myrmidons his steps
Attending) to his camp and to his fleet.
But Agamemnon order'd forth a bark,
A swift one, manned with twice ten lusty rowers;
He sent on board the Hecatomb:[24] he placed
Chryseïs with the blooming cheeks, himself,
And to Ulysses gave the freight in charge.
So all embarked, and plow'd their watery way.
Atrides, next, bade purify the host;
The host was purified, as he enjoin'd,
And the ablution cast into the sea.
Then to Apollo, on the shore they slew,
Of the untillable and barren deep,
Whole Hecatombs of bulls and goats, whose steam
Slowly in smoky volumes climbed the skies.
Thus was the camp employed; nor ceased the while
The son of Atreus from his threats denounced
At first against Achilles, but command
Gave to Taltbybius and Eurybates
His heralds, ever faithful to his will
Haste—Seek ye both the tent of Peleus' son
Achilles. Thence lead hither by the hand
Blooming Briseïs, whom if he withhold,
Not her alone, but other spoil myself
Will take in person—He shall rue the hour.
With such harsh message charged he them dismissed
They, sad and slow, beside the barren waste
Of Ocean, to the galleys and the tents
Moved of the Myrmidons. Him there they found
Beneath the shadow of his bark reclined,
Nor glad at their approach. Trembling they stood,
In presence of the royal Chief, awe-struck,
Nor questioned him or spake. He not the less
Knew well their embassy, and thus began.
Ye heralds, messengers of Gods and men,
Hail, and draw near! I bid you welcome both.
I blame not you; the fault is his alone
Who mends you to conduct the damsel hence
Briseïs. Go, Patroclus, generous friend!
Lead forth, and to their guidance give the maid.
But be themselves my witnesses before
The blessed Gods, before mankind, before
The ruthless king, should want of me be felt
To save the host from havoc[25]—Oh, his thoughts

Are madness all; intelligence or skill,
Forecast or retrospect, how best the camp
May be secured from inroad, none hath he.
He ended, nor Patroclus disobey'd,
But leading beautiful Brisëis forth
Into their guidance gave her; loth she went
From whom she loved, and looking oft behind.
Then wept Achilles, and apart from all,
With eyes directed to the gloomy Deep
And arms outstretched, his mother suppliant sought.
Since, mother, though ordain'd so soon to die,
I am thy son, I might with cause expect
Some honor at the Thunderer's hands, but none
To me he shows, whom Agamemnon, Chief
Of the Achnians, hath himself disgraced,
Seizing by violence my just reward.
So prayed he weeping, whom his mother heard
Within the gulfs of Ocean where she sat
Beside her ancient sire. From the gray flood
Ascending sudden, like a mist she came,
Sat down before him, stroked his face, and said.
Why weeps my son? and what is thy distress?
Hide not a sorrow that I wish to share.
To whom Achilles, sighing deep, replied.
Why tell thee woes to thee already known?
At Thebes, Eëtion's city we arrived,
Smote, sack'd it, and brought all the spoil away.
Just distribution made among the Greeks,
The son of Atreus for his lot received
Blooming Chrysëis. Her, Apollo's priest
Old Chryses followed to Achaia's camp,
That he might loose his daughter. Ransom rich
He brought, and in his hands the hallow'd wreath
And golden sceptre of the Archer God
Apollo, bore; to the whole Grecian host,
But chiefly to the foremost in command
He sued, the sons of Atreus; then, the rest
All recommended reverence of the Seer,
And prompt acceptance of his costly gifts.
But Agamemnon might not so be pleased,
Who gave him rude dismission; be in wrath
Returning, prayed, whose prayer Apollo heard,
For much he loved him. A pestiferous shaft
He instant shot into the Grecian best,
And heap'd the people died. His arrows swept
The whole wide camp of Greece, 'till at the last
A Seer, by Phœbus taught, explain'd the cause.
I first advised propitiation. Rage
Fired Agamemnon. Rising, he denounced
Vengeance, and hath fulfilled it. She, in truth,
Is gone to Chrysa, and with her we send
Propitiation also to the King
Shaft-arm'd Apollo. But my beauteous prize
Brisëis, mine by the award of all,
His heralds, at this moment, lead away.

But thou, wherein thou canst, aid thy own son!
Haste hence to Heaven, and if thy word or deed
Hath ever gratified the heart of Jove,
With earnest suit press him on my behalf.
For I, not seldom, in my father's hall
Have heard thee boosting, how when once the Gods,
With Juno, Neptune, Pallas at their head,
Conspired to bind the Thunderer, thou didst loose
His bands, O Goddess! calling to his aid
The Hundred-handed warrior, by the Gods
Briareus, but by men, Ægeon named.[26]
For he in prowess and in might surpassed
His father Neptune, who, enthroned sublime,
Sits second only to Saturnian Jove,
Elate with glory and joy. Him all the Gods
Fearing from that bold enterprise abstained.
Now, therefore, of these things reminding Jove,
Embrace his knees; entreat him that he give
The host of Troy his succor, and shut fast
The routed Grecians, prisoners in the fleet,
That all may find much solace[27] in their King,
And that the mighty sovereign o'er them all,
Their Agamemnon, may himself be taught
His rashness, who hath thus dishonor'd foul
The life itself, and bulwark of his cause.
To him, with streaming eyes, Thetis replied.
Born as thou wast to sorrow, ah, my son!
Why have I rear'd thee! Would that without tears,
Or cause for tears (transient as is thy life,
A little span) thy days might pass at Troy!
But short and sorrowful the fates ordain
Thy life, peculiar trouble must be thine,
Whom, therefore, oh that I had never borne!
But seeking the Olympian hill snow-crown'd,
I will myself plead for thee in the ear
Of Jove, the Thunderer. Meantime at thy fleet
Abiding, let thy wrath against the Greeks
Still burn, and altogether cease from war.
For to the banks of the Oceanus,[28]
Where Æthiopia fields a feast to Jove,[29]
He journey'd yesterday, with whom the Gods
Went also, and the twelfth day brings them home.
Then will I to his brazen-floor'd abode,
That I may clasp his knees, and much misdeem
Of my endeavor, or my prayer shall speed.
So saying she went; but him she left enraged
For fair Brisëis' sake, forced from his arms
By stress of power. Meantime Ulysses came
To Chrysa with the Hecatomb in charge.
Arrived within the havens[30] deep, their sails
Furling, they stowed them in the bark below.
Then by its tackle lowering swift the mast
Into its crutch, they briskly push'd to land,
Heaved anchors out, and moor'd the vessel fast.
Forth came the mariners, and trod the beach;

Forth came the victims of Apollo next,
And, last, Chrysëis. Her Ulysses led
Toward the altar, gave her to the arms
Of her own father, and him thus address'd.
O Chryses! Agamemnon, King of men,
Hath sent thy daughter home, with whom we bring
A Hecatomb on all our host's behalf
To Plœbus, hoping to appease the God
By whose dread shafts the Argives now expire.
So saying, he gave her to him, who with Jove
Received his daughter. Then, before the shrine
Magnificent in order due they ranged
The noble Hecatomb.[31] Each laved his hands
And took the salted meal, and Chryses made
His fervent prayer with hands upraised on high.
God of the silver bow, who with thy power
Encirclest Chrysa, and who reign'st supreme
In Tenedos, and Cilla the divine!
Thou prov'dst propitious to my first request,
Hast honor'd me, and punish'd sore the Greeks;
Hear yet thy servant's prayer; take from their host
At once the loathsome pestilence away!
So Chryses prayed, whom Phœbus heard well-pleased;
Then prayed the Grecians also, and with meal
Sprinkling the victims, their retracted necks
First pierced, then flay'd them; the disjointed thighs
They, next, invested with the double caul,
Which with crude slices thin they overspread.
The priest burned incense, and libation poured
Large on the hissing brands, while, him beside,
Busy with spit and prong, stood many a youth
Trained to the task. The thighs with fire consumed,
They gave to each his portion of the maw,
Then slashed the remnant, pierced it with the spits,
And managing with culinary skill
The roast, withdrew it from the spits again.
Their whole task thus accomplished, and the board
Set forth, they feasted, and were all sufficed.
When neither hunger more nor thirst remained
Unsatisfied, boys crown'd the beakers high
With wine delicious, and from right to left
Distributing the cups, served every guest.
Thenceforth the youths of the Achaian race
To song propitiatory gave the day,
Pæans[32] to Phœbus; Archer of the skies,
Chanting melodious. Pleased, Apollo heard.
But, when, the sun descending, darkness fell,
They on the beach beside their hawsers slept;
And, when the day-spring's daughter rosy-palm'd
Aurora look'd abroad, then back they steer'd
To the vast camp. Fair wind, and blowing fresh,
Apollo sent them; quick they rear'd the mast,
Then spread the unsullied canvas to the gale,
And the wind filled it. Reared the sable flood
Around the bark, that ever as she went

Dash'd wide the brine, and scudded swift away.
Thus reaching soon the spacious camp of Greece,
Their galley they updrew sheer o'er the sands
From the rude surge remote, then propp'd her sides
With scantlings long,[33] and sought their several tents.
But Peleus' noble son, the speed-renown'd
Achilles, he, his well-built bark beside,
Consumed his hours, nor would in council more,
Where wise men win distinction, or in fight
Appear, to sorrow and heart-withering we
Abandon'd; though for battle, ardent, still
He panted, and the shout-resounding field.
But when the twelfth fair morrow streak'd the East,
Then all the everlasting Gods to Heaven
Resorted, with the Thunderer at their head,
And Thetis, not unmindful of her son,
From the salt flood emerged, seeking betimes
Olympus and the boundless fields of heaven.
High, on the topmost eminence sublime
Of the deep-fork'd Olympian she perceived
The Thunderer seated, from the Gods apart.
She sat before him, clasp'd with her left hand
His knees, her right beneath his chin she placed,
And thus the King, Saturnian Jove, implored.
Father of all, by all that I have done
Or said that ever pleased thee, grant my suit.
Exalt my son, by destiny short-lived
Beyond the lot of others. Him with shame
The King of men both overwhelmed, by force
Usurping his just meed; thou, therefore, Jove,
Supreme in wisdom, honor him, and give
Success to Troy, till all Achaia's sons
Shall yield him honor more than he both lost!
She spake, to whom the Thunderer nought replied,
But silent sat long time. She, as her hand
Had grown there, still importunate, his knees
Clasp'd as at first, and thus her suit renew'd.[34]
Or grant my prayer, and ratify the grant,
Or send me hence (for thou best none to fear)
Plainly refused; that I may know and feel
By how much I am least of all in heaven.
To whom the cloud-assembler at the last
Spoke, deep-distress'd. Hard task and full of strife
Thou best enjoined me; Juno will not spare
For gibe and taunt injurious, whose complaint
Sounds daily in the ears of all the Gods,
That I assist the Trojans; but depart,
Lest she observe thee; my concern shall be
How best I may perform thy full desire.
And to assure thee more, I give the sign
Indubitable, which all fear expels
At once from heavenly minds. Nought, so confirmed,
May, after, be reversed or render'd vain.
He ceased, and under his dark brows the nod

Vouchsafed of confirmation. All around
The Sovereign's everlasting head his curls
Ambrosial shook,[35] and the huge mountain reeled.
Their conference closed, they parted. She, at once,
From bright Olympus plunged into the flood
Profound, and Jove to his own courts withdrew.
Together till the Gods, at his approach,
Uprose; none sat expectant till he came,
But all advanced to meet the Eternal Sire.
So on his throne he sat. Nor Juno him
Not understood; she, watchful, had observed,
In consultation close with Jove engaged
Thetis, bright-footed daughter of the deep,
And keen the son of Saturn thus reproved.
Shrewd as thou art, who now hath had thine ear?
Thy joy is ever such, from me apart
To plan and plot clandestine, and thy thoughts,
Think what thou may'st, are always barred to me.
To whom the father, thus, of heaven and earth.
Expect not, Juno, that thou shalt partake
My counsels at all times, which oft in height
And depth, thy comprehension far exceed,
Joye's consort as thou art. When aught occurs
Meet for thine ear, to none will I impart
Of Gods or men more free than to thyself.
But for my secret thoughts, which I withhold
From all in heaven beside, them search not thou
With irksome curiosity and vain.
Him answer'd then the Goddess ample-eyed.[36]
What word both passed thy lips, Saturnian Jove,
Thou most severe! I never search thy thoughts,
Nor the serenity of thy profound
Intentions trouble; they are safe from me:
But now there seems a cause. Deeply I dread
Lest Thetis, silver-footed daughter fair
Of Ocean's hoary Sovereign, here arrived
At early dawn to practise on thee, Jove!
I noticed her a suitress at thy knees,
And much misdeem or promise-bound thou stand'st
To Thetis past recall, to exalt her son,
And Greeks to slaughter thousands at the ships.
To whom the cloud-assembler God, incensed.
All subtle I ever teeming with surmise,
And fathomer of my concealed designs,
Thy toil is vain, or (which is worse for thee,)
Shall but estrange thee from mine heart the more.
And be it as thou sayest,—I am well pleased
That so it should be. Be advised, desist.
Hold thou thy peace. Else, if my glorious hands
Once reach thee, the Olympian Powers combined
To rescue thee, shall interfere in vain.
He said,—whom Juno, awful Goddess, heard
Appall'd, and mute submitted to his will.
But through the courts of Jove the heavenly Powers
All felt displeasure; when to them arose

Vulcan, illustrious artist, who with speech
Conciliatory interposed to sooth
His white-armed mother Juno, Goddess dread.
  Hard doom is ours, and not to be endured,
If feast and merriment must pause in heaven
While ye such clamor raise tumultuous here
For man's unworthy sake: yet thus we speed
Ever, when evil overpoises good.
But I exhort my mother, though herself
Already warn'd, that meekly she submit
To Jove our father, lest our father chide
More roughly, and confusion mar the feast
For the Olympian Thunderer could with ease
Us from our thrones precipitate, so far
He reigns to all superior. Seek to assuage
His anger therefore; so shall he with smiles
Cheer thee, nor thee alone, but all in heaven.
  So Vulcan, and, upstarting, placed a cup
Full-charged between his mother's hands, and said,
  My mother, be advised, and, though aggrieved,
Yet patient; lest I see thee whom I love
So dear, with stripes chastised before my face,
Willing, but impotent to give thee aid.[37]
Who can resist the Thunderer? Me, when once
I flew to save thee, by the foot he seized
And hurl'd me through the portal of the skies.
"From morn to eve I fell, a summer's day,"
And dropped, at last, in Lemnos. There half-dead
The Sintians found me, and with succor prompt
And hospitable, entertained me fallen.
  So He; then Juno smiled, Goddess white-arm'd,
And smiling still, from his unwonted hand[38]
Received the goblet. He from right to left
Rich nectar from the beaker drawn, alert
Distributed to all the powers divine.
Heaven rang with laughter inextinguishable
Peal after peal, such pleasure all conceived
At sight of Vulcan in his new employ.
  So spent they in festivity the day,
And all were cheered; nor was Apollo's harp
Silent, nor did the Muses spare to add
Responsive melody of vocal sweets.
But when the sun's bright orb had now declined,
Each to his mansion, wheresoever built
By the lame matchless Architect, withdrew.[39]
Jove also, kindler of the fires of heaven,
His couch ascending as at other times
When gentle sleep, approach'd him, slept serene,
With golden-sceptred Juno at his side.

Notes

1. "Latona's son and Jove's" was Apollo, the tutelary deity of the Dorians. The Dorians had not, however at this early age, become the predominant race in Greece proper. They had spread along the eastern shores of the Archipelago into the islands, especially Crete, and had every where signalized themselves by the Temples of Apollo, of which there seems to have been many in and about Troy. These temples were schools of art, and prove the Dorians to have been both intellectual and powerful. Homer was an Ionian, and therefore not deeply acquainted with the nature of the Dorian god. But to a mind like his, the god of a people so cultivated, and associated with what was most grand in art, must have been an imposing being, and we find him so represented. Throughout the *Iliad*, he appears and acts with splendor and effect, but always against the Greeks from mere partiality to Hector. It would perhaps be too much to say, that in this partiality to Hector, we detect the spirit of the Dorian worship, the only Paganism of antiquity that tended to perfect the individual,—Apollo being the expression of the moral harmony of the universe, and the great spirit of the Dorian culture being to make a perfect man, an incarnation of the κοσμος. This Homer could only have known intuitively.

   In making Apollo author of the plague, he was confounded with Helios, which was frequent afterwards, but is not seen elsewhere in Homer. The arrows of Apollo were "silent as light," and their emblem the sun's rays. The analogies are multitudinous between the natural and intellectual sun; but Helios and Apollo were two.—E. P. P.
2. There is something exceedingly venerable in this appearance of the priest. He comes with the ensigns of the gods to whom he belongs, with the laurel wreath, to show that he was a suppliant, and a golden sceptre, which the ancients gave in particular to Apollo, as they did one of silver to Diana.
3. The art of this speech is remarkable. Chryses considers the army of Greeks, as made up of troops, partly from the kingdoms and partly from democracies, and therefore begins with a distinction that includes all. Then, as priest of Apollo, he prays that they may obtain the two blessings they most desire—the conquest of Troy and a safe return. As he names his petition, he offers an extraordinary ransom, and concludes with bidding them fear the god if they refuse it; like one who from his office seems to foretell their misery, and exhorts them to shun it. Thus he endeavors to work by tho art of a general application, by religion, by interest, said the insinuation of danger.
4. Homer is frequently eloquent in his silence. Chryses says not a word in answer to the insults of Agamemnon, but walks pensively along the shore. The melancholy flowing of the verse admirably expresses the condition of the mournful and deserted father.
5. [So called on account of his having saved the people of Troas from a plague of mice, sminthos in their language meaning a mouse.—Tr.]
6. Apollo had temples at Chrysa, Tenedos, and Cilla, all of which lay 'round the bay of Troas. Müller remarks, that "the temple actually stood in the situation referred to, and that the appellation of Smintheus was still preserved in the district. Thus far actual circumstances are embodied in the mythus. On the other hand, the action of the deity as such, is purely ideal, and can have no other foundation than the belief that Apollo sternly resents ill usage of his priests, and that too in the way here represented, viz., by sending plagues. This belief is in perfect harmony with the idea generally entertained of the power and agency of Apollo; and it is manifest that the idea placed in combination with certain events, gave birth to the story so far as relates to the god. We have not yet the means of ascertaining whether it is to be regarded as a historical tradition, or an invention, and must therefore leave that question for the present undecided."
7. The poet is careful to leave no prayer unanswered that has justice on its side, He who prays either kills his enemy, or has signs given him that he has been heard.
8. [For this singular line the Translator begs to apologize, by pleading the strong desire he felt to produce an English line, if possible, somewhat resembling in its effect the famous original one. Δεινὴ δὲ κλαγγὴ γενετ΄ αργυρεõιο Βιõιο—Tr.]
9. The plague in the Grecian camp was occasioned perhaps by immoderate heats and gross exhalations. Homer takes occasion from it, to open the scene with a beautiful allegory. He supposes that such afflictions are sent from Heaven for the punishment of evil actions; and because the sun was the principal agent, he says it was sent to punish Agamemnon for despising that god, and injuring his priest.
10. Hippocrates observes two things of plagues; that their cause is in the air, and that different animals are differently affected by them, according to their nature and nourishment. This philosophy is referred to

the plagues here mentioned. First, the cause is in the air by means of the darts or beams of Apollo; second, the mules and dogs are said to die sooner than the men, partly from their natural quickness of smell, and partly from their feeding so near the earth whence the exhalations arise.

11. Juno, queen of Olympus, sides with the Grecians. Mr. Coleridge (in his disquisition upon the Prometheus of Æschylus, published in his Remains) shows very clearly by historical criticism, that Juno, in the Grecian religion, expressed the spirit of conservatism. Without going over his argument we assume it here, for Homer always attributes to Juno everything that may be predicated of this principle. She is persistent, obstinate, acts from no idea, but often uses a superficial reasoning, and refers to Fate, with which she upbraids Jupiter. Jupiter is the intellectual power or Free Will, and by their union, or rather from their antagonism, the course of things proceeds with perpetual vicissitude, but with a great deal of life.—E. P. P.

12. Observe this Grecian priest. He has no political power, and commands little reverence. In Agamemnon's treatment of him, as well as Chryses, is seen the relation of the religion to the government. It was neither master nor slave.—E. P. P.

13. A district of Thessaly forming a part of the larger district of Phthiotls. Phthiotls, according to Strabo, included all the southern portion of that country as far as Mount Œta and the Maliac Gulf. To the west it bordered on Dolopia, and on the east reached the confines of Magnesia. Homer comprised within this extent of territory the districts of Phthia and Hellas properly so called, and, generally speaking, the dominions of Achilles, together with those of Protesilaus and Eurypylus.

14. κυνῶπα

15. μεγὰιαιδὲς

16. Agamemnon's anger is that of a lover, and Achilles' that of a warrior. Agamemnon speaks of Chryseïs as a beauty whom he values too much to resign. Achilles treats Briseïs as a slave, whom he is anxious to preserve in point of honor, and as a testimony of his glory. Hence he mentions her only as "his spoil," "the reward of war," etc.; accordingly he relinquishes her not in grief for a favorite whom he loses, but in sullenness for the injury done him.—DACIER.

17. Jupiter, in the disguise of an ant, deceived Eurymedusa, the daughter of Cleitos. Her son was for this reason called Myrmidon (from, μὺρμηξ, an ant), and was regarded as the ancestor of the Myrmidons in Thessaly.—SMITH.

18. According to the belief of the ancients, the gods were supposed to have a peculiar light in their eyes. That Homer was not ignorant of this opinion appears from his use of it in other places.

19. Minerva is the goddess of the art of war rather than of war itself. And this fable of her descent is an allegory of Achilles restraining his wrath through his consideration of martial law and order. This law in that age, prescribed that a subordinate should not draw his sword upon the commander of all, but allowed a liberty of speech which appears to us moderns rather out of order.—E. P. P.

20. [The shield of Jupiter, made by Vulcan, and so called from its covering, which was the skin of the goat that suckled him.—TR.]

21. Homer magnifies the ambush as the boldest enterprise of war. They went upon those parties with a few only, and generally the most daring of the army, and on occasions of the greatest hazard, when the exposure was greater than in a regular battle. Idomeneus, in the 13th book, tells Meriones that the greatest courage appears in this way of service, each man being in a manner singled out to the proof of it.

22. In the earlier ages of the world, the sceptre of a king was nothing more than his walking-staff, and thence had the name of sceptre. Ovid, in speaking of Jupiter, describes him as resting on his sceptre.—SPENCE.

    From the description here given, it would appear to have been a young tree cut from the root and stripped of its branches. It was the custom of kings to swear by their sceptres.

23. For an account of the contest between the Centaurs and Lapiths here referred to, see Grecian and Roman Mythology.

24. In antiquity, a sacrifice of a hundred oxen, or beasts of the same kind; hence sometimes indefinitely, any sacrifice of a large number of victims.

25. (The original is here abrupt, and expresses the precipitancy of the speaker by a most beautiful aposiopesis.—TR.)

26. The *Iliad*, in its connection, is, we all know, a glorification of Achilles by Zeus; for the Trojans only prevail because Zeus wishes to show that the reposing hero who sits in solitude, can alone conquer them.

But to leave him this glorification entirely unmixed with sorrow, the Grecian sense of moderation forbids. The deepest anguish must mingle with his consciousness of fame, and punish his insolence. That glorification is the will of Zeus; and in the spirit of the ancient mythus, a motive for it is assigned in a divine legend. The sea-goddess Thetis, who was, according to the Phthioic mythus, wedded to the mortal Peleus, saved Zeus, by calling up the giant Briareus or Ægæon to his rescue. Why it was Ægæon, is explained by the fact that this was a great sea-demon, who formed the subject of fables at Poseidonian Corinth, where even the sea-god himself was called Ægæon who, moreover, was worshipped at several places in Eubœa, the seat of Poseidon Ægæus; and whom the Theogony calls the son-in-law of Poseidon, and near of the genealogists, especially Eumelus in the Titanomachy, brought into relation with the sea. There is therefore good reason to be found in ancient belief, why Thetis called up Ægæon of all others to Jove's assistance. The whole of the story, however, is not detailed—it is not much more than indicated—and therefore it would be difficult even now to interpret it in a perfectly satisfactory manner. It bears the same relation to the *Iliad*, that the northern fables of the gods, which serve as a background to the legend of Nibelungen, bear to our German ballad, only that here the separation is much greater still.—MULLER.

Homer makes use of this fable, without reference to its meaning as an allegory. Briareus seems to symbolize a navy, and the fable refers to rome event in remote history, when the reigning power was threatened in his autocracy, and strengthened by means of his association with the people against some intermediate class.—E. P. P.

27. ἐπαύρωται.

28. [A name by which we are frequently to understand the Nile in Homer.—TR.]

29. Around the sources of the Nile, and thence southwest into the very heart of Africa, stretching away indefinitely over its mountain plains, lies the country which the ancients called Ethiopia, rumors of whose wonderful people found their way early into Greece, and are scattered over the pages of her poets and historians. Homer wrote at least eight hundred years before Christ, and his poems are well ascertained to be a most faithful mirror of the manners of his times and the knowledge of his age. * * * * * *

    Homer never wastes an epithet. He often alludes to the Ethiopians also where, and always in terms of admiration and praise, as being the most just of men, and the favorites of the gods. The same allusions glimmer through the Greek mythology, and appear in the verses of almost all the Greek poets, ere yet the countries of Italy and Sicily were even discovered. The Jewish Scriptures and Jewish literature abound in allusions to this distant and mysterious people, the annals of the Egyptian priests are full of them, and uniformly, the Ethiopians are there lauded as among the best, the most religious, and most civilized of men.—CHRISTIAN EXAMINER.

    The Ethiopians, says Diodorus, are said to be the inventors of pomps, sacrifices, solemn meetings, and other honors paid to the gods. From hence arose their character of piety, which is here celebrated by Homer. Among these there was an annual feast at Diospolis, which Eustathius mentions when they carried about the statues of Jupiter and other gods, for twelve days, according to their number; to which, if we add the ancient custom of setting meat before statues, it will appear to be a rite from which this fable might easily have arisen.

30. [The original word (πολυβενθέος) seems to express variety of soundings, an idea probably not to be conveyed in an English epithet.—TR.]

31. The following passage gives the most exact account of the ancient sacrifices that we have left us. There is first, the purification by the washing of hands; second, the offering up of prayers; third, the barley-cakes thrown upon the victim; fourth, the manner of killing it; with the head turned upwards; fifth, selecting the thighs and fat for their gods, as the best of the sacrifice, and disposing about them pieces cut from every part for a representation of the whole (hence the thighs are frequently spoken of in Homer and the Greek poets as the whole victim); sixth, the libation of wine; seventh, consuming the thighs in the fire of the altar; eighth, the sacrificers dressing and feasting on the rest with joy and hymns to the gods.

32. The *Pæan* (originally sung in honor of Apollo) was a hymn to propitiate the god, and also a song of thanksgiving, when freed from danger. It was always of a joyous nature. Both tune and sound expressed hope and confidence. It was sung by several persons, one of whom probably led the others, and the singers either marched onward, or sat together at table.

33. It was the custom to draw the ships entirely upon the shore and to secure them by long props.—FELTON.

34. Suppliants threw themselves at the feet of the person whom the supplication was addressed, and embraced his knees.—FELTON.
35. Ambrosia, the food of the gods, conferred upon them eternal youth and immortality, and was brought to Jupiter by pigeons. It was also used by the gods for anointing the body and hair. Hence the expression, ambrosial locks.
36. The original says,—"the ox-eyed goddess," which furnishes Coleridge with one of the hints on which he proceeds in historically identifying the Argive Juno with Io and Isis, &c. There is real wit in Homer's making her say to Jupiter, "I never search thy thoughts," &c. The principle of conservatism asks nothing of the intellectual power, but blindly contends reposing upon the instinct of a common sense, which leads her always to surmise that something is intended by the intellectual power that she shall not like.—E. P. P.
37. This refers to an old fable of Jupiter's hanging up Juno and whipping her. Homer introduces it without reference to its meaning, which was undoubtedly some physical truth connected with the ether and the atmosphere.—E. P. P.
38. [The reader, in order that he may partake with the gods in the drollery of this scene, should observe that the crippled and distorted Vulcan had thrust himself into an office at all other times administered either by Hebe or Ganymede.—TR.]
39. As Minerva or Wisdom was among the company, the poets making Vulcan act the part of peace-maker, would appear to have been from choice, knowing that a mirthful person may often stop a quarrel, by making himself the subject of merriment.

The first book contains the preliminaries to the commencement of serious action. First, the visit of the priest of Apollo to ransom his captive daughter, the refusal of Agamemnon to yield her up, and the pestilence sent by the god upon the Grecian army in consequence. Secondly, the restoration, the propitiation of Apollo, the quarrel of Agamemnon and Achilles, and the withdrawing of the latter from the Grecian army. Thirdly, the intercession of Thetis with Jupiter; his promise unwillingly given, to avenge Achilles; and the assembly of the gods, in which the promise is angrily alluded to by Juno, and the discussion peremptorily checked by Jupiter. The poet, throughout this book, maintains a simple, unadorned style but highly descriptive, and happily adapted to the nature of the subject.—FELTON.

Book XVIII

Thus burn'd the battle like devouring fire.
Meantime, Antilochus with rapid steps
Came to Achilles. Him he found before
His lofty barks, occupied, as he stood,
With boding fears of all that had befall'n.
He groan'd, and to his noble self he said.
 Ah! wo is me—why falls Achaia's host,
With such disorder foul, back on the fleet?
I tremble lest the Gods my anxious thoughts
Accomplish and my mother's words, who erst
Hath warn'd me, that the bravest and the best
Of all my Myrmidons, while yet I live,
Slain under Troy, must view the sun no more.
Brave Menœtiades is, doubtless, slain.
Unhappy friend! I bade thee oft, our barks
Deliver'd once from hostile fires, not seek
To cope in arms with Hector, but return.
 While musing thus he stood, the son approach'd
Of noble Nestor, and with tears his cheeks
Bedewing copious, his sad message told.
 Oh son of warlike Peleus! Thou shalt hear
Tidings of deeds which best had never been.
Patroclus is no more. The Grecians fight
For his bare corse, and Hector hath his arms.[1]
 Then clouds of sorrow fell on Peleus' son,
And, grasping with both hands the ashes, down
He pour'd them on his head, his graceful brows
Dishonoring, and thick and sooty shower
Descending settled on his fragrant vest.
Then, stretch'd in ashes, at the vast extent
Of his whole length he lay, disordering wild
With his own hands, and rending off his hair.
The maidens, captived by himself in war
And by Patroclus, shrieking from the tent
Ran forth, and hemm'd the glorious Chief around.[2]
All smote their bosoms, and all, fainting, fell.
On the other side, Antilochus the hands
Held of Achilles, mourning and deep groans
Uttering from his noble heart, through fear
Lest Peleus' son should perish self-destroy'd.
Loud groan'd the hero, whose loud groans within
The gulfs of ocean, where she sat beside
Her ancient sire, his Goddess-mother heard,
And hearing Shriek'd; around her at the voice
Assembled all the Nereids of the deep
Cymodoce, Thalia, Glauca came,

Nisæa, Spio, Thoa, and with eyes
Protuberant beauteous Halia; came with these
Cymothöe, and Actæa, and the nymph
Of marshes, Limnorea, nor delay'd
Agave, nor Amphithöe the swift,
Iæra, Doto, Melita, nor thence
Was absent Proto or Dynamene,
Callianira, Doris, Panope,
Pherusa or Amphinome, or fair
Dexamene, or Galatea praised
For matchless form divine: Nemertes pure
Came also, with Apseudes chrystal-bright,
Callianassa, Mæra, Clymene,
Janeira and Janassa, sister pair,
And Orithya, and with azure locks
Luxuriant, Amathea; nor alone
Came these, but every ocean-nymph beside,
The silver cave was fill'd; each smote her breast,
And Thetis, loud lamenting, thus began.
Ye sister Nereids, hear! that ye may all
From my own lips my boundless sorrow learn.
Ah me forlorn! ah me, parent in vain
Of an illustrious birth! who, having borne
A noble son magnanimous, the chief
Of heroes, saw him like a thriving plant
Shoot rigorous under my maternal care,
And sent him early in his gallant fleet
Embark'd, to combat with the sons of Troy.
But him from fight return'd I shall receive
Beneath the roof of Peleus, never more;
And while he lives, and on the sun his eyes
Opens, he mourns, nor, going, can I aught
Assist him; yet I go, that I may see
My darling son, and from his lips be taught
What grief both now befallen him, who close
Abiding in his tent shares not the war.
So saying she left the cave, whom all her nymphs
Attended weeping, and where'er they pass'd
The breaking billows open'd wide a way.
At fruitful Troy arrived, in order fair
They climb'd the beach, where by his numerous barks
Encompass'd, swift Achilles sighing lay.
Then, drawing nigh to her afflicted son,
The Goddess-mother press'd between her palms
His temples, and in accents wing'd inquired.
Why weeps my son? what sorrow wrings thy soul?
Speak, hide it not. Jove hath fulfill'd the prayer
Which erst with lifted hands thou didst prefer,
That all Achaia's host, wanting thy aid,
Might be compell'd into the fleet, and foul
Disgrace incur, there prison'd for thy sake.
To whom Achilles, groaning deep, replied.
My mother! it is true; Olympian Jove
That prayer fulfils; but thence, what joy to me,
Patroclus slain? the friend of all my friends

Whom most I loved, dear to me as my life—
Him I have lost. Slain and despoil'd he lies
By Hector of his glorious armor bright,
The wonder of all eyes, a matchless gift
Given by the Gods to Peleus on that day
When thee they doom'd into a mortal's arms.
Oh that with these thy deathless ocean-nymphs
Dwelling content, thou hadst my father left
To espouse a mortal bride, so hadst thou 'scaped
Pangs numberless which thou must now endure
For thy son's death, whom thou shalt never meet
From Troy return'd, in Peleus' mansion more!
For life I covet not, nor longer wish
To mix with human kind, unless my spear
May find out Hector, and atonement take
By slaying him, for my Patroclus slain.
    To whom, with streaming tears, Thetis replied.
Swift comes thy destiny as thou hast said,
For after Hector's death thine next ensues.
    Then answer, thus, indignant he return'd.
Death, seize me now! since when my friend was slain,
My doom was, not to succor him. He died
From home remote, and wanting me to save him.
Now, therefore, since I neither visit more
My native land, nor, present here, have ought
Avail'd Patroclus or my many friends
Whom noble Hector hath in battle slain,
But here I sit unprofitable grown,
Earth's burden, though of such heroic note,
If not in council foremost (for I yield
That prize to others) yet in feats of arms,
Such as none other in Achaia's host,
May fierce contention from among the Gods
Perish, and from among the human race,
With wrath, which sets the wisest hearts on fire;
Sweeter than dropping honey to the taste,
But in the bosom of mankind, a smoke![3]
Such was my wrath which Agamemnon roused,
The king of men. But since the past is fled
Irrevocable, howsoe'er distressed,
Renounce we now vain musings on the past,
Content through sad necessity. I go
In quest of noble Hector, who hath slain
My loved Patroclus, and such death will take
As Jove ordains me and the Powers of Heaven
At their own season, send it when they may.
For neither might the force of Hercules,
Although high-favored of Saturnian Jove,
From death escape, but Fate and the revenge
Restless of Juno vanquish'd even Him.
I also, if a destiny like his
Await me, shall, like him, find rest in death;
But glory calls me now; now will I make
Some Trojan wife or Dardan with both hands
Wipe her soft cheeks, and utter many a groan.

Long time have I been absent from the field,
And they shall know it. Love me as thou may'st,
Yet thwart me not, for I am fixt to go.
    Whom Thetis answer'd, Goddess of the Deep.
Thou hast well said, my son! it is no blame
To save from threaten'd death our suffering friends.
But thy magnificent and dazzling arms
Are now in Trojan hands; them Hector wears
Exulting, but ordain'd not long to exult,
So habited; his death is also nigh.
But thou with yonder warring multitudes
Mix not till then behold me here again;
For with the rising sun I will return
To-morrow, and will bring thee glorious arms,
By Vulcan forged himself, the King of fire.[4]
    She said, and turning from her son aside,
The sisterhood of Ocean thus address'd.
    Plunge ye again into the briny Deep,
And to the hoary Sovereign of the floods
Report as ye have heard. I to the heights
Olympian haste, that I may there obtain
From Vulcan, glorious artist of the skies,
Arms of excelling beauty for my son.
    She said; they plunged into the waves again,
And silver-footed Thetis, to the heights
Olympian soaring swiftly to obtain
Arms for renown'd Achilles, disappeared.
    Meantime, with infinite uproar the Greeks
From Hector's hero-slaying arm had fled
Home to their galleys station'd on the banks
Of Hellespont. Nor yet Achaia's sons
Had borne the body of Patroclus clear
From flight of darts away, but still again
The multitude of warriors and of steeds
Came on, by Priameian Hector led
Rapid as fire. Thrice noble Hector seized
His ancles from behind, ardent to drag
Patroclus, calling to his host the while;
But thrice, the two Ajaces, clothed with might,
Shock'd and repulsed him reeling. He with force
Fill'd indefatigable, through his ranks
Issuing, by turns assail'd them, and by turns
Stood clamoring, yet not a step retired;
But as the hinds deter not from his prey
A tawny lion by keen hunger urged,
So could not both Ajaces, warriors bold,
Intimidate and from the body drive
Hector; and he had dragg'd him thence and won
Immortal glory, but that Iris, sent
Unseen by Jove and by the powers of heaven,
From Juno, to Achilles brought command
That he should show himself. Full near she drew,
And in wing'd accents thus the Chief address'd.
    Hero! most terrible of men, arise!
Protect Patroclus, for whose sake the war

Stands at the fleet of Greece. Mutual prevails
The slaughter, these the dead defending, those
Resolute hence to drag him to the gates
Of wind-swept Ilium. But beyond them all
Illustrious Hector, obstinate is bent
To win him, purposing to lop his head,
And to exhibit it impaled on high.
Thou then arise, nor longer on the ground
Lie stretch'd inactive; let the thought with shame
Touch thee, of thy Patroclus made the sport
Of Trojan dogs, whose corse, if it return
Dishonor'd home, brings with it thy reproach.
To whom Achilles matchless in the race.
Iris divine! of all the Gods, who sent thee?
Then, thus, the swift ambassadress of heaven.
By Juno sent I come, consort of Jove.
Nor knows Saturnian Jove high-throned, himself,
My flight, nor any of the Immortal Powers,
Tenants of the Olympian heights snow-crown'd.
Her answer'd then Pelides, glorious Chief.
How shall I seek the fight? they have my arms.
My mother charged me also to abstain
From battle, till she bring me armor new
Which she hath promised me from Vulcan's hand.
Meantime, whose armor else might serve my need
I know not, save perhaps alone the shield
Of Telamonian Ajax, whom I deem
Himself now busied in the stormy van,
Slaying the Trojans in my friend's defence.
To whom the swift-wing'd messenger of heaven.
Full well we know thine armor Hector's prize.
Yet, issuing to the margin of the foss,
Show thyself only. Panic-seized, perchance,
The Trojans shall from fight desist, and yield
To the o'ertoil'd though dauntless sons of Greece
Short respite; it is all that war allows.
So saying, the storm-wing'd Iris disappear'ed.
Then rose at once Achilles dear to Jove,
Athwart whose shoulders broad Minerva cast
Her Ægis fringed terrific, and his brows
Encircled with a golden cloud that shot
Fires insupportable to sight abroad.
As when some island, situate afar
On the wide waves, invested all the day
By cruel foes from their own city pour'd,
Upsends a smoke to heaven, and torches shows
On all her turrets at the close of eve
Which flash against the clouds, kindled in hope
Of aid from neighbor maritime allies,
So from Achilles' head light flash'd to heaven.
Issuing through the wall, beside the foss
He stood, but mix'd not with Achaia's host,
Obedient to his mother's wise command.
He stood and shouted; Pallas also raised
A dreadful shout and tumult infinite

Excited throughout all the host of Troy.
Clear as the trumpet's note when it proclaims
A numerous host approaching to invest
Some city close around, so clear the voice
Rang of Æacides, and tumult-toss'd
Was every soul that heard the brazen tone.
With swift recoil the long-maned coursers thrust
The chariots back, all boding wo at hand.
And every charioteer astonish'd saw
Fires, that fail'd not, illumining the brows
Of Peleus' son, by Pallas kindled there.
Thrice o'er the trench Achilles sent his voice
Sonorous, and confusion at the sound
Thrice seized the Trojans, and their famed allies.
Twelve, in that moment of their noblest died
By their own spears and chariots, and with joy
The Grecians from beneath a hill of darts
Dragging Patroclus, placed him on his bier.
Around him throng'd his fellow-warriors bold,
All weeping, after whom Achilles went
Fast-weeping also at the doleful sight
Of his true friend on his funereal bed
Extended, gash'd with many a mortal wound,
Whom he had sent into the fight with steeds
And chariot but received him thence no more.
    And now majestic Juno sent the sun,
Unwearied minister of light, although
Reluctant, down into the Ocean stream.[5]
So the sun sank, and the Achaians ceased
From the all-wasting labors of the war.
On the other side, the Trojans, from the fight
Retiring, loosed their steeds, but ere they took
Thought of refreshment, in full council met.
It was a council at which no man sat,
Or dared; all stood; such terror had on all
Fallen, for that Achilles had appear'd,
After long pause from battle's arduous toil.
First rose Polydamas the prudent son
Of Panthus, above all the Trojans skill'd
Both in futurity and in the past.
He was the friend of Hector, and one night
Gave birth to both. In council one excell'd
And one still more in feats of high renown.
Thus then, admonishing them, he began.
    My friends! weigh well the occasion. Back to Troy
By my advice, nor wait the sacred morn
Here, on the plain, from Illium's walls remote.
So long as yet the anger of this Chief
'Gainst noble Agamemnon burn'd, so long
We found the Greeks less formidable foes,
And I rejoiced, myself, spending the night
Beside their eery barks, for that I hoped
To seize them; but I now tremble at thought
Of Peleus' rapid son again in arms.
A spirit proud as his will scorn to fight

Here, on the plain, where Greeks and Trojans take
Their common share of danger and of toil,
And will at once strike at your citadel,
Impatient till he make your wives his prey.
Haste—let us home—else thus shall it befall
Night's balmy influence in his tent detains
Achilles now, but rushing arm'd abroad
To-morrow, should he find us lingering here,
None shall mistake him then; happy the man
Who soonest, then, shall 'scape to sacred Troy!
Then, dogs shall make and vultures on our flesh
Plenteous repast. Oh spare mine ears the tale
But if, though troubled, ye can yet receive
My counsel, thus assembled we will keep
Strict guard to-night; meantime, her gates and towers
With all their mass of solid timbers, smooth
And cramp'd with bolts of steel, will keep the town.
But early on the morrow we will stand
All arm'd on Ilium's towers. Then, if he choose,
His galleys left, to compass Troy about,
He shall be task'd enough; his lofty steeds
Shall have their fill of coursing to and fro
Beneath, and gladly shall to camp return.
But waste the town he shall not, nor attempt
With all the utmost valor that he boasts
To force a pass; dogs shall devour him first.
To whom brave Hector louring, and in wrath.
Polydamas, I like not thy advice
Who bidd'st us in our city skulk, again
Imprison'd there. Are ye not yet content?
Wish ye for durance still in your own towers?
Time was, when in all regions under heaven
Men praised the wealth of Priam's city stored
With gold and brass; but all our houses now
Stand emptied of their hidden treasures rare.
Jove in his wrath hath scatter'd them; our wealth
Is marketed, and Phrygia hath a part
Purchased, and part Mæonia's lovely land.
But since the son of wily Saturn old
Hath given me glory now, and to inclose
The Grecians in their fleet hemm'd by the sea,
Fool! taint not with such talk the public mind.
For not a Trojan here will thy advice
Follow, or shall; it hath not my consent.
But thus I counsel. Let us, band by band,
Throughout the host take supper, and let each,
Guarded against nocturnal danger, watch.
And if a Trojan here be rack'd in mind
Lest his possessions perish, let him cast
His golden heaps into the public maiw,[6]
Far better so consumed than by the Greeks.
Then, with the morrow's dawn, all fair array'd
In battle, we will give them at their fleet
Sharp onset, and if Peleus' noble son
Have risen indeed to conflict for the ships,

The worse for him. I shall not for his sake
Avoid the deep-toned battle, but will firm
Oppose his utmost. Either he shall gain
Or I, great glory, Mars his favors deals
Impartial, and the slayer oft is slain.
So counsell'd Hector, whom with shouts of praise
The Trojans answer'd:—fools, and by the power
Of Pallas of all sober thought bereft!
For all applauded Hector, who had given
Advice pernicious, and Polydamas,
Whose counsel was discreet and wholesome none.
So then they took repast. But all night long
The Grecians o'er Patroclus wept aloud,
While, standing in the midst, Pelides led
The lamentation, heaving many a groan,
And on the bosom of his breathless friend
Imposing, sad, his homicidal hands.
As the grim lion, from whose gloomy lair
Among thick trees the hunter hath his whelps
Purloin'd, too late returning mourns his loss,
Then, up and down, the length of many a vale
Courses, exploring fierce the robber's foot,
Incensed as he, and with a sigh deep-drawn
Thus to his Myrmidons Achilles spake.
How vain, alas! my word spoken that day
At random, when to soothe the hero's fears
Menœtius, then our guest, I promised him
His noble son at Opoeis again,
Living and laden with the spoils of Troy!
But Jove performs not all the thoughts of man,
For we were both destined to tinge the soil
Of Ilium with our blood, nor I shall see,
Myself, my father in his mansion more
Or Thetis, but must find my burial here.
Yet, my Patroclus! since the earth expects
Me next, I will not thy funereal rites
Finish, till I shall bring both head and arms
Of that bold Chief who slew thee, to my tent,
I also will smite off, before thy pile,
The heads of twelve illustrious sons of Troy,
Resentful of thy death. Meantime, among
My lofty galleys then shalt lie, with tears
Mourn'd day and night by Trojan captives fair
And Dardan compassing thy bier around,
Whom we, at price of labor hard, ourselves
With massy spears toiling in battle took
From many an opulent city, now no more.
So saying, he bade his train surround with fire
A tripod huge, that they might quickly cleanse
Patroclus from all stain of clotted gore.
They on the blazing hearth a tripod placed
Capacious, fill'd with water its wide womb,
And thrust dry wood beneath, till, fierce, the flames
Embraced it round, and warm'd the flood within.
Soon as the water in the singing brass

Simmer'd, they bathed him, and with limpid oil
Anointed; filling, next, his ruddy wounds
With unguent mellow'd by nine circling years,
They stretch'd him on his bed, then cover'd him
From head to feet with linen texture light,
And with a wide unsullied mantle, last.[7]
All night the Myrmidons around the swift
Achilles stood, deploring loud his friend,
And Jove his spouse and sister thus bespoke.
So then, Imperial Juno! not in vain
Thou hast the swift Achilles sought to rouse
Again to battle; the Anchaians, sure,
Are thy own children, thou best borne them all.
To whom the awful Goddess ample-eyed.
What word both pass'd thy lips, Jove, most severe?
A man, though mortal merely, and to me
Inferior in device, might have achieved
That labor easily. Can I who boast
Myself the chief of Goddesses, and such
Not by birth only, but as thine espoused,
Who art thyself sovereign of all the Gods,
Can I with anger burn against the house
Of Priam, and want means of just revenge?
Thus they in heaven their mutual conference held.
Meantime, the silver-footed Thetis reach'd
The starr'd abode eternal, brazen wall'd
Of Vulcan, by the builder lame himself
Uprear'd, a wonder even in eyes divine.
She found him sweating, at his bellows huge
Toiling industrious; tripods bright be form'd
Twenty at once, his palace-wall to grace
Ranged in harmonious order. Under each
Two golden wheels he set, on which (a sight
Marvellous!) into council they should roll
Self-moved, and to his house, self-moved, return.
Thus far the work was finish'd, but not yet
Their ears of exquisite design affixt,
For them he stood fashioning, and prepared
The rivets. While he thus his matchless skill
Employ'd laborious, to his palace-gate
The silver-footed Thetis now advanced,
Whom Charis, Vulcan's well-attired spouse,
Beholding from the palace portal, flow
To seize the Goddess' hand, and thus inquired.
Why, Thetis! worthy of all reverence
And of all love, comest thou to our abode,
Unfrequent here? But enter, and accept
Such welcome as to such a guest is due.
So saying, she introduced and to a seat
Led her with argent studs border'd around
And foot-stool'd sumptuously;[8] then, calling forth
Her spouse, the glorious artist, thus she said.
Haste, Vulcan! Thetis wants thee; linger not.
To whom the artist of the skies replied.

A Goddess then, whom with much cause I love
And venerate is here, who when I fell
Saved me, what time my shameless mother sought
To cast me, because lame, out of all sight;
Then had I been indeed forlorn, had not
Eurynome the daughter of the Deep
And Thetis in their laps received me fallen.
Nine years with them residing, for their use
I form'd nice trinkets, clasps, rings, pipes, and chains,
While loud around our hollow cavern roar'd
The surge of the vast deep, nor God nor man,
Save Thetis and Eurynome, my life's
Preservers, knew where I was kept conceal'd.
Since, therefore, she is come, I cannot less
Than recompense to Thetis amber-hair'd
With readiness the boon of life preserved.
Haste, then, and hospitably spread the board
For her regale, while with my best dispatch
I lay my bellows and my tools aside.
He spake, and vast in bulk and hot with toil
Rose limping from beside his anvil-stock
Upborne, with pain on legs tortuous and weak.
First, from the forge dislodged he thrust apart
His bellows, and his tools collecting all
Bestow'd them, careful, in a silver chest,
Then all around with a wet sponge he wiped
His visage, and his arms and brawny neck
Purified, and his shaggy breast from smutch;
Last, putting on his vest, he took in hand
His sturdy staff, and shuffled through the door.
Beside the King of fire two golden forms
Majestic moved, that served him in the place
Of handmaids; young they seem'd, and seem'd alive,
Nor want they intellect, or speech, or force,
Or prompt dexterity by the Gods inspired.
These his supporters were, and at his side
Attendant diligent, while he, with gait
Uncouth, approaching Thetis where she sat
On a bright throne, seized fast her hand and said.
Why, Thetis! worthy as thou art of love
And of all reverence, hast thou arrived,
Unfrequent here? Speak—tell me thy desire,
Nor doubt my services, if thou demand
Things possible, and possible to me.
Then Thetis, weeping plenteously, replied.
Oh Vulcan! Is there on Olympius' heights
A Goddess with such load of sorrow press'd
As, in peculiar, Jove assigns to me?
Me only, of all ocean-nymphs, he made
Spouse to a man, Peleus Æacides,
Whose bed, although reluctant and perforce,
I yet endured to share. He now, the prey
Of cheerless age, decrepid lies, and Jove
Still other woes heaps on my wretched head.
He gave me to bring forth, gave me to rear

A son illustrious, valiant, and the chief
Of heroes; he, like a luxuriant plant
Upran[9] to manhood, while his lusty growth
I nourish'd as the husbandman his vine
Set in a fruitful field, and being grown
I sent him early in his gallant fleet
Embark'd, to combat with the sons of Troy;
But him from fight return'd I shall receive,
Beneath the roof of Peleus, never more,
And while he lives and on the sun his eyes
Opens, affliction is his certain doom,
Nor aid resides or remedy in me.
The virgin, his own portion of the spoils,
Allotted to him by the Grecians—her
Atrides, King of men, resumed, and grief
Devour'd Achilles' spirit for her sake.
Meantime, the Trojans shutting close within
Their camp the Grecians, have forbidden them
All egress, and the senators of Greece
Have sought with splendid gifts to soothe my son.
He, indisposed to rescue them himself
From ruin, sent, instead, Patroclus forth,
Clad in his own resplendent armor, Chief
Of the whole host of Myrmidons. Before
The Scæan gate from morn to eve they fought,
And on that self-same day had Ilium fallen,
But that Apollo, to advance the fame
Of Hector, slew Mencatius' noble son
Full-flush'd with victory. Therefore at thy knees
Suppliant I fall, imploring from thine art
A shield and helmet greaves of shapely form
With clamps secured, and corselet for my son.
For those, once his, his faithful friend hath lost,
Slain by the Trojans, and Achilles lies,
Himself, extended mournful on the ground.
    Her answer'd then the artist of the skies.
Courage! Perplex not with these cares thy soul.
I would that when his fatal hour shall come,
I could as sure secrete him from the stroke
Of destiny, as he shall soon have arms
Illustrious, such as each particular man
Of thousands, seeing them, shall wish his own.
    He said, and to his bellows quick repair'd,
Which turning to the fire he bode them heave.
Full twenty bellows working all at once
Breathed on the furnace, blowing easy and free
The managed winds, now forcible, as best
Suited dispatch, now gentle, if the will
Of Vulcan and his labor so required.
Impenetrable brass, tin, silver, gold,
He cast into the forge, then, settling firm
His ponderous anvil on the block, one band
With his huge hammer fill'd, one with the tongs.
    [10]He fashion'd first a shield massy and broad
Of labor exquisite, for which he form'd

A triple border beauteous, dazzling bright,
And loop'd it with a silver brace behind.
The shield itself with five strong folds he forged,
And with devices multiform the disk
Capacious charged, toiling with skill divine.
There he described the earth, the heaven, the sea,
The sun that rests not, and the moon full-orb'd.
There also, all the stars which round about
As with a radiant frontlet bind the skies,
The Pleiads and the Hyads, and the might
Of huge Orion, with him Ursa call'd,
Known also by his popular name, the Wain,
That spins around the pole looking toward
Orion, only star of these denied
To slake his beams in ocean's briny baths.
Two splendid cities also there he form'd
Such as men build. In one were to be seen
Rites matrimonial solemnized with pomp
Of sumptuous banquets; from their chambers forth
Leading the brides they usher'd them along
With torches through the streets, and sweet was heard
The voice around of Hyrmenæal song.
Here striplings danced in circles to the sound
Of pipe and harp, while in the portals stood
Women, admiring, all, the gallant show.
Elsewhere was to be seen in council met
The close-throng'd multitude. There strife arose.
Two citizens contended for a mulet
The price of blood. This man affirm'd the fine
All Paid,[11] haranguing vehement the crowd,
That man denied that lie had ought received,
And to the judges each made his appeal
Eager for their award. Meantime the people,
As favor sway'd them, clamor'd loud for each.
The heralds quell'd the tumult; reverend sat
On polished stones the elders in a ring,
Each with a herald's sceptre in his hand,
Which holding they arose, and all in turn
Gave sentence. In the midst two talents lay
Of gold, his destined recompense whose voice
Decisive should pronounce the best award.
The other city by two glittering hosts
Invested stood, and a dispute arose
Between the hosts, whether to burn the town
And lay all waste, or to divide the spoil.
Meantime, the citizens, still undismay'd,
Surrender'd not the town, but taking arms
Secretly, set the ambush in array,
And on the walls their wives and children kept
Vigilant guard, with all the ancient men.
They sallied; at their head Pallas and Mars
Both golden and in golden vests attired
Advanced, proportion each showing divine,
Large, prominent, and such as Gods beseem'd.
Not such the people, but of humbler size.

Arriving at the spot for ambush chosen,
A river's side, where cattle of each kind
Drank, down they sat, all arm'd in dazzling brass.
Apart from all the rest sat also down
Two spies, both looking for the flocks and herds.
Soon they appear'd, and at their side were seen
Two shepherd swains, each playing on his pipe
Careless, and of the danger nought apprized.
Swift ran the spies, perceiving their approach,
And intercepting suddenly the herds
And flocks of silver fleece, view also those
Who fed them. The besiegers, at that time
In council, by the sound alarm'd, their steeds
Mounted, and hasted, instant to the place;
Then, standing on the river's brink they fought
And push'd each other with the brazen lance.
There Discord raged, there Tumult, and the force
Of ruthless Destiny; she now a Chief
Seized newly wounded, and now captive hold
Another yet unhurt, and now a third
Dragg'd breathless through the battle by his feet,
And all her garb was dappled thick with blood.
Like living men they traversed and they strove,
And dragg'd by turns the bodies of the slain.
He also grayed on it a fallow field
Rich, spacious, and well-till'd. Plowers not few,
There driving to and fro their sturdy teams,
Labor'd the land; and oft as in their course
They came to the field's bourn, so oft a man
Met them, who in their hands a goblet placed
Charged with delicious wine. They, turning, wrought
Each his own furrow, and impatient seem'd
To reach the border of the tilth, which black
Appear'd behind them as a globe new-turn'd,
Though golden. Sight to be admired by all!
There too he form'd the likeness of a field
Crowded with corn, in which the reapers toil'd
Each with a sharp-tooth'd sickle in his hand.
Along the furrow here, the harvest fell
In frequent handfuls, there, they bound the sheaves.
Three binders of the sheaves their sultry task
All plied industrious, and behind them boys
Attended, filling with the corn their arms
And offering still their bundles to be bound.
Amid them, staff in hand, the master stood
Silent exulting, while beneath, an oak
Apart, his heralds busily prepared
The banquet, dressing a well-thriven ox
New slain, and the attendant maidens mix'd
Large supper for the hinds of whitest flour.
There also, laden with its fruit he form'd
A vineyard all of gold; purple he made
The clusters, and the vines supported stood
By poles of silver set in even rows.
The trench he color'd sable, and around

Fenced it with tin. One only path it show'd
By which the gatherers when they stripp'd the vines
Pass'd and repass'd. There, youths and maidens blithe
In frails of wicker bore the luscious fruit,
While, in the midst a boy on his shrill harp
harmonious play'd, still as he struck the chord
Carolling to it with a slender voice.
They smote the ground together, and with song
And sprightly reed came dancing on behind.[12]
There too a herd he fashion'd of tall beeves
Part gold, part tin. They, lowing, from the stalls
Rush'd forth to pasture by a river-side
Rapid, sonorous, fringed with whispering reeds.
Four golden herdsmen drove the kine a-field
By nine swift dogs attended. Dreadful sprang
Two lions forth, and of the foremost herd
Seized fast a bull, Him bellowing they dragg'd,
While dogs and peasants all flow to his aid.
The lions tore the hide of the huge prey
And lapp'd his entrails and his blood. Meantime
The herdsmen, troubling them in vain, their hounds
Encouraged; but no tooth for lions' flesh
Found they, and therefore stood aside and bark'd.
There also, the illustrious smith divine
Amidst a pleasant grove a pasture form'd
Spacious, and sprinkled o'er with silver sheep
Numerous, and stalls and huts and shepherds' tzents.
To these the glorious artist added next,
With various skill delineated exact,
A labyrinth for the dance, such as of old
In Crete's broad island Dædalus composed
For bright-hair'd Ariadne.[13] There the youths
And youth-alluring maidens, hand in hand,
Danced jocund, every maiden neat-attired
In finest linen, and the youths in vests
Well-woven, glossy as the glaze of oil
These all wore garlands, and bright falchions, those,
Of burnish'd gold in silver trappings hung:—[14]
They with well-tutor'd step, now nimbly ran
The circle, swift, as when, before his wheel
Seated, the potter twirls it with both hands
For trial of its speed,[15] now, crossing quick
They pass'd at once into each other's place.
On either side spectators numerous stood
Delighted, and two tumblers roll'd themselves
Between the dancers, singing as they roll'd.
Last, with the might of ocean's boundless flood
He fill'd the border of the wondrous shield.
When thus the massy shield magnificent
He had accomplish'd, for the hero next
He forged, more ardent than the blaze of fire,
A corselet; then, a ponderous helmet bright
Well fitted to his brows, crested with gold,
And with laborious art divine adorn'd.
He also made him greaves of molten tin.

The armor finish'd, bearing in his hand
The whole, he set it down at Thetis' feet.
She, like a falcon from the snowy top
Stoop'd of Olympus, bearing to the earth
The dazzling wonder, fresh from Vulcan's hand.

Notes

1. This speech of Antilochus may serve as a model for its brevity.
2. This form of manifesting grief is frequently alluded to in the classical writers, and sometimes in the Bible. The lamentation of Achilles is in the spirit of the heroic times, and the poet describes it with much simplicity. The captives join in the lamentation, perhaps in the recollection of his gentleness, which has before been alluded to.—FELTON.
3. [Here it is that the drift of the whole poem is fulfilled. The evil consequent on the quarrel between him and Agamemnon, at last teaches Achilles himself this wisdom—that wrath and strife are criminal and pernicious; and the confession is extorted from his own lips, that the lesson may be the more powerfully inculcated. To point the instruction to leaders of armies only is to narrow its operation unnecessarily.]—TR.
4. The promise of Thetis to present her son with a suit of armor, was the most artful method of hindering him from putting immediately in practice his resolution of fighting, which, with his characteristic violence, he would otherwise have done.
5. [The sun is said to set with reluctance, because his setting-time was not yet come. Jupiter had promised Hector that he should prevail till the sun should go down, and sacred darkness cover all. Juno therefore, impatient to arrest the victor's progress, and having no other means of doing it, shortens the time allotted him.]—TR.
6. Καταδημοβορῆσαι.
7. This custom of washing the dead is continued among the Greeks to this day, and is performed by the dearest friend or relative. The body is then annointed with a perfume, and covered with linen, exactly in the manner here indicated.
8. Among the Greeks, visitors of rank are still honored in the same manner, by being set apart from the rest of the company, on a high seat, with a footstool.
9. Ανεδραμε
10. The description of the shield of Achilles is one of the noblest passages in the *Iliad*. It is elaborated to the highest finish of poetry. The verse is beautifully harmonious and the language as nicely chosen and as descriptive as can be conceived. But a still stronger interest belongs to this episode when considered as an exact representation of life at a very early period of the world, as it undoubtedly was designed by the pact.

    It is certainly a most remarkable passage for the amount of information it conveys relative to the state of arts, and the general condition of life at that period. From many intimations in the ancient authors, it may be gathered, that shields were often adorned by deities of figures in bas-relief similar to those here described. In particular, see Æscliyius in the Seven against Thebes. A close examination of the whole passage will lead to many curious inductions and inferences relative to the ancient world, and throw much light upon points which are elsewhere left in great obscurity.—FELTON.
11. Murder was not always punished with death or even banishment. But on the payment of a fine, the criminal was allowed to remain in the city.
12. Linus was the most ancient name in poetry, the first upon record as the inventor of verse and measure among the Grecians. There was a solemn custom among the Greeks, of bewailing annually their first poet. Pausanias informs us, that before the yearly sacrifice to the Muses on Mount Helicon, the obsequies of Linus were performed, who had a statue and altar erected to him in that place. In this passage Homer is supposed to allude to that custom.

13. There were two kids of dance—the Pyrrhic, and the common dance; both are here introduced. The Pyrrhic, or military, is performed by youths wearing swords, the other by the virgins crowned with garlands. The Grecian dance is still performed in this manner in the oriental nations. The youths and maidens dance in a ring, beginning slowly; by degrees the music plays in quicker time, till at last they dance with the utmost swiftness; and towards the conclusion, they sing in a general chorus.
14. The point of comparison is this. When the potter first tries the wheel to see "if it will run," he moves it much faster than when at work. Thus it illustrates the rapidity of the dance.—FELTON.

Book XXII

Thus they, throughout all Troy, like Hunted fawns
Dispersed, their trickling limbs at leisure cool'd,
And, drinking, slaked their fiery thirst, reclined
Against the battlements. Meantime, the Greeks
Sloping their shields, approach'd the walls of Troy,
And Hector, by his adverse fate ensnared,
Still stood exposed before the Scæan gate.
Then spake Apollo thus to Peleus' son.
  Wherefore, thyself mortal, pursuest thou me
Immortal? oh Achilles! blind with rage,
Thou know'st not yet, that thou pursuest a God.
Unmindful of thy proper task, to press
The flying Trojans, thou hast hither turn'd
Devious, and they are all now safe in Troy;
Yet hope me not to slay; I cannot die.
  To whom Achilles swiftest of the swift,
Indignant. Oh, of all the Powers above
To me most adverse, Archer of the skies
Thou hast beguiled me, leading me away
From Ilium far, whence intercepted, else,
No few bad at this moment gnaw'd the glebe.
Thou hast defrauded me of great renown,
And, safe thyself, hast rescued *them* with ease.
Ah—had I power, I would requite thee well.
  So saying, incensed he turned toward the town
His rapid course, like some victorious steed
That whirls, at stretch, a chariot to the goal,
Such seem'd Achilles coursing light the field,
  Him first, the ancient King of Troy perceived
Scouring the plain resplendent as the star
Autumnal, of all stars in dead of night
Conspicuous most, and named Orion's dog;
Brightest it shines, but ominous, and dire
Disease portends to miserable man;[1]
So beam'd Achilles' armor as he flew
Loud wail'd the hoary King: with lifted hands
His head he smote, and, uttering doleful cries
Of supplication sued to his own son,
He, fixt before the gate, desirous stood
Of combat with Achilles, when his sire
With arms outstretch'd toward him, thus began.
  My Hector! wait not, oh my son! the approach
Of this dread Chief, alone, lest premature
Thou die, this moment by Achilles slain,
For he is strongest far. Oh that the Gods
Him loved as I! then soon should vultures rend
And dogs his carcase, and my grief should cease.
He hath unchilded me of many a son,

All valiant youths, whom he hath slain or sold
To distant Isles, and even now, I miss
Two sons, whom since the shutting of the gates
I find not, Polydorus and Lycaon
My children by Laothöe the fair,
If they survive prisoners in yonder camp,
I will redeem them with the gold and brass
By noble Eltes to his daughter given,
Large store, and still reserved. But should they both,
Already slain, have journey'd to the shades,
We, then, from whom they sprang have cause to mourn
And mourn them long, but shorter shall the grief
Of Ilium prove, If thou escape and live.
Come then my son! enter the city-gate
That thou may'st save us all, nor in thy bloom
Of life cut off, enhance Achilles' fame.
Commiserate also thy unhappy sire
Ere yet distracted, whom Saturnian Jove
Ordains to a sad death, and ere I die
To woes innumerable; to behold
Sons slaughter'd, daughters ravish'd torn and stripp'd
The matrimonial chamber, infants dash'd
Against the ground in dire hostility,[2]
And matrons dragg'd by ruthless Grecian hands.
Me, haply, last of all, dogs shall devour
In my own vestibule, when once the spear
Or falchion of some Greek hath laid me low.
The very dogs fed at my table-side,
My portal-guards, drinking their master's blood
To drunkenness, shall wallow in my courts,
Fair falls the warlike youth in battle slain,
And when he lies torn by the pointed steel,
His death becomes him well; he is secure,
Though dead, from shame, whatever next befalls
But when the silver locks and silver beard
Of an old man slain by the sword, from dogs
Receive dishonor, of all ills that wait
On miserable man, that sure is worst.
　So spake the ancient King, and his grey hairs
Pluck'd with both hands, but Hector firm endured.
On the other side all tears his mother stood,
And lamentation with one hand she bared,
And with the other hand produced her breast,
Then in wing'd accents, weeping, him bespake.
　My Hector! reverence this, and pity me
If ever drawing forth this breast, thy griefs
Of infancy I soothed, oh now my son!
Acknowledge it, and from within the walls
Repulse this enemy; stand not abroad
To cope with *him,* for he is savage-fierce,
And should he slay thee, neither shall myself
Who bore thee, nor thy noble spouse weep o'er
Thy body, but, where we can never come,
Dogs shall devour it in the fleet of Greece.

So they with prayers importuned, and with tears
Their son, but him sway'd not; unmoved he stood,
Expecting vast Achilles now at hand.
As some fell serpent in his cave expects
The traveler's approach, batten'd with herbs
Of baneful juice to fury,[3] forth he looks
Hideous, and lies coil'd all around his den
So Hector, fill'd with confidence untamed,
Fled not, but placing his bright shield against
A buttress, with his noble heart conferr'd.
[4]Alas for me! should I repass the gate,
Polydamas would be the first to heap
Reproaches on me, for he bade me lead
The Trojans back this last calamitous night
In which Achilles rose to arms again.
But I refused, although to have complied,
Had proved more profitable far; since then
By rash resolves of mine I have destroy'd
The people, how can I escape the blame
Of all in Troy? The meanest there will say—
By his self-will he hath destroy'd us all.
So shall they speak, and then shall I regret
That I return'd ere I had slain in fight
Achilles, or that, by Achilles slain,
I died not nobly in defense of Troy.
But shall I thus? Lay down my bossy shield,
Put off my helmet, and my spear recline
Against the city wall, then go myself
To meet the brave Achilles, and at once
Promise him Helen, for whose sake we strive
With all the wealth that Paris in his fleet
Brought home, to be restored to Atreus' sons,
And to distribute to the Greeks at large
All hidden treasures of the town, an oath
Taking beside from every senator,
That he will nought conceal, but will produce
And share in just equality what stores
Soever our fair city still includes!
Ah airy speculations, questions vain!
I may not sue to him: compassion none
Will he vouchsafe me, or my suit respect,
But, seeing me unarm'd, will sate at once
His rage, and womanlike I shall be slain.
It is no time from oak or hollow rock
With him to parley, as a nymph and swain,
A nymph and swain[5] soft parley mutual hold,
But rather to engage in combat fierce
Incontinent; so shall we soonest learn
Whom Jove will make victorious, him or me.
Thus pondering he stood; meantime approach'd
Achilles, terrible as fiery Mars,
Crest-tossing God, and brandish'd as he came
O'er his right shoulder high the Pelian spear.

Like lightning, or like flame, or like the sun
Ascending, beam'd his armor. At that sight
Trembled the Trojan Chief, nor dared expect
His nearer step, but flying left the gates
Far distant, and Achilles swift pursued.
As in the mountains, fleetest fowl of air,
The hawk darts eager at the dove; she scuds
Aslant, he screaming, springs and springs again
To seize her, all impatient for the prey,
So flew Achilles constant to the track
Of Hector, who with dreadful haste beneath
The Trojan bulwarks plied his agile limbs.
Passing the prospect-mount where high in air
The wild-fig waved,[6] they rush'd along the road,
Declining never from the wall of Troy.
And now they reach'd the running rivulets clear,
Where from Scamander's dizzy flood arise
Two fountains,[7] tepid one, from which a smoke
Issues voluminous as from a fire,
The other, even in summer heats, like hail
For cold, or snow, or crystal-stream frost-bound.
Beside them may be seen the broad canals
Of marble scoop'd, in which the wives of Troy
And all her daughters fair were wont to lave
Their costly raiment,[8] while the land had rest
And ere the warlike sons of Greece arrived.
By these they ran, one fleeing, one in chase.
Valiant was he who fled, but valiant far
Beyond him lie who urged the swift pursuit;
Nor ran they for a vulgar prize, a beast
For sacrifice, or for the hide of such,
The swift foot-racer's customary need,
But for the noble Hector's life they ran.
As when two steeds, oft conquerors, trim the goal
For some illustrious prize, a tripod bright
Or beauteous virgin, at a funeral game,
So they with nimble feet the city thrice
Of Priam compass'd. All the Gods looked on,
And thus the Sire of Gods and men began.
　Ah—I behold a warrior dear to me
Around the walls of Ilium driven, and grieve
For Hector, who the thighs of fatted bulls
On yonder heights of Ida many-valed
Burn'd oft to me, and in the heights of Troy:[9]
But him Achilles, glorious Chief, around
The city walls of Priam now pursues.
Consider this, ye Gods! weigh the event.
Shall we from death save Hector? or, at length,
Leave him, although in battle high renown'd,
To perish by the might of Peleus' son?
　Whom answer'd thus Pallas cerulean-eyed.
Dread Sovereign of the storms! what hast thou said?
Wouldst thou deliver from the stroke of fate
A mortal man death-destined from of old?

Do it; but small thy praise shall be in heaven.
Then answer thus, cloud-gatherer Jove return'd.
Fear not, Tritonia, daughter dear! that word
Spake not my purpose; me thou shalt perceive
Always to thee indulgent. What thou wilt
That execute, and use thou no delay.
So roused he Pallas of herself prepared,
And from the heights Olympian down she flew
With unremitting speed Achilles still
Urged Hector. As among the mountain-height
The hound pursues, roused newly from her lair
The flying fawn through many a vale and grove;
And though she trembling skulk the shrubs beneath,
Tracks her continual, till he find the prey,
So 'scaped not Hector Peleus' rapid son.
Oft as toward the Dardan gates he sprang
Direct, and to the bulwarks firm of Troy,
Hoping some aid by volleys from the wall,
So oft, outstripping him, Achilles thence
Enforced him to the field, who as he might,
Still over stretch'd toward the walls again.
As in a dream,[10] pursuit hesitates oft,
This hath no power to fly, that to pursue,
So these—one fled, and one pursued in vain.
How, then, had Hector his impending fate
Eluded, had not Phœbus, at his last,
Last effort meeting him, his strength restored,
And wing'd for flight his agile limbs anew?
The son of Pelcus, as he ran, his brows,
Shaking, forbad the people to dismiss
A dart at Hector, lest a meaner hand
Piercing him, should usurp the foremost praise.
But when the fourth time to those rivulets
They came, then lifting high his golden scales,
Two lots the everlasting Father placed
Within them, for Achilles one, and one
For Hector, balancing the doom of both.
Grasping it in the midst, he raised the beam.
Down went the fatal day of Hector, down
To Ades, and Apollo left his side.
Then blue-eyed Pallas hasting to the son
Of Peleus, in wing'd accents him address'd.
Now, dear to Jove, Achilles famed in arms!
I hope that, fierce in combat though he be,
We shall, at last, slay Hector, and return
Crown'd with great glory to the fleet of Greece.
No fear of His deliverance now remains,
Not even should the King of radiant shafts,
Apollo, toil in supplication, roll'd
And roll'd again[11] before the Thunderer's feet.
But stand, recover breath; myself, the while,
Shall urge him to oppose thee face to face.
So Pallas spake, whom joyful he obey'd,
And on his spear brass-pointed lean'd. But she,
(Achilles left) to noble Hector pass'd,

And in the form, and with the voice loud-toned
Approaching of Deiphobus, his ear
In accents, as of pity, thus address'd.
  Ah brother! thou art overtask'd, around
The walls of Troy by swift Achilles driven;
But stand, that we may chase him in his turn.[12]
  To whom crest-tossing Hector huge replied.
Deiphobus! of all my father's sons
Brought forth by Hecuba, I ever loved
Thee most, but more than ever love thee now,
Who hast not fear'd, seeing me, for my sake
To quit the town, where others rest content.
  To whom the Goddess, thus, cerulean-eyed.
Brother! our parents with much earnest suit
Clasping my knees, and all my friends implored me
To stay in Troy, (such fear hath seized on all)
But grief for thee prey'd on my inmost soul.
Come—fight we bravely—spare we now our spears
No longer; now for proof if Peleus' son
Slaying us both, shall bear into the fleet
Our arms gore-stain'd, or perish slain by thee.
  So saying, the wily Goddess led the way.
They soon, approaching each the other, stood
Opposite, and huge Hector thus began.
  Pelides! I will fly thee now no more.
Thrice I have compass'd Priam's spacious walls
A fugitive, and have not dared abide
Thy onset, but my heart now bids me stand
Dauntless, and I will slay, or will be slain.
But come. We will attest the Gods; for they
Are fittest both to witness and to guard
Our covenant. If Jove to me vouchsafe
The hard-earn'd victory, and to take thy life,
I will not with dishonor foul insult
Thy body, but, thine armor stripp'd, will give
Thee to thy friends, as thou shalt me to mine.
  To whom Achilles, lowering dark, replied.
Hector! my bitterest foe! speak not to me
Of covenants! as concord can be none
Lions and men between, nor wolves and lambs
Can be unanimous, but hate perforce
Each other by a law not to be changed,
So cannot amity subsist between
Thee and myself; nor league make I with thee
Or compact, till thy blood in battle shed
Or mine, shall gratify the fiery Mars.
Rouse all thy virtue; thou hast utmost need
Of valor now, and of address in arms.
Escape me more thou canst not; Pallas' hand
By mine subdues thee; now will I avenge
At once the agonies of every Greek
In thy unsparing fury slain by thee.
  He said, and, brandishing the Pelian ash,
Dismiss'd it; but illustrious Hector warn'd,
Crouched low, and, overflying him, it pierced

The soil beyond, whence Pallas plucking it
Unseen, restored it to Achilles' hand,
And Hector to his godlike foe replied.
    Godlike Achilles! thou bast err'd, nor know'st
At all my doom from Jove, as thou pretend'st,
But seek'st, by subtlety and wind of words,
All empty sounds, to rob me of my might.
Yet stand I firm. Think not to pierce my back.
Behold my bosom! if the Gods permit,
Meet me advancing, and transpierce me there.
Meantime avoid my glittering spear, but oh
May'st thou receive it all! since lighter far
To Ilium should the toils of battle prove,
Wert thou once slain, the fiercest of her foes.
    He said, and hurling his long spear with aim
Unerring, smote the centre of the shield
Of Peleus' son, but his spear glanced away.
He, angry to have sent it forth in vain,
(For he had other none) with eyes downcast
Stood motionless awhile, then with loud voice
Sought from Deiphobus, white-shielded Chief,
A second; but Deiphobus was gone.
Then Hector understood his doom, and said.
    Ah, it is plain; this is mine hour to die.
I thought Deiphobus at hand, but me
Pallas beguiled, and he is still in Troy.
A bitter death threatens me, it is nigh,
And there is no escape; Jove, and Jove's son
Apollo, from the first, although awhile
My prompt deliverers, chose this lot for me,
And now it finds me. But I will not fall
Inglorious; I will act some great exploit
That shall be celebrated ages hence.
    So saying, his keen falchion from his side
He drew, well-temper'd, ponderous, and rush'd
At once to combat. As the eagle darts
Right downward through a sullen cloud to seize
Weak lamb or timorous hare, so brandishing
His splendid falchion, Hector rush'd to fight.
Achilles, opposite, with fellest ire
Full-fraught came on; his shield with various art
Celestial form'd, o'erspread his ample chest,
And on his, radiant casque terrific waved
The bushy gold of his resplendent crest,
By Vulcan spun, and pour'd profuse around,
Bright as, among the stars, the star of all
Most radiant, Hesperus, at midnight moves,
So, is the right hand of beam'd
His brandish'd spear, while mediatating wo
To Hector, he explored his noble form,
Seeking where he was vulnerable most,
But every part, his dazzling armor torn
From brave Patroclus' body, well secured,
Save where the circling key-bone from the neck
Disjoins the shoulder; there his throat appear'd

Whence injured life with swiftest flight escapes;
Achilles, plunging in that part his spear,
Impell'd it through the yielding flesh beyond
The ashen beam his power of utterance left
Still unimpair'd, but in the dust he fell,
And the exulting conqueror exclaim'd.
  But Hector thou hadst once fair other hopes,
And, stripping slain Patroclus, thought'st thee safe,
Nor caredst for absent me. Fond dream and vain!
I was not distant far; in yonder fleet
He left one able to avenge his death,
And he hath slain thee. Thee the dogs shall rend
Dishonorably, and the fowls of air,
But all Achaia's host shall him entomb.
  To whom the Trojan Chief languid replied.
By thy own life, by theirs who gave thee birth,
And by thy knees,[13] oh let not Grecian dogs
Rend and devour me, but in gold accept
And brass a ransom at my father's hands,
And at my mother's an illustrious price ;
Send home my body, grant me burial rites
Among the daughters and the sons of Troy.
  To whom with aspect stern Achilles thus.
Dog! neither knees nor parents name to me.
I would my fierceness of revenge were such,
That I could carve and eat thee, to whose arms
Such griefs I owe; so true it is and sure,
That none shall save thy carcass from the dogs.
No, trust me, would thy parents bring me weigh'd
Ten—twenty ransoms, and engage on oath
To add still more; would thy Dardanian Sire
Priam, redeem thee with thy weight in gold,
Not even at that price would I consent
That she who bare should place thee on thy bier
With lamentation; dogs and ravening fowls
Shall rend thy body while a scrap remains.
  Then, dying, warlike Hector thus replied.
Full well I knew before, how suit of mine
Should speed preferr'd to thee. Thy heart is steel.
But oh, while yet thou livest, think, lest the Gods
requite thee on that day, when pierced thyself
By Paris and Apollo, thou shalt fall,
Brave as thou art, before the Scæan gate.
  He ceased, and death involved him dark around.
His spirit, from his limbs dismiss'd, the house
Of Ades sought, mourning in her descent
Youth's prime and vigor lost, disastrous doom
But him though dead, Achilles thus bespake.
  Die thou. My death shall find me at what hour
Jove gives commandment, and the Gods above.
  He spake, and from the dead drawing away
His brazen spear, placed it apart, then stripp'd
His arms gore-stain'd. Meantime the other sons
Of the Achaians, gathering fast around,

The bulk admired, and the proportion just
Of Hector; neither stood a Grecian there
Who pierced him not, and thus the soldier spake.
Ye Gods ! how far more patient of the touch
Is Hector now, than when he fired the fleet!
Thus would they speak, then give him each a stab.
And now, the body stripp'd, their noble Chief
The swift Achilles standing in the midst,
The Grecians in wing'd accents thus address'd.
Friends, Chiefs and Senators; of Argos' host!
Since, by the will of heaven, this man is slain
Who harm'd us more than all our foes beside,
Essay we next the city, so to learn
The Trojan purpose, whether (Hector slain)
They will forsake the citadel, or still
Defend it, even though of him deprived.
But wherefore speak I thus? Still undeplored,
Unburied in my fleet Patroclus lies;
Him never, while alive myself, I mix
With living men and move, will I forget.
In Ades, haply, they forget the dead,
Yet will not I Patroclus, even there.
Now chanting pæans, ye Achaian youths!
Return we to the fleet with this our prize;
We have achieved great glory,[14] we have slain
Illustrious Hector, him whom Ilium praised
In all her gates, and as a God revered.
He said; then purposing dishonor foul
To noble Hector, both his feet he bored
From heel to ancle, and, inserting thongs,
Them tied behind his chariot, but his head
Left unsustain'd to trail along the ground.
Ascending next, the armor at his side
He placed, then lash'd the steeds; they willing flew.
Thick dust around the body dragg'd arose,
His sable locks all swept the plain, and all
His head, so graceful once, now track'd the dust
For Jove had given it into hostile hands
That they might shame it in his native soil.[15]
Thus, whelm'd in dust, it went. The mother Queen
Her son beholding, pluck'd her hair away,
Cast far aside her lucid veil, and fill'd
With shrieks the air. His father wept aloud,
And, all around, long, long complaints were heard
And lamentations in the streets of Troy,
Not fewer or less piercing, than if flames
Had wrapt all Ilium to her topmost towers.
His people scarce detain'd the ancient King
Grief-stung, and resolute to issue forth
Through the Dardanian gates; to all he kneel'd
In turn, then roll'd himself in dust, and each
By name solicited to give him way.
Stand off, my fellow mourners! I would pass
The gates, would seek, alone, the Grecian fleet.
I go to supplicate the bloody man,

Yon ravager; he may respect, perchance,
My years, may feel some pity of my age
For, such as I am, his own father is,
Peleus, who rear'd him for a curse to Troy,
But chiefly rear'd him to myself a curse,
So numerous have my sons in prime of youth
Fall'n by his hand, all whom I less deplore
(Though mourning all) than one; my agonies
For Hector soon shall send me to the shades.
Oh had he but within these arms expired,
The hapless Queen who bore him, and myself
Had wept him, then, till sorrow could no more!
    So spake he weeping, and the citizens
All sigh'd around; next, Hecuba began
Amid the women, thus, her sad complaint.
    Ah wherefore, oh my son! wretch that I am,
Breathe I forlorn of thee? Thou, night and day,
My glory wast in Ilium, thee her sons
And daughters, both, hail'd as their guardian God,
Conscious of benefits from thee received,
Whose life prolong'd should have advanced them all
To high renown. Vain boast! thou art no more.
    So mourn'd the Queen. But fair Andromache
Nought yet had heard, nor knew by sure report
Hector's delay without the city gates.
She in a closet of her palace sat,
A twofold web weaving magnificent,
With sprinkled flowers inwrought of various hues,
And to her maidens had commandment given
Through all her house, that compassing with fire
An ample tripod, they should warm a bath
For noble Hector from the fight return'd.
Tenderness ill-inform'd! she little knew
That in the field, from such refreshments far,
Pallas had slain him by Achilles' hand.
She heard a cry of sorrow from the tower;
Her limbs shook under her, her shuttle fell,
And to her bright-hair'd train, alarm'd, she cried.
    Attend me two of you, that I may learn
What hath befallen. I have heard the voice
Of the Queen-mother; my rebounding heart
Chokes me, and I seem fetter'd by a frost.
Some mischief sure o'er Priam's sons impends.
Far be such tidings from me! but I fear
Horribly, lest Achilles, cutting off
My dauntless Hector from the gates alone,
Enforce him to the field, and quell perhaps
The might, this moment, of that dreadful arm
His hinderence long; for Hector near was wont
To seek his safety in the ranks, but flew
First into battle, yielding place to none
    So saying, she rush'd with palpitating heart
And frantic air abroad, by her two maids
Attended; soon arriving at the tower,
And at the throng of men, awhile she stood

Down-looking wistful from the city-wall,
And, seeing him in front of Ilium, dragg'd
So cruelly toward the fleet of Greece,
O'erwhelm'd with sudden darkness at the view
Fell backward, with a sigh heard all around.
Far distant flew dispersed her head-attire,
Twist, frontlet, diadem, and even the veil
By golden Venus given her on the day
When Hector led her from Eëtion's house
Enrich'd with nuptial presents to his home.
Around her throng'd her sisters of the house
Of Priam, numerous, who within their arms
Fast held her[16] loathing life; but she, her breath
At length and sense recovering, her complaint
Broken with sighs amid them thus began.
Hector! I am undone; we both were born
To misery, thou in Priam's house in Troy,
And I in Hypoplacian Thebes wood-crown'd
Beneath Eëtion's roof. He, doom'd himself
To sorrow, me more sorrowfully doom'd,
Sustain'd in helpless infancy, whom oh
That he had ne'er begotten! Thou descend'st
To Pluto's subterraneous dwelling drear,
Leaving myself destitute, and thy boy,
Fruit of our hapless loves, an infant yet,
Never to be hereafter thy delight,
Nor love of thine to share or kindness more.
For should he safe survive this cruel war,
With the Achaians penury and toil
Mast be his lot, since strangers will remove
At will his landmarks, and possess his fields.
Thee lost, he loses all, of father, both,
And equal playmate in one day deprived,
To sad looks doom'd, and never-ceasing tears.
He seeks, necessitous his father's friends,
One by his mantle pulls, one by his vest,
Whose utmost pity yields to his parch'd lips
A thirst-provoking drop, and grudges more;
Some happier child, as yet untaught to mourn
A parent's loss, shoves rudely from the board
My son, and, smiting him, reproachful cries
Away—thy father is no guest of ours—
Then, weeping, to his widow'd mother comes
Astyanax, who on his father's lap
Ate marrow only, once, and fat of lambs,[17]
And when sleep took him, and his crying fit
Had ceased, slept ever on the softest bed,
Warm in his nurse's arms, fed to his fill
With delicacies, and his heart at rest.
But now, Astyanax (so named in Troy
For thy sake, guardian of her gates and towers)
His Mother lost, must many a pang endure.
And as for thee, cast naked forth among

Yon galleys, where no parent's eye of thine
Shall find thee, when the dogs have torn thee once
Till they are sated, worms shall eat thee next.
Meantime, thy graceful raiment rich, prepared
By our own maidens, in thy palace lies;
But I will burn it, burn it all, because
Useless to thee, who never, so adorn'd,
Shalt slumber more; yet every eye in Troy
Shall see, how glorious once was thy attire.[18]
So, weeping, she; to whom the multitude
Of Trojan dames responsive sigh'd around.

Notes

1. This simile is very striking. It not only describes the appearance of Achilles, but is peculiarly appropriate because the star was supposed to be of evil omen, and to bring with it disease and destruction. So Priam beholds Achilles, splendid with the divine armor, and the destined slayer of his son.—FELTON.
2. The usual cruelties practised in the sacking of towns. Isaiah foretells to Babylon, that her children shall be dashed in pieces by the Medes. David says to the same city, "Happy shall he be that taketh and dasheth thy little ones against the stones."—Ps. cxxxvii. 9.
3. It was supposed that venomous serpents were accustomed to eat poisonous roots and plants before attacking their victims—FELTON.
4. This speech of Hector shows the fluctuation of his mind, with much discernment on the part of the poet. He breaks out, after having apparently meditated a return to the city. But the imagined reproaches of Polydamus, and the anticipated scorn of the Trojans forbid it. He soliloquizes upon the possibility of coming to terms with Achilles, and offering him large concessions but the character of Achilles precludes all hope of reconciliation. It Is a fearful crisis with him, and his mind wavers, as if presentient of his approaching doom.—FELTON.
5. [The repetition follows the original, and the Scholiast is of the opinion that Homer uses it here that he may express more emphatically the length to which such conferences are apt to proceed.]—TR
6. [It grew near to the tomb of Ilus.]
7. The Scamander ran down the eastern side of Ida, and at the distance of three stadia from Troy, making a subterraneous dip, it passed under the walls and rose again in the form of the two fountains here described—from which fountains these rivulets are said to have proceeded.
8. It was the custom of that age to have cisterns by the side of rivers and fountains, to which the women, including the wives and daughters of kings and princes, resorted to wash their garments.
9. Sacrifices were offered to the gods upon the hills and mountains, or, in the language of scripture, upon the *high places*, for the people believed that the gods inhabited such eminences.
10. [The numbers in the original are so constructed as to express the painful struggle that characterizes such a dream.]—TR.
11. [προπροκυλινδόμενος.]
12. The whole circumference of ancient Troy is said to have measured sixty stadia. A stadium measured one hundred and twenty-five paces.
13. [The knees of the conqueror were a kind of sanctuary to which the vanquished fled for refuge.]—TR.
14. [The lines of which these three are a translation, are supposed by some to have been designed for the Επινικιον, or song of victory sung by the whole army.—TR.

15. [It was a custom in Thessaly to drag the slayer around the tomb of the slain; which custom was first begun by Simon, whose brother being killed by Eurydamas, he thus treated the body of the murderer. Achilles therefore, being a Thessallan, when he thus dishonors Hector, does it merely in compliance with the common practice of his country.]—TR.
16. (It is an observation of the Scholiast, that two more affecting spectacles cannot be imagined, than Priam struggling to escape into the field, and Andromache to cast herself from the wall.]—TR.
17. A figurative expression. In the style of the Orientals, marrow and fatness are taken for whatever is best most tender, and most delicious.
18. Homer is in nothing more excellent than in the distinction of characters, which he maintains throughout the poem. What Andromache here says cannot be said with propriety by any one but Andromache.

Book XXIV

The games all closed, the people went dispersed
Each to his ship; they, mindful of repast,
And to enjoy repose; but other thoughts
Achilles' mind employ'd: he still deplored
With tears his loved Patroclus, nor the force
Felt of all-conquering sleep, but turn'd and turn'd
Restless from side to side, —mourning the loss
Of such a friend, so manly, and so brave.
Their fellowship in toil; their hardships oft
Sustain'd in fight laborious, or o'ercome
With difficulty on the perilous deep—
Remembrance busily retracing themes
Like these, drew down his cheeks continual tears.
Now on his side he lay, now lay supine,
Now prone, then starting from his couch he roam'd
Forlorn the beach, nor did the rising morn
On seas and shores escape his watchful eye,
But joining to his chariot his swift steeds,
He fasten'd Hector to be dragg'd behind.
Around the tomb of Menœtiades
Him thrice he dragg'd; then rested in his tent,
Leaving him at his length stretch'd in the dust.
Meantime Apollo with compassion touch'd
Even of the lifeless Hector, from all taint
Saved him, and with the golden ægis broad
Covering, preserved him, although dragg'd, untorn.
While he, indulging thus his wrath, disgraced
Brave Hector, the immortals at that sight
With pity moved, exhorted Mercury
The watchful Argicide, to steal him thence.
That counsel pleased the rest, but neither pleased
Juno, nor Neptune, nor the blue-eyed maid.
They still, as at the first, held fast their hate
Of sacred Troy, detested Priam still,
And still his people, mindful of the crime
Of Paris, who when to his rural hut
They came, those Goddesses affronting,[1] praise
And admiration gave to her alone
Who with vile lusts his preference repaid.
But when the twelfth ensuing morn arose,
Apollo, then, the immortals thus address'd.
Ye Gods, your dealings now injurious seem
And cruel. Was not Hector wont to burn
Thighs of fat goats and bullocks at your shrine?
Whom now, though dead, ye cannot yet endure
To rescue, that Andromache once more
Might view him, his own mother, his own son,
His father and the people, who would soon

Yield him his just demand, a funeral fire.
But, oh ye Gods! your pleasure is alone
To please Achilles, that pernicious chief,
Who neither right regards, nor owns a mind
That can relent, but as the lion, urged
By his own dauntless heartland savage force,
Invades without remorse the rights of man,
That he may banquet on his herds and flocks,
So Peleus' son all pity from his breast
Hath driven, and shame, man's blessing or his curse.[2]
For whosoever hath a loss sustain'd
Still dearer, whether of his brother born
From the same womb, or even of his son,
When he hath once bewail'd him, weeps no more,
For fate itself gives man a patient mind.
Yet Peleus' son, not so contented, slays
Illustrious Hector first, then drags his corse
In cruel triumph at his chariot-wheels
Around Patroclus' tomb; but neither well
He acts, nor honorably to himself,
Who may, perchance, brave though he be, incur
Our anger, while to gratify revenge
He pours dishonor thus on senseless clay.
To whom, incensed, Juno white-arm'd replied.
And be it so; stand fast this word of thine,
God of the silver bow! if ye account
Only such honor to Achilles due
As Hector claims; but Hector was by birth
Mere man, and suckled at a woman's breast.
Not such Achilles; him a Goddess bore,
Whom I myself nourish'd, and on my lap
Fondled, and in due time to Peleus gave
in marriage, to a chief beloved in heaven
Peculiarly; ye were yourselves, ye Gods!
Partakers of the nuptial feast, and thou
Wast present also with thine harp in hand,
Thou comrade of the vile! thou faithless ever!
Then answer thus cloud-gatherer Jove return'd.
Juno, forbear. Indulge not always wrath
Against the Gods. They shall not share alike,
And in the same proportion our regards.
Yet even Hector was the man in Troy
Most favor'd by the Gods, and him no less
I also loved, for punctual were his gifts
To us; mine altar never miss'd from him
Libation, or the steam of sacrifice,
The meed allotted to us from of old.
But steal him not, since by Achilles' eye
Unseen ye cannot, who both day and night
Watches[3] him, as a mother tends her son.
But call ye Thetis hither, I would give
The Goddess counsel, that, at Priam's hands
Accepting gifts, Achilles loose the dead.
He ceased. Then Iris tempest-wing'd arose.
Samos between, and Imbrus rock-begirt,

She plunged into the gloomy flood; loud groan'd
The briny pool, while sudden down she rush'd
As sinks the bull's[4] horn with its leaden weight,
Death bearing to the raveners of the deep.
Within her vaulted cave Thetis she found
By every nymph of Ocean, round about
Encompass'd; she, amid them all, the fate
Wept of her noble son ordain'd to death
At fertile Troy, from Phthia far remote.
Then, Iris, drawing near, her thus address'd.
  Arise, O Thetis! Jove, the author dread
Of everlasting counsels, calls for thee.
  To whom the Goddess of the silver feet.
Why calls the mighty Thunderer me? I fear,
Oppress'd with countless sorrows as I am,
To mingle with the Gods. Yet I obey—
No word of his can prove an empty sound.
  So saying, the Goddess took her sable veil
(Eye ne'er beheld a darker) and began
Her progress, by the storm-wing'd Iris led.
On either hand the billows open'd wide
A pass before them; they, ascending soon
The shore, updarted swift into the skies.
They found loud-voiced Saturnian Jove around
Environ'd by the ever-blessed Gods
Convened in full assembly; she beside
Her Father Jove (Pallas retiring) sat.
Then, Juno, with consolatory speech,
Presented to her hand a golden cup,
Of which she drank, then gave it back again,
And thus the sire of Gods and men began.
  Goddess of ocean, Thetis! thou hast sought
Olympus, bearing in thy bosom grief
Never to be assuaged, as well I know.
Yet shalt thou learn, afflicted as thou art,
Why I have summon'd thee. Nine days' the Gods,
Concerning Hector's body and thy own
Brave city-spoiler son, have held dispute,
And some have urged oftentimes the Argicide
Keen-sighted Mercury, to steal the dead.
But I forbade it for Achilles' sake,
Whom I exalt the better to insure
Thy reverence and thy friendship evermore.
Haste, therefore, seek thy son, and tell him thus,
The Gods resent it, say (but most of all
Myself am angry) that he still detains
Amid his fleet, through fury of revenge,
Unransom'd Hector; so shall he, at length,
Through fear of me, perchance, release the slain.
Myself to generous Priam will, the while,
Send Iris, who shall bid him to the fleet
Of Greece, such ransom bearing as may soothe
Achilles, for redemption of his son.
  So spake the God, nor Thetis not complied.
Descending swift from the Olympian heights

She reach'd Achilles' tent. Him there she found
Groaning disconsolate, while others ran
To and fro, occupied around a sheep
New-slaughter'd, large, and of exuberant fleece.
She, sitting close beside him, softly strok'd
His cheek, and thus, affectionate, began.
How long, my son! sorrowing and mourning here,
Wilt thou consume thy soul, nor give one thought.
Either to food or love? Yet love is good,
And woman grief's best cure; for length of days
Is not thy doom, but, even now, thy death
And ruthless destiny are on the wing.
Mark me,—I come a lieger sent from Jove.
The Gods, he saith, resent it, but himself
More deeply than the rest, that thou detain'st
Amid thy fleet, through fury of revenge,
Unransom'd Hector. Be advised, accept
Ransom, and to his friends resign the dead.
To whom Achilles, swiftest of the swift.
Come then the ransomer, and take him hence;
If Jove himself command it,—be it so.
So they, among the ships, conferring sat
On various themes, the Goddess and her son
Meantime Saturnian Jove commanded down
His swift ambassadress to sacred Troy.
Hence, rapid Iris! leave the Olympian heights.
And, finding noble Priam, bid him haste
Into Achaia's fleet, bearing such gifts
As may assuage Achilles, and prevail
To liberate the body of his son.
Alone, he must; no Trojan of them all
May company the senior thither, save
An ancient herald to direct his mules
And his wheel'd litter, and to bring the dead
Back into Ilium, whom Achilles slew.
Let neither fear of death nor other fear
Trouble him aught, so safe a guard and sure
We give him; Mercury shall be his guide
Into Achilles' presence in his tent.
Nor will himself Achilles slay him there,
Or even permit his death, but will forbid
All violence; for he is not unwise
Nor heedless, no—nor wilful to offend,
But will his suppliant with much grace receive.[5]
He ceased; then Iris tempest-wing'd arose.
Jove's messenger, and, at the gates arrived
Of Priam, wo and wailing found within.
Around their father, in the hall, his sons
Their robes with tears water'd, while them amidst
The hoary King sat mantled, muffled close,
And on his venerable head and neck
Much dust was spread, which, rolling on the earth,
He had shower'd on them with unsparing hands.
The palace echoed to his daughters' cries,
Arid to the cries of matrons calling fresh

Into remembrance many a valiant chief
Now stretch'd in dust, by Argive hands destroy'd.
The messenger of Jove at Priam's side
Standing, with whispered accents low his ear
Saluted, but he trembled at the found.
    Courage, Dardanian Priam! fear thou nought;
To thee no prophetess of ill, I come;
But with kind purpose: Jove's ambassadress
Am I, who though remote, yet entertains
Much pity, and much tender care for thee.
Olympian Jove commands thee to redeem
The noble Hector, with an offering large
Of gifts that may Achilles' wrath appease.
Alone, thou must; no Trojan of them all
Hath leave to attend thy journey thither, save
An ancient herald to direct thy mules
And thy wheel'd litter, and to bring the dead
Back into Ilium, whom Achilles slew.
Let neither fear of death nor other fear
Trouble thee aught, so safe a guard and sure
He gives thee; Mercury shall be thy guide
Even to Achilles' presence in his tent.
Nor will himself Achilles slay thee there,
Or even permit thy death, but will forbid
All violence; for he is not unwise
Nor heedless, no—nor wilful to offend,
But will his suppliant with much grace receive.
    So spake the swift ambassadress, and went.
Then, calling to his sons, he bade them bring
His litter forth, and bind the coffer on,
While to his fragrant chamber he repair'd
Himself, with cedar lined and lofty-roof'd,
A treasury of wonders into which
The Queen he summon'd, whom he thus bespake.
    Hecuba! the ambassadress of Jove
Hath come, who bids me to the Grecian fleet,
Bearing such presents thither as may soothe
Achilles, for redemption of my son.
But say, what seems this enterprise to thee?
Myself am much inclined to it, I feel
My courage prompting me amain toward
The fleet, and into the Achaian camp.
    Then wept the Queen aloud, and thus replied.
Ah! whither is thy wisdom fled, for which
Both strangers once, and Trojans honor'd thee
How canst thou wish to penetrate alone
The Grecian fleet, and to appear, before
His face, by whom so many valiant sons
Of thine have fallen? Thou hast an iron heart!
For should that savage man and faithless once
Seize and discover thee, no pity expect
Or reverence at his bands. Come—let us weep
Together, here sequester'd; for the thread
Spun for him by his destiny severe
When he was born, ordain'd our son remote

From us his parents to be food for hounds
In that chief's tent. Oh I clinging to his side,
How I could tear him with my teeth! His deeds,
Disgraceful to my son, then should not want
Retaliation; for he slew not him
Skulking, but standing boldly for the wives,
The daughters fair, and citizens of Troy,
Guiltless of flight,[6] and of the wish to fly.
Whom godlike Priam answer'd, ancient King.
Impede me not who willing am to go,
Nor be, thyself, a bird of ominous note
To terrify me under my own roof,
For thou shalt not prevail. Had mortal man
Enjoin'd me this attempt, prophet, or priest,
Or soothsayer, I had pronounced him false
And fear'd it but the more. But, since I saw
The Goddess with these eyes, and heard, myself,
The voice divine, I go; that word shall stand
And, if my doom be in the fleet of Greece
To perish, be it so; Achilles' arm
Shall give me speedy death, and I shall die
Folding my son, and satisfied with tears.
So saying, he open'd wide the elegant lids
Of numerous chests, whence mantles twelve he took
Of texture beautiful; twelve single cloaks
As many carpets, with as many robes,
To which he added vests, an equal store.
He also took ten talents forth of gold,
All weigh'd, two splendid tripods, caldrons four,
And after these a cup of matchless worth
Given to him when ambassador in Thrace;
A noble gift, which yet the hoary King
Spared not, such fervor of desire he felt
To loose his son. Then from his portico,
With angry taunts he drove the gathered crowds.
Away! away! ye dregs of earth, away!
Ye shame of human kind!. Have ye no griefs
At home, that ye come hither troubling me?
Deem ye it little that Saturnian Jove
Afflicts me thus, and of my very best,
Best boy deprives me? Ah! ye shall be taught
Yourselves that loss, far easier to be slain
By the Achaians now, since he is dead.
But I, ere yet the city I behold
Taken and pillaged, with these aged eyes,
Shall find safe hiding in the shades below.
He said, and chased them with his staff; they left
In haste the doors, by the old King expell'd.
Then, chiding them aloud, his sons he call'd,
Helenus, Paris, noble Agathon,
Pammon, Antiphonus, and bold in fight
Polites, Dios of illustrious fame,
Hippothoüs and Deiphobus—all nine
He call'd, thus issuing, angry, his commands.

Quick! quick! ye slothful in your father's cause,
Ye worthless brood I would that in Hector's stead
Ye all had perish'd in the fleet of Greece!
Oh altogether wretched! in all Troy
No man had sons to boast valiant as mine,
And I have lost them all. Mestor is gone
The godlike, Troilus the steed-renown
And Hector, who with other men compared
Seem'd a Divinity, whom none had deem'd
From mortal man derived, but from a God.
These Mars hath taken, and hath left me none
But scandals of my house, void of all truth,
Dancers, exact step-measurers,[7] a band
Of public robbers, thieves of kids and lambs.
Will ye not bring my litter to the gate
This moment, and with all this package quick
Charge it, that we may hence without delay?
He said, and by his chiding awed, his sons
Drew forth the royal litter, neat, new-built,
And following swift the draught, on which they bound
The coffer; next, they lower'd from the wall
The sculptured boxen yoke with its two rings;[8]
And with the yoke its furniture, in length
Nine cubits; this to the extremest end
Adjusting of the pole, they cast the ring
Over the ring-bolt; then, thrice through the yoke
They drew the brace on both sides, made it fast
With even knots, and tuck'd[9] the dangling ends.
Producing, next, the glorious ransom-price.
Of Hector's body, on the litter's floor
They heap'd it all, then yoked the sturdy mules,
A gift illustrious by the Mysians erst
Conferr'd on Priam to the chariot, last,
They led forth Priam's steeds, which the old King
(In person serving them) with freshest corn
Constant supplied meantime, himself within
The palace, and his herald, were employ'd
Girding[10] themselves, to go; wise each and good.
And now came mournful Hecuba, with wine
Delicious charged, which in a golden cup
She brought, that not without libation due
First made, they might depart. Before the steeds
Her steps she stay'd, and Priam thus address'd.
Take this, and to the Sire of all perform
Libation, praying him a safe return
From hostile bands' since thou art urged to seek
The Grecian camp, though not by my desire.
Pray also to Idæan Jove cloud-girt,
Who oversees all Ilium, that he send
His messenger or ere thou go, the bird
His favorite most, surpassing all in strength,
At thy right hand; him seeing, thou shalt tend
With better hope toward the fleet of Greece.
But should loud-thundering Jove his lieger swift
Withhold, from me far be it to advise

This journey, howsoe'er thou wish to go.
To whom the godlike Priam thus replied.
This exhortation will I not refuse,
O Queen! for, lifting to the Gods his hands
In prayer for their compassion, none can err.
So saying, he bade the maiden o'er the rest,
Chief in authority, pour on his hands
Pure water, for the maiden at his side
With ewer charged and laver, stood prepared.
He laved his hands; then, taking from the Queen
The goblet, in his middle area stood
Pouring libation with his eyes upturn'd
Heaven-ward devout, and thus his prayer preferr'd.
Jove, great and glorious above all, who rulest,
On Ida's summit seated, all below!
Grant me arrived within Achilles' tent
Kindness to meet and pity, and oh send
Thy messenger or ere I go, the bird
Thy favorite most, surpassing all in strength,,
At my right hand, which seeing, I shall tend
With better hope toward the fleet of Greece.
He ended, at whose prayer, incontinent,
Jove sent his eagle, surest of all signs,
The black-plumed bird voracious, Morphnos[11] named,
And Percnos.[11] Wide as the well-guarded door
Of some rich potentate his vans he spread
On either side; they saw him on the right,
Skimming the towers of Troy; glad they beheld
That omen, and all felt their hearts consoled.
Delay'd not then the hoary King, but quick.
Ascending to his seat, his coursers urged
Through vestibule and sounding porch abroad.
The four-wheel'd litter led, drawn by the mules
Which sage Idæus managed, behind whom
Went Priam, plying with the scourge his steeds
Continual through the town, while all his friends,
Following their sovereign with dejected hearts,
Lamented him as going to his death.
But when from Ilium's gate into the plain
They had descended, then the sons-in-law
Of Priam, and his sons, to Troy return'd.
Nor they, now traversing the plain, the note
Escaped of Jove the Thunderer he beheld
Compassionate the venerable King,
And thus his own son Mercury bespake.
Mercury! (for above all others thou
Delightest to associate with mankind
Familiar, whom thou wilt winning with ease
To converse free) go thou, and so conduct
Priam into the Grecian camp, that none
Of all the numerous Danai may see
Or mark him, till he reach Achilles' tent.
He spake, nor the ambassador of heaven
The Argicide delay'd, but bound in haste

His undecaying sandals to his feet,
Golden, divine, which waft him o'er the floods
Swift as the wind, and o'er the boundless earth
He took his rod with which he charms to sleep
All eyes, and theirs who sleep opens again.
Arm'd with that rod, forth flew the Argicide.
At Ilium and the Hellespontic shores
Arriving sudden, a king's son he seem'd,
Now clothing first his ruddy cheek with down,
Which is youth's loveliest season; so disguised,
His progress he began. They now (the tomb
Magnificent of Ilus past) beside
The river stay'd the mules and steeds to drink,
For twilight dimm'd the fields. Idæus first
Perceived him near, and Priam thus bespake.
Think, son of Dardanus! for we have need
Of our best thought. I see a warrior. Now,
Now we shall die; I know it. Turn we quick
Our steeds to flight; or let us clasp his knees
And his compassion suppliant essay.
Terror and consternation at that sound
The mind of Priam felt; erect the hair
Bristled his limbs, and with amaze he stood
Motionless. But the God, meantime, approach'd,
And, seizing ancient Priam's hand, inquired.
Whither, my father! in the dewy night
Drivest thou thy mules and steeds, while others sleep?
And fear'st thou not the fiery host of Greece,
Thy foes implacable, so nigh at hand
Of whom should any, through the shadow dun
Of flitting night, discern thee bearing forth
So rich a charge, then what wouldst thou expect?
Thou art not young thyself, nor with the aid
Of this thine ancient servant, strong enough
Force to repulse, should any threaten force.
But injury fear none or harm from me;
I rather much from harm by other hands
Would save thee, thou resemblest so my sire.
Whom answer'd godlike Priam, hoar with age.
My son! well spoken. Thou hast judged aright.
Yet even me some Deity protects
Thus far to whom I owe it that I meet
So seasonably one like thee, in form
So admirable, and in mind discreet
As thou art beautiful. Blest parents, thine!
To whom the messenger of Heaven again,
The Argicide. Oh ancient and revered!
Thou hast well spoken all. Yet this declare,
And with sincerity; bear'st thou away
Into some foreign country, for the sake
Of safer custody this precious charge
Or, urged by fear, forsake ye all alike
Troy's sacred towers! since he whom thou hast lost,
Thy noble son, was of excelling worth
In arms, and nought inferior to the Greeks.

Then thus the godlike Priam, hoary King.
But tell me first who *Thou* art, and from whom
Descended, loveliest youth! who hast the fate
So well of my unhappy son rehearsed?
To whom the herald Mercury replied,
Thy questions, venerable sire! Proposed
Concerning noble Hector, are design'd
To prove me. Him, not seldom, with these eyes
In man-ennobling fight I have beheld
Most active; saw him when he thinn'd the Greeks
With his sharp spear, and drove them to the ships.
Amazed we stood to notice him; for us,
Incensed against the ruler of our host,
Achilles suffer'd not to share the fight.
I serve Achilles; the same gallant bark
Brought us, and of the Myrmidons am I,
Son of Polyctor; wealthy is my sire,
And such in years as thou; six sons he hath,
Beside myself the seventh, and (the lots cast
Among us all) mine sent me to the wars.
That I have left the ships, seeking the plain,
The cause is this; the Greeks, at break of day,
Will compass, arm'd, the city, for they loathe
To sit inactive, neither can the chiefs
Restrain the hot impatience of the host.
Then godlike Priam answer thus return'd.
If of the band thou be of Peleus' son,
Achilles, tell me undisguised the truth.
My son, subsists he still, or hath thy chief
Limb after limb given him to his dogs?
Him answer'd then the Herald of the skies.
Oh venerable sir! him neither dogs
Have eaten yet, nor fowls, but at the ships
His body, and within Achilles' tent
Neglected lies. Twelve days he so hath lain;
Yet neither worm which diets on the brave
In battle fallen, hath eaten him, or taint
Invaded. He around Patroclus' tomb
Drags him indeed pitiless, oft as day
Reddens the cast, yet safe from blemish still
His corse remains. Thou wouldst, thyself, admire
Seeing how fresh the dew-drops, as he lies,
Rest on him, and his blood is cleansed away
That not a stain is left. Even his wounds
(For many a wound they gave him) all are closed,
Such care the blessed Gods leave of thy son,
Dead as he is, whom living much they loved.
So he; then, glad, the ancient King replied.
Good is it, oh my son! to yield the Gods
Their just demands. My boy, while yet he lived,
Lived not unmindful of the worship due
To the Olympian powers, who, therefore, him
Remember, even in the bands of death.
Come then—this beauteous cup take at my hand—
Be thou my guard, and, if the Gods permit,

My guide, till to Achilles' tent I come.
  Whom answer'd then the messenger of heaven;
Sir! thou perceivest me young, and art disposed
To try my virtue; but it shall not fail.
Thou bidd'st me at thine hand a gift accept,
Whereof Achilles knows not; but I fear
Achilles, and on no account should dare
Defraud him, lest sonic evil find me next.
But thee I would with pleasure hence conduct
Even to glorious Argos, over sea
Or over land, nor any, through contempt
Of such a guard, should dare to do thee wrong.
  So Mercury, and to the chariot seat
Upspringing, seized at once the lash and reins,
And with fresh vigor mules and steeds inspired.
Arriving at the foss and towers, they found
The guard preparing now their evening cheer,
All whom the Argicide with sudden sleep
Oppress'd, then oped the gates, thrust back the bars,
And introduced, with all his litter-load
Of costly gifts, the venerable King,
But when they reached the tent for Peleus' son
Raised by the Myrmidons (with trunks of pine
They built it, lopping smooth the boughs away,
Then spread with shaggy mowings of the mead
Its lofty roof, and with a spacious court
Surrounded it, all fenced with driven stakes;
One bar alone of pine secured the door,
Which ask'd three Grecians with united force
To thrust it to its place, and three again
To thrust it back, although Achilles oft
Would heave it to the door himself alone;)
Then Hermes, benefactor of mankind,
That bar displacing for the King of Troy,
Gave entrance to himself and to his gifts
For Peleus' son design'd, and from the seat
Alighting, thus his speech to Priam turn'd.
  Oh ancient Priam! an immortal God
Attends thee I am Hermes, by command
Of Jove my father thy appointed guide.
But I return. I will not, entering here,
Stand in Achilles' sight; immortal Powers
May not so unreservedly indulge
Creatures of mortal kind. But enter thou,
Embrace his knees, and by his father both
And by his Goddess mother sue to him,
And by his son, that his whole heart may melt.
  So Hermes spake, and to the skies again
Ascended. Then leap'd Priam to the ground,
Leaving Idæus; he, the mules and steeds
Watch'd, while the ancient King into the tent
Proceeded of Achilles dear to Jove.
Him there he found, and sitting found apart
His fellow-warriors, of whom two alone
Served at his side, Aleimus, branch of Mars

And brave Automedon; he had himself
Supp'd newly, and the board stood unremoved.
Unseen of all huge Priam enter'd, stood
Near to Achilles, clasp'd his knees, and kiss'd
Those terrible and homicidal hands
That had destroy'd so many of his sons.
As when a fugitive for blood the house
Of some chief enters in a foreign land,
All gaze, astonish'd at the sudden guest,
So gazed Achilles seeing Priam there,
And so stood all astonish'd, each his eyes
In silence fastening on his fellow's face.
But Priam kneel'd, and suppliant thus began.
Think, oh Achilles, semblance of the Gods!
On thy own father full of days like me,
And trembling on the gloomy verge of life.[12]
Some neighbor chief, it may be, even now
Oppresses him, and there is none at hand,
No friend to succor him in his distress.
Yet, doubtless, bearing that Achilles lives,
He still rejoices, hoping, day by day,
That one day he shall see the face again
Of his own son from distant Troy return'd.
But me no comfort cheers, whose bravest sons,
So late the flower of Ilium, all are slain.
When Greece came hither, I had fifty sons;
Nineteen were children of one bed, the rest
Born of my concubines. A numerous house!
But fiery Mars hath thinn'd it. One I had,
One, more than all my sons the strength of Troy,
Whom standing for his country thou hast slain—
Hector—his body to redeem I come
Into Achaia's fleet, bringing, myself,
Ransom inestimable to thy tent.
Reverence the Gods, Achilles! recollect
Thy father; for his sake compassion show
To me more pitiable still, who draw
Home to my lips (humiliation yet
Unseen on earth) his hand who slew my son.
So saying, he waken'd in his soul regret
Of his own sire; softly, he placed his hand
On Priam's hand, and pushed him gently away.
Remembrance melted both. Rolling before
Achilles' feet, Priam his son deplored
Wide-slaughtering Hector, and Achilles wept
By turns his father, and by turns his friend
Patroclus; sounds of sorrow fill'd the tent.
But when, at length satiate, Achilles felt
His heart from grief, and all his frame relieved,
Upstarting from his seat, with pity moved
Of Priam's silver locks and silver beard,
He raised the ancient father by his hand,
Whom in wing'd accents kind he thus bespake.
Wretched indeed! ah what must thou have felt!
How hast thou dared to seek alone the fleet

Of the Achaians, and his face by whom
So many of thy valiant sons have fallen!
Thou hast a heart of iron, terror-proof.
Come—sit beside me—let us, if we may,
Great mourners both, bid sorrow sleep awhile.
There is no profit of our sighs and tears;
For thus, exempt from care themselves, the Gods
Ordain man's miserable race to mourn.
Fast by the threshold of Jove's courts are placed
Two casks, one stored with evil, one with good,
From which the God dispenses as he wills.
For whom the glorious Thunderer mingles both,
He leads a life checkered with good and ill
Alternate; but to whom he gives unmix
The bitter cup, he makes that man a curse,
His name becomes a by-word of reproach,
His strength is hunger-bitten, and he walks
The blessed earth, unblest, go where he may.
So was my father Pelcus at his birth
Nobly endowed with plenty and with wealth
Distinguish'd by the Gods past all mankind,
Lord of the Myrmidons, and, though a man
Yet unmatch'd from heaven with an immortal bride.
But even him the Gods afflict, a son
Refusing him, who might possess his throne
Hereafter; for myself, his only heir,
Pass as a dream and while I live, instead
Of solacing his age, here sit, before
Your distant walls, the scourge of thee and thine.
Thee also, ancient Priam, we have heard
Reported, once possessor of such wealth
As neither Lesbos, seat of Macar, owns,
Nor eastern Phrygia, nor yet all the ports
Of Hellespont, but thou didst pass them all
In riches, and in number of thy sons.
But since the Powers of heaven brought on thy land
This fatal war, battle and deeds of death
Always surround the city where thou reign'st.
Cease, therefore, from unprofitable tears,
Which, ere they raise thy son to life again,
Shall, doubtless, find fresh cause for which to flow.
    To whom the ancient King godlike replied.
Hero, forbear. No seat is here for me,
While Hector lies unburied in your camp.
Loose him, and loose him now, that with these eyes
I may behold my son; accept a price
Magnificent, which may'st thou long enjoy,
And, since my life was precious in thy sight,
May'st thou revisit safe thy native shore!
    To whom Achilles, lowering, and in wrath,[13]
Urge me no longer, at a time like this,
With that harsh note; I am already inclin'd
To loose him. Thetis, my own mother came
Herself on that same errand, sent from Jove.
Priam! I understand thee well. I know

That by some God conducted, thou hast reach'd
Achaia's fleet; for, without aid divine,
No mortal even in his prime of youth,
Had dared the attempt; guards vigilant as ours
He should not easily elude, such gates,
So massy, should not easily unbar.
Thou, therefore, vex me not in my distress,
Lest I abhor to see thee in my tent,
And, borne beyond all limits, set at nought
Thee, and thy prayer, and the command of Jove.
He said; the old King trembled, and obey'd
Then sprang Plides like a lion forth,
Not sole, but with his two attendant friends
Alcimus and Automedon the brave,
For them (Patroclus slain) he honor'd most
Of all the Myrmidons. They from the yoke
Released both steeds and mules, then introduced
And placed the herald of the hoary King.
They lighten'd next the litter of its charge
Inestimable, leaving yet behind
Two mantles and a vest, that, not unveil'd,
The body might be borne back into Troy.
Then, calling forth his women, them he bade
Lave and anoint the body, but apart,
Lest haply Priam, noticing his son,
Through stress of grief should give resentment scope,
And irritate by some affront himself
To slay him, in despite of Jove's commands.[14]
They, therefore, laving and anointing first
The body, cover'd it with cloak and vest
Then, Peleus' son disposed it on the bier,
Lifting it from the ground, and his two friends
Together heaved it to the royal wain.
Achilles, last, groaning, his friend invoked.
Patroclus! should the tidings reach thine ear,
Although in Ades, that I have released
The noble Hector at his father's suit,
Resent it not; no sordid gifts have paid
His ransom-price, which thou shalt also share.
So saying, Achilles to his tent return'd
And on the splendid couch whence he had risen
Again reclined, opposite to the seat
Of Priam, whom the hero thus bespake.
Priam! at thy request thy son is loosed,
And lying on his bier; at dawn of day
Thou shalt both see him and convey him hence
Thyself to Troy. But take we now repast;
For even bright-hair'd Niobe her food
Forgat not, though of children twelve bereft,
Of daughters six, and of six blooming sons.
Apollo these struck from his silver bow,
And those shaft-arm'd Diana, both incensed
That oft Latona's children and her own
Numbering, she scorn'd the Goddess who had borne
Two only, while herself had twelve to boast.

Vain boast! those two sufficed to slay them all.
Nine days they welter'd in their blood, no man
Was found to bury them, for Jove had changed
To stone the people; but themselves, at last,
The Powers of heaven entomb'd them on the tenth.
Yet even she, once satisfied with tears,
Remember'd food; and now the rocks among
And pathless solitudes of Sipylus,
The rumor'd cradle of the nymphs who dance
On Acheloüs' banks, although to stone
Transform'd she broods her heaven-inflicted woes.
Come, then my venerable guest! Take we
Refreshment also; once arrived in Troy
With thy dear son, thou shalt have time to weep
Sufficient, nor without most weighty cause.
So spake Achilles, and, upstarting slew
A sheep white-fleeced which his attendants flay'd,
And busily and with much skill their task
Administ'ring, first scored the viands well,
Then pierced them with the spits, and when the roast
Was finish'd, drew them from the spits again.
And now, Automedon dispensed around
The polish'd board bread in neat baskets piled,
Which done, Achilles portion'd out to each
His share, and all assail'd the ready feast.
But when nor hunger more nor thirst they felt,
Dardanian Priam, wond'ring at his bulk
And beauty (for he seem'd some God from heaven)
Gazed on Achilles, while Achilles held
Not less in admiration of his looks
Benign, and of his gentle converse wise,
Gazed on Dardanian Priam, and at length
(The eyes of each gratified to the full)
The ancient King thus to Achilles spake.
Hero! Dismiss us now each to our bed,
That there at ease reclined, we may enjoy
Sweet sleep; for never have these eyelids closed
Since Hector fell and died, but without cease
I mourn, and nourishing unnumber'd woes,
Have roll'd me in the ashes of my courts.
But I have now both tasted food and given
Wine to my lips, untasted till with thee.
So he, and at his word Achilles bade
His train beneath his portico prepare
With all dispatch two couches, purple rugs,
And arras, and warm mantles over all.
Forth went the women bearing lights, and spread
A couch for each, when feigning needful fear,[15]
Achilles thus his speech to Priam turn'd.
My aged guest beloved; sleep thou without;
Lest some Achaian chief (for such are wont
Ofttimes, here sitting, to consult with me)
Hither repair; of whom should any chance
To spy thee through the gloom, he would at once
Convey the tale to Agamemnon's ear,

Whence hindrance might arise, and the release
Haply of Hector's body be delay'd.
But answer me with truth. How many days
Wouldst thou assign to the funereal rites
Of noble Hector, for so long I mean
Myself to rest, and keep the host at home?
Then thus the ancient King, godlike replied.
If thou indeed be willing that we give
Burial to noble Hector, by an act
So generous, O Achilles! me thou shalt
Much gratify; for we are shut, thou know'st,
In Ilium close, and fuel must procure
From Ida's side remote; fear, too, hath seized
On all our people. Therefore thus I say.
Nine days we wish to mourn him in the house;
To his interment we would give the tenth,
And to the public banquet; the eleventh
Shall see us build his tomb; and on the twelfth
(If war we must) we will to war again.
To whom Achilles, matchless in the race.
So be it, ancient Priam! I will curb
Twelve days the rage of war, at thy desire.[16]
He spake, and at his wrist the right hand grasp'd
Of the old sovereign, to dispel his fear.
Then in the vestibule the herald slept
And Priam, prudent both, but Peleus' son
In the interior tent, and at his side
Brisëis, with transcendent beauty adorn'd.
Now all, all night, by gentle sleep subdued,
Both Gods and chariot-ruling warriors lay,
But not the benefactor of mankind,
Hermes; him sleep seized not, but deep he mused
How likeliest from amid the Grecian fleet
He might deliver by the guard unseen
The King of Ilium; at his head he stood
In vision, and the senior thus bespake.
Ah heedless and secure! Has thou no dread
Of mischief, ancient King, that thus by foes
Thou sleep'st surrounded, lull'd by the consent
And sufferance of Achilles? Thou hast given
Much for redemption of thy darling son,
But thrice that sum thy sons who still survive
Must give to Agamemnon and the Greeks
For *thy* redemption, should they know thee here.
He ended; at the sound alarm'd upsprang
The King, and roused his herald. Hermes yoked
Himself both mules and steeds, and through the camp
Drove them incontinent, by all unseen.
Soon as the windings of the stream they reach'd,
Deep-eddied Xanthus, progeny of Jove,
Mercury the Olympian summit sought,
And saffron-vested morn o'erspread the earth.
They, loud lamenting, to the city drove
Their steeds; the mules close follow'd with the dead.
Nor warrior yet, nor cinctured matron knew

Of all the Illum aught of their approach
Cassandra sole except. She, beautiful
As golden Venus, mounted on the height
Of Pergamus, her father first discern'd
Borne on his chariot-seat erect, and knew
The herald heard so oft in echoing Troy;
Him also on his bier outstretched she mark'd,
Whom the mules drew. Then shrieking, through the streets
She ran of Troy, and loud proclaim'd the sight.
Ye sons of Ilium and ye daughters, haste,
Haste all to look on Hector, if ye e'er
With joy beheld him, while he yet survived,
From fight returning; for all Ilium erst
In him, and all her citizens rejoiced.
She spake. Then neither male nor female more
In Troy remain'd, such sorrow seized on all.
Issuing from the city gate, they met
Priam conducting, sad, the body home,
And wife of Hector to the bier, on which
Their torn-off tresses with unsparing hands
They shower'd while all the people wept around.
All day, and to the going down of day
They thus had mourn'd the dead before the gates,
Had not their Sovereign from his chariot-seat
Thus spoken to the multitude around.
Fall back on either side, and let the mules
Pass on' the body in my palace once
Deposited, ye then may weep your fill.
He said; they opening, gave the litter way.
Arrived within the royal house, they sretch'd
The breathless Hector on a sumptuous bed,
And singers placed beside him, who should chant
The strain funereal; they with many a groan
The dirge began, and still at every close,
The female train with many a groan replied.
Then, in the midst, Andromache white-arm'd
Between her palms the dreadful Hector's head
Pressing her lamentation thus began.
[17] My hero! thou hast fallen in prime of life,
Me leaving here desolate, and the fruit
Of our ill-fated loves, a helpless child,
Whom grown to manhood I despair to see.
For ere that day arrive, down from her height
Precipitated shall this city fall,
Since thou hast perish'd once her sure defence,
Faithful protector of her spotless wives,
And all their little ones. Those wives shall soon
In Grecian barks capacious hence be borne,
And I among the rest. But thee, my child!
Either thy fate shall with thy mother send
Captive into a land where thou shalt serve
In sordid drudgery some cruel lord,
Or haply some Achaian here, thy hand
Seizing, shall hurl thee from a turret-top
To a sad death, avenging brother, son,

Or father by the hands of Hector slain;
For be made many a Grecian bite the ground.
Thy father, boy, bore never into fight
A milky mind, and for that self-same cause
Is now bewail'd in every house of Troy.
Sorrow unutterable thou hast caused
Thy parents, Hector! but to me hast left
Largest bequest of misery, to whom,
Dying, thou neither didst thy arms extend
Forth from thy bed, nor gavest me precious word
To be remember'd day and night with tears.
So spake she weeping, whom her maidens all
With sighs accompanied, and her complaint
Mingled with sobs Hecuba next began.
Ah Hector! dearest to thy mother's heart
Of all her sons, much must the Gods have loved
Thee living, whom, though dead, they thus preserve.
What son soever of our house beside
Achilles took, over the barren deep
To Samos, Imbrus, or to Lemnos girt
With rocks inhospitable, him he sold;
But thee, by his dread spear of life deprived,
He dragg'd and dragg'd around Patroclus' tomb,
As if to raise again his friend to life
Whom thou hadst vanquish'd yet he raised him not.
But as for thee, thou liest here with dew
Besprinkled, fresh as a young plant,[18] and more
Resemblest some fair youth by gentle shafts
Of Phœbus pierced, than one in battle slain.
So spake the Queen, exciting in all hearts
Sorrow immeasurable, after whom
Thus Helen, third, her lamentation pour'd.
[19]Ah dearer far than all my brothers else
Who brought me (would I had first died!) to Troy,
I call thy brothers mine; since forth I came
From Sparta, it is now the twentieth year,
Yet never heard I once hard speech from thee.
Or taunt morose, but if it ever chanced,
That of thy father's house female or male
Blamed me, and even if herself the Queen
(For in the King, whate're befell, I found
always a father) thou hast interposed
Thy gentle temper and thy gentle speech
To soothe them; Therefore, with the same sad drops
Thy fate, oh Hector! And my own I weep;
For other friend within the ample bounds
Of Ilium have I none, nor hope to hear
Kind word again, with horror view'd by all.
So Helen spake weeping, to whom with groans
The countless multitude replied, and thus
Their ancient sovereign next his people charged.
Ye Trojans, now bring fuel home, nor fear
Close ambush of the Greeks; Achilles' self
Gave me at my dismission from his fleet
Assurance, that from hostile force secure

We shall remain, till the twelfth dawn arise.
 All, then their mules and oxen to the wains
Join'd speedily, and under Ilium's walls
Assembled numerous; nine whole days they toil'd,
Bringing much fuel home, and when the tenth
Bright morn, with light for human kind, arose,
Then bearing noble Hector forth, with tears
Shed copious, on the summit of the pile
They placed him, and the fuel fired beneath.
 But when Aurora, daughter of the Dawn,
Redden'd the cast, then thronging forth, all Troy
Encompass'd noble Hector's pile around.
The whole vast multitude convened, with wine
They quench'd the pile throughout, leaving no part
Unvisited, on which the fire had seized.
His brothers, next collected, and his friends,
His white bones, mourning, and with tears profuse
Watering their cheeks; then in a golden urn
They placed them, which with mantles soft they veil'd
Mæonian-hued, and delving, buried it,
And overspread with stones the spot adjust.
Lastly, short time allowing to the task,
They heap'd his tomb, while posted on all sides,
Suspicious of assault, spies watch'd the Greeks.
The tomb once heap'd assembling all again
Within the palace, they a banquet shared
Magnificent, by godlike Priam given.

Such burial the illustrious Hector found[20]

Notes

[I cannot take my leave of this noble poem, without expressing how much I am struck with this plain conclusion of it. It is like the exit of a great man out of company whom he has entertained magnificently; neither pompous nor familiar; not contemptuous, yet without much ceremony. I recollect nothing, among the works of mere man, that exemplifies so strongly the true style of great antiquity.]—TR.

1. This Is the first allusion in the *Iliad* to the Judgment of Paris, which gave mortal offence to Minerva and Juno. On this account it has been supposed by some that these lines are spurious, on the ground that Homer could not have known the fable, or he would have mentioned it earlier in the poem.—FELTON.
2. [His blessing, if he is properly influenced by it; his curse in its consequences if he is deaf to its dictates.] —TR.
3. [This is the sense preferred by the Scholiast; for it is not true that Thetis was always present with Achilles, as is proved by the passage immediately ensuing.]—TR.
4. [The angler's custom was, in those days, to guard his line above the hook from the fishes' bite, by passing it through a pipe of horn.]—TR.
5. [Jupiter justifies him against Apollo's charge, affirming him to be free from those rental defects which chiefly betray men into sin, folly, improvidence, and perverseness.]—TR.
6. [But, at first, he did fly. It is therefore spoken as the Scholiast observes, φιλοϛοργῶς, and must be understood as the language of strong maternal affection.]—TR.
7. [κοροιτυπιῆσιν ἀριϛοι.]
8. [Through which the reins were passed.]—TR.

9. [The yoke being flat at the bottom, and the pole round, there would of course be a small aperture between the band and the pole on both sides, through which, according to the Scholium in Villoisson, they thrust the ends of the tackle lest they should dangle.]-TR.

10. [The text here is extremely intricate; as it stands now, the sons are, first, said to yoke the horses, then Priam and Idæus are said to do it, and in the palace too. I have therefore adopted an alteration suggested by Clarke, who with very little violence to the copy, proposes instead of ζευγνυσθην to read—ζωννύσθην.]—TR.

11. [The words both signify—sable.]—TR.

12. Priam begins not with a display of the treasures he has brought for the redemption of Hector's body, but with a pathetic address to the feelings of Achilles. Homer well knew that neither gold nor silver would influence the heart of a young and generous warrior, but that persuasion would. The old king therefore, with a judicious abruptness avails himself of his most powerful plea at once, and seizes the sympathy of the hero, before he has time to recollect who it is that addresses him.

13. [Mortified to see his generosity, after so much kindness shown to Priam, still distrusted, and that the impatience of the old king threatened to deprive him of all opportunity to do gracefully what he could not be expected to do willingly.]—TR.

14. [To control anger argues a great mind—and to avoid occasions that may betray one into it, argues a still greater. An observation that should suggest itself to us with no little force, when Achilles, not remarkable either for patience or meekness, exhorts Priam to beware of provoking him; and when having cleansed the body of Hector and covered it, he places it himself in the litter, lest his father, seeing how indecently he had treated it, should be exasperated at the sight, and by some passionate reproach exasperate himself also. For that a person so singularly irascible and of a temper harsh as his, should not only be aware of his infirmity, but even guard against it with so much precaution, evidences a prudence truly wonderful. —Plutarch.]—TR.

15. ['Επικερτομέων. Clarke renders the word in this place, *falso metû ludens*, and Eustathius says that Achilles suggested such cause of fear to Priam, to excuse his lodging him in an exterior part of the tent. The general import of the Greek word is sarcastic, but here it signifies rather—to intimidate. See also Dacier.] —TR.

16. The poet here shows the importance of Achilles in the army. Agamemnon is the general, yet all the chief commanders appeal to him for advice, and on his own authority he promises Priam a cessation of arms, giving his hand to confirm the promise, agrees with the custom of the present day.

17. This lament of Andromache may be compared to her pathetic address to Hector in the scene at the Scæan gate. It forms indeed a most beautiful and eloquent pendant to that.—FELTON

18. [This, according to the Scholiast, is a probable sense of προσφατος—He derives it απο των νεωςι πεφασ–μενων εκ γης φυτων—See Villoisson.]—TR.

19. Helen is throughout the *Iliad* a genuine lady, graceful in motion and speech, noble in her associations, full of remorse for a fault for which higher powers seem responsible, yet grateful and affectionate towards those with whom that fault had connected her. I have always thought the following speech in which Helen laments Hector and hints at her own invidious and unprotected situation in Troy, as almost the sweetest passage in the poem—COLERIDGE

20. ['Ως διγ' αμφιεπον ταφον 'Εκτορς ιπποδαμοιο.]

The *Odyssey:* Background

The *Odyssey* is Homer's companion epic to the *Iliad*. Ten long years after the Trojan War, Odysseus journeys home. Odysseus, unlike Achilles, is a hero known for his shrewdness. As a world-weary traveler, he suggests an insatiable quest for life. In his experiences, frequently hindered and helped by the gods, he is a more mature hero than Achilles is. Achilles' quest is to avenge his friend's death, which is more personal than national. Odysseus' quest is to return home, which suggests the major concerns of family, community, and nation. In many ways, Odysseus combines characteristics of both the old and new hero: he is both a warrior and thinker. Odysseus is also one of the earliest epic heroes to travel to the Underworld in the Western tradition.

In Book XI Odysseus travels to the Underworld to consult the blind seer Teiresias about his future. This journey is necessary; if he does not take it, it has been foretold that Odysseus can never return home. Here he encounters his mother, old war companions, such as Achilles and Agamemnon, and a host of others. The last characters whom he meets in the Underworld are Tityos, Tantalus, Sisyphus, and Herakles. These figures are punished for serious trangressions against the gods. Odysseus learns that he must revere the gods. In the plight of these figures and others, Odysseus sees a reality that includes transitoriness, destruction, and corporality. No more poignant plea is made than in Achilles' address to Odysseus. Achilles, who "ranked with immortals," makes Odysseus see that he can know nothing of death.

The Odyssey

IX

The Story Told to Alcinoüs—The Cyclops

Then wise Odysseus answered him and said: "Mighty Alcinoüs, renowned of all, surely it is a pleasant thing to hear a bard like this, one who is even like the gods in voice. For happier occasion I think there cannot be than when good cheer possesses a whole people, and feasting through the houses they listen to a bard, seated in proper order, while beside them stand the tables supplied with bread and meat, and, dipping wine from out the mixer, the pourer bears it round and fills the cups. That is a sight most pleasing. But your heart bids you learn my grievous woes, and so to make me weep and sorrow more. What shall I tell you first, then, and what last? For many are the woes the gods of heaven have given me. First, I will tell my name, that you, like all, may know it; and I accordingly, seeking deliverance from my day of doom, may be your guest-friend, though my home is far away. I am Odysseus, son of Laërtes, who for all craft am noted among men, and my renown reaches to heaven. My home is Ithaca, a land far seen; for on it is the lofty height of Neriton, covered with waving woods. Around lie many islands, very close to one another, Doulichion, Same, and woody Zacynthus. Ithaca itself lies low along the sea, far to the west,—the others stretching eastward, toward the dawn,—a rugged land, and yet a kindly nurse. A sweeter spot than my own land I shall not see. Calypso, a heavenly goddess, sought to keep me by her side within her hollow grotto, desiring me to be her husband; so too Aeaean Circe, full of craft, detained me in her palace, desiring me to be her husband; but they never beguiled the heart within my breast. Nothing more sweet than home and parents can there be, however rich one's dwelling far in a foreign land, cut off from parents. But let me tell you of the grievous journey home which Zeus ordained me on my setting forth from Troy.

"The wind took me from Ilios and bore me to the Ciconians, to Ismarus. There I destroyed the town and slew its men; but from the town we took the women and great stores of treasure, and parted all, that none might go lacking his proper share. This done, I warned our men swiftly to fly; but they, in utter folly, did not heed. Much wine was drunk, and they slaughtered on the shore a multitude of sheep and swing-paced, crook-horned oxen. Meanwhile, escaped Ciconians began to call for aid on those Ciconians who were their neighbors and more numerous and brave than they,—a people dwelling inland, skillful at fighting in chariot or on foot, as need might be. Accordingly at dawn they gathered, thick as leaves and flowers appear in spring. And now an evil fate from Zeus beset our luckless men, causing us many sorrows; for setting the battle in array by the swift ships, all fought and hurled their brazen spears at one another. While it was morning and the day grew stronger, we steadily kept them off and held our ground, though they were more than we; but as the sun declined, toward stalling-time, then the Ciconians turned our men and routed the Achaeans. Six of the crew of every ship fell in their harness there; the rest fled death and doom.

"Thence we sailed on with aching hearts, glad to be clear of death, though missing our dear comrades; yet the curved ships did not pass on till we had called three times to each poor comrade who died upon the plain, cut off by the Ciconians. But now cloud-gathering Zeus sent the north wind against our ships in a fierce tempest, and covered with his clouds both land and sea; night broke from heaven. The ships drove headlong onward, their sails torn into tatters by the furious wind. These sails we lowered, in terror for our lives, and rowed the ships themselves hurriedly toward the land. There for two nights and days continuously we lay, gnawing our hearts because of toil and trouble. But when the fair-haired dawn brought the third day, we set our masts, and hoisting the white sails we sat us down, while wind and helmsmen kept us steady. And now I should have come unharmed to my own land, but that the swell and current, in doubling Maleia, and northern winds turned me aside and drove me past Cythera.

"Thence for nine days I drifted before the deadly blasts along the swarming sea; but on the tenth we touched the land of Lotus-eaters, men who make food of flowers. So here we went ashore and drew us water, and soon by the swift ships my men prepared their dinner. Then after we had tasted food and drink, I sent some sailors forth to go and learn what men who live by bread dwelt in the land,—selecting two, and joining with them a herald as a third. These straightway went and mingled with the Lotus-eaters. These Lotus-eaters had no thought of harm against our men; indeed, they gave them lotus to taste; but whosoever of them ate the lotus' honeyed fruit wished to bring tidings back no more and never to leave the place, but with the Lotus-eaters there desired to stay, to feed on lotus and forget his going home. These men I brought back weeping to the ships by very force, and dragging them under the benches of our hollow ships I bound them fast, and bade my other trusty men to hasten and embark on the swift ships, that none of them might eat the lotus and forget his going home. Quickly they came aboard, took places at the pins, and sitting in order smote the foaming water with their oars.

"Thence we sailed on with aching hearts, and came to the land of the Cyclops, a rude and lawless folk, who, trusting to the immortal gods, plant with their hands no plant, nor ever plough, but all things spring unsown and without ploughing,—wheat, barley, and grape-vines with wine in their heavy clusters, for rain from Zeus makes the grape grow. Among this people no assemblies meet; they have no stable laws. They live on the tops of lofty hills in hollow caves; each gives the law to his own wife and children, and cares for no one else.

"Now a rough island stretches along outside the harbor, not close to the Cyclops' coast nor yet far out, covered with trees. On it innumerable wild goats breed; no tread of man disturbs them; none comes here to follow hounds, to toil through woods and climb the crests of hills. The island is not held for flocks or tillage, but all unsown, untilled, it evermore is bare of men and feeds the bleating goats. Among the Cyclops are no red-cheeked ships, nor are there shipwrights who might build the well-benched ships to do them service, sailing to foreign towns, as men are wont to cross the sea in ships to one another. With ships they might have worked the well-placed island; for it is not at all a worthless spot, but would bear all things duly. For here are meadows on the banks of the gray sea, moist, with soft soil; here vines could never die; here is smooth ploughing-land; a very heavy crop, and always well in season, might be reaped, for the under soil is rich. Here is a quiet harbor, never needing moorings,—throwing out anchor-stones or fastening cables,—but merely to run in and wait awhile till sailor hearts are ready and the winds are blowing. Just at the harbor's head a spring of sparkling water flows from beneath a cave; around it poplars grow. Here we sailed in, some god our guide, through murky night; there was no light to see, for round the ships was a dense fog. No moon looked out from heaven; it was shut in with clouds. So no one saw the island; and the long waves rolling on the shore we did not see until we beached our well-benched ships. After the ships were beached, we lowered all our sails and forth we went ourselves upon the shore; where falling fast asleep we awaited sacred dawn.

"But when the early rosy-fingered dawn appeared, in wonder at the island we made a circuit round it, and nymphs, daughters of aegis-bearing Zeus, started the mountain goats, to give my men a meal. Forthwith we took our bending bows and our long hunting spears from out the ships, and parted in three bands began to shoot; and soon God granted ample game. Twelve ships were in my train; to each there fell nine goats, while ten they set apart for me alone. Then all throughout the day till setting sun we sat and feasted on abundant meat and pleasant wine. For the ruddy wine of our ships was not yet spent; some still was left, because our crews took a large store in jars the day we seized the sacred citadel of the Ciconians. And now we looked across to the land of the neighboring Cyclops, and marked the smoke, the sounds of men, the bleat of sheep and goats; but when the sun went down and darkness came, we laid us down to sleep upon the beach. Then as the early rosy-fingered dawn appeared, holding a council, I said to all my men:

"'The rest of you, my trusty crews, stay for the present here; but I myself, with my own ship and my own crew, go to discover who these men may be,—if they are fierce and savage, with no regard for right, or kind to strangers and reverent toward the gods.'

"When I had spoken thus, I went on board my ship, and called my crew to come on board and loose the cables. Quickly they came, took places at the pins, and sitting in order smote the foaming water with their oars. But when we reached the neighboring shore, there at the outer point, close to the sea, we found a cave, high, overhung with laurel. Here many flocks of sheep and goats were nightly housed. Around was built a yard with a high wall of deep-embedded stone, tall pines, and crested oaks. Here a man-monster slept, who shepherded his flock alone and far apart; with others he did not mingle, but quite aloof followed his lawless ways. Thus had he grown to be a marvelous monster; not like a man who lives by bread, but rather like a woody peak of the high hills, seen single, clear of others.

"Now to my other trusty men I gave command to stay there by the ship and guard the ship; but I myself chose the twelve best among my men and sallied forth. I had a goat-skin bottle of the dark sweet wine given me by Maron, son of Evanthes, priest of Apollo, who watches over Ismarus. He gave me this because we guarded him and his son and wife, through holy fear; for he dwelt within the shady grove of Phoebus Apollo. He brought me splendid gifts: of fine-wrought gold he gave me seven talents, gave me a mixing-bowl of solid silver, and afterwards filled me twelve jars with wine, sweet and unmixed, a drink for gods. None knew that wine among the slaves and hand-maids of his house, none but himself, his own dear wife, and one sole house-dame. Whenever they drank the honeyed ruddy wine, he filled a cup and poured it into twenty parts of water, and still from the bowl came a sweet odor of a surprising strength; then to refrain had been no easy matter. I filled a large skin full of this and took it with me, and also took provision in a sack; for my stout heart suspected I soon should meet a man arrayed in mighty power, a savage, ignorant of rights and laws.

"Quickly we reached the cave, but did not find him there; for he was tending his fat flock afield. Entering the cave, we looked around. Here crates were standing, loaded down with cheese, and here pens thronged with lambs and kids. In separate pens each sort was folded: by themselves the older, by themselves the later born, and by themselves the younglings. Swimming with whey were all the vessels, the well-wrought pails and bowls in which he milked. Here my men pressed me strongly to take some cheeses and go back; then later, driving the kids and lambs to our swift ship out of the pens, to sail away over the briny water. But I refused,—far better had I yielded,—hoping that I might see him and he might offer gifts. But he was to prove, when seen, no pleasure to my men.

"Kindling a fire here, we made burnt offering and we ourselves took of the cheese and ate; and so we sat and waited in the cave until he came from pasture. He brought a ponderous burden of dry wood to use at supper time, and tossing it down inside the cave raised a great din. We hurried off in terror to a corner of the cave. But into the wide-mouthed cave he drove his sturdy flock, all that he milked; the males, both rams and goats, he left outside in the high yard. And now he set in place the huge door-stone, lifting it high in air, a ponderous thing; no two and twenty carts, staunch and four-wheeled, could start it from the ground; such was the rugged rock he set against the door. Then sitting down, he milked the ewes and bleating goats, all in due order, and underneath put each one's young. Straightway he curdled half of the white milk, and gathering it in wicker baskets, set it by; half he left standing in the pails, ready for him to take and drink, and have it for his supper. So after he had busily performed his tasks, he kindled a fire, noticed us, and asked:

"'Ha, strangers, who are you? Where do you come from, sailing the watery ways? Are you upon some business? Or do you rove at random, as the pirates roam the seas, risking their lives and bringing ill to strangers?'

"As he thus spoke, our very souls were crushed within us, dismayed by the heavy voice and by the monster's self; nevertheless I answered thus and said:

"'We are from Troy, Achaeans, driven by shifting winds out of our course across the great gulf of the sea; homeward we fared, but through strange ways and wanderings are come hither; so Zeus was pleased to purpose. Subjects of Agamemnon, son of Atreus, we boast ourselves to be, whose fame is now the widest under heaven; so great a town he sacked, so many people slew. But chancing here, we come before your knees to ask that you will offer hospitality, and in other ways as well will give the gift which is the stranger's due. O mighty one, respect the gods. We are your suppliants, and Zeus is the avenger of the suppliant and the stranger; he is the stranger's friend, attending the deserving.'

"So I spoke, and from a ruthless heart he straightway answered: 'You are simple, stranger, or come from far away, to bid me dread the gods or shrink before them. The Cyclops pay no heed to aegis-bearing Zeus, nor to the blessed gods; because we are much stronger than themselves. To shun the wrath of Zeus, I would not spare you or your comrades, did my heart not bid. But tell me where you left your staunch ship at your coming. At the far shore, or near? Let me but know.'

"He thought to tempt me, but he could not cheat a knowing man like me; and I again replied with words of guile: 'The Earth-shaker, Poseidon, wrecked my ship and cast her on the rocks at the land's end, drifting her on a headland; the wind blew from the sea; and I with these men here escaped from utter ruin.'

"So I spoke, and from a ruthless heart he answered nothing, but starting up laid hands on my companions. He seized on two and dashed them to the ground as if they had been dogs. Their brains ran out upon the floor, and wet the earth. Tearing them limb from limb, be made his supper, and ate as does a mountain lion, leaving nothing, entrails, or flesh, or marrow bones. We in our tears held up our hands to Zeus, at sight of his cruel deeds; helplessness held our hearts. But when the Cyclops had filled his monstrous maw by eating human flesh and pouring down pure milk, he laid himself in the cave full length among his flock. And I then formed the plan within my daring heart of closing on him, drawing my sharp sword from my thigh, and stabbing him in the breast where the midriff holds the liver, feeling the place out with my hand. Yet second thoughts restrained me, for then we too had met with utter ruin; for we could never with our hands have pushed from the tall door the enormous stone which he had set against it. Thus then with sighs we awaited sacred dawn.

But when the early rosy-fingered dawn appeared, he kindled a fire, milked his goodly flock, all in due order, and underneath put each one's young. Then after he had busily performed his tasks, seizing once more two men, he made his morning meal. And when the meal was ended, he drove from the cave his sturdy flock, and easily moved the huge door-stone; but afterwards put it back as one might put the lid upon a quiver. Then to the hills, with many a call, he steered his sturdy flock, while I was left behind brooding on evil and thinking how I might have vengeance, would but Athene grant my prayer. And to my mind this seemed the wisest way. There lay beside the pen a great club of the Cyclops, an olive stick still green, which he had cut to be his staff when dried. Inspecting it, we guessed its size, and thought it like the mast of a black ship of twenty oars,—some broad-built merchantman which sails the great gulf of the sea; so huge it looked in length and thickness. I went and cut away a fathom's length of this, laid it before my men, and bade them shape it down. They made it smooth. I then stood by to point the tip and, laying hold, I charred it briskly in the blazing fire. The piece I now put carefully away, hiding it in the dung which lay about the cave in great abundance; and then I bade my comrades fix by lot who the bold men should be to help me raise the stake and grind it in his eye, when pleasant sleep should come. Those drew the lot whom I myself would fain have chosen; four were they, for a fifth I counted in myself. He came toward evening, shepherding the fleecy flock, and forthwith drove his sturdy flock into the wide-mouthed cave, all with much care; he did not leave a sheep in the high yard outside, either through some suspicion, or God bade him so to do. Again he set in place the huge door-stone, lifting it high in air, and, sitting down, he milked the ewes and bleating goats, all in due order, and underneath put each one's young. Then after he had busily performed his tasks, he seized once more two men and made his supper. And now it was that drawing near the Cyclops I thus spoke, holding within my hands an ivy bowl filled with dark wine:

"'Here, Cyclops, drink some wine after your meal of human flesh, and see what sort of liquor our ship held. I brought it as an offering, thinking that you might pity me and send me home. But you are mad past bearing. Reckless! How should a stranger come to you again from any people, when you do not act with decency?'

"So I spoke; he took the cup and drank it off, and mightily pleased he was with the taste of the sweet liquor, and thus he asked me for it yet again:

"'Give me some more, kind sir, and straightway tell me you name, that I may give a stranger's gift with which you shall be pleased. Ah yes, the Cyclops' fruitful fields bear wine in their heavy clusters, for rain from Zeus makes the grape grow; but this is a bit of ambrosia and nectar.'

"So he spoke, and I again offered the sparkling wine. Three times I brought and gave; three times he drank it in his folly. Then as the wine began to dull the Cyclops' senses, in winning words I said to him:

"'Cyclops, you asked my noble name, and I will tell it; but do you give the stranger's gift, just as you promised. My name is Noman. Noman I am called by mother, father, and by all my comrades.'

"So I spoke, and from a ruthless heart he straight way answered: 'Noman I eat up last, after his comrades; all the rest first; and that shall be the stranger's gift for you.'

"He spoke, and sinking back fell flat; and there he lay, lolling his thick neck over, till sleep, that conquers all, took hold upon him. Out of his throat poured wine and scraps of human flesh; heavy with wine, he spewed it forth. And now it was I drove the stake under a heap of ashes, to bring it to a heat, and with my words emboldened all my men, that none might flinch through fear. Then when the olive stake, green though it was, was ready to take fire, and through and through was all aglow, I snatched it from the fire, while my men stood around and heaven inspired us with great courage. Seizing the olive stake, sharp at the tip, they plunged it in his eye, and I, perched up above, whirled it around. As when a man bores ship-beams with a drill, and those below keep it in motion with a strap held by the ends, and steadily it runs; even so we seized the fire-pointed stand and whirled it in his eye. Blood bubbled round the heated thing. The vapor singed off all the lids around the eye, and even the brows, as the ball burned and its roots crackled in the flame. As when a smith dips a great axe or adze into cold water, hissing loud, to temper it,—for that is strength to steel,—so hissed his eye about the olive stake. A hideous roar he raised; the rock resounded; we hurried away in terror. He wrenched the stake from out his eye, all dabbled with the blood, and flung it off in frenzy. Then he called loudly on the Cyclops who dwelt about him in the caves, along the windy heights. They heard his cry, and ran from every side, and standing by the cave they asked what ailed him:

"'What has come on you, Polyphemus, that you scream so in the immortal night, and so keep us from sleeping? Is a man driving off your flocks in spite of you? Is a man murdering you by craft or force?'

"Then in his turn from out the cave big Polyphemus answered: 'Friends, Noman is murdering me by craft. Force there is none.'

"But answering him in winged words they said: 'If no man harms you then and you are alone, illness which comes from mighty Zeus you cannot fly. Nay, make your prayer to your father, lord Poseidon.'

"This said, they went their way, and in my heart I laughed, my name, that clever notion, so deceived them. But now the Cyclops, groaning and in agonies of anguish, by groping with his hands took the stone off the door, yet sat himself inside the door with hands outstretched, to catch whoever ventured forth among the sheep; for he probably hoped in his heart that I should be so silly. But I was planning how it all might best be ordered that I might win escape from death both for my men and me. So many a plot and scheme I framed, as for my life; great danger was at hand. Then to my mind this seemed the wisest way: some rams there were of a good breed, thick in the fleece, handsome and large, which bore a dark blue wool. These I quietly bound together with the twisted willow withes on which the giant Cyclops slept,—the brute,—taking three sheep together. One, in the middle, carried the man; the other two walked by the sides, keeping my comrades safe. Thus three sheep bore each man. Then for myself, there was a ram, by far the best of all the flock, whose back I grasped, and curled beneath his shaggy belly there I lay, and with my hands twisted in that enormous fleece I steadily held on, with patient heart. Thus then with sighs we awaited sacred dawn.

"Soon as the early rosy-fingered dawn appeared, the rams hastened to pasture, but the ewes bleated unmilked about the pens, for their udders were well-nigh bursting. Their master, racked with grievous pains, felt over the backs of all the sheep as they stood up, but foolishly did not notice how under the breasts of the woolly sheep men had been fastened. Last of the flock, the ram stalked to the door, cramped by his fleece and me the crafty plotter; and feeling him over, big Polyphemus said:

"'What, my pet ram! Why do you move across the cave hindmost of all the flock? Till now you never lagged behind, but with your long strides you were always first to crop the tender blooms of grass; you were the first to reach the running streams, and first to wish to turn to the stall at night: yet here you are the last. Alternative hypothesis, but you miss your master's eye, which a villain has put out,—he and his vile companions—blunting my wits with wine. Noman it was,—not, I assure him, safe from destruction yet. If only you could sympathize and get the power of speech to say where he is skulking from my rage, then should that brain of his be knocked about the cave and dashed upon the ground. So might my heart recover from the ills which miserable Noman brought upon me.'

"So saying, from his hand he let the ram go forth, and after we were come a little distance from the cave and from the yard, first from beneath the ram I freed myself and then set free my comrades. So at quick pace we drove away those long-legged sheep, heavy with fat, many times turning round, until we reached the ship. A welcome sight we seemed to our dear friends, as men escaped from death. Yet for the others they began to weep and wail; but this I did not suffer; by my frowns I checked their tears. Instead, I bade them straightway toss the many fleecy sheep into the ship, and sail away over the briny water. Quickly they came, took places at the pins, and sitting in order smote the foaming water with their oars. But when I was as far away as one can call, I shouted to the Cyclops in derision:

"'Cyclops, no weakling's comrades you were destined to devour in the deep cave, with brutal might. But it was also destined your bad deeds should find you out, audacious wretch, who did not hesitate to eat the guests within your house! For this did Zeus chastise you, Zeus and the other gods.'

"So I spoke, and he was angered in his heart the more; and tearing off the top of a high hill, he flung it at us. It fell before the dark-bowed ship a little space, but failed to reach the rudder's tip. The sea surged underneath the stone as it came down, and swiftly toward the land the wash of water swept us, like a flood-tide from the deep, and forced us back to shore. I seized a setting-pole and shoved the vessel off; then inspiriting my men, I bade them fall to their oars that we might flee from danger,—with my head making signs,—and bending forward, on they rowed. When we had traversed twice the distance on the sea, again to the Cyclops would I call; but my men, gathering round, sought with soft words to stay me, each in his separate wise:

"'O reckless man, why seek to vex this savage, who even now, hurling his missile in the deep, drove the ship back to shore? We verily thought that we were lost. And had he heard a man make but a sound or speak, he would have crushed our heads and our ships' beams, by hurling jagged granite; for he can throw so far.'

"So they spoke, but did not move my daring spirit; again I called aloud out of an angry heart: 'Cyclops, if ever mortal man asks you the story of the ugly blinding of your eye, say that Odysseus made you blind, the spoiler of cities, Laërtes' son, whose home is Ithaca.'

"So I spoke, and with a groan he answered: 'Ah, surely now the ancient oracles are come upon me! Here once a prophet lived, a prophet brave and tall, Telemus, son of Eurymus, who by his prophecies obtained renown and in prophetic works grew old among the Cyclops. He told me it should come to pass in aftertime that I should lose my sight by means of one Odysseus; but I was always watching for the coming of some tall and comely person, arrayed in mighty power; and now a little miserable feeble creature blinded me of my eye, overcoming me with wine. Nevertheless, come here, Odysseus, and let me give the stranger's gift, and beg the famous Land-shaker to aid you on your way. His son am I; he calls himself my father. He, if he will, shall heal me; none else can, whether among the blessed gods or mortal men.'

"So he spoke, and answering him said I: 'Ah, would I might as surely strip you of life and being and send you to the house of Hades, as it is sure the Earth-shaker will never heal your eye!'

"So I spoke, whereat he prayed to lord Poseidon, stretching his hands forth toward the starry sky: 'Hear me, thou girder of the land, dark-haired Poseidon! If I am truly thine, and thou art called my father, vouchsafe no coming home to this Odysseus, spoiler of cities, Laërtes' son, whose home is Ithaca. Yet if it be his lot to see his friends once more, and reach his stately house and native land, late let him come, in evil plight, with loss of all his crew, on the vessel of a stranger, and may he at his home find trouble.'

So spoke he in his prayer, and the dark-haired god gave ear. Then once more picking up a stone much larger than before, the Cyclops swung and sent it, putting forth stupendous power. It fell behind the dark-bowed ship a little space, but failed to reach the rudder's tip. The sea surged underneath the stone as it came down, but the wave swept us forward and forced us to the shore.

"Now when we reached the island where our other well-benched ships waited together, while their crews sat round them sorrowing, watching continually for us, as we ran in we beached our ship among the sands, and forth we went ourselves upon the shore. Then taking the Cyclops' sheep out of the hollow ship, we parted all, that none might go lacking his proper share. The ram my mailed companions gave to me alone, a mark of special honor in the division of the flock; and on the shore I offered him to Zeus of the dark cloud, the son of Kronos, who is the lord of all, burning the thighs. He did not heed the sacrifice. Instead, he purposed that my well-benched ships should all be lost, and all my trusty comrades. But all throughout that day till setting sun we sat and feasted on abundant meat and pleasant wine; and when the sun went down and darkness came, we laid us down to sleep upon the beach. Then as the early rosy-fingered dawn appeared, inspiriting my men, I bade them come on board and loose the cables. Quickly they came, took places at the pins, and sitting in order smote the foaming water with their oars.

"Thence we sailed on, with aching hearts, glad to be clear of death, though missing our dear comrades."

X

Aeolus, the Laestrygonians, and Circe

"Soon we drew near the island of Aeolia, Where Aeolus, the son of Hippotas, dear to immortal gods, dwelt on a floating island. All round it is a wall of bronze, not to be broken through, and smooth and steep rises the rocky shore. Within the house of Aeolus, twelve children have been born, six daughters and six sturdy sons, and here he gave his daughters to his sons to be their wives. Here too with their loved father and honored mother they hold continual feast; before them countless viands lie. By day the steaming house resounds even to its court; by night they sleep by their chaste wives under the coverlets on well-bored bedsteads. Their city it was we reached, their goodly dwelling. For a full month here Aeolus made me welcome, and he questioned me of all, of Ilios, the Argive ships, and the return of the Achaeans. So I related all the tale in its due order. And when I furthermore asked him about my journey and entreated him for aid, he did not say me nay, but made provision for my going. He gave me a sack,—flaying therefor a nine-year ox,—and in it bound the courses of the blustering winds; for the son of Kronos made him steward of the winds, to stay or rouse which one he would. Upon my hollow ship he tied the sack with a bright cord of silver, that not a breath might stir, however little. Then for my aid he sent the west wind forth, to blow and bear along my ships and men. But it was not to be; by our folly we were lost.

"Nine days we sailed, as well by night as day. Upon the tenth our native fields appeared, so close at hand that we could see men tending fires. Then sweet sleep overcame me, wearied as I was; for I had all the time managed the vessel's sheet and yielded it to no one else among the crew, that so we might the sooner reach our native land. Meanwhile my men began to talk with one another, and to tell how I was bringing gold and silver home as gifts from Aeolus, the generous son of Hippotas; and glancing at his neighbor one would say:

"'Lo, how this man is welcomed and esteemed by all mankind, come to whose town and land he may! He brings a store of goodly treasure out of the spoils of Troy, while we, who toiled along the selfsame road, come home with empty hands. Now Aeolus gives him friendly gifts. Come, then, and let us quickly see what there is here, and how much gold and silver the sack holds.'

"Such was their talk, and the ill counsel of the crew prevailed; they loosed the sack, and out rushed all the winds. Straightway a sweeping storm bore off to sea my weeping comrades, far from their native land. And I, awaking, hesitated in my gallant heart whether to cast myself out of the ship into the sea and perish there, or saying nothing to endure and bide among the living. I forced myself to stay; covering my head, I laid me down, the while the ships were driven by the cruel storm of wind back to the island of Aeolia, my comrades sighing sore.

"So here we went ashore and drew us water, and soon by the swift ships my men prepared a meal. Then after we had tasted food and drink, taking a herald and a comrade with me, I turned me toward the lordly house of Aeolus. I found him at the feast, beside his wife and children. We entered the hall and on the threshold by the doorposts sat us down; and they all marveled in their hearts and questioned:

"'How came you here, Odysseus? What hostile power assailed you? With care we sent you forth, to let you reach your land and home or anywhere you pleased.'

"So they spoke, and with an aching heart I answered: 'A wicked crew betrayed me—they and a cruel sleep. But heal my woes, my friends, for you have power.'

"So I spoke, addressing them in humble words. Then all the rest were silent, but the father answered thus: 'Out of the island instantly, vilest of all that live! I may not aid or send upon his way a man detested by the blessed gods. Begone! for you are here because detested by the immortals.'

"Therewith he turned me loud lamenting from his door. Thence we sailed on, with aching hearts. Worn was the spirit of my men under the heavy rowing, caused by our folly too; aid on our way appeared no more.

"Six days we sailed, as well by night as day, and on the seventh came to the steep citadel of Lamos, Telepylus in Laestrygonia, where one shepherd leading home his flock calls to another, and the other answers as he leads his own flock forth. Here a man who never slept might earn a double wage: this, herding kine; that, tending silvery sheep; so close are the outgoings of the night and day. Now when we reached the splendid harbor,—round which the rock runs steep, continuous all the way, and the projecting cliffs, facing each other, stretch forward at the mouth, and narrow is the entrance,—into the basin all the rest steered their curved ships, and so the ships lay in the hollow harbor close-anchored, side by side; for no wave swelled within it, large or small, but a clear calm was all around. I alone posted my black ship without the harbor, there at the point, lashing my cables to the rock. Then climbing up, I took my stand on a rugged point of outlook. From it no work of man or beast was to be seen, only we saw some smoke ascending from the ground. So I sent sailors forth to go and learn what men who live by bread dwelt in the land,—selecting two, and joining with them a herald as a third. Leaving the ship, they took a beaten road where carts brought timber from the lofty hills down to the town below. Before the town they met a maiden drawing water, the stately daughter of the Laestrygonian Antiphates. She had come down to the clear-flowing fountain of Artacia, from which they used to fetch the water for the town. So my men, drawing near, addressed her and inquired who was the king of the folk here and whom he ruled; whereat she pointed to her father's high-roofed house. But when they entered the lordly hall, they found a woman there huge as a hilltop; at her they were aghast. Forthwith she called from the assembly noble Antiphates, her husband, who sought to bring upon my men a miserable end. Straight seizing one, he made his meal of him; and the two others, dashing off, came flying to the ships. Thereat he raised a cry throughout the town, and hearing it, the mighty Laestrygonians gathered from here and there, seeming not men but giants. Then from the rocks they hurled down ponderous stones; and soon among the ships arose a dreadful din of dying men and crashing ships. As men spear fish, they gathered in their loathsome meal. But while they slaughtered these in the deep harbor, I drew my sharp sword from my thigh and cut the cables of my dark-bowed ship; and quickly inspiriting my men, I bade them fall to their oars, that we might flee from danger. They all tossed up the water, in terror for their lives, and cheerily to sea, away from the beetling cliff, my ship sped on; but all the other ships went down together there.

"Thence we sailed on with aching hearts, glad to be clear of death, though missing our dear comrades. And now we reached the island of Aeaea, where fair-haired Circe dwelt, a mighty goddess, human of speech. She was own sister of the sorcerer Aeetes; both were the children of the beaming Sun and of a mother Perse, the daughter of Oceanus. Here we bore landward with our ship and ran in silence into a sheltering harbor, God our guide. Landing, we lay two days and nights, gnawing our hearts because of toil and trouble; but when the fair-haired dawn brought the third day, I took my spear and my sharp sword, and from the ship walked briskly up to a place of distant view, hoping to see some work of man or catch some voice. So climbing up, I took my stand on a rugged point of outlook, and smoke appeared rising from open ground at Circe's dwelling, through some oak thickets and a wood. Then for a time I doubted in my mind and heart whether to go and search the matter while I saw the flaring smoke. Reflecting thus, it seemed the better way first to return to the swift ship and to the shore; there give my men their dinner, and send them forth to search.

"But on my way, as I drew near to the curved ship, some god took pity on me all forlorn, and sent a high-horned deer into my very path. From feeding in the wood he came to the stream to drink, for the sun's power oppressed him. As he stepped out, I struck him in the spine midway along the back; the bronze spear pierced him through; down in the dust he fell with a moan, and his life flew away. Setting my foot upon him, I drew from the wound the brazen spear and laid it on the ground; then I plucked twigs and osiers, and wove a rope a fathom long, twisted from end to end, with which I bound together the monstrous creature's legs. So with him upon my back I walked to the black ship leaning upon my spear, because it was not possible to hold him with my hand upon my shoulder; for the beast was very large. Before the ship I threw him down and then with cheering words aroused my men, standing by each in turn:

"'We shall not, friends, however sad, go to the halls of Hades until our destined day. But while there still is food and drink in the swift ship, let us attend to eating, not waste away with hunger.'

"So I spoke, and my words they quickly heeded. Throwing their coverings off upon the shore beside the barren sea, they gazed upon the deer; for the beast was very large. Then after they had satisfied their eyes with gazing, they washed their hands and made a glorious feast. Thus all throughout the day till setting sun we sat and feasted on abundant meat and pleasant wine; and when the sun went down and darkness came, we laid us down to sleep upon the beach. Then as the early rosy-fingered dawn appeared, holding a council, I said to all my men:

"'My suffering comrades, hearken to my words: for since, my friends, we do not know the place of dusk or dawn, the place at which the beaming sun goes under ground nor where he rises, let us at once consider if a wise course be left. I do not think there is; for I saw, on climbing to a rugged outlook, an island which the boundless deep encircles like a crown. Low in the sea it lies; midway across, I saw a smoke through some oak thickets and a wood.'

"As I thus spoke, their very souls were crushed within them, remembering the deeds of Laestrygonian Antiphates and the cruelty of the daring Cyclops, the devourer of men. They cried aloud and let the big tears fall; but no good came to them from their lamenting.

"Now the whole body of my mailed companions I told off in two bands, and to each band assigned a leader: the one I led, godlike Eurylochus the other. Straightway we shook the lots in a bronze helmet, and the lot of bold Eurylochus leapt out the first. So he departed, two and twenty comrades following, all in tears; and us they left in sorrow too behind. Within the glades they found the house of Circe, built of smooth stone upon commanding ground. All round about were mountain wolves and lions, which Circe had charmed by giving them evil drugs. These creatures did not spring upon my men, but stood erect, wagging their long tails, fawning. As hounds fawn round their master when he comes from meat, because he always brings them dainties that they like, so round these men the strong-clawed wolves and lions fawned. Still my men trembled at the sight of the strange beasts. They stood before the door of the fair-haired goddess, and in the house heard Circe singing with sweet voice, while tending her great imperishable loom and weaving webs, fine, beautiful, and lustrous as are the works of gods. Polites was the first to speak, one ever foremost, and one to me the nearest and the dearest of my comrades:

"'Ah, friends, somebody in the house is tending a great loom and singing sweetly; all the pavement rings. A god it is or woman. Then let us quickly call.'

"He spoke, the others lifted up their voice and called; and suddenly coming forth, she opened the shining doors and bade them in. The rest all followed, heedless. Only Eurylochus remained behind, suspicious of a snare. She led them in and seated them on couches and on chairs, and made a potion for them,—cheese, barley, and yellow honey, stirred into Pramnian wine,— but mingled with the food pernicious drugs, to make them quite forget their native land. Now after she had given the cup and they had drunk it off, straight with a wand she smote them, and penned them up in sties; and they took on the heads of swine, the voice, the bristles, and even the shape, yet was their reason as sound as heretofore. Thus, weeping, they were penned; and Circe flung them acorns, chestnuts, and cornel-fruit to eat, such things as swine that wallow in the mire are wont to eat.

"Eurylochus, meanwhile, came to the swift black ship to bring me tidings of my men and tell their bitter fate. Strive as he might, he could not speak a word, so stricken was he to the soul with sore distress; his eyes were filled with tears, his heart felt anguish. But when we all in great amazement questioned him, then he described the loss of all his men:

"'We went, as you commanded, noble Odysseus, through the thicket and found within the glades a beautiful house, built of smooth stone upon commanding ground. There somebody was tending a great loom and loudly singing, some god or woman. The others lifted up their voice and called; and suddenly coming forth, she opened the shining doors and bade them in. The rest all followed, heedless; but I remained behind, suspicious of a snare. They vanished, one and all; not one appeared again, though long I sat and watched.'

"So he spoke; I slung my silver-studded sword about my shoulders,—large it was and made of bronze,—and my bow with it, and bade him lead me back the selfsame way. But he, clasping my knees with both his hands, entreated me, and sorrowfully said in winged words:

"'O heaven-descended man, bring me not there against my will, but leave me here; for well I know you never will return, nor will you bring another of your comrades. Rather, with these now here, let us speed on; for we might even yet escape the evil day.'

"So he spoke, and answering him said I: 'Eurylochus, remain then here yourself, eating and drinking by the black hollow ship; but I will go, for strong necessity is on me.'

"Saying this, I passed up from the ship and from the sea. But when, in walking up the solemn glades, I was about to reach the great house of the sorceress Circe, there I was met, as I approached the house, by Hermes of the golden wand, in likeness of a youth, the first down on his lip,—a time of life most pleasing. He held my hand and spoke, and thus addressed me:

"'Where are you going, hapless man, along the hills alone, ignorant of the land? Your comrades yonder, at the house of Circe, are penned like swine and kept in fast-closed sties. You come to free them? Nay, I am sure you will return no more, but there, like all the rest, you too will stay. Still, I can keep you clear of harm and give you safety. Here, take this potent herb and go to Circe's house; this shall protect your life against the evil day. And I will tell you all the magic arts of Circe: she will prepare for you a potion and cast drugs into your food; but even so, she cannot charm you, because the potent herb which I shall give will not permit it. And let me tell you more: when Circe turns against you her long wand, then drawing the sharp sword from your thigh spring upon Circe as if you meant to slay her. In terror she will bid you to her bower. And do not you refuse the goddess's bower, that so she may release your men and care for you. But bid her swear the blessed ones' great oath that she is not meaning now to plot you a fresh woe and when you are defenceless make you feeble and unmanned.'

"As he thus spoke, the Speedy-comer gave the herb, drawing it from the ground, and pointed out its nature. Black at the root it is, like milk its blossom, and the gods call it moly. Hard is it for a mortal man to dig; with gods all things may be.

"Hermes departed now to high Olympus, along the woody island. I made my way to Circe's house, and as I went my heart grew very dark. But I stood at the gate of the fair-haired goddess, stood there and called, and the goddess heard my voice. Suddenly coming forth, she opened the shining doors and bade me in; I followed her with aching heart. She led me in and placed me on a silver-studded chair, beautiful, richly wrought, with a footstool for the feet, and she prepared a potion in a golden cup for me to drink, but put therein a drug, with wicked purpose in her heart. Now after she had given the drink and I had drunk it off, and yet it had not charmed me, smiting me with her wand, she spoke these words and cried: 'Off to the sty, and lie there with your fellows!'

"She spoke; I drew the sharp blade from my thigh and sprang upon Circe as if I meant to slay her. With a loud cry, she cowered and clasped my knees, and sorrowfully said in winged words:

"'Who are you? Of what people? Where is your town and kindred? I marvel much that drinking of these drugs you were not charmed. None, no man else, ever withstood these drugs who tasted them, so soon as they had passed the barrier of his teeth; but in your breast there is a mind which cannot be beguiled. Surely you are adventurous Odysseus, who the god of the golden wand, the Speedy-comer, always declared would come upon his way from Troy,—he and his swift black ship. Nay, then, put up your blade within its sheath, and let us now turn to my bower, that there we two may know our love and learn to trust each other.'

"So she spoke, and answering her said I: 'Circe, why ask me to be gentle toward you when you have turned my comrades into swine within your halls, and here detain me and with treacherous purpose invite me to your bower and to approach your side that when I am defenceless you may make me feeble and unmanned? But I will never willingly approach your bower till you consent, goddess, to swear a solemn oath that you are not meaning now to plot me a new woe.'

"So I spoke, and she then took the oath which I required. So after she had sworn and ended all that oath, then I approached the beauteous bower of Circe.

"Meanwhile attendants plied their work about the halls,—four maids, who were the serving-women of the palace. They are the children of the springs and groves and of the sacred streams that run into the sea. One threw upon the chairs beautiful cloths; purple she spread above, linen below. The next placed silver tables by the chairs and set forth golden baskets. A third stirred in a bowl the cheering wine—sweet wine in silver—and filled the golden cups. A fourth brought water and kindled a large fire under a great kettle, and let the water warm. Then when the water in the glittering copper boiled, she seated me in the bath and bathed me from the kettle about the head and shoulders, tempering the water well, till from my joints she drew the sore fatigue. And after she had bathed me and anointed me with oil and put upon me a goodly coat and tunic, she led me in and placed me on a silver-studded chair, beautiful, richly wrought, with a footstool for the feet, and water for the hands a servant brought me in a beautiful pitcher made of gold, and poured it out over a silver basin for my washing, and spread a polished table by my side. Then the grave housekeeper brought bread and placed before me, setting out food of many a kind, freely giving of her store, and bade me eat. But that pleased not my heart; I sat with other thoughts; my heart foreboded evil.

"When Circe marked me sitting thus, not laying hands upon my food but cherishing sore sorrow, approaching me she said in winged words: 'Why do you sit, Odysseus, thus, like one struck dumb, gnawing your heart, and touch no food nor drink? Do you suspect some further guile? You have no cause for fear, for even now I swore to you a solemn oath.'

"So she spoke, and answering her said I: 'Ah, Circe, what upright man could bring himself to taste of food or drink before he had released his friends and seen them with his eyes? But if you in sincerity will bid me drink and eat, then set them free; that I with my own eyes may see my trusty comrades.'

"So I spoke, and from the hall went Circe, wand in hand. She opened the sty doors, and forth she drove what seemed like nine-year swine. A while they stood before her, and, passing along the line, Circe anointed each one with a counter-charm. So from their members fell the hair which at the first the accursed drug which potent Circe gave had made to grow; and once more they were men, men younger than before, much fairer too and taller to behold. They knew me, and each grasped my hand, and from them all passionate sobs burst forth, and all the house gave a sad echo. The goddess pitied us, even she, and standing by my side the heavenly goddess said:

"'High-born son of Laërtes, ready Odysseus, go now to your swift ship and to the shore, and first of all draw up your ship upon the land, and store within the caves your goods and all your gear, and then come back yourself and bring your trusty comrades.'

"So she spoke, and my high heart assented. I went to the swift ship and to the shore, and found by the swift ship my trusty comrades in bitter lamentation, letting the big tears fall. As the stalled calves skip round a drove of cows returning to the barn-yard when satisfied with grazing; with one accord they all bound forth, the folds no longer hold them, but with continual bleat they frisk about their mothers; so did these men, when they caught sight of me, press weeping round. To them it seemed as if they had already reached their land, their very town of rugged Ithaca where they were bred and born; and through their sobs they said in winged words:

"'Now you have come, O heaven-descended man, we are as glad as if we were approaching Ithaca, our native land. But tell about the loss of all our other comrades.'

"So they spoke; I in soft words made answer: 'Let us now first of all draw up our ship upon the land and store within the caves our goods and all our gear; then hasten all of you to follow me, and see your comrades in the magic house of Circe drinking and eating, holding constant cheer.'

"So I spoke, and my words they quickly heeded. Eurylochus alone tried to hold back my comrades, and speaking in winged words he said: 'Poor fools, where are we going? Why are you so in love with ill that you will go to Circe's hall and let her turn us all to swine and wolves and lions, that we may then keep watch at her great house, perforce? Such deeds the Cyclops did when to his lair our comrades came, and with them went this reckless man, Odysseus; for through his folly those men also perished.'

"As he thus spoke, I hesitated in my heart whether to draw my keen-edged blade from my stout thigh and by a blow bring down his head into the dust, near as he was by tie of marriage; but with soft words my comrades stayed me, each in his separate wise:

"'High-born Odysseus, we will leave him, if you like, here by the ship to guard the ship; but lead us to the magic house of Circe.'

"Saying this, they passed up from the ship and from the sea. Yet did Eurylochus not tarry by the hollow ship; he followed, for he feared my stern rebuke.

"But in the mean while to my other comrades at the palace Circe had given a pleasant bath, anointed them with oil, and put upon them fleecy coats and tunics; merrily feasting in her halls we found them all. When the men saw and recognized each other, they wept aloud and the house rang around; and standing by my side the heavenly goddess said:

"'High-born son of Laërtes, ready Odysseus, let not this swelling grief rise further now. I myself know what hardships you have borne upon the swarming sea and how fierce men harassed you on the land. Come, then, eat food, drink wine, until you find once more that spirit in the breast which once was yours when you first left your native land of rugged Ithaca. Now, worn and spiritless, your thoughts still dwell upon your weary wandering. This many a day your heart has not been glad, for sorely have you suffered.'

"So she spoke, and our high hearts assented. Here, then, day after day, for a full year, we sat and feasted on abundant meat and pleasant wine. But when the year was gone and the round of the seasons rolled, as the months waned and the long days were done, then calling me aside my trusty comrades said:

"'Ah, sir, consider now your native land, if you are destined ever to be saved and reach your stately house and native land.'

"So they spoke, and my high heart assented. Yet all throughout that day till setting sun we sat and feasted on abundant meat and pleasant wine; and when the sun went down and darkness came, my men lay down to sleep throughout the dusky halls. But I, on coming to the beauteous bower of Circe, made supplication to her by her knees, and to my voice the goddess hearkened; and speaking in winged words, I said:

"'Circe, fulfill the promise made to send me home; for now my spirit stirs, with that of all my men, who vex my heart with their complaints when you are gone away.'

"So I spoke, and straight the heavenly goddess answered: 'High-born son of Laërtes, ready Odysseus stay no longer at my home against your will. But you must first perform a different journey, and go to the halls of Hades and of dread Persephone, there to consult the spirit of Teiresias of Thebes,—the prophet blind, whose mind is steadfast still. To him, though dead, Persephone has granted reason, to him alone sound understanding; the rest are flitting shadows.'

"As she thus spoke, my very soul was crushed within me, and sitting on the bed I fell to weeping; my heart no longer cared to live and see the sun. But when of weeping and of writhing I had had my fill, then thus I answered her and said: 'But, Circe, who will be my pilot on this journey? None by black ship has ever reached the land of Hades.'

"So I spoke, and straight the heavenly goddess answered: 'High-born son of Laërtes, ready Odysseus, let not the lack of pilot for your ship disturb you, but set the mast, spread the white sail aloft, and sit you down; the breath of Boreas shall bear her onward. When you have crossed by ship the Ocean-stream to where the shore is rough and the grove of Persephone stands,—tall poplars and seed-shedding willows, there beach your ship by the deep eddies of the Ocean-stream, but go yourself to the mouldering house of Hades. There is a spot where into Acheron run Pyriphlegethon and Cocytus, a stream which is an offshoot of the waters of the Styx; a rock here forms the meeting-point of the two roaring rivers. To this spot then, hero, draw nigh, even as I bid; and dig a pit, about a cubit either way, and round its edges pour an offering to all the dead,—first honey mixture, next sweet wine, and thirdly water, and over all strew the white barley-meal. Make many supplications also to the strengthless dead, vowing when you return to Ithaca to take the barren cow that is your best and offer it in your hall, heaping the pyre with treasure; and to Teiresias separately to sacrifice a sheep, for him alone, one wholly black, the very choicest of your flock. So when with vows you have implored the illustrious peoples of the dead, offer a ram and a black ewe, bending their heads toward Erebus, but turn yourself away facing the river's stream; to you shall gather many spirits of those now dead and gone. Then forthwith call your men, and bid them take the sheep now lying there slain by the ruthless sword, and flay and burn them, and call upon the gods,—on powerful Hades and on dread Persephone,—while you yourself, drawing your sharp sword from your thigh, sit still and do not let the strengthless dead approach the blood till you have made inquiry of Teiresias. Thither the seer will quickly come, O chief of men, and he will tell your course, the stages of your journey, and of your homeward way, how you may pass along the swarming sea.'

"Even as she spoke, the gold-throned morning came. On me she put a coat and tunic for my raiment; and the nymph dressed herself in a long silvery robe, fine spun and graceful; she bound a beautiful golden girdle round her waist, and put a veil upon her head. Then through the house I passed and roused my men with cheering words, standing by each in turn:

"'Sleep no more now, nor drowse in pleasant slumber, but let us go, for potent Circe has at last made known the way.'

"So I spoke, and their high hearts assented. Yet even from there I did not bring away my men in safety. There was a certain Elpenor, the youngest of them all, a man not very firm in fight nor sound of understanding, who, parted from his mates, lay down to sleep upon the magic house of Circe, seeking for coolness when overcome with wine. As his companions stirred, hearing the noise and tumult, he suddenly sprang up and quite forgot how to come down again by the long ladder, but fell headlong from the roof; his neck was broken in its socket, and his soul went down to the house of Hades.

"As my men mustered there, I said to them: 'You think, perhaps, that you are going home to your own native land; but Circe has marked out for us a different journey, even to the halls of Hades and of dread Persephone, there to consult the spirit of Teiresias of Thebes.'

"As I thus spoke, their very souls were crashed within them, and sitting down where each one was they moaned and tore their hair; but no good came to them from their lamenting.

"Now while we walked to the swift ship and to the shore, in sadness, letting the big tears fall, Circe went on before, and there by the black ship tied a black ewe and ram, passing us lightly by. When a god does not will, what man can spy him moving to and fro?"

XI

The Land of the Dead

"Now when we came down to the ship and to the sea, we in the first place launched our ship into the sacred sea, put mast and sail in the black ship, then took the sheep and drove them in, and we ourselves embarked in sadness, letting the big tears fall. And for our aid behind our dark-bowed ship came a fair wind to fill our sail, a welcome comrade, sent us by fair-haired Circe, the mighty goddess, human of speech. So when we had done our work at the several ropes about the ship we sat us down, while wind and helmsman kept her steady; and all day long the sail of the running ship was stretched. Then the sun sank, and all the ways grew dark.

"And now she reached earth's limits, the deep stream of the Ocean, where the Cimmerian people's land and city lie, wrapt in a fog and cloud. Never on them does the shining sun look down with his beams, as he goes up the starry sky or as again toward earth he turns back from the sky, but deadly night is spread abroad over these hapless men. On coming here, we beached our ship and set the sheep ashore, then walked along the Ocean-stream until we reached the spot foretold by Circe.

"Here Perimedes and Eurylochus held fast the victims, while drawing my sharp blade from my thigh, I dug a pit, about a cubit either way, and round its edges poured an offering to all the dead,—first honey-mixture, next sweet wine, and thirdly water, and over all I strewed white barley-meal; and I made many supplications to the strengthless dead, vowing when I returned to Ithaca to take the barren cow that was my best and offer it in my hall, heaping the pyre with treasure; and to Teiresias separately to sacrifice a sheep, for him alone, one wholly black, the choicest of my flock. So when with prayers and vows I had implored the peoples of the dead, I took the sheep and cut their throats over the pit, and forth the dark blood flowed. Then gathered there spirits from out of Erebus of those now dead and gone,—brides, and unwedded youths, and worn old men, delicate maids with hearts but new to sorrow, and many pierced with brazen spears, men slain in fight, wearing their bloodstained armor. In crowds around the pit they flocked from every side, with awful wail. Pale terror seized me. Nevertheless, inspiriting my men, I bade them take the sheep now lying there slain by the ruthless sword, and flay and burn them, and call upon the gods,—on powerful Hades and on dread Persephone,—while I myself, drawing my sharp sword from my thigh, sat still and did not let the strengthless dead approach the blood till I had made inquiry of Teiresias.

"First came the spirit of my man, Elpenor. He had not yet been buried under the broad earth; for we left his body at the hall of Circe, unwept, unburied, since another task then pressed. I wept to see him and pitied him from my heart, and speaking in winged words I said:

"'Elpenor, how came you in this murky gloom? Faster you came on foot than I in my black ship.'

"So I spoke, and with a groan he answered: 'Highborn son of Laërtes, ready Odysseus, Heaven's cruel doom destroyed me, and excess of wine. After I went to sleep on Circe's house, I did not notice how to go down again by the long ladder, but fell headlong from the roof; my neck was broken in its socket, and my soul came down to the house of Hades. Now I entreat you by those left behind, not present here, by your wife, and by the father who cared for you when little, and by Telemachus whom you left at home alone,—for I know, as you go hence out of the house of Hades, you will touch with your staunch ship the island of Aeaea,—there then, my master, I charge you, think of me. Do not, in going, leave me behind, unwept, unburied, deserting me, lest I become a cause of anger to the gods against you; but burn me in the armor that was mine, and on the shore of the foaming sea erect the mound of an unhappy man, that future times may know. Do this for me, and fix upon my grave the oar with which in life I rowed among my comrades.'

"So he spoke, and answering him said I: 'Unhappy man, this will I carry out and do for you.'

"In such sad words talking with one another, there we sat,—I on the one side, holding my blade over the blood, while the spectre of my comrade, on the other, told of his many woes.

"Now came the spirit of my dead mother, Anticleia, daughter of brave Autolycus, whom I had left alive on setting forth for sacred Ilios. I wept to see her and pitied her from my heart; but even so, I did not let her—deeply though it grieved me—approach the blood till I had made inquiry of Teiresias.

"Now came the spirit of Teiresias of Thebes, holding his golden sceptre. He knew me, and said to me: 'Highborn son of Laërtes, ready Odysseus, why now, unhappy man, leaving the sunshine, have you come here to see the dead and this forbidding place? Nay, draw back from the pit and turn your sharp blade from the blood, that I may drink and speak what will not fail.'

"So he spoke, and drawing back I thrust my silver studded sword into its sheath. And after he had drunk of the dark blood, then thus the blameless seer addressed me:

"'You are looking for a joyous journey home, glorious Odysseus, but a god will make it hard; for I do not think you will elude the Land-shaker, who bears a grudge against you in his heart, angry because you blinded his dear son. Yet even so, by meeting hardship you may still reach home, if you will curb the passions of yourself and crew when once you bring your staunch ship to the Thrinacian island, safe from the dark blue sea, and find the pasturing kine and sturdy sheep of the Sun, who all things oversees, all overhears. If you leave these unharmed and heed your homeward way, you still may come to Ithaca, though you shall meet with hardship. But if you harm them, then I predict the loss of ship and crew; and even if you yourself escape, late shall you come, in evil plight, with loss of all your crew, on the vessel of a stranger. At home you shall find trouble, bold men devouring your living, wooing your matchless wife, and offering bridal gifts. Nevertheless, on your return, you surely shall avenge their crimes. But after you have slain the suitors in your halls, whether by stratagem or by the sharp sword boldly, then journey on, bearing a shapely oar, until you reach the men who know no sea and do not eat food mixed with salt. These therefore have no knowledge of the red-cheeked ships, nor of the shapely oars which are the wings of ships. And I will name a sign easy to be observed, which shall not fail you: when another traveler, meeting you, shall say you have a winnowing fan on your white shoulder, there fix in the ground your shapely oar, and make fit offerings to lord Poseidon a ram, a bull, and the sow's mate, a boar,—and turning homeward offer sacred hecatombs to the immortal gods who hold the open sky, all in the order due. Upon yourself death from the sea shall very gently come and cut you off bowed down with hale old age. Round you shall be a prosperous people. I speak what shall not fail.'

"So he spoke, and answering him said I: 'Teiresias, these are the threads of destiny the gods themselves have spun. Nevertheless, declare me this, and plainly tell: I see the spirit of my dead mother here; silent she sits beside the blood and has not, although I am her son, deigned to look in my face or speak to me. Tell me, my master, how may she know that it is I?'

"So I spoke, and straightway answering me said he: 'A simple saying I will tell and fix it in your mind: whomever among these dead and gone you let approach the blood, he shall declare the truth. But whomsoever you refuse, he shall turn back again.'

"So saying, into the house of Hades passed the spirit of the great Teiresias, after telling heaven's decrees; but I still held my place until my mother came and drank of the dark blood. She knew me instantly, and sorrowfully said in winged words:

"'My child, how came you in this murky gloom, while still alive? Awful to the living are these sights. Great rivers are between, and fearful floods,—mightiest of all, the Ocean-stream, not to be crossed on foot, but only on a strong-built ship. Are you but now come here, upon your way from Troy, wandering a long time with your ship and crew? Have you not been in Ithaca, nor seen your wife at home?'

"So she spoke, and answering her said I: 'My mother, need brought me to the house of Hades, here to consult the spirit of Teiresias of Thebes. I have not yet been near Achaea nor once set foot upon my land, but have been always wandering and meeting sorrow since the first day I followed royal Agamemnon to Ilios, famed for horses, to fight the Trojans there. But now declare me this and plainly tell: what doom of death that lays men low o'erwhelmed you? Some long disease? Or did the huntress Artemis attack and slay you with her gentle arrows? And tell me of my father and the son I left; still in their keeping are my honors? Or does at last an alien hold them, while people say that I shall come no more? Tell me, moreover, of my wedded wife, her purposes and thoughts. Is she abiding by her child and keeping all in safety? Or was she finally married by some chief of the Achaeans?'

"So I spoke, and straight my honored mother answered: 'Indeed she stays with patient heart within your hall, and wearily the nights and days are wasted with her tears. Nobody yet holds your fair honors; in peace Telemachus farms your estate, and sits at equal feasts where it befits the lawgiver to be a guest; for all give him a welcome. Your father stays among the fields, and comes to town no more. Bed has he none, bedstead, nor robes, nor brightened rugs; but through the winter he sleeps in the house where servants sleep, in the dust beside the fire, and wears upon his body sorry clothes. Then when the summer comes and fruitful autumn, wherever he may be about his slope of vineyard-ground a bed is piled of leaves fallen on the earth. There lies he in distress, woe waxing strong within, longing for your return; and hard old age comes on. Even so I also died and met my doom: not that at home the sure-eyed huntress attacked and slew me with her gentle arrows; nor did a sickness come, which oftentimes by sad decay steals from the limbs the life; but longing for you—your wise ways, glorious Odysseus, and your tenderness,—took joyous life away.'

"As she thus spoke, I yearned, though my mind hesitated, to clasp the spirit of my mother, even though dead. Three times the impulse came; my heart urged me to clasp her. Three times out of my arms like a shadow or a dream she flitted, and the sharp pain about my heart grew only more; and speaking in winged words, I said:

"'My mother, why not stay for me who long to clasp you, so that in the very house of Hades, throwing our arms round one another, we two may take our fill of piercing grief? Or is it a phantom high Persephone has sent, to make me weep and sorrow more?'

"So I spoke, and straight my honored mother answered: 'Ah, my own child, beyond all men ill-fated! In no wise is Persephone, daughter of Zeus, beguiling you, but this is the way with mortals when they die: the sinews then no longer hold the flesh and bones together; for these the strong force of the blazing fire destroys, when once the life leaves the white bones, and like a dream the spirit flies away. Nay now, press quickly on into the light, and of all this take heed, to tell your wife hereafter.'

"So we held converse there; but now the women came—for high Persephone had sent them—who were great men's wives and daughters. Round the dark blood in throngs they gathered, and I considered how to question each. Then to my mind this seemed the wisest way: I drew my keen-edged blade from my stout thigh and did not let them all at once drink the dark blood, but one by one they came, and each declared her lineage, and I questioned all.

"There I saw Tyro first, of noble ancestry, who told of being sprung from gentle Salmoneus; told how she was the wife of Cretheus, son of Aeolus. She loved a river-god, divine, Enipeus, who flows the fairest of all streams on earth. So she would walk by the fair currents of Enipeus, and in his guise the Land-shaker, who girds the land, met her at the outpouring of the eddying stream. The heaving water compassed them, high as a hill and arching, and hid the god and mortal woman. He touched the maiden and she fell asleep. Then on departing he took her hand and spoke and thus addressed her:

"'Be happy, lady, in my love. In the revolving year you shall bear noble children; for the love of the immortals is not barren. Rear them yourself and cherish them. And now go home. Hold fast and speak it not. I am Poseidon, the shaker of the land.'

"So saying, he plunged into the surging sea. She then bore Pelias and Neleus, who both became strong ministers of mighty Zeus. Pelias dwelt in the open country of Iolcas, rich in flocks, the other at sandy Pylos. And sons to Cretheus also this queen of women bore—Aeson, and Pheres, and Amythaon, the charioteer.

"And after her I saw Antiope, Asopus' daughter, who boasted she had been the spouse of Zeus himself. To him she bore two sons, Amphion and Zethus, who first laid the foundations of seven-gated Thebes and fortified it; because, unfortified, they could not dwell in open Thebes, for all their power.

"And after her I saw Alcinene, wife of Amphitryon, her who bore dauntless Hercules, the lion-hearted, as spouse of mighty Zeus; and Megara, harsh Creon's daughter, whom the tireless son of Amphitryon took to wife.

"The mother of Oedipus I saw, fair Epicaste, who did a monstrous deed through ignorance of heart, in marrying her son. He, having slain his father, married her; and soon the gods made the thing known to men. In pain at pleasant Thebes he governed the Cadmeians, through the gods' destroying purpose; and she went down to Hades, the strong gaoler, fastening a fatal noose to the high rafter, abandoned to her grief. To him she left the many woes which the avengers of a mother bring.

"Beautiful Chloris, too, I saw, whom Neleus once married for her beauty after making countless gifts, the youngest daughter of that Amphion, son of Iasus, who once held sway at Minyan Orchomenus. She was the queen of Pylos and bore Neleus famous children, Nestor and Chromius and Periclymenus the headstrong. And beside these she bore that stately Pero, the marvel of mankind, whom all her neighbors wooed. But to none would Neleus give her save to him who should drive from Phylace the crook-horned, broad-browed kine of haughty Iphiclus, and dangerous kine were they. A blameless seer alone would undertake to drive them; but cruel doom of God prevented, harsh bonds and clownish herdsmen. Yet after days and months were spent, as the year rolled and other seasons came, then haughty Iphiclus released him on his telling all the oracles. The will of Zeus was done.

"Leda I saw, the wife of Tyndareus, who bore to Tyndareus two stalwart sons: Castor, the horseman, and Polydeuces, good at boxing. These in a kind of life the nourishing earth now holds, and even beneath the ground they have from Zeus the boon that to-day they be alive, to-morrow dead; and they are allotted honors like the gods.

"Iphimedeia I saw, wife of Aloëus, who said she had been once loved by Poseidon. She bore two children, but short-lived they proved,—Otus, the godlike, and the far-famed Ephialtes,—whom the fruitful earth made grow to be the tallest and most beautiful of men, after renowned Orion; for at nine years they were nine cubits broad, and in height they reached nine fathoms. Therefore they even threatened the immortals with raising on Olympus the din of furious war. Ossa they strove to set upon Olympus, and upon Ossa leafy Pelion, that so the heavens might be scaled. And this they would have done, had they but reached their period of full vigor; but the son of Zeus whom fair-haired Leto bore destroyed them both before below their temples the downy hair had sprung and covered their chins with the fresh beard.

"Phaedra and Procris, too, I saw, and beautiful Ariadne, daughter of wizard Minos, whom Theseus tried to bring from Crete to the slopes of sacred Athens. But he gained naught thereby; before she came, Artemis slew her in sea-girt Dia,—prompted by the report of Dionysus.

"Maera and Clymene I saw, and odious Eriphyle who took a bribe of gold as the price of her own husband. But all I cannot tell, nor even name the many heroes' wives and daughters whom I saw; ere that, the immortal night would wear away. Already it is time to sleep, at the swift ship among the crew or here. My journey hence rests with the gods and you."

As thus he ended, all were hushed to silence, held by the spell throughout the dusky hall. White-armed Arete was the first to speak: "Phaeacians, how seems to you this man in beauty, height, and balanced mind within? My guest indeed he is, but each one shares the honor. Be not in haste then to dismiss him, nor stint your gifts to one so much in need. By favor of the gods great wealth is in your houses."

Then also spoke the old lord Echeneüs, who was the oldest of Phaeacian men: "My friends, not wide of the mark, nor of her reputation, speaks the wise queen; therefore give heed. Yet word and work zest with Alcinoüs here."

Then answered him Alcinoüs and said: "Even as she speaks that word shall be, if I be now the living lord of oar-loving Phaeacians! But let our guest, however much he longs for home, consent to stay at all events until to-morrow, till I shall make our gift complete. To send him hence shall be the charge of all, especially of me; for power within this land rests here."

Then wise Odysseus answered him and said: "Mighty Alcinoüs, renowned of all, if you should bid me stay a year and then should send me forth, giving me splendid gifts, that is what I would choose; for much more to my profit would it be with fuller hands to reach my native land. Then should I be regarded more and welcomed more by all who saw me coming home to Ithaca."

Then answered him Alcinoüs and said: "Odysseus, we judge you by your looks to be no cheat or thief; though many are the men the dark earth breeds, and scatters far and wide, who fashion falsehoods out of what no man can see. But you have a grace of word and a noble mind within, and you told your tale as skillfully as if you were a bard, relating all the Argives' and your own sore troubles. But now declare me this and plainly tell: did you see any of the god-like comrades who went with you to Ilios and there met doom? The night is very long; yes, vastly long. The hour for sleeping at the hall is not yet come. Tell me the wondrous story. I could be well content till sacred dawn, if you were willing in the hall to tell us of your woes."

Then wise Odysseus answered him and said: "Lord Alcinoüs, renowned of all, there is a time for stories and a time for sleep; yet if you wish to listen longer, I would not shrink from telling tales more pitiful than these, the woes of my companions who died in aftertime, men who escaped the grievous war-cry of the Trojans to die on their return through a wicked woman's will.

"When, then, chaste Persephone had scattered here and there those spirits of tender women, there came the spirit of Agamemnon, son of Atreus, sorrowing. Around thronged other spirits of men who by his side had died in the house of Aegisthus and there had met their doom. He knew me as soon as he had drunk of the dark blood; and then he cried aloud and let the big tears fall, and stretched his hands forth eagerly to grasp me. But no, there was no strength or vigor left, such as was once within his supple limbs. I wept to see him, and pitied him from my heart, and speaking in winged words I said:

"'Great son of Atreus, Agamemnon, lord of men, what doom of death that lays men low o'erwhelmed you? Was it on shipboard that Poseidon smote you, raising unwelcome blasts of cruel wind? Or did fierce men destroy you on the land, while you were cutting off their kine or their fair flocks of sheep, or while you fought to win their town and carry off their women?

"So I spoke, and straightway answering me said he: 'No, high-born son of Laërtes, ready Odysseus, on shipboard Poseidon did not smite me, raising unwelcome blasts of cruel wind, nor did fierce men destroy me on the land; it was Aegisthus, plotting death and doom, who slew me, aided by my accursed wife, when he had bidden me home and had me at the feast, even as one cuts the ox down at his stall. So thus I died a lamentable death, and all my men, with no escape, were slain around me; like white-toothed swine at some rich, powerful man's wedding, or banquet, or gay festival. You have yourself been present at the death of many men,—men slain in single combat and in the press of war; yet here you would have felt your heart most touched with pity, to see how round the mixing-bowl and by the loaded tables we lay about the hall, and all the pavement ran with blood. Saddest of all, I heard the cry of Priam's daughter, Cassandra, whom crafty Clytaemnestra slew beside me; and I, on the ground, lifted my hands and clutched my sword in dying. But she, the brutal woman, turned away and did not deign, though I was going to the house of Hades, to draw with her and my eyelids down and press my lips together. Ah, what can be more horrible and brutish than a woman when she admits into her thoughts such deeds as these! And what a shameless deed she plotted, to bring about the murder of the husband of her youth! I used to think how glad my coming home would be, even to my children and my slaves; but she, intent on such extremity of crime, brought shame upon herself and all of womankind who shall be born hereafter, even on well-doers too.'

"So he spoke, and answering him said I: 'Alas! The house of Atreus far-seeing Zeus has sorely plagued with women's arts, from the beginning: for Helen's sake how many of us died; and Clytaemnestra plotted for you while absent.'

"So I spoke, and straightway answering me said he: 'Never be you, then, gentle to your wife, nor speak out all you really mean; but tell a part and let a part be hid. And yet on you, Odysseus, no violent death shall ever fall from your wife's hand; for truly wise and of an understanding heart is the daughter of Icarius, heedful Penelope. As a young bride we left her, on going to the war. A child was at her breast, an infant then, who now perhaps sits in the ranks of men, and happy too; for his dear father, coming home, will see him, and he will meet his father with embrace, as children should. But my wife did not let me feast my eyes upon my son; before he came, she slew me. Nay, this I will say further: mark it well. By stealth, not openly, bring in your ship to shore, for there is no more faith in woman. But now declare me this and plainly tell if you hear my son is living still—at Orchomenus, perhaps, or sandy Pylos, or at the home of Menelaus in broad Sparta; for surely nowhere on earth has royal Orestes died.'

"So he spoke, and answering him said I: 'O son of Atreus, why question me of this? Whether he be alive or dead I do not know. To speak vain words is ill.'

"In such sad words talking with one another mournfully we stood, letting the big tears fall. And now there came the spirit of Achilles, son of Peleus, and of Patroclus too, of gallant Antilochus, and of Ajax who was first in beauty and in stature of all the Danaäns after the gallant son of Peleus. But the spirit of swift footed Aeacides knew me, and sorrowfully said in winged words:

"'High-born son of Laërtes, ready Odysseus, rash as you are, what will you undertake more desperate than this! How dared you come down hither to the house of Hades, where dwell the senseless dead, spectres of toil-worn men?'

"So he spoke, and answering him said I: 'Achilles, son of Peleus, foremost of the Achaeans, I came for consultation with Teiresias, hoping that he might give advice for reaching rugged Ithaca. I have not yet been near Achaea nor once set foot upon my land, but have had constant trouble; while as for you, Achilles, no man was in the past more fortunate, nor in the future shall be; for formerly, during your life, we Argives gave you equal honor with the gods, and now you are a mighty lord among the dead when here. Then do not grieve at having died, Achilles.'

"So I spoke, and straightway answering me said he: 'Mock not at death, glorious Odysseus. Better to be the hireling of a stranger, and serve a man of estate whose living is but small, than be the ruler over all these dead and gone. No, tell me tales of my proud son, whether or not he followed to the war to be a leader; tell what you know of gallant Peleus, whether he still has honor in the cities of the Myrmidons; or do they slight him now in Hellas and in Phthia, because old age has touched his hands and feet? I am myself no longer in the sunlight to defend him, nor like what I once was when on the Trojan plain I routed a brave troop in succoring the Argives. If once like that I could but come, even for a little space, into my father's house, frightful should be my might and my resistless hands to any who are troubling him and keeping him from honor.'

"So he spoke, and answering him said I: 'Indeed, of gallant Peleus I know nothing. But about your dear son Neoptolemus, I will tell you all the truth, as you desire; for it was I, in my trim hollow ship, who brought him from Scyros to the mailed Achaeans. And when encamped at Troy we held a council, he always was the first to speak, and no word missed its mark; godlike Nestor and I alone surpassed him. Moreover, on the Trojan plain, when we Achaeans battled, he never tarried in the throng nor at the rallying-place, but pressed before us all, yielding to none in courage. Many a man he slew in mortal combat. Fully I cannot tell, nor even name the host he slew in fighting for the Argives; but how he vanquished with his sword the son of Telephus, Eurypylus the hero! Many of that Ceteian band fell with their leader, destroyed by woman's bribes. So goodly a man as he I never saw, save kingly Memnon.

"'Then when we entered the horse Epeius made,—we chieftains of the Argives,—and it lay all with me to shut or open our close ambush, other captains and councilors of the Danaäns would wipe away a tear, and their limbs shook beneath them; but watching him, at no time did I see his fair skin pale, nor from his cheeks did he wipe tears away. Often he begged to leave the horse; he fingered his sword-hilt and his bronze-tipped spear, longing to vex the Trojans. Yet after we overthrew the lofty town of Priam, he took his share of spoil and an honorable prize, and went on board unharmed, not hit by brazen point nor wounded in close combat, as for the most part happens in war; hap-hazard Ares rages.'

"So I spoke, and the spirit of swift-footed Aeacides departed with long strides across the field of asphodel, pleased that I said his son was famous.

"But the other spirits of those dead and gone stood sadly there; each asked for what he loved. Only the spirit of Ajax, son of Telamon, held aloof, still angry at the victory I gained in the contest at the ships for the armor of Achilles. The goddess mother of Achilles offered the prize, and the sons of the Trojans were the judges,—they and Pallas Athene. Would I had never won in such a strife, since thus the earth closed round the head of Ajax, who in beauty and achievement surpassed all other Danaäns save the gallant son of Peleus. To him I spoke in gentle words and said:

"'Ajax, son of gallant Telamon, will you not, even in death, forget your wrath about the accursed armor? To plague the Argives the gods gave it, since such a tower as you were lost thereby. For you as for Achilles, son of Peleus, do we Achaeans mourn unceasingly. None was to blame but Zeus, who, fiercely hating all the host of Danaän spearmen, brought upon you this doom. Nay, king, draw near, that you may listen to our voice and hear our words. Abate your pride and haughty spirit.'

"I spoke; he did not answer, but went his way after the other spirits of those dead and gone, on into Erebus. Yet then, despite his wrath, he should have spoken, or I had spoken to him, but that the heart within my breast wished to see other spirits of the dead.

"There I saw Minos, the illustrious son of Zeus, a golden sceptre in his hand, administering justice to the dead from where he sat, while all around men called for judgment from the king, sitting and standing in the wide-doored hall of Hades.

"Next I marked huge Orion drive through the field of asphodel the game that in his life he slew on the lonely hills. He held a club of solid bronze that never can be broken.

"And Tityus, I saw, the son of far-famed Gaia, stretched on the plain; across nine roods he stretched. Two vultures sat beside him, one upon either hand, and tore his liver, piercing the caul within. Yet with his hands he did not keep them off; for he did violence to Leto, the honored wife of Zeus, as she was going to Pytho through pleasant Panopeus.

"Tantalus, too, I saw in grievous torment and standing in a pool. It touched his chin. He strained for thirst, but could not take and drink; for as the old man bent, eager to drink, the water always was absorbed and disappeared, and at his feet the dark earth showed, God made it dry. Then leafy-crested trees drooped down their fruit,—pears, pomegranates, apples with shining fruit, sweet figs, and thrifty olives. But when the old man stretched his hand to take, a breeze would toss them toward the dusky clouds.

"And Sisyphus I saw in bitter pains, forcing a monstrous stone along with both his hands. Tugging with hand and foot, he pushed the stone upward along a hill. But when he thought to heave it on clean to the summit, a mighty power would turn it back, and so once more down to the ground the wicked stone would tumble. Again he strained to push it back; sweat ran from off his limbs, and from his head a dust cloud rose.

"And next I marked the might of Hercules,—his phantom form; for he himself is with the immortal gods reveling at their feasts, wed to fair-ankled Hebe, child of great Zeus and golden-sandaled Here. Around him rose a clamor of the dead, like that of birds, fleeing all ways in terror; while he, like gloomy night, with his bare bow and arrow on the string, glared fearfully, as if forever shooting. Terrible was the baldric round about his breast, a golden belt where marvelous devices had been wrought, bears and wild boars and fierce-eyed lions, struggles and fights, murders and blood-sheddings. Let the artificer design no more who once achieved that sword-belt by his art. Soon as he saw, he knew me, and sorrowfully said in winged words:

"'High-born son of Laërtes, ready Odysseus, so you, poor man, work out a cruel task such as I once endured when in the sunlight. I was the son of Kronian Zeus, yet I had pains unnumbered; for to one very far beneath me I was bound, and he imposed hard labors. He even sent me here to carry off the dog, for nothing he supposed could be a harder labor. I brought the dog up hence, and dragged him forth from Hades. Hermes was my guide, he and clear-eyed Athene.'

"So saying, back he went into the house of Hades, while I still held my place, hoping there yet might come some other heroes who died long ago. And more of the men of old I might have seen, as I desired,—

Theseus and Peirithoüs, famous children of the gods;—but ere they came, myriads of the people of the dead gathered with awful cry. Pale terror seized me; I thought perhaps the Gorgon head of some fell monster, high Persephone might send out of the house of Hades. So, turning to my ship, I called my crew to come on board and loose the cables. Quickly they came, took places at the pins, and down the Ocean-stream the flowing current bore us, with oarage first and then a pleasant breeze."

Aesop (6th Century BC)

Anecdotes about the African Aesop are as interesting as his fables. A number of references identify him as a Phrygian slave. According to one account, Aesop was a mute hunchback to whom the goddess Isis gave speech as a reward for his devotion to her. He then went on to outwit his masters, gain freedom, and advise kings. Another account finds Aesop falsely accused of theft, convicted by the citizens of Delphi, and thrown from a cliff. A third account claims that Aesop was serving as Croesus' ambassador in Delphi. Aesop was to distribute gold among the Delphians, but he was so irritated by the citizens' covetousness that he returned the money to Croesus. Seeking revenge, the Delphians denounced Aesop as a public criminal and executed him. This third version of Aesop's life adds that after his death, the Delphians experienced various calamities, and "the blood of Aesop" became a popular adage to indicate that evil would be punished. However, an authoritative source for Aesop's biographical information is Herodotus' *History*. Herodotus, during the fifth century BC, wrote that Aesop, a slave belonging to a Samian citizen, lived during the reign of the Egyptian pharaoh Amasis (the middle of the sixth century BC) and died in Delphi. The fact that Herodotus assumed the details of Aesop's death to be common knowledge indicates that the writer was well known. Aesop, by the end of the fifth century BC, now a familiar name in Greece, was referred to as the author of fables. Among other ancient writers who mention Aesop are Aristotle, Aristophanes, and Plato. Plato, for example, reported that Socrates spent his pre-execution days transforming Aesop's fables into verse. More than two thousand years later, Aesop remains a man of mystery, yet he has bequeathed a rich legacy of fables to young and old.

Aesop's Fables

Though Aesop was not the inventor of the fable, which had been employed by Hesiod before him, his name nevertheless comes to mind when most people think of fables. The author of many concise narratives, Aesop frequently featured animals as characters with human virtues and vices whose exploits teach moral lessons, often by means of the oral tradition. His fables are timeless "primers" on how to live life. Though today Aesopian fables are considered children's literature, in Aesop's time they were often sophisticated, political and social satire. The fact that these stories are accessible to and enjoyed by both children and adults across many centuries attests to their evocative power.

The Fox and the Grapes

A fox looked and beheld the grapes that grew upon a huge vine, the which grapes he much desired for to eat them. And when he saw that none he might get, he turned his sorrow into joy, and said, "These grapes are sour, and if I had some I would not eat them."

He is wise which faineth not to desire the thing the which he may not have.

The Ant and the Grasshopper

A grasshopper in the wintertime went and demanded of the ant some of her corn for to eat. And then the ant said to the grasshopper, "What hast thou done all the summer last past?" And the grasshopper answered, "I have sung." And after said the ant to her, "Of my corn shalt thou none have, and if thou hast sung all the summer, dance now in winter."

There is one time for to do some labor and work, and one time for to have rest, for he that worketh not nor does no good shall have oft at his teeth great cold, and lack at his need.

The Hart, the Sheep, and the Wolf

A hart, in the presence of a wolf, demanded of a sheep that she should pay a bushel of corn, and the wolf commanded to the sheep to pay it. And when the day of payment was come, the hart came and demanded of the sheep his corn. And the sheep said to him, "The covenants and pacts made by dread and force ought not to be holding. For it was forced on me, being before the wolf, to promise and grant to give to thee that which thou never lent to me. And therefore thou shalt have right nought of me."

Sometimes it is good to make promise of something for to eschew greater damage or loss, for the things which are done by force have none fidelity.

The Dog and His Shadow

In time past was a dog that went over a bridge, and held in his mouth a piece of meat, and as he passed over the bridge, he perceived and saw the shadow of himself and of his piece of meat within the water. And he, thinking that it was another piece of meat, forthwith thought to take it. And as he opened his mouth, the piece of meat fell into the water, and thus he lost it.

He that desires to have another man's good often loses his own.

The Frogs Who Wanted a King

There were frogs which were in ditches and ponds at their liberty. They all together of one assent and of one will made a request to Jupiter that he would give them a king. And Jupiter began thereof to marvel. And for their king he cast to them a great piece of wood, which made a great sound and noise in the water, whereof all the frogs had a great dread and feared much. And after, they approached to their king for to make obeisance unto him. And when they perceived that it was but a piece of wood, they turned again to Jupiter, praying him sweetly that he would give to them another king. And Jupiter gave to them the heron for to be their king. And then the heron began to enter into the water and eat them one after another. And when the frogs saw that their king destroyed and ate them thus, they began tenderly to weep, saying in this manner to the god Jupiter, "Right high and right mighty god Jupiter, please thee to deliver us from the throat of this dragon and false tyrant which eateth us the one after another." And he said to them, "The king which you have demanded shall be your master. For when men have that which men ought to have, they ought to be joyful and glad. And he that has liberty ought to keep it well, for nothing is better than liberty."

Liberty should not be well sold for all the gold and silver of all the world.

The Lion and the Horse

A lion saw a horse which ate grass in a meadow. And to find some subtlety and manner to eat and devour him, approached to him and said, "God keep thee, my brother. I am a leech and withal a good physician. And because I see that thou hast a sore foot, I am come hither for to heal thee of it." And the horse knew well all his evil thought, and said to the lion, "My brother, I thank thee greatly, and thou art welcome to me. I pray thee that thou wilt make my foot whole." And then the lion said to the horse, "Let me see thy foot." And as the lion looked on it, the horse smote him on the forehead in such wise that he broke his head and went full out of his mind and fell to the ground, and so wondrously was he hurt that almost he might not rise up again. And then said the lion in himself, "I am well worthy to have had this, for he that searcheth evil, evil cometh to him."

None ought to feign himself other than such as he is.

The Rat, the Frog, and the Kite

As a rat went in pilgrimage, he came by a river, and demanded help of a frog for to pass and go over the water. And then the frog bound the rat's foot to her foot, and thus swam unto the middle of the river. And as they were there the frog stood still, to the end that the rat should be drowned. And in the meanwhile came a kite upon them and bare them both with him.

He that thinketh evil against good, the evil that he thinketh shall fall upon himself.

The Frog and the Ox

A frog was in a meadow when she espied and saw an ox which pastured. She would make herself as great and as mighty as the ox, and by her great pride she began to swell against the ox, and demanded of her children if she was not as great as the ox and as mighty. And her children answered and said, "Nay Mother, for to look and behold on the ox it seemeth of you to be nothing." And then the frog began more to swell. And when the ox saw her pride, he trod and threshed her with his foot, and broke her belly.

Swell not thyself to the end that thou break not.

The Ass and the Boar

While the dull ass the sturdy boar derides,
The boar, whose passion sounder reason guides,
Replies. "Dull villain, that the world may see
How much I slight thy scoffs, although from me
Thou just revenge deservst, jest on thy fill,
Thy baseness guards thee, and withholds my will."

Do not enraged at all aspersions grow
Lest false untruths like verities may show.

The Wolf and the Lamb

A thirsty lamb walks to the river's side,
Where she is by a ravenous wolf espied,
Whose currish nature (still on mischief bent)
Thus picks a quarrel with the innocent
And harmless beast; "What villain moved thee thus
Just in our presence (as in scorn of us)
Ere we could drink, to foul the crystal spring?"
The lamb, afflighted at his menacing,
Replied, "Great sir, the cause of my offense
Was through my ignorance, not insolence;
Nor did I know, that you were present here;"
At which the wolf'gins more to domineer,
And answers, "Slave thou liest; have not I seen
How ready thou, and all thy friends have been,
To cross us still? for which (without delay)
Thy blood for all those former wrongs shall pay."

So great men often times o'ersway with might
The poor, against respect of law or right.

Plato (428?–347 BC)

Plato (c. 428–347 B.C.), a philosopher, politician, essayist, poet, and teacher, was born in Athens, or perhaps Aegina, from an old, distinguished family. His father, Ariston, died when Plato was a child. His mother, Perictione, then married her uncle, Pyrilampes, a close friend of Pericles (the famous statesman). Plato was reared in their home. His adolescent and young adult years were uneventful. As a young man, he had entertained political ambitions, particularly after his uncle Charmides and his cousin Critias, who had established themselves as dictators after their participation in Sparta's defeat of Athens, asked Plato to help them rule. However, because of their ruthless and immoral practices, Plato declined their offer. Some time later, he made two trips to Sicily. In 389 B.C., he returned to Athens and founded the Academy (by some accounts the first university), where astronomy, the biological sciences, mathematics, and political science were taught. When Critias and Charmides were deposed in 403 B.C., Plato reconsidered entering politics but again refrained from doing so when Socrates, his friend and teacher, was brought to trial in 399 B.C., and fatally poisoned. Plato spent the remainder of his years as head of the Athenian Academy.

Plato, who was first a student of Cratylus,[1] then later, of Socrates, wrote six different types of texts: (1) the *Letters*, for which he is given credit for having written thirteen, though some believe that he actually wrote only one; (2) the *Apology*, an idealized monologue of Socrates' trial; (3) the *Dialogues*, which are forty-two dramatized conversations in dialectal form that Plato allegedly wrote, though he probably wrote only twenty-six. The most well-known of these dialogues are the *Phaedo,* containing his theory on immortality, the *Symposium*, consisting of his theory of love, the *Crito,* giving his beliefs on respect for the law, the *Republic*, outlining his ideas of an ideal state founded on justice; (4) the *Georgias*, conveying his ideas of truth and justice prevailing over evil, falsehood and injustice in the material world and of rewards and punishments meted out in the afterlife; (5) the *Phaedrus*, a defense of true versus false rhetoric; and (6) the *Epigrams.*[2]

The dialogues have been divided into three types: the early ones (composed of inquiries), the middle ones (consisting of speculations), and the late ones (comprised of criticism, appraisal and application). The first set of early dialogues have been further subdivided into three subsets. The first set of early subdivided dialogues (*Lycis, Charmides* and *Laches)* contains a defense (called an Apology) of Plato's teacher and friend, Socrates against the charges that Socrates was corrupting the youth, that he was impious and that he was a Sophist. The *Apology,* containing Socrates' trial and execution, is found in the second subgroup of early dialogues. It is in the middle dialogues, e.g., the *Symposium,* the *Phaedrus* and the *Republic,* that Plato's theory of Forms (Ideas), of the soul, of ethics and of government and society are developed. Plato believed that true reality consists of an absolute, eternal and unchanging hierarchy of Forms, also called intellectual concepts or Ideas, with the idea of Good at the top. The material world is one of "appearances" or shadows of reality that the senses perceive.[3] Only reason and argument can lead the individual to grasp true reality, though absolute reality may perhaps be attained by the soul only after death. Real forms reside not in the time-space continuum but elsewhere.

He says that forms are quite different from the ordinary shadows which humans perceive as solid objects in the sensible word of things. The form is the real identity of each thing. It is also an interconnected system with each form including and excluding some of the other forms. These interconnections, inclusions and exclusions are shared by the shadow-things in the world of form. Humans are naturally attracted to forms. This natural affection humans experience as love or desire. Humans yearn for love on earth, yet when they experience earthly love, this love seems incomplete or faulty because of their dim recollection of an eternal love that can only be found in the realm of form.

There are forms for abstractions as well as for objects in the objective world. Ordinary abstractions are relative and can change from one person to another, and both abstractions or objects are inferior shadows that imperfectly approximate their forms. Things can change but their forms are immutable. For example, the size or shape of a triangle may change, but the ideal abstraction of triangularity, which is common to all triangles and which permits humans to recognize them as such, does not change. Likewise, when humans attempt to define justice, they have to look at what is common in a list of just acts that allows humans to recognize them as just; that common characteristic is the essence of justice, its archetype or first, perfect and unchanging form, pattern or ideal.

In metaphysics, Plato states that the soul consists of three parts: (1) reason (intellect), (2) spirit (will), and (3) appetite (desire). In a healthy soul, reason should control desire with the help of the spirit.[4] The three aspects of soul are often in conflict. He believes that, though the body dies and returns to dust, the soul—the center of will, self-motivation and knowing—is immortal. While the soul is imprisoned in the body, it yearns for immortality, which, in its corporeal form, is beyond its reach. After the body's demise, the soul returns to the realm of pure form. After some time, it returns to the material world by reincarnating into another body. Learning, Plato says, is the individual's recollection of the synthesis of the soul's experiences while residing in the domain of forms.

Plato begins his dialogue on ethics by stating that the soul must be healthy before an individual can experience true happiness, naturally. A healthy soul, one that is morally virtuous, can transform a diseased (immoral) soul into a healthy one. Therefore, Plato reasons, all who desire happiness (and all people do) must first live an ethical and virtuous life. Because citizens do not know that virtue naturally begets happiness, they do not seek a virtuous life. For Plato, therefore, the basic ethical problem that confronts humans is one of ignorance. He contends that a person would logically behave more virtuously if he or she knew how to find happiness.

Both Plato's philosopy of ethics and his ideal state are patterned after his soul theory. He advocates, not a democratic, oligarchic or despotic state, but a half-communal state based on justice. Like the soul, society consists of three components or classes: those who rule (the philosopher-kings who represent the intellect), those who maintain law and order as well as defend society against threats from within and without its borders (the police or "guardians" who represent the will), and those who supply society's needs (ordinary humans who represent the appetite or desire).

Though Plato himself considered his founding and organization of the Academy his greatest contribution to posterity, for later generations, it was his philosophical writings that continue to make of him one of the greatest writers the world has ever had.

Notes

1. Cratylus, a follower of Heraclites, believed that the external world was in a constant state of flux, that the word *true* is not an adjective that can be used to describe things in perpetual change because, by the time the word is uttered, the thing(s) will have changed. Words, therefore, falsify reality by acknowledging stability where none exists.
2. Thirty-three of these epigrams were collected and included in *The Greek Anthology* by Agathius.
3. See Plato's "Allegory of the Cave" where this belief is concretely illustrated.
4. This belief is similar to Freud's concepts of the id (controlled by the pleasure principle), the ego (controlled by the reality principle) and the superego (controlled by the morality principle). The ego checks and balances the id, and if the ego is dysfunctional, then the superego exerts its control over both.

The Apology: Background

According to Plato, Socrates believed that a person can arrive at truth and can learn only through shared inquiry, i.e., question-answer sessions or debates. For this reason, Plato structures his works in the literary form known as the dialogue, a conversation between two or more persons. Plato's dialogues contain characters who present, critique, then show conflicts in philosophical ideas. Plato shows Socrates realistically introducing philosophical problems and then debating opposing facets of an issue. These debates often take the form of "dramas of ideas" not only because of the views of the characters but also because of the way the characters interact. One such famous dialogue found in the second of three subgroups of the early dialogues is *The Apology,* which contains Socrates' trial and execution.[1]

In these three dialogues, Plato makes several Socratic points: one, that Socrates is sincere; two, that he has moral integrity; three, that his purpose is a serious one; and four, that he believes his own doctrine. Socrates knows his ancient and recent accusers well. He contends that he has three types of enemies: the poets (led by Meletus), the rhetoricians (led by Anytus), and the artisans (led by Lycon).

We are unsure of the extent to which Plato embellishes Socrates' thought or to what degree Plato articulates his own ideas. Also evident is Socrates' belief that virtue (goodness) depends on knowledge, that the sufferer is better than the perpetrator of evil, that no evil can come to a virtuous human being either in his or her physical or spiritual existence and, most importantly, that the unexamined life is not worth living.

Note

1. The other two dialogues in this grouping are the *Euthyphro* and the *Crito.*

The Apology

CHARACTERS

SOCRATES
MELETUS

SCENE—The Court of Justice

SOCRATES. I do not know what impression my accusers have made upon you, Athenians. But I do know that they nearly made me forget who I was, so persuasive were they. And yet they have scarcely spoken one single word of truth. Of all their many falsehoods, the one which astonished me most was their saying that I was a clever speaker, and that you must be careful not to let me deceive you. I thought that it was most shameless of them not to be ashamed to talk in that way. For as soon as I open my mouth they will be refuted, and I shall prove that I am not a clever speaker in any way at all—unless, indeed, by a clever speaker they mean someone who speaks the truth. If that is their meaning, I agree with them that I am an orator not to be compared with them. My accusers, I repeat, have said little or nothing that is true, but from me you shall hear the whole truth. Certainly you will not hear a speech, Athenians, dressed up, like theirs, with fancy words and phrases. I will say to you what I have to say, without artifice, and I shall use the first words which come to mind, for I believe that what I have to say is just; so let none of you expect anything else. Indeed, my friends, it would hardly be right for me, at my age, to come before you like a schoolboy with his concocted phrases. But there is one thing, Athenians, which I do most earnestly beg and entreat of you. Do not be surprised and do not interrupt with shouts if in my defense I speak in the same way that I am accustomed to speak in the market place, at the tables of the money-changers, where many of you have heard me, and elsewhere. The truth is this: I am more than seventy, and this is the first time that I have ever come before a law court; thus your manner of speech here is quite strange to me. If I had really been a stranger, you would have forgiven me for speaking in the language and the manner of my native country. And so now I ask you to grant me what I think I have a right to claim. Never mind the manner of my speech—it may be superior or it may be inferior to the usual manner. Give your whole attention to the question, whether what I say is just or not? That is what is required of a good judge, as speaking the truth is required of a good orator.

I have to defend myself, Athenians, first against the older false accusations of my old accusers, and then against the more recent ones of my present accusers. For many men have been accusing me to you, and for very many years, who have not spoken a word of truth; and I fear them more than I fear Anytus and his associates, formidable as they are. But, my friends, the others are still more formidable, since they got hold of most of you when you were children and have been more persistent in accusing me untruthfully, persuading you that there is a certain Socrates, a wise man, who speculates about the heavens, who investigates things that are beneath the earth, and who can make the worse argument appear the stronger. These men, Athenians, who spread abroad this report are the accusers whom I fear; for their hearers think that persons who pursue such inquiries never believe in the gods. Besides they are many, their attacks have been going on for a long time, and they spoke to you when you were most ready to believe them, since you were all young, and some of you were children. And there was no one to answer them when they attacked me. The most preposterous thing of all is that I do not even know their names: I cannot tell you who they are except when one happens to be a comic poet. But all the rest who have persuaded you, from motives of resentment and prejudice, and sometimes, it may be, from conviction, are hardest to cope with. For I cannot call any one of them forward in court to cross-examine him. I have, as it were, simply to spar with shadows in my defense, and to put questions which there is no one to answer. I ask you, therefore, to believe that, as I say, I have been attacked by two kinds of accusers—first, by Meletus and his associates, and, then, by those older ones of whom I have spoken. And, with your leave, I will defend myself first against my old accusers, since you heard their accusations first, and they were much more compelling than my present accusers are.

Well, I must make my defense, Athenians, and try in the short time allowed me to remove the prejudice which you have been so long a time acquiring. I hope that I may manage to do this, if it be best for you and for me, and that my defense may be successful; but I am quite aware of the nature of my task, and I know that it is a difficult one. Be the outcome, however, as is pleasing to god, I must obey the law and make my defense.

Let us begin from the beginning, then, and ask what is the accusation that has given rise to the prejudice against me, on which Meletus relied when he brought his indictment. What is the prejudice which my enemies have been spreading about me? I must assume that they are formally accusing me, and read their indictment. It would run somewhat in this fashion: "Socrates is guilty of engaging in inquiries into things beneath the earth and in the heavens, of making the weaker argument appear the stronger, and of teaching others these same things." That is what they say. And in the comedy of Aristophanes you yourselves saw a man called Socrates swinging around in a basket and saying that he walked on air, and sputtering a great deal of nonsense about matters of which I understand nothing at all. I do not mean to disparage that kind of knowledge if there is anyone who is wise about these matters. I trust Meletus may never be able to prosecute me for that. But the truth is, Athenians, I have nothing to do with these matters, and almost all of you are yourselves my witnesses of this. I beg all of you who have ever heard me discussing, and they are many, to inform your neighbors and tell them if any of you have ever heard me discussing such matters at all. That will show you that the other common statements about me are as false as this one.

But the fact is that not one of these is true. And if you have heard that I undertake to educate men, and make money by so doing, that is not true either, though I think that it would be a fine thing to be able to educate men, as Gorgias of Leontini, and Prodicus of Ceos, and Hippias of Elis do. For each of them, my friends, can go into any city, and persuade the young men to leave the society of their fellow citizens, with any of whom they might associate for nothing, and to be only too glad to be allowed to pay money for the privilege of associating with themselves. And I believe that there is another wise man from Paros residing in Athens at this moment. I happened to meet Callias, the son of Hipponicus, a man who has spent more money on sophists than everyone else put together. So I said to him (he has two sons), "Callias, if your two sons had been foals or calves, we could have hired a trainer for them who would have trained them to excel in doing what they are naturally capable of. He would have been either a groom or a farmer. But whom do you intend to take to train them, seeing that they are men? Who understands the excellence which a man and citizen is capable of attaining? I suppose that you must have thought of this, because you have sons. Is there such a person or not?" "Certainly there is," he replied. "Who is he," said I, "and where does he come from, and what is his fee?" "Evenus, Socrates," he replied, "from Paros, five minae." Then I thought that Evenus was a fortunate person if he really understood this art and could teach so cleverly. If I had possessed knowledge of that kind, I should have been conceited and disdainful. But, Athenians, the truth is that I do not possess it.

Perhaps some of you may reply: "But, Socrates, what is the trouble with you? What has given rise to these prejudices against you? You must have been doing something out of the ordinary. All these rumors and reports of you would never have arisen if you had not been doing something different from other men. So tell us what it is, that we may not give our verdict arbitrarily." I think that that is a fair question, and I will try to explain to you what it is that has raised these prejudices against me and given me this reputation.

Listen, then. Some of you, perhaps, will think that I am joking, but I assure you that I will tell you the whole truth. I have gained this reputation, Athenians, simply by reason of a certain wisdom. But by what kind of wisdom? It is by just that wisdom which is perhaps human wisdom. In that, it may be, I am really wise. But the men of whom I was speaking just now must be wise in a wisdom which is greater than human wisdom, or else I cannot describe it, for certainly I know nothing of it myself, and if any man says that I do, he lies and speaks to arouse prejudice against me. Do not interrupt me with shouts, Athenians, even if you think that I am boasting. What I am going to say is not my own statement. I will tell you who says it, and he is worthy of your respect. I will bring the god of Delphi to be the witness of my wisdom, if it is wisdom at all, and of its nature. You remember Chaerephon. From youth upwards he was my comrade; and also a partisan of your democracy, sharing your recent exile and returning with you. You remember, too, Chaerephon's character—how impulsive he was in carrying through whatever he took in hand. Once he went to Delphi and ventured to put this question to the oracle—I entreat you again, my friends, not to interrupt me with your shouts—he asked if there was anyone who was wiser than I. The priestess answered that there was no one. Chaerephon himself is dead, but his brother here will witness to what I say.

Now see why I tell you this, I am going to explain to you how the prejudice against me has arisen. When I heard of the oracle I began to reflect: What can the god mean by this riddle? I know very well that I am not wise, even in the smallest degree. Then what can he mean by saying that I am the wisest of men? It cannot be that he is speaking falsely, for he is a god and cannot lie. For a long time I was at a loss to understand his meaning. Then, very reluctantly, I turned to investigate it in this manner: I went to a man who was reputed to be wise, thinking that there, if anywhere, I should prove the answer wrong, and meaning to point out to the oracle its mistake, and to say, "You said that I was the wisest of men, but this man is wiser than I am," So I examined the man—I need not tell you his name, he was a politician—but this was the result, Athenians. When I conversed with him I came to see that, though a great many persons, and most of all he himself, thought that he was wise, yet he was not wise. Then I tried to prove to him that he was not wise, though he fancied that he was. By so doing I made him indignant, and many of the bystanders. So when I went away, I thought to myself, "I am wiser than this man: neither of us knows anything that is really worth knowing, but he thinks that he has knowledge when he has not, while I, having no knowledge, do not think that I have. I seem, at any rate, to be a little wiser than he is on this point: I do not think that I know what I do not know." Next I went, to another man who was reputed to be still wiser than the last with exactly the same result. And there again I made him, and many other men, indignant.

Then I went on to one man after another, realizing that I was arousing indignation every day, which caused me much pain and anxiety. Still I thought that I must set the god's command above everything. So I had to go to every man who seemed to possess any knowledge, and investigate the meaning of the oracle. Athenians, I must tell you the truth; I swear, this was the result of the investigation which I made at the god's command: I found that the men whose reputation for wisdom stood highest were nearly the most lacking in it, while others who were looked down on as common people were much more intelligent. Now I must describe to you the wanderings which I undertook, like Herculean labors, to prove the oracle irrefutable. After the politicians, I went to the poets, tragic, dithyrambic, and others, thinking that there I should find myself manifestly more ignorant than they. So I took up the poems on which I thought that they had spent most pains, and asked them what they meant, hoping at the same time to learn something from them. I am ashamed to tell you the truth, my friends, but I must say it. Almost any one of the bystanders could have talked about the works of these poets better than the poets themselves. So I soon found that it is not by wisdom that the poets create their works, but by a certain instinctive inspiration, like soothsayers and prophets, who say many fine things, but understand nothing of what they say. The poets seemed to me to be in a similar situation. And at the same time I perceived that, because of their poetry, they thought that they were the wisest of men in other matters too, which they were not. So I went away again, thinking that I had the same advantage over the poets that I had over the politicians.

Finally, I went to the artisans, for I knew very well that I possessed no knowledge at all worth speaking of, and I was sure that I should find that they knew many fine things. And in that I was not mistaken. They knew what I did not know, and so far they were wiser than I. But, Athenians, it seemed to me that the skilled artisans had the same failing as the poets. Each of them believed himself to be extremely wise in matters of the greatest importance because he was skillful in his own art: and this presumption of theirs obscured their real wisdom. So I asked myself, on behalf of the oracle, whether I would choose to remain as I was, without either their wisdom or their ignorance, or to possess both, as they did. And I answered to myself and to the oracle that it was better for me to remain as I was.

From this examination, Athenians, has arisen much fierce and bitter indignation, and as a result a great many prejudices about me. People say that I am "a wise man." For the bystanders always think that I am wise myself in any matter wherein I refute another. But, gentlemen, I believe that the god is really wise, and that by this oracle he meant that human wisdom is worth little or nothing. I do not think that he meant that Socrates was wise. He only made use of my name, and took me as an example, as though he would say to men, "He among you is the wisest who, like Socrates, knows that his wisdom is really worth nothing at all." Therefore I still go about testing and examining every man whom I think wise, whether he be a citizen or a stranger, as the god has commanded me. Whenever I find that he is not wise, I point out to him, on the god's behalf, that he is not wise. I am so busy in this pursuit that I have never had leisure to take any part worth mentioning in public matters or to look after my private affairs. I am in great poverty as the result of my service to the god.

Besides this, the young men who follow me about, who are the sons of wealthy persons and have the most leisure, take pleasure in hearing men cross-examined. They often imitate me among themselves; then they try their hands at cross-examining other people. And, I imagine, they find plenty of men who think that they know a great deal when in fact they know little or nothing. Then the persons who are cross-examined get angry with me instead of with themselves, and say that Socrates is an abomination and corrupts the young. When they are asked, "Why, what does he do? What does he teach?" they do not know what to say. Not to seem at a loss, they repeat the stock charges against all philosophers, and allege that he investigates things in the air and under the earth, and that he teaches people to disbelieve in the gods, and to make the worse argument appear the stronger. For, I suppose, they would not like to confess the truth, which is that they are shown up as ignorant pretenders to knowledge that they do not possess. So they have been filling your ears with their bitter prejudices for a long time, for they are ambitious, energetic, and numerous; and they speak vigorously and persuasively against me. Relying on this, Meletus, Anytus, and Lycon have attacked me. Meletus is indignant with me on behalf of the poets, Anytus on behalf of the artisans and politicians, and Lycon on behalf of the orators. And so, as I said at the beginning, I shall be surprised if I am able, in the short time allowed me for my defense, to remove from your minds this prejudice which has grown so strong. What I have told you, Athenians, is the truth: I neither conceal nor do I suppress anything, trivial or important. Yet I know that it is just this outspokenness which rouses indignation. But that is only a proof that my words are true, and that the prejudice against me, and the causes of it, are what I have said. And whether you investigate them now or hereafter, you will find that they are so.

What I have said must suffice as my defense against the charges of my first accusers. I will try next to defend myself against Meletus, that "good patriot," as he calls himself, and my later accusers. Let us assume that they are a new set of accusers, and read their indictment, as we did in the case of the others. It runs thus: Socrates is guilty of corrupting the youth, and of believing not in the gods whom the state believes in, but in other new divinities. Such is the accusation. Let us examine each point in it separately. Meletus says that I am guilty of corrupting the youth. But I say, Athenians, that he is guilty of playing a solemn joke by casually bringing men to trial, and pretending to have a solemn interest in matters to which he has never given a moment's thought. Now I will try to prove to you that this is so.

Come here, Meletus. Is it not a fact that you think it very important that the young should be as good as possible?

MELETUS. It is.

SOCRATES. Come, then, tell the judges who improves them. You care so much, you must know. You are accusing me, and bringing me to trial, because, as you say, you have discovered that I am the corrupter of the youth. Come now, reveal to the gentlemen who improves them. You see, Meletus, you have nothing to say; you are silent. But don't you think that this is shameful? Is not your silence a conclusive proof of what I say—that you have never cared? Come, tell us, my good man, who makes the young better?

MEL. The laws.

SOCR. That, my friend, is not my question. What man improves the young, who begins by knowing the laws?

MEL. The judges here, Socrates.

SOCR. What do you mean, Meletus? Can they educate the young and improve them?

MEL. Certainly.

SOCR. All of them? Or only some of them?

MEL. All of them.

SOCR. By Hera, that is good news! Such a large supply of benefactors! And do the members of the audience here improve them, or not?

MEL. They do.

SOCR. And do the councilors?

MEL. Yes.

SOCR. Well, then, Meletus, do the members of the assembly corrupt the young or do they again all improve them?

MEL. They, too, improve them.

SOCR. Then all the Athenians, apparently, make the young into good men except me, and I alone corrupt them. Is that your meaning?

MEL. Certainly, that is my meaning.

SOCR. You have discovered me to be most unfortunate. Now tell me: do you think that the same holds good in the case of horses? Does one man do them harm and everyone else improve them? On the contrary, is it not one man only, or a very few—namely, those who are skilled with horses—who can improve them, while the majority of men harm them if they use them and have anything to do with them? Is it not so, Meletus, both with horses and with every other animal? Of course it is, whether you and Anytus say yes or no. The young would certainly be very fortunate if only one man corrupted them, and everyone else did them good. The truth is, Meletus, you prove conclusively that you have never thought about the young in your life. You exhibit your carelessness in not caring for the very matters about which you are prosecuting me.

Now be so good as to tell us, Meletus, is it better to live among good citizens or bad ones? Answer, my friend, I am not asking you at all a difficult question. Do not the bad harm their associates and the good do them good?

MEL. Yes.

SOCR. Is there anyone who would rather be injured than benefited by his companions? Answer, my good man; you are obliged by the law to answer. Does anyone like to be injured?

MEL. Certainly not.

SOCR. Well, then, are you prosecuting me for corrupting the young and making them worse, voluntarily or involuntarily?

MEL. For doing it voluntarily.

SOCR. What, Meletus? Do you mean to say that you, who are so much younger than I, are yet so much wiser than I that you know that bad citizens always do evil, and that good citizens do good, to those with whom they come in contact, while I am so extraordinarily ignorant as not to know that, if I make any of my companions evil, he will probably injure me in some way? And you allege that I do this voluntarily? You will not make me believe that, nor anyone else either, I should think. Either I do not corrupt the young at all or, if I do, I do so involuntarily, so that you are lying in either case. And if I corrupt them involuntarily, the law does not call upon you to prosecute me for an error which is involuntary, but to take me aside privately and reprove and educate me. For, of course, I shall cease from doing wrong involuntarily, as soon as I know that I have been doing wrong. But you avoided associating with me and educating me; instead you bring me up before the court, where the law sends persons, not for education, but for punishment.

The truth is, Athenians, as I said, it is quite clear that Meletus has never cared at all about these matters. However, now tell us, Meletus, how do you say that I corrupt the young? Clearly, according to your indictment, by teaching them not to believe in the gods the state believes in, but other new divinities instead. You mean that I corrupt the young by that teaching, do you not?

MEL. Yes, most certainly I mean that.

SOCR. Then in the name of these gods of whom we are speaking, explain yourself a little more clearly to me and to these gentlemen here. I cannot understand what you mean. Do you mean that I teach the young to believe in some gods, but not in the gods of the state? Do you accuse me of teaching them to believe in strange gods? If that is your meaning, I myself believe in some gods, and my crime is not that of complete atheism. Or do you mean that I do not believe in the gods at all myself, and that I teach other people not to believe in them either?

MEL. I mean that you do not believe in the gods in any way whatever.

SOCR. You amaze me, Meletus! Why do you say that? Do you mean that I believe neither the sun nor the moon to be gods, like other men?

MEL. I swear he does not, judges. He says that the sun is a stone, and the moon earth.

SOCR. My dear Meletus, do you think that you are prosecuting Anaxagoras? You must have a very poor opinion of these men, and think them illiterate, if you imagine that they do not know that the works of Anaxagoras of Clazomenae are full of these doctrines. And so young men learn these things from me, when they can often buy them in the theater for a drachma at most, and laugh at Socrates were he to pretend that these doctrines, which are very peculiar doctrines, too, were his own. But please tell me, do you really think that I do not believe in the gods at all?

MEL. Most certainly I do. You are a complete atheist.

SOCR. No one believes that, Meletus, not even you yourself. It seems to me, Athenians, that Meletus is very insolent and reckless, and that he is prosecuting me simply out of insolence, recklessness, and youthful bravado. For he seems to be testing me, by asking me a riddle that has no answer. "Will this wise Socrates," he says to himself, "see that I am joking and contradicting myself? Or shall I deceive him and everyone else who hears me?" Meletus seems to me to contradict himself in his indictment: it is as if he were to say, "Socrates is guilty of not believing in the gods, but believes in the gods." This is joking.

Now, my friends, let us see why I think that this is his meaning. You must answer me, Meletus, and you, Athenians, must remember the request which I made to you at the start, and not interrupt me with shouts if I talk in my usual manner.

Is there any man, Meletus, who believes in the existence of things pertaining to men and not in the existence of men? Make him answer the question, gentlemen, without these interruptions. Is there any man who believes in the existence of horsemanship and not in the existence of horses? Or in flute playing and not in flute players? There is not, my friend. If you will not answer, I will tell both you and the judges. But you must answer my next question. Is there any man who believes in the existence of divine things and not in the existence of divinities?

MEL. There is not.

SOCR. I am very glad that these gentlemen have managed to extract an answer from you. Well then, you say that I believe in divine things, whether they be old or new, and that I teach others to believe in them. At any rate, according to your statement, I believe in divine things. That you have sworn in your indictment. But if I believe in divine things, I suppose it follows necessarily that I believe in divinities. Is it not so? It is. I assume that you grant that, as you do not answer. But do we not believe that divinities are either gods themselves or the children of the gods? Do you admit that?

MEL. I do.

SOCR. Then you admit that I believe in divinities. Now, if these divinities are gods, then, as I say, you are joking and asking a riddle, and asserting that I do not believe in the gods, and at the same time that I do, since I believe in divinities. But if these divinities are the illegitimate children of the gods, either by the nymphs or by other mothers, as they are said to be, then, I ask, what man could believe in the existence of the children of the gods, and not in the existence of the gods? That would be as absurd as believing in the existence of the offspring of horses and asses, and not in the existence of horses and asses. You must have indicted me in this manner, Meletus, either to test me or because you could not find any act of injustice that you could accuse me of with truth. But you will never contrive to persuade any man with any sense at all that a belief in divine things and things of the gods does not necessarily involve a belief in divinities, and in the gods.

But in truth, Athenians, I do not think that I need say very much to prove that I have not committed the act of injustice for which Meletus is prosecuting me. What I have said is enough to prove that. But be assured it is certainly true, as I have already told you, that I have aroused much indignation. That is what will cause my condemnation if I am condemned; not Meletus nor Anytus either, but that prejudice and resentment of the multitude which have been the destruction of many good men before me, and I think will be so again. There is no prospect that I shall be the last victim.

Perhaps someone will say: "Are you not ashamed, Socrates, of leading a life which is very likely now to cause your death?" I should answer him with justice, and say: "My friend, if you think that a man of any worth at all ought to reckon the chances of life and death when he acts, or that he ought to think of anything but whether he is acting justly or unjustly, and as a good or a bad man would act, you are mistaken. According to you, the demigods who died at Troy would be foolish, and among them Achilles, who thought nothing of danger when the alternative was disgrace. For when his mother—and she was a goddess—addressed him, when he was resolved to slay Hector, in this fashion, 'My son, if you avenge the death of your comrade Patroclus and slay Hector, you will die yourself, for fate awaits you next after Hector.' When he heard this, he scorned danger and death; he feared much more to live a coward and not to avenge his friend. 'Let me punish the evil-doer and afterwards die,' he said, 'that I may not remain here by the beaked ships jeered at, encumbering the earth.'" Do you suppose that he thought of danger or of death? For this, Athenians, I believe to be the truth. Wherever a man's station is, whether he has chosen it of his own will, or whether he has been placed at it by his commander, there it is his duty to remain and face the danger without thinking of death or of any other thing except disgrace.

When the generals whom you chose to command me, Athenians, assigned me my station during the battles of Potidaea, Amphipolis, and Delium, I remained where they stationed me and ran the risk of death, like other men. It would be very strange conduct on my part if I were to desert my station now from fear of death or of any other thing when the god has commanded me—I am persuaded that he has done—to spend my life in searching for wisdom, and in examining myself and others. That would indeed be a very strange thing. Then certainly I might with justice be brought to trial for not believing in the gods, for I should be disobeying the oracle, and fearing death and thinking myself wise when I was not wise. For to fear death, my friends, is only to think ourselves wise without really being wise, for it is to think that we know what we do not know. For no one knows whether death may not be the greatest good that can happen to man. But men fear it as if they knew quite well that it was the greatest of evils. And what is this but that shameful ignorance of thinking that we know what we do not know? In this matter, too, my friends, perhaps I am different from the multitude. And if I were to claim to be at all wiser than others, it would be because, not knowing very much about the other world, I do not think I know. But I do know very well that it is evil and disgraceful to do an unjust act, and to disobey my superior, whether man or god. I will never do what I know to be evil, and shrink in fear from what I do not know to be good or evil. Even if you acquit me now, and do not listen to Anytus' argument that, if I am to be acquitted, I ought never to have been brought to trial at all, and that, as it is, you are bound to put me to death because, as he said, if I escape, all your sons will be utterly corrupted by practicing what Socrates teaches. If you were therefore to say to me, "Socrates, this time we will not listen to Anytus. We will let you go, but on the condition that you give up this investigation of yours, and philosophy. If you are found following these pursuits again, you shall die." I say, if you offered to let me go on these terms, I should reply: "Athenians, I hold you in the highest regard and affection, but I will be persuaded by the god rather than you. As long as I have breath and strength I will not give up philosophy and exhorting you and declaring the truth to every one of you whom I meet, saying, as I am accustomed, 'My good friend, you are a citizen of Athens, a city which is very great and very famous for its wisdom and power—are you not ashamed of caring so much for the making of money and for fame and prestige, when you neither think nor care about wisdom and truth and the improvement of your soul?'" If he disputes my words and says that he does care about these things, I shall not at once release him and go away: I shall question him and cross-examine him and test him. If I think that he has not attained excellence, though he says that he has, I shall reproach him for undervaluing the most valuable things, and overvaluing those that are less valuable. This I shall do to everyone whom I meet, young or old, citizen or stranger, but especially to citizens, since they are more closely related to me. This, you must recognize, the god has commanded me to do. And I think that no greater good has ever befallen you in the state than my service to the god. For I spend my whole life in going about and persuading you all to give your first and greatest care to the improvement of your souls, and not till you have done that to think of your bodies or your wealth. And I tell you that wealth does not bring excellence, but that wealth, and every other good thing which men have, whether in public or in private, comes from excellence. If then I corrupt the youth by this teaching, these things must be harmful. But if any man says that I teach anything else, there is nothing in what he says. And therefore, Athenians, I say, whether you are persuaded by Anytus or not, whether you acquit me or not, I shall not change my way of life; no, not if I have to die for it many times.

Do not interrupt me, Athenians, with your shouts. Remember the request which I made to you, and do not interrupt my words. I think that it will profit you to hear them. I am going to say something more to you, at which you may be inclined to protest, but do not do that. Be sure that if you put me to death, I who am what I have told you that I am, you will do yourselves more harm than me. Meletus and Anytus can do me no harm: that is impossible, for I am sure it is not allowed that a good man be injured by a worse. He may indeed kill me, or drive me into exile, or deprive me of my civil rights. Perhaps Meletus and others think those things great evils. But I do not think so. I think it is a much greater evil to do what he is doing now, and to try to put a man to death unjustly. And now, Athenians, I am not arguing in my own defense at all, as you might expect me to do, but rather in yours in order you may not make a mistake about the gift of the god to you by condemning me. For if you put me to death, you will not easily find another who, if I may use a ludicrous comparison, clings to the state as a sort of gadfly to a horse that is large and well-bred but rather sluggish because of its size, so that it needs to be aroused. It seems to me that the god has attached me like that to the state, for I am constantly alighting upon you at every point to arouse, persuade, and reproach each of you all day long. You will not easily find anyone else, my friends, to fill my place; and if you are persuaded by me, you will spare my life. You are indignant, as drowsy persons are when they are awakened, and, of course, if you are persuaded by Anytus, you could easily kill me with a single blow, and then sleep on undisturbed for the rest of your lives, unless the god in his care for you sends another to arouse you. And you may easily see that it is the god who has given me to your city; for it is not human, the way in which I have neglected all my own interests and allowed my private affairs to be neglected for so many years, while occupying myself unceasingly in your interests, going to each of you privately, like a father or an elder brother, trying to persuade him to care for human excellence. There would have been a reason for it, if I had gained any advantage by this, or if I had been paid for my exhortations; but you see yourselves that my accusers, though they accuse me of everything else without shame, have not had the shamelessness to say that I ever either exacted or demanded payment. To that they have no witness. And I think that I have sufficient witness to the truth of what I say—my poverty.

Perhaps it may seem strange to you that, though I go about giving this advice privately and meddling in others' affairs, yet I do not venture to come forward in the assembly and advise the state. You have often heard me speak of my reason for this, and in many places: it is that I have a certain divine guide, which is what Meletus has caricatured in his indictment. I have had it from childhood. It is a kind of voice which, whenever I hear it, always turns me back from something which I was going to do, but never urges me to act. It is this which forbids me to take part in politics. And I think it does well to forbid me. For, Athenians, it is quite certain that, if I had attempted to take part in politics, I should have perished at once and long ago without doing any good either to you or to myself. And do not be indignant with me for telling the truth. There is no man who will preserve his life for long, either in Athens or elsewhere, if he firmly opposes the multitude, and tries to prevent the commission of much injustice and illegality in the state. He who would really fight for justice must do so as a private citizen, not as a political figure, if he is to preserve his life, even for a short time.

I will prove to you that this is so by very strong evidence, not by mere words, but by what you value more—actions. Listen, then, to what has happened to me, that you may know that there is no man who could make me consent to commit an unjust act from the fear of death, but that I would perish at once rather than give way. What I am going to tell you may be commonplace in the law court; nevertheless, it is true. The only office that I ever held in the state, Athenians, was that of councilor. When you wished to try the ten admirals who did not rescue their men after the battle of Arginusan as a group, which was illegal, as you all came to think afterwards, the executive committee was composed of members of the tribe Antiochis, to which I belong. On that occasion I alone of the committee members opposed your illegal action and gave my vote against you. The orators were ready to impeach me and arrest me; and you were clamoring and urging them on with your shouts. But I thought that I ought to face the danger, with law and justice on my side, rather than join with you in your unjust proposal, from fear of imprisonment or death. That was when the state was democratic. When the oligarchy came in, The Thirty sent for me, with four others, to the council-chamber, and ordered us to bring Leon the Salaminian from Salamis, that they might put him to death. They were in the habit of frequently giving similar orders to many others, wishing to implicate as many as possible in their crimes. But then I again proved, not by mere words, but by my actions, that, if I may speak bluntly, I do not care a straw for death; but that I do care very much indeed about not doing anything unjust or impious: That government with all its power did not terrify me into doing anything unjust. When we left the council-chamber, the other four went over to Salamis and brought Leon across to Athens; I went home. And if the rule of The Thirty had not been overthrown soon afterwards, I should very likely have been put to death for what I did then. Many of you will be my witnesses in this matter.

Now do you think that I could have remained alive all these years if I had taken part in public affairs, and had always maintained the cause of justice like a good man, and had held it a paramount duty, as it is, to do so? Certainly not, Athenians, nor could any other man. But throughout my whole life, both in private and in public, whenever I have had to take part in public affairs, you will find I have always been the same and have never yielded unjustly to anyone; no, not to those whom my enemies falsely assert to have been my pupils. But I was never anyone's teacher. I have never withheld myself from anyone, young or old, who was anxious to hear me converse while I was making my investigation; neither do I converse for payment, and refuse to converse without payment. I am ready to ask questions of rich and poor alike, and if any man wishes to answer me, and then listen to what I have to say, he may. And I cannot justly be charged with causing these men to turn out good or bad, for I never either taught or professed to teach any of them any knowledge whatever. And if any man asserts that he ever learned or heard anything from me in private which everyone else did not hear as well as he, be sure that he does not speak the truth.

Why is it, then, that people delight in spending so much time in my company? You have heard why, Athenians. I told you the whole truth when I said that they delight in hearing me examine persons who think that they are wise when they are not wise. It is certainly very amusing to listen to. And, as I have said, the god has commanded me to examine men, in oracles and in dreams and in every way in which the divine will was ever declared to man. This is the truth, Athenians, and if it were not the truth, it would be easily refuted. For if it were really the case that I have already corrupted some of the young men, and am now corrupting others, surely some of them, finding as they grew older that I had given them bad advice in their youth, would have come forward today to accuse me and take their revenge. Or if they were unwilling to do so themselves, surely their relatives, their fathers or brothers, or others, would, if I had done them any harm, have remembered it and taken their revenge. Certainly I see many of them in court. Here is Crito, of my own district and of my own age, the father of Critobulus; here is Lysanias of Sphettus, the father of Aeschines; here is also Antiphon of Cephisus, the father of Epigenes. Then here are others whose brothers have spent their time in my company—Nicostratus, the son of Theozotides and brother of Theodotus—and Theodotus is dead, so he at least cannot entreat his brother to be silent; here is Paralus, the son of Demodocus and the brother of Theages; here is Adeimantus, the son of Ariston, whose brother is Plato here; and Aeantodorus, whose brother is Aristodorus. And I can name many others to you, some of whom Meletus ought to have called as witnesses in the course of his own speech; but if he forgot to call them then, let him call them now—I will yield the floor to him—and tell us if he has any such evidence. No, on the contrary, my friends, you will find all these men ready to support me, the corrupter who has injured their relatives, as Meletus and Anytus call me. Those of them who have been already corrupted might perhaps have some reason for supporting me, but what reason can their relatives have who are grown up, and who are uncorrupted, except the reason of truth and justice—that they know very well that Meletus is lying, and that I am speaking the truth?

Well, my friends, this, and perhaps more like this, is pretty much all I have to offer in my defense. There may be some one among you who will be indignant when he remembers how, even in a less important trial than this, he begged and entreated the judges, with many tears, to acquit him, and brought forward his children and many of his friends and relatives in court in order to appeal to your feelings; and then finds that I shall do none of these things, though I am in what he would think the supreme danger. Perhaps he will harden himself against me when he notices this; it may make him angry, and he may cast his vote in anger. If it is so with any of you—I do not suppose that it is, but in case it should be so—I think that I should answer him reasonably if I said: "My friend, I have relatives, too, for, in the words of Homer, I am 'not born of an oak or a rock' but of flesh and blood." And so, Athenians, I have relatives, and I have three sons, one of them nearly grown up, and the other two still children. Yet I will not bring any of them forward before you and implore you to acquit me. And why will I do none of these things? It is not from arrogance, Athenians, nor because I lack respect for you—whether or not I can face death bravely is another question—but for my own good name, and for your good name, and for the good name of the whole state. I do not think it right, at my age and with my reputation, to do anything of that kind. Rightly or wrongly, men have made up their minds that in some way Socrates is different from the multitude of men. And it will be shameful if those of you who are thought to excel in wisdom, or in bravery, or in any other excellence, are going to act in this fashion. I have often seen men of reputation behaving in an extraordinary way at their trial, as if they thought it a terrible fate to be killed, and as though they expected to live for ever if you did not put them to death. Such men seem to me to bring shame upon the state, for any stranger would suppose that the best and most eminent Athenians, who are selected by their fellow citizens to hold office, and for other honors, are no better than women. Those of you, Athenians, who have any reputation at all ought not to do these things, and you ought not to allow us to do them. You should show that you will be much more ready to condemn men who make the state ridiculous by these pathetic performances than men who remain quiet.

But apart from the question of reputation, my friends, I do not think that it is right to entreat the judge to acquit us, or to escape condemnation in that way. It is our duty to teach and persuade him. He does not sit to give away justice as a favor, but to pronounce judgment; and he has sworn, not to favor any man whom he would like to favor, but to judge according to law. And, therefore, we ought not to encourage you in the habit of breaking your oaths; and you ought not to allow yourselves to fall into this habit, for then neither you nor we would be acting piously. Therefore, Athenians, do not require me to do these things, for I believe them to be neither good nor just nor pious; especially, do not ask me to do them today when Meletus is prosecuting me for impiety. For were I to be successful and persuade you by my entreaties to break your oaths, I should be clearly teaching you to believe that there are no gods, and I should be simply accusing myself by my defense of not believing in them. But, Athenians, that is very far from the truth. I do believe in the gods as no one of my accusers believes in them; and to you and to the god I commit my cause to be decided as is best for you and for me.

(He is found guilty by 281 votes to 220.)

I am not indignant at the verdict which you have given, Athenians, for many reasons. I expected that you would find me guilty; and I am not so much surprised at that as at the numbers of the votes. I certainly never thought that the majority against me would have been so narrow. But now it seems that if only thirty votes had changed sides, I should have escaped. So I think that I have escaped Meletus, as it is; and not only have I escaped him, for it is perfectly clear that if Anytus and Lycon had not come forward to accuse me, too, he would not have obtained the fifth part of the votes, and would have had to pay a fine of a thousand drachmae.

So he proposes death as the penalty. Be it so. And what alternative penalty shall I propose to you, Athenians? What I deserve, of course, must I not? What then do I deserve to pay or to suffer for having determined not to spend my life in ease? I neglected the things which most men value, such as wealth, and family interests, and military commands, and public oratory, and all the civic appointments, and social clubs, and political factions, that there are in Athens; for I thought that I was really too honest a man to preserve my life if I engaged in these affairs. So I did not go where I should have done no good either to you or to myself. I went, instead, to each one of you privately to do him, as I say, the greatest of benefits, and tried to persuade him not to think of his affairs until he had thought of himself and tried to make himself as good and wise as possible, nor to think of the affairs of Athens until he had thought of Athens herself; and to care for other things in the same manner. Then what do I deserve for such a life? Something good, Athenians, if I am really to propose what I deserve; and something good which it would be suitable for me to receive. Then what is a suitable reward to be given to a poor benefactor who requires leisure to exhort you? There is no reward, Athenians, so suitable for him as receiving; free meals in the prytaneum. It is a much more suitable reward for him than for any of you who has won a victory at the Olympic games with his horse or his chariots. Such a man only makes you seem happy, but I make you really happy; he is not in want, and I am. So if I am to propose the penalty which I really deserve, I propose this—free meals in the prytaneum.

Perhaps you think me stubborn and arrogant in what I am saying now, as in what I said about the entreaties and tears. It is not so, Athenians. It is rather that I am convinced that I never wronged any man voluntarily, though I cannot persuade you of that, since we have conversed together only a little time. If there were a law at Athens, as there is elsewhere, not to finish a trial of life and death in a single day, I think that I could have persuaded you; but now it is not easy in so short a time to clear myself of great prejudices. But when I am persuaded that I have never wronged any man, I shall certainly not wrong myself, or admit that I deserve to suffer any evil, or propose any evil for myself as a penalty. Why should I? Lest I should suffer the penalty which Meletus proposes when I say that I do not know whether it is a good or an evil? Shall I choose instead of it something which I know to be an evil, and propose that as a penalty? Shall I propose imprisonment? And why should I pass the rest of my days in prison, the slave of successive officials? Or shall I propose a fine, with imprisonment until it is paid? I have told you why I will not do that. I should have to remain in prison, for I have no money to pay a fine with. Shall I then propose exile? Perhaps you would agree to that. Life would indeed be very dear to me if I were unreasonable enough to expect that strangers would cheerfully tolerate my discussions and arguments when you who are my fellow citizens cannot endure them, and have found them so irksome and odious to you that you are seeking now to be relieved of them. No, indeed, Athenians, that is not likely. A fine life I should lead for an old man if I were to withdraw from Athens and pass the rest of my days in wandering from city to city, and continually being expelled. For I know very well that the young men will listen to me wherever I go, as they do here. If I drive them away, they will persuade their elders to expel me; if I do not drive them away, their fathers and other relatives will expel me for their sakes.

Perhaps someone will say, "Why cannot you withdraw from Athens, Socrates, and hold your peace?" It is the most difficult thing in the world to make you understand why I cannot do that. If I say that I cannot hold my peace because that would be to disobey the god, you will think that I am not in earnest and will not believe me. And if I tell you that no greater good can happen to a man than to discuss human excellence every day and the other matters about which you have heard me arguing and examining myself and others, and that an unexamined life is not worth living, then you will believe me still less. But that is so, my friends, though it is not easy to persuade you. And, what is more, I am not accustomed to think that I deserve anything evil. If I had been rich, I would have proposed as large a fine as I could pay: that would have done me no harm. But I am not rich enough to pay a fine unless you are willing to fix it at a sum within my means. Perhaps I could pay you a mina, so I propose that. Plato here, Athenians, and Crito, and Critobulus, and Apollodorus bid me propose thirty minae, and they guarantee its payment. So I propose thirty minae. Their security will be sufficient to you for the money.

(*He is condemned to death.*)

You have not gained very much time, Athenians, and at the price of the slurs of those who wish to revile the state. And they will say that you put Socrates, a wise man, to death. For they will certainly call me wise, whether I am wise or not, when they want to reproach you. If you had waited for a little while, your wishes would have been fulfilled in the course of nature; for you see that I am an old man, far advanced in years, and near to death. I am saying this not to all of you, only to those who have voted for my death. And to them I have something else to say. Perhaps, my friends, you think that I have been convicted because I was wanting in the arguments by which I could have persuaded you to acquit me, if I had thought it right to do or to say anything to escape punishment. It is not so. I have been convicted because I was wanting, not in arguments, but in impudence and shamelessness—because I would not plead before you as you would have liked to hear me plead, or appeal to you with weeping and wailing, or say and do many other things which I maintain are unworthy of me, but which you have been accustomed to from other men. But when I was defending myself, I thought that I ought not to do anything unworthy of a free man because of the danger which I ran, and I have not changed my mind now. I would very much rather defend myself as I did, and die, than as you would have had me do, and live. Both in a lawsuit and in war, there are some things which neither I nor any other man may do in order to escape from death. In battle, a man often sees that he may at least escape from death by throwing down his arms and falling on his knees before the pursuer to beg for his life. And there are many other ways of avoiding death in every danger if a man is willing to say and to do anything. But, my friends, I think that it is a much harder thing to escape from wickedness than from death, for wickedness is swifter than death. And now I, who am old and slow, have been overtaken by the slower pursuer: and my accusers, who are clever and swift, have been overtaken by the swifter pursuer—wickedness. And now I shall go away, sentenced by you to death; they will go away, sentenced by truth to wickedness and injustice. And I abide by this award as well as they. Perhaps it was right for these things to be so. I think that they are fairly balanced.

And now I wish to prophesy to you, Athenians, who have condemned me. For I am going to die, and that is the time when men have most prophetic power. And I prophesy to you who have sentenced me to death that a far more severe punishment than you have inflicted on me will surely overtake you as soon as I am dead. You have done this thing, thinking that you will be relieved from having to give an account of your lives. But I say that the result will be very different. There will be more men who will call you to account, whom I have held back, though you did not recognize it. And they will be harsher toward you than I have been, for they will be younger, and you will be more indignant with them. For if you think that you will restrain men from reproaching you for not living as you should, by putting them to death, you are very much mistaken. That way of escape is neither possible nor honorable. It is much more honorable and much easier not to suppress others, but to make yourselves as good as you can. This is my parting prophecy to you who have condemned me.

With you who have acquitted me I should like to discuss this thing that has happened, while the authorities are busy, and before I go to the place where I have to die. So, remain with me until I go: there is no reason why we should not talk with each other while it is possible. I wish to explain to you, as my friends, the meaning of what has happened to me. An amazing thing has happened to me, judges—for I am right in calling you judges. The prophetic guide has been constantly with me all through my life till now, opposing me even in trivial matters if I were not going to act rightly. And now you yourselves see what has happened to me—a thing which might be thought, and which is sometimes actually reckoned, the supreme evil. But the divine guide did not oppose me when I was leaving my house in the morning, nor when I was coming up here to the court, nor at any point in my speech when I was going to say anything; though at other times it has often stopped me in the very act of speaking. But now, in this matter, it has never once opposed me, either in my words or my actions. I will tell you what I believe to be the reason. This thing that has come upon me must be a good; and those of us who think that death is an evil must needs be mistaken. I have a clear proof that that is so; for my accustomed guide would certainly have opposed me if I had not been going to meet with something good.

And if we reflect in another way, we shall see that we may well hope that death is a good. For the state of death is one of two things: either the dead man wholly ceases to be and loses all consciousness or, as we are told, it is a change and a migration of the soul to another place. And if death is the absence of all consciousness, and like the sleep of one whose slumbers are unbroken by any dreams, it will be a wonderful gain. For if a man had to select that night in which he slept so soundly that he did not even dream, and had to compare with it all the other nights and days of his life, and then had to say how many days and nights in his life he had spent better and more pleasantly than this night, I think that a private person, nay, even the Great King of Persia himself, would find them easy to count, compared with the others. If that is the nature of death, I for one count it a gain. For then it appears that all time is nothing more than a single night. But if death is a journey to another place, and what we are told is true—that all who have died are there—what good could be greater than this, my judges? Would a journey not be worth taking, at the end of which, in the other world, we should be delivered from the pretended judges here and should find the true judges who are said to sit in judgment below, such as Minos and Rhadamanthus and Acacus and Triptolemus, and the other demigods who were just in their own lives? Or what would you not give to converse with Orpheus and Musaeus and Hesiod and Homer? I am willing to die many times if this be true. And for my own part I should find it wonderful to meet there Palamedes, and Ajax the son of Telamon, and the other men of old who have died through an unjust judgment, and to compare my experiences with theirs. That I think would be no small pleasure. And, above all, I could spend my time in examining those who are there, as I examine men here and in finding out which of them is wise, and which of them thinks himself wise when he is not wise. What would we not give, my judges, to be able to examine the leader of the great expedition against Troy, or Odysseus, or Sisyphus, or countless other men and women whom we could name? It would be an inexpressible happiness to converse with them and to live with them and to examine them. Assuredly there they do not put men to death for doing that. For besides the other ways in which they are happier than we are, they are immortal, at least if what we are told is true.

And you too, judges, must face death hopefully, and believe this one truth, that no evil can happen to a good man, either in life or after death. His affairs are not neglected by the gods; and what has happened to me today has not happened by chance. I am persuaded that it was better for me to die now, and to be released from trouble; and that was the reason why the guide never turned me back. And so I am not at all angry with my accusers or with those who have condemned me to die. Yet it was not with this in mind that they accused me and condemned me, but meaning to do me an injury. So far I may blame them.

Yet I have one request to make of them. When my sons grow up, punish them, my friends, and harass them in the same way that I have harassed you, if they seem to you to care for riches or for any other thing more than excellence; and if they think that they are something when they are really nothing, reproach them, as I have reproached you, for not caring for what they should, and for thinking that they are something when really they are nothing. And if you will do this, I myself and my sons will have received justice from you.

But now the time has come, and we must go away—I to die, and you to live. Which is better is known to the god alone.

Terence (190?–159 BC)

Roman playwright Publius Terentius Afer was born in Carthage, North Africa. During his childhood, he was taken to Rome, where he became the slave of Publius Terentius Lucanus, a senator who educated and emancipated him. Terence was a member of the Roman general Scipio Africanus the Younger's Scipionic Circle, a group that promoted Greek culture in Rome and was concerned with improving the Latin language. Under the Scipionic Circle's patronage, Terence, one of the earliest known dramatists of African descent, wrote at least six plays approximately 160 years before the birth of Christ. One year after production of his last extant play, the *Brothers,* Terence died in Greece.

Few details are known about Terence's life, yet more than two thousand years later, individuals interested in Terence's works have access to his six extant plays: *Andria* (the *Girl from Andros); Hecrya* (the *Mother-in-Law* or the *Step-Mother), Heautontimorumenos* (the *Self Tormentor*); *Eunuchus* (the *Eunuch),* his most popular play during his lifetime; *Phormio (a Parasite)*; and the *Brothers,* his most profound work. Terence's plays are adaptations of Greek dramas; while he borrowed content from playwrights Menander and Apollodorus, he added plot complexity (including subplot), refined dialogue, subtle humor, and proverbial wisdom. Consequently, Terence's plays, appreciated for his stylistic contributions, influenced a number of European dramatists of the fourteenth through eighteenth centuries, especially the seventeenth-century French dramatist Molière.

All of Terence's extant plays are *comedies* (literary works, usually dramatic, with happy or amusing endings). Terence, along with the Greek dramatists Aristophanes and Menander and his fellow Roman countryman and predecessor Plautus, established the European comic tradition. Terence's plays are trailblazers for the modern *comedy of manners* (a play that satirizes the extremes of fashion and society). His comedies, which enjoyed great popularity during the Middle Ages and the Renaissance, continue to amuse contemporary readers and audiences.

The Step-Mother: Background

Terence's the *Step-Mother,* an adaptation of Menander's *Arbitration,* was first performed in 165 BC. The comedy, also known as *Hecyra* or The *Mother-in-Law,* revolves around a young man and his family. Pamphilus is in love with Bacchis, a courtesan, yet he agrees to marry Philumena in order to please his father, Laches. By the time Pamphilus becomes disenchanted with Bacchis and falls in love with Philumena, his bride has left him. Unaware of the truth, confusion controls Pamphilus, Philumena, and their parents until the character least likely to restore harmony among the relatives does so.

The *Step-Mother* is the only play among Terence's six extant comedies that lacks a double plot; Terence's plays, known for their plot complexity, usually involve two love affairs interwoven such that when the denouement is revealed, one couple's fate depends upon that of another couple. While Terence does not write a double plot in the *Step-Mother,* this comedy does have a subplot. In each of Terence's comedies, the subplot allows the audience to discern various characters' reactions to a significant event. Thus in the *Step-Mother,* the audience views the reactions of Pamphilus, his parents, and his in-laws to Philumena's departure; plot suspense is built as members of the audience, now cognizant of the characters' perspectives on Pamphilus and Philumena's separation, anticipate the *Step-Mother*'s final outcome. Suspense also mounts as the audience waits for Philumena's entrance. Her husband, parents, and in-laws voice their concerns about the separation, but as a feature of Terence's plot, the bride is silent.

Though a classical play, the *Step-Mother* addresses topics that are still pertinent two thousand years later including marital relationships, parental interference, gender issues, and aging. Several moral questions are raised about rape, premarital sex, and infidelity, yet no answers are provided. Providing such responses is not Terence's purpose as a writer of comedy.

The Step-Mother

PERSONS REPRESENTED

PROLOGUE.	*SOSTRATA.*
LACHES.	*MYRRHINA.*
PHIDIPPUS.	*BACCHIS.*
PAMPHILUS.	*PHILOTIS.*
PARMENO.	*SYRA.*
SOSIA.	*NURSE, Servants to Bacchis, etc.*
BOY, and other Servants.	

SCENE, ATHENS.

PROLOGUE.

This play is call'd the STEP-MOTHER. When first
It was presented, such a hurricane,
A tumult so uncommon interven'd,
It neither could be seen nor understood:
So taken were the people, so engag'd
By a rope-dancer!—It is now brought on
As a new piece: and he who wrote the play
Suffer'd it not to be repeated then,
That he might profit by a second sale.
Others, his plays, you have already known;
Now then, let me beseech you, now this too.

ANOTHER PROLOGUE.

I come a pleader, in the shape of prologue:
Let me then gain my cause, and now grown old,
Experience the same favor as when young;
Who then recover'd many a lost play,
Breath'd a new life into the scenes, and sav'd
The author and his writings from oblivion.
Of those which first I studied of Cæcilius,
In some I was excluded; and in some
Hardly maintain'd my ground. But knowing well
The variable fortunes of the scene,
I was content to hazard certain toil
For an uncertain gain. I undertook
To rescue those same plays from condemnation,
And labor'd to reverse your sentence on them;
That the same Poet might afford me more,
And no ill fortune damp young Genius in him.
My cares prevail'd; the plays were heard; and thus
Did I restore an Author, nearly lost
Through the malevolence of adversaries,
To study, labor, and the Poet's art.
But had I at that time despis'd his plays,
Or labor'd to deter him from the task,

It had been easy to have kept him idle,
And to have scar'd him from attempting more:
For my sake, therefore, deign to hear with candor
The suit I mean to you now.
Once more I bring the STEP-MOTHER before you,
Which yet in silence I might never play;
So did confusion crush it: which confusion
Your prudence may allay, if it will deign
To second our endeavors.—When I first
Began to play this piece, the sturdy Boxers,
(The dancers on the rope expected too,)
Th' increasing crowds, the noise and women's clamor,
Oblig'd me to retire before my time.
I, upon this occasion, had recourse
To my old way. I brought it on again.
In the first act I please: meanwhile there spreads
A rumor of the Gladiators: then
The people flock together, riot, roar,
And fight for places. I meanwhile *my* place
Could not maintain—To-day there's no disturbance;
All's silence and attention; a clear stage:
'Tis yours to give these games their proper grace.
Let not, oh let not the Dramatic Art
Fall to a few! let your authority
Assist and second mine! if I for gain
Ne'er overrated my abilities,
If I have made it still my only care
To be obedient to your will, oh grant
That he who hath committed his performance
To my defense, and who hath thrown himself
On your protection, be not giv'n to scorn,
And foul derision of his envious foes!
Admit this plea for my sake, and be silent;
That other Poets may not fear to write,
That I too may hereafter find it meet
To play new pieces bought at my expense.

ACT THE FIRST.
SCENE I.
PHILOTIS, SYRA.

PHI. Now, by my troth, a woman of the town
Scarce ever finds a faithful lover, Syra.
This very Pamphilus, how many times
He swore to Bacchis, swore so solemnly
One could not but believe him that he never
Would, in her lifetime, marry. See! he's married.
SYRA. I warn you, therefore, and most earnestly
Conjure you, to have pity upon none.
But plunder, fleece, and beggar ev'ry man
That falls into your pow'r.
PHI. What! spare none?
SYRA. None.
For know, there is not one of all your sparks
But studies to cajole you with fine speeches,

And have his will as cheaply as he can.
Should not you, then, endeavor to fool them?

PHI. But to treat all alike is wrong.

SYRA. What! wrong?
To be reveng'd upon your enemies?
Or to snare those who spread their snares for you?
—Alas! why have not I your youth and beauty,
Or you my sentiments?

SCENE II.

Enter PARMENO.

PAR. (*to* SCRITUS *within*). If our old gentleman
Asks for me, tell him I'm this very moment
Gone to the Port to seek for Pamphilus.
D'ye understand my meaning, Scritus? If he asks,
Tell him that; if he should not ask, say nothing;
That this excuse may serve another time.
(*Comes forward*.)
—But is not that Philotis? Whence comes she?
Philotis, save you!

PHI. Save you, Parmeno!

SYRA. Save you, good Parmeno!

PAR. And save you, Syra!
—Tell me, Philotis, where have you been gadding?
Taking your pleasure this long time?

PHI. I've taken
No pleasure, Parmeno, indeed. I went
With a most brutal Captain hence to Corinth,
There have I led a wretched life with him
For two whole years.

PAR. Aye, aye, I warrant you
That you have often wish'd to be in Athens;
Often repented of your journey.

PHI. Oh,
'Tis quite impossible to tell how much
I long'd to be at home, how much I long'd
To leave the Captain, see you, revel with you,
After the good old fashion, free and easy.
For there I durst not speak a single word,
But what, and when the mighty Captain pleas'd.

PAR. 'Twas cruel in him thus to tie your tongue:
At least, I'll warrant, that you thought it so.

PHI. But what's this business, Parmeno? this story
That Bacchis have been telling me within?
I could not have believ'd that Pamphilus
Would in her lifetime marry.

PAR. Marry truly!

PHI. Why he is married: is not he?

PAR. He is.
But I'm afraid 'twill prove a crazy match,
And will not hold together long.

PHI. Heav'n grant it.
So it turn out to Bacchis's advantage!
But how can I believe this, Parmeno?
Tell me.

PAR. It is not fit it should be told.
Inquire no more.
PHI. For fear I should divulge it?
Now Heav'n so prosper me, as I inquire,
Not for the sake of telling it again,
But to rejoice within myself.
PAR. All these
Fair words, Philotis, sha'n't prevail on me
To trust my back to your discretion.
PHI. Well;
Don't tell me, Parmeno.—As if you had not
Much rather tell this secret than I hear it.
PAR. She's in the right: I am a blab, 'tis true,
It is my greatest failing.—Give your word
You'll not reveal it, and I'll tell you.
PHI. Now
You're like yourself again. I give my word.
Speak.
PAR. Listen then.
PHI. I'm all ear.
PAR. Pamphilus
Doted on Bacchis still as much as ever,
When the old gentleman began to tease him
To marry, in the common cant of fathers;
—"That he was now grown old; and Pamphilus
His only child; and that he long'd for heirs,
As props of his old age." At first my master
Withstood his instances, but as his father
Became more hot and urgent, Pamphilus
Began to waver in his mind, and felt
A conflict betwixt love and duty in him.
At length, by hammering on marriage still,
And daily instances, th' old man prevail'd,
And made a match with our next neighbor's daughter.
Pamphilus did not take it much to heart,
Till just upon the very brink of wedlock:
But when he saw the nuptial rites prepar'd,
And, without respite, he must marry; then
It came so home to him, that even Bacchis,
Had she been present, must have pitied him.
Whenever he could steal from company,
And talk to me alone,—"Oh Parmeno,
What have I done?" he'd cry.—"I'm lost forever.
Into what ruin have I plung'd myself!
I can not bear it, Parmeno. Ah wretch!
I am undone."
PHI. Now all the powers of heav'n
Confound you, Laches, for thus teasing him?
PAR. In short, he marries, and brings home this wife.
The first night he ne'er touch'd her! nor the next.
PHI. How! he a youth, and she a maidenhead!
Tipsy, and never touch her! 'Tis not likely;
Nor do I think it can be true.
PAR. No wonder.

For they that come to you come all desire:
But he was bound to her against his will.
PHI. What followed upon this?
PAR. A few days after,
Pamphilus, taking me aside, informs me,
"That the maid still remain'd a maid for him;
That he had hop'd, before he brought her home,
He might have borne the marriage:—but resolving
Within myself not to retain her long,
I held it neither honesty in me,
Nor of advantage to the maid herself,
That I should throw her off to scorn:—but rather
Return her to her friends, as I receiv'd her,
Chaste and inviolate."
PHI. Worthy youth,
And of great modesty!
PAR. "To make this public
Would not, I think, do well: and to return her
Upon her father's hands, no crime alleg'd,
As arrogant: but she, I hope, as soon
As she perceives she can not live with me,
Will of her own accord depart."
PHI. But tell me;
Went he meanwhile to Bacchis?
PAR. Every day.
But she, as is the way you know, perceiving
He was another's property, became
More cross and mercenary.
PHI. Troth, no wonder.
PAR. Aye, but 'twas that detach'd him chiefly from her.
For when he had examined well himself,
Bacchis, and her at home; and had compar'd
Their different manners; seeing that his bride,
After the fashion of a lib'ral mind,
Was decent, modest, patient of affronts,
And anxious to conceal the wrongs he did her;
Touch'd partly with compassion for his wife,
And partly tir'd with t'others insolence,
He by degrees withdrew his heart from Bacchis,
Transferring it to her, whose disposition
Was so congenial to his own. Meanwhile
An old relation of the family
Dies in the isle of Imbrus. His estate
Comes by the law to them; and our old man
Dispatching thither, much against his will,
The now-fond Pamphilus, he leaves his wife
Here with his mother. The old gentleman
Retir'd into the country, and but seldom
Comes up to town.
PHI. But what is there in this
That can affect the marriage?
PAR. You shall hear
Immediately. At first, for some few days,
The woman seem'd to live on friendly terms:
Till all at once the bride, forsooth, conceiv'd

A wonderful disgust to Sostrata:
And yet there was no open breach between them,
And no complaints on either side.

PHI. What then?

PAR. If Sostrata, for conversation' sake,
Went to the bride, she instantly withdrew,
Shunning her company. At length, not able
To bear it any longer, she pretends
Her mother had sent for her to assist
At some home-sacrifice. Away she went.
After a few days' absence, Sostrata
Sent for her back. They made some lame excuse,
I know not what. She sends again. No lady.
Then after several messages, at last
They say the gentlewoman's sick. My mistress
Goes on a visit to her: not let in.
Th' old gentleman, inform'd of all this, came
On this occasion yesterday to town;
And waited on the father of the bride.
What pass'd between them, I as yet can't tell;
And yet I long to know the end of this.
—There's the whole business. Now I'll on my way.

PHI. And I: for there's a stranger here, with whom
I have an assignation.

PAR. Speed the plow!

PHI. Parmeno, fare you well!

PAR. Farewell, Philotis! (*Exeunt severally.*)

ACT THE SECOND.
SCENE I.
LACHES, SOSTRATA.

LACH. Oh heav'n and earth, what animals are women!
What a conspiracy between them all,
To do or not do, love or hate alike!
Not one but has the sex so strong in her,
She differs nothing from the rest. Step-mothers
All hate their Step-daughters: and every wife
Studies alike to contradict her husband,
The same perverseness running through them all.
Each seems train'd up in the same school of mischief:
And of that school, if any such there be,
My wife, I think, is schoolmistress.

SOSTRA. Ah me!
Who know not why I am accus'd.

LACH. Not know?

SOSTRA. No, as I hope for mercy! as I hope
We may live long together!

LACH. Heav'n forbid!

SOSTRA. Hereafter, Laches, you'll be sensible
How wrongfully you have accus'd me.

LACH. I?
Accuse you wrongfully?—Is't possible
To speak too hardly of your late behavior?

Disgracing me, yourself, and family;
Laying up sorrow for your absent son;
Converting into foes his new-made friends,
Who thought him worthy of their child in
marriage.
You've been our bane, and by your shrewishness
Brew'd this disturbance.

SOSTRA. I?

LACH. You, woman, you!
Who take me for a stone, and not a man.
Think ye, because I'm mostly in the country,
I'm ignorant of your proceedings here?
No, no; I know much better what's done here,
Than where I'm chiefly resident. Because
Upon my family at home depends
My character abroad. I knew long since
Philumena's disgust to you;—no wonder!
Nay, 'twere a wonder, had it not been so.
Yet I imagin'd not her hate so strong,
'Twould vent itself upon the family:
Which had I dream'd of, she should have remain'd,
And you pack'd off.—Consider, Sostrata,
How little cause you had to vex me thus.
In complaisance to you, and husbanding
My fortune, I retir'd into the country:
Scraping, and laboring beyond the bounds
Of reason, or my age, that my estate
Might furnish means for your expense and
pleasure.
—Was it not then your duty, in return,
To see that nothing happen'd here to vex me?

SOSTRA. 'Twas not my doing, nor my fault indeed.

LACH. 'Twas your fault, Sostrata; your fault alone.
You was sole mistress here; and in your care
The house, though I had freed you of all other
cares.
A woman, an old woman too, and quarrel
With a green girl! oh shame upon't!—You'll say
That 'twas her fault.

SOSTRA. Not I indeed, my Laches.

LACH. 'Fore Heav'n, I'm glad on't! on my son's account.
For as for you, I'm well enough assur'd,
No fault can make you worse.

SOSTRA. But prithee, husband,
How can you tell that her aversion to me
Is not a mere pretense, that she may stay
The longer with her mother?

LACH. No such thing.
Was not your visit yesterday a proof,
From their denial to admit you to her?

SOSTRA. They said she was so sick she could not see me.

LACH. Sick of your humors; nothing else, I fancy.
And well she might: for there's not one of you
But want your sons to take a wife: and that's
No sooner over, but the very woman

Which, by your instigation, they have married,
They, by your instigation, put away.

SCENE II.
Enter PHIDIPPUS.

PHID. (*to* PHILUMENA *within*). Although, Philumena, I know
My power
To force you to comply with my commands;
Yet yielding to paternal tenderness,
I e'en give way, nor cross your humor.

LACH. See,
Phidippus in good time! I'll learn from him
The cause of this.—(*Going up to him.*) Phiddipus, though I own
Myself indulgent to my family,
Yet my complacency and easiness
Runs not to that extreme, that my good-nature
Corrupts their morals. Would you act like me,
'Twould be of service to both families.
But you, I see, are wholly in their power.

PHID. See there!

LACH. I waited on you yesterday
About your daughter: but I went away
No wiser than I came. It is not right,
If you would have the alliance last between us,
To smother your resentment. If we seem
In fault, declare it; that we may refute,
Or make amends for our offense: and you
Shall carve the satisfaction out yourself.
But if her sickness only is the cause
Of her remaining in your family,
Trust me, Phidippus, but you do me wrong,
To doubt her due attendance at my house.
For, by the pow'rs of heav'n, I'll not allow
That you, although her father, wish her better
Than I. I love her on my son's account;
To whom, I'm well convinc'd, she is as dear
As he is to himself: and I can tell
How deeply 'twill affect him, if he knows this.
Wherefore I wish she should come home again,
Before my son's return.

PHID. My good friend Laches,
I know your care, and your benevolence;
Nor doubt that all is as you say; and hope
That you'll believe I wish for her return,
So I could but effect it.

LACH. What prevents it?
Tell me, Phidippus! does she blame her husband?

PHID. Not in the least. For when I urg'd it home,
And threaten'd to oblige her to return,
She vow'd most solemnly she could not bear
Your house, so long as Pamphilus was absent.
—All have their failings: I am of so soft

A nature, I can't thwart my family.
LACH. Ha, Sostrata! (*To* SOSTRATA, *apart.*)
SOSTRA. Wretch that I am! Ah me! (*Aside.*)
LACH. And her return's impossible? (*To* PHIDIPPUS.)
PHID. At present.
—Would you aught else with me? for I have business
That calls me to the Forum.
LACH. I'll go with you. (*Exeunt.*)

SCENE III.
Manet SOSTRATA.

SOSTRA. How unjustly
Do husbands stretch their censures to all wives
For the offenses of a few, whose vices
Reflect dishonor on the rest!—For, Heaven
So help me, as I'm wholly innocent
Of what my husband now accuses me!
But 'tis no easy task to clear myself;
So fix'd and rooted is the notion in them,
That Step-Mothers are all severe.—Not I;
For I have ever lov'd Philumena
As my own daughter; nor can I conceive
What accident has drawn her hatred on me.
My son's return, I hope, will settle all;
And, ah, I've too much cause to wish his coming.
(*Exit.*)

ACT THE THIRD.
SCENE I.
Enter PAMPHILUS *and* PARMENO.

PAM. Never did man experience greater ills,
More miseries in love than I.—Distraction!
Was it for this I held my life so dear?
For this was I so anxious to return?
Better, much better were it to have liv'd
In any place, than come to this again!
To feel and know myself a wretch!—For when
Mischance befalls, us, all the interval
Between its happening, and our knowledge of it,
May be esteem'd clear gain.
PAR. But as it is,
You'll sooner be deliver'd from your troubles:
For had you not return'd, the breach between them
Had been made wider. But now, Pamphilus,
Both will, I doubt not, reverence your presence.
You'll know the whole, make up their difference,
And reconcile them to each other.—These
Are all mere trifles, which you think so grievous.
PAM. Ah, why will you attempt to comfort me?
Was ever such a wretch?—Before I married,
My heart, you know, was wedded to another.
—But I'll not dwell upon that misery,

Which may be easily conceiv'd: and yet
I had not courage to refuse the match
My father forc'd upon me.—Scarcely wean'd
From my old love, my lim'd soul scarcely freed
From Bacchis, and devoted to my wife,
Than, lo, a new calamity arises,
Threatening to tear me from Philumena.
For either I shall find my mother faulty,
Or else my wife: In either case unhappy.
For duty, Parmeno, obliges me
To bear with all the failings of a mother:
And then I am so bounden to my wife,
Who, calm as patience, bore the wrongs I did her,
Nor ever murmur'd a complaint.—But sure
'Twas somewhat very serious, Parmeno,
That could occasion such a lasting quarrel.

PAR. Rather some trifle, if you knew the truth.
The greatest quarrels do not always rise
From deepest injuries. We often see
That what would never move another's spleen
Renders the choleric your worst of foes.
Observe how lightly children squabble.—Why?
Because they're govern'd by a feeble mind.
Women, like children, too, are impotent,
And weak of soul. A single word, perhaps,
Has kindled all this enmity between them.

PAM. Go, Parmeno, and let them know I'm come.
(*Noise within.*)

PAR. Ha! what's all this?

PAM. Hush!

PAR. I perceive a bustle,
And running to and fro.—Come this way, Sir!
—To the door!—nearer still!—There, there, d'ya hear?
(*Noise continues.*)

PAM. Peace; hush! (*Shriek within.*) Oh Jupiter, I heard a shriek!

PAR. You talk yourself, and bid me hold my tongue.

MYRRHINA (*within*). Hush, my dear child, for Heaven's sake!

PAM. It seem'd
The voice of my wife's mother. I am ruin'd!

PAR. How so?

PAM. Undone!

PAR. And why?

PAM. Ah Parmeno,
They hide some terrible misfortune from me!

PAR. They said your wife Philumena was ill:
Whether 'tis that, I can not tell.

PAM. Death, Sirrah!
Why did you not inform me that before?

PAR. Because I could not tell you all at once.

PAM. What's her disorder?

PAR. I don't know.

PAM. But tell me,
Has she had no physician?

PAR. I don't know.

PAM. But why do I delay to enter straight,
That I may learn the truth, be what it will?
—Oh my Philumena, in what condition
Shall I now find thee?—If there's danger of thee,
My life's in danger too. (*Exit*)

SCENE II

PARMENO *alone.*

It were not good
That I should follow him into the house:
For all our family are odious to them.
That's plain from their denying Sostrata
Admittance yesterday.—And if by chance
Her illness should increase (which Heav'n forbid,
For my poor master's sake!), they'll cry directly,
"Sostrata's servant came into the house:"
Swear,—"that I brought the plague along with me,
Put all their lives in danger, and increas'd
Philumena's distemper."—By which means
My mistress will be blam'd, and I be beaten.

SCENE III.

Enter SOSTRATA.

SOSTRA. Alas, I hear a dreadful noise within.
Philumena, I fear, grows worse and worse:
Which Æsculapius, and thou, Health, forbid!
But now I'll visit her. (*Goes toward the house.*)

PAR. Ho, Sostrata!

SOSTRA. Who's there?

PAR. You'll be shut out a second time.

SOSTRA. Ha, Parmeno, are you there?—Wretched woman!
What shall I do?—Not visit my son's wife,
When she lies sick at next door!

PAR. Do not go;
No, nor send any body else; for they
That love the folks, to whom themselves are odious,
I think are guilty of a double folly:
Their labor proves but idle to themselves,
And troublesome to those for whom 'tis meant.
Besides, your son, the moment he arriv'd,
Went in to visit her.

SOSTRA. How, Parmeno!
Is Pamphilus arriv'd?

PAR. He is.

SOSTRA. Thank Heav'n!
Oh, how my comfort is reviv'd by that!

PAR. And therefore I ne'er went into the house.
For if Philumena's complaints abate,
She'll tell him, face to face, the whole affair,
And what has pass'd between you to create
This difference.—But here he comes—how sad!

Scene IV.
Enter Pamphilus.

Sostra. My dear boy, Pamphilus!
Pam. My mother, save you! (*Disordered.*)
Sostra. I'm glad to see you safe return'd—How does
Your wife!
Pam. A little better.
Sostra. Grant it, Heav'n!
—But why d'ye weep, and why are you so sad?
Pam. Nothing, good mother.
Sostra. What was all that bustle?
Tell me, did pain attack her suddenly?
Pam. It did.
Sostra. And what is her complaint?
Pam. A fever.
Sostra. What! a quotidian?
Par. So they say.—But in,
Good mother, and I'll follow.
Sostra. Be it so. (*Exit*)
Pam. Do you run, Parmeno, to meet the servants,
And give your help in bringing home the baggage.
Par. As if they did not know the road!
Pam. Away! (*Exit* Parmeno.)

Scene V.
Pamphilus *alone.*

Which way shall I begin the wretched tale
Of my misfortunes, which have fall'n upon me

These very eyes have seen, these ears have heard?
And which, discover'd, drove me out o'doors.
Cover'd with deep confusion?—For but now
As I rush'd in, all anxious for my wife,
And thinking to have found her visited,
Alas! with a far different complaint;
Soon as her women saw me, at first sight
Struck and o'erjoy'd, they all exclaim'd, "He's
come!"
And then as soon each countenance was chang'd,
That chance had brought me so unseasonably.
Meanwhile one of them ran before, to speak
Of my arrival. I, who long'd to see her,
Directly follow'd; and no sooner enter'd,
Than her disorder was, alas! too plain:
For neither had they leisure to disguise it,
Nor could she silence the loud cries of travail.
Soon as I saw it, "Oh shame, shame!" I cried,
And rushed away in tears and agony,
O'erwhelm'd with horror at a stroke so grievous.
The mother follows me, and at the threshold
Falls on her knees before me all in tears.
This touch'd me to the soul. And certainly
'Tis in the very nature of our minds,

To rise and fall according to our fortunes.
Thus she adderss'd me.—"Oh, my Pamphilus,
The cause of her removal from your house
You've now discover'd. To my virgin-daughter
Some unknown villain offer'd violence;
And she fled hither to conceal her labor
From you and from your family."—Alas!
When I but call her earnest prayers to mind,
I can not choose but weep.—"Whatever chance,"
Continued she, "whatever accident,
Brought you to-day thus suddenly upon us,
By that we both conjure you—if in justice
And equity we may—to keep in silence,
And cover her distress.—Oh, Pamphilus,
If e'er you witness'd her affection for you,
By that affection she implores you now
Not to refuse us!—for recalling her,
Do as your own discretion shall direct.
That she's in labor now, or has conceiv'd
By any other person, is a secret
Known but to you alone. For I've been told,
The two first months you had no commerce with
her,
And it is now the seventh since your union.
Your sentiments on this are evident.
But now, my Pamphilus, if possible,
I'll call it a miscarriage: no one else
But will believe, as probable, 'tis yours.
The child shall be immediately expos'd.
No inconvenience will arise to you;
While thus you shall conceal the injury
That my poor girl unworthily sustain'd."
—I promis'd her; and I will keep my word.
But to recall her would be poor indeed:
Nor will I do it, though I love her still.
And former commerce binds me strongly to her.
—I can't but weep, to think how sad and lonely
My future life will be.—Oh fickle fortune!
How transient are they smiles!—But I've been
school'd
To patience by my former hapless passion,
Which I subdued by reason: and I'll try
By reason to subdue this too.—But yonder
Comes Parmeno, I see, with th' other slaves!
He must by no means now be present, since
To him alone I formerly reveal'd
That I abstain'd from her when first we married:
And if he hears her frequent cries, I fear
That he'll discover her to be in labor.
I must dispatch him on some idle errand,
Until Philumena's deliver'd.

SCENE VI.

Enter at a distance PARMENO, SOSIA, *and other slaves with baggage.*

PAR. (*to* SOSIA). Aye?
And had you such a wretched voyage, say yon?
SOSIA. Oh Parmeno, words can't express how wretched
A sea-life is.
PAR. Indeed?
SOSIA. Oh happy Parmeno!
You little know the dangers you've escap'd,
Who've never been at sea.—For not to dwell
On other hardships, only think of this!
I was on shipboard thirty days or more,
In constant fear of sinking all the while,
The winds so contrary, such stormy weather!
PAR. Dreadful!
SOSIA. I found it so, I promise you.
In short, were I assur'd I must return,
'Fore Heaven, Parmeno, I'd run away,
Rather than go on board a ship again.
PAR. You have been apt enough to think of that
On slighter reasons, Sosia, before now.
—But yonder's my young master Pamphilus
Standing before that door.—Go in! I'll to him,
And see if he has any business for me.
(*Exeunt* SOSIA, *and the rest of the slaves with the baggage*.)
Master, are you here still? (*To* PAMPHILUS.)
PAM. Oh Parmeno!
I waited for you.
PAR. What's your pleasure, Sir?
PAM. Run to the Citadel.
PAR. Who?
PAM. You.
PAR. The Citadel!
For what?
PAM. Find out one Callidemides,
My landlord of Mycone, who came over
In the same ship with me.
PAR. A plague upon it!
Would not one swear that he had made a vow
To break my wind, if he came home in safety,
With running on his errands?
PAM. Away, Sirrah!
PAR. What message? must I only find him out?
PAM. Yes; tell him that it is not in my power
To meet him there to-day, as I appointed;
That he mayn't wait for me in vain.—Hence; fly!
PAR. But I don't know him, if I see him, Sir.
PAM. (*impatiently*). Well; I'll describe him, so you can not miss him.
—A large, red, frizzle-pated, gross, blear-eyed,
I'll-looking fellow.
PAR. Plague on him, say I!
—What if he should not come, Sir, must I wait

Till evening for him?
PAM. Wait.—Be quick!
PAR. Be quick?
I can't be quick,—I'm so much tir'd. *(Exit.)*

SCENE VII.
PAMPHILUS *alone.*

He's gone.
What shall I do? Alas! I scarcely know
How to conceal, as Myrrhina desir'd,
Her daughter's labor. Yet I pity her;
And what I can, I am resolv'd to do,
Consistent with my duty: for my parents
Must be obey'd before my love.—But see!
My father and Phidippus come this way.
How I shall act, Heav'n knows.

SCENE VIII.
Enter at a distance LACHES *and* PHIDIPPUS.

LACH. Did not you say
She only waited my son's coming?
PHID. Aye.
LACH. They say that he's arriv'd. Let us return then!
PAM. (*behind*). What reason I shall frame to give my father,
For not recalling her, I can not tell.
LACH. (*overhearing*). Whose voice was that?
PAM. (*to himself*). And yet I am resolv'd
To stand to my first purpose.
LACH. (*seeing* PAMPHILUS). He himself,
Whom I was speaking of!
PAM. (*going up*). My father, save you!
LACH. Save you, my son!
PHID. Pamphilus, welcome home!
I'm glad to see you safe, and in good health.
PAM I do believe it.
LACH. Are you just now come?
PAM. Just now, Sir.
LACH. Well; and tell me, Pamphilus,
What has our kinsman Phania left us?
PAM. Ah, Sir,
He, his whole lifetime, was a man of pleasure,
And such men seldom much enrich their heirs.
Yet he has left at least this praise behind him,
"While he liv'd he liv'd well."
LACH. And have you brought
Nothing home with you but this single sentence?
PAM. What he has left, though small, is of advantage.
LACH. Advantage? No, it is a disadvantage:
For I could wish he was alive and well.
PHID. That you may safely; for your wishing for't
Will never bring the man to life again:

Yet I know well enough which you'd like best.
(*Aside.*)

LACH. (*to* PAMPHILUS). Phidippus order'd that Philumena
Should be sent over to him yesterday.
—Say that you order'd it. (*Aside to* PHIDDIPPUS, *thrusting him.*)

PHID. (*aside to* LACHES). Don't thrust me so.—
I did. (*Aloud.*)

LACH. But now he'll send her home again.

PHID. I will.

PAM. Nay, nay, I know the whole affair.
Since my arrival, I have heard it all.

LACH. Now plague upon these envious tale-bearers,
Who are so glad to fetch and carry news!

PAM. (*to* PHIDIPPUS). That I've endeavor'd to deserve no blame
From any of the family, I'm conscious.
Were it my inclination to relate
How true I've been, how kind and gentle tow'rd her,
I well might do it: but I rather choose
You should collect it from herself. For when
She, although now there's enmity between us,
Bespeaks me fair, you will the sooner credit
My disposition tow'rd her. And I call
The Gods to witness that this separation
Has not arisen from my fault. But since
She thinks it is beneath her to comply
With Sostrata, and bear my mother's temper;
And since no other means are to be found
Of reconciliation, I, Phidippus,
Must leave my mother or Philumena.
Duty then calls me to regard my mother.

LACH. My Pamphilus, I can not be displeas'd
That you prefer to all the world a parent.
But take heed your resentment don't transport you
Beyond the bounds of reason, Pamphilus.

PAM. Ah, what resentment can I bear to her,
Who ne'er did any thing I'd wish undone,
But has so often deserv'd well of me?
I love her, own her worth, and languish for her;
For I have known her tenderness of soul;
And Heaven grant that with some other husband
She find that happiness she miss'd in me;
From whom the strong hand of necessity
Divorces her forever!

PHID. That event
'Tis in your pow'r to hinder.

LACH. If you're wise,
Take your wife home again!

PAM. I can not, father.
I must not slack my duty to my mother. (*Going.*)

LACH. Where are you going? (*Exit* PAMPHILUS.)

SCENE IX.
Manent LACHES *and* PHIDIPPUS.

PHID. How perverse is this! (*Angrily.*)
LACH. Did not I say he'd take it ill, Phidippus,
And therefore begg'd you to send back your daughter?
PHID. 'Fore Heaven I did not think him such a churl.
What! does he fancy I'll go cringing to him?
No;—if he'll take his wife he may:—if not,
Let him refund her portion;—there's an end!
LACH. See there now! you're as fractious as himself.
PHID. You're come back obstinate and proud enough
In conscience, Pamphilus! (*Angrily.*)
LACH. This anger will subside,
Though he has had some cause to be disturb'd.
PHID. Because you've had a little money left you,
Your minds are so exalted!
LACH. What, d'ye quarrel
With me too?
PHID. Let him take to-day to think on't,
And send me word if he shall have her home
Or not: that if she don't remain his wife,
She may be given to another. (*Exit hastily.*)

SCENE X.
LACHES *alone.*

Stay!
Hear me! one word, Phidippus! Stay!—He's gone.
—What is't to me? (*Angrily.*) E'en let them settle it
Among themselves; since nor my son, nor he
Take my advice, nor mind one word I say.
—This quarrel shall go round, I promise them:
I'll to my wife, the author of this mischief,
And vent my spleen and anger upon her. (*Exit.*)

ACT THE FOURTH.
SCENE I.
Enter MYRRHINA *hastily.*

MYRR. What shall I do?—Confusion!—which way turn?
Alas! what answer shall I make my husband?
For I dare say he heard the infant's cries,
He ran so hastily, without a word,
Into my daughter's chamber. If he finds
That she has been deliver'd, what excuse
To make, for having thus conceal'd her labor,
I can't devise.—But our door creaks!—'tis he.
I am undone.

SCENE II.
Enter PHIDIPPUS.

PHID. Soon as my wife perceiv'd
That I was going to my daughter's chamber,
She stole directly out o'doors.—But there
She stands.—Why, how now, Myrrhina?
Holo, I say! (*She affects not to see him.*)
MYRR. D'ye call me, husband?
PHID. Husband!
Am I your husband? am I ev'n a man?
For had you thought me to be either, woman,
You would not dare to play upon me thus.
MYRR. How!
PHID. How?—My daughter has been brought to bed.
—Ha! are you dumb?—By whom?
MYRR. Is that a question
For you, who are her father, to demand?
Alas! by whom d'ye think, unless her husband?
PHID. So I believe: nor is it for a father
To suppose otherwise. But yet I wonder
That you have thus conceal'd her labor from us,
Especially as she has been deliver'd
At her full time, and all is as it should be.
What! Is there such perverseness in your nature,
As rather to desire the infant's death,
Than that his birth should knit the bond of friendship
Closer betwixt us; rather than my daughter,
Against your liking, should remain the wife
Of Pamphilus?—I thought all this
Had been their fault, while you're alone to blame.
MYRR. How wretched am I!
PHID. Would to Heav'n you were!
—But now I recollect your conversation
When first we made this match, you then declar'd
You'd not endure she should remain the wife
Of Pamphilus, who follow'd mistresses,
And pass'd the nights abroad.
MYRR. I had much rather
He should think any reason than the true one. (*Aside.*)
PHID. I knew he kept a mistress; knew it long
Ere you did, Myrrhina; but I could never
Think that offense so grievous in a youth,
Seeing 'tis natural to them all: and soon
The time shall come when he'll stand self-reprov'd.
But you, perverse and willful as at first,
Could take no rest till you had brought away
Your daughter, and annull'd the match I made:
There's not a circumstance but loudly speaks
Your evil disposition to the marriage.
MYRR. D'ye think me then so obstinate, that I,
Who am her mother, should betray this spirit,
Granting the match were of advantage to us?

PHID. Is it for you then to foresee, or judge
What's of advantage to us? You perhaps
Have heard from some officious busy-body,
That they have seen him going to his mistress,
Or coming from her house: and what of that,
So it were done discreetly, and but seldom?
Were it no better that we should dissemble
Our knowledge of it, than pry into things
Which to appear to know would make him hate us?
For could he tear her from his heart at once,
To whom he'd been so many years attach'd,
I should not think he were a man, or likely
To prove a constant husband to my daughter.

MYRR. No more of Pamphilus or my offense;
Since you will have it so!—Go, find him out;
Confer with him alone, and fairly ask him,
Will he, or no, take back Philumena?
If he avows his inclination to't,
Restore her; but if he refuses it,
Allow, I've ta'en good counsel for my child.

PHID. Grant, he should prove repugnant to the match,
Grant, you perceiv'd this in him, Myrrhina;
Was not I present! had not I a right
To be consulted in't?—It makes me mad.
That you should dare to act without my order:
And I forbid you to remove the child
Out of this house.—But what a fool am I,
Enjoining her obedience to my orders!
I'll in, and charge the servants not to suffer
The infant to be carried forth. (*Exit.*)

SCENE III.
MYRRHINA *alone.*

No woman more unhappy than myself:
For how he'd bear it, did he know the whole,
When he has taken such offense at this,
Which is of much less consequence, is plain.
Nor by what means to reconcile him to it,
Can I devise. After so many ills,
This only misery there yet remain'd,
To be oblig'd to educate the child,
Ignorant of the father's quality.
For he, the cruel spoiler of her honor,
Taking advantage of the night and darkness,
My daughter was not able to discern
His person; nor to force a token from him,
Whereby he might be afterward discover'd:
But he, at his departure, pluck'd by force
A ring from off her finger.—I fear too,
That Pamphilus will not contain himself,
Nor longer keep our secret, when he finds
Another's child acknowledg'd for his own. (*Exit.*)

Scene IV.
Sostrata, Pamphilus.

Sostra. Dear son, I'm not to learn that you suppose,
Though you dissemble your suspicious to me,
That my ill-humor caus'd your wife's departure.
But by my trust in Heav'n, and hopes in you,
I never knowingly did any thing
To draw her hatred and disgust upon me.
I always thought you lov'd me, and to-day
You have confirm'd my faith: for even now
Your father has been telling me within,
How much you held me dearer than your love.
Now therefore, on my part, I am resolv'd
To equal you in all good offices;
That you may know your mother ne'er withholds
The just rewards of filial piety;
Finding it then both meet for your repose,
My Pamphilus, as well as my good name,
I have determin'd to retire directly
From hence into the country with your father;
So shall my presence be no obstacle,
Nor any cause remain, but that your wife
Return immediately.

Pam. What thoughts are these?
Shall her perverseness drive you out of town?
It shall not be: Nor will I draw, good mother,
That censure on me, that my obstinacy,
Not your good-nature, was the cause.—Besides,
That you should quit relations, friends, diversions,
On my account, I can't allow.

Sostra. Alas!
Those things have no allurements for me now.
While I was young, and 'twas the season for them,
I had my share, and I am satisfied.
'Tis now my chief concern to make my age
Easy to all, that no one may regret
My lengthen'd life, nor languish for my death.
Here, although undeservedly, I see
My presence odious: I had best retire:
So shall I best cut off all discontent,
Absolve myself from this unjust suspicion,
And humor them. Permit me then to shun
The common scandal thrown upon the sex.

Pam. How fortunate in every thing but one,
Having so good a mother,—such a wife!

Sostra. Patience, my Pamphilus! Is't possible
You can't endure one inconvenience in her?
If in all else, as I believe, you like her,
Dear son, be rul'd by me, and take her home!

Pam. Wretch that I am!
For this grieves me, my son, no less than you.

SCENE V.
Enter LACHES.

LACH. I have been standing at a distance, wife,
And overheard your conversation with him.
You have done wisely to subdue your temper,
And freely to comply with what, perhaps,
Hereafter must be done.
SOSTRA. And let it be!
LACH. Now then retire with me into the country:
There I shall bear with you, and you with me.
SOSTRA. I hope we shall.
LACH. Go in then, and pack up
The necessaries you would carry with you.
Away!
SOSTRA. I shall obey your orders. (*Exit.*)
PAM. Father!
LACH. Well, Pamphilus?
PAM. My mother leave the town?
By no means.
LACH. Why?
PAM. Because I'm yet uncertain
What I shall do about my wife.
LACH. How's that?
What *would* you do but take her home again?
PAM. 'Tis what I wish for, and can scarce forbear it.
But I'll not alter what I first design'd.
What's best I'll follow: and I'm well convinc'd
That there's no other way to make them friends,
But that I should not take her home again.
LACH. You don't know that: but 'is of no importance
Whether they're friends or not, when Sostrata
Is gone into the country. We old folks
Are odious to the young. We'd best retire.
In short, we're grown a by-word, Pamphilus,
"The old man and old woman."—But I see
Phidippus coming in good time. Let's meet him!

SCENE VI.
Enter PHIDIPPUS.

PHID. (*to* PHILUMENA *within*). I'm angry with you—'fore
Heaven, very angry,
Philumena!—You've acted shamefully.
Though you indeed have some excuse for't, seeing
Your mother urg'd you to't; but she has none.
LACH. You're come upon us in good time, Phidippus;
Just in the time we wanted you.
PHID. What now?
PAM. What answer shall I give them! how explain!
(*Aside.*)
LACH. Inform your daughter, Sostrata will hence
Into the country; so Philumena
Need not dread coming home again.
PHID. Ah, friend!

Your wife has never been in fault at all:
All this has sprung from my wife Myrrhina.
The case is alter'd. She confounds us, Laches.

PAM. So that I may not take her home again,
Confound affairs who will! (*Aside.*)

PHID. I, Pamphilus,
Would fain, if possible, make this alliance
Perpetual between our families.
But if you can not like it, take the child.

PAM. He knows of her delivery. Confusion! (*Aside.*)

LACH. The child! what child?

PHID. We've got a grandson, Laches.
For when my daughter left your house, she was
With child, it seems, although I never knew it
Before this very day.

LACH. 'Fore Heav'n, good news!
And I rejoice to hear a child is born,
And that your daughter had a safe delivery.
But what a woman is your wife, Phidippus?
Of what a disposition? to conceal
Such an event as this? I can't express
How much I think she was to blame.

PHID. This pleases me no more than you, good Laches.

PAM. Although my mind was in suspense before,
My doubts all vanish now. I'll ne'er recall her,
Since she brings home with her another's child.
(*Aside.*)

LACH. There is no room for choice now, Pamphilus.

PAM. Confusion! (*Aside.*)

LACH. We've oft wish'd to see the day
When you should have a child to call you father.
That day's now come. The Gods be thank'd!

PAM. Undone! (*Aside.*)

LACH. Recall your wife, and don't oppose my will.

PAM. If she had wish'd for children by me, father,
Or to remain my wife, I'm very sure
She never would have hid this matter from me:
But now I see her heart divorc'd from me,
And think we never can agree hereafter,
Wherefore should I recall her?

LACH. A young woman
Did as her mother had persuaded her.
Is that so wonderful? and do you think
To find a woman without any fault?
—Or is't because the *men* are ne'er to blame?
(*Ironically.*)

PHID. Consider with yourselves then, gentlemen,
Whether you'll part with her, or call her home.
What my wife does, I can not help, you know.
Settle it as you please, you've my consent,
But for the child, what shall be done with him?

LACH. A pretty question truly! come what may,
Send his own bantling home to him of course,
That we may educate him.

PAM. When his own
Father abandons him, I educate him?

LACH. What said you? how! not educate him, say you?
Shall we expose him rather, Pamphilus?
What madness is all this?—My breath and blood!
I can contain no longer. You oblige me
To speak, against my will, before Phidippus:
Think you I'm ignorant whence flow those tears?
Or why you're thus disorder'd and distress'd?
First, when you gave as a pretense, *you could not*
Recall your wife from reverence to your mother,
She promis'd to retire into the country.
But now, since that excuse is taken from you,
You've made *her private lying-in* another.
You are mistaken if you think me blind
To your intentions—That you might at last
Bring home your stray affections to your wife,
How long a time to wean you from your mistress
Did I allow! your wild expense upon her
How patiently I bore? I press'd, entreated,
That you would take a wife. 'Twas time, I said.
At my repeated instances, you married,
And, as in duty heart is gone abroad again
After your mistress, whom to gratify,
You throw this wanton insult on your wife.
For I can plainly see you are relaps'd
Into your former life again.

PAM. Me?

LACH. You.
And 'tis base in you to invent false causes
Of quarrel with your wife, that you may live
In quiet with your mistress, having put
This witness from you. This your wife perceiv'd.
For was there any other living reason
Wherefore she should depart from you?

PHID. He's right,
That was the very thing.

PAM. I'll take my oath
'Twas none of those that you have mention'd.

LACH. Ah!
Recall your wife: or tell me why you will not.

PAM. 'Tis not convenient now.

LACH. Take home the child then;
For *he* at least is not in fault. I'll see
About the mother afterward.

PAM. (*to himself*). Ev'ry way
I am a wretch, nor know I what to do:
My father has me in the toils, and I,
By struggling to get loose, am more entangled.
I'll hence, since present I shall profit little.
For I believe they'll hardly educate
The child against my will; especially
Seeing my step-mother will second me. (*Exit.*)

SCENE VII.
Manent PHIDIPPUS, LACHES.

LACH. Going? how's that? and give me no plain answer!
—D'ye think he's in his senses?—Well—send home
The child to me, Phidippus. I'll take care on't.

PHID. I will.—I can not wonder that my wife
Took this so ill. Women are passionate,
And can't away with such affronts as these.
This was their quarrel: nay she told me so,
Though before him I did not care to speak on't:
Nor did I credit it at first; but now
'Tis evident, and I can plainly see
He has no stomach to a wife.

LACH. Phidippus,
How shall I act? What's your advice?

PHID. How act?
I think 'twere best to seek this wench, his mistress,
Let us expostulate the matter with her,
Speak to her roundly, nay, e'en threaten her,
If she has aught to do with him hereafter.

LACH. I'll follow your advice.—Ho, boy! (*Enter a boy*) run over
To Bacchis. Tell her to come forth to me. (*Exit boy.*)
—I must beseech you also to continue
Your kind assistance to me in this business.

PHID. Ah, Laches! I have told you all along,
And I repeat it now, that 'tis my wish
To render our alliance firm and lasting,
If possible, as I have hopes it will be.
—But would you have me present at your conference
With Bacchis?

LACH. No; go, seek the child a nurse.
(*Exit* PHIDIPPUS.)

SCENE VIII.
Enter BACCHIS *attended by her Women.*

BACCH. (*to herself*). 'Tis not for nothing Laches wants to see me;
And, or I'm much deceiv'd, I guess the cause.

LACH. (*to himself*). I must take care my anger don't transport me
Beyond the bounds of prudence, which may hinder
My gaining my design on her, and urge me
To do what I may afterward repent.
I'll to her.—(*Going up.*) Save you, Bacchis!

BACCH. Save you, Laches!

LACH. Bacchis, I do not doubt but you're surpris'd
That I should send the boy to call you forth.

BACCH. Aye, and I'm fearful too, when I reflect
Both who and what I am: lest my vocation
Should prejudice me in your good opinion.
My conduct I can fully justify.

LACH. If you speak truth, you're in no danger, woman.
For I'm arriv'd at that age when a trespass
Would not be easily forgiven in me.
Wherefore I study to proceed with caution,
And to do nothing rashly. If you act,
And will continue to act honestly,
It were ungenerous to do you wrong,
And seeing you deserve it not, unjust.
BACCH. Truly, this conduct asks my highest thanks;
For he who does the wrong, and then asks pardon,
Makes but a sorry reparation for it.
But what's your pleasure?
LACH. You receive the visits
Of my sons Pamphilus—
BACCH. Ah!—
LACH. Let me speak.
Before he married I endur'd your love.
—Stay! I've not finish'd all I have to say.—
He is now married. You then, while 'tis time,
Seek out another and more constant friend.
For he will not be fond of you forever,
Nor you, good faith, forever in your bloom.
BACCH. Who tells you that I still receive the visits
Of Pamphilus?
LACH. His step-mother.
BACCH. I?
LACH. You.
And therefore has withdrawn her daughter:
therefore
Meant secretly to kill the new-born child.
BACCH. Did I know any thing, to gain your credit,
More sacred than an oath, I'd use it, Laches,
In solemn protestation to assure you
That I have had no commerce with your son
Since he was married.
LACH. Good girl! but d'ye know
What I would farther have you to do?
BACCH. Inform me.
LACH. Go to the women here, and offer them
The same oath. Satisfy their minds, and clear
Yourself from all reproach in this.
BACCH. I'll do't.
Although I'm sure no other of my calling
Would show herself before a married woman
Upon the same occasion.—But it hurts me
To see your son suspected on false grounds;
And that, to those who owe him better thoughts,
His conduct should seem light. For he deserves
All my best offices.
LACH. Your conversation has much wrought upon me,
Gain'd my good-will, and alter'd my opinion.
For not the women only thought thus of you,
But I believ'd it too. Now therefore, since
I've found you better than my expectation,
Prove still the same, and make my friendship sure.

If otherwise—But I'll contain myself. I'll not
Say any thing severe.—But I advise you,
Rather experience what a friend I am,
Than what an enemy.

BACCH. I'll do my best.

SCENE IX.

Enter PHIDIPPUS *and a Nurse.*

PHID. (*to the Nurse*). Nay, you shall want for nothing at my house;
I'll give you all that's needful in abundance;
But when you've eat and drank your fill yourself,
Take care to satisfy the infant too.

LACH. I see the father of Philumena
Coming this way. He brings the child a nurse.
—Phidippus, Bacchis swears most solemnly—

PHID. Is this she?

LACH. Aye.

PHID. They never mind the Gods,
Nor do I think the Gods mind them.

BACCH. Here are
My waiting-women: take them, and extort
By any kind of torment the truth from them.
—Our present business is, I take it, this:
That I should win the wife of Pamphilus
To return home; which so I but effect,
I sha'n't regret the same of having done
What others of my calling would avoid.

LACH. Phidippus, we've discover'd that in fact
We both suspected our wives wrongfully.
Let's now try her: for if your wife perceives
Her own suspicions also are unjust,
She'll drop her anger. If my son's offended
Because his wife conceal'd her labor from him,
That's but a trifle; he'll be soon appeas'd.
—And truly I see nothing in this matter
That need occasion a divorce.

PHID. 'Fore Heaven,
I wish that all may end well.

LACH. Here she is:
Examine her; she'll give you satisfaction.

PHID. What needs all this to Me! You know my mind
Already, Laches: do but make them easy.

LACH. Bacchis, be sure you keep your promise with me.

BACCH. Shall I go in then for that purpose?

LACH. Aye.
Go in; remove their doubts, and satisfy them.

BACCH. I will; although I'm very sure my presence
Will be unwelcome to them; for a wife,
When parted from her husband, to a mistress
Is a sure enemy.

LACH. They'll be your friends,
When once they know the reason of your coming.

PHID. Aye, aye, they'll be your friends, I promise you,

When they once learn your errand; for you'll free
Them from mistake, yourself from all suspicion.

BACCH. I'm cover'd with confusion. I'm asham'd
To see Philumena.—(*To her women.*) You two in
after me.

(*Exeunt* PHIDIPPUS, BACCHIS, etc.)

LACHES *alone.*

What is there that could please me more than this,
That Bacchis, without any loss, should gain
Favor from them, and do me service too?
For if she really has withdrawn herself
From Pamphilus, it will increase, she knows,
Her reputation, interest, and honor:
Since by this generous act she will at once
Oblige my son, and make us all her friends. (*Exit.*)

ACT THE FIFTH.

SCENE I.

PARMENO *alone.*

I' faith my master holds my labor cheap,
To send me to the Citadel for nothing,
Where I have waited the whole day in vain
For his Myconian, Callidemides.
There was I siting, gaping like a fool,
And running up, if any one appear'd,
—"Are you, Sir, a Myconian?"—"No, not I."—
—"But your name's Callidemides?"—"Not it."—
"And have not you a guest here of the name
Of Pamphilus?"—All answer'd, No.
In short, I don't believe there's such a man.
At last I grew asham'd, and so sneak'd off.
—But is't not Bacchis that I see come forth
From our new kinsman? What can she do there?

SCENE II.

Enter BACCHIS.

BACCH. Oh Parmeno, I'm glad I've met with you.
Run quick to Pamphilus.

PAR. On what account?

BACCH. Tell him that I desire he'd come.

PAR. To you?

BACCH. No; to Philumena.

PAR. Why? what's the matter?

BACCH. Nothing to you; so ask no questions.

PAR. Must I
Say nothing else?

BACCH. Yes; tell him too,
That Myrrhina acknowledges the ring,
Which formerly he gave me, as her daughter's.

PAR. I understand you. But is that all?

BACCH. All.
He'll come the moment that you tell him that.
What! do you loiter?

PAR. No, i' faith, not I.
I have not had it in my pow'r, I've been
So bandied to and fro, sent here and there,
Trotting, and running up and down all day. (*Exit.*)

SCENE III.
BACCHIS *alone.*

What joy have I procur'd to Pamphilus
By coming here to-day! what blessings brought him!
And from how many sorrows rescued him!
His son, by his and their means nearly lost,
I've sav'd; a wife he meant to put away,
I have restor'd; and from the strong suspicions
Of Laches and Phidippus set him free.
—Of all these things the ring has been the cause.
For I remember, near ten months ago,
That he came running home to me one evening,
Breathless, alone, and much inflam'd with wine,
Bringing this ring. I was alarm'd at it.
"Prithee, my dearest Pamphilus, said I,
Whence comes all this confusion? whence this
ring?
Tell me, my love."—He put me off at first:
Perceiving this, it made me apprehend
Something of serious import, and I urg'd him
More earnestly to tell me.—He confess'd
That, as he came along, he had committed
A rape upon a virgin—whom he knew not—
And as she struggled, forc'd from her that ring:
Which Myrrhina now seeing on my finger,
Immediately acknowledg'd, and inquir'd
How I came by it. I told all this story:
Whence 'twas discover'd that Philumena
Was she who had been ravish'd, and the child
Conceiv'd from that encounter.—That I've been
The instrument of all these joys I'm glad,
Though other courtesans would not be so;
Nor is it for our profit and advantage
That lovers should be happy in their marriage.
But never will I, for my calling's sake,
Suffer ingratitude to taint my mind.
I found him while occasion gave him leave,
Kind, pleasant, and good-humor'd: and this
marriage
Happen'd unluckily, I must confess.
Yet I did nothing to estrange his love;
And since I have receiv'd much kindness from him,
'Tis fit I should endure this one affliction.

SCENE IV.
Enter at a distance PAMPHILUS *and* PARMENO.

PAM. Be sure you prove this to me, Parmeno;
Prithee, be sure on't. Do not bubble me

	With false and short-liv'd joy.
PAR.	'Tis even so.
PAM.	For certain?
PAR.	Aye, for certain.
PAM.	I'm in heaven, If this be so.
PAR.	You'll find it very true.
PAM.	Hold, I beseech you.—I'm afraid I think One thing, while you relate another.
PAR.	Well?
PAM.	You said, I think, "that Myrrhina discover'd The ring on Bacchis' finger was her own."
PAR.	She did.
PAM.	"The same I gave her formerly. —And Bacchis bade you run and tell me this." Is it not so?
PAR.	I tell you, Sir, it is.
PAM.	Who is more fortunate, more bless'd than I? —What shall I give you for this news? what? what? I don't know.
PAR.	But I know.
PAM.	What?
PAR.	Just nothing. For I see nothing of advantage to you, Or in the message, or myself.
PAM.	Shall I Permit you to go unrewarded; you, Who have restor'd me ev'n from death to life? Ah, Parmeno, d'ye think me so ungrateful? —But yonder's Bacchis standing at the door. She waits for me, I fancy. I'll go to her.
BACCH.	(*seeing him*). Pamphilus, save you
PAM.	Bacchis! my dear Bacchis! My guardian! my protectress!
BACCH.	All is well: And I'm o'erjoy'd at it.
PAM.	Your actions speak it. You're still the charming girl I ever found you. Your presence, company, and conversation, Come where you will, bring joy and pleasure with them.
BACCH.	And you, in faith, are still the same as ever, The sweetest, most engaging man on earth.
PAM.	Ha! ha! ha! that speech from you, dear Bacchis?
BACCH.	You lov'd your wife with reason, Pamphilus: Never that I remember, did I see her Before to-day; and she's a charming woman.
PAM.	Speak truth.
BACCH.	So Heaven help me, Pamphilus!
PAM.	Say, have you told my father any part Of this tale?
BACCH.	Not a word.
PAM.	Nor is there need. Let all be hush! I would not have it here, As in a comedy, where every thing

Is known to every body. Here those persons
Whom it concerns already know it; they,
Who 'twere not meet should know it, never shall.

BACCH. I promise you it may with ease be hid.
Myrrhina told Phidippus that my oath
Convinc'd her, and she held you clear.

PAM. Good! good!
All will be well, and all, I hope, end well.

PAR. May I know, Sir, what good I've done to-day?
And what's the meaning of your conversation?

PAM. No.

PAR. I suspect, however.—"I restore him
From death to life"—which way?—

PAM. Oh, Parmeno,
You can't conceive the good you've done to-day;
From what distress you have deliver'd me.

PAR. Ah, but I know, and did it with design.

PAM. Oh, I'm convinced of that. (*Ironically*.)

PAR. Did Parmeno
Ever let slip an opportunity
Of doing what he ought, Sir?

PAM. Parmeno,
In after me!

PAR. I follow.—By my troth,
I've done more good to-day, without design,
Than ever with design in all my life.—

Clap your hands!

Gaius Valerius Catullus (84?–54? BC)

Catullus was born in Verona, Italy where his wealthy family provided him with an excellent education. Catullus, attracted by the excitement of Rome, went there in his twenties. Family friends introduced him to the most fashionable circles of society, and in that sophisticated atmosphere, he met Clodia, a beautiful, intelligent aristocrat, whom he calls Lesbia in his poems. Catullus fell in love with her, but she had no real affection for him. Catullus traces the whole tragic story of this misplaced love in the poems of Lesbia. His love poems indicate that there is first a period of happiness between Lesbia and himself, only to be followed soon after by his intense bitterness and despair at her rejection of his love and her infidelity. Catullus' love poems reveal that his love has turned into an obsession, and he tries to free himself from his deep infatuation and despair. As Catullus begins to suspect her infidelity, the rapture of his early poems becomes clouded with doubt. After Catullus recognizes Lesbia's true nature, he still vacillates between love and hatred, unable for a long time to make the final renunciation.

The Poetry of Catullus: Background

Gaius Valerius Catullus was the first Roman poetic genius. In fact, the Roman tradition of lyric poetry practically began with Catullus. Prior to him, Roman poetry was ornate, artificial, and impersonal. In contrast, his poetry provides a vivid and lively account of Roman life which markedly offsets the actual violent and chaotic turmoil of Rome during Julius Caesar's tempestuous tenure. When Catullus and his contemporaries began writing c. 70 BC, they rejected Roman poetic tradition in favor of the Greek.

His single surviving manuscript was discovered in his hometown of Verona, Italy. Preserved are some 116 poems which cover a wide variety of themes, meters, and tones. The most popular group of his poems tells of his great love for Clodia, who was in real life married to a prominent Roman politician. Notorious for her liaisons with younger men, Clodia became the infamous Lesbia ("woman from the island of Lesbos") in his passionate love poems. He wrote about their affair from its spontaneous inception to its final disillusionment and impassioned end. Her name clearly recalls Sappho, the Greek poet and famous woman of Lesbos.

Undoubtedly using Sappho as a model, Catullus wrote intensely personal love lyrics that were often sensual, even erotic. This intentional rebellion against tradition was unprecedented. While the modern reader expects the poet's voice to be personal and introspective, this was not the case in antiquity, particularly in Rome. Catullus' admiration and imitation of Sappho, including his use of the Sapphic stanza, gave the Latin language a new lyrical power. His love poetry is filled with the raw emotions of a passionate yet doomed relationship, and there is an appealing candor in his ability to speak truthfully in first person, a distinctly Greek lyrical convention. Catullus vacillates between ecstasy and misery, sincere love and stormy infatuation, confidence and doubt, love and hate. The Lesbia of the early poems is a portrait of earthly perfection, whereas the Lesbia of the latter poems is a perfectly drawn "femme fatale." Some of the last poems in the series might even be described as invective, which leads to the second largest group of his poems.

Catullus even goes as far as to present not a few political heavyweights in unfavorable light. For example, he once launched a biting attack of corruption against a high-ranking and popular administrator under Julius Caesar. Moreover, during the turbulent years of the Republic, Catullus joined the faction that opposed Julius Caesar and referred to him as a "pathic Romulus" in one of his scorching satires. Remarkably, the poet was later pardoned by Julius Caesar for this obscenity. Other notable figures such as Socrates were similarly defiled in his verse. One recurring method of demeaning his political foes was to insult them sexually or to equate them with "mere women," a clear indication of the sexism of the times. In short, Catullus is as well known for his finely polished violations of good taste as he is for his sensitive celebration of the object of his affection.

If traditional Roman poetry was supposed to be didactic and focused on the Republic and its leaders, Catullus broke tradition to celebrate all that was un-Roman. For instance, rather than reinforce conventional morality, he wrote of extravagant living and of private pleasures and pain. Genuine grief and tenderness are present in his touching lament "the Farewell," addressed to his dead brother; it ends with the immortal phrase of *ave atque vale*, "hail and farewell." In all of his work is a sincere quality of self-revelation based on opposites that cause him to not only rage and rail but also love and lament. He can be the vengeful lover and contemptible critic or the genial friend and captivating charmer, extremes which seem to capture the poet perpetually. His realistic exuberance and polished simplicity have endeared him to modern readers. It is no wonder that Catullus' poetry has endured.

Selected Bibliography

Lee, Guy. *The Poems of Catullus*. Oxford: Oxford UP, 1990.

Wheeler, Arthur Leslie. *Catullus and the Traditions of Ancient Poetry*. Berkeley: U of California P, 1974.

Let Us Live and Love, My Lesbia

LET us live and love, my Lesbia, and a farthing for all the talk of morose old sages! Suns may set and rise again; but we, when once our brief light has set, must sleep through a perpetual night. Give me a thousand kisses, then a hundred, then another thousand, then a second hundred, then still another thousand, then a hundred. Then when we shall have made up many thousands, we will confuse the reckoning, so that we ourselves may not know their amount, nor any spiteful person have it in his power to envy us when he knows that our kisses were so many.

You Ask How Many Kisses of Yours, Lesbia, May Be Enough

YOU ask how many kisses of yours, Lesbia, may be enough for me, and more? As the numerous sands that lie on the spicy shores of Cyrene, between the oracle of sultry Jove and the sacred tomb of old Battus; or as the many stars that in the silence of night behold men's furtive amours; to kiss you with so many kisses is enough and more for madly fond Catullus; such a multitude as prying gossips can neither count, nor bewitch with their evil tongues.

Wretched Catullus, Cease Your Folly

WRETCHED Catullus, cease your folly, and look upon that as lost which you see has perished. Fair days shone once for you, when you bent your constant steps whither that girl drew them, who was loved by us as none ever will be loved. There all these merry things were done which you desired, and to which she was nothing loth. Fair days indeed shone for you *then*. Now she is not willing, be you too self-possessed, and follow not one who shuns you, nor lead a miserable life, but bear all with obstinacy, be obdurate. Farewell, girl; Catullus is now obdurate: he will neither seek you more, nor solicit your unwilling favours. But you will grieve, false one, when you shall not be entreated for a single night. What manner of life now remains for you? Who will visit you? Who will think you charming? Whom will you love now? Whose will you be called? Whom will you kiss? Whose lips will you bite? But you, Catullus, be stubbornly obdurate.

Were I Allowed to Kiss Your Sweet Eyes

WERE I allowed to kiss your sweet eyes without stint, I would kiss on and on up to three hundred thousand times; nor even then should I ever have enough, not though our crop of kissing were thicker than the dry ears of the corn-field.

He Seems to Me To Be Equal to a God

He seems to me to be equal to a god, he seems to me, if it be meet, to surpass the gods, who, sitting opposite thee, at once beholds thee and hears thy sweet laughter; but this takes away all my senses, wretch that I am; for, as soon as I have looked upon thee, Lesbia, there remains to me [*no voice*], but my tongue is paralysed; a subtle flame flows down through my limbs; my ears ring with their own sound; both my eyes are veiled in night.

Ease is baneful to thee, Catullus; thou revellest and delightest to excess in ease; *love of* ease has ere now destroyed kings and prosperous cities.

Wherefore, Catullus, Wherefore Dost Thou Delay?

Wherefore, Catullus, wherefore dost thou delay to die? Struma Nonius sits in the curule chair; Vatinius perjures himself in the consulship. Wherefore, Catullus, wherefore dost thou delay to die?

You Used Once To Say, Lesbia

You used once to say, Lesbia, that you knew none but *your own* Catullus, and that you would not prefer even Jove to me. I loved you then not merely as men commonly love a mistress, but as a father loves his sons and his sons-in-law. Now I know you. Wherefore though I burn for you more vehemently than ever, yet are you much more despicable and worthless in my eyes. How can this be? you ask. Because such wrongs *as mine* compel a lover to love more, but to like less.

No Woman Can Say Truly She Has Been Loved

No woman can say truly she has been loved so well as thou, my Lesbia, hast been loved by me. Never was so much faith observed in any compact as hath been manifested on my part in my love for thee. Now is my mind brought to this pass by thy perfidy, my Lesbia, and has so lost itself in its devotion to thee, that I can neither like thee, shouldst thou become faultless, nor cease to love thee, do what thou wilt.

If There Be Any Pleasure to a Man

IF there be any pleasure to a man in the remembrance of former good deeds, when he considers that his conduct is upright, and that be has not broken sacred faith, or abused the sanction of the gods, in any compact, to the deception of men; many delights remain in store for thee, Catullus, for long years to come, out of that ill-requited love of thine. For all the kindness that men can show to any one by word or deed, has been evinced in thy words and deeds; but all has been lavished in vain on a thankless mind. Why then torture thyself more? Why not summon up resolution enough to withdraw utterly from that *illusion*, and cease to be wretched in defiance of the gods? It is hard to put off suddenly a long-cherished love: it is hard, but do it how thou mayest. This is thine only safety; this must be achieved by thee; this thou shalt do, be it possible or impossible. O ye gods, if it is your attribute to have pity, or if ever you granted aid to mortals in the very crisis of mortal agony, look upon my misery; and if I have led a pure life, pluck from me this plague and destruction, which, creeping like a lethargy through every fibre of my frame, has expelled all gladness from my breast. I do not now ask that she may love me in return, or, what is impossible, that she should be chaste; I desire myself to be healed, and to cast off this dire disease. Grant me this, O gods, in reward of my piety.

Lesbia Says All Sorts of Abusive Things

LESBIA says all sorts of abusive things of me, when her husband is by, and this is a great delight to that numskull. Ass! do you not see that if she forgot me and said nothing, she would be all right? Whereas now she snarls and rails, she not only remembers, but what is worse, she is angry: that is to say, she is on fire and she speaks.

If Ever Any One Who Desires and Longs for Anything

IF ever any one who desires and longs for anything, but has no hope of it, obtains the object of his wishes, then is it peculiarly welcome to his soul: therefore it is welcome to me, and more precious than gold, that you, Lesbia, restore yourself to my longing breast. You restore yourself, and of your own accord give yourself back to me unexpectedly. O day of whiter mark! Who can say what happier man lives than I, or what there is more to be desired in. life than this?

If Your Hoary Age, Cominius

IF your hoary age, Cominius, defiled by foul habits, were to perish by the sentence of the people, I make no doubt but that your tongue, so hostile to the good, would be cut out and thrown to a vulture; the crow would pick out your eyes and swallow them down its black throat; dogs would devour your intestines, and wolves the rest of your carcase.

My Life, My Lesbia, You Profess That This Love

MY life, my Lesbia, you profess that this love of ours shall be mutually fond and perpetual. Great gods! grant that she may be able to promise truly, and that she say this sincerely and from her soul; that we may be permitted to maintain throughout our lives this hallowed bond of affection.

Virgil (70–19 BC)

Born on the 15th of October in the year 70 BC in a small township of northern Italy near Mantua, Publius Vergilius Maro grew up to be Rome's most celebrated poet. Virgil, as he is popularly known, produced his great epic the *Aeneid*, which is considered the national epic of Rome as well as a masterpiece of world literature.

Virgil's well-to-do father provided him with a liberal education in schools at Cremona, Milan, and Naples. He studied Greek literature, philosophy, and sciences. Virgil later studied rhetoric and philosophy at Rome. In his youth he wrote the "Ecologues" or "Bucolics" and quickly became known for his polished pastoral poetry. He was quite the man of culture. However, after losing his estate during civil war, Virgil was forced to depend upon the patronage of the governor. Even after his property was restored, Virgil was indebted to men in power. By then Virgil was living in Rome or Naples and had become one of the literary men who gathered in the circle of Maecenas, a powerful patron of the arts and something of an advisor to the young Octavian. After introducing Virgil to the future emperor, Maecenas urged him to begin writing patriotic poems. The result was the four books of the "Georgics," didactic poems on types of agriculture filled with the idealization of the Italian country and the states.

During Virgil's lifetime, Julius Caesar was murdered, and Augustus Caesar (Octavian) became the first of Rome's emperors. Virgil's association with the emperor, who also became a patron, profoundly influenced his fortunes and his career. The period which followed was a time of tremendous prosperity, peace, and expansion for Rome, and the era became known as the "Augustan Age" or the golden years of Rome. Virgil's genius and fortunes also reached a high point; in 30 BC during Virgil's fortieth year, he began writing his masterpiece the *Aeneid.* Almost a Roman bible, its purpose was to show that Rome's rise to power was part of a divine plan, that Augustus was a divinely appointed leader, and that, according to Virgil, Rome's mission was to usher in peace and civilization to the world.

For over a decade the poet continually revised the *Aeneid* while the literary circle and the emperor himself watched Virgil's progress with exceptional interest. Sadly, however, Virgil did not live to reap the rewards of his labor. He had become ill while visiting Greece and died on September 21st 19 BC before the *Aeneid* was completed. Deeply dissatisfied with what he considered the imperfection of the text, Virgil left precise instructions to burn the manuscript after his death. The intervention of Augustus Caesar prevented the poem from being destroyed, and Virgil's friends Varius and Tucca prepared the manuscript for publication. Its "political correctness" and literary merits catapulted the work to the stature of Rome's national epic, named after the hero Aeneas.

Selected Bibliography

Levi, Peter. *Virgil: His Life and Times.* New York: St. Martins, 1999.

Martindale, Charles. *The Cambridge Companion to Virgil.* Port Chester, NY: Cambridge UP, 1997.

The *Aeneid*: Background

If people were to reach into their wallets, pull out a dollar bill, and look closely at the back, they would encounter the Roman poet, Virgil. Notice the Latin inscriptions: "*novus ordo seclorum*" (new world order) and "e pluribus unum" (one from many). Written in the language that dominated Western learning for two thousand years, these quotes suggest a new world's ordering, an auspicious beginning for a new society which makes many cultures one political body. On the dollar, the words of the Great Seal of the United States are made the coin of the realm, the ideals which Americans want to believe and propagate. They are "propaganda" in the original Latin sense of the word. In many ways, Virgil's intent in writing them is a similar propaganda, an idealized account of the genesis, glory, power, and destiny of Caesar Augustus' Eternal Rome.

Virgil's subject in the *Aeneid* is the destruction of Troy, the seven-year wanderings of Aeneas, his settlement in Italy, the war he wages against the native tribes, and the events leading to the establishment of Rome. All of this is presented as the Manifest Destiny of a people selected by the gods for conquest and rule. As an epic, the *Aeneid* is modeled on Homer's the *Iliad* and the *Odyssey*, simply reversing, as many have said, the sequence of Homer's epics. Thus the *Aeneid* begins with an odyssey: the travels, the tales of adventures, marvels, temptations, and heroic deeds of its hero, Aeneas. A refugee in search of a homeland, Aeneas, like Odysseus, overcomes temptations and dangers with steadfast courage. Unlike the Homeric hero, Aeneas sacrifices his great passion, Dido, to his greater duty to Rome. The second half of the poem, like the *Iliad*, is an epic of battle, a war between the Trojans led by Aeneas and the Latins under Turnus. Virgil, with Homer as a model, created a new genre, the literary epic. Its inspirations are not the pre-existing oral folk traditions but self consciously modeled on classicaliterary sources. The poet thus simultaneously traces his literary roots to Homer even as the poem itself creates a Roman genealogy legitimized by Greek legend and divine authority. On a number of occasions, Virgil uses the *Aeneid* to comment directly on the power and glory of Rome's Golden Age under Augustus. On his journey through the underworld, for example, Aeneas is given glimpses of the future. He is shown Augustus Caesar, who will renew Latinium's golden age. Rome's way, Aeneas is told, will not be that of poets or priests but the way of warriors, conquerors, and administrators. It is in the tragic irony of Aeneas' vision that readers can perhaps best relate Virgil's "e pluribus unum" to the current century. Must there be a conquering to teach peace? Is dominance the same as or equivalent to peace? For the Romans, it was a one-way street. Virgil gives a second symbolic history lesson engraved on the shield the gods fashion for Aeneas. Here, in the center Augustus is triumphant. Around the edge are the conquered peoples of the Empire—yes, under the protective shield of Rome but at the cost of their freedom.

The Aeneid

Book IV

Now felt the Queen the sharp, slow-gathering pangs
Of love; and out of every pulsing vein
Nourished the wound and fed its viewless fire.
Her hero's virtues and his lordly line
Keep calling to her soul; his words, his glance
Cling to her heart like lingering, barbèd steel,
And rest and peace from her vexed body fly.

A new day's dawn with Phoebus' lamp divine
Lit up all lands, and from the vaulted heaven
Aurora had dispelled the dark and dew;
When thus unto the ever-answering heart
Of her dear sister spoke the stricken Queen:
"Anna, my sister, what disturbing dreams
"Perplex me and alarm? What guest is this
"New-welcomed to our house? How proud his mien!
"What dauntless courage and exploits of war!
"Sooth, I receive it for no idle tale
"That of the gods he sprang. 'Tis cowardice
"Betrays the base-born soul. Ah me! How fate
"Has smitten him with storms! What dire extremes
"Of war and horror in his tale he told!
"O, were it not immutably resolved
"In my fixed heart, that to no shape of man
"I would be wed again (since my first love
"Left me by death abandoned and betrayed);
"Loathed I not so the marriage torch and train,
"I could—who knows?—to this one weakness yield.
"Anna, I hide it not! But since the doom
"Of my ill-starred Sichæus, when our shrines
"Were by a brother's murder dabbled o'er,
"This man alone has moved me; he alone
"Has shaken my weak will. I seem to feel
"The motions of love's lost, familiar fire.
"But may the earth gape open where I tread,
"And may almighty Jove with thunder-scourge
"Hurl me to Erebus' abysmal shade,
"To pallid ghosts and midnight fathomless,
"Before, O Chastity! I shall offend
"Thy holy power, or cast thy bonds away!
"He who first mingled his dear life with mine
"Took with him all my heart. 'Tis is his alone
"O, let it rest beside him in the grave!"

She spoke: the bursting tears her breast o'erflowed.

"O dearer to thy sister than her life,"
Anna replied, "wouldst thou in sorrow's weed
"Waste thy long youth alone, nor ever know
"Sweet babes at thine own breast, nor gifts of love?
"Will dust and ashes, or a buried ghost,
"Reck what we do? 'T is true thy grieving heart
"Was cold to earlier wooers, Libya's now,
"And long ago in Tyre. Iarbas knew
"Thy scorn, and many a prince and captain bred
"In Afric's land of glory. Why resist
"A love that makes thee glad? Hast thou no care
"What alien lands are these where thou dost reign?
"Here are Gætulia's cities and her tribes
"Unconquered ever; on thy borders rove
"Numidia's uncurbed cavalry; here too
"Lies Syrtis' cruel shore, and regions wide
"Of thirsty desert, menaced everywhere
"By the wild hordes of Barca. Shall I tell
"Of Tyre's hostilities, the threats and rage
"Of our own brother? Friendly gods, I trow,
"Wafted the Teucrian ships, with Juno's aid,
"To these our shores. O sister, what a throne,
"And what imperial city shall be thine,
"If thus espoused! With Trojan arms allied
"How far may not our Punic fame extend
"In deeds of power? Call therefore on the gods
"To favor thee; and, after omens fair,
"Give queenly welcome, and contrive excuse
"To make him tarry, while yon wintry seas
"Are loud beneath Orion's stormful star,
"And on his battered ships the season frowns."

So saying, she stirred a passion-burning breast
To love more madly still; her words infused
A doubting mind with hope, and bade the blush
Of shame begone. First to the shrines they went
And sued for grace; performing sacrifice,
Choosing an offering of unblemished ewes,
To law-bestowing Ceres, to the god
Of light, to sire Lyæus, lord of wine;
But chiefly unto Juno, patroness
Of nuptial vows. There Dido, beauteous Queen,
Held forth in her right hand the sacred bowl,
And poured it full between the lifted horns
Of the white heifer; or on temple floors
She strode among the richly laden shrines,
The eyes of gods upon her, worshipping
With many a votive gift; or, peering deep
Into the victims' cloven sides, she read
The fate-revealing tokens trembling there.
How blind the hearts of prophets be! Alas!
Of what avail be temples and fond prayers
To change a frenzied mind? Devouring ever,
Love's fire burns inward to her bones; she feels
Quick in her breast the viewless, voiceless wound.

Ill-fated Dido ranges up and down
The spaces of her city, desperate,
Her life one flame—like arrow-stricken doe,
Through Cretan forest rashly wandering,
Pierced by a far-off shepherd, who pursues
With shafts, and leaves behind his light-winged steel,
Not knowing; while she scours the dark ravines
Of Dicte and its woodlands; at her heart
The mortal barb irrevocably clings.
Around her city's battlements she guides
Æneas, to make show of Sidon's gold,
And what her realm can boast; full oft her voice
Essays to speak and trembling dies away:
Or, when the daylight fades, she spreads anew
A royal banquet, and once more will plead,
Mad that she is, to hear the Trojan sorrow;
And with oblivious ravishment once more
Hangs on his lips who tells; or when her guests
Are scattered, and the wan moon's fading horn
Bedims its ray, while many a sinking star
Invites to slumber, there she weeps alone
In the deserted hall, and casts her down
On the cold couch he pressed. Her love from far
Beholds her vanished hero and receives
His voice upon her ears; or to her breast,
Moved by a father's image in his child,
She clasps Ascanius, seeking to deceive
Her unblest passion so. Her enterprise
Of tower and rampart stops: her martial host
No longer she reviews, nor fashions now
Defensive haven and defiant wall;
But idly all her half-built bastions frown,
And enginery of sieges, high as heaven.

But soon the chosen spouse of Jove perceived
The Queen's infection; and because the voice
Of honor to such frenzy spoke not, she,
Daughter of Saturn, unto Venus turned
And counselled thus: "How noble is the praise,
"How glorious the spoils of victory,
"For thee and for thy boy! Your names should be
"In lasting, vast renown—that by the snare
"Of two great gods in league one woman fell!
"It 'scapes me not that my protected realms
"Have ever been thy fear, and the proud halls
"Of Carthage thy vexation and annoy.
"Why further go? Prithee, what useful end
"Has our long war? Why not from this day forth
"Perpetual peace and nuptial amity?
"Hast thou not worked thy will? Behold and see
"How love-sick Dido burns, and all her flesh
"The madness feels! So let our common grace
"Smile on a mingled people! Let her serve
"A Phrygian husband, while thy hands receive
"Her Tyrian subjects for the bridal dower!"

In answer (reading the dissembler's mind
Which unto Libyan shores were fain to shift
Italia's future throne) thus Venus spoke:
"'Twere mad to spurn such favor, or by choice
"Be numbered with thy foes. But can it be
"That fortune on thy noble counsel smiles?
"To me Fate shows but dimly whether Jove
"Unto the Trojan wanderers ordains
"A common city with the sons of Tyre,
"With mingling blood and sworn, perpetual peace.
"His wife thou art; it is thy rightful due
"To plead to know his mind. Go, ask him, then!
"For humbly I obey!"

With instant word

Juno the Queen replied: "Leave that to me!
"But in what wise our urgent task and grave
"May soon be sped, I will in brief unfold
"To thine attending ear. A royal hunt
"In sylvan shades unhappy Dido gives
"For her Æneas, when to-morrow's dawn
"Uplifts its earliest ray and Titan's beam
"Shall first unveil the world. But I will pour
"Black storm-clouds with a burst of heavy hail
"Along their way; and as the huntsmen speed
"To hem the wood with snares, I will arouse
"All heaven with thunder. The attending train
"Shall scatter and be veiled in blinding dark,
"While Dido and her hero out of Troy
"To the same cavern fly. My auspices
"I will declare—if thou alike wilt bless;
"And yield her in true wedlock for his bride.
"Such shall their spousal be!" To Juno's will
Cythéra's Queen inclined assenting brow:
And laughed such guile to see.

Aurora rose,

And left the ocean's rim. The city's gates
Pour forth to greet the morn a gallant train
Of huntsmen, bearing many a woven snare
And steel-tipped javelin; while to and fro
Run the keen-scented dogs and Libyan squires.
The Queen still keeps her chamber; at her doors
The Punic lords await; her palfrey, brave
In gold and purple housing, paws the ground
And fiercely champs the foam-flecked bridle-rein.
At last, with numerous escort, forth she shines:
Her Tyrian pall is bordered in bright hues,
Her quiver, gold; her tresses are confined
Only with gold; her robes of purple rare
Meet in a golden clasp. To greet her come
The noble Phrygian guests; among them smiles
The boy Iulus; and in fair array
Æneas, goodliest of all his train.
In such a guise Apollo (when he leaves
Cold Lycian hills and Xanthus' frosty stream

To visit Delos to Latona dear)
Ordains the song, while round his altars cry
The choirs of many islands, with the pied,
Fantastic Agathyrsi; soon the god
Moves o'er the Cynthian steep; his flowing hair
He binds with laurel garland and bright gold;
Upon his shining shoulder as he goes
The arrows ring:—not less uplifted mien
Æneas wore; from his illustrious brow
Such beauty shone.
Soon to the mountains tall
The cavalcade comes nigh, to pathless haunts
Of woodland creatures; the wild goats are seen,
From pointed crag descending leap by leap
Down the steep ridges; in the vales below
Are routed deer, that scour the spreading plain,
And mass their dust-blown squadrons in wild flight,
Far from the mountain's bound. Ascanius,
Flushed with the sport, spurs on a mettled steed
From vale to vale, and many a flying herd
His chase outspeeds; but in his heart he prays
Among these tame things suddenly to see
A tusky boar, or, leaping from the hills,
A growling mountain-lion, golden-maned.

Meanwhile low thunders in the distant sky
Mutter confusedly; soon bursts in full
The storm-cloud and the hail. The Tyrian troop
Is scattered wide; the chivalry of Troy,
With the young heir of Dardan's kingly line,
Of Venus sprung, seek shelter where they may,
With sudden terror; down the deep ravines
The swollen torrents roar. In that same hour
Queen Dido and her hero out of Troy
To the same cavern fly. Old Mother-Earth
And wedlock-keeping Juno gave the sign;
The flash of lightnings on the conscious air
Lit them the bridal bed; along the hills
The wailing wood-nymphs sobbed a wedding song.
Such was that day of death, the source and spring
Of many a woe. For Dido took no heed
Of honor and good-name; nor did she mean
Her loves to hide; but called the lawless deed
A marriage, and with phrases veiled her shame.

Swift through the Libyan cities Rumor sped.
Rumor! What evil can surpass her speed?
In movement she grows mighty, and achieves
Strength and dominion as she swifter flies.
Small first, because afraid, she soon exalts
Her stature skyward, stalking through the lands
And mantling in the clouds her baleful brow.
The womb of Earth, in anger at high Heaven,
Bore her, they say, last of the Titan spawn,
Sister to Cœus and Enceladus.

Feet swift to run and pinions like the wind
The dreadful monster wears; her carcase huge
Is feathered, and at root of every plume
A peering eye abides; and, strange to tell,
An equal number of vociferous tongues,
Foul, whispering lips, and ears, that catch at all.
At night she spreads midway 'twixt earth and heaven
Her pinions in the darkness, hissing loud,
Nor e'er to happy slumber gives her eyes:
But with the morn she takes her watchful throne
High on the housetops or on lofty towers,
To terrify the nations. She can cling
To vile invention and malignant wrong,
Or mingle with her word some tidings true.

She now with changeful story filled men's ears,
Exultant, whether false or true she sung:
How, Trojan-born Æneas having come,
Dido, the lovely widow, looked his way,
Deigning to wed; how all the winter long
They passed in revel and voluptuous ease,
To dalliance given o'er; naught heeding now
Of crown or kingdom—shameless! lust-enslaved!
Such tidings broadcast on the lips of men
The filthy goddess spread; and soon she hied
To King Iarbas, where her hateful song
To newly-swollen wrath his heart inflamed.
Him the god Ammon got by forced embrace
Upon a Libyan nymph; his kingdoms wide
Possessed a hundred ample shrines to Jove,
A hundred altars whence ascended ever
The fires of sacrifice, perpetual seats
For a great god's abode, where flowing blood
Enriched the ground, and on the portals hung
Garlands of every flower. The angered King,
Half-maddened by malignant Rumor's voice,
Unto his favored altars came, and there,
Surrounded by the effluence divine,
Upraised in prayer to Jove his suppliant hands.
"Almighty Jupiter, to whom each day,
"At banquet on the painted couch reclined,
"Numidia pours libation! Do thine eyes
"Behold us? Or when out of yonder heaven,
"O sire, thou launchest the swift thunderbolt,
"Is it for naught we fear thee? Do the clouds
"Shoot forth blind fire to terrify the soul
"With wild, unmeaning roar? O, look upon
"That woman, who was homeless in our realm,
"And bargained where to build her paltry town,
Receiving fertile coastland for her farms,
By hospitable grant! She dares disdain
Our proffered nuptial vow. She has proclaimed
"Æneas partner of her bed and throne.
"And now that Paris, with his eunuch crew,
"Beneath his chin and fragrant, oozy hair

"Ties the soft Lydian bonnet, boasting well
"His stolen prize. But we to all these fanes,
"Though they be thine, a fruitless offering bring,
"And feed on empty tales our trust in thee."

As thus he prayed and to the altars clung,
Th' Omnipotent gave ear, and turned his gaze
Upon the royal dwelling, where for love
The amorous pair forgot their place and name.
Then thus to Mercury he gave command:
"Haste thee, my son, upon the Zephyrs call,
"And take thy wingèd way! My mandate bear
"Unto that prince of Troy who tarries now
"In Tyrian Carthage, heedless utterly
"Of empire Heaven-bestowed. On wingèd winds
"Hasten with my decrees. Not such the man
"His beauteous mother promised; not for this
"Twice did she shield him from the Greeks in arms:
"But that he might rule Italy, a land
"Pregnant with thrones and echoing with war;
"That he of Teucer's seed a race should sire,
"And bring beneath its law the whole wide world.
"If such a glory and event supreme
"Enkindle not his bosom; if such task
"To his own honor speak not; can the sire
"Begrudge Ascanius the heritage
"Of the proud name of Rome? What plans he now?
"What mad hope bids him linger in the lap
"Of enemies, considering no more
"The land Lavinian and Ausonia's sons.
"Let him to sea! Be this our final word:
"This message let our herald faithful bear."
He spoke. The god a prompt obedience gave
To his great sire's command. He fastened first
Those sandals of bright gold, which carry him
Aloft o'er land or sea, with airy wings
That race the fleeting wind; then lifted he
His wand, wherewith he summons from the grave
Pale-featured ghosts, or, if he will, consigns
To doleful Tartarus; or by its power
Gives slumber or dispels; or quite unseals
The eyelids of the dead: on this relying,
He routs the winds or cleaves th' obscurity
Of stormful clouds. Soon from his flight he spied
The summit and the sides precipitous
Of stubborn Atlas, whose star-pointing peak
Props heaven; of Atlas, whose pine-wreathèd brow
Is girdled evermore with misty gloom
And lashed of wind and rain; a cloak of snow
Melts on his shoulder; from his aged chin
Drop rivers, and ensheathed in stiffening ice
Glitters his great grim beard.

Here first was stayed

The speed of Mercury's well-poising wing;
Here making pause, from hence he headlong flung

His body to the sea; in motion like
Some sea-bird's, which along the levelled shore
Or round tall crags where rove the swarming fish,
Flies low along the waves: o'er-hovering so
Between the earth and skies, Cyllene's god
Flew downward from his mother's mountain-sire,
Parted the winds and skimmed the sandy marge
Of Libya. When first his wingèd feet
Came nigh the clay-built Punic huts, he saw
Æneas building at a citadel,
And founding walls and towers; at his side
Was girt a blade with yellow jaspers starred,
His mantle with the stain of Tyrian shell
Flowed purple from his shoulder, broidered fair
By opulent Dido with fine threads of gold,
Her gift of love; straightway the god began:
"Dost thou for lofty Carthage toil, to build
"Foundations strong? Dost thou, a wife's weak thrall,
"Build her proud city? Hast thou, shameful loss!
"Forgot thy kingdom and thy task sublime?
"From bright Olympus, I. He who commands
"All gods, and by his sovran deity
"Moves earth and heaven—he it was who bade
"Me bear on wingèd winds his high decree.
"What plan is thine? By what mad hope dost thou
"Linger so long in lap of Libyan land?
"If the proud guerdon of thy destined way
"Move not thy heart, if all the arduous toil
"To thine own honor speak not, look upon
"Iulus in his bloom, thy hope and heir
"Ascanius. It is his rightful due
"In Italy o'er Roman lands to reign."
After such word Cyllene's wingèd god
Vanished, and e'er his accents died away
Dissolved in air before the mortal's eyes.

Æneas at the sight stood terror-dumb
With choking voice and horror-rising hair.
He fain would fly at once and get him gone
From that voluptuous land, much wondering
At Heaven's wrathful word. Alas! how stir?
What cunning argument can plead his cause
Before th' infuriate Queen? How break such news?
Flashing this way and that, his startled mind
Makes many a project and surveys them all.
But, pondering well, his final counsel stopped
At this resolve: he summoned to his side
Mnestheus, Sergestus, and Serestus bold,
And bade them fit the fleet, all silently
Gathering the sailors and collecting gear,
But carefully dissembling what emprise
Such novel stir intends: himself the while
(Since high-born Dido dreamed not love so fond
Could have an end) would seek an audience,
At some indulgent time, and try what shift

Such matters may require. With joy they heard,
And wrought, assiduous, at their prince's plan.

But what can cheat true love? The Queen foreknew
His stratagem, and all the coming change
Perceived ere it began. Her jealous fear
Counted no hour secure. That unclean tongue
Of Rumor told her fevered heart the fleet
Was fitting forth, and hastening to be gone.
Distractedly she raved, and passion-tossed
Roamed through her city, like a Mænad roused
By the wild rout of Bacchus, when are heard
The third year's orgies, and the midnight scream
To cold Cithæron calls the frenzied crew.
Finding Æneas, thus her plaint she poured:
"Didst hope to hide it, false one, that such crime
"Was in thy heart,—to steal without farewell
"Out of my kingdom? Did our mutual joy
"Not move thee; nor thine own true promise given
"Once on a time? Nor Dido, who will die
"A death of sorrow? Why compel thy ships
"To brave the winter stars? Why off to sea
"So fast through stormy skies? O, cruelty!
"If Troy still stood, and if thou wert not bound
"For alien shore unknown, wouldst steer for Troy
"Through yonder waste of waves? Is it from me
"Thou takest flight? O, by these flowing tears,
"By thine own plighted word (for nothing more
"My weakness left to miserable me),
"By our poor marriage of imperfect vow,
"If aught to me thou owest, if aught in me
"Ever have pleased thee—O, be merciful
"To my low-fallen fortunes! I implore,
"If place be left for prayer, thy purpose change!
"Because of thee yon Libyan savages
"And nomad chiefs are grown implacable,
"And my own Tyrians hate me. Yes, for thee
"My chastity was slain and honor fair,
"By which alone to glory I aspired,
"In former days. To whom dost thou in death
"Abandon me? my guest!—since but this name
"Is left me of a husband! Shall I wait
"Till fell Pygmalion, my brother, raze
"My city walls? Or the Gætulian king,
"Iarbas, chain me captive to his car?
"O, if, ere thou hadst fled, I might but bear
"Some pledge of love to thee, and in these halls
"Watch some sweet babe Æneas at his play,
"Whose face should be the memory of thine own—
"I were not so forsaken, lost, undone!"

She said. But he, obeying Jove's decree,
Gazed steadfastly away; and in his heart
With strong repression crushed his cruel pain;
Then thus the silence broke: "O Queen, not one

"Of my unnumbered debts so strongly urged
"Would I gainsay. Elissa's memory
"Will be my treasure long as memory holds,
"Or breath of life is mine. Hear my brief plea!
"'Twas not my hope to hide this flight I take,
"As thou hast dreamed. Nay, I did never light
"A bridegroom's torch, nor gave I thee the vow
"Of marriage. Had my destiny decreed,
"That I should shape life to my heart's desire,
"And at my own will put away the weight
"Of toil and pain, my place would now be found
"In Troy, among the cherished sepulchres
"Of my own kin, and Priam's mansion proud
"Were standing still; or these my loyal hands
"'Had rebuilt Ilium for her vanquished sons.
"But now to Italy Apollo's power
"Commands me forth; his Lycian oracles
"Are loud for Italy. My heart is there,
"And there my fatherland. If now the towers
"Of Carthage and thy Libyan colony
"Delight thy Tyrian eyes; wilt thou refuse
"To Trojan exiles their Ausonian shore?
"I too by Fate was driven, not less than thou,
"To wander far a foreign throne to find.
"Oft when in dewy dark night hides the world,
"And flaming stars arise, Anchises' shade
"Looks on me in my dreams with angered brow.
"I think of my Ascanius, and the wrong
"To that dear heart, from whom I steal away
"Hesperia, his destined home and throne.
"But now the wingèd messenger of Heaven,
"Sent down by Jove (I swear by thee and me!),
"Has brought on wingèd winds his sire's command.
"My own eyes with unclouded vision saw
"The god within these walls; I have received
"With my own ears his word. No more inflame
"With lamentation fond thy heart and mine.
"'Tis is not my own free act seeks Italy."

She with averted eyes and glance that rolled
Speechless this way and that, had listened long
To his reply, till thus her rage broke forth:
"No goddess gave thee birth. No Dardanus
"Begot thy sires. But on its breast of stone
"Caucasus bore thee, and the tigresses
"Of fell Hyrcania to thy baby lip
"Their udders gave. Why should I longer show
"A lying smile? What worse can I endure?
"Did my tears draw one sigh? Did he once drop
" His stony stare? or did he yield a tear
"To my lament, or pity this fond heart?
"Why set my wrongs in order? Juno, now,
"And Jove, the son of Saturn, heed no more
" Where justice lies. No trusting heart is safe
"In all this world. That waif and castaway

"I found in beggary and gave him share—
"Fool that I was!—in my own royal glory.
"His lost fleet and his sorry crews I steered
"From death away. O, how my fevered soul
"Unceasing raves! Forsooth Apollo speaks!
"His Lycian oracles! and sent by Jove
"The messenger of Heaven on fleeting air
"The ruthless bidding brings! Proud business
"For gods, I trow, that such a task disturbs
"Their still abodes! I hold thee back no more,
"Nor to thy cunning speeches give the lie.
"Begone! Sail on to Italy, thy throne,
"Through wind and wave! I pray that, if there be
"Any just gods of power, thou mayest drink down
"Death on the mid-sea rocks, and often call
"With dying gasps on Dido's name—while I
"Pursue with vengeful fire. When cold death rends
"The body from the breath, my ghost shall sit
"Forever in thy path. Full penalties
"Thy stubborn heart shall pay. They'll bring me news
"In yon deep gulf of death of all thy woe."

Abrupt her utterance ceased; and sick at heart
She fled the light of day, as if to shrink
From human eyes, and left Æneas there
Irresolute with horror, while his soul
Framed many a vain reply. Her swooning shape
Her maidens to a marble chamber bore
And on her couch the helpless limbs reposed.

Æneas, faithful to a task divine,
Though yearning sore to remedy and soothe
Such misery, and with the timely word
Her grief assuage, and though his burdened heart
Was weak because of love, while many a groan
Rose from his bosom, yet no whit did fail
To do the will of Heaven, but of his fleet
Resumed command. The Trojans on the shore
Ply well their task and push into the sea
The lofty ships. Now floats the shining keel,
And oars they bring all leafy from the grove,
With oak half-hewn, so hurried was the flight.
Behold them how they haste—from every gate
Forth-streaming!—just as when a heap of corn
Is thronged with ants, who, knowing winter nigh,
Refill their granaries; the long black line
Runs o'er the levels, and conveys the spoil
In narrow pathway through the grass; a part
With straining and assiduous shoulder push
The kernels huge; a part array the file,
And whip the laggards on; their busy track
Swarms quick and eager with unceasing toil.
O Dido, how thy suffering heart was wrung,
That spectacle to see! What sore lament
Was thine, when from the towering citadel

The whole shore seemed alive, the sea itself
In turmoil with loud cries! Relentless Love,
To what mad courses may not mortal hearts
By thee be driven? Again her sorrow flies
To doleful plaint and supplication vain;
Again her pride to tyrant Love bows down,
Lest, though resolved to die, she fail to prove
Each hope of living: "O Anna, dost thou see
"Yon busy shore? From every side they come.
"Their canvas wooes the winds, and o'er each prow
"The merry seamen hang their votive flowers.
"Dear sister, since I did forebode this grief,
"I shall be strong to bear it. One sole boon
"My sorrow asks thee, Anna! Since of thee,
"Thee only, did that traitor make a friend,
"And trusted thee with what he hid so deep—
"The feelings of his heart; since thou alone
"Hast known what way, what hour the man would
yield
"To soft persuasion—therefore, sister, haste,
"And humbly thus implore our haughty foe:
"'I was not with the Greeks what time they swore
"'At Aulis to cut off the seed of Troy;
"'I sent no ships to Ilium. Pray, have I
"'Profaned Anchises' tomb, or vexed his shade?'
"Why should his ear be deaf and obdurate
"To all I say? What haste? May he not make
"One last poor offering to her whose love
"Is only pain? O, bid him but delay
"Till flight be easy and the winds blow fair.
"I plead no more that bygone marriage-vow
"By him forsworn, nor ask that he should lose
"His beauteous Latium and his realm to be.
"Nothing but time I crave! to give repose
"And more room to this fever, till my fate
"Teach a crushed heart to sorrow. I implore
"This last grace. (To thy sister's grief be kind!)
"I will requite with increase, till I die."

Such plaints, such prayers, again and yet again,
Betwixt the twain the sorrowing sister bore.
But no words move, no lamentations bring
Persuasion to his soul; decrees of Fate
Oppose, and some wise god obstructs the way
That finds the hero's ear. Oft-times around
The aged strength of some stupendous oak
The rival blasts of wintry Alpine winds
Smite with alternate wrath: loud is the roar,
And from its rocking top the broken boughs
Are strewn along the ground; but to the crag
Steadfast it ever clings; far as toward heaven.
Its giant crest uprears, so deep below
Its roots reach down to Tartarus:—not less
The hero by unceasing wail and cry
Is smitten sore, and in his mighty heart

Has many a pang, while his serene intent
Abides unmoved, and tears gush forth in vain.

Then wretched Dido, by her doom appalled,
Asks only death. It wearies her to see
The sun in heaven. Yet that she might hold fast
Her dread resolve to quit the light of day,
Behold, when on an incense-breathing shrine
Her offering was laid—O fearful tale!—
The pure libation blackened, and the wine
Flowed like polluting gore. She told the sight
To none, not even to her sister's ear.
A second sign was given: for in her house
A marble altar to her husband's shade,
With garlands bright and snowy fleeces dressed,
Had fervent worship; here strange cries were heard
As if her dead spouse called while midnight reigned,
And round her towers its inhuman song
The lone owl sang, complaining o'er and o'er
With lamentation and long shriek of woe.
Forgotten oracles by wizards told
Whisper old omens dire. In dreams she feels
Cruel Æneas goad her madness on,
And ever seems she, friendless and alone,
Some lengthening path to travel, or to seek
Her Tyrians through wide wastes of barren lands.
Thus frantic Pentheus flees the stern array
Of the Eumenides, and thinks to see
Two noonday lights blaze o'er his doubled Thebes;
Or murdered Agamemnon's haunted son,
Orestes, flees his mother's phantom scourge
Of flames and serpents foul, while at his door
Avenging horrors wait.

Now sorrow-crazed
And by her grief undone, resolved on death,
The manner and the time her secret soul
Prepares, and, speaking to her sister sad,
She masks in cheerful calm her fatal will:
"I know a way—O, wish thy sister joy!—
"To bring him back to love, or set me free.
"On Ocean's bound and next the setting sun
"Lies the last Æthiop land, where Atlas tall
"Lifts on his shoulder the wide wheel of heaven,
"Studded with burning stars. From thence is come
"A witch, a priestess, a Numidian crone,
"Who guards the shrine of the Hesperides
"And feeds the dragon; she protects the fruit
"Of that enchanting tree, and scatters there
"Her slumb'rous poppies mixed with honey-dew.
"Her spells and magic promise to set free
"What hearts she will, or visit cruel woes
"On men afar. She stops the downward flow
"Of rivers, and turns back the rolling stars;
"On midnight ghosts she calls: her vot'ries hear
"Earth bellowing loud below, while from the hills

"The ash-trees travel down. But, sister mine,
"Thou knowest, and the gods their witness give,
"How little mind have I to don the garb
"Of sorcery. Depart in secret, thou,
"And bid them build a lofty funeral pyre
"Inside our palace-wall, and heap thereon
"The hero's arms, which that blasphemer hung
"Within my, chamber; every relic bring,
"And chiefly that ill-omened nuptial bed,
"My death and ruin! For I must blot out
"All sight and token of this husband vile.
"'Tis what the witch commands." She spoke no more,
And pallid was her brow. Yet Anna's mind
Knew not what web of death her sister wove
By these strange rites, nor what such frenzy dares;
Nor feared she worse than when Sichæus died,
But hied her forth the errand to fulfil.

Soon as the funeral pyre was builded high
In a sequestered garden, looming huge
With boughs of pine and faggots of cleft oak,
The queen herself enwreathed it with sad flowers
And boughs of mournful shade; and crowning all
She laid on nuptial bed the robes and sword
By him abandoned; and stretched out thereon
A mock Æneas;—but her doom she knew.
Altars were there; and with loose locks unbound
The priestess with a voice of thunder called
Three hundred gods, Hell, Chaos, the three shapes
Of triple Hecate, the faces three
Of virgin Dian. She aspersed a stream
From dark Avernus drawn, she said; soft herbs
Were cut by moonlight with a blade of bronze,
Oozing, black poison-sap; and she had plucked
That philter from the forehead of new foal
Before its dam devours. Dido herself,
Sprinkling the salt meal, at the altar stands;
One foot unsandalled, and with cincture free,
On all the gods and fate-instructed stars,
Foreseeing death, she calls. But if there be
Some just and not oblivious power on high,
Who heeds when lovers plight unequal vow,
To that god first her supplications rise.

Soon fell the night, and peaceful slumbers breathed
On all earth's weary creatures; the loud seas
And babbling forests entered on repose;
Now midway in their heavenly course the stars
Wheeled silent on; the outspread lands below
Lay voiceless; all the birds of tinted wing,
And flocks that haunt the marge of waters wide
Or keep the thorny wold, oblivious lay
Beneath the night so still; the stings of care
Ceased troubling, and no heart its burden knew.
Not so the Tyrian Queen's deep-grieving soul!

To sleep she could not yield; her eyes and heart
Refused the gift of night; her suffering
Redoubled, and in full returning tide
Her love rebelled, while on wild waves of rage
She drifted to and fro. So, ceasing not
From sorrow, thus she brooded on her wrongs:
"What refuge now? Shall I invite the scorn
"Of my rejected wooers, or entreat
"Of some disdainful, nomad blackamoor
"To take me to his bed—though many a time
"Such husbands I made mock of? Shall I sail
"On Ilian ships away, and sink to be
"The Trojans' humble thrall? Do they rejoice
"That once I gave them bread? Lives gratitude
"In hearts like theirs for bygone kindnesses?
"O who, if so I stooped, would deign to bear
"On yon proud ships the scorned and fallen Queen?
"Lost creature! Woe betide thee! Knowest thou not
"The perjured children of Laomedon?
"What way is left? Should I take flight alone
"And join the revelling sailors? Or depart
"With Tyrians, the whole attending train
"Of my own people? Hard the task to force
"Their hearts from Sidon's towers; how once more
"Compel to sea, and bid them spread the sail?
"Nay, perish! Thou hast earned it. Let the sword
"From sorrow save thee! Sister of my blood—
"Who else but thee,—by my own tears borne down,
"Didst heap disaster on my frantic soul,
"And fling me to this foe? Why could I not
"Pass wedlock by, and live a blameless life
"As wild things do, nor taste of passion's pain?
"But I broke faith! I cast the vows away
"Made at Sichæus' grave." Such loud lament
Burst from her breaking heart with doleful sound.

Meanwhile Æneas on his lofty ship,
Having made ready all, and fixed his mind
To launch away, upon brief slumber fell.
But the god came; and in the self-same guise
Once more in monitory vision spoke,—
All guised as Mercury,—his voice, his hue,
His golden locks, and young limbs strong and fair.
"Hail, goddess-born! Wouldst linger on in sleep
"At such an hour? Nor seest thou the snares
"That hem thee round? Nor hearest thou the voice
"Of friendly zephyrs calling? Senseless man!
"That woman's breast contrives some treachery
"And horrid stroke; for, resolute to die,
"She drifts on swollen floods of wrath and scorn.
"Wilt thou not fly before the hastening hour
"Of flight is gone? To-morrow thou wilt see
"Yon waters thronged with ships, the cruel glare
"Of fire-brands, and yonder shore all flame,
"If but the light of morn again surprise

"Thee loitering in this land. Away! Away!
"Stay not! A mutable and shifting thing
"Is woman ever."
Such command he spoke,
Then melted in. the midnight dark away.
Æneas, by that fleeting vision struck
With an exceeding awe, straightway leaped forth
From slumber's power, and to his followers cried:
"Awake, my men! Away! Each to his place
"Upon the thwarts! Unfurl at once the sails!
"A god from heaven a second time sent down
"Urges our instant flight, and bids us cut
"The twisted cords. Whatever be thy name,
"Behold, we come, O venerated Power!
"Again with joy we follow! Let thy grace
"Assist us as we go! And may thy power
"Bring none but stars benign across our sky."
So saying, from its scabbard forth he flashed
The lightning of his sword, with naked blade
Striking the hawsers free. Like ardor seized
On all his willing men, who raced and ran;
And, while their galleys shadowed all the sea,
Clean from the shore they scudded, with strong
strokes
Sweeping the purple waves and crested foam.

Aurora's first young beams to earth were pouring
As from Tithonus' saffron bed she sprang;
While from her battlements the wakeful Queen
Watched the sky brighten, saw the mated sails
Push forth to sea, till all her port and strand
Held not an oar or keel. Thrice and four times
She smote her lovely breast with wrathful hand,
And tore her golden hair. "Great Jove," she cries,
"Shall that departing fugitive make mock
"Of me, a queen? Will not my men-at-arms
"Draw sword, give chase, from all my city thronging?
"Down from the docks, my ships! Out, out! Begone!
"Take fire and sword! Bend to your oars, ye slaves!
"What have I said? Where am I? What mad thoughts
"Delude this ruined mind? Woe unto thee,
"Thou wretched Dido, now thy impious deeds
"Strike back upon thee. Wherefore struck they not,
"As was most fit, when thou didst fling away
"Thy sceptre from thy hand? O lying oaths!
"O faith forsworn! of him who brings, they boast,
"His father's gods along, and bowed his back
"To lift an age-worn sire! Why dared I not
"Seize on him, rend his body limb from limb,
"And hurl him piecemeal on the rolling sea?
"Or put his troop of followers to the sword,
"Ascanius too, and set his flesh before
"That father for a feast? Such fearful war
"Had been of doubtful issue. Be it so!
"What fears a woman dying? Would I had

"Attacked their camp with torches, kindled flame
"From ship to ship, until that son and sire,
"With that whole tribe, were unto ashes burned
"In one huge holocaust—myself its crown!
"Great orb of light whose holy beam surveys
"All earthly deeds! Great Juno, patroness
"Of conjugal distress, who knowest all!
"Pale Hecate, whose name the witches cry
"At midnight crossways! O avenging furies!
"O gods that guard Queen Dido's dying breath!
"Give ear, and to my guiltless misery
"Extend your power. Hear me what I pray!
"If it be fated that yon creature curst
"Drift to the shore and happy haven find,
"If Father Jove's irrevocable word
"Such goal decree—there may he be assailed
"By peoples fierce and bold. A banished man,
"From his Iulus' kisses sundered far,
"May his own eyes see miserably slain
"His kin and kind, and sue for alien arms.
"Nor when he basely bows him to receive
"Terms of unequal peace, shall he be blest
"With sceptre or with life; but perish there
"Before his time, and lie without a grave
"Upon the barren sand. For this I pray.
"This dying word is flowing from my heart
"With my spilt blood. And—O ye Tyrians!
"Sting with your hatred all his seed and tribe
"Forevermore. This is the offering
"My ashes ask. Betwixt our nations twain,
"No love! No truce or amity! Arise,
"Out of my dust, unknown Avenger, rise!
"To harry and lay waste with sword and flame
"Those Dardan settlers, and to vex them sore,
"To-day, to-morrow, and as long as power
"Is thine to use! My dying curse arrays
"Shore against shore and the opposing seas
"In shock of arms with arms. May living foes
"Pass down from sire to son insatiate war!"

She said. From point to point her purpose flew,
Seeking without delay to quench the flame
Of her loathed life. Brief bidding she addressed
To Barce then, Sichæus' nurse (her own
Lay dust and ashes in a lonely grave
Beside the Tyrian shore), "Go, nurse, and call
"My sister Anna! Bid her quickly bathe
"Her limbs in living water, and procure
"Due victims for our expiating fires.
"Bid her make haste. Go, bind on thy own brow
"The sacred fillet. For to Stygian Jove
"It is my purpose now to consummate
"The sacrifice ordained, ending my woe,
"And touch with flame the Trojan's funeral pyre."

The aged crone to do her bidding ran
With trembling zeal. But Dido (horror-struck
At her own dread design, unstrung with fear,
Her bloodshot eyes wide-rolling, and her cheek
Twitching and fever-spotted, her cold brow
Blanched with approaching death)—sped past the doors
Into the palace garden; there she leaped,
A frenzied creature, on the lofty pyre
And drew the Trojan's sword; a gift not asked
For use like this! When now she saw the garb
Of Ilian fashion, and the nuptial couch
She knew too well, she lingered yet awhile
For memory and tears, and, falling prone
On that cold bed, outpoured a last farewell:
"Sweet relics! Ever dear when Fate and Heaven
"Upon me smiled, receive my parting breath,
"And from my woe set free! My life is done.
"I have accomplished what my lot allowed;
"And now my spirit to the world of death
"In royal honor goes. The founder I
"Of yonder noble city, I have seen
"Walls at my bidding rise. I was avenged
"For my slain husband: I chastised the crimes
"Of our injurious brother. Woe is me!
"Blest had I been, beyond deserving blest,
"If but the Trojan galleys ne'er had moored
"Upon my kingdom's bound!" So saying, she pressed
One last kiss on the couch. "Though for my death
No vengeance fall, O, give me death!" she cried.
"O thus! O thus! it is my will to take
"The journey to the dark. From yonder sea
"May his cold Trojan eyes discern the flames
"That make me ashes! Be this cruel death
"His omen as he sails!"

She spoke no more.

But almost ere she ceased, her maidens all
Thronged to obey her cry, and found their Queen
Prone fallen on the sword, the reeking steel
Still in her bloody hands. Shrill clamor flew
Along the lofty halls; wild rumor spread
Through the whole smitten city; loud lament,
Groans and the wail of women echoed on
From roof to roof, and to the dome of air
The noise of mourning rose. Such were the cry
If a besieging, host should break the walls
Of Carthage or old Tyre, and wrathful flames
O'er towers of kings and worshipped altars roll.
Her sister heard. Half in a swoon, she ran
With trembling steps, where thickest was the throng,
Beating her breast, while with a desperate hand
She tore at her own face, and called aloud
Upon the dying Queen. "Was it for this
"My own true sister used me with such guile?
"O, was this horrid deed the dire intent

"Of altars, lofty couch, and funeral fires?
"What shall I tell for chiefest of my woes?
"Lost that I am! Why, though in death, cast off
"Thy sister from thy heart? Why not invite
"One mortal stroke for both, a single sword,
"One agony together? But these hands
"Built up thy pyre; and my voice implored
"The blessing of our gods, who granted me
"That thou shouldst perish thus—and I not know!"
"In thy self-slaughter, sister, thou hast slain
"Myself, thy people, the grave counsellors
"Of Sidon, and yon city thou didst build
"To be thy throne!—Go, fetch me water, there!
"That I may bathe those gashes! If there be
"One hovering breath that stays, let my fond lips
"Discover and receive!"
So saying, she sprang up
From stair to stair, and, clasping to her breast
Her sister's dying form, moaned grievously,
And staunched the dark blood with her garment's fold.
Vainly would Dido lift her sinking eyes,
But backward fell, while at her heart the wound
Opened afresh; three times with straining arm
She rose; three times dropped helpless, her dimmed eyes
Turned skyward, seeking the sweet light of day,
Which when she saw, she groaned.
Great Juno then
Looked down in mercy on that lingering pain
And labor to depart: from realms divine
She sent the goddess of the rainbow wing,
Iris, to set the struggling spirit free
And loose its fleshly coil. For since the end
Came not by destiny, nor was the doom
Of guilty deed, but of a hapless wight
To sudden madness stung, ere ripe to die,
Therefore the Queen of Hades had not shorn
The fair tress from her forehead, nor assigned
That soul to Stygian dark. So Iris came
On dewy, saffron pinions down from heaven,
A thousand colors on her radiant way,
From the opposing sun. She stayed her flight
Above that pallid brow: "I come with power
"To make this gift to Death. I set thee free
From thy frail body's bound." With her right hand
She cut the tress: then through its every limb
The sinking form grew cold; the vital breath
Fled forth, departing on the viewless air.

Medieval Literature

Although the Middle Ages are generally regarded to span the years AD 500–1500, from the collapse of the Roman Empire to the discovery of the Americas and the invention of the printing press, medieval poetry flourished in Europe during the latter part of that period, from the eleventh century—the time of the Norman conquest of England and the Crusades—to the late fourteenth or early fifteenth century. Thematically, the poetry reflected the Christian dominance of European civilization, including the consideration of humankind's place in the divinely created universe and the importance of personal devotion to God. The pagan warrior-hero of earlier ages, the Anglo-Saxon hero Beowulf and the Norse hero Sigemund, had been transformed into the hero of the *Song of Roland,* who was now fighting in the Crusades or the knight of the courtly romance, who practiced Christianity, courtesy, and honor. In addition, the partial fusion of Anglo-Saxon, Germanic, Norman (French), and Italian cultures, which had taken place through conquest and commerce, produced an international art and literature; tradesmen, monks, and civil servants traveled freely throughout Europe and were influenced by foreign cultures. Chaucer (1340–1400), for example, journeyed several times to France and Italy as the king's envoy. In later years he translated the French allegorical romance *Roman de la Rose* and borrowed the light didacticism and style of the work for his own *House of Fame* and *Parliament of Fowles* and used Boccaccio's *Il Filostrato* as a source for *Troilus and Crysede.* There was also a renewed interest in classical Greek and Roman culture; as a result, the period's greatest writers used classical characters and themes as bases for their own unique poetic works. Dante (1265–1321), in fact, held the Roman poet Virgil in such esteem that he used the poet's ghost as the narrator's guide to the underworld realms in the *Divine Comedy.* Finally, the Medieval Period marked the development or evolution of a number of literary forms, among them the ballade, the sonnet, the allegory, and the romance. The ballade and the sonnet codified the forms in which the personal lyric was written, while the allegory and romance, sometimes interconnected genres, redefined the nature of the extended narrative which, in its most extreme form, had been the epic.

Medieval Theater

There are many reasons for the theater being less than a dominant literary form during the Medieval Period. In the transition from the Heroic Age to the Medieval Age, the most important shift in focus is from the warrior or knight to the saint. The Church set its rigid standards to enforce orthodoxy, and theater was associated with paganism. Yet, ironically, it was the Church that led to a rebirth of theater in the Medieval World. In the re-enactments of special holidays in the Church calendar, the Church adapted the theater for its own uses. These liturgical dramas, such as the Ascension, the Nativity or the Easter Passion, eventually moved out of the Church and became a part of the theater of the people. The language of the Church, Latin, was mixed with the vernacular. The Church used dramas to educate a large public that could not read. In 1264, Pope Urban IV, upon his death, instituted the festival of Corpus Christi in honor of the Blessed Sacrament. The Church had now begun its fruitful tradition as a patron of the arts. These sacred stories presented, dramatically developed, into the first drama of the Medieval World. Theater became one of the most effective and compelling ways to teach moral lessons.

Two types of dramas were written during the Medieval Period, both growing out of the ritual of the Mass itself as a kind of drama. *Miracles* was the general name for plays based on the Scriptures. *Moralities* developed later and were more didactic religious allegories. Miracle plays are dramas associated with particular locales such as the *Cornwall Cycle* (late 13th century), the *York Cycle* (1350–1440), the *Chester Cycle* (1475–1500) and the *Wakefield Cycle* (mid-fifteenth century). The most famous morality play is *Everyman*. Other titles are the *Castle of Perseverance* (c.1425), *Mankind* (c. 1475), and John Skelton's *Magnyfycence* (1516).

Everyman: Background

Everyman is an English *morality* play, a type of play which reached its vogue during the fifteenth and sixteenth centuries. Although drama was not a dominant literary form during the Medieval Period, in England drama was quite popular. Its earliest forms were associated with the liturgy of the Church. Thus, there were plays about the Nativity or some other church feast holiday. Since these plays were based closely on the stories of the Bible, they are known as *miracle* plays. England produced both miracle plays and morality plays. Originating in France, morality plays also developed about the same time, but they differ from miracle plays in that they dramatize the sermons or homilies of the Church. Although morality plays have a religious intent, they are more poetic in nature. As an early form of poetic drama, morality plays depict characters as personifications of abstract qualities, or they are generalizations. Thus, morality plays can be thought of as an allegorized drama.

Everyman is the best known morality play. It depicts man's progress through life; he is "every" man and represents all humanity. The characters he meets are personified virtues and vices. Although this might suggest a certain dullness, the reader should realize that the characters are both representations of "abstractions" and yet convincingly "realistic."

The morality play became less popular during the Elizabethan period. The sparseness of which *Everyman* is so indicative became less apparent in later morality plays. They were loaded down with much farcical material that would later give birth to the tradition of English comedy.

Everyman

CHARACTERS

MESSENGER
GOD
DEATH
EVERYMAN
FELLOWSHIP
COUSIN
KINDRED
GOODS
DOCTOR
GOOD DEEDS
KNOWLEDGE
CONFESSION
BEAUTY
STRENGTH
DISCRETION
FIVE WITS
ANGEL

Here beginneth a treatise how the High Father of Heaven sendeth Death to summon every creature to come and give account of their lives in this world, and is in manner of a moral play

[*Enter* MESSENGER *as Prologue.*]

MESSENGER. I pray you all give your audience,
And hear this matter with reverence,
By figure a moral play;
The *Summoning of Everyman* called it is,
That of our lives and ending shows
How transitory we be all day.
This matter is wondrous precious,
But the intent of it is more gracious,
And sweet to bear away.
The story saith: Man, in the beginning,
Look well, and take good heed to the ending,
Be you never so gay!
Ye think sin in the beginning full sweet,
Which in the end causeth thy soul to weep,
When the body lieth in clay.
Here shall you see how Fellowship and jollity,
Both Strength, Pleasure, and Beauty,
Will fade from thee as flower in May.
For ye shall hear how our Heaven King
Calleth Everyman to a general reckoning.
Give audience, and hear what he doth say.
[*Exit.*]

[GOD *speaketh*]

GOD. I perceive here in my majesty,
How that all creatures be to me unkind,
Living without dread in worldly prosperity;
Of ghostly sight the people be so blind,
Drowned in sin, they know me not for their God.
In worldly riches is all their mind,
They fear not my rightwiseness, the sharp rod;
My love that I showed when I for them died
They forget clean, and shedding of my blood red;
I hanged between two, it cannot be denied;

To get them life I suffered to be dead;
I healed their feet, with thorns hurt was my head.
I could do no more than I did, truly;
And now I see the people do clean forsake me.
They use the seven deadly sins damnable;
As pride, covetise, wrath, and lechery,
Now in the world be made commendable;
And thus they leave of angels the heavenly
company.
Everyman liveth so after his own pleasure,
And yet of their life they be nothing sure.
I see the more that I them forbear
The worse they be from year to year;
All that liveth appaireth fast.
Therefore I will in all the haste
Have a reckoning of Everyman's person;
For and I leave the people thus alone
In their life and wicked tempests,
Verily they will become much worse than beasts;
For now one would by envy another up eat;
Charity they all do clean forget.
I hoped well that Everyman
In my glory should make his mansion,
And thereto I had them all elect;
But now I see, like traitors deject,
They thank me not for the pleasure that I to them
meant,
Nor yet for their being that I them have lent.
I proffered the people great multitude of mercy,
And few there be that asketh it heartily;
They be so cumbered with worldly riches,
That needs on them I must do justice,
On Everyman living without fear.
Where art thou, Death, thou mighty messenger?
[*Enter* DEATH.]

DEATH. Almighty God, I am here at your will,
Your commandment to fulfil.

GOD. Go thou to Everyman,
And show him, in my name,
A pilgrimage he must on him take,
Which he in no wise may escape;
And that he bring with him a sure reckoning
Without delay or any tarrying.

DEATH. Lord, I will in the world go run over all,
And cruelly out search both great and small.
Every man will I beset that liveth beastly
Out of God's laws, and dreadeth not folly,
He that loveth riches I will strike with my dart,
His sight to blind, and from heaven to depart,
Except that alms-deeds be his good friend.
In hell for to dwell, world without end.
[EVERYMAN *enters, at a distance.*]
Lo, yonder I see Everyman walking;
Full little he thinketh on my coming;
His mind is on fleshly lusts and his treasure,

And great pain it shall cause him to endure
Before the Lord, Heaven King.
Everyman, stand still; whither art thou going
Thus gaily? Hast thou thy Maker forgot?

EVERYMAN. Why askest thou?
Wouldest thou wete?

DEATH. Yea, sir, I will show you;
In great haste I am sent to thee
From God, out of his majesty.

EVERYMAN. What, sent to me?

DEATH. Yea, certainly.
Though thou have forgot him here,
He thinketh on thee in the heavenly sphere,
As, ere we depart, thou shalt know.

EVERYMAN. What desirest God of me?

DEATH. That shall I show thee;
A reckoning he will needs have
Without any longer respite.

EVERYMAN. To give a reckoning longer leisure I crave;
This blind matter troubleth my wit.

DEATH. On thee thou must take a long journey,
Therefore thy book of count with thee thou bring;
For turn again thou can not by no way.
And look thou be sure of thy reckoning;
For before God thou shalt answer, and show
Thy many bad deeds, and good but a few,
How thou hast spent thy life, and in what wise,
Before the chief Lord of paradise.
Have ado that we were in that way,
For, wete thou well, thou shalt make none attournay.

EVERYMAN. Full unready I am such reckoning to give.
I know thee not. What messenger art thou?

DEATH. I am Death, that no man dreadeth.
For every man I rest and no man spareth;
For it is God's commandment
That all to me should be obedient.

EVERYMAN. O Death, thou comest when I had thee least in mind;
In thy power it lieth me to save,
Yet of my good will I give thee, if ye will be kind;
Yea, a thousand pound shalt thou have,
And defer this matter till another day.

DEATH. Everyman, it may not be by no way;
I set not by gold, silver, nor riches,
Nor by pope, emperor, king, duke, nor princes.
For and I would receive gifts great,
All the world I might get;
But my custom is clean contrary.
I give thee no respite. Come hence, and not tarry.

EVERYMAN. Alas, shall I have no longer respite?
I may say Death giveth no warning.
To think on thee, it maketh my heart sick,
For all unready is my book of reckoning.
But twelve year and I might have abiding,

My counting-book, I would make so clear,
That my reckoning I should not need to fear.
Wherefore, Death, I pray thee, for God's mercy,
Spare me till I be provided of remedy.

DEATH. Thee availeth not to cry, weep, and pray;
But haste thee lightly that you were gone the journey,
And prove thy friends if thou can.
For, wete thou well, the tide abideth no man;
And in the world each living creature
For Adam's sin must die of nature.

EVERYMAN. Death, if I should this pilgrimage take,
And my reckoning surely make,
Show me, for saint charity,
Should I not come again shortly?

DEATH. No, Everyman; and thou be once there,
Thou mayst never more come here,
Trust me verily.

EVERYMAN. O gracious God, in the high seat celestial,
Have mercy on me in this most need;
Shall I have no company from this vale terrestrial
Of mine acquaintance that way me to lead?

DEATH. Yea, if any be so hardy,
That would go with thee and bear thee company.
Hie thee that you were gone to God's magnificence,
Thy reckoning to give before his presence.
What, weenest thou thy life is given thee,
And thy worldly goods also?

EVERYMAN. I had weened so, verily.

DEATH. Nay, nay; it was but lent thee;
For as soon as thou art gone,
Another a while shall have it, and then go therefrom
Even as thou hast done.
Everyman, thou art mad; thou hast thy wits five,
And here on earth will not amend thy life;
For suddenly I do come.

EVERYMAN. O wretched caitiff, whither shall I flee,
That I might 'scape this endless sorrow!
Now, gentle Death, spare me till tomorrow,
That I may amend me
With good advisement.

DEATH. Nay, thereto I will not consent,
Nor no man will I respite,
But to the heart suddenly I shall smite
Without any advisement.
And now out of thy sight I will me hie;
See thou make thee ready shortly,
For thou mayst say this is the day
That no man living may 'scape away. *[Exit.]*

EVERYMAN. Alas, I may well weep with sighs deep;
Now have I no manner of company
To help me in my journey and me to keep;
And also my writing is full unready.

How shall I do now for to excuse me?
I would to God I had never be gete!
To my soul a full great profit it had be;
For now I fear pains huge and great.
The time passeth; Lord, help, that all wrought;
For though I mourn it availeth naught.
The day passeth, and is almost a-gone;
I wot not well what for to do.
To whom were I best my complaint to make?
What and I to Fellowship thereof spake,
And showed him of this sudden chance?
For in him is all mine affiance;
We have in the world so many a day
Been good friends in sport and play.
I see him' yonder, certainly;
I trust that he will bear me company;
Therefore to him will I speak to ease my sorrow.
[*Enter* FELLOWSHIP.]
Well met, good Fellowship, and good morrow!

FELLOWSHIP. Everyman, good morrow; by this day,
Sir, why lookest thou so piteously?
If any thing be amiss, pray thee, me say,
That I may help to remedy.

EVERYMAN. Yea, good Fellowship, yea,
I am in great jeopardy.

FELLOWSHIP. My true friend, show to me your mind;
I will not forsake thee, unto my life's end, In the way of good company.

EVERYMAN. That is well spoken, and lovingly.

FELLOWSHIP. Sir, I must needs know your heaviness;
I have pity to see you in any distress;
If any have you wronged ye shall revenged be,
Though I on the ground be slain for thee,
Though that I know before that I should die.

EVERYMAN. Verily, Fellowship, gramercy.

FELLOWSHIP. Tush! by thy thanks I set not a straw.
Show me your grief, and say no more.

EVERYMAN. If I my heart should to you break,
And then you to turn your mind from me,
And would not me comfort when you hear me speak,
Then should I ten times sorrier be.

FELLOWSHIP. Sir, I say as I will do in deed.

EVERYMAN. Then be you a good friend at need;
I have found you true here before.

FELLOWSHIP. And so ye shall evermore;
For, in faith, and thou go to hell
I will not forsake thee by the way!

EVERYMAN. Ye speak like a good friend; I believe you well;
I shall deserve it, and I may.

FELLOWSHIP. I speak of no deserving, by this day.
For he that will say and nothing do
Is not worthy with good company to go;
Therefore show me the grief of your mind,
As to your friend most loving and kind.

EVERYMAN. I shall show you how it is;
Commanded I am to go a journey,
A long way, hard and dangerous,
And give a strait count without delay
Before the high judge Adonai.
Wherefore, I pray you, bear me company,
As ye have promised, in this journey.

FELLOWSHIP. That is matter indeed! Promise is duty;
But, and I should take such a voyage on me.
I know it well, it should be to my pain.
Also it maketh me afeared, certain.
But let us take counsel here as well as we can,
For your words would fear a strong man.

EVERYMAN. Why, ye said if I had need,
Ye would me never forsake, quick nor dead,
Though it were to hell, truly.

FELLOWSHIP. So I said, certainly,
But such pleasures be set aside, thee sooth to say.
And also, if we took such a journey,
When should we come again?

EVERYMAN. Nay, never again till the day of doom.

FELLOWSHIP. In faith, then will not I come there!
Who hath you these tidings brought?

EVERYMAN. Indeed, Death was with me here.

FELLOWSHIP. Now, by God that all hath bought,
If Death were the messenger,
For no man that is living today
I will not go that loath journey—
Not for the father that begat me!

EVERYMAN. Ye promised otherwise, pardie.

FELLOWSHIP. I wot well I said so, truly;
And yet if thou wilt eat, and drink, and make some good cheer,
Or haunt to women the lusty company,
I would not forsake you while the day is dear,
Trust me verily!

EVERYMAN. Yea, thereto ye would be ready;
To go to mirth, solace, and play,
Your mind to folly will sooner apply
Than to bear me company in my long journey.

FELLOWSHIP. Nay, in good faith, I will not that way.
But and thou wilt murder, or any man kill,
In that I will help thee with a good will!

EVERYMAN. O that is a simple advice indeed!
Gentle fellow, help me in my necessity;
We have loved long, and now I need,
And now, gentle Fellowship, remember me.

FELLOWSHIP. Whether ye have loved me or no,
By Saint John, I will not with thee go.

EVERYMAN. Yet, I pray thee, take the labor, and do so much for me
To bring me forward, for saint charity,
And comfort me till I come without the town.

FELLOWSHIP. Nay, and thou would give me a new gown,
I will not a foot with thee go;

But, and you had tarried, I would not have left thee so.
And as now, God speed thee in thy journey,
For from thee I will depart as fast as I may.

EVERYMAN. Whither away, Fellowship? Wilt thou forsake me?

FELLOWSHIP. Yea, by my fay, to God I betake thee.

EVERYMAN. Farewell, good Fellowship; for thee my heart is sore;
Adieu, I shall never see thee no more.

FELLOWSHIP. In faith, Everyman, farewell now at the end;
For you I will remember that parting is mourning.
[Exit.]

EVERYMAN. Alack! shall we thus depart indeed?
O, Lady, help, without any more comfort,
Lo, Fellowship, forsaketh me in my most need.
For help in this world whither shall I resort?
Fellowship herebefore with me would merry make,
And now little sorrow for me doth he take.
It is said, in prosperity men friends may find,
Which in adversity be full unkind.
Now whither for succor shall I flee,
Sith that Fellowship hath forsaken me?
To my kinsmen I will, truly,
Praying them to help me in my necessity;
I believe that they will do so,
For kind will creep where it may not go.
I will go say, for yonder I see them go.
Where be ye now, my friends and kinsmen?
[Enter KINDRED *and* COUSIN.*]*

KINDRED. Here we be now at your commandment.
Cousin, I pray you show us your intent
In any wise, and do not spare.

COUSIN. Yea, Everyman, and to us declare
If ye be disposed to go any whither,
For wot you well, we will live and die together.

KINDRED. In wealth and woe we will with you hold,
For over his kin a man may be bold.

EVERYMAN. Gramercy, my friends and kinsmen kind.
Now shall I show you the grief of my mind.
I was commanded by a messenger
That is an high King's chief officer;
He bade me go a pilgrimage to my pain,
But I know well I shall never come again;
Also I must give a reckoning straight,
For I have a great enemy that hath me in wait,
Which intendeth me for to hinder.

KINDRED. What account is that which ye must render?
That would I know.

EVERYMAN. Of all my works I must show
How I have lived and my days spent;
Also of ill deeds that I have used
In my time, sith life was me lent;
And of all virtues that I have refused.
Therefore I pray you go thither with me,
To help to make mine account, for saint charity.

COUSIN. What, to go thither? Is that the matter?
Nay, Everyman, I had liefer fast bread and water
All this five year and more.
EVERYMAN. Alas, that ever I was born!
For now shall I never be merry
If that you forsake me.
KINDRED. Ah, sir, what, ye be a merry man!
Take good heart to you, and make no moan.
But one thing I warn you, by Saint Anne,
As for me, ye shall go alone.
EVERYMAN. My Cousin, will you not with me go?
COUSIN. No, by our Lady; I have the cramp in my toe.
Trust not to me, for, so God me speed,
I will deceive you in your most need.
KINDRED. It availeth not us to dice.
Ye shall have my maid with all my heart;
She loveth to go to feasts, there to be nice,
And to dance, and abroad to start;
I will give her leave to help you in that journey,
If that you and she may agree.
EVERYMAN. Now show me the very effect of your mind.
Will you go with me, or abide behind?
KINDRED. Abide behind? yea, that will I and I may!
Therefore farewell until another day. *[Exit.]*
EVERYMAN. How should I be merry or glad?
For fair promises men to me do make,
But when I have most need, they me forsake.
I am deceived; that maketh me sad.
COUSIN. Cousin Everyman, farewell now,
For verily I will not go with you;
Also of mine own life an unready reckoning
I have to account; therefore I make tarrying.
Now, God keep thee, for now I go. *[Exit.]*
EVERYMAN. Ah, Jesus, is all come hereto?
Lo, fair words make fools feign;
They promise and nothing will do certain.
My kinsmen promised me faithfully
For to abide with me steadfastly,
And now fast away do they flee:
Even so Fellowship promised me.
What friend were best me of to provide?
I lose my time here longer to abide.
Yet in my mind a thing there is;
All my life I have loved riches;
If that my Good now help me might,
It would make my heart full light.
I will speak to him in this distress.
Where art thou, my Goods and riches?
[GOODS speaks from within.]
GOODS. Who calleth me? Everyman? What! haste thou hast?
I lie here in corners, trussed and piled so high,
And in chests I am locked so fast,
Also sacked in bags, thou mayst see with thine eye,
I cannot stir; in packs low I lie.

What would ye have? Lightly me say.
EVERYMAN. Come hither, Good, in all the haste thou may.
For of counsel I must desire thee.
[Enter GOODS.*]*
GOODS. Sir, and ye in the world have trouble or adversity,
That can I help you to remedy shortly.
EVERYMAN. It is another disease that grieveth me;
In this world it is not, I tell thee so.
I am sent for, another way to go,
To give a strait count general
Before the highest Jupiter of all;
And all my life I have had joy and pleasure in thee.
Therefore I pray thee go with me,
For peradventure, thou mayst before God
Almighty
My reckoning help to clean and purify;
For it is said ever among,
That money maketh all right that is wrong.
GOODS. Nay, Everyman, I sing another song,
I follow no man in such voyages;
For and I went with thee
Thou shouldst fare much the worse for me;
For because on me thou did set thy mind,
Thy reckoning I have made blotted and blind,
That thine account thou cannot make truly;
And that hast thou for the love of me.
EVERYMAN. That would grieve me full sore,
When I should come to that fearful answer.
Up, let us go thither together.
GOODS. Nay, not so, I am too brittle, I may not endure;
I will follow no man one foot, be thou sure.
EVERYMAN. Alas, I have thee loved, and had great pleasure
All my life-days on good and treasure.
GOODS. That is to thy damnation without lesing,
For my love is contrary to the love everlasting.
But if thou had me loved moderately during,
As to the poor to give part of me,
Then shouldst thou not in this dolor be,
Nor in this great sorrow and care.
EVERYMAN. Lo, now was I deceived ere I was ware,
And all I may wyte my spending of time.
GOODS. What, weenest thou that I am thine?
EVERYMAN. I had weened so.
GOODS. Nay, Everyman, I say no;
As for a while I was lent thee,
A season thou hast had me in prosperity.
My condition is man's soul to kill;
If I save one, a thousand I do spill;
Weenest thou that I will follow thee?
Nay, not from this world verily.
EVERYMAN. I had weened otherwise.
GOODS. Therefore to thy soul Good is a thief;
For when thou art dead, this is my guise—
Another to deceive in the same wise
As I have done thee, and all to his soul's reprief.

EVERYMAN. O false Good, cursed thou be!
Thou traitor to God, that hast deceived me
And caught me in thy snare.
GOODS. Marry, thou brought thyself in care;
Whereof I am glad.
I must needs laugh, I cannot be sad.
EVERYMAN. Ah, Good, thou hast had my heartly love;
I gave thee that which should be the Lord's above.
But wilt thou not go with me in deed?
I pray thee truth to say.
GOODS. No, so God me speed,
Therefore farewell, and have good day. *[Exit.]*
EVERYMAN. O, to whom shall I make my moan
For to go with me in that heavy journey?
First Fellowship said he would with me go;
His words were very pleasant and gay,
But afterward he left me alone.
Then spake I to my kinsmen all in despair,
And also they gave me words fair,
They lacked no fair speaking,
But all forsake me in the ending.
Then went I to my Goods, that I loved best,
In hope to have comfort, but there had I least;
For my Goods sharply did me tell
That he bringeth many into hell.
Then of myself I was ashamed,
And so I am worthy to be blamed;
Thus may I well myself hate.
Of whom shall I now counsel take?
I think that I shall never speed
Till that I go to my Good Deed.
But alas! she is so weak
That she can neither go nor speak.
Yet will I venture on her now.
My Good Deeds, where be you?
*[*GOOD DEEDS *speaks from the ground.]*
GOOD DEEDS. I lie cold in the ground.
Thy sins hath me so sore bound,
That I cannot stir.
EVERYMAN. O Good Deeds, I stand in fear;
I must you pray of counsel,
For help now should come right well.
GOOD DEEDS. Everyman, I have understanding
That ye be summoned account to make
Before Messias, of Jerusalem king;
And you do by me, that journey with you will I take.
EVERYMAN. Therefore I come to you my moan to make;
I pray you that ye will go with me.
GOOD DEEDS. I would full fain, but I cannot stand, verily.
EVERYMAN. Why, is there anything on you fall?
GOOD DEEDS. Yea, sir, I may thank you of all;
If ye had perfectly cheered me,
Your book of count now full ready had be.
Look, the books of your works and deeds eke;

Behold how they lie under the feet,
To your soul's heaviness.

EVERYMAN. Our Lord Jesus, help me!
For one letter herein can I not see.

GOOD DEEDS. There is a blind reckoning in time of distress!

EVERYMAN. Good Deeds, I pray you, help me in this need,
Or else I am for ever damned indeed;
Therefore help me to make my reckoning
Before the Redeemer of all thing,
That king is, and was, and ever shall.

GOOD DEEDS. Everyman, I am sorry of your fall,
And fain would I help you, and I were able.

EVERYMAN. Good Deeds, your counsel I pray you give me.

GOOD DEEDS. That shall I do verily;
Though that on my feet I may not go,
I have a sister that shall with you also,
Called Knowledge, which shall with you abide,
To help you to make that dreadful reckoning.

[Enter KNOWLEDGE.*]*

KNOWLEDGE. Everyman, I will go with thee, and be thy guide,
In thy most need to go by thy side.

EVERYMAN. In good condition I am now in every thing,
And am wholly content with this good thing;
Thanked be God my creator.

GOOD DEEDS. And when he hath brought thee there,
Where thou shalt heal thee of thy smart,
Then go you with your reckoning and your Good Deeds together
For to make you joyful at the heart
Before the blessèd Trinity.

EVERYMAN. My Good Deeds, I thank thee heartily;
I am well content, certainly,
With your words sweet.

KNOWLEDGE. Now go we thither lovingly
To Confession, that cleansing river.

EVERYMAN. For joy I weep; I would we were there;
But, I pray you to instruct me by intellection
Where dwelleth that holy virtue, Confession.

KNOWLEDGE. In the house of salvation;
We shall find him in that place,
That shall us comfort by God's grace.

[Enter CONFESSION.*]*

Lo, this is Confession. Kneel down and ask mercy,
For he is in good conceit with God almighty.

EVERYMAN. O glorious fountain, that all uncleanness doth clarify,
Wash from me the spots of vice unclean,
That on me no sin may be seen.
I come with Knowledge for my redemption,
Repent with hearty and full contrition;
For I am commanded a pilgrimage to take,
And great accounts before God to make.
Now, I pray you, Shrift, mother of salvation,
Help my good deeds for my piteous exclamation.

CONFESSION. I know your sorrow well, Everyman.

Because with Knowledge ye come to me,
I will you comfort as well as I can,
And a precious jewel I will give thee,
Called penance, voider of adversity;
Therewith shall your body chastised be,
With abstinence, and perseverance in God's
service.
Here shall you receive that scourge of me,
[Gives EVERYMAN *a scourge.]*
Which is penance strong, that ye must endure
To remember thy Savior was scourged for thee
With sharp scourges, and suffered it patiently;
So must thou, ere thou 'scape that painful
pilgrimage.
Knowledge, keep him in this voyage,
And by that time Good Deeds will be with thee.
But in any wise be sure of mercy,
For your time draweth fast, and we will saved be;
Ask God mercy, and He will grant truly;
When with the scourge of penance man doth him
bind,
The oil of forgiveness then shall he find.
[Exit.]

EVERYMAN. Thanked be God for his gracious work!
For now I will my penance begin;
This hath rejoiced and lighted my heart,
Though the knots be painful and hard within.

KNOWLEDGE. Everyman, look your penance that ye fulfil,
What pain that ever it to you be,
And Knowledge shall give you counsel at will
How your accounts ye shall make clearly.
*[*EVERYMAN *kneels.]*

EVERYMAN. O eternal God, O heavenly figure,
O way of righteousness, O goodly vision,
Which descended down in a virgin pure
Because he would Everyman to redeem,
Which Adam forfeited by his disobedience.
O blesséd Godhead, elect and high divine,
Forgive me my grievous offence;
Here I cry thee mercy in this presence.
O ghostly treasure, O ransomer and redeemer,
Of all the world hope and conductor,
Mirror of joy, and founder of mercy,
Which illumineth heaven and earth thereby,
Hear my clamorous complaint, though it late be.
Receive my prayers of thy benignity
Though I be a sinner most abominable,
Yet let my name be written in Moses' table.
O Mary, pray to the Maker of all thing,
Me for to help at my ending,
And save me from the power of my enemy,
For Death assaileth me strongly.
And, Lady, that I may by means of thy prayer
Of your Son's glory to be partaker,
By the means of his passion I it crave;

I beseech you, help my soul to save. *[He rises.]*
Knowledge, give me the scourge of penance.
My flesh therewith shall give a quittance.
I will now begin, if God give me grace.

KNOWLEDGE. Everyman, God give you time and space.
Thus I bequeath you in the hands of our Savior,
Thus may you make your reckoning sure.

EVERYMAN. In the name of the Holy Trinity,
My body sore punished shall be.
[Scourges himself.]
Take this, body, for the sin of the flesh;
Also thou delightest to go gay and fresh,
And in the way of damnation you did me-bring;
Therefore suffer now strokes and punishing.
Now of penance I will wade the water clear,
To save me from hell and from the fire.
*[*GOOD DEEDS *rises.]*

GOOD DEEDS. I thank God, now I can walk and go,
And am delivered of my sickness and woe.
Therefore with Everyman I will go, and not spare;
His good works I will help him to declare.

KNOWLEDGE. Now, Everyman, be merry and glad;
Your Good Deeds cometh now; ye may not be sad;
Now is your Good Deeds whole and sound,
Going upright upon the ground.
Everyman. My heart is light, and shall be evermore.
Now will I smite faster than I did before.

GOOD DEEDS. Everyman, pilgrim, my special friend,
Blesséd be thou without end;
For thee is prepared the eternal glory.
Ye have me made whole and sound,
Therefore I will bide by thee in every stound.

EVERYMAN. Welcome, my Good Deeds; now I hear thy voice,
I weep for very sweetness of love.

KNOWLEDGE. Be no more sad, but ever rejoice;
God seeth thy living in his throne above.
Put on this garment to thy behoof,
Which with your tears is now all weet,
Lest before God you be it unsweet,
When you to your journey's end come shall.

EVERYMAN. Gentle Knowledge, what do ye it call?

KNOWLEDGE. It is the garment of sorrow;
From pain it will you borrow;
Contrition it is
That getteth forgiveness;
It pleaseth God passing well.

GOOD DEEDS. Everyman, will you wear it for your heal?

EVERYMAN. Now blesséd be Jesu, Mary's Son!
[Puts on garment of contrition.]
For now have I on true contrition.
And let us go now without tarrying;
Good Deeds, have we clear our reckoning?

GOOD DEEDS. Yea, indeed I have it here.

EVERYMAN. Then I trust we need not fear.
Now, friends, let us not part in twain.

Knowledge. Nay, Everyman, that will we not, certain.
Good Deeds. Yet must thou lead with thee
Three persons of great might.
Everyman. Who should they be?
Good Deeds. Discretion and Strength they hight,
And thy Beauty may not abide behind.
Knowledge. Also ye must call to mind
Your Five Wits as for your counselors.
Good Deeds. You must have them ready at all hours.
Everyman. How shall I get them hither?
Knowledge. You must call them all together,
And they will hear you incontinent.
Everyman. My friends, come hither and be present;
Discretion, Strength, my Five Wits, and Beauty.
[*Enter* Discretion, Strength, Five Wits, *and* Beauty.]
Beauty. Here at your will we be ready.
What would ye that we should do?
Good Deeds. That ye would with Everyman go,
And help him in his pilgrimage.
Advise you, will ye with him or not in that voyage?
Strength. We will bring him all thither,
To his help and comfort, ye may believe me.
Discretion. So will we go with him all together.
Everyman. Almighty God, lovéd may thou be,
I give thee laud that I have hither brought
Strength, Discretion, Beauty, and Five Wits; lack I naught;
And my Good Deeds, with Knowledge clear,
All be in company at my will here.
I desire no more to my business.
Strength. And I, Strength, will by you stand in distress,
Though thou would in battle fight on the ground.
Five Wits. And though it were through the world round,
We will not depart for sweet nor sour.
Beauty. No more will I, unto death's hour,
Whatsoever thereof befall.
Discretion. Everyman, advise you first of all;
Go with a good advisement and deliberation.
We all give you a virtuous monition
That all shall be well.
Everyman. My friends, hearken what I will tell:
I pray God reward you in his heavenly sphere.
Now hearken, all that be here,
For I will make my testament
Here before you all present.
In alms half my good I will give with my hands twain
In the way of charity, with good intent,
And the other half still shall remain
In quethe to be returned there it ought to be.
This I do in despite of the fiend of hell,
To go quite out of his peril
Ever after and this day.
Knowledge. Everyman, hearken what I say;

Go to Priesthood, I you advise,
And receive of him in any wise
The holy sacrament and ointment together;
Then shortly see ye turn again hither;
We will all abide you here.

FIVE WITS. Yea, Everyman, hie you that ye ready were.
There is no emperor, king, duke, nor baron,
That of God hath commission
As hath the least priest in the world being;
For of the blesséd sacraments pure and benign
He beareth the keys, and thereof hath he cure
For man's redemption, it is ever sure;
Which God for our soul's medicine
Gave us out of his heart with great pain;
Here in this transitory life, for thee and me
The blesséd sacraments seven there be,
Baptism, confirmation, with priesthood good,
And the sacrament of God's precious flesh and blood,
Marriage, the holy extreme unction, and penance.
These seven be good to have in remembrance,
Gracious sacraments of high divinity.

EVERYMAN. Fain would I receive that holy body
And meekly to my ghostly father I will go.

FIVE WITS. Everyman, that is the best that ye can do.
God will you to salvation bring,
For priesthood exceedeth all other thing;
To us Holy Scripture they do teach,
And converteth man from sin heaven to reach;
God hath to them more power given,
Than to any angel that is in heaven.
With five words he may consecrate
God's body in flesh and blood to take,
And handleth his Maker between his hands.
The priest bindeth and unbindeth all bands,
Both in earth and in heaven;
Thou ministers all the sacraments seven;
Though we kist thy feet, thou wert worthy;
Thou art the surgeon that cureth sin deadly:
No remedy we find under God
But all only priesthood.
Everyman, God gave priests that dignity,
And setteth them in his stead among us to be;
Thus be they above angels in degree.
[EVERYMAN goes out to receive the last rites of the church.]

KNOWLEDGE. If priests be good it is so surely;
But when Jesus hanged on the cross with great smart,
There he gave out of his blesséd heart
The same sacrament in great torment.
He sold them not to us, that Lord omnipotent.
Therefore Saint Peter the apostle doth say
That Jesus' curse hath all they
Which God their Savior do buy or sell,

	Or they for any money do take or tell.
	Sinful priests giveth the sinners example bad.
Five Wits.	I trust to God no such may we find.
	Therefore let us priesthood honor,
	And follow their doctrine for our souls' succor.
	We be their sheep, and they shepherds be
	By whom we all be kept in surety.
	Peace, for yonder I see Everyman come,
	Which hath made true satisfaction.
Good Deeds.	Methinketh it is he indeed.
	[Re-enter Everyman.*]*
Everyman.	Now Jesu be your alder speed.
	I have received the sacrament for my redemption,
	And mine extreme unction.
	Blesséd be all they that counseled me to take it!
	And now, friends, let us go without longer respite.
	I thank God that ye have tarried so long.
	Now set each of you on this rod your hand,
	And shortly follow me.
	I go before, there I would be. God be our guide.
Strength.	Everyman, we will not from you go,
	Till ye have gone this voyage long.
Discretion.	I, Discretion, will bide by you also.
Knowledge.	And though this pilgrimage be never so strong
	I will never part you fro.
	Everyman, I will be as sure by thee
	As ever I did by Judas Maccabee.
	[They approach the grave.]
Everyman.	Alas, I am so faint I may not stand,
	My limbs under me do fold.
	Friends, let us not turn again to this land,
	Not for all the world's gold;
	For into this cave must I creep
	And turn to earth and there to sleep.
Beauty.	What, into this grave? Alas!
Everyman.	Yea, there shall you consume, more and less.
Beauty.	And what, should I smother here?
Everyman.	Yea, by my faith, and never more appear.
	In this world live no more we shall,
	But in heaven before the highest Lord of all.
Beauty.	I cross out all this; adieu by Saint John;
	I take my cap in my lap and am gone.
Everyman.	What, Beauty, whither will ye?
Beauty.	Peace, I am deaf. I look not behind me,
	Not and thou would give me all the gold in thy chest. *[Exit.]*
Everyman.	Alas, whereto may I trust?
	Beauty goeth fast away and from me;
	She promised with me to live and die.
Strength.	Everyman, I will thee also forsake and deny.
	Thy game liketh me not at all.
Everyman.	Why, then ye will forsake me all!
	Sweet Strength, tarry a little space.
Strength.	Nay, sir, by the rood of grace,
	I will hie me from thee fast,

Though thou weep till thy heart to-brast.
EVERYMAN. Ye would ever bide by me, ye said.
STRENGTH. Yea, I have you far enough conveyed;
Ye be old enough, I understand,
Your pilgrimage to take on hand.
I repent me that I hither came.
EVERYMAN. Strength, you to displease I am to blame;
Will you break promise that is debt?
STRENGTH. In faith, I care not;
Thou art but a fool to complain.
You spend your speech and waste your brain;
Go thrust thee into the ground. *[Exit.]*
EVERYMAN. I had weened surer I should you have found.
He that trusteth in his Strength
She him deceiveth at the length.
Both Strength and Beauty forsaketh me,
Yet they promised me fair and lovingly.
DISCRETION. Everyman, I will after Strength be gone;
As for me I will leave you alone.
EVERYMAN. Why, Discretion, will ye forsake me?
DISCRETION. Yea, in faith, I will go from thee;
For when Strength goeth before
I follow after evermore.
EVERYMAN. Yet, I pray thee, for the love of the Trinity,
Look in my grave once piteously.
DISCRETION. Nay, so nigh will I not come.
Farewell, every one! *[Exit.]*
EVERYMAN. O all thing faileth, save God alone;
Beauty, Strength, and Discretion;
For when Death bloweth his blast
They all run from me full fast.
FIVE WITS. Everyman, my leave now of thee I take;
I will follow the other, for here I thee forsake.
EVERYMAN. Alas! then may I wail and weep,
For I took you for my best friend.
FIVE WITS. I will no longer thee keep;
Now farewell, and there an end. *[Exit.]*
EVERYMAN. O Jesu, help, all hath forsaken me!
GOOD DEEDS. Nay, Everyman, I will bide with thee,
I will not forsake thee indeed;
Thou shalt find me a good friend at need.
EVERYMAN. Gramercy, Good Deeds; now may I true friends see;
They have forsaken me every one;
I loved them better than my Good Deeds alone.
Knowledge, will ye forsake me also?
KNOWLEDGE. Yea, Everyman, when ye to death do go;
But not yet for no manner of danger.
EVERYMAN. Gramercy, Knowledge, with all my heart.
KNOWLEDGE. Nay, yet I will not from hence depart
Till I see where ye shall be come.
EVERYMAN. Methinketh, alas, that I must be gone
To make my reckoning and my debts pay,
For I see my time is nigh spent away.
Take example, all ye that this do hear or see,

How they that I loved best do forsake me,
Except my Good Deeds that bideth truly,

GOOD DEEDS. All earthly thing is but vanity.
Beauty, Strength, and Discretion do man forsake,
Foolish friends and kinsmen, that fair spake,
All fleeth save Good Deeds, and that am I.

EVERYMAN. Have mercy on me, God most mighty;
And stand by me, thou Mother and Maid, holy Mary!

GOOD DEEDS. Fear not, I will speak for thee.

EVERYMAN. Here I cry God mercy.

GOOD DEEDS. Short our end, and minis hour pain.
Let us go and never come again.

EVERYMAN. Into thy hands, Lord, my soul I commend.
Receive it, Lord, that it be not lost.
As thou me boughtest, so me defend,
And save me from the fiend's boast,
That I may appear with that blesséd host
That shall be saved at the day of doom.
In manus tuas—of might's most,
Forever—*commendo spiritum meum.*

*[*EVERYMAN *and* GOOD DEEDS *descend into the grave.]*

KNOWLEDGE. Now hath he suffered that we all shall endure;
Thy Good Deeds shall make all sure.
Now hath he made ending.
Methinketh that I hear angels sing
And make great joy and melody
Where Everyman's soul received shall be.

ANGEL *(within)*. Come, excellent elect spouse to Jesu.
Here above thou shalt go
Because of thy singular virtue.
Now the soul is taken the body fro,
Thy reckoning is crystal-clear.
Now shalt thou into the heavenly sphere,
Unto the which all ye shall come
That liveth well before the day of doom.

[Exit KNOWLEDGE.*]*

[Enter DOCTOR *as Epilogue.]*

DOCTOR. This moral men may have in mind;
Ye hearers, take it of worth, old and young,
And forsake pride, for he deceiveth you in the end,
And remember Beauty, Five Wits, Strength, and Discretion,
They all at the last do Everyman forsake,
Save his Good Deeds there doth he take.
But beware, for and they be small
Before God he hath no help at all.
None excuse may be there for Everyman.
Alas, how shall he do then?
For after death amends may no man make,
For then mercy and pity do him forsake.
If his reckoning be not clear when he do come,
God will say—*ite maledicti in ignem æternum.*
And he that hath his account whole and sound,

High in heaven he shall be crowned.
Unto which place God bring us all thither,
That we may live body and soul together.
Thereto help the Trinity,
Amen, say ye, for saint charity.

AMEN

Dante Alighieri (1265–1321)

Italian poet, prose writer, literary theorist, moral philosopher, and political thinker, Dante Alighieri was born to a Florentine family of noble ancestry. He grew up in Florence, Italy. Dante married in 1285, but his life was given its direction by his spiritual love for Beatrice Portinari, whom he first saw when she was a child and he but nine years old. Dante was her ardent admirer, but it is doubtful that she was aware of him for she married Simone de Bardi shortly before her death in 1290. She becomes the subject of his *Vita Nuova* (the New Life) and in the *Divine Comedy,* serves as his guide through Paradise. In the *Vita Nuova,* Dante concentrates on his love for Beatrice. She remained his ideal lady, the inspiration of his poetry and of his Christian devotion. She became a life-long symbol for him of Divine Love and perfection.

A member of the White Guelf party, he played a major part in the political struggles that divided the city. Dante was a politician who served for a time as a member of the Council of Six which governed Florence. Dante's Italy was one of political chaos and unrest. Italy consisted of numerous city-states which were in constant rivalry and warfare with each other. Two political factions struggled for power within the country. The Ghibellines were opposed to papal domination and anticipated the conquest and unification of Italy by the Holy Roman Empire. On the other hand, the Guelfs opposed the authority of the Holy Roman Empire and preferred the independence of the city-states. When these two parties disappeared—the Guelfs in 1260 and the Ghibellines in 1266—two new parties, the Whites and Blacks, emerged to take their places. The political confusion was further heightened by the constant intervention of the Roman Catholic Church which was corrupt, at that time, and anxious to gain as much profit and prestige as possible.

In 1300 when Pope Boniface VIII claimed the City of Florence, Dante went to Rome in an effort to persuade the Pope to reverse his decision. The Pope refused and gave the city to the brother of the King of France. Dante attempted, with several others, a revolution, and Dante and his associates were exiled. The government in power sentenced Dante to death in absentia and confiscated his property. He never again entered Florence though his family remained there. He wandered throughout Italy sustained only by hope that the country would be united bringing an end to the political turmoil. He plunged deeply into the study of philosophy and theology, both as a means of escape and preparation for his writing.

Dante Alighieri represents both the epitome of scholarship in the Middle Ages and a foreshadowing of the humanism which was to characterize the Renaissance. He ranks among those literary giants of many talents who were able to indulge in all aspects of contemporary life. Dante spent his last years in exile in Ravenna, where he acquired honor and fame before his death in 1321.

The Divine Comedy: Background

Dante's the *Divine Comedy* is an epic of mankind's search for perfection, and it reflects nearly all phases of medieval life: religion, culture, science, society. The term *comedy* is used here in its medieval meaning of a work which begins in misery (Dante begins in the Dark Wood of Error) and ends in happiness (Dante ends in Paradise). The adjective "Divine" was added to the title in the sixteenth century by those who felt that the narrative was a sacred poem. Since then, the *Divine Comedy* has been considered the greatest poem of the Middle Ages.

The three divisions of the poem are Hell, Purgatory, and Paradise. Each division consists of a symbolic number of cantos. The first part has thirty-four, and the other two have thirty-three. These numbers signify the fact that Christ died at the age of thirty-three in his thirty-fourth year. The three divisions correspond in number to the Trinity. This numerlogical structure illustrates the fact that the complexity of the *Divine Comedy* arises from levels of allegory and symbolism. An *allegory* is a story which can be read on several levels: literal, moral, political, and anagogical. The literal is the basic story level of the poem without regard to symbolism. It concerns the state of souls after death and describes Dante's journey though Hell, Purgatory, and Paradise. The moral level is concerned with the understanding or recognition of sin (Hell), the process of moral redemption (Purgatory), and ultimate spiritual salvation (Paradise). The political level depicts the chaotic conditions with the Church and the empire in contemporary Italy and predicts the establishment of an independent, purified Church and a universal empire. Dante's political views form the basis of political allegory in the *Divine Comedy.* The anagogical is the spiritual or mystical level which presents a glimpse of what the Divine Plan for the world is. The Divine Plan is to remove the living from the state of misery and lead them to the state of happiness. This plan is temporarily unrealized on earth because of man's sin and corruption. What Dante advocates is not new. He models his ideal coexistent Church and state upon the Church and empire, which were coexistent in Virgil's day.

The poem's symbolism is represented through its characters and places. Virgil, serving as Dante's guide through Hell and Purgatory, portrays human reason and the wisdom of antiquity. Beatrice, guiding Dante through Paradise, epitomizes Divine Love and perfection. Hell is filled with images of ruin and examples of sin. It represents the state of corrupt man and unregenerate Italy. Purgatory illustrates man's pathway to repentance if he is guided by reason and inspired by revelation. Paradise leads to ultimate redemption and Divine Love. The *Divine Comedy* seeks to present a universally true picture of life. During Dante's journey through Hell, Purgatory, and Paradise, he reflects upon human actions and their ultimate consequences, and he learns to judge human experience in light of eternal principles.

Inferno

Canto I.

Midway upon the journey of our life
I found myself within a forest dark,
For the straightforward pathway had been lost.
Ah me! how hard a thing it is to say
What was this forest savage, rough, and stem,
Which in the very thought renews the fear.
So bitter is it, death is little more;
But of the good to treat, which there I found,
Speak will I of the other things I saw there.
I cannot well repeat how there I entered,
So full was I of slumber at the moment
In which I had abandoned the true way.
But after I had reached a mountain's foot,
At that point where the valley terminated,
Which had with consternation pierced my heart,
Upward I looked, and I beheld its shoulders,
Vested already with that planet's rays
Which leadeth others right by every road.
Then was the fear a little quieted
That in my heart's lake had endured throughout
The night, which I had passed so piteously.
And even as he, who, with distressful breath,
Forth issued from the sea upon the shore,
Turns to the water perilous and gazes;
So did my soul, that still was fleeing onward,
Turn itself back to re-behold the pass
Which never yet a living person left.
After my weary body I had rested,
The way resumed I on the desert slope,
So that the firm foot ever was the lower.
And lo! almost where the ascent began,
A panther light and swift exceedingly,
Which with a spotted skin was covered o'er!
And never moved she from before my face,
Nay, rather did impede so much my way,
That many times I to return had turned.
The time was the beginning of the morning,
And up the sun was mounting with those stars
That with him were, what time the Love Divine
At first in motion set those beauteous things;
So were to me occasion of good hope,
The variegated skin of that wild beast,
The hour of time, and the delicious season;
But not so much, that did not give me fear
A lion's aspect which appeared to me.

He seemed as if against me he were coming
With head uplifted, and with ravenous hunger,
So that it seemed the air was afraid of him;
And a she-wolf, that with all hungerings
Seemed to be laden in her meagreness,
And many folk has caused to live forlorn!
She brought upon me so much heaviness,
With the affright that from her aspect came,
That I the hope relinquished of the height.
And as he is who willingly acquires,
And the time comes that causes him to lose,
Who weeps in all his thoughts and is despondent,
E'en such made me that beast withouten peace,
Which, coming on against me by degrees
Thrust me back thither where the sun is silent.
While I was rushing downward to the lowland,
Before mine eyes did one present himself,
Who seemed from long-continued silence hoarse.
When I beheld him in the desert vast,
"Have pity on me," unto him I cried,
"Whiche'er thou art, or shade or real man!"
He answered me: "Not man; man once I was,
And both my parents were of Lombardy,
And Mantuans by country both of them.
Sub Julio was I born, though it was late,
And lived at Rome under the good Augustus,
During the time of false and lying gods.
A poet was I, and I sang that just
Son of Anchises, who came forth from Troy,
After that Ilion the superb was burned.
But thou, why goest thou back to such annoyance?
Why climb'st thou not the Mount Delectable,
Which is the source and cause of every joy?"
"Now, art thou that Virgilius and that fountain
Which spreads abroad so wide a river of speech
I made response to him with bashful forehead.
"O, of the other poets honour and light,
Avail me the long study and great love
That have impelled me to explore thy volume
Thou art my master, and my author thou,
Thou art alone the one from whom I took
The beautiful style that has done honour to me.
Behold the beast, for which I have turned back;
Do thou protect me from her, famous Sage,
For she doth make my veins and pulses tremble."
"Thee it behoves to take another road,"
Responded he, when he beheld me weeping,
"If from this savage place thou wouldst escape;
Because this beast, at which thou criest out,
Suffers not any one to pass her way,
But so doth harass him, that she destroys him
And has a nature so malign and ruthless,
That never doth she glut her greedy will,
And after food is hungrier than before.
Many the animals with whom she weds,

And more they shall be still, until the Greyhound
Comes, who shall make her perish in her pain.
He shall not feed on either earth or pelf,
But upon wisdom, and on love and virtue;
'Twixt Feltro and Feltro shall his nation be;
Of that low Italy shall he be the saviour,
On whose account the maid Camilla died,
Euryalus, Turnus, Nisus, of their wounds;
Through every city shall he hunt her down,
Until he shall have driven her back to Hell,
There from whence envy first did let her loose.
Therefore I think and judge it for thy best
Thou follow me, and I will be thy guide,
And lead thee hence through the eternal place,
Where thou shalt hear the desperate lamentations,
Shalt see the ancient spirits disconsolate,
Who cry out each one for the second death;
And thou shalt see those who contented are
Within the fire, because they hope to come,
Whene'er it may be, to the blessed people;
To whom, then, if thou wishest to ascend,
A soul shall be for that than I more worthy;
With her at my departure I will leave thee;
Because that Emperor, who reigns above,
In that I was rebellious to his law,
Wills that through me none come into his city.
He governs everywhere, and there he reigns;
There is his city and his lofty throne;
O happy he whom thereto he elects!"
And I to him: "Poet, I thee entreat,
By that same God whom thou didst never know,
So that I may escape this woe and worse,
Thou wouldst conduct me there where thou hast said,
That I may see the portal of Saint Peter,
And those thou makest so disconsolate."
Then he moved on, and I behind him followed.

Canto II.

Day was departing, and the embrowned air
Released the animals that are on earth
From their fatigues; and I the only one
Made myself ready to sustain the war,
Both of the way and likewise of the woe,
Which memory that errs not shall retrace.
O Muses, O high genius, now assist me!
O memory, that didst write down what I saw,
Here thy nobility shall be manifest!
And I began: "Poet, who guidest me,
Regard my manhood, if it be sufficient,
Ere to the arduous pass thou dost confide me.
Thou sayest, that of Silvius the parent,
While yet corruptible, unto the world
Immortal went, and was there bodily.

But if the adversary of all evil
Was courteous, thinking of the high effect
That issue would from him, and who, and what,
To men of intellect unmeet it seems not;
For he was of great Rome, and of her empire
In the empyreal heaven as father chosen;
The which and what, wishing to speak the truth,
Were stablished as the holy place, wherein
Sits the successor of the greatest Peter.
Upon this journey, whence thou givest him vaunt,
Things did he hear, which the occasion were
Both of his victory and the papal mantle.
Thither went afterwards the Chosen Vessel,
To bring back comfort thence unto that Faith,
Which of salvation's way is the beginning.
But I, why thither come, or who concedes it?
I not Æneas am, I am not Paul,
Nor I, nor others, think me worthy of it.
Therefore, if I resign myself to come,
I fear the coming may be ill-advised
Thou'rt wise, and knowest better than I speak."
And as he is, who unwills what he willed,
And by new thoughts doth his intention change,
So that from his design he quite withdraws,
Such I became, upon that dark hillside,
Because, in thinking, I consumed the emprise,
Which was so very prompt in the beginning.
"If I have well thy language understood,"
Replied that shade of the Magnanimous,
"Thy soul attainted is with cowardice,
Which many times a man encumbers so,
It turns him back from honoured enterprise,
As false sight doth a beast, when he is shy.
That thou mayst free thee from this apprehension,
I'll tell thee why I came, and what I heard
At the first moment when I grieved for thee.
Among those was I who are in suspense,
And a fair, saintly Lady called to me
In such wise, I besought her to command me.
Her eyes where shining brighter than the Star;
And she begin to say, gentle and low,
With voice angelical, in her own language:
'O spirit courteous of Mantua,
Of whom the fame still in the world endures,
And shall endure, long-lasting as the world;
A friend of mine, and not the friend of fortune,
Upon the desert slope is so impeded
Upon his way, that he has turned through terror,
And may, I fear, already be so lost,
That I too late have risen to his succour,
From that which I have heard of him in Heaven.
Bestir thee now, and with thy speech ornate,
And with what needful is for his release,
Assist him so, that I may be consoled.
Beatrice am I, who do bid thee go;

I come from there, where I would fain return
Love moved me, which compelleth me to speak.
When I shall be in presence of my Lord,
Full often will I praise thee unto him.'
Then paused she, and thereafter I began:
'O Lady of virtue, thou alone through whom
The human race exceedeth all contained
Within the heaven that his the lesser circles,
So grateful unto me is thy commandment,
To obey, if 'twere already done, were late
No farther need'st thou ope to me thy wish.
But the cause tell me why thou dost not shun
The here descending down into this centre,
From the vast place thou burnest to return to.'
'Since thou wouldst fain so inwardly discern,
Briefly will I relate,' she answered me,
'Why I am not afraid to enter here.
Of those things only should one be afraid
Which have the power of doing others harm;
Of the rest, no; because they are not fearful.
God in his mercy such created me
That misery of yours attains me not,
Nor any flame assails me of this burning.
A gentle Lady is in Heaven, who grieves
At this impediment, to which I send thee,
So that stern judgment there above is broken.
In her entreaty she besought Lucìa,
And said, "Thy faithful one now stands in need
Of thee, and unto thee I recommend him."
Lucìa, foe of all that cruel is,
Hastened away, and came unto the place
Where I was sitting with the ancient Rachel.
"Beatrice," said she, "the true praise of God,
Why succourest thou not him, who loved thee so,
For thee he issued from the vulgar herd?
Dost thou not hear the pity of his plaint?
Dost thou not see the death that combats him
Beside that flood, where ocean has no vaunt?"
Never were persons in the world so swift
To work their weal and to escape their woe,
As I, after such words as these were uttered,
Came hither downward from my blessed seat,
Confiding in thy dignified discourse,
Which honours thee, and those who've listened to it.'
After she thus had spoken unto me,
Weeping, her shining eyes she turned away;
Whereby she made me swifter in my coming;
And unto thee I came, as she desired;
I have delivered thee from that wild beast,
Which barred the beautiful mountain's short ascent.
What is it, then? Why, why dost thou delay?
Why is such baseness bedded in thy heart?
Daring and hardihood why hast thou not,

Seeing that three such Ladies benedight
Are caring for thee in the court of Heaven,
And so much good my speech doth promise thee?"
Even as the flowerets, by nocturnal chill,
Bowed down and closed, when the sun whitens them,
Uplift themselves all open on their stems;
Such I became with my exhausted strength,
And such good courage to my heart there coursed,
That I began, like an intrepid person:
"O she compassionate, who succoured me,
And courteous thou, who hast obeyed so soon
The words of truth which she addressed to thee
Thou hast my heart so with desire disposed
To the adventure, with these words of thine,
That to my first intent I have returned.
Now go, for one sole will is in us both,
Thou Leader, and thou Lord , and Master thou."
Thus said I to him; and when he had moved,
I entered on the deep and savage way.

Canto III.

"Through me the way is to the city dolent;
Through me the way is to eternal dole ;
Through me the way among the people lost.
Justice incited my sublime Creator;
Created me divine Omnipotence,
The highest Wisdom and the primal Love.
Before me there were no created things,
Only eterne, and I eternal last.
All hope abandon, ye who enter in!"
These words in sombre colour I beheld
Written upon the summit of a gate;
Whence I: "Their sense is, Master, hard to me!"
And he to me, as one experienced:
"Here all suspicion needs must be abandoned,
All cowardice must needs be here extinct.
We to the place have come, where I have told thee
Thou shalt behold the people dolorous
Who have foregone the good of intellect."
And after he had laid his band on mine
With joyful mien, whence I was comforted,
He led me in among the secret things.
There sighs, complaints, and ululations loud
Resounded through the air without a star,
Whence I, at the beginning, wept thereat.
Languages diverse, horrible dialects,
Accents of anger, words of agony,
And voices high and hoarse, with sound of hands,
Made up a tumult that goes whirling on
For ever in that air for ever black,
Even as the sand doth, when the whirlwind breathes.

And I, who had my head with horror bound,
Said: "Master, what is this which now I hear?
What folk is this, which seems by pain so
vanquished?"
And he to me: "This miserable mode
Maintain the melancholy souls of those
Who lived withouten infamy or praise.
Commingled are they with that caitiff choir
Of Angels, who have not rebellious been,
Nor faithful were to God, but were for self,
The heavens expelled them, not to be less fair;
Nor them the nethermore abyss receives,
For glory none the damned would have from
them."
And I: "O Master, what so grievous is
To these, that maketh them lament so sore?"
He answered: "I will tell thee very briefly.
These have no longer any hope of death;
And this blind life of theirs is so debased,
They envious are of every other fate.
No fame of them the world permits to be
Misericord and justice both disdain them.
Let us not speak of them, but look, and pass."
And I, who looked again, beheld a banner,
Which, whirling round, ran on so rapidly,
That of all pause it seemed to me indignant;
And after it there came so long a train
Of people, that I ne'er would have believed
That ever Death so many had undone.
When some among them I had recognised.
I looked, and I beheld the shade of him
Who made through cowardice the great refusal.
Forthwith I comprehended, and was certain,
That this the sect was of the caitiff wretches
Hateful to God and to his enemies.
These miscreants, who never were alive,
Were naked, and were stung exceedingly
By gadflies and by hornets that were there.
These did their faces irrigate with blood,
Which, with their tears commingled, at their feet
By the disgusting worms was gathered up.
And when to gazing farther I betook me.
People I saw on a great river's bank;
Whence said I: "Master, now vouchsafe to me,
That I may know who these are, and what law
Makes them appear so ready to pass over,
As I discern athwart the dusky light."
And he to me: "These things shall all be known
To thee, as soon as we our footsteps stay
Upon the dismal shore of Acheron."
Then with mine eyes ashamed and downward cast,
Fearing my words might irksome be to him,
From speech refrained I till we reached the river.
And lo! towards us coming in a boat
An old man, hoary with the hair of eld,

Crying: "Woe unto you, ye souls depraved!
Hope nevermore to look upon the heavens;
I come to lead you to the other shore,
To the eternal shades in heat and frost.
And thou, that yonder standest, living soul,
Withdraw thee from these people, who are dead!"
But when he saw that I did not withdraw,
He said: "By other ways, by other ports
Thou to the shore shalt come, not here, for passage;
A lighter vessel needs must carry thee."
And unto him the Guide: "Vex thee not, Charon;
It is so willed there where is power to do
That which is willed; and farther question not."
Thereat were quieted the fleecy cheeks
Of him the ferryman of the livid fen,
Who round about his eyes had wheels of flame.
But all those souls who weary were and naked
Their colour changed and gnashed their teeth
together.
As soon as they had heard those cruel words.
God they blasphemed and their progenitors,
The human race, the place, the time, the seed
Of their engendering and of their birth!
Thereafter all together they drew back,
Bitterly weeping, to the accursed shore,
Which waiteth every man who fears not God.
Charon the demon, with the eyes of glede,
Beckoning to them, collects them all together,
Beats with his oar whoever lags behind.
As in the autumn-time the leaves fall off,
First one and then another, till the branch
Unto the earth surrenders all its spoils
In similar wise the evil seed of Adam
Throw themselves from that margin one by one,
At signals, as a bird unto its lure.
So they depart across the dusky wave,
And ere upon the other side they land,
Again on this side a new troop assembles.
"My son," the courteous Master said to me,
"All those who perish in the wrath of God
Here meet together out of every land
And ready are they to pass o'er the river,
Because celestial justice spurs them on,
So that their fear is turned into desire.
This way there never passes a good soul;
And hence if Charon doth complain of thee,
Well mayst thou know now what his speech
imports."
This being finished, all the dusk champaign
Trembled so violently, that of that terror
The recollection bathes me still with sweat.
The land of tears gave forth a blast of wind,
And fulminated a vermilion light,
Which overmastered in me every sense,
And as a man whom sleep hath seized I fell.

Canto IV.

Broke the deep lethargy within my head
A heavy thunder, so that I upstarted,
Like to a person who by force is wakened;
And round about I moved my rested eyes,
Uprisen erect, and steadfastly I gazed,
To recognise the place wherein I was.
True is it, that upon the verge I found me
Of the abysmal valley dolorous,
That gathers thunder of infinite ululations.
Obscure, profound it was, and nebulous,
So that by fixing on its depths my sight
Nothing whatever I discerned therein.
"Let us descend now into the blind world,"
Began the Poet, pallid utterly;
"I will be first, and thou shalt second be."
And I, who of his colour was aware,
Said: "How shall I come, if thou art afraid,
Who'rt wont to be a comfort to my fears?"
And he to me: "The anguish of the people
Who are below here in my face depicts
That pity which for terror thou hast taken.
Let us go on, for the long way impels us."
Thus he went in, and thus he made me enter
The foremost circle that surrounds the abyss.
There, as it seemed to me from listening,
Were lamentations none, but only sighs,
That tremble made the everlasting air.
And this arose from sorrow without torment,
Which the crowds had, that many were and great,
Of infants and of women and of men.
To me the Master good: "Thou dost not ask
What spirits these, which thou beholdest, are?
Now will I have thee know, ere thou go farther,
That they sinned not; and if they merit had,
'Tis not enough, because they had not baptism
Which is the portal of the Faith thou holdest;
And if they were before Christianity,
In the right manner they adored not God;
And among such as these am I myself.
For such defects, and not for other guilt,
Lost are we, and are only so far punished,
That without hope we live on in desire."
Great grief seized on my heart when this I heard,
Because some people of much worthiness
I knew, who in that Limbo were suspended.
"Tell me, my Master, tell me, thou my Lord,"
Began I, with desire of being certain
Of that Faith which o'ercometh every error,
"Came any one by his own merit hence,
Or by another's, who was blessed thereafter?"
And he, who understood my covert speech,
Replied: "I was a novice in this state,

When I saw hither come a Mighty One,
With sign of victory incoronate.
Hence he drew forth the shade of the First Parent,
And that of his son Abel, and of Noah,
Of Moses the lawgiver, and the obedient
Abraham, patriarch, and David, king,
Israel with his father and his children,
And Rachel, for whose sake he did so much,
And others many, and he made them blessed;
And thou must know, that earlier than these
Never were any human spirits saved."
We ceased not to advance because he spake,
But still were passing onward through the forest,
The forest, say I, of thick-crowded ghosts.
Not very far as yet our way had gone
This side the summit, when I saw a fire
That overcame a hemisphere of darkness.
We were a little distant from it still,
But not so far that I in part discerned not
That honourable people held that place.
"O thou who honourest every art and science,
Who may these be, which such great honour have,
That from the fashion of the rest it parts them?"
And he to me: "The honourable name,
That sounds of them above there in thy life,
Wins grace in Heaven, that so advances them."
In the mean time a voice was heard by me:
"All honour be to the pre-eminent Poet;
His shade returns again, that was departed."
After the voice had ceased and quiet was,
Four mighty shades I saw approaching us
Semblance had they nor sorrowful nor glad.
To say to me began my gracious Master:
"Him with that falchion in his hand behold,
Who comes before the three, even as their lord.
That one is Homer, Poet sovereign;
He who comes next is Horace, the satirist;
The third is Ovid, and the last is Lucan.
Because to each of these with me applies
The name that solitary voice proclaimed,
They do me honour, and in that do well."
Thus I beheld assemble the fair school
Of that lord of the song pre-eminent,
Who o'er the others like an eagle soars.
When they together had discoursed somewhat,
They turned to me with signs of salutation,
And on beholding this, my Master smiled;
And more of honour still, much more, they did me,
In that they made me one of their own band;
So that the sixth was I, mid so much wit.
Thus we went on as far as to the light,
Things saying 'tis becoming to keep silent,
As was the saying of them where I was.
We came unto a noble castle's foot,
Seven times encompassëd with lofty walls,

Defended round by a fair rivulet;
This we passed over even as firm ground
Through portals seven I entered with these Sages;
We came into a meadow of fresh verdure.
People were there with solemn eyes and slow,
Of great authority in their countenance;
They spake but seldom, and with gentle voices.
Thus we withdrew ourselves upon one side
Into an opening luminous and lofty,
So that they all of them were visible.
There opposite, upon the green enamel,
Were pointed out to me the mighty spirits,
Whom to have seen I feel myself exalted.
I saw Electra with companions many,
'Mongst whom I knew both Hector and Æneas,
Cæsar in armour with gerfalcon eyes
I saw Camilla and Penthesilea
On the other side, and saw the King Latinus,
Who with Lavinia his daughter sat;
I saw that Brutus who drove Tarquin forth,
Lucretia, Julia, Marcia, and Cornelia,
And saw alone, apart, the Saladin.
When I had lifted up my brows a little,
The Master I beheld of those who know,
Sit with his philosophic family.
All gaze upon him, and all do him honour.
There I beheld both Socrates and Plato,
Who nearer him before the others stand;
Democritus, who puts the world on chance,
Diogenes, Anaxagoras, and Thales,
Zeno, Empedocles, and Heraclitus;
Of qualities I saw the good collector,
Hight Dioscorides; and Orpheus saw I,
Tully and Livy, and moral Seneca,
Euclid, geometrician, and Ptolemy,
Galen, Hippocrates, and Avicenna,
Averroes, who the great Comment made.
I cannot all of them pourtray in full,
Because so drives me onward the long theme,
That many times the word comes short of fact.
The sixfold company in two divides;
Another way my sapient Guide conducts me
Forth from the quiet to the air that trembles;
And to a place I come where nothing shines.

Canto V.

Thus I descended out of the first circle
Down to the second, that less space begirds,
And so much greater dole, that goads to wailing.
There standeth Minos horribly, and snarls;
Examines the transgressions at the entrance;
Judges, and sends according as he girds him.
I say, that when the spirit evil-born

Cometh before him, wholly it confesses;
And this discriminator of transgressions
Seeth what place in Hell is meet for it;
Girds himself with his tail as many times
As grades he wishes it should be thrust down.
Always before him many of them stand;
They go by turns each one unto the judgment;
They speak, and hear, and then are downward
hurled.
"O thou, that to this dolorous hostelry
Comest," said Minos to me, when he saw me,
Leaving the practice of so great an office,
"Look how thou enterest, and in whom thou trustest;
Let not the portal's amplitude deceive thee."
And unto him my Guide: "Why criest thou too?
Do not impede his journey fate-ordained;
It is so willed there where is power to do
That which is willed; and ask no further question."
And now begin the dolesome notes to grow
Audible unto me; now am I come
There where much lamentation strikes upon me.
I came into a place mute of all light,
Which bellows as the sea does in a tempest,
If by opposing winds 't is combated.
The infernal hurricane that never rests
Hurtles the spirits onward in its rapine
Whirling them round, and smiting, it molests them.
When they arrive before the precipice,
There are the shrieks, the plaints, and the laments,
There they blaspheme the puissance divine.
I understood that unto such a torment
The carnal malefactors were condemned,
Who reason subjugate to appetite.
And as the wings of starlings bear them on
In the cold season in large band and full,
So doth that blast the spirits maledict;
It hither, thither, downward, upward, drives them;
No hope doth comfort them for evermore,
Not of repose, but even of lesser pain.
And as the cranes go chanting forth their lays,
Making in air a long line of themselves,
So saw I coming, uttering lamentations,
Shadows borne onward by the aforesaid stress.
Whereupon said I: "Master, who are those
People, whom the black air so castigates?"
"The first of those, of whom intelligence
Thou fain wouldst have," then said he unto me,
"The empress was of many languages.
To sensual vices she was so abandoned,
That lustful she made licit in her law,
To remove the blame to which she had been led.
She is Semiramis, of whom we read
That she succeeded Ninus, and was his spouse;
She held the land which now the Sultan rules.
The next is she who killed herself for love,

And broke faith with the ashes of Sichæus;
Then Cleopatra the voluptuous."
Helen I saw, for whom so many ruthless
Seasons revolved; and saw the great Achilles,
Who at the last hour combated with Love.
Paris I saw, Tristan; and more than a thousand
Shades did he name and point out with his finger,
Whom Love had separated from our life.
After that I had listened to my Teacher,
Naming the dames of eld and cavaliers,
Pity prevailed, and I was nigh bewildered.
And I began: "O Poet, willingly
Speak would I to those two, who go together,
And seem upon the wind to be so light."
And he to me: "Thou'lt mark, when they shall be
Nearer to us; and then do thou implore them
By love which leadeth them, and they will come."
Soon as the wind in our direction sways them,
My voice uplift I: "O ye weary souls!
Come speak to us, if no one interdicts it."
As turtle-doves, called onward by desire,
With open and steady wings to the sweet nest
Fly through the air by their volition borne,
So came they from the band where Dido is,
Approaching us athwart the air malign,
So strong was the affectionate appeal.
"O living creature gracious and benignant,
Who visiting goest through the purple air
Us, who have stained the world incarnadine,
If were the King of the Universe our friend,
We would pray unto him to give thee peace,
Since thou hast pity on our woe perverse.
Of what it pleases thee to hear and speak,
That will we hear, and we will speak to you,
While silent is the wind, as it is now.
Sitteth the city, wherein I was born,
Upon the sea-shore where the Po descends
To rest in peace with all his retinue.
Love, that on gentle heart doth swiftly seize,
Seized this man for the person beautiful
That was ta'en from me, and still the mode offends me.
Love, that exempts no one beloved from loving,
Seized me with pleasure of this man so strongly,
That, as thou seest, it doth not yet desert me;
Love has conducted us unto one death;
Caïna waiteth him who quenched our life!
These words were borne along from them to us.
As soon as I had heard those souls tormented,
I bowed my face, and so long held it down
Until the Poet said to me: "What thinkest?"
When I made answer, I began: "Alas!
How many pleasant thoughts, how much desire,
Conducted these unto the dolorous pass!"
Then unto them I turned me, and I spake,
And I began: "Thine agonies, Francesca,

Sad and compassionate to weeping make me.
But tell me, at the time of those sweet sighs,
By what and in what manner Love conceded,
That you should know your dubious desires?"
And she to me: "There is no greater sorrow
Than to be mindful of the happy time
In misery, and that thy Teacher knows.
But, if to recognise the earliest root
Of love in us thou hast so great desire,
I will do even as he who weeps and speaks.
One day we reading were for our delight
Of Launcelot, how Love did him enthral.
Alone we were and without any fear.
Full many a time our eyes together drew
That reading, and drove the colour from our faces;
But one point only was it that o'ercame us.
When as we read of the much-longed-for smile
Being by such a noble lover kissed,
This one, who ne'er from me shall be divided,
Kissed me upon the mouth all palpitating.
Galeotto was the book and he who wrote it.
That day no farther did we read therein."
And all the while one spirit uttered this,
The other one did weep so, that, for pity,
I swooned away as if I had been dying,
And fell, even as a dead body falls.

Canto XXXIV.

"Vexilla Regis prodeunt Inferni
Towards us; therefore look in front of thee,"
My Master said, "if thou discernest him."
As, when there breathes a heavy fog, or when
Our hemisphere is darkening into night,
Appears far off a mill the wind is turning,
Methought that such a building then I saw;
And, for the wind, I drew myself behind
My Guide, because there was no other shelter.
Now was I, and with fear in verse I put it,
There where the shades were wholly covered up,
And glimmered through like unto straws in glass.
Some prone are lying, others stand erect,
This with the head, and that one with the soles;
Another, bow-like, face to feet inverts.
When in advance so far we had proceeded,
That it my Master pleased to show to me
The creature who once had the beauteous
semblance,
He from before me moved and made me stop,
Saying: "Behold Dis, and behold the place
Where thou with fortitude must arm thyself."
How frozen I became and powerless then,
Ask it not, Reader, for I write it not,
Because all language would be insufficient.

I did not die, and I alive remained not;
Think for thyself now, hast thou aught of wit,
What I became, being of both deprived.
The Emperor of the kingdom dolorous
From his mid-breast forth issued from the ice;
And better with a giant I compare
Than do the giants with those arms of his;
Consider now how great must be that whole,
Which unto such a part conforms itself.
Were he as fair once, as he now is foul,
And lifted tip his brow against his Maker,
Well may proceed from him all tribulation.
O, what a marvel it appeared to me,
When I beheld three faces on his head!
The one in front, and that vermilion was;
Two were the others, that were joined with this
Above the middle part of either shoulder,
And they were joined together at the crest;
And the right-hand one seemed 'twixt white and yellow;
The left was such to look upon as those
Who come from where the Nile falls valley-ward.
Underneath each came forth two mighty wings,
Such as befitting were so great a bird
Sails of the sea I never saw so large.
No feathers had they, but as of a bat
Their fashion was; and he was waving them,
So that three winds proceeded forth therefrom.
Thereby Cocytus wholly was congealed.
With six eyes did he weep, and down three chins
Trickled the tear-drops and the bloody drivel.
At every mouth be with his teeth was crunching
A sinner, in the manner of a brake,
So that he three of them tormented thus.
To him in front the biting was as naught
Unto the clawing, for sometimes the spine
Utterly stripped of all the skin remained.
"That soul up there which has the greatest pain,"
The Master said, "is Judas Iscariot;
With head inside, be plies his legs without.
Of the two others, who head downward are,
The one who hangs from the black jowl is Brutus;
See how he writhes himself, and speaks no word.
And the other, who so stalwart seems, is Cassius.
But night is reascencling, and 'tis time
That we depart, for we have seen the whole."
As seemed him good, I clasped him round the neck,
And he the vantage seized of time and place,
And when the wings were opened wide apart,
He laid fast hold upon the shaggy sides;
From fell to fell descended downward then
Between the thick hair and the frozen crust.
When we were come to where the thigh revolves
Exactly on the thickness of the haunch,
The Guide, with labour and with hard-drawn breath,

Turned round his head where he had had his legs,
And grappled to the hair, as one who mounts,
So that to Hell I thought we were returning.
"Keep fast thy hold, for by such stairs as these,"
The Master said, panting as one fatigued,
"Must we perforce depart from so much evil."
Then through the opening of a rock he issued,
And down upon the margin seated me;
Then tow'rds me he outstretched his wary step.
I lifted up mine eyes and thought to see
Lucifer in the same way I had left him;
And I beheld him upward hold his legs.
And if I then became disquieted,
Let stolid people think who do not see
What the point is beyond which I had passed.
"Rise up," the Master said, "upon thy feet;
The way is long, and difficult the road,
And now the sun to middle-tierce returns."
It was not any palace corridor
There where we were, but dungeon natural,
With floor uneven and unease of light.
"Ere from the abyss I tear myself away,
My Master," said I when I had arisen,
"To draw me from an error speak a little;
Where is the ice?" and how is this one fixed
Thus upside down? and how in such short time
From eve to morn has the sun made his transit
And he to me: "Thou still imaginest
Thou art beyond the centre, where I grasped
The hair of the fell worm, who mines the world.
That side thou wast, so long is I descended;
When round I turned me, thou didst pass the point
To which things heavy draw from every side,
And now beneath the hemisphere art come
Opposite that which overhangs the vast
Dry-land, and 'neath whose cope was put to death
The Man who without sin was born and lived.
Thou hast thy feet upon the little sphere
Which makes the other face of the Judecca.
Here it is morn when it is evening there;
And he who with his hair a stairway made us
Still fixed remaineth as he was before.
Upon this side he fell down out of heaven
And all the land, that whilom here emerged,
For fear of him made of the sea a veil,
And came to our hemisphere; and peradventure
To flee from him, what on this side appears
Left the place vacant here, and back recoiled."
A place there is below, from Beelzebub
As far receding as the tomb extends,
Which not by sight is known, but by the sound
Of a small rivulet, that there descendeth
Through chasm within the stone, which it has gnawed
With course that winds about and slightly falls.

The Guide and I into that hidden road
Now entered, to return to the bright world.;
And without care of having any rest
We mounted up, he first and I the second,
Till I beheld through a round aperture
Some of the beauteous things that Heaven doth bear
Thence we came forth to rebehold the stars.

Geoffrey Chaucer (1340?–1400)

Geoffrey Chaucer, the most distinguished English poet of the Middle Ages, was born about 1340 in London, England, where he spent most of his life. He grew up in a middle-class family as the son of John Chaucer, a successful vintner, and Agnes de Compton. Chaucer witnessed some of the devastating effects of the Black Death (bubonic plague) on London around 1348 and later.

Although there are no records of Chaucer's formal education, some scholars believe that Chaucer probably received his early learning at Saint Paul's Almonry, where he may have studied English, Latin, French, and arithmetic. Chaucer, a prodigious reader, became well versed in many subjects, such as theology, music, astronomy, philosophy, and the Latin classics. Later, he served as a page to Elizabeth, Countess of Ulster and wife of Prince Lionel, from 1357 to 1358. In 1359 he was a soldier with the English in France, and during the siege of Reims, he was made prisoner; however, in 1360 he was ransomed by King Edward III. Then he returned to England. Subsequently, in 1366 he married Philippa de Roet, Sir Paon de Roet's daughter. It is said that Chaucer was the father of two sons, Thomas and Lewis.

Chaucer's education and experiences were crucial to his diversified public career, which included controller of customs, 1374–1386; justice of the peace, 1385; member of Parliament, 1386; clerk of the King's Works, 1389–1391, and shortly, thereafter, Deputy Forester of the Royal Forest of North Petherton. As a diplomat, Chaucer's duties required him to travel extensively in France, Flanders, Italy, and Spain. Consequently, he came in contact with the works of several literary figures, whose writings had a tremendous influence on him.

Chaucer's works are usually divided into three periods. The first period is dominated by French influence (about 1359–72). Some of the poets who influenced Chaucer were Machaut, Deschamps, and Froissart. Works included in this period are *Roman de la Rose,* an extant translation in fragments, partly ascribed to Chaucer; *Book of the Lyon,* a lost translation; and the *Book of the Duchess,* a dream-allegory (the conventional fourteen-century French genre), which is considered the most significant poem of this period. It was written to commemorate Blanche, the deceased first wife of John Gaunt, Duke of Lancaster. The second period is characterized by Italian influence (about 1372–86). Some writers who had a profound effect on Chaucer were Boccaccio, Dante, and Petrarch. Included in this period are two occasional poems, the *House of Fame* and the *Parliament of Fowls;* Boethius's *Consolation of Philosophy,* a prose translation; *Legend of Good Women,* unfinished; and *Troilus and Criseyde,* a magnificent narrative poem consisting of 8,000 lines, based on Boccaccio's *Filostrato.* The third period is the English (1386–1400). Portraying contemporary England in a realistic setting, Chaucer wrote his masterpiece, the *Canterbury Tales,* which is a collection of stories told by twenty-nine pilgrims on their way to the shrine of Thomas à Becket in Canterbury, a shrine associated with miracles. Although the *Canterbury Tales* was written during the English period, French, Latin and Italian influences are still evident.

Recognized as the most significant writer in the English language prior to Shakespeare, Chaucer died October 25, 1400, and is buried in the Poets' Corner in Westminster Abbey. Critics, scholars, teachers, and students alike have continued to admire this literary giant for his noteworthy contributions to English literature.

Selected Bibliography

Bloom, Harold, ed. *Geoffrey Chaucer.* New York: Chelsea, 1985.

Magnusson, Maynus, ed. *Cambridge Biographical Dictionary*. Cambridge, NY: Press Syndicate of the U of Cambridge, 1990.

Richmond, Velma Bourgeois. *Geoffrey Chaucer.* New York: Continum, 1992.

The "Prologue" of the *Canterbury Tales:* Background

The "Prologue" to the *Canterbury Tales* is the official roster of Chaucer's twenty-nine travelers who make the pilgrimage to Canterbury. They are all his contemporaries, and they represent a cross section of late fourteenth-century English middle class society. Chaucer sets the mood of the poem by opening with a vivid description of the English countryside in the springtime, the most popular time of the year for pilgrimages. The annual pilgrimage was a common feature of medieval life, and the Shrine of the martyr, St. Thomas á Becket at Canterbury was a frequent destination. As well as having a religious objective, these popular excursions provided a welcomed break from the monotony of daily life. Chaucer joins the congenial group gathered at the Tabard Inn in Southwark and describes his fellow travelers. Chaucer reveals the kind of people the pilgrims are, their rank in society, and their appearance. More than typical representations of class, the sketches are insightfully enriched, implicitly or explicitly, by exposure of the best and worst of humanity. Members of the group are classified as good, worldly, or depraved. The good live sustained by their faith. The worldly cannot resist wealth, power, and carnal temptations, while the depraved live completely immoral lives.

The pilgrims are a microcosm of middle class English society. The Prioress, Monk, and Friar are members of religious orders. The Merchant, Oxford Student, Lawyer, Franklin, Skipper, Doctor of Physics, the five Guildsmen, Cook, and Wife of Bath represent professions and trades. The Parson, the Plowman, his brother, and the Oxford student are idealized types, and the Miller, Manciple, Reeve, Summoner, and Pardoner are scoundrels and rogues. The clergy, both sacred and secular, are included. Although royalty and nobility are not a part of the pilgrimage, Chaucer's Knight expresses the mind and manner of courtly society; the Squire is the typical courtly lover. Many of the travelers are described as individuals as well as flawed types. The Wife of Bath has widespread teeth, the Knight's tunic is dirty, and the Miller has a wart; these and other minute actualities suggest the reality of each pilgrim and allow Chaucer to show individual character types.

The "Prologue" introduces two motifs that add to the unity of the *Canterbury Tales*. The first is the literary persona of the poet who provides Chaucer's individual voice and allows him to make objective commentary. The second motif is the personage of the Host who proposes a game, a storytelling contest. The *Canterbury Tales* is a frame tale, and Chaucer creates a frame in which many types of narratives including romance, fabliau, homily, beast fable, exemplum, Saint's legend, and religious treatise. The "Prologue" introduces a unique group of characters and provides structure to the stories that follow. Each tale expresses the personality of the pilgrim who tells it. For Chaucer, the frame tale is a literary tool which permits him to be an objective recorder. An active participant, Chaucer, the narrator, is the accurate recorder of what he hears his fellow pilgrims say. Indeed, the presence of Chaucer the pilgrim, narrator, observer, and participant, enhances the frame structure and unity of the entire work. Sometimes dramatic exchange or interchange between the pilgrims adds to the development of stylistic contrasts between the tales. A drunken Miller, for example, preempts the order of storytelling to tell his tale, a tale which sharply contrasts to the Knight's tale.

The overriding focus which permeates much of medieval literature is Christianity/spirituality. The church was a dominant force, for it controlled education and significantly influenced the government. Most people came in frequent contact with some aspect of church affairs. Although more of Chaucer's pilgrims are secular than sacred, many of the stories are related to the church in some way, presenting a disordered Christian society in need of reform. Greatly influenced by the things of this world, the pilgrims, some of whom are seriously flawed, have the potential for virtue, although it is never realized.

Chaucer originally planned to have one hundred and twenty stories in the *Canterbury Tales*, two told by each pilgrim on the journey to Canterbury and two told on the return. The best storyteller would receive a free supper at the Tabard Inn. What actually exists is twenty-three tales and the beginning of a twenty-fourth being told by the Cook. Chaucer died before completing the task. At the end of the "Prologue," Harry Bailey, the host at the Inn, includes himself in the group, takes over as the unofficial person in charge, and convinces the pilgrims to tell stories for amusement as they travel to Canterbury. The Knight draws the lot to tell the first tale.

Selected Bibliography

Bloom, Harold, ed. *Geoffrey Chaucer: Modern Critical Views*. New York: Chelsea, 1985.

Donald, Howard. *Chaucer: His Life, His Works, His World*. New York: Dutton, 1987.

Payne, Robert. *Geoffrey Chaucer*. 2nd ed. Boston: Twayne, 1986.

The Canterbury Tales

Here beginneth the Book of the Tales of Canterbury.

The Prologue

When the sweet showers of April have pierced to the root the dryness of March, and bathed every vein in moisture whose quickening brings forth the flowers; when Zephyr also with his sweet breath has quickened the tender new shoots in holt and moor, and the young sun has run his half-course in the Ram, and little birds make melody and sleep all night with eyes open, so nature pricks them in their hearts: then folk long to go on pilgrimage to renowned shrines in sundry distant lands, and palmers to seek strange shores. And especially from every shire's end in England they go their way to Canterbury, to seek the holy blessed martyr who helped them when they were sick.

On a day in that season, as I was biding at the Tabard Inn at Southwark, about to make my pilgrimage with devout heart to Canterbury, it befell that there came at night to that hostelry a company of full nine-and-twenty sundry folk, who by chance had fallen into fellowship. All were pilgrims, riding to Canterbury. The chambers and the stables were wide, and we were right well lodged. But in brief, when the sun had gone to rest, I had spoken with every one of them and was soon of their company, and agreed to rise early to take our way whither I have told you. Nevertheless, whilst I have time and space, before this tale goes farther, I think it is reason to tell you all the quality of each of them, as they appeared to me, what sort of folk they were, of what station and how they were accoutred. With a knight I will begin.

There was a *Knight* and that a worthy, who, from the time when he first rode abroad, loved knighthood, faithfulness and honor, liberality and courtesy. He was full valiant in his lord's war and had campaigned, no man farther, both in Christendom and in heathen lands, ever honored for his worth. He was at Alexandria when it was won; many a time in Prussia he had headed the board, before all the foreign knights; he had fought in Lithuania and in Russia, no Christian man of his degree oftener; he had been in Granada at the siege of Algeciras and in Belmaria; he was at Lyeys and in Attalia when they were won, and had landed with many a noble army in tile Levant. He had been in fifteen mortal battles, and had thrice fought for our faith in the lists at Tremessen and ever slain his foe; he had been also, long before, with the lord of Palathia against another heathen host in Turkey; and ever he had exceeding renown. And though he was valorous he was prudent, and as meek as a maid of his bearing. In all his life he never yet spoke discourtesy to any living creature, but was truly a perfect gentle knight. To tell you of his equipment, his horses were good but he was not gaily clad. He wore a jerkin of fustian all begrimed by his coat of mail, for he had just returned from his travels and went to do his pilgrimage.

His son was with him, a young *Squire*, a lover and a lusty young soldier. His locks were curled as if laid in a press. He may have been twenty years of age, middling in height, wondrous nimble and great of strength. He had been, upon a time in a campaign in Flanders, Artois, and Picardy, and had borne him well, in so little time, in hope to stand in his lady's grace. His clothes were embroidered, red and white, as it were a meadow full of fresh flowers. All the day long he was singing or playing upon the flute; he was as fresh as the month of May. His coat was short, with long, wide sleeves. Well could he sit a horse and ride, make songs, joust and dance, draw and write. He loved so ardently that at night-time he slept no more than a nightingale. He was courteous, modest and helpful, and carved before his father at table.

They had a *Yeoman* with them; on that journey they would have none other servants. He was clad in coat and hood of green, and in his hand bore a mighty bow and under his belt a neat sheaf of arrows, bright and sharp, with peacock feathers. He knew how to handle his gear like a good yeoman; his arrows flew not aslant with feathers trailing. His head was cropped and his visage brown. He understood well all the practice of wood-craft. He wore a gay arm-guard of leather and at one side a sword and buckler; at the other a fine dagger, well accoutred and as sharp as a spear-point; on his breast a St. Christopher in bright silver, and over his shoulder a horn on a green baldric. He was a woodman indeed, I trow.

There was also a nun, a *Prioress*, full quiet and simple in her smiling; her greatest oath was but by Saint Loy. She was named Madame Eglantine. Well she sang divine service, intoned full seemly in her nose, and spoke French elegantly, after the manner of Stratford-le-Bow, for Parisian French she knew naught of. She had been well taught the art of eating, and let no morsel fall from her lips, and wet but her finger-tips in the sauce. She knew how to lift and how to hold a bit so that not a drop fell upon her breast. Her pleasure was all in courtesy. She wiped her upper lip so well that no film of grease was to be seen in her cup after she had drunk; and very dainty she was in reaching for her food. In truth she was full diverting, pleasant and amiable of bearing. She took pains to imitate court manners, to be stately in her demeanor and to be held worthy of reverence. But to tell you of her character, she was so charitable and so tender-hearted she would weep if she saw a mouse caught in a trap if it were dead or bleeding. She had certain small dogs, which she fed upon roasted meat or milk and finest wheaten bread. She would weep sore if one of them died or was struck at sharply with a stick. She was all warm feeling and tender heart. Her wimple was plaited neatly. Her nose was slender, her eyes gray as glass, her mouth small and soft and red withal. Certainly she had a fine forehead, almost a span high,—verily she was not undersized. Her cloak was neatly made, I was ware. About her arm was a coral rosary, the larger beads of green, upon which hung a brooch of shining gold; on it was engraved first an *A* with a crown, and after that *Amor vincit omnia.*

Another *Nun*, her chaplain, was with her, and three *Priests*.

There was a *Monk*, exceeding fine and imposing, a great rider about the country-side and a lover of hunting, a manly man withal, fit to be an abbot. He had many a blooded horse in his stable, and when he rode, men could hear his bridle jingling in a whistling wind as clear and loud as the chapel-bell where this lord was prior. Because the rule of St. Maur or of St. Bennet was old and something austere, this same monk let such old things pass and followed the ways of the newer world: He gave not a plucked hen for the text that hunters are not holy, or that a careless monk (that is to say, one out of his cloister) is like a fish out of water; for that text he would not give a herring. And I said his opinion was right; why should he study and lose his wits ever poring over a book in the cloister, or toil with his hands and labor as St. Austin bids? How shall the world be served? Let St. Austin have his work to himself. Therefore he rode hard, followed greyhounds as swift as birds on the wing. All his pleasure was in riding and hunting the hare, and he spared no cost thereon. I saw his sleeves edged at the wrist with fine dark fur, the finest in the country, and to fasten his hood under his chin he had a fine-wrought brooch of gold; in the larger end was a love-knot. His bald head shone like glass; so did his face, as if it had been anointed. He was a sleek, fat lord. His bright eyes rolled in his head, glowing like the fire under a cauldron. His boots were of rich soft leather, his horse in fine fettle. Now certainly he was a fair prelate. He was not pale, like a wasted ghost; best of any viand he loved a fat roasted swan. His palfrey was as brown as a berry.

There was a begging *Friar*, wanton and jolly, a very self-important fellow. In all the four orders is not one so skilled in gay and flattering talk. He had, at his own expense, married off many a young woman; he was a noble pillar of his order! He was well beloved and familiar amongst franklins everywhere in his country-side, and eke with worthy town women, for he had, as he said himself, more virtue as confessor than a parson, for he held a papal license. Full sweetly he heard confession, and his absolution was pleasant; he was an easy man to give penance, when he looked to have a good dinner. Gifts to a poor order are a sign that a man has been well shriven, he maintained; if a man gave, he knew he was contrite. For many a man is so stern of heart that he cannot weep though he suffer sore; therefore, instead of weeping and praying, men may give silver to the poor friars. His tippet was stuffed full of knives and pins as presents to comely women. And certainly he had a pleasant voice in singing, and well could play the fiddle; in singing ballads he bore off the prize. His neck was as white as the flower-deluce, and he was as strong as a champion. He knew all the town taverns, and every inn-keeper and bar-maid, better than the lepers arid beggar-women. For it accorded not with a man of his importance to have acquaintance with sick lepers; it was not seemly, it profited not, to deal with any such poor trash, but all with rich folk and sellers of victual. But everywhere that advantage might follow he was courteous, lowly and serviceable. Nowhere was any so capable; he was the best beggar in his convent, and gave a certain yearly payment that none of his brethren might trespass on his routes. Though a widow might not have an old shoe to give, so pleasant was his "In principio," he would have his farthing ere he went. He gained more from his begging than from his property, I trow! He would romp about like a puppy-dog. In love-days he was right efficacious, for he was not like a cloister-monk or a poor scholar with a threadbare cope, but like a Master of Arts or a cardinal. His half-cope was of double worsted and came from the clothes-press rounding out like a bell. He pleased his whim by lisping a little, to make his English sound sweet upon his tongue, and in his harping and singing his eyes twinkled in his head as the stars on a frosty night. This worthy friar was named Hubert.

There was a *Merchant* with a forked beard, in parti-colored garb. High he sat upon his horse, a Flanders beaver-hat on his head, and boots fastened neatly with rich clasps. He uttered his opinions pompously, ever tending to the increase of his own profit; at any cost he would the sea were safeguarded betwixt Middleburg and Orwell. In selling crown pieces he knew how to profit by the exchange. This worthy man employed his wit full cunningly; no wight knew that he was in debt, so stately he was of demeanor in bargaining and borrowing. He was a worthy man withal, but, to say the truth, I know not his name.

There was also an Oxford *Clerk* who had long gone to lectures on logic. His horse was as lean as a rake, and he was not right fat, I trow, but looked hollow-cheeked, and grave likewise. His little outer cloak was threadbare, for he had no worldly craft to beg office, and as yet had got him no benefice. He would rather have had at his bed's head twenty volumes of Aristotle and his philosophy, bound in red or black, than rich robes or a fiddle or gay psaltery. Albeit he was a philosopher, he had but little gold in his money-box! But all that he could get from his friends he spent on books and learning, and would pray diligently for the souls of them that gave him wherewith to stay at the schools. Of study he took most heed and care. Not a word spoke he more than was needful, and that little was formal and modest, in utterance short and quick, and full of high matter. All that he said tended toward moral virtue. Above all things he loved to learn and to teach.

There was also a *Sergeant of the Law*, an excellent man, wary and wise, a frequenter of the porch of Paul's Church. He was discreet and of great distinction; or seemed such, his words were so sage. He had been Judge at assizes, by patent and full commission; with his learning and great repute he had earned many a fee and robe. Such a man as he for acquiring goods there never was; aught that he desired could be shown to be held in fee-simple, and none could find a flaw in his deeds. Nowhere was there so busy a man, and yet he seemed busier than he was. He knew in precise terms every case and judgment since King William the Conqueror, and every statute fully, word for word, and none could chide at his writing. He rode in homely style in a coat of mixed stuff and a girdle of silk with small cross-bars. Of his appearance I will not make a longer story.

A *Franklin* was travelling with him, bearded white as a daisy, ruddy of face and sanguine of temper. Well he loved a sop in wine of a morning. He was ever wont to live in pleasure, for he was a very son of Epicurus, who held the opinion that perfect felicity stands in pleasure alone. He ever kept open house, as a very St. Julian in his own country-side. His bread and his wine were ever alike of the best; never were a man's wine-vaults better stored. His house was never without a huge pasty of fish or flesh-meat; in his house it snowed meat and drink, and every dainty that a man could dream of. According to the season of the year he varied his meats and his suppers. Many a fat partridge was in his mew and many a bream and pike in his fish-pond. Woe to his cook unless his sauces were pungent and sharp, and his gear ever in order! All the long day stood a great table in his hall ready laid. When the justices met at sessions, there he lorded it full grandly, and many a time he sat as knight of the shire in parliament. A dagger hung at his girdle, and a pouch of taffeta, white as morning's milk. He had been sheriff and auditor; nowhere was so worthy a vassal.

A *Haberdasher*, a *Carpenter*, a *Weaver*, a *Dyer* and an *Upholsterer* were with us eke, all in the same livery of a great and splendid guild. All fresh and new was their gear. Their knives were not tipped with brass but all with fine-wrought silver, like their girdles and their pouches. Each of them seemed a fair burgess to sit in a guildhall on a dais. Each for his discretion was fit to be alderman of his guild, and had goods and income sufficient therefor. Their wives would have consented, I trow! And else were they to blame; it is a full fair thing to be called *madame*, and to walk ahead of other folks to vigils, and to have a mantle carried royally before them.

They had a *Cook* with them for that journey, to boil chickens with the marrow-bones and tart powder-merchant and cyperus-root. Well he knew a draught of London ale! He could roast and fry and broil and stew, make dainty pottage and bake pies well. It was a great pity, methought, that he had a great sore on his shin, for he made capon-in-cream with the best of them.

There was a *Shipman*, from far in the West; for aught I know, he was from Dartmouth. He rode a nag, as well as he knew how, in a gown of frieze to the knee. He had a dagger hanging on a lace around his neck and under his arm. The hot summer had made his hue brown. Of a truth he was a good fellow:

many a draught of wine had he drawn at Bordeaux whilst the merchant slept. He paid no heed to nice conscience; on the high seas, if he fought and had the upper hand, he made his victims walk the plank. But in skill to reckon his moon, his tides, his currents and dangers at hand, his harbors and steersmanship, there was none such from Hull to Carthage. In an emprise he was bold and shrewd. His beard had been shaken by many a tempest. He knew the harbors well from Gothland to Cape Finisterre, and every creek in Spain and in Brittany, His ship was called the *Maudelayne*.

With us was a *Doctor of Physic*; for skill in medicine and in surgery was not his peer in all this world. He watched sharply for favorable hours and an auspicious ascendent for his patients' treatment, for he was full well grounded in astrology. He knew the cause of each malady, were it from a humor hot, cold, dry or moist, whence it had sprung and of what humor. He was a thorough and a perfect practitioner. Having found the cause and source of his trouble, anon he had ready the sick man's physic. He had his apothecaries all prepared to send him electuaries and drugs, for each helped the other's gain; their friendship was not formed of late! He knew well the old Æsculapius, Dioscorides and Rufus, Hippocrates, Haly and Galen, Serapion, Rhasis and Avicenna, Averroes, Damascene and Constantine, Bernard, Gatisden and Gilbertine. His own diet was moderate, with no superfluity, but nourishing and simple to digest. His study was but little on Scripture. He was clad in sanguine and light blue, lined with taffeta and sarcenet. Yet he was but moderate in spending, and kept what he won during the pestilence. Gold is a cordial in physic; doubtless that was why he loved gold above all else.

There was a *Goodwife* from near Bath, but she was somewhat deaf and that was pity. She was so skilled in making cloth that she passed them of Ypres and Ghent. In all the parish was no wife who should march up to make an offering before her, and if any did, of a truth so wroth she was that she was out of all charity. Her kerchiefs were full fine of texture; and I durst swear they weighed ten pound that were on her head of a Sunday. Her hose were of a fine scarlet and tightly fastened, and her shoes full soft and new. Her face was bold and fair and red. All her life she was a worthy woman; she had had five husbands at church-door, besides other company in her youth, but thereof it needs not speak now. She had thrice been at Jerusalem; many a distant stream had she crossed; she had been on pilgrimages to Boulogne and to Rome, to Santiago in Galicia and to Cologne. This wandering by the way had taught her sundry things. Sooth to say, she was gap-toothed; she sat full easily on an ambling horse, wearing a fair wimple and on her head a hat as broad as a buckler or target. About her broad hips was a short riding skirt and on her feet a pair of sharp spurs. Well could she laugh and prate in company. Love and its remedies she knew all about, I dare be bound, for she had been through the old game.

There was a good man of religion, a poor *Parson*, but rich in holy thought and deed. He was also a learned man, a clerk, and would faithfully preach Christ's gospel and devoutly instruct his parishioners. Benign, wondrous diligent, and patient in adversity, such he was oftentimes proved. Right loath he was to excommunicate for unpaid tithes, but rather would give to his poor parishioners out of the church alms and eke of his own substance; in little he found sufficiency. His parish was wide and the houses far apart, but for thunder or rain he neglected not to visit the farthest, great or small, in sickness or misfortune, going a-foot, a staff in his hand. This noble example he gave to his sheep, that first he wrought and afterward taught; these words he took out of the gospel, and this similitude he added eke, that if gold rust, what shall iron do? For if a priest upon whom we trust be foul, no wonder though an ignorant layman be corrupt; and it is shame (if a priest will but heed it) that a shepherd should be defiled and the sheep clean. A priest should give good ensample by his cleanness how his sheep should live. He would not farm out his benefice, nor leave his sheep stuck fast in the mire, whilst he ran to London to St. Paul's, to get an easy office of chantry-priest, or to be retained by some guild, but dwelt at home and guarded his fold full well, so that the wolf made it not miscarry. He was no hireling, but a shepherd. And though he were holy and virtuous, he was not pitiless to sinful men, nor cold or haughty of speech, but both discreet and benign in his teaching; to draw folk up to heaven by his fair life and good ensample, this was his care. But when a man were stubborn, whether of high or low estate, he would chide him sharply. There was nowhere a better priest than he. He looked for no pomp and reverence, nor yet was his conscience overnice; but the teaching of Christ and his apostles he taught, and first he followed it himself.

With him was his brother, a *Ploughman*, who had drawn many a cartload of dung. He was a faithful and good toiler, living in peace and perfect charity. He loved God best at all times with all his whole heart, in good and ill fortune, and then his neighbor even as himself. He would thresh and ditch and delve for every poor person without pay, but for Christ's sake, if it lay in his might. He paid his tithes fairly and well on both his produce and his goods. He wore a ploughman's frock and rode upon a mare.

There was a *Reeve* also and a *Miller*, a *Sumner* and a *Pardoner*, a *Manciple* and myself. There were no more.

The *Miller* was a stout fellow, full big of bones and brawn; and well he showed them, for everywhere he came to a wrestling match he would ever carry off the prize ram. He was short-shouldered and broad, a thick, knotty fellow. There was no door that he could not heave off its hinges, or break with his head at a running. His beard was as red as any sow or fox, and eke broad like a spade. Upon the very tip of his nose he had a wart, and on it stood a tuft of red hair like the bristles on a sow's ears, and his nostrils were black and wide. At his thigh hung a sword and buckler. His mouth was as great as a great furnace. He was a loud prater and a ribald jester, and it was mostly of sin and scurrility. He knew well to steal corn and take his toll of meal three times over; and yet he had a golden thumb, perdy! He wore a white coat and a blue hood. He could blow and play the bagpipe well, and with its noise he brought us out of town.

There was a gentle *Manciple* of an Inn of Court, of whom other stewards might take ensample for craftiness in buying victual. Whether he paid in cash or took on credit, he was so watchful in his buying that he was ever before others and in good case. Now is it not a full fair gift of God that the wit of such an unlettered man shall pass the wisdom of a great body of learned men? He had more than a score of masters, expert and diligent in law, of whom in that house there were a dozen worthy to be stewards of lands and revenues of any lord in England, to let him live upon his income, honorably, free from debt, unless he were mad, or live as plainly as he would; or able to help a whole shire in any case which might befall. And yet this Manciple hoodwinked all of them.

The *Reeve* was a slender, bilious man. His beard was shaven as close as could be, his hair was cut short around his ears and docked in front like a priest's. His legs were full long and lean like a stick; I could see no calf. He could well keep a bin and a garner and no inspector could get the best of him. In the drought or in the wet he could foretell the yield of his grain and seed. His lord's sheep, poultry and cattle, his dairy and swine and horses and all his stock, this Reeve had wholly under his governance, and submitted his accounts thereon ever since his lord was twenty years of age; and none could ever find him out in arrears. There was no bailiff nor herdsman nor other churl whose tricks and craftiness he knew not. They were as afraid of him as of the plague. His dwelling-place was a pleasant one on a heath, all shaded with green trees. Better than his lord he knew how to pick up wealth, and had a rich privy hoard; he knew how to please his master cunningly by giving and lending him out of what was his master's by right, and to win thanks therefor, and a cast coat and hood withal. In his youth he had learned a good trade and was a full good carpenter and wright. This Reeve sat upon a fine dapple gray cob named Scot. He wore a long surcoat of blue and at his side a rusty blade. He was from Norfolk, near a town they call Baldeswell. His coat was tucked up around him like a friar's, and he ever rode last of us all.

A *Sumner* was with us there, a fire-red cherubim-faced fellow, salt-phlegmed and pimply, with slits for eyes, scabby black eyebrows and thin ragged beard, and, as hot and lecherous as a sparrow. Children were terrified at his visage. No quicksilver, white-lead, brimstone, borax nor ceruse, no cream of tartar nor any ointment that would clean and burn, could help his white blotches or the knobs on his chaps. He loved garlic, onions and leeks too well, and to drink strong wine as red as blood, and then he would talk and cry out like mad. And after drinking deep of wine he would speak no word but Latin, in which he had a few terms, two or three, learned out of some canon. No wonder was that, for he heard it all day long, and you know well how a jay can call 'Wat,' after long hearing it, as well as the pope could. But if he were tested in any other point, his learning was found to be all spent. *Questio quid juris*, he was ever crying. He was a kind rogue and a gentle, a better fellow I never knew; for a quart of wine he would suffer a good fellow to have his paramour a twelvemonth and utterly wink at it, and privily he practised the same himself! And if anywhere he found a good fellow, he would teach him in such case to have no fear of the archdeacon's excommunication, unless a man's soul is in his purse, for it was in his purse he should be punished. 'The Archdeacon's hell is your purse,' he said. But well I wot he lied in his teeth; every guilty man should fear the church's curse, for it will slay even as absolution saves,—and also let him beware of a *significavit*. Within his jurisdiction on his own terms he held all the young folk of the diocese, and knew their guilty secrets and was their chief adviser. He had a garland on his head large enough for an ale-house sign, and carried a round loaf of bread as big as a buckler.

With him rode a gentle *Pardoner*, of Roncesvalles, his friend and crony, come straight from the court of Rome. He sang full loudly,

'Come hither, love, to me,'

whilst the Sumner bore him a stiff bass; never was trumpet of half such a sound. This Pardoner had waxy-yellow hair, hanging smooth, like a hank of flax, spread over his shoulders in thin strands. For sport he wore no hood, which was trussed up in his wallet; riding with his hair dishevelled, bareheaded save for his cap, he thought he was all in the newest fashion. His eyes were glaring like a hare's. He had a vernicle sewed on his cap, and his wallet, brimful of pardons hot from Rome, lay before him on his saddle. His voice was as small as a goat's. He had no beard nor ever would have, his face was as smooth as if lately shaven; I trow he was a mare or a gelding. But as for his trade, from Berwick to Dover there was not such another pardoner. In his bag he had a pillow-case which he said was our Lady's kerchief, and a small piece of the sail which he said St. Peter had when he walked upon the sea and Jesu Christ caught him. He had a cross of latten, set full of false gems, and pigs' bones in a glass. But with these relics, when he found a poor parson dwelling in the country, in one day he gat him more money than the parson gat in two months. And thus, with flattering deceit and tricks, he made the parson and the people his dupes. But to give him his due, after all he was a noble ecclesiastic in church; he could read well a lesson or legend and best of all sing an offertory. For he knew well that when that was done he must preach and file his tongue smooth, to win silver as he well knew how. Therefore he sang merrily and loud.

Now I have told you in few words the station, the array, the number of this company and eke why they were assembled in Southwark, at this noble hostelry the Tabard, hard by the Bell. But now it is time to say how we bore us that same even, when we had alighted at that hostelry; and afterward I will tell you of our journey and the remnant of our pilgrimage. But first I pray that of your courtesy ye ascribe it not to mine ill manners if I speak plainly in this matter, telling you their words and cheer, and if I speak their very words as they were. For this ye know as well as I, that whoso tells a tale that another has told, he must repeat every word, as near as he can, although he speak never so rudely and broad. Else he must tell his tale falsely, or feign, or find new words. He may not spare any, were it his own brother; he is bound to say one word as well as the next. Christ himself spoke full plainly in Holy Writ and ye know well that it is no baseness. And Plato says, whoever can read him, that the word must be cousin to the act. I also pray you to forgive me though I have not set folk here in this tale according to their station, as they should be. My wit is short, ye can well understand.

Our host made us all great cheer, and anon brought us to supper and served us with the best of victual. The wine was strong and right glad we were to drink. Our *Host* was a seemly man, fit to be marshal in a banquet-hall, a large man with bright eyes, bold in speech, wise and discreet, lacking naught of manhood: there is not a fairer burgess in Cheapside. He was withal a right merry fellow, and after supper, when we had paid our scores, he began to jest and speak of mirth amongst other things. 'Now lordings,' he said, 'verily you are right heartily welcome to me, for by my troth, if I shall say sooth, I have not seen this year so merry a company at this inn at once. I would fain make mirth if I but knew how. And I have even now bethought me of a mirthful thing to give you pleasure, which shall cost nothing. You go to Canterbury,—God speed you, and the blessed martyr duly reward you! I know full well, along the way you mean to tell tales and make sport, for in truth it is no comfort nor mirth to ride by the way dumb as a stone. And therefore, as I said, I will make you sport. If it please you all by common consent to stand by my words and to do as I shall tell you, now by my father's soul (and he is in heaven) to-morrow as you ride along, if you be not merry, I will give you my head. Hold up your hands, without more words!'

Our mind was not long to seek. We thought it not worth debating, and agreed with him without more thought, and bade him to say his verdict as he would.

'Lordings,' quoth he, 'pray hearken now, but take it not, I pray you, disdainfully. To speak briefly and plainly, this is the point, that each of you for pastime shall tell two tales in this journey to Canterbury, and two others on the way home, of chances that have befallen whilom. And whichever of you bears him best, that is to say, that tells now tales most instructive and diverting, shall have a supper at the expense of us all, sitting here in this place, beside this post, when we come back from Canterbury. And to add to your sport, I will gladly go with you at mine own cost, and be your guide. And whoever opposes my judgment shall pay all that we spend on the way. If you agree that this be so, tell me now, without more words, and straightway I will, plan therefor.'

We agreed to this thing and pledged our word with glad hearts, and prayed him to do so, and to be our ruler and to remember and judge our tales, and to appoint a supper at a certain price. We would be ruled at his will in great and small, and thus with one voice we agreed to his judgment. Thereupon the wine was fetched, and we drank and then each went to rest without longer stay.

On the morrow, when the day began to spring, our host arose and played Chanticleer to us all, and gathered us in a flock. Forth we rode, a little faster than a walk, to St. Thomas-a-Waterings. There our Host drew up his horse and said, 'Hearken, lordings, if you will. You know your agreement; I remind you of it. If evensong and matins accord, let see who shall tell the first tale. So may I ever drink beer or wine, whoso rebels against my judgment shall pay all that is spent on the journey. Now draw cuts, ere we separate further; he who has the shortest shall begin the tales. Sir Knight, my master and my lord,' quoth he, 'now draw your lot, for this is my will. Come nearer, my lady Prioress, and you, sir Clerk, be not shamefast, study not; lay hand to, every man of you.'

Anon every one began to draw, and in short, were it by chance or not, the truth is, the lot fell to the Knight, at which every one was full blithe and glad; he must tell his tale, as was reason, according to the agreement which ye have heard,—what need of more words? When this good man saw it was so, as one discreet and obedient to his free promise he said, 'Since I begin the sport, what! in God's name, welcome be the cut! Now let us ride on, and hearken to what I say.'

And at that word we rode forth on our journey. And he began his tale anon with right glad cheer, and spoke in this wise.

The "Pardoner's Tale": Background

Under the guise of holiness, a thoroughly depraved, self-seeking Pardoner tells a tale which illustrates the very vice he practices. It is an exemplum or an illustrative example, and its theme, which addresses the evils of greed, is used by the Pardoner in all of his sermons. He, however, personifies the very sins against which he preaches. Portrayed as a consummate hypocrite in Chaucer's the *Canterbury Tales*, the Pardoner openly acknowledges the weakness of his character which is greed. He is a skilled, self-confident preacher who has perfected his "con" to convince the unsuspecting to give money to him.

The Pardoner is not what he should be neither spiritually nor physically. He is a lay employee of the church, and he should not preach or collect offerings at all. Papal indulgences sold by honest pardoners were to release people only from the punishment of sin. The Pardoner, however, claims he can absolve sinners completely. He sells admittedly worthless relics which he claims will absolve sinners from the punishment and the guilt of sin. The Pardoner shrewdly manipulates parishioners by convincing them that he will not sell pardons to those who are extremely sinful. Those who do not participate in his scam are suspected of being sinners by those who do. Proficient in arousing emotions by manipulating language, the Pardoner's sermons are performances rampant with fraudulent acts; and he shares with his fellow pilgrims his true intent to deceive them. Physically, the Pardoner is portrayed as effeminate in appearance with a high pitched voice. Chaucer suggests that he is a eunuch, a description which parallels his spiritual sterility. However, the Pardoner, however, boasts of his sexual prowess, further indicating the height of his hypocrisy.

The Pardoner demonstrates that a good sermon can come from a sinful mouth. Offering both theory and practice, he precedes his tale by discussing four major sins and showing the relation of one to the other: gluttony, gambling, false oaths, and blasphemy. The focus of the story is the consequence of committing these deadly sins. The characters in his story unwittingly engage in all of the sins condemned by the Pardoner. Ironically the tale emphasizes and illustrates the wages of sin.

Selected Bibliography

Bloom, Harold, ed. *Geoffrey Chaucer*. New York: Chelsea, 1985.

Faulkner, Dewey R., ed. *Twentieth Century Interpretations of the Pardoner's Tale.* Englewood Cliffs, NJ: Prentice Hall, 1973.

Lawler, Traugott. *The One and the Many in the Canterbury Tales.* Hamden, CT: Anchor, 1980.

Pardoner's Tale

Here Followeth the Prologue of the Pardoner's Tale.

Radix malorum est; Ad Thimotheum, sexto.

'Lordings,' quoth he, 'when I preach in churches, I strive after a high-resounding voice, and I ring it out as round as a bell, for I know by rote all that I say. My theme is and ever was one and the same,—*Radix malorum est cupiditas*. First I pronounce whence I come, and then I show my bulls, one and all, but first the seal of our liege lord the king upon my patent,—that I show first to secure my body, lest any man, priest or clerk, be so bold as to disturb me in Christ's holy labors. After that I say forth my say, and show bulls of popes and cardinals and patriarchs and bishops, and in Latin I speak a few words to give a savor to my preaching and to stir men to devotion. Then I show forth my long crystal boxes, crammed full of clouts and bones; all the folk ween that they are holy relics. I have a shoulder-bone set in latten which came from an holy Jew's sheep. "Good men," I say, "mark my words; wash this bone in any spring, and if a cow or calf or sheep or ox swell up that has been stung or bitten by any serpent, take water from this spring and wash its tongue and it will he whole anon. And moreover, every sheep that drinks a draught from this spring shall be whole of pox or scabs or sore. And mark what I say. If the goodman that owns the beasts will drink, fasting, a draught from this spring every week ere cock-crow, as this holy Jew taught our forefathers, his beasts and his stock shall multiply. And sirs, it will cure jealousy also; though a man be fallen into a jealous fury, only make his pottage with this water and he will nevermore mistrust his wife, though he know the very truth of her fault,—though she had taken two or three priests. "Here too is a mitten. He that will put his hand in this mitten shall see his grain multiply, be it wheat or barley; so he offer pence, or else groats.

"But, good men and women, of one thing I warn you; if any wight is now in this church who has done a horrible sin and dares not be shriven of it for shame, or if any woman, old or voting, has made her husband a cuckold, such folk shall have no power or grace to make offerings here to my relics. But whoso knows him to be free from such fault, let him comeup and offer in the name of God, and I will assoil him by the authority granted me by bull."

'With this trickery I have won a hundred marks, year by year, since I have been a pardoner. I stand like a cleric in my pulpit, and when the lay folk are sat down I preach as you have heard and tell a hundred false cozening quips beside. Then I take pains to stretch out my neck and bob my head east and west over the people, like a dove perched upon a barn. My hands and tongue go so briskly that it is a joy to see my diligence. All my preaching is of avarice and such cursedness, to make them large in giving their pence and especially to me. My aim is all for gain and not at all for correction of sin. I reck not, when they are underground, though their souls go a-blackberrying! Certes, many a sermon arises from an ill intent, how to please and flatter folk and to aim for promotion through hypocrisy, now from vain glory and again from hate. For when I dare not otherwise have it out with a man, then I sting him with my bitter tongue as I preach, so that he cannot escape being falsely defamed, if he have trespassed against me or my brethren. For though I tell not his name, men shall know whom I mean by hints and other circumstances. Thus I requite folk who do us ill-turns, and thus I spit out my venom under the guise of holiness, seeming holy and faithful. I say again, in few words, I preach for no motive but avarice; wherefore my theme is and ever was, *Radix malorum est cupiditas*. Thus can I preach against that same vice which I practice, covetousness. But though myself be guilty of it, I can make other folk depart from avarice and repent full sore. But that is not my chiefest purpose, I preach for naught but covetousness; and this should suffice for this matter.

'Then I tell them many an ensample from old stories of long ago. For simple people love old tales; such things they can well remember and repeat.

'What!—trow you so long as I can preach and gain gold and silver by discoursing, that I shall live in poverty willingly? Nay, nay, truly I never thought of it! I will preach and beg everywhere I go; I will not labor with my hands nor make baskets to live by, only because I will not be an idle beggar. I will imitate none of the apostles. I will have wool, wheat, cheese, and money, were it given by the poorest lad or widow in a village, though her children pine and starve! I will have a merry wench in every town and drink liquor from the vine.

'But hearken, lordings, in conclusion. Your will is that I tell a tale. Now that I have drunk a good draught of malty beer, by the Lord I hope I shall tell you a thing that ought by reason to be to your liking. For though myself be a vicious man, yet I know how to tell you a moral tale which I am wont to tell in my money-getting homilies. Now hold your peace, and I will begin.'

Here Beginneth the Pardoner's Tale.

Whilom there dwelt in Flanders a company of young folk who followed after folly, as riotous living and gaming in stews and taverns, where with harps, lutes and citterns they danced and played at dice day and night, and ate and drank inordinately. Thus they did service to the Devil in cursed fashion within those Devil's temples by abominable superfluity. Their oaths were so great and so damnable that it was grisly to hear them swear; they rent our blessed Lord's body in pieces anew (as if the Jews had not rent him enough!), and each laughed at the others' sins. And anon came dancing girls, graceful and slim young fruit-wenches, singers with harps, bawds and confectioners, who are all very officers of the Devil to kindle and blow that fire of lust that is near allied to gluttony. I take Holy Writ to witness that in wine and drunkenness are excess and lust. Lo, how drunken Lot sinned against nature, not knowing what he did; he was so drunk he knew not what he wrought. Herod (let any one look up the history), when he was full of wine at his feast, gave command at his own table to slay the Baptist John guiltless. Seneca also of a surety says a good word; he says he can find no difference betwixt a man that is out of his mind and him who is drunken, except that madness, when it attacks an ill-conditioned fellow, endures longer than drunkenness. Oh cursed gluttony, first cause of our undoing, origin of our damnation, until Christ redeemed us with His blood! Only think how dearly was this cursed sin paid for; this whole world was ruined by gluttony! Our father Adam and his wife in verity were driven from Paradise to labor and woe for that vice. For whilst Adam fasted I read that he was in Paradise, and when he ate of the forbidden fruit of the tree, he was cast out to woe and pain. O gluttony, well mar we accuse thee! If a man but knew how many maladies follow low from gluttony and excess, he would be more moderate of his diet as he sits at table. Alas! for the tender mouth and the short throat, east and west and south and north men labor in the earth and air and water to get dainty meat and drink for a glutton. On this, O Paul, well canst thou discourse. 'Meat unto belly and belly unto meat,—God shall destroy both,' as Paul says. Alas! foul is it to say, by my faith, but fouler is the act, when a man drinks so of the white and red that he makes a jakes of his throat through this accursed excess. The apostle, weeping, says piteously, 'There walk many of whom I have told you, and I say it now weeping and with a piteous voice, they are enemies of the cross of Christ, their end is death, their god is their belly. O belly, foul bag, full of corruption! what labor and cost to provide for thee! How these cooks pound and strain and grind, and turn substance into accident, to satisfy all thy greedy taste! Out of the hard bones they knock the marrow, and cast away naught that may go through the gullet soft and sweet. Of spicery and bark, root and leaf, is made the glutton's delicious sauce, to get him ever a new appetite. But he that follows after such delights, certes, is dead whilst he lives in those vices.

Wine is a lecherous thing, and drunkenness is full of wretchedness and of contention. O drunken man, thy face is disfigured, thy breath is sour, thou art foul to clasp in arms, and the sound through thy drunken nose seems as if thou saidest ever, 'Sam-soun, Sam-soun!' And yet Samson drank never wine, God wot. Thou fallest like a stuck pig, thy tongue is lost and all thy care for honest things, for drunkenness is the very sepulchre of man's wit and discretion. He over whom drink has dominion can keep no counsel, of a surety. Now keep you from the wine white and red, and chiefly from the white wine of Lepe for sale in Fish Street, or Cheapside. This Spanish wine subtly creeps through other wines growing hard by, and such fumes arise therefrom that after two or three draughts, though a man deem himself to be at home in Cheapside, he is even at the town of Lepe in Spain, not at Rochelle nor at Bordeaux; and then he will say, *'Sam-soun, Sam-soun!'*

But hearken to one word, I pray you, lordings all; the supreme acts of victory in the Old Testament, I dare be bound, were done through the help of the true omnipotent God in prayer and abstinence. Look into the Bible and there you may see it. Look too at Attila, the great conqueror, who died in shame and disgrace, bleeding at his nose in a drunken sleep. A great captain should live soberly. And moreover, consider right carefully what was commanded to Lemuel,—not Samuel, I say, but Lemuel; read the Bible and find it expressly set down as to giving wine to them that have oversight of justice. But no more now, for this may suffice.

Now that I have spoken of gluttony, I will forbid you gaming, which is the very mother of lies, deceit, and cursed forswearing, of blasphemy of Christ, manslaughter and waste of money and of time; and furthermore, it is a disgrace and against all honor to be known as a common gamester. And ever the higher a man's estate, the more abandoned he is held to be. If a prince practise hazard, by all temperance and public policy common opinion will hold him the lower in reputation. Stilbon, the wise ambassador, was sent to Corinth in great pomp from Lacedaemon to make an alliance; and when he came he chanced to find all the greatest men of that land playing at hazard. Wherefore, as soon as might be, he stole home again to his country and said, 'I will not lose my good name there, nor will I take on me such a shame as to ally you to gamblers. Send otherwise ambassadors; for by my troth I would rather die than ally you with gamesters. For you who be so glorious in honors shall not be allied with gamesters by my will, or treaty of my making.' Thus spake this wise philosopher. Look also how the king of the Parthians, as the book tells us, sent in scorn a set of golden dice to King Demetrius because he had practised gambling; wherefore he held at no value his glory and renown. Lords may find other kinds of virtuous diversion to pass the day with.

Now I will speak a word or two of false and great oaths that old books treat of. Violent swearing is an abominable thing, and false swearing is yet more to be blamed. The high God, as witness Matthew, forbade swearing at all; but especially the holy Jeremy says of swearing, 'Thou shalt say thine oaths in sooth, and not lie, and swear in righteousness and judgment.' But idle swearing is a cursedness. Behold how in the first table of the high God's glorious commandments the second commandment is, 'Take not my name amiss or in vain.' Lo, He forbids such swearing earlier than He forbids homicide or many other cursed things. I say that it stands in this order, as any one knows who knows the commandments, how that is the second commandment. And moreover I tell you flatly that vengeance will not depart from the house of him who is too outrageous of his oaths. 'By God's precious heart and by the nails of His cross, by the blood of Christ in the abbey of Hales, my chance is seven; yours is five and three. By God's arms, if you play falsely, this dagger shall go through your heart!' This is the fruit that comes of the two dice-bones, forswearing, ire, falseness, murder. Now for the love of Christ Who died for us, forsake your oaths, great and small. But, sirs, I will now tell on my tale.

These three rioters of whom I speak, long before any bell had rung for prime, were set down in a tavern to drink. And as they sat, they heard a bell tinkle that was carried before a corpse to his grave. One of them called to his boy, 'Off with you, and ask straightway what corpse it is passing by and see you report his name aright.'

'Sir,' quoth the boy, 'it needs not. It was told me two hours before you came here; he was an old fellow of yours, perdy, and he was slain suddenly in the night, as he sat very drunk on his bench. A privy thief men call Death, that slays all the people in this country-side, came with his spear and smote his heart in two, and went his way without a word. He has slain a thousand in this pestilence; and master, ere you come before him, methinks you were best be warned of such an adversary. Be ready to meet him ever; thus my mother taught me, I can say no more.'

'The child speaks truth, by St. Mary,' said the taverner, 'for over a mile hence, in a large village, he has slain both woman, child, churl and knave. I trow his habitation be there. It were great wisdom, a man to be on his guard lest he do him a hurt.'

'Yea, God's arms!' quoth this reveller, 'is it such peril to meet with him? I vow to God's bones I will seek him in the highways and the byways. Hearken, fellows, we are all as one; let each of us hold up his hand and become the others' brother, and slay this false traitor Death. He shall be slain ere night that slays so many, by God's dignity!'

These three plighted their troth together, each to live and die for the rest as he were their sworn brother, and up they all started in this drunken fury, and forth they went toward that village of which the taverner had spoken; and many a grisly oath they swore, and Christ's blessed body they rent to pieces,—'Death shall be dead if they can but catch him.'

When they had gone but a little way, even as they were treading over a stile, an old man and poor met them, and greeted them full meekly, and said, 'Now, lordings, God be with you!'

The proudest of these three revellers answered, 'What, churl, bad luck to you! Why are you all wrapped up save your face? Why live you so long and so decrepit?'

This old man began to peer into his visage, and said, 'Because I cannot find a man, though I walked from hence to India, in hamlet or in city, who will exchange his youth for mine age. And therefore I must keep mine old age as long as it is God's will. Alas, death will not take me! Thus I walk, a restless caitiff, and thus morn and night I knock with my staff upon the ground, which is my mother's gate, and say, "Dear mother, let me in. Lo, how I vanish away, flesh and skin and blood! Alas, when shall my bones be at peace? Mother, I would exchange my chest with you, which has been long time in my chamber, yea, for an hair-cloth shroud to wrap me in!" But still she will not do me that favor; wherefore my face is full pale awl withered.—But sirs, it is not a courteous thing to speak churlishly to an old man, unless he trespass in act or word. You may read yourselves in Holy Writ, "Before an old hoaryhead man ye shall arise;" wherefore I counsel you, do no harm now to an old man, no more than you would that it were done to you in your old age, if you abide so long. And now God be with you, wherever you go or be; I must go whither I have to go.'

'Nay, old churl, not so fast, by God,' said this second gamester straightway. 'By St. John, you part not so lightly! You spoke even now of that traitor Death who slays all our friends in this country-side. By my troth, you are his spy! Tell where he is, or by God and the Holy Sacrament you shall all pay for it. Truly you are of his consent to slay us young folk, false thief.'

'Now sirs,' quoth he, 'if you are so fain to find Death, turn up this crooked path; for by my faith I left him in that grove tinder a tree, and there he will tarry, nor for all your bluster will he hide him. See you that oak? There you shall find him. May God, Who redeemed mankind, save you and amend you!' Thus spoke this old wight.

And each of these revellers ran till he came to that tree, and there they found wellnigh eight bushels, as it seemed to them, of florins coined of fine round gold. No longer sought they then after Death, but each was so glad at the sight of the precious hoard that they sat them down by the fair shining florins. The worst of them spoke the first word. 'Brethren,' he said, 'heed what I say; though I jest oft and make sport, I have a pretty headpiece. Now Fortune has given us this treasure that we may live the rest of our lives in mirth and jollity, and lightly as it comes, so we will spend it. Eh! God's precious dignity! Who would have weened to-day that we should have so fair a grace! Could this gold be but carried hence to my house or else to yours,—for you know well all this gold is ours,—then were we in high felicity. But truly it may not be done by day. Folk would call us sturdy thieves and hang us for our own treasure. It must be carried by night, as wisely and slyly as may be. Therefore I advise that we draw cuts amongst us all, and he that draws the shortest shall run with a blithe heart to the town and that forthwith, and privily bring us wine and bread. And two of us shall cunningly guard this treasure, and at night, if he delay us not, we will carry it where we all agree is safest.'

One of them brought the cuts in his fist and bade them look where the lot should fill. It fell to the youngest of them and he straightway went forth toward the town. So soon as he was gone, the second said to the third, 'You well know you are my sworn brother, and now I will tell you somewhat to your advantage. Here is gold great plenty, to divide amongst the three of us; and you know well our fellow is gone. Now if I can shape it so that it be divided amongst the two of us, had I not done you a friendly turn?'

'I wot not how that may be,' the other answered, 'he knows the gold is left with us two. What shall we do ? What shall we say to him?'

'Shall it be a secret?' said the first villain. I shall tell you in few words what we shall do to bring it about.'

'I assent,' said the other, 'not to betray you, by my troth.'

Now quoth the first , 'you know well we be two and that two shall be stronger than one. Look when he is set down; do you arise and scuffle with him as in sport, and I will rive him through the two sides' and look that you do the same with your dagger. And then shall all this gold be shared betwixt you and me, dear friend. Then may we both fulfill all our lusts, and play at dice at our own pleasure.' And thus were these two villains accorded to slay the third as I have said.

The youngest, going to the town, revolved full often in his heart the beauty of those bright new florins. 'O Lord,' quoth he, 'if so be I could have all this treasure to myself, no man living under God's throne should live so merry as I!' And at last the fiend, our enemy, put it into his thought to buy poison with which to slay his two fellows; for the fiend found him in such a way of life that he had leave to bring him to perdition, for utterly his full purpose was to slay them both and never to repent. And forth he went without delay into the town to an apothecary, and prayed him to sell him some poison that he might kill his rats; and eke there was a pole-cat in his yard, he said, which had killed his capons, and he would fain wreak him upon the vermin, that ruined him by night. 'And you shall have such a thing,' answered the apothecary, 'that, so may God save my soul, no creature in all this world can eat or drink of this compound the amount of a grain of wheat, but he shall die anon. Yea, he shall die the death, and that in less time than you can walk a mile, this poison is so violent.'

This cursed man gripped the box of poison in his hand, and then ran into the next street to a shop and borrowed three large bottles. Into two of them he poured his poison, but the third he kept clean for his own drink, for he planned to labor all night long carrying away the gold. And when this reveller, the Devil take him!, had filled his three great bottles with wine, he repaired again to his fellows.

What need to discourse about it more? For as they had planned his death, even so they slew him, and that anon. When this was done, one of the two said, 'Now let us sit and drink and make merry, and then we will bury his body.' And with that word he chanced to take one of the bottles where the poison was, and he drank and gave his fellow to drink also. Wherefore anon they both died. And certes Avicenna wrote never in any canon or any chapter more wondrous signs of empoisoning than these trio wretches showed ere they died. Thus ended these two murderers, and eke the false poisoner also.

O cursed sin, full of cursedness! O treacherous homicide! O gluttony, lust and gaming! Thou blasphemer of Christ with insult and great oaths habitual and proud! Alas mankind, how may it be that to thy Creator Who made thee, and redeemed thee with His precious heart's blood, thou art so false and unkind, alas!

Now, good men, God forgive you your trespasses and guard you from the sin of avarice. My holy pardon will cure you all, so you offer nobles and other sterling coin, or else silver rings brooches, spoons. Bow your heads, bow them under this holy bull! Come up, wives, offer of your yarn! See, I enter your name here in my roll; you shall enter into heaven's bliss; I assoil you by mine high power, you that will make offerings, as clear and clean as when you were born—(lo sirs, thus I preach). And may Jesu Christ, our soul's physician, grant you to receive His pardon; for that is better than mine, I will not deceive you.

But sirs, one word I have forgot to say. Here in my wallet I have relics and indulgences as fair as any man's in Britain, that were given me by the pope's own hand. If any of you of devotion will make an offering and have mine absolution, come forth now and kneel down here and take meekly my pardon; or else take pardons all new and fresh as you go along, at every town's end, so you ever anew offer nobles and pence which be good and sound. It is an honor to every wight here to have a competent pardoner to absolve you as you ride through the lonely country, in case of misadventure which might befall. Peradventure one or two may fall down off their horses and break their necks in two. Look what a security it is to you all that I fell into your company, who may assoil you all, high and low, when the soul shall pass from the body! I counsel that our Host here be the first, for he is most enveloped in sin. Come forth, Sir Host, and offer first, and you shall kiss all the relics, yea, for a groat; straightway unbuckle your purse!

'Nay, nay, may I have Christ's malison if I do,' quoth he. 'Let be; it shall not be, on my soul. You would make me kiss your old breech and swear it were a saint's relic, be it never so foul! But by the holy cross and St. Helen, I would I had your guts in my hand instead of relics or halidom; pull them out, I will help you carry them. They shall be shrined in a hog's belly!'

This Pardoner answered not a word; so wroth he was, he would not speak.

'Now,' quoth our Host, 'I will not talk with you longer, nor with any other angry man.'

But anon when the worthy Knight saw all the people laughing, he said, 'Enough, no more of this. Sir Pardoner, be of merry cheer, and I pray you, Sir Host, that are so dear to me, kiss the Pardoner. And Pardoner, I pray you draw near again, and let us laugh and make sport as we did before.' And forthwith they kissed and rode on.

Here is ended the Pardoner's Tale.

"The Wife of Bath's Tale": Background

It might be useful to distinguish between Chaucer's purpose in writing "the Wife of Bath's Tale" and the Wife's purpose in telling the tale. Chaucer's purpose in writing the Wife's tale, as it is throughout the *Canterbury Tales,* is to delight his readers. He does this more fully by writing tales which are not only entertaining in themselves but also reflecting the characters and interests of the tellers.

Some of the characters on Chaucer's pilgrimage are intent on enjoying themselves. And so, the Wife of Bath enjoys pilgrimages and spends much of her time on them. Much of her delight in making pilgrimages derives from putting on her best clothes and being seen by men. So she goes on the pilgrimage to Canterbury dressed flamboyantly in order to attract men. Her tale, then, can be considered part of a process of self-advertisement. Its purpose, as far as the Wife is concerned, is to commend herself to her fellow pilgrims as an attractive, vivacious and lusty woman to gain her ambition of a sixth husband.

In her story, an ugly, old woman captures a lusty, young knight and convinces him that her age and ugliness do not matter and indeed are positive advantages in a marriage. This is certainly a broad hint to the lusty young bachelors on the pilgrimage. Furthermore, the old woman in her tale is miraculously restored to youth and beauty, things which the Wife would dearly love to regain. The Wife of Bath truly indulges in some wishful thinking. The reader must remember that the Wife is a self-confessed prevaricator who lies to her husbands. The reader should therefore be wary of taking her story as a true confession of her way of life. It would be safer to regard it as the story of how she would like to have acted and what she would like the other pilgrims to believe about her.

Overall, "the Wife of Bath's Tale" is Chaucer's reworking of the popular story of the Loathly Lady. There are many versions of the story throughout medieval literature. In Chaucer's version, the knight is offered the choice of having the woman fair by day and virtuous, not both. The tale clinches the argument that a man's true happiness lies in allowing his wife to do as she chooses. But the relevance of the tale to the Wife's situation goes further. She, like the old woman, has been transformed from a beautiful girl into an ugly old woman. In the Wife's case, the transformation has been wrought, not by a magic spell, but by the natural process of growing old. Nevertheless, she would love to be retransformed. No doubt she would love some lusty but submissive young knight to be her next husband.

Selected Bibliography

Donaldson, E.B. *Speaking of Chaucer*. London: Athlone, 1992.

Millan, Robert. *Chaucer: Sources and Backgrounds*. New York: Oxford UP, 1987.

The Wife of Bath's Tale

Here beginneth the Tale of the Wife of Bath.

In the old days of King Arthur, of whom Britons speak great glory, this land was all filled with fairy power. The elf-queen danced full oft, with her merry company, in many a green mead; this was the belief of old, as I find in books. I speak of many hundred years ago; but in our times no man can see elves any more. For now the great charity and the prayers of limiters and of other holy friars, who reach every land and every brook, as thick as motes in a sunbeam, blessing halls, towers, chambers, kitchens, cities, burgs, castles, thorps, dairies, barns, stables, bowers,—this brings it to pass that there be no elves. For where a fairy was wont to walk, there walks the limiter himself now, of mornings or of afternoons, and says his matins and his holy things as he goes in his mendicancy. Women may go up and down in safety; in every bush, under every tree, save him, there is none incubus,—and he will do them nought but dishonor.

And so befell that this King Arthur had a lusty young knight in his court, who on a day came riding from the river; and it happed that he saw a maid walking ahead alone as she was born, and her he ravished. For this violation there was such clamor and such appeal unto King Arthur, that the knight was condemned by course of law to die; and peradventure, such was the statute then, he would have lost his head, but that the queen and other ladies so long prayed the king for grace, till he granted him his life thereupon, and gave him over to the queen's will, to choose whether she would save him or let him die.

The queen thanked the king right heartily; and after this, upon a day when she saw her time, she spake thus to the knight: 'You stand yet,' quoth she, 'in such case that you have even now no assurance of your life. I grant you life, if you can tell me what thing it is that women desire most. Beware, and guard your neckbone from iron! And if you cannot tell it forthwith, I will give you yet leave to go for a twelvemonth and a day, to search out and learn an answer sufficient for this point. And ere you depart, I will have security that you will yield up your body in this place.'

Woe was this knight, and he sighed sorrowfully. But what! He might not do even as he list. And at last he chose to go and come again even at the year's end, with such reply as God should purvey him; and he took his leave and went his way forth.

He sought every house and place where he hoped to find such luck as to learn what women chiefly love. But he could arrive at no coast where he could find two creatures agreeing together on this thing. Some said that women best love riches; some said honor; some said mirth; some, rich array; some, lusty husbands, and to be widowed and wedded often. Some said that our hearts are most eased when we be flattered and gratified. They came full nigh the truth; a man shall best win us by flattery, I will not deny it, and by attentiveness and diligence we are caught, both great and small. And some said how we love best to be free and to do even as we will, and that no man reprove us for our faults, but say that we be wise and never foolish at all. For in sooth there is none amongst us, if any wight claw us on a sore place, that will not kick, because he tells us the truth. Try, and lie shall find it out who does so. For be we never so sinful within, we would be held for wise, and clean of evil-doing.

And some said that we have great delight to be accounted stable and eke trustworthy and steadfast in one purpose, and never bewraying what men tell us. But that tale is not worth a rake-handle, perdy! We women can conceal nothing, as witness Midas; will ye hear the tale?

Ovid, amongst other small stories, says that Midas had two ass's ears growing upon his head under his long hair, which blemish he hid full cunningly from every man's sight, as best he could, so that none wist of it save his wife. He loved her most and trusted her; and he prayed her to tell of his disfigurement to no creature. She swore to him., 'Nay, not to gain all the world she would not do that villainy and sin, to bring her husband so foul a name; for her own honor she would not do it. But nevertheless she felt she should die, to hide a secret so long; it swelled so sore about her heart, it seemed to her, that some word must needs burst from her. And since she durst tell it to no human creature, she ran down to a marsh hard by; her heart was ablaze till she came there. And ever as a bittern bumbles in the mire, she laid her mouth down unto the water: 'Thou water, bewray me not with thy sound,' quoth she; 'I tell it to thee, and to none else. Mine husband hath two long ass's ears. Now my heart is whole and well again; now it is out.

In very truth I could keep it in no longer.' By this you may see that though we bide a time, we can conceal no secret forever; it must out. If you will hear the remnant of the tale, read Ovid; there you may learn it.

This knight, of whom is my tale chiefly, when he saw he could not come by it—that is to say, what women most love—full sorrowful was the spirit within his breast. But home he went, he might not tarry; the day was come when he must turn homeward. And as he went, deep in care, it befell that he rode under a forest-side, where he saw four-and-twenty ladies and yet more go on a dance. Full eagerly he drew toward this dance, in hope of learning some piece of wisdom. But in truth, ere he fully came there, the dance was vanished—where, he wist not; and he discerned no living creature, save that he saw sitting on the green an old wife, a fouler wight none could imagine.

At the approach of the knight this old wife arose and said, 'Sir knight, by this way lies no path. Tell me, by your faith, what seek you? Peradventure it may be the better for you; these old folk know many a thing.'

'My dear mother,' quoth this knight, 'in truth I am but a dead man, unless I can say what thing it is that women desire most. Could you instruct me, I would well pay you your reward.'

'Plight me your troth,' quoth she, 'on my hand here, that you will do the first thing that I require of you, if it lie in your power; and ere it be night I will tell it you.'

'Take my pledge here,' said the knight, 'I agree.'

'Then,' quoth she, 'I dare be bound your life is safe; for upon my soul I will stand to it that the queen will say as I do. Let see the proudest kerchief or caul of the whole court, who dares say nay to what I shall teach you. Let us go on, without further words.'

Then she whispered a word in his ear, and bade him be glad and have no dread.

When they were come to the court, this knight said 'he had kept his day, as he had promised, and ready was his answer.' Then were assembled to hear his answer full many a noble wife, and many a maiden, and many a widow,—because they be wise; and the queen herself sat as justicer. And then this knight was summoned. Silence was commanded to every wight, and the knight was bidden tell in full audience what thing mortal women most love. This knight stood not like a dumb beast, but anon answered the question with manly voice, that all the court heard it. 'My liege lady,' quoth he, 'over all this world women wish to have sovereignty over their husbands as well as over their lovers, and to be in mastership above them. This is your chiefest desire, though you slay me for the word; do as you list, I am here at your will.'

In all the court there was neither wife nor maid nor widow to gainsay what he replied, but all declared he was worthy to have his freedom. And at that word, the old woman started up whom the knight had seen sitting on the green.

'Your favor, my sovereign lady!' quoth she. 'Do me justice, ere your court break up. I taught the knight this answer, for which he plighted me his faith that he would do the first thing I should require of him, if it lay in his power. Before the court, then, I pray you, sir knight,' quoth she, 'that you take me to wife, for you well know that I have saved your neck. If I speak falsely, say me nay, upon your faith!'

This knight answered, 'I wot full well that such was my promise, alas and alack! But for the love of God, pray choose another request! Take all my goods; let my body go.'

'Nay, then,' answered she, 'I beshrew us both. For though I be foul, poor, and old, I would none of all the metal or ore that is buried under the earth or lies upon it, but I were thy wife, and thy love eke.'

'My love!' quoth he, 'nay, my damnation! Alas that any of my kindred should be so foully mismated!'

But all this was for nought. This is the conclusion, that he was constrained, and needs must wed her. And he took his old wife and went to his chamber.

Now peradventure some men would say that of my negligence I take no care to tell you all the rejoicing and pomp which was at the celebration that day. To which thing I shall briefly answer, and say there was no joy nor celebration at all; but only heaviness and much sorrow. For he wedded her privily on a morn; and such was his woe, hid him all day after like an owl, his wife looked so ugly.

Great was his misery when he was alone with his wife; he tossed about and turned to and fro. His old wife lay evermore smiling, and said, 'Ah, *benedicite*, dear husband! fares every knight thus with his wife as you do? Is this the way of King Arthur's household? Is every knight of his so distant? I am your own love and your wife eke, and I have saved your neck, and certes, I have never yet done you a wrong.

Why do you so this first night? You fare as a man who has lost his wit. What is my guilt? Tell it me, for the love of God, and if I have the power, it shall be amended.'

'Amended!' quoth this knight. 'Alas, nay, nay; it cannot be amended forevermore! You are so loathly and so old, and eke come of so low a lineage, that it is small wonder though I toss and turn. Would God my heart would burst!'

'Is this the cause of your unquiet?'

'Yea, certainly, and no wonder,' quoth he.

'Now, sir,' she replied, 'I could amend all this ere three days were gone, if I list, so you bear yourself toward me well.

'But when you speak of such gentility as is descended from ancient wealth, so that therefor you knights are men of breeding,—such arrogance is not worth a hen. Look who is ever most virtuous, openly and privily, and ever most inclines to do what gentle deeds he may; take him for the gentlest man. Christ wills that we claim our gentility from him, not from our ancestors' ancient wealth. For though all their heritage, by reason whereof we claim high station, descend to us, yet they cannot at all bequeath to any of us their virtuous living, which made them to be called gentle men and to bid us follow them and do in like manner. The wise poet of Florence, who is named Dante, has a noble saying on this matter; lo, in such rhyme is Dante's saying:—

"Seldom into the branches of the tree
Mounts worth of man, for He that gives it to us
Wills that of Him we claim nobility."

For we may claim naught as from our ancestors save temporal things which men may injure and impair. Every wight eke knows this as well as I, that if nobility were planted by nature in a certain family all down the line, then would they never cease to do the fair offices of nobility, both privately and before the world; they could never do villainy or sin. Take fire and bear it into the darkest house betwixt here and the mount of Caucasus, and let men shut the doors and go thence, nevertheless the fire will burn and blaze as fairly as though twenty thousand men beheld it; on peril of my life, it will hold to its natural office till it die! Here you may well see how nobility hangs not from ancient possessions, since folk perform not alway its works, as does the fire, lo! according to its nature. For, God wot, men may full often see a lord's son do shame and baseness; and he that will have esteem for gentility because he was born of a noble house and had virtuous and noble ancestors, and yet himself will not perform the deeds of gentility nor follow after his gentle ancestor who is dead, he is not noble, be he duke or baron; for base sinful deeds make a churl. For gentility then were but renown of your ancestors for their high worthiness, which is full extraneous to your person. Your gentility comes only from God. Then comes our true gentility of divine grace, and was in no wise bequeathed to us with our earthly station.

'Think how noble was that Tullius Hostilius, as Valerius tells, who rose out of poverty to high nobility. Read Seneca, and Boethius eke; there you shall see expressly that he who does noble deeds is noble. And therefore, dear husband, I conclude thus: albeit mine ancestors were untutored, yet may the high God—and so I hope—grant me grace to live virtuously. Then I am noble, when I begin to live virtuously and to abandon evil.

'And you reproach me for poverty; but the high God on whom we believe chose freely to live in poverty. And certes every mail, maid or wife, may well know that Jesus, King of Heaven, would not choose an ill manner of living. Verily, cheerful poverty is an honorable thing, so will Seneca say and other clerks. Whoso holds him content with his poverty, I count him rich, though he have not a shirt! He who covets is a poor wight, for he would have that which is not within his power. But he that has naught, nor covets to have, is rich, albeit you count him but a serving-lad. True poverty, it sings by nature. Juvenal says merrily, concerning poverty:—

"The poor man as he strides along
Before the thieves may sing a song."

Poverty is a hateful good, and a full great ridder from cares I trow, and eke a great teacher of wisdom to him that takes it in patience. All this is poverty, though it seem wretched; and a possession which no wight will challenge. When a mail is humbled, full often poverty makes him to know his God and himself eke. Poverty methinks is a perspective glass through which he may see who are his true friends. And therefore, sir, I pray, so I grieve you not, upbraid me no more for my poverty.

'Now, sir, you reproach me for mine old age. And certes, sir, though there were no authority in any book to tell you so, yet you honorable gentlefolk say that men should do courtesy to an old wight, and for your gentle manners call him Father. And I could find authorities for this, I trow. Now you say I am old and foul—then dread you not to be a cuckold. For ugliness and age, on my life, are great wardens over chastity. But nevertheless, since I know what it is you would have, I shall fulfil your worldly will.

'Choose,' quoth she, 'one of these two things, to have me foul and old till I die, and to you a true, humble wife, never in all my days displeasing you; or else to have me young and fair, and take your adventure of the resorting to your house—or mayhap to some other place—which there will be for my sake. Now choose yourself which you will have.'

This knight took counsel with himself and sighed sore; but at last he spake after this manner: 'My lady and love, and my dear wife, I put me in your wise governance. Do you choose which may be greatest pleasure and greatest honor to you and me also; I care not which of the two, for it suffices me as it pleases you.'

'Then have I got the mastery over you,' quoth she, 'since I may make choice, and control as I list?'

'Yea, certes, wife,' quoth he; 'I hold that for the best.'

Quoth she, 'Kiss me, we be angered no longer. For by my faith I will be both unto you—that is to say, both fair, yea, and good. I pray to God that I may die mad, but I be as good and faithful as ever wife was since the world was new. And except I be in the morn as fair to see as any lady, queen or empress, betwixt the east and the west, do with my life and death as you will. Cast up the curtain, look how it is.'

And when the knight saw verily that she was so fair and likewise so young, he clasped her in his two arms for joy, his heart bathed in a bath of bliss. A thousand times together he kissed her.

And she obeyed him in all which might cause him delight or pleasure. And thus they lived in perfect, joy to the end of their lives. And may Jesu Christ send us husbands meek, young, and lusty, and grace to overlive them that we wed. And eke I pray Jesu to shorten their days that will not be ruled by their wives. And old, angry niggards of money, God send them betimes a very pestilence!

Here endeth the Wife of Bath's Tale.

Greco-Roman and Medieval Painting, Sculpture and Architecture

The art of the West, from classical Greece to the Renaissance, was humanistic in the broadest sense, centered on the representation of the human body and its place in the cosmos. It answers, differently at different times and places, in a concrete and embodied form, the ultimate humanist question, "What is man?" This act, one could say obligation, of representation has placed the artist at the center of a series of tensions or dichotomies that define Western culture: reason and emotion, science and religion, induction and deduction, innovation and tradition, real and ideal, individual and society, mind and body, man and nature. Never resolved, these tensions are thus always available for political and cultural delineation. They give to the art of the West a vibrant and dynamic quality that separates it from the more massive and eternal structures of Egypt and the Near East.

One early example of this difference is the bronze Apollo of Piombino (Figure 32), dating from early in the fifth century BC. The sculpture coincides with beginnings of classical Athenian civilization and reflects a time when philosophers were questioning the old gods and statesmen about the nature of political life. It belongs to a generation that witnessed the birth of Greek political freedom, the growth of science and the classical theater. Like these cultural expressions, the Apollo evidences this inquisitive attitude. Thus, while there are strong and unmistakable Egyptian influences, the Greek artist has begun to experiment. The Egyptian artist models from a past tradition of representation; the Athenian looks at nature: the hint of a smile in the lips, the effort to understand the muscles of the knee, the positioning of the feet and hands to suggest a balance of muscle and tension rather than an abstract design. There is a shift from deductive tradition to scientific induction and innovation. Yet this increased sense of scientific observation and drawing from nature is not designed to be "realistic." This is not a portrait of an individual but an ideal. Serenity surrounds the sculpture; there is not a narrative or delineation of passion but the human form idealized. The Apollo represents not so much a deity or religious ideal as a moral truth—a belief in human perfectibility.

The increased presence of a scientific and secular world view can be seen in the representation of Athena and the Warriors, completed only a few years later. This is the era of the Greek tragedies, and the human figures are no longer heroic but tragic ideals. They are vulnerable, mortal, sculpted on the same scale as Athena but with greater intensity. Scientific observation and accuracy serve an emotive end. The artistic work does not capture a timeless ideal but a tragic narrative. Later in the century, the details of the folds in the drapery and the pensive expression of Penelope (460–450 BC) further the humanized and individual representation of the human body (Figure 33). If the vacant, stylized faces of Egyptian and Near Eastern sculpture suggest an other-worldliness, Penelope's pose is natural and connected to the earth. The folds of drapery are depicted with observed scientific accuracy, and her thoughtful expression invites the viewer to respond to a very human emotional context.

Even in their representation of the Olympus immortals, then, the Greeks idealize the human form. The sculpture of Demeter, after Phidias in the fourth century BC, is a celebration of the Greek ideals of balance and proportion, both as an abstract composition and in its representation of the human form. The folds of drapery, the feet, and positioning of the hands—all create the sensation of muscular tension and control, simultaneously real and ideal, scientifically observed and emotive.

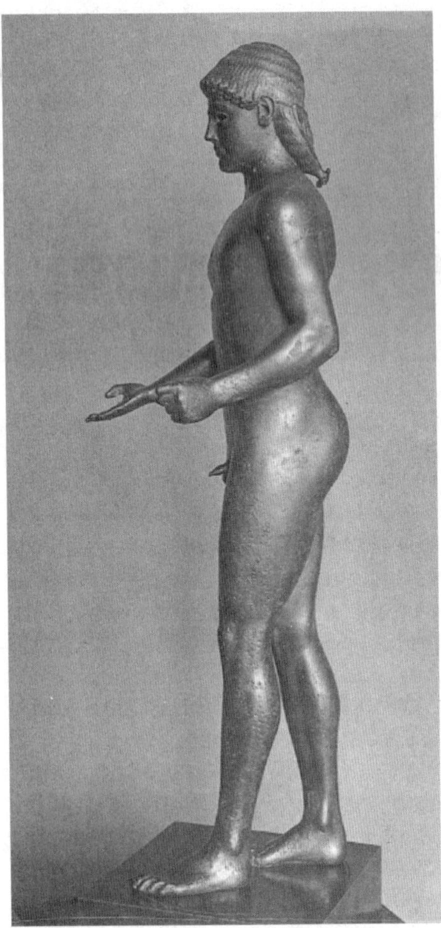

Figure 32. Apollo of Piombino. Louvre Museum.
Photograph © Giraudon/Art Resource, NY.

Figure 33. Penelope. Vatican Museum.
Photograph © Alinari/Art Resource, NY.

By the end of the fourth century BC, civil wars and social unrest had redefined, both politically and artistically, the values and ideals of the Greek city-states. Athens was no longer politically powerful and independent, although still a seat of culture and learning in Alexander's far flung empire. As befits a "world city" and seat of empire, Greek art in the Hellenistic period is increasingly sophisticated, self-consciously stylized, and individualistic. Thus, the second century BC Laokoon (Figure 34), from the workshop of Hagesandros, Polydoros, and Athanadoros, calls attention to itself as a unique work of art and to its sculptor as an artist expressing himself, not merely following a tradition. The Laokoon is simultaneously a scientific analysis of passion and an operatic heightening of its design to create in the viewer a sensation of horror. The central figure, the Trojan priest Laokoon, has just warned his countrymen of "Greeks bearing gifts." He cautions them to burn the monstrous horse statue left behind by the departing Greeks rather than take it into the city. As he speaks, the gods send serpents to attack him and his sons. As the horrified citizenry watch, Laokoon and his family are destroyed for challenging fate—the will of the gods. The Laokoon reveals the artist in complete control, both technically and emotively. Technically, this is no longer a static composition; in its compositional grouping of interconnected figures, it captures the dramatic moment of a life and death struggle. Likewise, the goal here is not religious or public/civic but the artist's personal conception of what true horror must be. The sculpture celebrates its own artistry, beauty, and emotive power simply as art—the artist's ability to convince viewers emotionally and intellectually of the dramatized moment. Art is no longer an act of worship or reverence but an individual artist's attempt to understand the human's place in the cosmos.

By Roman times, the art of the West had become highly individualized, to the point of scientific portraiture. The statue of the Emperor Augustus (Figure 35), for example, realistically represents the Emperor in the military garb of a Roman general, impressing the observer with the active nature of its subject. While realistic, the sculpture is by no means neutral or simply an objective representation of reality. It is art in service to the state, art celebrating the power of imperial Rome. Individuality exists but only for the Emperor as the embodiment of Rome. Augustus' breastplate chronicles his conquests, his arm holds a weapon of force and strength, and beside him the world is as helpless and dependent as an infant. His face is intelligent, thoughtful, and stern. His outstretched hand leads to a future only he controls. The truth and beauty that the Greeks invested into the Apollo are here the sole property of Rome, incarnate in Augustus. Everything else disappears. With the fall of Rome, however, this celebration of the individual realistically represented through an art designed to capture the inner, unique personality, will disappear until the Renaissance.

Figure 34. Laokoon. Vatican Museum.
Photograph © Archivi Alinari, 1991. Courtesy of Art Resource, NY.

Similarly dynamic distinctions can be seen in the characteristic architecture of the Greco-Roman world. In scale, proportion, simplicity, and clear arrangement, the Parthenon in Athens is a perfect example of Greek humanism. Built in the style of the early wooden Doric temples, the Parthenon still impresses viewers with the harmony of its lines. The columns, for example, are ever so slightly bowed outward at the center; an effect often likened to humans effortlessly supporting the load. Indeed, the Parthenon's human scale suggests a building designed and constructed for human use—not massive, not other worldly, not authoritarian, but human. Even today, the lines of the Parthenon are echoed in our public buildings.

The theater of Dionysus, located on the Acropolis near the Parthenon, is equally suggestive of the humanistic spirit of Greek art. As it developed in the fourth century BC, the Greek theater is an excellent example of how the Greeks can suggest universal truths through abstract shapes—the circle, the cube, and the cone. Typically, the theater is constructed around the circle, the dancing place, or *orchestra*. Behind the circle is the simple cubic stage or *skene*, and in front, cut into the hillside, the truncated cone of audience seats. On the stage, the principle drama is enacted; in the *orchestra*, the chorus, representing the communal voice, interacts with the actors on stage, comments on their actions, and itself becomes an audience lens into the drama. Because of the fine acoustics, much of the Athenian population gathered to view the plays. The basic format of the Greek theater is preserved in the modern stage.

Figure 35. Augustus of Primaporta, c. 20 BC.
Photo courtesy of Art Resource, NY.

Roman architecture, like Roman sculpture, borrowed heavily from the Greeks; in fact, most of the artisans in Rome were of Greek origin. Although the Romans themselves were content to reproduce Greek styles and patterns, they adapted them, through technological breakthroughs in civil engineering, to a variety of useful structures. The Coliseum (Figure 36), the massive amphitheater in the center of Rome, is probably the most famous. The seats of this vast stadium were supported with three stories of arches. The columns themselves were Greek; what is new is the use of the arch, which enabled the Romans to construct the bridges, aqueducts, and vaulted domes that were the marvels of the ancient world.

Although the representation of the human figure in its physical space continued to define Western art, the terms in which artists conceived their work altered radically in AD 311, when the Emperor Constantine adopted Christianity as the religion of the Roman Empire. In both the representational arts and in architecture, the problem was in adapting existing classical forms to the new needs of the church. In the representational arts, the church's position was well articulated by Pope Gregory the Great. Noting that many Christians could neither read nor write, he regarded painting as a means of communicating with the illiterate. Hence, churches were to become illustrated Bibles, allegorical mirrors of the world.

A look at paintings from the fifth and sixth centuries of the Christian Era illustrates this process. Each of these paintings contains a central figure and a cluster of followers: Dido and her servants (a classical theme), the Empress Theodora and her ladies of the court (contemporary secular portraiture), and Christ enthroned amidst his Apostles (Christian adaptation). In many ways, the Theodora artist follows in the classical traditions, considering the positioning of the feet and heads. Yet it is also clear that the artist follows a tradition and no longer looks at nature. Unlike the classical Dido, the bodies in the later painting just float in space, and the heads are just a row of beads. There is almost no individuality in the faces or gestures, and the representation of the draping clothes lacks the realism of its classical models. In addition, the artist borrows from the newly forming Christian symbols, framing the Empress with a halo-like effect. The mosaic "Christ Enthroned with the Apostles" from the Church of Santa Pudenziana in Rome shows the classical style fully adapted to Christian representation. The figure of Christ is now centered, not only within a balanced representation of other figures but also in the way Christ's halo dominates the

Figure 36. Roman Coliseum.

center stage, and with the background cross, stretches from earth to the heavens. This mosaic is still rooted in classical forms. Each figure is humanized (i.e., given mass, weight, individuality, and emotion) like the Hellenic Penelope of a thousand years earlier and unlike the more contemporary Theodora. The depictions of Greco-Roman architecture in the background, with their columns and arches, clearly shows how Christ now dominates the classical landscape.

Once set, these traditions would endure virtually unchanged for a millennium in the Byzantine or Eastern Christian Church. The "Enthroned Madonna and Child" (Color Figure 15), painted in Constantinople around 1200, shows little stylistic variation from the "Christ Enthroned" which predates it by eight centuries. While the Byzantine Madonna still preserves many of the innovations and achievements of the Greeks—the angle of the head, the shadowing of the face, and the folds of the drapery all look back to the fourth century Penelope, but—compared to its ancient predecessor, the painting is static. It is an iconic representation, not a slice of life. Symbolism, not the natural world, orders the representation of the Christ Child, and the individuality and experimentation of the earlier artist have all but disappeared.

In architecture, too, the major Byzantine and early medieval structural innovations resulted from adapting classical traditions to the needs of the Christian community. Greek and Roman temples, for example, were primarily shrines or homes for the gods where one went to make offerings or seek wisdom. They were not designed to meet the ceremonial and devotional needs of large congregations. The early churches, then, were based in public halls and royal courts called basilicas. These large buildings domed in the Roman manner became the foundations for the architectural style that would flourish in early medieval Europe—the Romanesque. As the church grew into the dominant institution of the medieval world, the simple basilica churches of Roman times no longer seemed sufficient. By the eleventh century a small but significant building boom started. The Romanesque, if anything, was a period of great experimentation and innovation, and successful alterations in one area soon spread to neighboring regions. Additions were made to the basilica's basic structure: expanding the floor plan into a large Latin cross, adding an ambulatory with radiating chapels to curve around the apse, and erecting the fortress-like towers that still dominate the landscapes of European villages and towns. All of this mass was now supported in a series of vaulted arches, first in the Roman form and later in the ribbed style of Norman France. These ribbed vaults, like those in the twelfth century cathedral at Canterbury (Figure 37), focus and balance the cathedral's weight on a series of interior pillars. The result is massive, solid, heavy—a feudal fortress that stands as a symbol of the Church Militant.

The Gothic style's beginnings in the twelfth century are the result of this continued experimentation. As vaulted, cross ribbed arches replaced rounded Roman ones, churches could expand upward even as the outward walls grew lighter and thinner. This transition was greatly encouraged by another technological breakthrough, the flying buttress. Supports for columns could be put on the outside of the building, allowing an interior transformation from the dark, fortress-like crypt in the Canterbury Cathedral, to the soaring lightness of Notre Dame in Paris. These technological experiments led to a totally new religious experience. The Romanesque church was a fortress, a sanctuary in a world of danger and temptation. To walk into a Gothic cathedral like Notre Dame or Chartres was to glimpse Heaven, a vivid incarnation of the promised salvation described in the Bible: ". . . coming down out of heaven from God, having the glory of God, her light was like unto a stone most precious . . . and the building of the wall thereof was jasper and the city was pure gold like unto pure glass" (*Revelation* 21). The new structural support methods allowed for walls filled with stained glass, and churches flooded with light and color. Illuminated by divine brightness, the holy personages of the Bible came vividly alive for the faithful, and the visual impact of the huge rose windows helped to foster the period's mystical proclivities.

Not only were the interiors of the Gothic churches transformed to reflect the growing religious spirit of the twelfth century, but the exteriors, too, celebrated man's divine aspirations with soaring church spires that towered over the landscape. From below, the towers of Chartres must have seemed to reach heaven; from above, they offered a new, unique and God-like perspective on the human condition.

The Gothic cathedral, with its statuary and stained glass, is as representative of its world as was the Athenian Parthenon with its marble friezes. For the Greeks, a temple to the immortals becomes a venue to idealize the mortal body and celebrate man's human potential for moral virtue. The medieval cathedral offers a different ideal, spiritual rather than physical, allowing its congregation, as they gaze in wonder, to experience their place in the Christian cosmology. Yet, seventeen centuries apart, they also share

Figure 37. Crypt of Canterbury Cathedral.
CORBIS/Angelo Hornak.

the artistic tensions that define Western art. Both are a balance of tradition and innovation. The sense of lightness supporting the roof of Athena's temple, its symmetry and simplicity, has its counterpart in the glass-filled walls of Our Lady's cathedral. Both, too, appeal to the rational mind with their unity of form and function, even as they touch individuals spiritually with their exuberant sense of human potential.

Classical and Medieval Music

Nineteenth century English poet John Keats, in his poem, "Ode on a Grecian Urn," describes a typical piece of Greek craftsmanship (in this case an urn) ornamented with illustrations of people engaged in the various activities of life, including the playing of musical instruments as others dance. Reflecting on the fact that contemporary men and women cannot know what that music would have sounded like because the Greeks did not devise a system of musical notation, Keats finds Greek melodies (which are "unheard") to be "sweeter" than those which it was possible for him to hear. For Keats, the sound of the actual Greek music could not rival the imaginary music of individuals' minds as they think of the Greeks, look at their art (which includes many images of musicians), and read their literature which are the only sources of speculation about this art form.

It is hard to believe that if Keats could somehow have come upon a recording of actual Greek music, he would have refused to listen, preferring his "unheard melodies," but he certainly is right in suggesting that the glimpses of Greek musical life are tantalizing. Take, for instance, Homer's description (Book XVIII of the *Iliad*) of people celebrating the harvest of grapes while a young boy performed on his lyre a song so exquisite that it simultaneously broke the heart of the rapt listeners and served as a haunting dirge for the dying year.

What is known about Greek music is that it included singing, drumming, and the playing of both string instruments like the lyre and reed instruments such as the *aulos*. The Greeks divided music into different modes or groups of notes. Each mode was thought to have a different effect on listeners. The Dorian mode, for instance, inspired determination and courage, while the Phrygian mode induced passionate feelings. Philosophers, such as Pythagarus, Plato, and Aristotle were struck by the mathematical qualities in the proportions of vibrations in musical notes. For these thinkers, simple, austere melodies could connect the mind to the eternal patterns behind the illusory flux of everyday life, assisting people in quiet meditation on the nature of Being.

In Euripides' tragedy, the *Bacchae*, on the other hand, music is used by Dionysus's followers to induce ecstasy as dancers abandon themselves to wild revelries. The same purpose can be witnessed in the paintings of Pieter Breughel the Elder some two millennia later, in his depictions of north-European peasants dancing to the music of folk musicians. There has always been a popular current within music that lends itself to a kind of revelry that may not be sanctioned by the official or "high" culture. The power of such music is perhaps symbolized by the Greek god, Orpheus, who was supposed to have been able to uproot trees, shatter rocks, and control wild animals with his music. Because of its explosive power, Plato would have prohibited most forms of music from his Republic or ideal state.

It is worth noting that a number of important twentieth century composers have felt the allure of those "unheard melodies" of the Greeks and have composed music perhaps to recapture this ancient flavor. Russian composer Igor Stravinsky, for instance, composed an opera in 1927 based on Sophocles' play, *Oedipus the King*. Stravinsky's music may not sound like the actual music of the Ancient Greeks, but it at least reminds listeners that the Greek tragedies were what today are called multi-media performances, with masks, costumes, choral singing, drumming, and dance, combining for a stirring overall effect. Other composers who have created works inspired by the Greeks include the British composer Harrison Birtwistle, American Elliott Carter, and modern Greek Iannis Xenakis.

While several modern composers have been inspired, then, by the idea of Ancient music, other contemporary composers, such as Estonian Arvo Pärt and British composer John Tavener, have been influenced more by Medieval music. However, one's understanding of Medieval music naturally differs from the grasp of music in Ancient Greece; listeners can know what Medieval music sounds like. In the eleventh century, Benedictine monks at Cluny devised a system of musical notation, which was developed and improved in future generations. Thus, Gregorian chant, one of the earliest forms of music that was written down in the new notation, can be performed today and sounds much as it did in the Middle Ages. In fact, Gregorian chant, which features an almost floating melodic line, has become immensely popular again in the last decade or so and has even led to some best-selling recordings. The same is true of the music of Hildegaard of Bingen, perhaps the first important woman composer, as well as a significant philosopher. Her music, likewise, has been much recorded lately and sells well at record stores.

Gregorian chant is monophonic, that is, it has one melodic line. It was not long before polyphony or music of two or more melodic lines was developed. By the time one gets to the music of the thirteenth century French composer Guillame de Machaut, one deals with compositions of great complexity and sophistication. De Machaut's *Masse de Notre Dame* is built on a beautiful weaving together of different parts of the choir. In this way it is "architecturally" similar to the great Medieval cathedrals or to the great literary masterpiece of the Middle Ages, like Dante's *Divine Comedy*. All of these art forms include rich localized details within a large, interlocking structure suggesting the majesty and order of God's creation. Nevertheless, the goal of de Machaut's compositions remains very close to what Plato had understood the goal of music to be in Classical times (both Plato and Aristotle were very influential on Medieval thinkers, such as St. Augustine and St. Thomas Aquinas): to lift the spirit, through a contemplation of beautiful sounds beautifully structured, to a contemplation of the order and harmony of the universe.

Part III: The American Perspective

American Background: Pre-Columbian History and Culture

America originated as many as 11,000 to 35,000 years ago, at the zenith of the Ice Age, when Asian tribal hunters migrated across a land bridge that linked Siberia and Alaska. When the oceans rose at the end of the Ice Age, Americans were isolated from Asia and Europe for five hundred years prior to the first European explorations. The centuries of isolation witnessed the emergence of ancient America's three greatest civilizations: the Maya (250 BC–AD 1000), the Aztecs (1350–1521), and the Incas (1300?–1532).

The Maya empire encompassed the areas now known as the Yucatan Peninsula, Belize, Guatemala, parts of the Mexican states of Chiapas and Tabasco, and the western sections of Honduras and El Salvador. This Mesoamerican culture, at the height of its power from approximately AD 600 to 900, first flourished in Peten, now known as northern Guatemala, before its massive northern migration to the Yucatan. The Maya triumphed over a less than accommodating environment comprised of the rain forest, other areas with inadequate water supplies, and few natural resources. This group became the most ingenious and influential early Americans.

Reasons for the empire's decline are unknown, yet the Maya left a legacy that includes achievements in astronomy, mathematics, engineering, architecture, art, and writing. Astronomers studied planetary and celestial cycles, tracked planetary paths, and successfully predicted solar and lunar eclipses. Scientists shared their findings with kings because astronomy was regarded as vital for the rulers' protection of their people. Present-day travelers to the city of Chichen Itza, in the Yucatan, may view El Caracol, a building archaeologists have identified as an early observatory. Based on their keen astronomical and mathematical abilities as well as their perception of time as cyclical rather than linear, the Maya created two calendars: a 365-day farming calendar and a 260-day sacred calendar connected to their bloodletting rituals. The two calendars combined produced a cycle of 52 years (18,980 days). These calendars were used at least 1,200 years before Europeans created the Gregorian calendar. The Maya also invented complex systems of mathematics including ones that recognized zero, 1,000 years before the Hindus. Talented engineers and architects, the Maya used concrete for structural work as they built many important cities, such as Tikal, Copan, and Chichen Itza that contained palace-like residences, monasteries, sanctuaries, and domed-shape observatories. However, the temple-pyramids were the most magnificent architectural structures. Temples were constructed on the top of many steep steps, whose shapes resembled pyramids. A temple-pyramid in Chichen Itza has 911 steps on each of four sides, while a temple-pyramid in Tikal rises 212 feet above ground. Art work found among the ruins include carvings on jade and other pieces of precious stones, ceramics, stone mosaics, masks, jewelry, paintings, and sculpture. Much of the art work depicts ceremonies and images of god and war. Writing also flourished in the Maya empire. No ancient American culture invented an alphabet, yet a number of these civilizations created various systems of writing. The Maya, as well as other Mesoamericans, wrote in books made of fig-bark paper or deerskin that unfolded into screens. The Maya created a written language in the form of hieroglyphs. Although they produced a prodigious amount of hieroglyphic works recorded in books or stone, sixteenth-century Spanish colonizers and missionaries destroyed all of the works except four. Of the surviving works, the most complete creation myth is the *Popol Vuh,* which is the "Council Book" or "Council Paper" of the Maya-Quiche.

Most Mayan activities were dominated by religion. According to these polytheistic people, the universe contained three layers: the upper, middle, and underworlds. The upper world was viewed as the heavens. The Maya, who believed in life after death, thought that when kings or noblemen died, they then lived in the sky with the gods. Rulers were buried in magnificent tombs that contained food, clothing, and other essentials for the afterlife journey. The Maya believed that the middleworld of human activity with constant battles between good and evil had a different history of creations and destructions. Growing from the center of the middleworld was the Wacah Chan, a tree that extended into the underworld. Cardinal directions flowed from the Wacah Chan, and each direction had its own gods, symbols, colors, and birds. Kings were viewed as personifications of the Wacah Chan and as the link to the three levels of the universe, as they stood on temple-pyramids during rituals and were agents of their own bloodletting. The Maya believed that daily blood sacrifices kept their gods happy, insuring health, safety, and prosperity among the people. In addition to the kings' blood offerings, Mayan citizens volunteered to let their blood drip on paper that was burned as offerings to the gods.

A second mighty Mesoamerican culture were the Aztecs, who were the descendants of the Toltecs, a people credited with invention of a calendar and recognized as great warriors. The Toltecs were in power from AD 900 until the twelfth century. Then according to legend, the Aztecs or Mexica, as they referred to themselves, migrated from Aztlan and were nomads until their principal god Huitzilopochtli transformed himself into an eagle. When the Aztecs saw the eagle in the middle of Lake Texcoco, they claimed the area as their homeland. By 1376 the Aztecs were a monarchy rather than a society of clans. Their empire was surpassed in size only by the Incas. By 1441 when Moctezuma Ilhuicamina became the sixth emperor, the Aztecs considered themselves rulers of the world.

The Aztec capital was Tenochtitlan which they believed was the "Heart of the One World" and the "Place Where the Gods Reside." Tenochtitlan was located approximately thirty miles northeast of present-day Mexico City and covered more than eight square miles. The city was built on five islands in the middle of Lake Texcoco, a flooded volcano crater, and was connected to the mainland by three causeways. Centuries later, Spanish invaders called Tenochtitlan "the Venice of the New World." During the height of the Aztec empire, more than 200,000 people resided in the capital; thus its population surpassed that of any European city of the same period. Tenochtitlan's canals and roadways led to main plazas, paved with cement, and filled with temple-pyramids, palaces, residences, and other buildings. The capital's most impressive structure was the Sun Temple, a huge stepped pyramid designed like the temple-pyramids of the Maya; the Sun Temple was two hundred feet high with a base more than 650 feet long on each side. Among the other pyramids were ones dedicated to the moon and rain gods.

The Aztecs, like the Maya, engaged in activities of other ancient American cultures such as making religion dominant in their lives, generating calendars, keeping time, maintaining an interest in mathematics (the Aztecs developed a unique counting system), practicing astronomy; completing engineering projects (the Aztecs built canals, roads, aqueducts, sewers, dams, irrigation systems), creating art works (stone sculptures, stone friezes, carved wall sculptures, paintings, pottery, and gold and silver objects), and writing (via hieroglyphics). The Aztecs were especially fond of poetry, which they called "flower songs." Their painted scrolls represented poetry as a flowered scroll coming out of a mouth.

The Aztecs are noted for their stratified society, thriving economy that maintained trade with the Maya and other contemporaries, imperial political system, and agricultural advances. The Aztecs were preoccupied with war because they believed that the gods had granted them dominion over all Mexican territory, and because they wanted victims for sacrifice to their gods. The Aztecs were the first ancient Americans to use swords, and they also used bows, arrows, spears, as well as padded armor. The birth of males was celebrated with war cries by midwives prior to the infants' dedication to Huitzilopochtli, the war and sun god. Dying in battle was considered a great honor.

Like the Maya, the Aztecs believed human blood guaranteed the gods' good will. They were a polytheistic people who followed sixty major and many minor gods. Each god/goddess had its own culture as well as hierarchy of priests, and each ruled one or more human or nature activity. While the Maya practiced bloodletting, the Aztecs cut out their victims' hearts. Thousands of captives were taken to Tenochtitlan, led to sacrificial altars at the top of temple-pyramids, and held down while drums rolled. Then priests cut open the captives' chests, took out their hearts, and held them up for viewing.

The Aztec empire ended in 1521. Because of the Spaniards' use of firearms, thousands of Aztec warriors were defeated by five hundred Spanish soldiers and approximately ten thousand American allies who joined forces with conqueror Hernando Cortes' army in retaliation against previous devastation by the Aztecs. After the collapse of the Aztec empire, only one great ancient civilization remained—that of the Incas.

The Incas of Peru were the Aztecs' contemporaries. The Inca empire, extending from the southern portion of present-day Columbia to northern Chile and Argentina, and included the entire central Andes region and Peru. At its height, the empire, regarded as the largest, richest and most sophisticated ancient American culture, contained an estimated sixteen million people. The Inca lifestyle was dominated by worship of the sun god. Inca legend, like the Aztec eagle legend, reveals divine intervention. The sun god created a son and daughter, placed them on an island in Lake Titicaca with a gold staff, and told them to settle where the staff disappeared in the ground. The siblings traveled north of Lake Titicaca to a village between the Andes mountains; there the staff disappeared in the ground. Thus Cuzco, the legend concludes, was founded by the future king Manco Capac and queen Mama Ocilo.

Cuzco, the capital city, probably rivaled Tenochtitlan in magnificence. The Incas considered Cuzco the center of the universe. Four roads emanated from the city, dividing the empire into four quadrants. Hence, the Incas referred to their kingdom as Tawantinsuyu, "Land of the Four Quarters." The emperor, who was called Sapa Inca and was worshiped as a descendent of the sun god, resided in Cuzco even though there were additional palaces for him in every city of the empire. Present-day visitors to Cuzco can view the ruins of a huge temple dedicated to the sun god. Similarly, modern-day visitors to Machu Picchu, known as the fabled "Lost City of the Inca," can see a superior Inca accomplishment. Tourists marvel at the design of the stone city amid majestic, natural rock walls rising out of the jungle. The city's buildings required decades to finish because the stonework was completed with precision and without mortar. Archaeologists assume that Machu Picchu was a religious retreat and regard the city as the best extant example of Inca architecture. Machu Picchu's location high in the Andes, northwest of Cuzco, helped save it from destruction during the Spanish conquest.

The Incas, like the Aztecs, borrowed from earlier American civilizations, such as the Maya, calendars, temples, weaving, metalwork, and stone carvings, pottery, and ceramics. Unlike the Aztecs and Maya, the Incas did not use hieroglyphs. Yet in order to facilitate record-keeping of maize production, other stored goods, or the available workforce, the Incas created *quipu,* which was a color-coded, complex system of representing numbers via knotted strings, similar to a Chinese abacus.

The Incas' extraordinary success is attributed to advances in agriculture, storage, administration, politics, engineering, and communication. Increasing the amount of tillable land by terracing mountainsides and building irrigation systems ameliorated the harvesting of maize, the Incas' chief crop, as well as other grains and vegetables. Increased harvesting resulted in the need for improved food storage, so storehouses, many with special ventilation systems, were built to guarantee adequate food supplies in a climate that frequently led to crop failure. These storehouses, along with bureaucratic and manufacturing facilities, were located in several enormous administrative centers built throughout the empire in order to maintain the Incas' well-organized and well-run political system. The Incas demonstrated great engineering ability in the construction of their bureaucratic centers, cities, bridges, and roads. Administrators walked great distances on well-planned roads paved with flat stone. Communication was facilitated in the empire by a series of runners along the major roads who carried messages eight to fifteen miles to other messengers.

Religious sacrifice was also an important aspect of the Inca empire. Dead rulers were preserved as mummies, and their bodies were sealed in stone tombs where people prayed and offered animal or crop sacrifices. Human sacrifices were offered only during disaster. The Incas engaged in *capacocha,* a ritual where children were sacrificed and then worshiped as gods. Frequently, children of chiefs were sacrificed in order to insure the connection between chiefs and emperors. A 1999 discovery on an Argentine volcano, linking the ancient Incas to contemporary civilization, may be a result of *capacocha*. Archaeologists discovered three mummies (two girls and one boy) that have been frozen for half a millennium.

Francisco Pizarro's conquering of the Incas in 1532 marked the collapse of ancient America's third great empire. Other cultures existed prior to 1600 in Mesoamerica, Central America, and North America. For example there were approximately 240 tribes, including the Navajo, Kwakiutl, Crow, and Cherokee, in North America. Thus study of the Maya, Aztecs, and Incas, early America's dominant empires, along with their American neighbors, can provide a panoramic view of the lifestyles of ancient Americans.

Selected Bibliography

Baquedano, Elizabeth. *Aztecs, Inca and Maya.* New York: Knopf, 1993.

Bauer, Brian S. *The Development of the Inca State.* Austin: U of Texas P, 1992.

Boone, Elizabeth. *The Aztec World.* Montreal: St. Remy, 1994.

Carrasco, David with Scott Sessions. *Daily Life of the Aztecs: People of the Sun and Earth.* Westport, CT: Greenwood, 1998.

Clancy, Flora S., and Peter D. Harrison, eds. *Vision and Revision in Maya Studies.* Alburquerque: U of New Mexico P, 1990.

Clendinnen, Inga. *Aztecs: An Interpretation.* New York: Cambridge UP, 1993.

Coe, Michael D. *The Maya.* 5th ed. London: Thames and Hudson, 1994.

Josephy, Alvin M., Jr. *The Indian Heritage of America.* Rev. ed. Boston: Houghton Mifflin, 1991.

Malpass, Michael. A. *Daily Life in the Inca Empire.* Westport, CT: Greenwood, 1996.

Patterson, Thomas. *The Inca Empire: The Formation and Disintegration of a Pre-Capitalist State.* New York: Berg, 1991.

Sharer, Robert J. *Daily Life in Maya Civilization.* Westport, CT: Greenwood, 1996.

Smith, Michael E. *The Aztecs.* Oxford, UK: Blackwell, 1996.

Sullivan, William. *The Secret of the Incas' Mythology, Astronomy and the War Against Time.* New York: Crown, 1996.

Townsend, Richard. *The Aztecs.* London: Thames and Hudson, 1994.

Pre-Columbian Literature

Fewer than thirty years after Christopher Columbus' arrival in the "New World" in 1492, Hernan Cortes entered Tenochtitian, the center of the Aztec empire in what is now Mexico City. Two years later, in 1521, he completed the Spanish conquest of the Aztecs. By 1533, Francisco Pizarro had experienced similar success in overthrowing the Inca empire of South America. In each of these situations, the conquest of the Americans by the Spaniards occurred on several levels. Not only did the invaders introduce a new government and a new religion, Christianity, they also enacted a transformation of the literary traditions of the conquered people.

Indeed, for centuries before the arrival of the Europeans, the inhabitants of Mesoamerica, the region stretching roughly from the southern half of Mexico down through central America, had developed a variety of literary styles to preserve their most important thoughts. In Mexico, for example, the oldest forms of writing have been attributed to the Olmecs, a people who lived along the Gulf of Mexico almost a thousand years before Christ. Examples of their writing and calendar systems include recovered artifacts dating as early as 600 BC. The subject of their writings, as with most ancient literatures, was usually religious in nature and was portrayed by using a system of hieroglyphs and other symbols on stelae, large carved stone monuments.

The Olmecs had a considerable influence on the later, more developed Mexican civilizations that followed them. During what is considered the Classic Period in Mexico, consisting of the first nine centuries AD, three significant cultures developed. These included the residents of Teotihuacan, the City of the Gods, in the central plateau; the Zapotecs of Monte Alban (present-day Oaxaca); and the more famous Mayas, who inhabited the Northern Yucatan peninsula and the surrounding areas. These groups further developed the use of writing and calendars, using some of the same symbols and hieroglyphs the Olmecs had used as well as some that would be used by the Aztecs that followed them. Their writings took the form of inscriptions on stelae, like those left by the Olmecs, as well as in temples, palaces, and ceramics. These peoples also developed the use of codice or painted books, which would become central to the Aztec system of education. One of the most prevalent subjects for these writings were the gods that the Teotihacans worshiped, many of whom were invoked by later inhabitants of the Mexican territory. These included Tlaloc and Chalchiuhtlicue, the male and female ruler of the Waters; and Xiuhtecuhtli, the Lord of Fire; in addition to the Feathered Serpent, Quetzalcoatl; and the Prince of Flowers, Xochipilli.

Although most of them remain undeciphered, the hieroglyphics left by the Mayan people also reveal religious themes, in addition to a growing recognition of the importance of preserving memories of the past. Their hieroglyphic texts record dates, keep prophecies, and chronicle their important warriors, rulers, priests, and wise men. The Mayas also developed a more sophisticated calendar, with a year-count one ten-thousandth closer to the astronomical tropical year than the Gregorian calendar, as well as the concept and a symbol for zero, hundreds of years before any other civilization.

The Mayas continued to exert influence into the Post-classic Period, which occurred between AD 950 and 1150, although their prominence was superseded by that of other groups, including the Mixtecs, who succeeded the Zapotecs in Oaxaca; and the Toltecs, who reentered Central Mexico after the collapse of Teotihuacan. They settled in Tula, located fifty miles north of Mexico City, where they became followers of Quetzalcoatl, a priest and sage who derived his name from a god worshiped by the Teotihucuans. Several of the writings, which took the forms of glyphs, inscriptions, and codices were dedicated to this figure.

At the end of the eleventh century, Tula was abandoned by the Toltecs, who dispersed among the different regions of Mesoamerica, bringing their knowledge and arts with them. Some joined with the Mixtecs, who had left the largest number of pre-Columbian codices, displaying a style used later by the Aztecs. Others traveled to Yucatan and the Quiche and Cakchiquel regions of Guatemala, mixing with the Mayas of those areas to create a transformation of culture. The Toltec arrival in Guatemala is described in the *Popol Vuh* or "Book of Counsel," the sacred book of the Quiches.

After the abandonment of Tula, as with the earlier decline of Teotihucuan, new groups descended from the outlying regions to settle in central Mexico. Among these groups were the Nahuatlan tribes, including the Aztecs, who settled in the Valley of Mexico in 1325, establishing Tenochtitlan as their center. After a period of unrest, during which they had to contend with opposition from the Tepanecs of neighboring Azcapotzalco, the Aztecs were able to establish themselves as an independent and autonomous state in 1428. Unfortunately, one of the first official acts after this success was to establish a new version of their history, a goal which required them to burn their own books and those of the Tepanecs and write new ones in which they claimed a direct relationship to the noble Toltecs and elevated their patron god of war, Huitzilpochtli, to the same level as the ancient creator gods.

In order to perpetuate this history, the Aztecs developed an elaborate system of education, based on the memorization of codices containing myths, legends, historical discussion, and religious doctrines under the supervision of priestly teachers. In this respect, the literature of the Mesoamerican people was both oral and written in nature. The written texts utilized a combination of three types of writing. Pictograms, or schematic representations, were the simplest and involved a more direct representation of the subjects, including houses, bundles of corn, and priests. Ideograms, or symbolic representations, were more sophisticated and usually dealt with more abstract ideas such as time, movement, or divinity, with certain colors, for example, representing gender, royalty, or geographic direction. The Aztecs also used a partially phonetic form of script, principally for the names of specific people or places, using combinations of glyphs to signify specific sounds.

After the Spanish conquest of the Aztecs, most of the native texts were burned, although some of the Christian missionaries worked with the Americans to preserve their literature, a process that involved translating most of it from their native language of Nahuatl to Spanish or Latin. This was accomplished either by Nahuatl speakers dictating their stories to a translator who wrote them down in the European language or by Americans who learned the new languages and then wrote the translations themselves. This recording of texts continued until the end of the sixteenth century and included poetry, mythology, song, dramatic fragments, religious hymns, and folklore. Beginning with the seventeenth century, interest in the native literatures of Mesoamerica waned, and the texts were left unread in the basements of libraries and monasteries until the early twentieth century.

The literature of the indigenous people of South America was similar to that of the Mesoamericans in that it had both oral and written components, although theirs relied more heavily on oral tradition. The Incas, whose empire included present-day Peru, Bolivia, Ecuador, and parts of Colombia, Chile, and Argentina, created a great wealth of texts that were folkloric in nature and which served an official function in perpetuating the values of the ruling class. In fact, there were actually two types of artists, including the *amautas,* the state officials who recorded important historical events, celebrated Inca political and military successes and produced hymns to the state gods. The other group of artists, the *haravecs,* were popular poets who recorded the beliefs of the community. The texts created by these artists were perpetuated both orally and officially by *quipucamayocs,* the state archivists who used a system of colored strings to aid in the memory of the texts.

As the Aztecs did, the defeated Incas saw most of their texts disappear, though again, some chroniclers were able to transcribe examples from the oral tradition, including origin myths, historical narratives, and lyric poetry focusing on the topic of love. Most of these texts were translated from their native Quechua language to the language of the conquerors. Since that time, Quechua literature has experienced a fate similar to that of Mesoamerica, occupying a marginalized position, existing either in oral, folkloric form or in written texts only a relative minority can understand. It has only been in the last century that the works of both cultures have become more widely studied and accessible.

Selected Bibliography

Higgins, James. *A History of Peruvian Literature.* Liverpool: Francis Cairns, 1987.

Leon-Portilla, Miguel, ed. *Native Mesoamerican Spirituality: Ancient Myths, Discourses,Stories, Doctrines, Hymns, Poems, from the Aztec, Yucatec, Quiche-Maya, and Other Sacred Traditions.* New York: Paulist, 1980.

_____. *Pre-Columbian Literatures of Mexico.* Trans. Grace Lobano Miguel Lobanov and Miguel Leon-Portilla. Norman: U of Oklahoma P, 1969.

Pre-Columbian Poetry

The richly-textured poetic language of Mesoamerica creates patterns of images that reflect the highly-literate culture of several ancient societies in the New World. The geographical mapping of Mesoamerica combines central and southern Mexico with the central territory of the Mayas, along with the districts of the Quechua-speaking inhabitants of the Inca empire. Inca terrain stretched from Peru, Bolivia, Ecuador and parts of Colombia, Chile and Argentina. First among the various groups who inhabited these lands were the Olmecs, whose culture dates back to more than 900 BC. Writing was at the center of later groups, such as the Nahuatl or Aztecs, the Mixtecs and Zapotecs of Oaxaca, the Tarascans of Michoacan, and the Otomis of Central Mexico. The Mayas were found in Mexico and Honduras.

One of the key attributes of these societies was the importance given to the function of literature in evoking cultural memory. Poetry served a crucial role in conserving major events and in revitalizing those cultural relations that led to poetic expression. In this regard poems and the glyphs on steles shared the same symbolic function. In the schools and centers of higher learning, the chanting of poems was a mnemonic device that helped to conserve myths and other valued cultural texts.

As a result of its link with cultural memory, poetry crystalizes and vivifies the reactions of Nahuatl and Mayan citizens to the conquest of their cultural space by Europeans. European chroniclers describe in detail the cultural activity of the indigenous settlers. One of the unfortunate consequences of the initial contact between these cultures was the Catholic friars' determination to destroy all of the literary production of the conquered people. Bernardo de Sahagun rescued what he could of the Nahuatl books that were undergoing mass destruction. As a result of his efforts, several codices are on file at libraries throughout the world. In contrast, most of the books of lyric poetry of the Mayas were lost or destroyed in similar proselytizing campaigns. There are a few samples embedded in longer works alongside myths and historical texts, such as in the *Chilam Balam*. It is ironic that it was the same zeal for conversion that allowed the survival of Mayan language and the compilation of later collections; in addition to the *Chilam Balam* of Yucatan, the *Songs of Dzitbalche*, and lyrics interspersed in the *Popol Vuh* of the Quiche Mayas of Guatemala are basic examples. These later works were the result of the translations from Mayan into Spanish, under the tutelage of friars. Lacking anyone with the foresight of a Bernardo Sahagun, many of the works by popular poets of the Quechuan Empire were also lost. The reduced corpus has been archived in major world libraries, and there are some samples of poetry embedded in dramatic works, such as in the *Ollantay*, which was published at a later date.

Just as the poetry of the Nahuatl, Mayan, and Quechuan cultures was put in jeopardy by religious settlers who followed in the wake of the intrusion of the conquistadores, prior to the conquest, there were evident points poets shared. Principal among them was the elevated role of the poet in the society, as a sage whose purpose was to mediate between the divine and earthly realms. Perhaps this is best seen in the varied use of the following metaphors: flower and song, and the painted book. The poet who composed "Beginning and End" compares the writing of a codex with the divine creation of the manifest world. The Supreme Being writes with flowers and songs, for the creation is the result of sound and the repetition of songs. The poem suggests the vulnerability of humanity and a complete dependence on the Creator for existence and sustenance. Yet life is brought to an end with black ink that blots out human relationships. The book stands for the created world, and its destruction signifies the inevitability of death for all but the Supreme Being who is beyond the created realm.

The metaphorical use of "text as world" and of the transcendant power of the "flower and song" metaphor exemplify two of the poetic devices that pre-Columbian Nahuatl writers exploited. "Flower and song" is a polyvalent term that stands for a variety of meanings. It can signify the realm beyond this earth but most commonly connotes "art and symbolism." It is through art that the poet reaches the divine realms. This key metaphor is constituted by the juxtaposition of two nouns, which together create a third term. The combining of terms for a metaphorical function is common to the poetic art of Nahuatl writers; other similar terms are skirt-and-blouse to mean "female" and face-and-heart to connote "personality."

The poets were not always males, for there are several women's names listed in the codices as having authored poetry. There are no available samples of their work. In contrast, "Macuilxochitzin's Song," is a rare example of the poetic creativity of women in pre-Columbian societies. Having at hand a poem that bears the signature of a female author is rare indeed. Her name could possibly be symbolic of the day on which she was born, which was the 5-Flower of the Mexica calendar and which stands for the domicile of the god-goddess of art, songs and dance.

The theme of her poem chronicles the prowess of her father, but while praising his significant military contribution in battle, she mentions the active role of women in healing the wounded, and in her own compassionate appeal to her father, to ask that he spare the life of the Otomi "other."

In contrast to the vivid imagery and the inclusion of a personal voice in the Nahuatl poetic samples, the Quechuan hymn must depend on other techniques for its appeal. "The Hymn to Viracoha" appeals to the Creator of the universe. Rhetorical questions contribute to its cohesiveness in an effort to determine the nature of divinity. The resplendent quality of the Creator stands out as do the oppositions between images of diurnal and seasonal time. Thematically, the Inca poetry is as broadly-ranging as is the poetry by Nahuatls and Mayas. Yet having been the result of reconstructions at a later period, specialists suspect colonial influences on literary production, creating inversions.

Regardless of the destructive impacts of colonization on the educational systems of Nahuatl, Mayan, and Quechuan societies, and on the painted books themselves, a thematic treasure trove of beauty remains pressed between the pages of the codices. Pre-Columbian poetry evokes cultural memories that were essential for the harmonic functioning of these societies. The poet-sage translated intuited energies into enduring truths that resonate, like bird song, even today.

Selected Bibliography

Higgins, James. "The Native Tradition." *A History of Peruvian Literature.* Liverpool: Francis Cairns, 1987.

Leon-Portilla, Miguel. *Fifteen Poets of the Aztec World.* Norman: Oklahoma UP, 1992.

Aztec

Beginning and End

With flowers you write,
Oh Giver of Life!
With songs you give color,
with songs you shade
those who must live on the earth.

Later you will destroy
eagles and tigers;
we live only in your painting
here, on the earth.

With black ink you will blot out
all that was friendship,
brotherhood, nobility.

You give shading
to those who must live on the earth.

Later You will destroy
eagles and tigers;
we live only in your painting
here, on the earth.

Song of Tlaltecatzin, Cuauhchinanco

I come to guard the mountain,
somewhere is its story;
with flowers is painted
The Giver of life, the community.
You have been left in your home, you,
Tlaltecatzin, you suspire there, you speak.

I alone I sing,
to Him, who is my God,
in our place where the lords command,
the flowering chocolate drink is foaming,
the one which intoxicates men with its flowers.

I yearn,
my heart has tasted it,
my heart has been inebriated,
my heart knows it.

O red songbird of the supple neck!
Fresh and burning,
you show your garland of flowers.
You, mother!

Sweet woman,
precious flower of toasted maize,
you only lend yourself,
you will be abandoned,
you will have to go away,
there will be a defleshing.

Here you have come,
before the lords,
you marvelous being,
in an erect pose.
Upon the mat of yellow and blue feathers,
there you stand proudly.
But, precious flower of toasted maize,
You only lend yourself,
soon you must be abandoned,
you will have to go away,
there will be a defleshing.

The flowering chocolate drink is foaming,
the flower of tobacco is passed round,
if my heart would taste them,
my life would become inebriated.
But here on the earth,
you, O lords, O princes,
if my heart would taste them,
my life would become inebriated.

I only suffer and say:
may I not go
to the place of the fleshless.

My heart is a precious reality,
I am, I am only a singer
but golden flowers I carry,
I have to abandon them,
I only look at my house,
the flowers remain there.

Perhaps big jades,
broad plumages,
are my price?
Alone I must go,
sometime it will be,
alone I must go,
I will perish.
I abandon myself,
O my God, Giver of life,
I say: let me go,
my body will be a funerary bundle,
I a singer,
let thus it be.

Is anyone there who will become the owner of my heart?
Alone I must go,
my heart covered with flowers.
Quetzal feathers,
precious jades,
so perfectly polished,
will be destroyed.
Nowhere on earth is their model,
thus let it be,
but let it be without violence.

Song of Springtime

In the house of paintings
the singing begins,
song is practiced,
flowers are spread,
the song rejoices.

The song resounds,
little bells are heard,
to these answer
our flowery timbrels.
Flowers are spread,
the song rejoices.

Above the flowers is singing
the radiant pheasant;
his song unfolds
into the midst of the waters.
To him reply
all manner of red birds,
the dazzling red bird
beautifully sings.

Your heart is a book of paintings,
you have come to sing,
to make your drums resound,
you are the singer.
Within the house of springtime,
You make the people happy.

You alone bestow
flowers that intoxicate,
precious flowers.
You are the singer.
Within the house of springtime,
you make the people happy.

Song of Macuilxochitl

I raise my songs,
I, Macuilxochitl,
with these I gladden the Giver of Life,
may the dance begin!

There Where-in-Someway-One-Exists,
to His house,
are these songs carried?
Or only here are your flowers?
May the dance begin!

The Matlatzinca,
you well deserve these people, Lord Itzcoatl.
Axayacatzin, you have conquered
the city of Tlacotepec!
There went to make forays
your flowers, your butterflies.
With this we rejoice.
The Matlatzinca are in Toluca, in Tlacotepec.

He makes offerings
of flowers and feathers
to the Giver of Life.
He puts the eagle shields
on the arms of the men,
there where the war rages,
in the midst of the plain,
as our songs,
as our flowers,
thus you, warrior of the shaven head,
give pleasure to the Giver of Life.
The flowers of the eagle
remain in your hands,
lord Axayacatl.

With divine flowers,
with flowers of war,
is covered,
with these becomes intoxicated
he who is on our side.

Above us open
the flowers of war,
in Ehecatepec, in Mexico,
with these becomes intoxicated
he who is on our side.

They have shown themselves fearless,
the princes,
those of Acolhuacan,
you, the Tepanec.

On every side Axayacatl
made conquests,
in Matlatzinco, in Malinalco,
In Ocuillan, in Tequaloya, in Xohcotitlan.
From here he went forth.
There in Xiquipilco was Axayacatl
wounded in the leg by an Otomi,
his name was Tlilatl.

That one went in search of his women,
he said to them:
"Prepare a breechcloth and a cape,
give these to your man."
And Axayacatl called out:
"Bring the Otomi
who wounded me in the leg."
The Otomi was afraid,
he said:
"Now truly they will kill me!"
Then he brought a large piece of wood
and a deerskin,
with these he bowed before Axayacatl.
He was full of fear, the Otomi,
but then his women made supplication for him to Axayacatl.

Quechua

Prayer to Virachocha

(Oh Viracocha, power behind all that exists!
"Let this be man,
let this be woman," you said.
Sacred . . . lord,
maker
of all light that dawns.
Who are you!
Where are you?
Might I not see you?
Is your powerful throne
in the world of above
or in the world of below
or beyond the world's edge?
From the celestial ocean
or the earthly seas wherein you dwell,
speak to me, say but "I hear!"
Pachacamac,
creator of man,
Lord, your servants
wish to see you
with their tainted eyes,
you.
When I am able to see,
when I am able to know,
when I am able to point,
when I am able to reflect,
you will see me,
you will understand me.
The sun, the moon,
day, night,
summer, winter
are not free,
they move to order;
they are designated
and arrive
at the appointed time.
Where, to whom
did you send
the shining sceptre?
Speak to me, say but "I hear!"
hear me
while I am still
not worn out,
dead.)

The *Popol Vuh:* Background

Like other holy texts, the *Popol Vuh,* the holy text of the Maya, is a reflection of cultural beliefs. Containing several creation stories and tales of the epic hero, the work reveals the society's polytheistic religious position along with its views of death and the afterlife. Additionally, the work vicariously reveals the Maya's history before and after the arrival of the Europeans. In the end, this is a work full of historical and anthropological information.

Before studying the mythical or literary value of such a work, one must consider how the *Popol Vuh* came to the attention of contemporary readers. The stories told in the *Popol Vuh* were passed orally from generation to generation and later transcribed in the Quiché language of the Maya. Subsequently, these works were translated by Spanish clerics. However, some of these translations raise certain issues of authenticity. With a translation one must first trust the translator, that he/she is actually capable of performing the task without error. The translator must exhibit a credible understanding of the indigenous language and culture. This type of language acquisition requires more translating time and knowledge than the Spanish translators of this text had. In addition to the issue of competence, one must be assured that the translator will be objective. What is known is that the Spanish desired to convert the native population to Catholicism. In attempting to do so, they destroyed many of the other Mayan holy texts because the Catholic friars considered them texts of the devil. This destruction reflects an obvious Eurocentrism. In the end, then, the modern reader cannot be certain whether similarities between *Popol Vuh* and the Bible are to be attributed to Jung's collective unconscious or to a corrupt Spanish translation.

These translation issues aside, the text still reveals a great deal of anthropological information, rich in revelation about the Maya. The subtle yet powerful anthropological information seems to be such that either the translators did not realize it was present, or they did not find it offensive, and therefore permitted it to remain in the text. The reader witnesses by means of the *Popol Vuh* a highly-developed civilization governed by religious and social laws and steeped in a vibrant historical tradition. The multiple creation stories probably reflect a society tolerant of diversity and change. Moreover, multiple creation stories allow Mayan gods to be more human and less perfect, presenting standards of conduct not too exalted for humans to attain. In societies in which the god structure or religious standard is too high, the people are doomed to destruction in some form or another. By permitting the gods to be imperfect, the people are allowed to make mistakes and still reap the rewards of the afterlife.

More than anthropological information, the different creation stories can be taken as sign posts in Mayan history. Mayan history is divided into three eras, moving from the most archaic to the most sophisticated, and the creation stories seem to replicate this sequence. In these tales, the gods use progressively more sophisticated means of producing various generations of human kind. The final version of humans emerges as close to perfection as the gods will make them; however, the *Popol Vuh* stresses that individuals are never perfected, but rather, they are left to evolve into what they must become.

Within this holy text is an immaculate-conception story somewhat similar to that of the Christian story. The newborn child has supernatural abilities and becomes an epic hero. He becomes a savior for his mother when his grandfather suspects her of acting dishonorably and orders her death. He convinces the servants, who are to kill his mother, of her innocence and together they work to free her.

The gods frequently embody values and concepts important to the community. As with the Greeks, Egyptians, or Mesopotamians, the gods represent forces of nature, and the *Popol Vuh* elucidates the mysterious dimensions of these forces. Mayan gods are limited not only by conditions in the physical world but also by the processes of death. The *Popol Vuh* allows the reader to infer that death is not the end but that it can be conquered. The very title of one of the episodes, "Victory over the Underworld," allows the reader to understand a notion of the Mayan people: that if the society follows its spiritual leaders, overcoming death is possible. In this portion of the story, also, one cannot help noticing the similarity to many of the other epic heroes who descend into the underworld, where they are tested, prove their worthiness, and return with the boon of knowledge for the people.

The reader also learns of the Mayan thoughts about the origin of man, how and why he came to be. The reader sees the organic connection that the Mayans have with their past. One sees how man came to be and how he was made from corn—an extremely important and symbolic crop for the Mayan peoples. The work ends with a logically-sequenced prayer for future generations. The *Popol Vuh* suggests that only by delving into the past does one understand the present and that in understanding the present, prayers must be offered for the future. Thus, for the Mayas, life is cyclical, continuous, and serious.

Selected Bibliography

Garfield, Evelyn Picon, and Ivan A. Schulman. *Literaturas Hispanicas: Introducción a su Estudio.* 3 vols. Detroit: Wayne State U, 1991.

Mayan

Popol Vuh[1]

From Part I

[Prologue, Creation]

This is the beginning of the Ancient Word, here in this place called Quiché. Here we shall inscribe, we shall implant the Ancient Word, the potential and source for everything done in the citadel of Quiché, in the nation of Quiché people.

And here we shall take up the demonstration, revelation, and account of how things were put in shadow and brought to light

by the Maker, Modeler, named Bearer, Begetter,
Hunahpu Possum, Hunahpu Coyote,
Great White Peccary, Tapir,
Sovereign Plumed Serpent,
Heart of the Lake, Heart of the Sea,
Maker of the Blue-Green Plate,
Maker of the Blue-Green Bowl,[2]

as they are called, also named, also described as

the midwife, matchmaker
named Xpiyacoc, Xmucane,
defender, protector,[3]
twice a midwife, twice a matchmaker,

as is said in the words of Quiché. They accounted for everything—and did it too—as enlightened beings, in enlightened words. We shall write about this now amid the preaching of God, in Christendom now. We shall bring it out because there is no longer a place to see it, a Council Book,

a place to see "The Light That Came from
Across the Sea,"
the account of "Our Place in the Shadows,"
a place to see "The Dawn of Life,"

as it is called. There is the original book and ancient writing, but he who reads and ponders it hides his face.[4] It takes a long performance and account to complete the emergence of all the sky-earth:

the fourfold siding, fourfold cornering
measuring, fourfold staking,
halving die cord, stretching the cord
in the sky, on the earth,
the four sides, the four corners,[5]
by the Maker, Modeler,
mother-father of life, of humankind,
giver of breath, giver of heart,
bearer, upbringer in the light that lasts
of those born in the light, begotten in the light;
worrier, knower of everything, whatever there is:
sky-earth, lake-sea.

This is the account, here it is:

Now it still ripples, now it still murmurs, ripples, it still sighs, still hums, and it is empty under the sky.

Here follow the first words, the first eloquence:

There is not yet one person, one animal, bird, fish, crab, tree, rock, hollow, canyon, meadow, forest. Only the sky alone is there; the face of the earth is not clear. Only the sea alone is pooled under all the sky; there is nothing whatever gathered together. It is at rest; not a single thing stirs. It is held back, kept at rest under the sky.

Whatever there is that might be is simply not there: only the pooled water, only the calm sea, only it alone is pooled.

Whatever might be is simply not there: only murmurs, ripples, in the dark, in the night. Only the Maker, Modeler alone, Sovereign Plumed Serpent the Bearers, Begetters are in the water, a glittering light. They are there, they are enclosed in quetzal feathers, in blue-green.

Thus the name, "Plumed Serpent." They are great knowers, great thinkers in their very being.

And of course there is the sky, and there is also die Heart of Sky. This is the name of the god, as it is spoken.

And then came his word, he came here to the Sovereign Plumed Serpent, here in the blackness, in the early dawn. He spoke with the Sovereign Plumed Serpent, and they talked, then they thought, then they worried. They agreed with each other, they joined their words, their thoughts. Then it was clear, then they reached accord in the light, and then humanity was clear, when they conceived the growth, the generation of trees, of bushes, and the growth of life, of humankind, in the blackness, in the early dawn, all because of the Heart of Sky, named Hurricane. Thunderbolt Hurricane comes first, the second is Newborn Thunderbolt, and the third is Raw Thunderbolt.[6]

So there were three of them, as Heart of Sky, who came to the Sovereign Plumed Serpent, when the dawn of life was conceived:

"How should it be sown, how should it dawn? Who is to be the provider, nurturer?"[7]

"Let it be this way, think about it this water should be removed, emptied out for the formation of the earth's own plate and platform, then comes the sowing, the dawning of the sky-earth. But there will be no high days and no bright praise for our work, our design, until the rise of the human work the human design," they said.

And then the earth arose because of them, it was simply their word that brought it forth. For the forming of the earth they said "Earth." It arose suddenly, just like a cloud, like a mist, now forming, unfolding. Then the mountains were separated from the water, all at once the great mountains came forth. By their genius alone, by their cutting edge[8] alone they carried out the conception of the mountain-plain, whose face grew instant groves of cypress and pine.

And the Plumed Serpent was pleased with this:

"It was good that you came, Heart of Sky, Hurricane, and Newborn Thunderbolt, Raw Thunderbolt. Our work, our design will turn out well," they said.

And the earth was formed first, the mountain-plain. The channels of water were separated; their branches wound their ways among the mountains. The waters were divided when the great mountains appeared.

Such was the formation of the earth when it was brought forth by the Heart of Sky, Heart of Earth, as they are called, since they were the first to think of it. The sky was set apart, and the earth was set apart in the midst of the waters.

Such was their plan when they thought, when they worried about the completion of their work.[9]

From Part 2

[The Twins Defeat Seven Macaw]

Here is the beginning of the defeat and destruction of The day of Seven Macaw by the two boys, the first named Hunahpu and the second named Xbalanque.[1] Being gods, the two of them saw evil in his attempt at selfmagnification before the Heart of Sky.

* * *

This is the great tree of Seven Macaw, a nance,[2] and this is the food of Seven Macaw. In order to eat the fruit of the nance he goes up the tree every day. Since Hunahpu and Xbalanque have seen where he feeds, they are now hiding beneath the tree of Seven Macaw, they are keeping quiet here, the two boys are in the leaves of the tree.

And when Seven Macaw arrived, perching over his meal, the nance, it was then that lie was shot by Hunahpu. The blowgun shot went right to his jaw, breaking his mouth. Then he went up over the tree and fell flat on the ground. Suddenly Hunahpu appeared, running. He set out to grab him, but actually it was the arm of Hunahpu that was seized by Seven Macaw. He yanked it straight back, he bent it back at the shoulder. Then Seven Macaw tore it right out of Hunahpu. Even so, the boys did well: the first round was not their defeat by Seven Macaw.

And when Seven Macaw had taken the arm of Hunahpu, he went home. Holding his jaw very carefully, he arrived:

"What have you got there?" said Chimalmat, the wife of Seven Macaw.

"What is it but those two tricksters! They've shot me, they've dislocated my jaw.[3] All my teeth are just loose, now they ache. But once what I've got is over the fire—hanging there, dangling over the fire—then they can just come and get it. They're real tricksters!" said Seven Macaw, then he hung up the arm of Hunahpu.

Meanwhile Hunahpu and Xbalanque were thinking. And then they invoked a grandfather, a truly white-haired grandfather, and a grandmother, a truly humble grandmother—just bent-over, elderly people. Great White Peccary is the name of the grandfather, and Great White Tapir is the name of the grandmother.[4] The boys said to the grandmother and grandfather:

"Please travel with us when we go to get our arm from Seven Macaw; we'll just follow right behind you. You'll tell him:

'Do forgive us our grandchildren, who travel with us. Their mother and father are dead, and so they follow along there, behind us. Perhaps we should give them away, since all we do is pull worms out of teeth.' So we'll seem like children to Seven Macaw, even though we're giving you the instructions," the two boys told them.

"Very well," they replied.

After that they approached the place where Seven Macaw was in front of his home. When the grandmother and grandfather passed by, the two boys were romping along behind them. When they passed below the lord's house, Seven Macaw was yelling his mouth off because of his teeth. And when Seven Macaw saw the grandfather and grandmother traveling with them:

"Where are you headed, our grandfather?" said the lord.

"We're just making our living, your lordship," they replied.

"Why are you working for a living? Aren't those your children traveling with you?"

"No, they're not, your lordship. They're our grandchildren, our descendants, but it is nevertheless *we* who take pity on *them*. The bit of food they get is the portion we give them, your lordship," replied the grandmother and grandfather. Since the lord is getting done in by the pain in his teeth, it is only with great effort that he speaks again:

"I implore you, please take pity on me! What sweets can you make, what poisons[5] can you cure? said the lord.

"We just pull the worms out of teeth, and we just cure eyes. We just set bones, your lordship," they replied.

"Very well, please cure my teeth. They really ache, every day. It's insufferable! I get no sleep because of them—and my eyes. They just shot me, those two tricksters! Ever since it started I haven't eaten because of it. Therefore take pity on me! Perhaps it's because my teeth are loose now."

"Very well, your lordship. It's a worm, gnawing at the bone.[6] It's merely a matter of putting in a replacement and taking the teeth out, sir."

"But perhaps it's not good for my teeth to come out—since I am, after all, a lord. My finery is in my teeth—and my eyes."

"But then we'll put in a replacement. Ground bone will be put back in." And this is the "ground bone": it's only white corn.

"Very well. Yank them out! Give me some help here!" he replied.

And when the teeth of Seven Macaw came out, it was only white corn that went in as a replacement for his teeth—just a coating shining white, that corn in his mouth. His face fell at once, he no longer looked like a lord. The last of his teeth came out, the jewels that had stood out blue from his mouth.

And then the eyes of Seven Macaw were cured. When his eyes were trimmed back the last of his metal came out.[7] Still he felt no pain; he just looked on while the last of his greatness left him. It was just as Hunahpu and Xbalanque had intended.

And when Seven Macaw died, Hunahpu got back his arm. And Chimalmat, the wife of Seven Macaw, also died.

Such was the loss of the riches of Seven Macaw: only the doctors got the jewels and gems that had made him arrogant, here on the face of the earth. The genius of the grandmother, the genius of the grandfather did its work when they took back their arm: it was implanted and the break got well again. Just as they had wished the death of Seven Macaw, so they brought it about. They had seen evil in his self-magnification.

After this the two boys went on again. What they did was simply the word of the Heart of Sky.

From Part 3

[Victory over the Underworld]

And now we shall name the name of the father of Hunahpu and Xbalanque. Let's drink to him, and let's just drink to the telling and accounting of the begetting of Hunahpu and Xbalanque. We shall tell just half of it, just a part of the account of their father. Here follows the account.

These are the names: One Hunahpu and Seven Hunahpu,[8] as they are called.

* * *

And One and Seven Hunahpu went inside Dark House.[9] And then their torch was brought, only one torch, already lit, sent by One and Seven Death, along with a cigar for each of them, also already lit, sent by the lords. When these were brought to One and Seven Hunahpu they were cowering, here in the dark. When the bearer of their torch and cigars arrived, the torch was bright as it entered; their torch and both of their cigars were burning. The bearer spoke:

"'They must be sure to return them in the morning—not finished, but just as they look now. They must return them intact,' the lords say to you," they were told, and they were defeated. They finished the torch and they finished the cigars that had been brought to them.

And Xibalba is packed with tests, heaps and piles of tests.

This is the first one: the Dark House, with darkness alone inside.

And the second is named Rattling House, heavy with cold inside, whistling with drafts, clattering with hail. A deep chill comes inside here.

And the third is named Jaguar House, with jaguars alone inside, jostling one another, crowding together, with gnashing teeth. They're scratching around; these jaguars are shut inside the house.

Bat House is the name of the fourth test, with bats alone inside the house, squeaking, shrieking, darting through the house. The bats are shut inside; they can't get out.

And the fifth is named Razor House, with blades alone inside. The blades are moving back and forth, ripping, slashing through the house.

These are the first tests of Xibalba, but One and Seven Hunahpu never entered into them, except for the one named earlier, the specified test house.

And when One and Seven Hunahpu went back before One and Seven Death, they were asked:

"Where are my cigars? What of my torch? They were brought to you last night!"

"We finished them, your lordship."

"Very well. This very day, your day is finished, you will die, you will disappear, and we shall break you off. Here you will hide your faces: you are to be sacrificed!" said One and Seven Death.

And then they were sacrificed and buried. They were buried at the Place of Ball Game Sacrifice,[1] as it is called. The head of One Hunahpu was cut off; only his body was buried with his younger brother.

"Put his head in the fork of the tree that stands by the road," said One and Seven Death.

And when his head was put in the fork of the tree, the tree bore fruit. It would not have had any fruit, had not the head of One Hunahpu been put in the fork of the tree.

This is the calabash tree, as we call it today, or "the head of One Hunahpu," as it is said.

And then One and Seven Death were amazed at the fruit of the tree. The fruit grows out everywhere, and it isn't clear where the head of One Hunahpu is; now it looks just the way the calabashes look. All the Xibalbans see this, when they come to look.

The state of the tree loomed large in their thoughts, because it came about at the same time the head of One Hunahpu was put in the fork. The Xibalbans said among themselves:

"No one is to pick the fruit, nor is anyone to go beneath the tree," they said. They restricted themselves; all of Xibalba held back.

It isn't clear which is the head of One Hunahpu; now it's exactly the same as the fruit of the tree. Calabash tree came to be its name, and much was said about it. A maiden heard about it, and here we shall tell of her arrival.

And here is the account of a maiden, the daughter of a lord named Blood Gatherer.[2]

And this is when a maiden heard of it, the daughter of a lord. Blood Gatherer is the name of her father, and Blood Woman is the name of the maiden.

And when he heard the account of the fruit of the tree, her father retold it. And she was amazed at the account:

"I'm not acquainted with that tree they talk about. '"Its fruit is truly sweet!" they say,' I hear," she said.

Next, she went all alone and arrived where the tree stood. It stood at the Place of Ball Game Sacrifice:

"What? Well! What's the fruit of this tree? Shouldn't this tree bear something sweet? They shouldn't die, they shouldn't be wasted. Should I pick one?" said the maiden.

And then the bone spoke; it was here in the fork of the tree:

"Why do you want a mere bone, a round thing in the branches of a tree?" said the head of One Hunahpu when it spoke to the maiden. "You don't want it," she was told.

"I do want it," said the maiden.

"Very well. Stretch out your right hand here, so I can see it," said the bone.

"Yes," said the maiden. She stretched out her right hand, up there in front of the bone.

And then the bone spit out its saliva, which landed squarely in the hand of the maiden.

And then she looked in her hand, she inspected it right away, but the bone's saliva wasn't in her hand.

"It is just a sign I have given you, my saliva, my spittle. This, my head, has nothing on it—just bone, nothing of meat. It's just the same with the head of a great lord: it's just the flesh that makes his face look good. And when he dies, people get frightened by his bones. After that, his son is like his saliva, his spittle, in his being, whether it be the son of a lord or the son of a craftsman, an orator. The father does not disappear, but goes on being fulfilled. Neither dimmed nor destroyed is the face of a lord, a warrior, craftsman, orator. Rather, he will leave his daughters and sons. So it is that I have done likewise through you. Now go up there on the face of the earth; you will not die. Keep the word. So be it," said the head of One and Seven Hunahpu—they were of one mind when they did it.

This was the word Hurricane, Newborn Thunderbolt, Raw Thunderbolt had given them. In the same way, by the time the maiden returned to her home, she had been given many instructions. Right away something was generated in her belly, from the saliva alone, and this was the generation of Hunahpu and Xbalanque.

And when the maiden got home and six months had passed, she was found out by her father. Blood Gatherer is the name of her father.

* * *

And they came to the lords.[3] Feigning great humility, they bowed their heads all the way to the ground when they arrived. They brought themselves low, doubled over, flattened out, down to the rags, to the tatters. They really looked like vagabonds when they arrived.

So then they were asked what their mountain[4] and tribe were, and they were also asked about their mother and father:

"Where do you come from?" they were asked.

"We've never known, lord. We don't know the identity of our mother and father. We must've been small when they died," was all they said. They didn't give any names.

"Very well. Please entertain us, then. What do you want us to give you in payment?" they were asked.

"Well, we don't want anything. To tell the truth, we're afraid," they told the lord.

"Don't be afraid. Don't be ashamed. Just dance this way: first you'll dance to sacrifice yourselves, you'll set fire to my house after that, you'll act out all the things you know. We want to be entertained. This is our heart's desire, the reason you had to be sent for, dear vagabonds. We'll give you payment," they were told.

So then they began their songs and dances, and then all the Xibalbans arrived, the spectators crowded the floor, and they danced everything: they danced the Weasel, they danced the Poorwill,[5] they danced the Armadillo. Then the lord said to them:

"Sacrifice my dog, then bring him back to life again," they were told.

"Yes," they said.

When they sacrificed the dog
  he then came back to life.
And that dog was really happy
  when he came back to life.
Back and forth he wagged his tail
  when he came back to life.

And the lord said to them:

"Well, you have yet to set my home on fire," they were told next, so then they set fire to the home of the lord. The house was packed with all the lords, but they were not burned. They quickly fixed it back again, lest the house of One Death be consumed all at once, and all the lords were amazed, and they went on dancing this way. They were overjoyed.

And then they were asked by the lord:

"You have yet to kill a person! Make a sacrifice without death!" they were told.

"Very well," they said.

And then they took hold of a human sacrifice.

And they held up a human heart on high.

And they showed its roundness to the lords.

And now One and Seven Death admired it, and now that person was brought right back to life. His heart was overjoyed when he came back to life, and the lords were amazed:

"Sacrifice yet again, even do it to yourselves! Let's see it! At heart, that's the dance we really want from you," the lords said now.

"Very well, lord," they replied, and then they sacrificed themselves.

And this is the sacrifice of Hunahpu by Xbalanque. One by one his legs, his arms were spread wide. His head came off, rolled far away outside. His heart, dug out, was smothered in a leaf,[6] and all the Xibalbans went crazy at the sight.

So now, only one of them was dancing there: Xbalanque.

"Get up!" he said, and Hunahpu came back to life. The two of them were overjoyed at this—and likewise the lords rejoiced, as if they were doing it themselves. One and Seven Death were as glad at heart as if they themselves were actually doing the dance.

And then the hearts of the lords were filled with longing, with yearning for the dance of Hunahpu and Xbalanque, so then came these words from One and Seven Death:

"Do it to us! Sacrifice us!" they said. "Sacrifice both of us!" said One and Seven Death to Hunahpu and Xbalanque.

"Very well. You ought to come back to life. After all, aren't you Death?[7] And aren't we making you happy, along with the vassals of your domain?" they told the lords.

And this one was the first to be sacrificed: the lord at the very top, the one whose name is One Death, the ruler of Xibalba.

And with One Death dead, the next to be taken was Seven Death. They did not come back to life.

And then the Xibalbans were getting up to leave, those who had seen the lords die. They underwent heart sacrifice there, and the heart sacrifice was performed on the two lords only for the purpose of destroying them.

As soon as they had killed the one lord without bringing him back to life, the other lord had been meek and tearful before the dancers. He didn't consent, he didn't accept it:

"Take pity on me!" he said when he realized. All their vassals took the road to the great canyon, in one single mass they filled up the deep abyss. So they piled up there and gathered together, countless ants, tumbling down into the canyon, as if they were being herded there. And when they arrived, they all bent low in surrender, they arrived meek and tearful.

Such was the defeat of the rulers of Xibalba. The boys accomplished it only through wonders, only through self-transformation.

* * *

Such was the beginning of their disappearance and the denial of their worship.

Their ancient day was not a great one,
these ancient people only wanted conflict,
their ancient names are not really divine,
but fearful is the ancient evil of their faces.
They are makers of enemies, users of owls,[8]
they are inciters to wrongs and violence,
they are masters of hidden intentions as well,
they are black and white,[9]
masters of stupidity, masters of perplexity,

as it is said. By putting on appearances they cause dismay.

Such was the loss of their greatness and brilliance. Their domain did not return to greatness. This was accomplished by Hunahpu and Xbalanque.

From Part 4

[Origin of Humanity, First Dawn]

And here is the beginning of the conception of humans, and of the search for the ingredients of the human body. So they spoke, the Bearer, Begetter, the Makers, Modelers named Sovereign Plumed Serpent:

"The dawn has approached, preparations have been made, and morning has come for the provider, nurturer, born in the light, begotten in the light. Morning has come for humankind, for the people of the face of the earth," they said. It all came together as they went on thinking in the darkness, in the night, as they searched and they sifted, they thought and they wondered.

And here their thoughts came out in clear light. They sought and discovered what was needed for human flesh. It was only a short while before the sun, moon, and stars were to appear above the Makers and Modelers. Broken Place, Bitter Water Place is the name: the yellow corn, white corn came from there.

And these are the names of the animals who brought the food: fox, coyote, parrot, crow. There were four animals who brought the news of the ears of yellow corn and white corn. They were coming from over there at Broken Place, they showed the way to the break.[1]

And this was when they found the staple foods.

And these were the ingredients for the flesh of the human work, the human design, and the water was for the blood. It became human blood, and corn was also used by the Bearer, Begetter.

And so they were happy over the provisions of the good mountain, filled with sweet things, thick with yellow corn, white corn, and thick with pataxte and cacao, countless zapotes, anonas, jocotes, nances, matasanos,[2] sweets—the rich foods filling up the citadel named Broken Place, Bitter Water Place. All the edible fruits were there: small staples, great staples, small plants, great plants. The way was shown by the animals.

And then the yellow corn and white corn were ground, and Xmucane did the grinding nine times. Corn was used, along with the water she rinsed her hands with, for the creation of grease; it became human fat when it was worked by the Bearer, Begetter, Sovereign Plumed Serpent, as they are called.

After that they put it into words:

the making, the modeling of our first mother-father,
with yellow corn, white corn alone for the flesh,
food alone for the human legs and arms,
for our first fathers, the four human works.

It was staples alone that made up their flesh.
These are the names of the first people who were made and modeled.

This is the first person: Jaguar Quitze.
And now the second: Jaguar Night
And now the third: Mahucutah.
And the fourth: True Jaguar.[3]

And these are the names of our first mother-fathers.[4] They were simply made and modeled, it is said; they had no mother and no father. We have named the men by themselves. No woman gave birth to them, nor were they begotten by the builder, sculptor, Bearer, Begetter. By sacrifice alone, by genius alone they were made, they were modeled by the Maker, Modeler, Bearer, Begetter, Sovereign Plumed Serpent. And when they came to fruition, they came out human:

They talked and they made words.
They looked and they listened.
They walked, they worked.

They were good people, handsome, with looks of the male kind. Thoughts came into existence and they gazed; their vision came all at once. Perfectly they saw, perfectly they knew everything under the sky, whenever they looked. The moment they turned around and looked around in the sky, on the earth, everything was seen without any obstruction. They didn't have to walk around before they could see what was under the sky; they just stayed where they were.

As they looked, their knowledge became intense. Their sight passed through trees, through rocks, through lakes, through seas, through mountains, through plains. Jaguar Quitze, Jaguar Night Mahucutah, and True Jaguar were truly gifted people.

And then they were asked by the builder and mason:

"What do you know about your being? Don't you look, don't you listen? Isn't your speech good, and your wall? So you must look, to see out under the sky. Don't you see the mountain-plain clearly? So try it," they were told.

And then they saw everything under the sky perfectly. After that, they thanked the Maker, Modeler.

"Truly now,
double thanks,
triple thanks
that we've been formed, we've been given
our mouths, our faces,
we speak, we listen,
we wonder, we move,
our knowledge is good, we've understood
what is far and near,
and we've seen what is great and small
under the sky, on the earth.
Thanks to you we've been formed,
we've come to be made and modeled,
our grandmother, our grandfather,"

they said when they gave thanks for having been made and modeled. They understood everything perfectly, they sighted the four sides, the four corners in the sky, on the earth, and this didn't sound good to the builder and sculptor:

"What our works and designs have said is no good:

'We have understood everything, great and small,' they say." And so the Bearer, Begetter took back their knowledge:

"What should we do with them now? Their vision should at least reach nearby, they should see at least a small part of the face of the earth, but what they're saying isn't good. Aren't they merely 'works' and 'designs' in their very names? Yet they'll become as great as gods, unless they procreate, proliferate at the sowing, the dawning, unless they increase."

"Let it be this way: now we'll take them apart just a little, that's what we need. What we've found out isn't good. Their deeds would become equal to ours, just because their knowledge reaches so far. They see everything," so said

the Heart of Sky, Hurricane,
Newborn Thunderbolt, Raw Thunderbolt,
Sovereign Plumed Serpent,
Bearer, Begetter,
Xpiyacoc, Xmucane,
Maker, Modeler,

as they are called. And when they changed the nature of their works, their designs, it was enough that the eyes be marred by the Heart of Sky. They were blinded as the face of a mirror is breathed upon. Their eyes were weakened. Now it was only when they looked nearby that things were clear.

And such was the loss of the means of understanding, along with the means of knowing everything, by the four humans. The root was implanted.

And such was the making, modeling of our first grandfather, our father, by the Heart of Sky, Heart of Earth.

And then their wives and women came into being. Again, the same gods thought of it. It was as if they were asleep when they received them, truly beautiful women were there with Jaguar Quitze, Jaguar Night Mahucutah, and True Jaguar. With their women there they became wider awake. Right away they were happy at heart again, because of their wives.

Celebrated Seahouse is the name of the wife of Jaguar Quitze.

Prawn House is the name of the wife of Jaguar Night.

Hummingbird House is the name of the wife of Mahucutah.

Macaw House is the name of the wife of True Jaguar.

So these are the names of their wives, who became ladies of rank, giving birth to the people of the tribes, small and great.

* * *

And here is the dawning and showing of the sun, moon, and stars. And Jaguar Quitze, Jaguar Night, Mahucutah, and True Jaguar were overjoyed when they saw the daybringer.[5] It came up first. It looked brilliant when it came up, since it was ahead of the sun.

After that they unwrapped their copal[6] incense, which came from the east, and there was triumph in their hearts when they unwrapped it. They gave their heartfelt thanks with three kinds at once:

Mixtam Copal is the name of the copal brought by Jaguar Quitze.

Cauiztan Copal, next, is the name of the copal brought by Jaguar Night.

Godly Copal, as the next one is called, was brought by Mahucutah.

The three of them had their copal, and this is what they burned as they incensed the direction of the rising sun. They were crying sweetly as they shook their burning copal,[7] the precious copal.

After that they cried because they had yet to see and yet to witness the birth of the sun.

And then, when the sun came up, the animals, small and great, were happy. They all came up from the rivers and canyons; they waited on all the mountain peaks. Together they looked toward the place where the sun came out.

So then the puma and jaguar cried out, but the first to cry out was a bird, the parrot by name. All the animals were truly happy. The eagle, the white vulture, small birds, great birds spread their wings, and the penitents and sacrificers knelt down.

From Part 5

[Prayer for Future Generations]

And this is the cry of their hearts, here it is:

"Wait! On this blessed day,
thou Hurricane, thou Heart of the Sky-Earth,
thou giver of ripeness and freshness,
and thou giver of daughters and sons,
spread thy stain, spill thy drops
of green and yellow;[8]
give life and beginning
to those I bear and beget,
that they might multiply and grow,
nurturing and providing for thee,
calling to thee along the roads and paths,
on rivers, in canyons,
beneath the trees and bushes;
give them their daughters and sons.

"May there be no blame, obstacle, want or misery;
let no deceiver come behind or before them,
may they neither be snared nor wounded,
nor seduced, nor burned,
nor diverted below the road nor above it;
may they neither fall over backward nor stumble;
keep them on the Green Road, the Green Path.

"May there be no blame or barrier for them
through any secrets or sorcery of thine;
may thy nurturers and providers be good
before thy mouth and thy face,
thou, Heart of Sky; thou, Heart of Earth;
thou, Bundle of Flames;[9]
and thou, Tohil, Auilix, Hacauitz,[1]
under the sky, on the earth,
the four sides, the four corners;
may there be only light, only continuity within,
before thy mouth and thy face, thou god."

Notes

1. Translated by Dennis Tedlock.
2. All thirteen names refer to the Creator or to a company of creators, a designation applicable clearly to the first four names and Sovereign Plumed Serpent, Heart of the Lake and Heart of the Sea also since the creators will later be described as "in the water," and somewhat obscurely, so does the pair of names (Plate and Bowl may be read as "earth" and "sky, respectively). Hunahpu Possum Hunahpu Coyote, Great White Peccary, and Tapir refer specifically to the grandparents of the gods, usually called Xpiyacoc and Xmucane.
3. Four names for Xpiyacoc and Xmucane.
4. The hieroglyphic source (Council Book) was suppressed by missionaries; it was said to have been brought to Quiché in ancient times from the far side of a lagoon (Sea). The reader hides his face to avoid the missionaries.

5. As though a farmer were measuring and staking a cornfield.
6. Alternate names for Heart of Sky, the deity who cooperates with Sovereign Plumed Serpent. The triple naming adapts the Christian trinity to native theology, perhaps more in the spirit of defiant preemption than of conciliation.
7. That is, humanity, which alone is capable of nurturing the gods with sacrifices.
8. When used together, *puz* ("cutting edge" or "sacrifice") and *naual* ("genius") are metonyms for shamanic power, referring to the ability to make genius or spiritual essence visible or audible by means of ritual [Translator's note].
9. That is, the creation of humans; an account of the first three, unsuccessful attempts at creating humans occupies the remainder of Part 1.
1. First mention of the twin hero gods (their origin is recounted in Part 3). Here they confront the false god Seven Mlacaw who has arisen during the time of primordial darkness. boasting, "My eyes are of metal; my teeth just glitter with jewels, and turquoise as well . . . I am like the sun and the moon." Note that ail the characters in Parts 1, 2, and 3 are supernatural; humans are not created until Part 4.
2. A pickle tree (*Byrsonima crassifolia*).
3. This is obviously the origin of the way a macaw's beak looks, with a huge tipper mandible and a much smaller and retreating lower one [Translator's note].
4. Animal names of the divine grandparents, Xpiyacoc and Xmucane, who are also the twins' genealogical grandparents.
5. Play on words as qui is translated as both "sweet" and "poison."
6. The present-day Quiché retain the notion that a toothache is caused by a worm gnawing at the bone [Translator's note].
7. This is clearly meant to be the origin of the large white eye patch and very small eyes of the scarlet macaw [Translator's note].
8. Twin sons of Xpiyacoc and Xmucane; the elder of twins, One Hunahpu, will become the father of Hunahpu and Xbalanque. "As for Seven Hunahpu," according to the text, "he has no wife. He's just a partner and just secondary; he just remains a boy."
9. The first of the "test" houses in Xibalba (the underworld) to which One and Seven Hunahpu, avid ballplayers, have been lured by the underworld lords, One and Seven Death; the lords have promised them a challenging ball game. The Mesoamerican ball game, remotely comparable to both basketball and soccer, was played on a rectangular court, using a ball of native rubber.
1. Probably not a place name, but rather a name for the altar where losing ball players were sacrificed [Translator's note].
2. Fourth-ranking lord of Xibalba, whose commission is to draw blood from people.
3. Forced to flee the underworld the maiden (Blood Woman) finds refuge on earth with Xmucane. There she gives birth to the twins, who, like their father and uncle, become ballplayers and are enticed to the underworld. Surviving the Dark House and other tests, they disguise themselves as vagabonds and earn a reputation as clever entertainers among the denizens of Xibalba; as such they are summoned to entertain the high lords.
4. A metonym for almost any settlement, but especially a fortified town or citadel, located on a defensible elevation [Translators note].
5. The goatsucker. The dances apparently were imitations of these animals and birds.
6. As a tamale is wrapped. In the typical Mesoamerican heart sacrifice the victim's arms and legs were stretched wide and the heart was excised and offered to a deity.
7. Evident sarcasm.
8. The lords had used owls as messengers to lure the ballplayers to Xibalba.
9. Contradictory, duplicitous.
1. In the widespread Mesoamerican story of the discovery of corn, one or more animals reveal that corn and other foods are hidden within a rock or a mountain, accessible through a cleft; in some versions the mountain is broken apart by lightning.

2. Quincelike fruits of the tree *Casimiroa edulis.* Pataxte (*Theobroma bicolor*) is a species of cacao that is inferior to cacao proper (*T. cacao*). Zapotes are fruits of the sapota tree (*Lucuma mammosa*). Anonas are custard apples (*genus Anona*). Jocotes are yellow plumlike fruits of the tree *Spondias purpurea.*
3. The four original Quiché males.
4. That is, parents, although only the first three founded lineages; True Jaguar had no son.
5. The morning star.
6. Resin used as incense.
7. Note that the Mesoamerican pottery censer must be shaken or swayed back and forth to keep the incense burning.
8. The imagery, denoting human offspring, alludes to semen and plant growth.
9. A sacred relic left to the Quiché lords by Jaguar Quitze; like the sacred bundles of the North American Indians, a sort of cloth-wrapped ark with mysterious contents [Translator's note].
1. Patron deities of the Quiché lineages.

Pre-Columbian Art and Architecture

Throughout Mesoamerica, the complex symbolism of the region's art and architecture almost equals the magnificence of the fine quality of their execution. To this day, specialists marvel at the Inca Machu Picchu settlement in Peru, built with rocks geometrically cut to perfection and assembled without mortar. No one can explain how they were moved from the quarry to the site. That early Incas were master builders becomes evident when one considers the stones of the Cathedral of Santo Domingo, in Cuzco. Erected on the base of the destroyed Temple of the Sun, the precise cutting of the masonry is glaringly evident. When speaking of pre-Columbian art and architecture, one might raise another question. For some anthropologists, pre-Columbian contacts between Africans and indigenous peoples explain architectural techniques and similarities, despite great geographical distances. It is likely that belief systems having an astronomical base could explain why the perimeters of the Great Pyramid of Giza and the pyramid of the Chaco canyon, on different continents, have identical measurements. American contacts with Africans could have taken place during the reign of Ramses III, during the Nubian era of the twenty-fifth dynasty, or during the Mandingo voyages of the fourteenth century. Documented testimonials of those who claim to have seen blacks in Mexico and the record of Columbus' having sent samples of gold-tipped spears back to Spain attest to the early intercontinental contacts. The giant sculpted Olmec heads with braided hair further support the possibility of intercontinental contacts, as does the array of later sculpted heads of Yucatan, with their Mandingo facial features, scarifications, and hairstyles. Mayan paintings reveal mastery in the ability to represent the human form. During the classic period calligraphy and paintings on pottery made no attempt to create the illusion of dimensions. Frequent depictions of scribes abounded on period pottery. Little distinction existed between writing and painting, which were executed with pictographs and ideographs. However beautiful the contoured ink renditions were, either of human forms of glyphs, architectural sculpture was perhaps the most distinctive of the Mayan arts. Through this medium the cycle of creation and the linear nature of history were displayed.

Chichen Itza (Figure 38) demonstrates the symbolically functional role of the four directions in Mayan architecture and thought. These directions were reflected in the design of cities and governance structures. For this reason, Chichen Itza had four parts. In addition to the four-sided Castillo, there was a round observatory named the Caracol, an immense ball court, and a Temple of the Warriors with the Sacred Cenote or Well of Sacrifice. Chichen means "mouth of the will of Itza," and Itza refers to "Water Wizards." The High Priest's grave at Chichen Itza depicts a monster around the door to symbolize a cave and a mountain. A mountain was believed to be a living being. Similarly, the cenote was a door to the valley of the underworld.

In a sense, many Mayan structures were architectural time-keepers. For example, glyphic records show the dates when the Itza established its confederacy and when it dedicated lintels, walls, and stelae. They recorded the years of settlement and resettlement. Also, in AD 83, a Maya group built the Caracol observatory to determine the exact date of important astronomical events, such as the nocturnal zenith of the Pleiades which signals the continued movement of time that avoided the feared end of the world. Time is also a feature in the design of the Castillo. When the rising equinoctial sun struck the balustrades, carved feathered serpents appeared to wriggle from heaven to earth. In order to accomplish this momentary and momentous descent of these serpents down the steps of the Kukulkan building, there had to be a well-orchestrated interactivity between astronomical, religious, architectural, sculptural and scenographic knowledge among Mayan priests.

Figure 38. Ruins of "The Church" at Chichen Itza.
CORBIS/Danny Lehman.

Not only were these structures elaborate time-keepers, but also they were the setting for blood sacrifices. Blood sacrifice was thought to mediate between humanity and the temporal divinity. The importance of such sacrifices may be deduced from the sheer magnitude of the space set aside for this purpose. The ball court at Chichen Itza is one of the largest in Mesoamerica, for it measures more than 500 feet long and 200 feet wide.

This blood ritual at Chichen Itza resembles that of other Mayan regions. In Palenque, designers arranged buildings so that sunlight would fall directly on the Temple of the Cross, one day per year. Similarly, in Yaxchilan, during the spring solstice, the sun's light brightened the temple at the precise point where the statue of the Bird Jaguar King stood, and for that brief moment, the king was ritualistically revived in a flood of light.

Art and architecture at Chichen Itza and in other Mesoamerican cultures vivify the past, to insure the continuity of life in the present. Myths were reenacted against architectural backdrops through an interplay of art and science no longer understood today.

Selected Bibliography

Adams, Richard E. W. *Prehistoric Mesoamerica.* Rev. ed. Norman: Oklahoma UP, 1991.

Donnan, Christopher B., and Donna McClelland. *The Burial Theme in Moche Iconography.* Washington, DC.: Dumbarton Oaks, Trustees of Harvard U, 1979.

Florescano, Enrique. *Memory, Myth and Time in Mexico: From the Aztecs to Independence.* Trans. Albert G. Bork and Kathryn R. Bork. Austin: Texas UP, 1994.

Hunter, C. Bruce. *A Guide to Ancient Maya Ruins.* Norman: Oklahoma UP, 1986.

Leon-Portilla, Miguel. *Time and Reality in the Thought of the Maya.* Boston: Beacon 1973.

Reents-Budet, Dorie. *Painting the Maya Universe: Royal Ceramics of the Classic Period.* Durham: Duke UP, 1994.

Schele, Linda, and Peter Mathews. *The Code of Kings: The Language of Seven Sacred Maya Temples and Tombs.* New York: Scribner, 1998.

Van Sertima, Ivan. *Early America Revisited.* New Brunswick: Transaction, 1998.

Wright, Ronald. *Time Among the Maya.* New York: Weidenfeld and Nicholson, 1989.

Part IV: The Asian Perspective

Asian Background: History and Culture

On the whole, it is impossible to arrive at compelling generalizations which could throw into relief the threads binding the disparate cultures of Asia today with the equally diverse civilizations of the past. Such threads, if they do exist, can be found in the recognition that the sweeping geographical, demographic, and religious diversity seen in Asia today are fruits of causes deeply rooted in the Asian ancient and pre-modern worlds. In making this assertion, the researcher is struck by four distinct phases of Asian history and culture: 1) that between the dawn of history and 3000 BC, which yields both fossil evidence of early man and indications of Asian ingenuity in the fashioning of early instruments and tools; 2) the period between 3000 BC and AD 200, witnessing the growth of the most influential Asian cultures—India and China; 3) the era between 200 BC and AD 600, bringing cross-fertilizations of philosophies and religions in Asia and portions of Europe; and 4) that between AD 600 and 1500, involving domination by both Islam and aggressive Mongol groups from the north.

The geographical, demographic, and religious diversity of Asia is obvious. Placed almost entirely in the northern hemisphere, Asia is the largest of earth's continents, encompassing nearly a third of the earth's land surface, though Asians themselves comprise about three-fifths of earth's inhabitants. When speaking of Asia, many scholars refer to a diverse group of countries, peoples, languages, and cultures largely of South and East Asia, such as China, Japan, India, Korea, Indonesia, and the Phillippines, whereas others include Arab countries and populations to the west and Russian provinces east of the Ural mountains. Taken in the broadest sense, then, one can divide Asia into five distinct areas: East Asia (e.g., China, Korea, Japan), Southeast Asia (e.g., Thailand, Vietnam, Indonesia, the Philippines), South Asia (e.g., India and Pakistan), Southwest Asia (e.g., Iran, Iraq, Israel, and Saudi Arabia), and finally Russian territory east of the Ural Mountains. Because much of the continent falls along latitudes similar to those of North America and Canada, climates and weather patterns vary considerably; as a result, one can encounter arctic, arid, and tropical conditions.

Just as Asia enjoys a diversity of geography and climate, so the peoples of Asia are the most diverse in the world. The population is frequently concentrated in relatively small land areas, particularly in the lower southeast quarter of the continent. Population density is a marked feature in China and Japan. It is not surprising that, because of the huge population of China itself, dispersed over much of Asia, the Chinese language or its variants are the most commonly spoken in Asia—even though Urdu or Hindi is spoken in South Asia in locations like Pakistan and northern India; Arabic, Persian (or Farsi), and Hebrew, in Southwest Asia; and Russian, in the Russian provinces.

In most of Southwest Asia, Islam is the dominant religion, although Christian and Jewish religious expression is also found. In India, the chief religion is Hinduism, and Buddhism flourishes in Thailand, South Korea, Vietnam, and Japan. The moral and social philosophy of Confucius dominated China (and in Russia, Orthodox Christianity) until the Communist revolutions in those countries. The Japanese have traditionally espoused Shinto, a religion which blends Buddhism, reverence towards ancestors, and celebration of spirits in nature. Roman Catholicism can also be encountered in a number of East Asian locales because of the influence of Roman Catholic missionaries. One can imagine that, amid this religious melting pot, religious conflict would not be unknown.

The period between the dawn of history and 3000 BC yields both fossil evidence of early man and indications of Asian ingenuity in the fashioning of early instruments and tools. Like the civilizations of Africa, those of Asia have been extremely influential in establishing the foundations of global culture; yet it is important to acknowledge that at no time was the culture of Asia homogeneous. On the contrary, the various cultures developed for the most part independently of one another; even so, there were a number of significant exchanges and cross-fertilizations. Some of the oldest evidence of human habitation in Asia was offered by the fossils of the Peking Man in China and the Java man in Indonesia. Further, Homo Erectus, ancestor of Homo Sapiens or modern mankind, emerged some 150,000 years ago—although other evidence places his arrival in Asia at about one million years ago, likely from Africa. The earliest known Asian civilizations appeared in parts of Southwest Asia and in portions of India and China, all having in common an increasingly robust agricultural economy, which became even more productive when the plow was introduced around 3000 BC. By 3000 BC, too, to the west in what are now Iraq and Syria, Mesopotamia, the so-called cradle of civilization, rose to prominence. The Sumerians, inhabitants of this region, irrigated their fields from precisely measured canals, employed bronze and polished stone-tools, made textiles and wheel-turned pottery, built temples and palaces, traveled in wheeled carts and sailing ships, constructed accurate calendars predicting seasons, invented cuneiform writing, worshiped a sun god, and lived under a written code of laws.

The period 3000–200 BC saw the expansion of Asian culture from the Indus Valley in India to the Yellow River in China. By 2300 BC, one saw the rise of the Indus Valley civilization of northwest India and southern Pakistan, which traded cotton and textiles with Mesopotamia. Here, inhabitants enjoyed straight streets lined with large, two-story homes equipped with plumbing; wheeled carts; creative jewelry; and written languages. Later, from 1500–1200 BC, the peoples of this region were invaded from the north by speakers of an Indo-Aryan language soon known as Sanskrit, in which the *Vedas*, sacred text of India, were written. These invaders destroyed the advanced cities of the Indus Valley and imposed a monarchial form of government and a caste system supported by Hindu doctrine. From 3000–1600 BC, Chinese civilization likewise developed along the Huang He or Yellow River, in the form of large farming communities, which traded with Central Asia. However, the Chinese did not adopt a system of written records until the sixteenth century BC. By 770–256 BC, Chinese territory had more than doubled, and China even then had witnessed the highest population concentration in the world. At this time, China made iron weapons, expanded irrigation, and built roads and canals to improve communication and commerce. During this period, the Zhou Dynasty fostered the rise of competent civil servants called mandarins, and witnessed the development of Chinese philosophy as seen in Confucianism, Taoism, and Legalism. This period was, in fact, later referred to as the classical period of Chinese philosophy. And, indeed, by AD 500 the major world religions and philosophies, with the exception of Islam, had flourished and spread far from their original birth places. The vibrancy of this religious and philosophical proliferation is indicated by Color Figure 16, showing a seated Buddha AD 50–320; Figure 39, a Bodhisattva from AD II–III centuries; and Figure 40, a dancing Shiva. Figure 41 depicts the great Umayyad Mosque built in AD eighth century.

From the sixth century BC to AD seventh century, the kingdom of Persia, created around the sixth century BC united the Iranian peoples, under kings Cyrus the Great and Darius I. During the latter's reign, there emerged a centralized government, as well as an historically important religion, Zoroastrianism—important because to it is frequently ascribed the notions of good and evil and heaven and hell possibly borrowed by Judaism, Christianity, and Islam. But by 330 BC, Persia had succumbed to the military challenge of Alexander the Great, who had sought to unite the cultures of east and west. Northern India, earlier conquered by the Persians, also fell under Alexander's military control. It is through this contact that Greek philosophers likely were influenced by both Hinduism and Buddhism. When inhabitants of Central Asia conquered north India during AD first century, Buddhism was further spread by them into Central Asia and China. Upon the rise of Hinduism in India, however, Buddhism became a persecuted religion. During the fourth and fifth centuries, under the influence of the Gupta Dynasty, Indian civilization reached an impressive height. From 200 BC to the early centuries AD, Chinese culture made its imprint on surrounding regions in Asia, among them Korea and Vietnam, the later of which was ruled by China for some 1000 years. During the Han Dynasty (206–200 BC), papermaking was invented, the arts and literature flowered, and engineering reached a significant level of competency, because of which fact China constructed roads and canals similar to those of the Romans. Though invasions from the north created some problems for China between AD fourth to seventh centuries, Chinese culture continued to spread, especially into

Figure 39. Bodhisattva, c. 2nd–3rd century.
Seattle Art Museum.

Figure 40. Shiva Nataraja.
Photograph © Otto E. Nelson. Courtesy of The Asia Society.

Figure 41. The Great Umayyad Mosque, Damascus.
Arab Information Center.

Korea, which adopted the Chinese writing system, Confucian governmental models, and Buddhism. Chinese influence reached as far as Japan, ruled by the Yamato Clan. Through contact with Korea, Japan imported Buddhism, the Chinese writing system, and other cultural innovations and amenities.

From the seventh to the fifteenth centuries, Asia was strongly influenced by both the spread of Islam and the military domination of the Mongols. In Arabia of the seventh century, there arose the Prophet Muhammad, who, according to legend, was approached by the angel Gabriel and told the will of God, whereupon Muhammad founded the religion of Islam. The codification of his spiritual revelations is the Koran. The missionary tendencies of Islamic doctrine led to the expansion of the faith into areas so disparate as India and Spain. Later, in the eleventh and twelfth centuries, much of Islam fell into war with the Christian Byzantine Empire. This, combined with the closing of Christian holy places in Palestine, provoked European Christians to launch military expeditions, called Crusades, into western Asia in defense of their religion. The Crusades lasted about 300 years but failed to dislodge the Muslims. Crusaders, however, returned to Europe with many elements of Islamic culture. Although Islamic influence was formidable, it did not succeed in affecting those countries like Korea, Vietnam, and China which had fallen under Chinese cultural influence. But Chinese control was somewhat affected by the Mongol invasions from the steppes of Asia, culminating in the campaigns of Genghis Khan against northern and western China and portions of Central Asia, extended by his sons later, into Turkistan, Iran, and Russia. Another such invader was Kublai Khan, who, conquering Korea and North China, established his own Yuan Dynasty (1279–1368). The Mongols were, however, open to the notion of foreign trade; and it was they who had invited the Italian Marco Polo to China. However, by the fourteenth and fifteenth centuries, the Mongol Empire had begun to disintegrate.

While the supposed connections between present effects and past causality may be tenuous, it is easy to see why Asia today is such a diverse culture and why the conflicts and competitions which observers now witness in Asia are inevitable—conflicts which are territorial, ethnic, and religious in origin. Yet in the resolving of these tensions, Asia may come to find a sound basis for unity, cooperation, and sharing.

One sees in Asia as many similarities as differences and expects that, in these similarities, Asia will find the keys to its future.

Selected Bibliography

Bowker, John Westerdale, ed. *World Religions*. New York: DK, 1997.

Clunas, Craig. *Oxford History of Art: Art in China*. New York: Oxford UP, 1997.

Kahn, Joel S., ed. *Southeast Asian Identities: Culture and the Politics of Representation in Indonesia, Malaysia, Singapore, and Thailand*. New York: St. Martin's, 1998.

Lambton, Ann K.S. *Continuity and Change in Medieval Persia: Aspects of Administrative, Economic and Social History, 11th–14th Century*. Albany, NY: Bibliotheca Persica, 1988.

Liu, Hsin-ju. *Ancient India and Ancient China: Trade and Religious Exchanges,* AD *1–600*. New York: Oxford UP, 1988.

Asian Literature

Agrarian societies of ancient civilizations thrived in the Fertile Crescent, that area carved out between the Tigris and Euphrates rivers, today's Iraq and Iran or the Middle East. Members of the ancient Middle East cultures wanted to discover life's ultimate meaning through their literature. They desired to create order out of chaos and find order in the production of religious poetry, ritual dramas, and myth.

Researchers discovered in the ancient Middle East fragments of approximately ten epics from Sumerian literature, as well as extant hymns and proverbs. However, the greatest single work to emerge from the ancient Middle East is the Babylonian epic poem *Gilgamesh* (ca. 2500–1500 BC), a work of art in historical narrative and myth. It is the saga of Gilgamesh, the superhuman half-god dictator and his exploits. The thematic representations explore a reading of the human condition, the delicate relationship between mortals and immortals, the depth of enduring friendship, and the complexity of civilization building.

Historical narrative also abounds in Hebrew or Old Testament literature but is not limited to that. The lyric, song, riddle, drama, short story, and biography embellish Hebrew literature. The Psalms, an anthology of sacred verse, contains some of the great poems of the period; and Job, a philosophical work, includes poetry, drama, impassioned dialogue, and the speeches of God, who manifests Himself as the Voice in the Whirlwind. Hebrew literature also includes the Proverbs, which is a compendium of wisdom; Ruth, which is an idyllic pastoral tale; and the Song of Songs, a collection of sensual love lyrics.

Much of the literature of the Hebrews captures their history, but glimpses into Islamic history only surface in the biography of Muhammad, the spiritual leader of Arabia. Prior to the coming of Muhammad, some fragmentary odes or epic plays survive, *Muallaqat (Golden Odes)*, but the compilations of the revelations of Muhammad into a book called the *Koran* is the sacred book of the Muslims and provides evidence of the skillful use of lyric poetry, which, in actuality, constitutes the words of the Prophet Himself. Another literary genre of Arab genius is prose fiction, depicted in the well-known *Alf Laylah wa-Laylah* (the *Arabian)*, a magnificent frame tale. Some of the best loved stories include the characters Aladin, Ali Baba, and Sinbad.

The Arabs influenced to a great degree the production of literature in Persia, but heterodoxy by the Persians led to their own unique literature. Prior to Persia's conversion to Mohammedanism, the country's religion was Zoroastrianism. The *Avesta* or *Zen-Avesta* is the book of scripture that identifies Ormazd as the lord of light and righteousness and Ahriman as the spirit of death and darkness. These represent the cosmic principles of good and evil which war against each other ceaselessly; however, when time ends, Ormazd emerges the victor and the judge of men, sending them to paradise or hell, depending on their earthly deeds. Later in Persian literary history, the poet Sa'di (1194–1292) penned *Bustan (Fruit Garden)*, philosophical poetry, and *Gulistan (Rose Garden)*, epigrams and aphorisms. The renown Persian poet Abu'l Qasim Firdausi (c. 940–1020) authored *Shah Nameh* or *Shah-namah (Book of Kings)*, an epic of major undertaking that attempts to chronicle all the significant Iranian heroes and the history of Persian rulers from Persia's beginnings to the seventh ccentury. Like many epics, it showcases the heroes' bravery in battle and pride in strict behavioral codes and the culture of a nation.

Indian literature, the literature of South Asia, aims to emphasize Hindu beliefs, making no distinction between the sacred and the secular. The *Mahabharata (Great Bharata/Story)*, India's long cultural and theological epic poem, tells the story of an ambitious feudal family that vies to control the Ganges Valley but after gaining control isolates itself in the Himalayas. This book also contains the most sacred work of the Hindus, the *Bhagavadgita (Song of the Blessed)*, which outlines the mysticism of Hinduism. Another long poem is the *Ramayana*, a love story about Prince Rama's pursuit for Sita, his love.

While South Asian literature is religious, East Asian literature is philosophical, especially the literature of China. Confucius, to many Chinese, is a deity, and his collected philosophies appear in the *Analects*, four books that are collections of sententiae. Confucius' followers are not limited to the Chinese border; his philosophical sayings touch the lives of many people all over the world. Other philosophical works include *Shih Ching (Book of Odes)*, a book of poetry, and *Hsi yu chi (Pilgrimage to the West)*. The lyric poem and philosophical prose are other Chinese literary forms. The Chinese developed intricate rules for their construction and limited subject matter to upper-class themes of life and love.

Because the Japanese succumbed to Buddhist influence from China, most writers used the Chinese language to express themselves because this language seemed more civilized to them. However, the Japanese soon adapted Chinese principles of life to their own needs. Instead of building on philosophical thoughts, the Japanese perfected their own forms of poetry and drama. The seventeen-syllable *haiku* and the thirty-one-syllable *tanka* are Japanese approaches to poetry. Their Noh drama with its dance, mime, and poetic language is a unique work of art. The highlight of Japanese prose contribution is Shikibu Murasaki's the *Tale of Genji*, a novel about the loves of Prince Genji and a psychological study of courtly society.

Southeast Asian literature is a composite of Asian literature in general. The primary religious influence is Theravada Buddhism, which emerges in the literature. It takes credit for *Jatakas*, stories of the previous lives of the Buddha, and a favorite poem of the Vietnamese, "Lament of a Warrior's Wife," was originally written in Chinese but later transcribed into the Vietnamese language and given recognition as a Vietnamese work of art.

Although much of Asian literature developed in the early centuries, a classical literary tradition evolved that came to represent the Asian canon. Asian literature remains valuable for its explorations into love, truth, and beauty.

Japanese Drama: Noh Play

The Noh play, created in the middle of the fourteenth century and reaching its zenith in the middle of the fifteenth century, is a classic Japanese dance-drama containing stylized action, a chorus, elaborate costumes, simple scenery, and a heroic theme. It is an examination in aesthetics, literature, and theater. Noh plays, composed in part-prose and part-verse and adapted from established literature already in the minds of the people, are in the vernacular of the Japanese Court of the fourteenth century. The two styles of Noh are *kotoba* (words) and *fushi* (melody). The performance of fushi is either *yowagin* (soft) or *tsuyogin* (strong), which appears in masculine and warrior scenes. Noh's adherence to tradition and its continued popularity are the genius of two men, Kwannami Kiyotsuga (1333–1384) and his son Zeami Motokiyo (1363–1444).

Kwannami was a Shinto priest of the Kasuga Temple near the city of Nara, an actor, and a writer of *sarugaku* (monkey music). The third Ashikaga shogun Yoshimitsu (1368–98), who ruled absolutely in Kyoto (formerly Heian) at the time, saw one of Kwannami's performances, admired his acting ability, took him under his protection, and became his patron. His patronage elevated Kwannami and his theatrical style to a new position, making Noh the official theater of the ruling class. Yoshimitsu was a devotee of Zen Buddhism, the religion of choice for many of the great patrons of the arts, and Kwannami merged sacred Zen Buddhism practices, theatrical conventions, and poetic forms to create Japan's classic art form, the Noh drama. His son Zeami refined the art form under Yoshimitsu's patronage, giving it seriousness and merit. He published *Kwadensho (Book of the Flower)*, which outlines the principles of Noh plays, illustrates the fundamentals of *mai* (dancing), *monomane* (miming), and *yokyoku* (song). Zeami insisted on perfection in these art forms. His purpose of perfecting these three theatrical forms is to achieve *yugen* or ultimate aesthetic expression, meaning "what lies beneath the surface." Yugen emphasizes suggestion rather than representation, subtlety rather than obviousness, implication rather than reality. The influence of Zen Buddhism with its dedication to allusion dominates the Noh drama as an art form.

Noh derives from three forms associated with the shrine, marketplace, and rusticity. They are *sarugaku* (monkey music), *sangaku* (acrobatic performance), and *dengaku* (field music). Sarugaku originally was a shrine pantomine ritual play which evolved into theater comedy. It also was a masquerade which was an escape from the solemn Shinto rituals. When Kwannami adapted other conventions into *sarugaku*, it became Sarugaku no Noh, which is now Noh. *Sangaku* grew out of the popularity of sarugaku. Acrobats of sangaku, marketplace performers, were always visible in Heian city life; Chinese acrobats later joined the sarugaku performance. Another influence, *dengaku*, was the ritualistic folk dances of the rice-planting labor class. It evolved into an opera-like theatrical performance that included dance and poetry. Other forms incorporate the Noh tradition. *Kusemai* (tune dance), various poetic forms, mystery plays, Buddhist liturgy, ballads, and the Chinese dances that were essential to the Japanese Court tradition contribute to the adaptation of the independent art form called Noh.

Zeami's principles of Noh attracted students who desired to abide by his tenets. As a result, Kanze, the first school of Noh, emerged, later followed by other schools, Hosho, Komparu, Kita, and Kongo. All the schools adhere to the strict construction of the Noh stage. The traditional Noh theater, originally constructed out of doors but built in an auditorium today, established its roots at Kyoto in 1464. A theater experience in Noh drama includes five Noh plays and three *kyogen* comedies. Kyogen comedies as a general rule exclude music but occasionally contain party songs or folk songs. The 240-play Noh repertoire, always performed accompanied by music, has five categories of characters: a god, a warrior, a woman, an insane woman or miscellaneous subjects, and a devil. The theatergoer sees one from each category.

A Noh play's actors are always men who also play the roles of females. The play's principal actor is the *shite,* and the play centers around him. He combines the decorum of Zen Buddhist priests and the movements of the martial arts in his interpretation of the character. The secondary actor or assistant is the *waki,* who comes on stage first to give an exposition of the shite's character and the reason he dances the central dance.

The structure of a Noh play contains the *Jo* (introduction), *Ha* (exposition), *Nakairi* (interlude), and *Kyu* (denouement). The musical ensemble contains the *nohkan* (flute) and the *ko-tsuzumi, o-tsuzumi,* and *taiko,* three types of drums. The singing style of the Noh chorus is a derivation of Buddhist chanting. The chorus, consisting of eight to twelve people, sings the *yokyoku* (also called *utai*). The *jigashira* (chorus leader) lengthens the sounds, thus managing the tempo of the chant. Another function of the chorus is to sing the shite's words when his dance steps prevent him from singing. Noh costumes (robes) are elaborate creations, originally from the Japanese Court, military, nobility, and priesthood. Their construction is of woven and embroidered silks with various color arrangements, continuous geometric ground patterns, and repeated motifs. The motifs are an indication of the function and dignity of the personality of the character portrayed in the Noh drama. The masks used in Noh drama are made of wood and covered the faces of only the shite and his subordinates. Although no single component of Noh drama is original, their combination into a finished mosaic forged a magnificent art form.

Ikkaku Sennin

Komparu Zenpo Motoyasu

CHARACTERS

IKKAKU SENNIN, *a wizard*
SHINDA, *a court official*
LADY SENDA, *a beautiful young girl*
TWO DRAGON GODS
CHORUS
LADY SENDA'S ATTENDANTS
STAGE ASSISTANTS

The play takes place in the Kingdom of Barana, India. The season is autumn. The auditorium and stage lights are up full before the audience enters and remain so during the performance to enable actors wearing masks to note their positions on stage through the pin-point eyeholes of the masks. The stage is a raised platform about twenty feet square, with square pillars at the four corners. The wooden surface of the stage has been rubbed smooth and is completely empty of scenery. The rear of the stage consists of a large wooden panel on which a beautiful twisted pine tree is painted. A passageway leads from the up right corner of the stage to the "mirror room." or dressing room, fifteen feet away. There is a low railing along the passageway, and three pine saplings are spaced along its length to mark the position of actors during their entrances or exits or during any action that may take them onto the passageway. A silk curtain of green, white, and red vertical stripes covers the door leading to the mirror room; it is raised and lowered by two bamboo poles attached to the bottom corners. Stage left there is a low door, the "hurry door," used for entrances and exits of the CHORUS and STAGE ASSISTANTS.

The play begins with two STAGE ASSISTANTS bringing on the first of the set props. The passageway curtain is lifted and a platform is brought down the passageway and placed lengthwise on the main stage left of center. The STAGE ASSISTANTS exit and return carrying two set props symbolic of the rock cave within which the DRAGON GODS are trapped. They are basket-woven and shaped in semicircles, covered with blue silk, and tied together lightly with white tapes. The ASSISTANTS lift the rock pieces carefully onto the platform as actors playing the DRAGON GODS step onto the platform from behind, unseen. The silk is adjusted to fully cover the hidden characters. The STAGE ASSISTANTS, dressed unobtrusively in their black divided trousers over black kimonos, exit silently through the small door left. The hermit's hut has been waiting backstage to be set with IKKAKU SENNIN already inside. A curtain has been hung on the hut and tied in back at the top and bottom. As the curtain is three inches longer than the hut, IKKAKU SENNIN's feet cannot be seen. The two ASSISTANTS lift the hut on either side and enter. The hut is placed upstage center, and the front is lifted slightly to tuck the front end of the curtain neatly under the hut. ASSISTANTS move upstage right, behind the hut, and kneel. The action of the play begins.

After a moment the music of a flute can be heard. On the first note of the music the passageway curtain lifts slowly, LADY SENDA enters on the passageway, followed by two ATTENDANTS holding a frame representing a canopy and by SHINDA, a court official. She wears a silk kimono of orange, green, and gold, tied with a sash of gold and orange, and over it a wide, split skirt of orange brocade. She wears a smooth black wig and the white mask of a beautiful, sweetly serene young woman. The mask is attached with a headband of gold and orange material decorated with an intricate bow at the back. She wears a delicate crown and carries a gold and orange folding dance-fan. Her ATTENDANTS wear wide, split trousers of white over green and brown kimonos. They do not carry fans nor do they wear masks. SHINDA is dressed similarly but with a green and gold outer jacket tied at the waist with a black and white sash. He wears no mask but carries a blue and white folding fan decorated with a fish design. All move slowly down the passageway, gliding their feet in the stylized walk of Noh. The procession lasts .a full two minutes. LADY

SENDA stops center stage, SHINDA, upstage right. The music ends. In a rich baritone voice SHINDA almost chants his speech, his face immobile, explaining to the audience who they are and what they hope to achieve.

SHINDA The prince I serve is a great prince,
he is the emperor of Barana,
with many lands along the Ganges.

Now in the country of this prince
there lives a hermit
and he is a wizard,
he was born from the womb of a deer
and he has one single long horn,
a horn that sprouts out of his forehead;
and therefore we have named this wizard
Ikkaku Sennin, holy hermit unicorn.
Once Ikkaku Sennin and the great dragon gods
had an affair of honor, and the wizard won;
he used his magic
to undo the dragon gods,
he drove them into a cave
and made them stay inside.
Away in that cave,
for many years they could not cause rain to fall.
Since then, my prince has come to grieve,
he sees that his whole countryside is dry,
and so now he knows
he has to free those dragon gods.

(SHINDA *pivots left slightly to face* LADY SENDA.)
Listen, this is the prince's plan,
this is the beautiful young girl
who is going to go up into the mountains,
there where the wizard lives,
the holy hermit unicorn,
and he may make a mistake
and think she's lost her way.
Then he may fall in love,
he may say this young girl is so beautiful,
he may lose his heart and art
and all the magic that he used to use.
It may work out that way,
that's what the prince is hoping for,
and so we're going to carry her up
to the unicorn.

ATTENDANTS (*still standing and holding the canopy frame over* LADY SENDA, *they sing the following travel song*)
Mountains and mountains and mountains,
mists that cover over all the weary travelers,
cold winds that blow through the open woods,
as we keep going,
no sleep on the mountainside,
no sweet dreams for us.

SHINDA (*pivots front and speaks*)
Day after day,
we've hurried on our way,

traveling on this old road
that no one knows about;
now we are lost, we are all worn out.
Look, there are many rocks,
all lying on the ground
and piled up in a mound,
I wonder why?
—how sweet the breezes
as they blow over the rock pile;
I can tell the smell of pine.
Perhaps this is where the wizard lives,
the holy hermit unicorn,
perhaps this is the place.
We could keep quiet
and get close to it,
slowly, slowly,
get close so we can see
if the wizard is hiding inside.

(During his speech the STAGE ASSISTANTS cross to the back of the hut unobtrusively and untie the curtain. They hold the curtain and wait for the proper moment to lower it. SHINDA turns again to LADY SENDA and asks her permission to stay.)

Gracious lady,
if your patience will permit it,
we would like to stay right here.

LADY SENDA shows no sign that she agrees. She moves slowly to the downstage corner of the dragon cave and sits. SHINDA moves to the upstage corner and sits. The ATTENDANTS lower the canopy frame, place it against the back wall of the stage, and kneel facing each other. The STAGE ASSISTANTS lower the hut's curtain slowly to reveal IKKAKU SENNIN sitting with right knee up and holding a fan in his right hand, which rests on his knee. He is an extraordinary sight as seen through the bamboo poles of the hut. His ornate brown-and-blue kimono is covered by a light overgarment of sheer black material. A leaf-shaped apron is tied at his waist. A huge black wig stands out around his face in great wisps. A single horn, fixed into the wig, protrudes from his forehead. He wears a mask with a face very old and gnarled but at the same time tender. His nonfolding Chinese fan is blue, gold, and orange. He is not frightening; rather, he gives the impression of wisdom. The ASSISTANT right passes the curtain of the hut to the ASSISTANT left, who exits with it through the small door left. The remaining ASSISTANT unobtrusively nudges IKKAKU SENNIN through the cagelike bars of the hut to cue him. In a deep, rumbling voice, which seems to come almost from the ground, IIKKAKU SENNIN tells SHINDA they should leave him to his solitary life.

IKKAKU SENNIN

I scoop water from deep streams
with my magic gourd,
I call forth all my art,
I lift up clouds that have folded over forests

and I make them boil swiftly,
then I play music.
But I play alone.
The mountains rise up high above river banks.
Green leaves suddenly become the color of blood.
I play music and I play alone in autumn.

On the last two lines of IKKAKU SENNIN's speech LADY SENDA and SHINDA rise from their position, kneeling on one knee, pivot slowly toward the hut, and move forward one step.

SHINDA
Listen to me,
listen, this is a traveler;
we have lost our way
and we want to speak to you.

IKKAKU SENNIN
Who's there?—
I thought I would be free in these mountains,
I thought I would be able to escape
from the human race,
and now someone comes—
O please leave, please leave
as fast as you can.

SHINDA *(pleads to be allowed to stay)*
No, listen to me, listen,
we are travelers
and we are lost,
and the sun is setting,
and the road is dark,
so won't you let us spend the night
right here?

IKKAKU SENNIN
No, no, I told you to go,
this is no place for you to stay,
so go;
I say you should go far from here.

SHINDA *(adamant)*
You say this is no place for us to stay,
and is that because
the holy hermit unicorn lives here?
Come out, I say, so we can see your face!

IKKAKU SENNIN *(as yet motionless)*
I am getting up,
I am coming out of here,
I am going to show myself
to all these travelers!

Slow music of flute and drums. As the CHORUS begins to sing with an almost sinister feeling, IKKAKU SENNIN slowly rises and opens the bamboo gate to the hut. He steps out, and his robe is adjusted as he does so.

CHORUS *(offstage)*
He takes the great grass gate

and swings it to one side,
(MUSICIANS *inject cries of "Iya," and we hear drums whack.)*
he takes the great grass gate
and swings it to one side,
now he is aroused—
look, look at his face!
Black hair snarled on his proud brow,
a single long horn
sprouting out of his forehead.
See how he stands here—
if he disappeared
we would still see him stand here,
strange and wonderful!

IKKAKU SENNIN has pivoted to face LADY SENDA and SHINDA, and on the last line of the CHORUS all three slowly sink to the floor. The music ends.

SHINDA Are you the hermit
we have heard about,
which they call
the holy hermit unicorn?
IKKAKU SENNIN
I am ashamed to say it
but I am he,
Ikkaku Sennin.
SHINDA Here is some sake which we brought along with us,
to cheer us up on our long journey.
My lady kindly offers it to you,
so do take a cup of this fine wine!
IKKAKU SENNIN
We hermits prefer
to eat the needles of pine trees,
the clothes we wear
are made of moss,
and we do not drink anything
but dew.
Year after year,
we do not age,
we do not change,
we do not even die.
And that is why I say
I do not want your sake.
SHINDA *(appealing to the* HERMITS *innate courtesy)*
You say you do not want our sake,
(He pivots on his knee to indicate LADY SENDA.)
but then would you take just a little
if my lady asks it as a special favor?

LADY SENDA opens her fan, holds it horizontally in front of her to represent the sake, rises, and takes a few steps toward IKKAKU SENNIN. In a clear, light voice she speaks her only line in the play.

LADY SENDA The young girl rises,
rises to pour out some wine;

she urges the hermit
to try some sake.

IKKAKU SENNIN *(unable to resist her beauty and charm)*
When travelers ask a favor,
how can anyone refuse?
—impossible,
only the devil would say no.

Music begins. As the CHORUS sings its song of wine to the haunting melody of the flute, LADY SENDA crosses to IKKAKU SENNIN. She kneels beside him, pantomimes—with her fan—pouring him some wine, then opens the fan and sweeps it up and out to the side in a wide, graceful arc.

CHORUS
A cup of wine is like the moon
in the night sky,
a cup of wine is like the moon
in the night sky.
The hermit reaches out
and takes the cup of wine,
just as a hermit once
plucked a chrysanthemum,
the dew dropped down to the ground.
O that was so long ago,
so long ago,
but I will love you for that long.

As there are no realistic movements in Noh, only a slight nod of the HERMIT's head indicates he has drunk the wine after raising his body from the low stool on which he has been resting and which the STAGE ASSISTANT now quickly removes. A moment later the HERMIT drops his left knee to the floor abruptly, and we realize he is now intoxicated.

IKKAKU SENNIN *(singing)*
O blessed ecstasy,
the cup of wine!

CHORUS *(continues the song of praise)*
O blessed ecstasy,
the cup of wine!
—it is like the moon
that circles in the night sky.
Red leaves on the autumn hills,
see the silk sleeves.
Two leaves move,
like two sleeves
that are dancing together,
dancing in a great court dance,
blessed ecstasy.

(Music begins and accompanies LADY SENDA's danced seduction of the HERMIT. LADY SENDA slowly rises from her kneeling position and crosses down center. There she bows ceremoniously, bringing both arms overhead. The music of the flute begins as she slides her feet smoothly on the mirrorlike floor. Her arms flow in beautiful movements, manipulating her fan. She dances alone until the CHORUS again is heard, accompanied by the dynamic sounds of the big drum. The HERMIT watches her seductive dance, and when she begins a second variation of steps, he rises to join her, always slightly behind in tempo. They dance together, sometimes in unison, sometimes in opposition.)

Dance to the music of flutes,
dance to the flute music.
Dance to the music of flutes,
dance to the flute music.
Pass the cup around, around,
pass the cup around, around.

(At the critical encounter of the dance the WIZARD places his left hand across the breast of LADY SENDA; she repulses him by stiffly lifting her right arm. The WIZARD staggers backward, then forward again; then he goes into a spin, takes two turns, and sinks to his knees. He raises his right arm so that the kimono sleeve covers his face, symbolizing that overcome by love and sake, he has fallen into a stupor.)

The hermit has fallen in love,
he has fallen in love.
See, his feet have grown weak,
and see how the hermit
is beginning to falter and fall,
he keeps turning in circles,
now he wraps his sleeve around him
and he sleeps.
The beautiful young girl is pleased;
she tells everyone to come away
and they all go down the mountain,
they go down the rough mountain road
until they are already at the court
of the prince.

(Quickly LADY SENDA closes her fan and turns upstage to SHINDA. The ATTENDANTS, having risen when the WIZARD began to falter, cross down to her and raise the canopy frame over her head. They all turn and move onto the passageway. There they pause momentarily, then cross swiftly off as the passageway curtain is lifted for their exit. The music ends. Suddenly there is a loud "thwack" of the drum, and the WIZARD awakens. The STAGE ASSISTANTS, who moved behind the rock cave when the procession went off, quickly untie the tapes that hold the two pieces of rock together and stand ready to push them apart.)

Rumble rumble rumble,
where is it coming from?
Rumbles thunder from deep
inside the cave,
rumbles cause earthquakes
and make all creation shake.

Ikkaku Sennin, kneeling, turns toward the cave and reproaches himself for his weakness.

Why have I been sleeping,
sleeping all this while?
—it was the wine,
it was the beautiful young girl,
it was the need for some sleep.
Rumble rumble rumble,
something's wrong,
what is it?

Dragon Gods *(unseen within the cave)*

Holy hermit unicorn Ikkaku Sennin,
you have let yourself get lost in lust,
and you confused your mind with wine.
No wonder now you do not know you are undone,
no wonder now you have no power.
Now the sky strikes you down,
Ikkaku, Sen-ni-in-n-n!

They vigorously announce that the Wizard, having succumbed to human temptation, has lost his power over them. Ending their chant with his name, they almost sing in elongated syllables. Music for their dance begins.

Ikkaku Sennin rises, advancing to the center of the stage, a sight cue for the Stage Assistants to push apart the two pieces of the rock cave in what seems to be an explosion. Ikkaku Sennin retreats up right to the edge of the passageway as the rock falls to the floor and is swept up and carried off through the small door left by the two Stage Assistants. Two Dragon Gods jump off the platform and move upstage center. They are an impressive sight with their flowing red wings topped with dragon headpieces. They wear dragon masks and carry wands. Jackets of blue and gold and wide, split trousers of orange and gold are worn over their kimonos—one of green, orange, and white and the other of orange, blue, and white. They begin an exciting and militant dance of strong, sweeping movements. Symbolizing heaven and earth, they raise their wings majestically, then turn, swoop down on one knee, and point their wands to the floor. They circle the stage in unison, always retaining three feet of space between them. In a final diagonal cross they move from up right to the platform and leap onto it, then turn to face the Wizard. Ikkaku Sennin speaks the final words of the play, intoning his self-doubt, stamping once for emphasis.

Ikkaku Sennin

Now, holy hermit unicorn,
I do not know what to do.

The Hermit accepts the challenge of the Dragon Gods. The music becomes faster. Ikkaku Sennin pivots by the passageway, receives a short wooden sword from a Stage Assistant at the same time that he passes the Assistant his fan, and without breaking the flow of his movement, moves toward center stage. The Dragon

GODS leap from the platform to the stage; they cross the HERMIT'S sword with their wands. IIKKAKU SENNIN fights courageously, but he cannot defeat them. To rapid beating of the drum, in a "big rhythm," he backs falteringly upstage. He drops to one knee and lets the sword fall from his hand. In an instant a STAGE ASSISTANT moves in to pick it up and carry it off left. The WIZARD crosses to the passageway, defeated. On the passageway, and considered to be invisible, he moves swiftly off as the curtain is lifted for his exit.

Triumphant, the DRAGON GODS dance to bring the rain that will end the drought. They swoop about the stage and finally cross to the passageway as if flying through the skies. They stop at the third small pine tree. They stamp, signifying the end of the dance. Then they jump, turning in the air, as if leaping into the sea and returning to their dragon home. They raise their left arm and flip the sleeve up and over to hide their face, in a movement which symbolizes their invisibility. The music ends with a flourish of the flute and the final cries of the MUSICIANS, "I-ya-o-o, i-ya-o-o!" The DRAGON GODS turn., and as the passageway curtain is raised for them, exit in silence.

The props are now removed in view of the audience and with no music. The STAGE ASSISSTANT who had exited with the HERMIT'S sword re-enters, and together the two ASSISTANTS lift the hut and carry it off down the passageway. They re-enter and remove the platform the same way. The play is finished. There are no curtain calls.

Japanese Poetry

For many readers, Japanese poetry means a school assignment to write haiku. That exercise, if successful, may have created an appreciation for the great variety possible within a prescribed form. While haiku came relatively late in the Japanese tradition, the use of strict forms is constant. Roughly ninety per cent of the over 4,500 works in the *Man'yo-shu* are *tanka*, poems of five lines and 31 syllables. This form proved capable of conveying almost all of the poetic expression of the seventh and eighth centuries, the first great age of Japanese civilization.

The *Man'yo-shu,* title of the earliest surviving collection of Japanese poetry, is variously translated as *Collection of 10,000 Leaves, Collection for Myriad Ages,* or *Collection for 10,000 Generations.* Collected on twenty scrolls, the poems are arranged chronologically as well as by subject, season, author, and source. Otomo no Yakamochi, the compiler of the collection, is also one of the most heavily represented of the 530 authors whose works are gathered in the *Man'yo-shu*. His father, Otomo no Tabito (surnames appear first, given names last) wrote often in praise of sake during his rule as governor-general of Kyushu. Sake may have offered solace, some argue, to a man unhappily serving far from the capital, his home, and experiencing the death of his wife during that period of service.

Tabito's half-sister, the Lady of Sakanoye, is here represented with a love poem; love is the most common subject matter of the *Man'yo-shu*. Her lines on the separated lovers and the strength of her heart can be read more clearly in the context of sex roles and relationships of the time. Matriarchal tradition was still strong, a legacy of the Polynesian peoples who had settled centuries earlier. Not only had Japan seen eight periods of Empress rule from 593–769, but women owned and inherited property, and suitors had to obtain maternal consent before marriage. Consent was often quite slow in coming, and the painful waiting of young lovers finds repeated poetic expression. Much later, as Buddhist and Confucian influences begin to dominate Japan, and as the warrior class begins to rule, women begin to be seen as inferiors whose lives must be controlled by men. At least in the eighth century, however, Japanese women exercised some power and expressed passion and power freely in poetry.

While the court society, including families such as the Otomo, had the greatest leisure and occasion for composing and sharing poetry, the *Man'yo-shu* represents the work of nameless commoners. Subjects range from celebration of divine sovereigns to a comic poem on excrement. The collection's earliest poem may date to the fifth century though the great majority of the work dates from 629–759. Most are from an oral tradition; only some of the later poems may have been written prior to their appearance in Yakamochi's compilation. The later collection, the *Kokinshu,* from which two poems are presented here, brought together some 1,100 poems of 130 authors. It was an imperially commissioned work and lacks the breadth of subject and source found in the *Man'yo-shu.*

Poetry often helps to shape a language, but the *Man'yo-shu* has the distinction of transforming Japanese from a spoken language only to a written one. Up to this time, Chinese was considered the language of "serious" poetry and lofty ideas; however, the desire to record and preserve national poetic tradition led to the development of a script called Man'yo-gana, combining Chinese characters used for the appropriate sounds of Japanese words along with some Chinese symbols used for their more familiar meanings. This written form of Japanese became obscure as early as the twelfth century. Modern English translations, therefore, vary widely and can only approximate in spirit the originals.

Selected Bibliography

Kato, Shuichi. *A History of Japanese Literature: The First Thousand Years*. Trans. David Chibbett. Tokyo: Kodansha International, 1979.

N ihon bungaku, Hisamatsu Sen' ichi., ed. *Japanese Literature: A Historical Outline*. Trans. Edward Putzar. Tucson: U of Arizona P, 1973.

Prusek, Jaroslav, ed. *Dictionary of Oriental Literatures*. Vol. 1: East Asia. New York: Basic, 1974.

Traditional Japanese Poetry: An Anthology. Trans. Steven D. Carter. Stanford: Stanford UP, 1991.

Written on Water: Five Hundred Poems from the Man'yo-shu. Trans. Takashi Kojima. Rutland, VT: Tuttle, 1995.

The Lady of Sakanoye [8th Century]

It is other people who have separated
You and me.
Come, my lord!
Do not dream of listening
To the between-words of people!
My heart, thinking
"How beautiful [he is]"
Is like a swift river
[Which] though one dams it and dams it,
Will still break through.

Ōtomo No Tabito [665–731]

To sit silent
And look wise
Is not to be compared with
Drinking saké
And making a riotous shouting.

The Priest Hakutsū [c. 704]

O pine-tree standing
At the [side of] the stone house,
When I look at you,
It is like seeing face to face
The men of old time.

Ki No Akimine [9th Century]

The beloved person must I think
Have entered
The summer mountain:
For the cuckoo is singing
With a louder note.

The Lady Eguchi [c. 890]

If only Life-and-Death
Were a thing.
Subject to our wills,
What would be the bitterness of parting?

Haiku: Background

Haiku are easy to spot for many students. They are the short poems, the descriptive ones. In fact, haiku's simple form is so distinctive that on first reading these poems may seem elementary or quaint to Westerners. What might be hard to understand is the vital role hiaku play in Japanese culture. Today there are over twenty million serious haiku poets in Japan, a sixth of the population; and every major newspaper publishes haiku columns daily, some on the front page. Poetry has long been prominent in daily Japanese life. Dating back to the ninth century, members of the court were expected to be skillful poets; and during the twelfth and thirteenth centuries men of all positions in society avidly participated in poetry contests. But when haiku became popular in the seventeenth century, it was seen as revolutionary—able to change how everyday experience was seen by everyone.

Sharing the Japanese appreciation for haiku requires an attuned sensitivity to daily life. People endure similar routines and gloss over the same mundane observations. Haiku draw from this shared experience to elevate the reader to a universal consciousness. Within the ordinary landscape of human activity are unique details that lure the poet into noticing life's qualities. Pursuing this single focus, the poet loses self-awareness, becoming submerged in the subject. The description that emerges is said to go into the heart of created things and become one with nature. This isolated emotion becomes both a personal discovery as well as a profound connector. Given this purpose, it may seem that haiku are limited to human responses to nature. However, haiku poets also contemplate the nature of human relations, such as love, which offers material for descriptions of common experience.

The power of these slight, unassuming poems is generated by their simplicity. The small details depicted in haiku are as precise as brush strokes in a painting. But the larger picture is never completed. The limited part revealed by the poet provides enough for readers to complete the scene. Discovery of the missing details becomes the most valuable part of the experience. Readers are led to create a larger moment that joins them with an experience that all can share.

Haiku poets use specific techniques to draw readers into the poet's inspirations. One might notice that haiku lines are spare and fragmentary, demanding that readers complete the thought to make the sentence clear. Also, haiku rely heavily on associative meanings. So few words comprise a haiku that ordinary words must be used metaphorically to ground readers in an experience that is both real and imaginary. Such precise use of plain language turns the words into the experience. Unfortunately, the intended double meanings are often difficult to translate into English. Form also contributes to the effect achieved by haiku. Since haiku reflect single moments, each poem is limited to the average number of syllables uttered in one breath—seventeen. The syllables also are arranged to suggest a single, unified experience. Breaking up the poem into three lines of five, seven, and five syllables produces a harmonious unit.

It is interesting to note that the aim of haiku corresponds neatly to the tenets of Buddhism. The poems are modest and unadorned, leading readers away from their encumbered lives into a blissful union with all of creation. One might also recognize a connection to Confucianism. Like the aphorisms in *Analects*, haiku direct one inward toward a discovery of one's potential. From either perspective, the poems rely on external descriptions to evoke an internal universe. The influence of such foreign Eastern beliefs may be precisely the barrier that keeps Westerners from fully enjoying this art form. On the other hand, haiku present possibly the most tangible access to Eastern culture. The lyric quality of haiku can translate grand Eastern philosophies into comprehensible human experience.

Preparing to read traditional haiku, one should know which themes the poets believed to be universal: beauty and sadness. These are not separate emotions. They are linked by the belief that perishability is a part of beauty. These poets aimed to capture the grief of lost beauty and love, while also being keenly aware that these feelings are made pleasurable because of their fragility.

Finally, readers should approach these poems with a reflective mood and allow for several readings. They should reread to fill in what may merely be implied. Readers can feel reassured that the discipline needed to engage in the poet's experience makes perusing haiku an art form.

Selected Bibliography

Keene, Donald. *Landscapes and Portraits: Appreciations of Japanese Culture.* Palo Alto: Kodansha International, 1971.

Kenning, Douglas. *The Romanticism of 17th Century Japanese Poetry*. Lesiston: Edwin Mellen, 1998.

Makoto, Ooka. *The Poetry and Poetics of Ancient Japan.* Honolulu: Katydid, 1997.

Matsuo Basho [1644–1694]

Many, many things
  they bring to mind—
    cherry-blossoms.

On a withered branch
  A crow has settled—
    autumn nightfall.

Around existence twine
  (Oh, bridge that hangs across the gorge!)
    ropes of twisted vine.

Cool it is, and still:
  just the tip of a crescent moon
  over Black-wing Hill.

The summer grasses grow.
  Of mighty warriors' splendid dreams
    the afterglow.

Old pond:
  frog-jump-in
    water-sound.

How rough a sea—
  and, stretching over Sado Isle,
    the Galaxy—

A village where they ring
  no bells!—Oh, what do they do
    at dusk in spring?

Some of them with staves,
  and white-haired—a whole family
    visiting the graves!

Fall of night
  over the sea—the wild-duck voices
    shadowy and white.

No rice?—In that hour
  we put into the gourd
    a maiden flower.

A lightning-gleam:
  into darkness travels
    a night-heron's scream.

Chinese Poetry

From 800 BC to AD 1200, Chinese poetry is essentially written in the "Shih" form—a song form or lyric in nature form of personal expression. Chinese poetry is a celebration of the beauties of nature, friendship, a medium of expressing grief, advancing courtship, or venting political opinions. Chinese poetry is a leveler—it is classless; it accommodates all levels of society. Poetry appeals to all levels of Chinese society, and anyone can engage in this art of expression. Chinese poetry is remarkable for its antiquity and continuity; it has a long and unbroken history.

It seems that what accounts for the enduring age of Chinese poetry is its accessibility. It is everybody's genre and deals with human issues. It is not the mouthpiece of any political faction or the drum beat of any warring armies. Furthermore, Chinese poetry is easy to read and comprehend because it concentrates largely on human concerns—issues that are of common interest to human beings everywhere in whatever time. These very qualities are responsible for making Chinese poetry of more than two thousand years still fresh and relevant today.

Another enduring quality of Chinese poetry is its personal and occasional nature. For the Chinese, poetry belongs to all. One does not have to belong to a particular group in society or have special talent or divine inspiration to write poetry. For scholars and government officials, poetry was a necessary part of daily life. Ordinary poems were written to entertain visitors at banquets and at picnics. Poems were also exchanged among friends at partings. A Chinese individual can write poems for any purposes [of which Yuan-Chen's poem "the Pitcher," which he uses as a symbol of lost love is a prime example]. Chinese occasional poetry, poems which commemorate special occasions, are more like their counterparts in the West. Unlike in the West, where a poem could have a life of its own apart from the poet's, more of the Chinese poems of this particular genre are read as a form of autobiography. For this reason, Chinese occasional poetry is purely personal in tone. It is this personal tone that makes Chinese poetry uniquely different in content among Ancient World poetry. Chinese poetry has a broad scope because its themes are not limited to religious issues and holy sentiments like the Vedas and the Psalms.

Traditional Chinese poetry celebrates the beauties of nature ["Clearing at Dawn"], especially as captured in a remote mountain side. This type of poetry is rich in symbolism whose suggestive meanings are derived from Chinese traditional outlook. For example, pines and cranes stand for long life; orchids signify an elderly gentleman of moral character. Plum blossoms, because of their early blooming , represent fortitude and symbolize integrity. As the wilderness is opened up for human habitation and farming and as cities emerge with their corrupting wealth and power, the mountains and their unspoiled landscape become sanctuaries of safety, peace, and freedom from turmoil. On the mountains one can practice meditation or contemplate the teaching of Tao or Buddha. This association of the city with its corrupting influences and the relaxing mountain with its calming atmosphere is the theme of Po Chu-I's poem.

Three distinguished Chinese poets, who lived and wrote during the eight and ninth centuries, are of special interest. Li Po (AD 701–762) and Tu Fu are two pre-modern poets who made Chinese poetry in the Shih form a powerful medium of expression. Unlike Tu Fu whose poetry was not acknowledged during his lifetime, Li Po enjoyed instant recognition. Li Po's poetry is appreciated by his countrymen, because he did not disturb the ground rules of poetry followed by his predecessors. About 1,000 poems are said to have been written by him. Of this number, one sixth are based on themes from old folk songs and are said to be written in "Yeh'fu" style. Li Po entitled the rest of his poems "Ku-feng," which means that the poems were written according to the old order. Although Li Po's poetry focuses on traditional themes, he treats them with remarkable grace and eloquence. Li Po is also given to playfulness, fantasy, and exaggeration in his tone. This makes his poetry interesting to read. Another quality of Li Po's poetry is his love of the carefree life of the recluse. The special love of nature and love of wine are clearly revealed in his poems.

In his twelve-line poem entitled, "Drinking Alone by Moonlight" Number II, written in blank verse, Li Po uses the first two lines to introduce imageries of wasted beauty. The speaker is despondent. In this situation he makes specific and concrete observations about place, season, and human condition which he attributes to God in the first six lines. From the speaker's reference to the Creator, he seems to be a believer in God. In the last six lines, the speaker sees an intake of wine as a form of induced forgetfulness. In this state of forgetfulness, he is happy and momentarily relieved of his depression and loneliness. The speaker does not reveal the cause of his loneliness. His depression, as he hints in the second line of the poem, is from the devastating waste of winter. Li Po's next poem, "Clearing at Dawn," is quite a contrast in tone with "Drinking Alone by Midnight." The "dawn" in the title says it all; it is morning , and the light is daylight. "Clearing at Dawn" is a celebration of spring with its life-invigorating colors. All living things—animals, birds, fish, as well as plants, shrubs, and flowers—join in this celebration. Every living thing is doing something lively and lovely in the poem, hence the use of personifications. In summary, the poem is a hymn of unrestrained enthusiasm and joy over the coming of spring.

Another poet is Po Chu-I (AD 772–846) who was one of the highly productive poets of the T'ang school. To make sure that his poetry was preserved for posterity, he personally compiled and arranged his works in one edition of seventy-five chapters. This volume contains about 2,800 poems and different genres. Although Po Chu-I worked as a government official throughout his life, his bold criticisms of the policies of government frequently brought him into disfavor. His narrative poems, "Songs of Everlasting Regret" and "Song of the Lute" and his simple style may be the reasons for his popularity. Po Chu-I had the habit of exchanging poems with his life-time friend Yuan Chen. He is also known for his dignified portrayal of old age and his reverential treatment of Buddhist themes.

"In Early Summer Lodging in a Temple to Enjoy the Moonlight" is a twenty-four line poem where the speaker, along with his two jobless companions, abandon the distractions of a summer day to meditate and find happiness in the teaching of Tao. They sit under the influence of the moon, presumably in meditation. Forgetting the boredom of unemployment by self meditation and prayer, the speaker and his jobless companions find consolation and inspiration in spiritual life. In the last two lines of the poem, the rhetorical question posed by the speaker ridicules Ch'ang-an, the worldly city with its preoccupation with profit, business success, and personal fame.

"Watching the Reapers" calls attention to the peak month of the farmers' labor. The speaker, who might be a government official, is a sympathetic observer of the toiling contributions of farmers. The poet intimates the rigid division of labor in ancient China, where workers are grouped according to gender. In the poem young males just carry food and wine to the females, working under the severe heat of the sun. Lines thirteen to sixteen present a sympathetic imagery of a mother with her child at her bosom, gleaning after the reapers. Here, the poet criticizes the society that has made this spectacle a common sight. The speaker has a moral conscience. He feels ashamed of living well and being paid abundantly at the expense of the working class and the poor. This is evident in the last six lines of the poem. He wonders why he should receive such preferential treatment. The speaker's functional use of the "d" sound in the last three lines emphasizes the apparent injustice to the poor in his society.

In "At the End of Spring" the persona, the voice speaking in the poem, uses the cyclical change of seasons as a backdrop of experience and contemplation over the passage of time. The processes of growing, aging, and reproducing provoke a rhetorical question about the benefit of religion. When time passes, what can religion teach the speaker? Religion teaches the speaker to accept the passage of time. It teaches him not to worry about growing old because, after all, the world is a dream. Though the speaker accepts the loss of time with patient resignation, he finds it hard to forget the memory of his friend, Yuan Chen. The forced separation is too much for him.

Po Chu-I's concern with old age again shines through in "the Chrysanthemums in the Eastern Garden," a poem of twenty-four lines. In the first twelve lines, the speaker is confronted with the imageries of waning light and withering growth, signifying old age. The speaker in the first five lines is sad because he is growing old and lonely. As winter approaches, old age is evident in the imageries he uses. As a lover of wine, the speaker fears that in old age, wine can no longer be a source of joy to him. This contrasts with his experience in his youth when the sight of wine gave him joy. However, in the last four lines, the late blooming flowers provide a lesson to the speaker to be cheerful while he is still alive. The speaker's fear that he would lose the capacity for drinking wine as he grows older reflects the importance of wine to a Chinese poet.

Of the three poets whose works are included, only Yuan Chen (AD 779–831) is an enigma as far as facts of his life are concerned. Po Chu-I's friendly association with him allows readers to infer about him. Po Chu-I's poem "At the End of Spring" is dedicated to Yuan Chen. Yuan Chen had been in exile in Chiang-ling before this poem was written in AD 810. This banishment of his friend is the cause of Po Chu-I's sorrow in this poem. The reasons for Yuan Chen's exile are not expressed, but as the two poets were good friends, readers may think that they have identical social views of their contemporary society. Po Chu-I was banished in 811 to Hsun-Yang for criticizing the policies of the government of which he was an official. It is not farfetched, therefore, to think that Yuan Chen's exile was the same circumstance as his friend's.

Yuan Chen's "the Pitcher," a thirty-line poem, recalls a nightmare. This nightmare is disturbingly in progress in the first fifteen lines of the poem. In the dream the speaker finds himself on a mountain wanting very much to have a drink of water. He has to scout around for water and finds a well in which there is a pitcher lying down below. He has no rope to pull the pitcher to the surface and have a drink. So he goes from village to village looking for men to help him raise the pitcher but to no avail. There are no men around; only their menacing dogs remain to harass the speaker. In desperation he returns to the well, crying profusely in his sleep, thereby waking up himself. The last fifteen lines present the speaker's attempt to make sense of his dream. He hears the midnight bell ring and speculates that the plain in his dream is the grave yard at Ch'ang-en where his love is buried. The pitcher at the bottom of the well represents his dead love. "The Pitcher" is full of imageries of lost love and helplessness. The speaker's helpless effort to raise the sunken pitcher symbolizes man's vain effort to overcome this type of loss. The speaker is superstitious. He talks about dead men leaving their graves and walking the earth at night. He also makes reference to the midnight bell. In medieval times the dead were said to wander the world, but they did not stay beyond their graves past the midnight.

A study of the background of Chinese poetry and three of its poets provides basic knowledge of Chinese poetic traditions that are universal and timeless. The seven poems included in this text may inspire comparisons with poetry from other cultures and times.

Selected Bibliography

Watson, Burton, trans. and ed. *The Columbia Book of Chinese Poetry: From Early Times to the Thirteenth Century*. New York: Columbia UP, 1984.

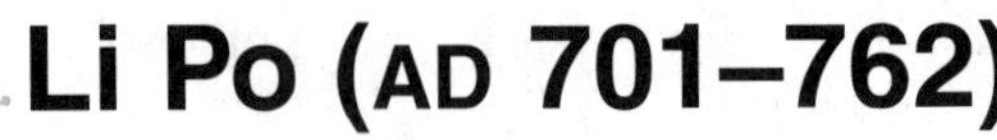

Li Po (AD 701–762)

Drinking Alone by Moonlight

. . . In the third month the town of Hsien-yang
Is thick-spread with a carpet of fallen flowers.
Who in Spring can bear to grieve alone?
Who, sober, look on sights like these?
Riches and Poverty, long or short life,
By the Maker of Things are portioned and disposed;
But a cup of wine levels life and death
And a thousand things obstinately hard to prove.
When I am drunk, I lose Heaven and Earth.
Motionless—I cleave to my lonely bed.
At last I forget that I exist at all,
And at *that* moment my joy is great indeed.

Clearing at Dawn

The fields are chill; the sparse rain has stopped;
The colours of Spring teem on every side.
With leaping fish the blue pond is full;
With singing thrushes the green boughs droop.
The flowers of the field have dabbled their powdered cheeks;
The mountain grasses are bent level at the waist.
By the bamboo stream the last fragment of cloud
Blown by the wind slowly scatters away.

Po Chu-I (AD 742–846)

In Early Summer Lodging in a Temple to Enjoy the Moonlight

[AD 805]

In early summer, with two or three more
That were seeking fame in the city of Ch'ang-an,
Whose low employ gave them less business
Than ever they had since first they left their homes,—
With these I wandered deep into the shrine of Tao,
For the joy we sought was promised in this place.
When we reached the gate, we sent our-coaches back;
We entered the yard with only cap and stick.
Still and clear, the first weeks of May,
When trees are green and bushes soft and wet;
When the wind has stolen the shadows of new leaves
And birds linger on the last boughs that bloom.
Towards evening when the sky grew clearer yet
And the South-east was still clothed in red,
To the western cloister we carried our jar of wine;
While we waited for the moon, our cups moved slow.
Soon, how soon her golden ghost was born,
Swiftly, as though she had waited for us to come.
The beam; of her light shone in every place,
Oh towers and halls dancing to and fro.
Till day broke we sat in her clear light
Laughing and singing, and yet never grew tired.
In Ch'ang-an, the place of profit and fame,
Such moods as this, how many men know?

At the End of Spring

To Yüan Chen. [AD 810]

The flower of the pear-tree gathers and turns to fruit;
The swallows' eggs have hatched into young birds.
When the Seasons' changes thus confront the mind
What comfort can the Doctrine of Tao give?
It will teach me to watch the days and months fly
Without grieving that Youth slips away;
If the Fleeting World is but a long dream,
It does not matter whether one is young or old.
But ever since the day that my friend left my side
And has lived an exile in the City of Chiang-ling,
There is one wish I cannot quite destroy:
That from time to time we may chance to meet again.

The Chrysanthemums in the Eastern Garden

[AD 812]

The days of my youth left me long ago;
And now in their turn dwindle my years of prime.
With what thoughts of sadness and loneliness
I walk again in this cold, deserted place!
In the midst of the garden long I stand alone;
The sunshine, faint; the wind and dew chill.
The autumn lettuce is tangled and turned to seed;
The fair trees are blighted and withered away.
All that is left are a few chrysanthemum-flowers
That have newly opened beneath the wattled fence.
I had brought wine and meant to fill my cup,
When the night of these made me stay my hand.

I remember, when I was young,
How easily my mood changed from sad to gay.
If I saw wine, no matter at what season,
Before I drank it, my heart was already glad.
But now that age comes,
A moment of joy is harder and harder to get.
And always I fear that when I am quite old
The strongest liquor will leave me comfortless.
Therefore I ask you, late chrysanthemum-flower
At this sad season why do you bloom alone?
Though well I know that it was not for my sake,
Taught by you, for a while I will open my face.

Yuan Chen (AD 779–831)

The Pitcher

[AD 779-831]

I dreamt I climbed to a high, high plain;
And on the plain I found a deep well.
My throat was dry with climbing and I longed to drink;
And my eyes were eager to look into the cool shaft.
I walked round it; I looked right down;
I saw my image mirrored on the face of the pool.
An earthen pitcher was sinking into the black depths;
There was no rope to pull it to the well-head.
I was strangely troubled lest the pitcher should be lost,
And started wildly running to look for help.
From village to village I scoured that high plain;
The men were gone: the dogs leapt at my throat.
I came back and walked weeping round the well;
Faster and faster the blinding tears flowed—
Till my own sobbing suddenly woke me up;
My room was silent; no one in the house stirred;
The flame of my candle flickered with a green smoke;
The tears I had shed glittered in the candle-light.
A bell sounded; I knew it was the midnight-chime;
I sat up in bed and tried to arrange my thoughts:
The plain in my dream was the graveyard at Ch'ang-an,
Those hundred acres of untilled land.
The soil heavy and the mounds heaped high;
And the dead below them laid in deep troughs.
Deep are the troughs, yet sometimes dead men
Find their way to the world above the grave.
And to-night my love who died long ago
Came into my dream as the pitcher sunk in the well.
That was why the tears suddenly streamed from my eyes,
Streamed from my eyes and fell on the collar of my dress.

India: The *Mahabharata*

The interesting story of the five Pandava brothers (Yudhistra, Bhima, Arjuna, Nakula, Sadevea) and their common wife, Draupadi, provides a view of the sophisticated civilization of the heroic period of Indian history. In its stories, legends, myths, and instructional passages, the *Mahabharata* treats all aspects of ancient Indian culture—religion, moral values, politics, economics, art, science, and mathematics.

The struggle of the Pandavas to overcome the external obstacles posed by their jealous cousins, the Kuravas, is part of the living culture of India. Every Hindu, whether rich or poor, educated or illiterate, is influenced by the story. Storytellers narrate its episodes in villages, priests recount them in temples, and mothers and grandmothers tell them in the homes. These stories have provided an ethical base in India for over three thousand years. The wisdom of the *Mahabharata* is also shared by the countries that fall within India's cultural sphere. The noble deeds of the characters are embodied in many of the stories, dances, drama, and art of Java, Sumatra, Cambodia, Thailand, and Malaysia. In general, the epic strongly indicates that humanity can realize its spiritual potential through education, meditation, and discipline. The *Mahabharata's* most famous section is the eighteen chapters of the *Bhagavad Gita.*

The *Mahabharata* is set in the kingdom of the Bharatas, which flourished along the upper course of the Ganges River in northern India. Although India (known as Bharat-varsha after the Bharatas) was divided into numerous small kingdoms, it was united by a common religion and cultural heritage. The Bharatas' highly advanced civilization was displayed at Hastinapur, the capital city. The kingdom was one of stability and prosperity. Economic security came from the fertile soil and vast natural resources, and social stability was insured by a system of four castes: priests, warriors and kings, merchants, and servants. In such a culture, intellectual and spiritual life flourished.

There is some disagreement among scholars regarding the dates when this Sanskrit epic was originally composed, but many agree that it reflects the development of Hindu thought from approximately 200 BC to AD 400. The historical fact on which the epic is based is a great war that took place between the Kuravas and the neighboring Panchalas, probably in the fourteenth or thirteenth century BC. The battle may not have been of the global proportion that the epic suggests, but it grew in magnitude as the account of heroic exploits was spread throughout India. Rivalry between two sets of cousins, the Pandavas and Kuravas, for the right to rule the kingdom gave rise to the war. The central theme that emerges from the epic is that of *dharma,* or righteousness in thoughts, actions, and goals. The behavior of the noble characters exemplifies that true heroism is not found in physical strength or political power but through following *dharma* or the duties associated with one's station in life. The third brother, Arjuna, sired by Indra, is skilled in every aspect of warfare, especially archery. He makes a journey to heaven and wins the favor of the gods Shiva and Indra, who give him their secret weapons, thus making him invincible on the battlefield. Yet, Arjuna is sensitive and reluctant to fight when he sees his relatives and the venerable elders on the battlefield. Arjuna would rather die in battle. He is induced to fight by the wise counsel of Krishna, who reminds him of the insults to Draupadi and the shameless killing of his son, Abhimanyu.

When Arjuna lays down his weapons and refuses to fight, Krishna appeals to his duties as a warrior. Krishna instructs him that each man attains perfection by doing his own duty with detachment—with no desire for reward. When pleasure and pain, gain and loss, victory and defeat are the same, a warrior may go into battle without sin. Similarly, when Yudhistra, the oldest brother, wants to relinquish his kingdom, the duties of the four castes are enumerated for him. The kingly duty of protection of the weak is considered the highest honor.

The transcendental nature of the soul which cannot be destroyed is also explained in the epic; hence, Arjuna and Yudhistra need not grieve for the dead because the latter's souls cannot be killed. These precepts form the religious instruction of Hindus even today. Western readers need not be disturbed by religious dogma and creed because the epic does not moralize. These values are presented more as "choices" the characters make when they are confronted with various situations. The epic ends on a philosophic and peaceful note. When the end of life is near, the Pandavas meditate on the transitory nature of military prowess, worldly wealth, and glory. In the end, Arjuna's divine weapons are powerless, and he cannot even protect the women and children of Krishna's kingdom. There is everlasting peace in heaven for all the major characters, who are finally free from anger, fear, jealousy, and revenge.

The *Mahabharata* consists of ninety thousand rhymed couplets. It is three times as long as the Bible and eight times as long as the *Iliad* and the *Odyssey* combined. The epic was part of the oral tradition of India before it was written in Sanskrit between AD 200 and 400. As the epic spread, legends of other princes, philosophy, religious treatises, political passages, and didactic episodes were deftly linked to the central theme. The epic became a repository of Indian culture and values, giving the people an identity and cohesiveness as a nation. It still provides modern Indians with a sense of continuity with the past.

The *Bhagavadgita:* Background

The *Bhagavadgita*, the most sacred text of the Hindus, was the inspiration for Mahatma Gandhi, the leader of the non-violent Indian resistance against the British. Through this sacred, prophetic, philosophical, and activist poem, he found the fortitude to stand in the gap for his people, taking them from bondage to independence.

As part of the Sanskrit epic the *Mahabharata*, the *Bhagavadgita* explores Vedanta philosophy in eighteen chapters and 700 verses. Its core section is chapters twenty-three to forty. The poem itself has eighteen cantos, focusing on the rivalry between the Pandava and Kuravas armies. The battlefield scenes are in medias res. A battle weary Pandava brother, Arjuna, one of five and the most highly respected, suddenly becomes unwilling to fight. His conscience tells him that to take life from family and friends is morally wrong, and he desires to remove himself from the whole sordid mess. Arjuna decides to become a religious hermit; however, Sri Krishna, the Hindu deity who is the incarnation of Vishnu and who later appears to Arjuna in His divine form (Chapter X), encourages him to live up to his responsibility as a prince and return to the battlefield. The deity's prompting causes Arjuna to ponder specific issues, and these issues become the embodiment of the epic. Essentially, it answers questions pertaining to the requirements of a good Hindu. What is dharma? How can a person know his/her dharma and respond to it? Is there conflict with dharma? Does dharma cause one to commit wrong acts? Is an individual's dharma chosen or destined? How does an individual attain moksa?

Brahman, in the cosmological theory of the *Bhagavadgita,* is the representation of the Godhead. Brahman is the epitome of life, knowledge, wisdom, understanding, love, mercy, truth, justice, purity, and happiness. Another identity given to Brahman is Atman, that is, omnipresent, existing within all things, living and nonliving. When Brahman is a personal God, he is Ishwara, creator of the universe but never destroyer. Communion with Ishwara is impossible unless a person achieves a super conscious state or union with Ishwara called *samadhi,* a meditative state that breaks consciousness with the physical world. Moreover, Ishwara performs three functions: Brahma, creation; Vishnu, preservation; and Shiva, destruction. Brahman's power is indicative of all mind and matter, called *Prakriti* or *Maya.* If Ishwara chooses to be born human, he forms a body for himself from Prakriti, but because he is Ishwara, he remains in control of Prakriti; the Hindus call this process a divine incarnation. Arjuna considers these things and more in the *Bhagavadgita.*

Chapter One, "The Sorrow of Arjuna," catalogues the events of the battle and shows Arjuna on the battlefield when he fully recognizes familiar faces. Because he seems to know everyone he battles against, he becomes despondent and throws down his weapons in an act of disgust. Arjuna experiences several yogas, approximately seventeen, as he undergoes his quest for mystical comprehension. They include the "yoga of knowledge" (Chapter II), "karma yoga" (Chapter III), "yoga of renunciation" (Chapter V, XVIII), "yoga of meditation" (Chapter VI), "yoga of mysticism" (Chapter IX), and "yoga of devotion" (Chapter XII). The yoga's purpose is to teach Arjuna to suppress the activity of his body, mind, and will in order to liberate himself from the cares of physical life. Instead of grasping the knowledge to which the yoga seems to be leading him through dialogue and discussion, Arjuna vacillates, unsure of the path he needs to take.

The remaining chapters of the *Bhagavadgita* are explorations into many states of Brahman. The epic suggests that union with God occurs in life and in death. It also suggests that the world is both a real and an unreal place. In terms of ritual worship, the poem emphasizes that sometimes such practices are desirable and, at other times, they are not. In the same manner, the epic espouses both orthodox and unorthodox religion. When Arjuna ponders the question about the moral right to take another life, Sri Krishna encourages him to fight and at the same time to be non-violent. Either way, he is one with God. Whether or not these opposites are inconsistent is difficult to determine. The Hindus see no reason to separate the sacred from the secular. They see the *Bhagavadgita* as practical and spiritual; thus union with God takes many avenues, including the paths of knowledge, action, and devotion.

II. The Yoga of Knowledge

SANJAYA:

Then his eyes filled with tears, and his heart grieved and was bewildered with pity. And Sri Krishna spoke to him, saying:

SRI KRISHNA:

Arjuna, is this hour of battle the time for scruples and fancies? Are they worthy of you, who seek enlightenment? Any brave man who merely hopes for fame or heaven would despise them.

What is this weakness? It is beneath you. Is it for nothing men call you the foe-consumer? Shake off this cowardice, Arjuna. Stand up.

ARJUNA:

Bhisma and Drona are noble and ancient, worthy of the deepest reverence. How can I greet them with arrows, in battle? If I kill them, how can I ever enjoy my wealth, or any other pleasure? It will be cursed with blood-guilt. I would much rather spare them, and eat the bread of a beggar.

Which will be worse, to win this war, or to lose it? I scarcely know. Even the sons of Dhritarashtra stand in the enemy ranks. If we kill them, none of us will wish to live.

Is this real compassion that I feel, or only a delusion? My mind gropes about in darkness. I cannot see where my duty lies. Krishna, I beg you, tell me frankly and clearly what I ought to do. I am your disciple. I put myself into your hands. Show me the way.

Not this world's kingdom,
Supreme, unchallenged,
No, nor the throne
Of the gods in heaven,
Could ease this sorrow
That numbs my senses!

SANJAYA:

When Arjuna, the foe-consuming, the never-slothful, had spoken thus to Govinda, ruler of the senses, he added: 'I will not fight,' and was silent.

Then to him who thus sorrowed between the two armies, the ruler of the senses spoke, smiling:

SRI KRISHNA:

Your words are wise, Arjuna, but your sorrow is for nothing. The truly wise mourn neither for the living nor for the dead.

There was never a time when I did not exist, nor you, nor any of these kings. Nor is there any future in which we shall cease to be.

Just as the dweller in this body passes through childhood, youth and old age, so at death he merely passes into another kind of body. The wise are not deceived by that.

Feelings of heat and cold, pleasure and pain, are caused by the contact of the senses with their objects. They come and they go, never lasting long. You must accept them.

A serene spirit accepts pleasure and pain with an even mind, and is unmoved by either. He alone is worthy of immortality.

That which is non-existent can never come into being, and that which is can never cease to be. Those who have known the inmost Reality know also the nature of *is* and *is not.*

That Reality which pervades the universe is indestructible. No one has power to change the Changeless.

Bodies are said to die, but That which possesses the body is eternal. It cannot be limited, or destroyed. Therefore you must fight.

Some say this Atman
Is slain, and others
Call It the slayer:
They know nothing.
How can It slay
Or who shall slay It?

Know this Atman
Unborn, undying,
Never ceasing,
Never beginning,
Deathless, birthless,
Unchanging for ever.
How can It die
The death of the body?

Knowing It birthless,
Knowing It deathless,
Knowing It endless,
For ever unchanging,
Dream not you do
The deed of the killer,
Dream not the power
Is yours to command it.

Worn-out garments
Are shed by the body:
Worn-out bodies
Are shed by the dweller
Within the body.
New bodies are donned
By the dweller, like garments.

Not wounded by weapons,
Not burned by fire,
Not dried by the wind,
Not wetted by water:
Such is the Atman,

Not dried, not wetted,
Not burned, not wounded,
Innermost element,
Everywhere, always,
Being of beings,
Changeless, eternal,
For ever and ever.

This Atman cannot be manifested to the senses, or thought about by the mind. It is not subject to modification. Since you know this, you should not grieve.

But if you should suppose this Atman to be subject to constant birth and death, even then you ought not to be sorry.

Death is certain for the born. Rebirth is certain for the dead. You should not grieve for what is unavoidable.

Before birth, beings are not manifest to our human senses. In the interim between birth and death, they are manifest. At death they return to the unmanifest again. What is there in all this to grieve over?

There are some who have actually looked upon the Atman, and understood It, in all Its wonder. Others can only speak of It as wonderful beyond their understanding. Others know of Its wonder by hearsay. And there are others who are told about It and do not understand a word.

He Who dwells within all living bodies remains for ever indestructible. Therefore, you should never mourn for any one.

Even if you consider this from the standpoint of your own caste-duty, you ought not to hesitate; for, to a warrior, there is nothing nobler than a righteous war. Happy are the warriors to whom a battle such as this comes: it opens a door to heaven.

But if you refuse to fight this righteous war, you will be turning aside from your duty. You will be a sinner, and disgraced. People will speak ill of you throughout the ages. To a man who values his honour, that is surely worse than death. The warrior-chiefs will believe it was fear that drove you from the battle; you will be despised by those who have admired you so long. Your enemies, also, will slander your courage. They will use the words which should never be spoken. What could be harder to bear than that?

Die, and you win heaven. Conquer, and you enjoy the earth. Stand up now, son of Kunti, and resolve to fight. Realize that pleasure and pain, gain and loss, victory and defeat, are all one and the same: then go into battle. Do this and you cannot commit any sin.

I have explained to you the true nature of the Atman. Now listen to the method of Karma Yoga. If you can understand and follow it, you will be able to break the chains of desire which bind you to your actions.

In this yoga, even the abortive attempt is not wasted. Nor can it produce a contrary result. Even a little practise of this yoga will save you from the terrible wheel of rebirth and death.

In this yoga, the will is directed singly toward one ideal. When a man lacks this discrimination, his will wanders in all directions, after innumerable aims.

Those who lack discrimination may quote the letter of the scripture, but they are really denying its inner truth. They are full of worldly desires, and hungry for the rewards of heaven. They use beautiful figures of speech. They teach elaborate rituals which are supposed to obtain pleasure and power for those who perform them. But, actually, they understand nothing except the law of Karma, that chains men to rebirth.

Those whose discrimination is stolen away by such talk grow deeply attached to pleasure and power. And so they are unable to develop that concentration of the will which leads a map to absorption in God.

The Vedas teach us about the three gunas and their functions. You, Arjuna, must overcome the three gunas. You must be free from the pain of opposites. Poise your mind in tranquility. Take care neither to acquire nor to hoard. Be established in the consciousness of the Atman, always.

When the whole country is flooded, the reservoir becomes superfluous. So, to the illumined seer, the Vedas are all superfluous.

You have the right to work, but for the work's sake only. You have no right to the fruits of work. Desire for the fruits of work must never, be your motive in working. Never give way to laziness, either.

Perform every action with your heart fixed on the Supreme Lord. Renounce attachment to the fruits. Be even-tempered in success and failure; for it is this evenness of temper which is meant by yoga.

Work done with anxiety about results is far Inferior to work done without such anxiety, in the calm of self-surrender. Seek refuge in the knowledge of Brahman. They who work selfishly for results are miserable.

In the calm of self-surrender you can free yourself from the bondage of virtue and vice during this very life. Devote yourself, therefore, to reaching union with Brahman. To unite the heart with Brahman and then to act: that is the secret of non-attached work. In the calm of self-surrender, the seas renounce the fruits of their actions, and so reach enlightenment. Then they are free from the bondage of rebirth, and pass to that state which is beyond all evil.

When your intellect has cleared itself of its delusions, you will become indifferent to the results of all action, present or future, At present, your intellect is bewildered by conflicting interpretations of the scriptures. When it can rest, steady and undistracted, in contemplation of the Atman, then you will reach union with the Atman.

ARJUNA:

Krishna, how can one identify a man who is firmly established and absorbed in Brahman? In what manner does an illumined soul speak? How does he sit? How does he walk?

SRI KRISHNA:

He knows bliss in the Atman
And wants nothing else.
Cravings torment the heart:
He renounces cravings.
I call him illumined.

Not shaken by adversity,
Not hankering after happiness:
Free from fear, free from anger,
Free from the things of desire.
I call him a seer, and illumined.
The bonds of his flesh are broken.
He is lucky, and does not rejoice:
He is unlucky, and does not weep.
I call him illumined.

The tortoise can draw in his legs:
The seer can draw in his senses.
I call him illumined.

The abstinent run away from what they desire
But carry their desires with them;
When a man enters Reality,
He leaves his desires behind him.

Even a mind that knows the path
Can be dragged from the path:
The senses are so unruly.
But he controls the senses
And recollects the mind
And fixes it on me.
I call him illumined.

Thinking about sense-objects
Will attach you to sense-objects;
Grow attached, and you become addicted;
Thwart your addiction, it turns to anger;
Be angry, and you confuse your mind;
Confuse your mind, you forget the lesson of experience;
Forget experience, you lose discrimination;
Lose discrimination, and you miss life's only purpose.

When he has no lust, no hatred,
A man walks safely among the things of lust and hatred.
To obey the Atman
Is his peaceful joy:
Sorrow melts
Into that clear peace:
His quiet mind

Is soon established in peace.
The uncontrolled mind
Does not guess that the Atman is present:
How can it meditate?
Without meditation, where is peace?
Without peace, where is happiness?

The wind turns a ship
From its course upon the waters:
The wandering winds of the senses
Cast man's mind adrift
And turn his better judgment from its course.
When a man can still the senses
I call him illumined.
The recollected mind is awake
In the knowledge of the Atman
Which is dark night to the ignorant:
The ignorant are awake in their sense-life
Which they think is daylight:
To the seer it is darkness.

Water flows continually into the ocean
But the ocean is never disturbed:
Desire flows into the mind of the seer
But he is never disturbed.
The seer knows peace:
The man who stirs up his own lusts
Can never know peace.
He knows peace who has forgotten desire.
He lives without craving:
Free from ego, free from pride.

This is the state of enlightenment in Brahman:
A man does not fall back from it
Into delusion.
Even at the moment of death
He is alive in that enlightenment:
Brahman and he are one.

X. Divine Glory

Sri Krishna:

Once more, warrior,
Hear this highest
Word of my wisdom:
Wishing your welfare,
To you I teach it
Since your heart
Delights in the telling.

How shall the mighty
Seers or the devas
Know my beginning?
I am the origin,
I the sustainer
Of seers and devas.

Who knows me birthless,
Never-beginning,
Lord of the worlds;
He alone among mortals
Is stainless of sin,
Unvexed by delusion.

All that makes Man
In his many natures:
Knowledge and power
Of understanding
Unclouded by error,
Truth, forbearance,
Calm of spirit,
Control of senses,
Happiness, sorrow,
Birth and destruction,
What fears, what is fearless,
What harms no creature,
The mind unshaken,
The heart contented,
The will austere,
The hand of the giver,
Fame and honour
And infamy also:
It is by me only
That these are allotted.
Forth from my thought
Came the seven Sages,

The Ancient Four
And at last the Manus:
Thus I gave birth

To the first begetters
Of all earth's children.

Who truly knows me,
In manifold Being
Everywhere present
And all-prevailing,
Dwells in my yoga
That shall not be shaken:
Of this be certain.

I am where all things began, the issuing-forth of the creatures,
Known to the wise in their love when they worship with hearts overflowing:
Mind and sense are absorbed, I alone am the theme of their discourse:
Thus delighting each other, they live in bliss and contentment
Always aware of their Lord are they, and ever devoted:
Therefore the strength of their thought is illumined and guided toward me.

There in the ignorant heart where I dwell, by the grace of my mercy,
I am knowledge, that brilliant lamp, dispelling its darkness.

ARJUNA:

You are Brahman, the highest abode, the utterly holy:
All the sages proclaim you eternal, Lord of the devas:
Saintly Narada anew you the birthless, the everywhere present:
Devala echoed your praise; Asita, too, and Vyasa;
Now I also have heard, for to me your own lips have confirmed it,
Krishna, this is the truth that you tell: my heart bids me believe you.

God of gods, Lord of the world, Life's Source, O King of all creatures:
How shall deva or titan know all the extent of your glory?
You alone know what you are, by the light of your innermost nature.
Therefore teach me now, and hold back no word in the telling,
All the sum of your shapes by which the three worlds are pervaded;
Tell me how you will make yourself known to my meditation;
Show me beneath what form and disguise I must

learn to behold you;
Number them all, your heavenly powers, your
manifestations:
Speak, for each word is immortal nectar; I never
grow weary.

SRI KRISHNA:

O Arjuna, I will indeed make known to you my divine manifestations; but I shall name the chief of these, only. For, of the lesser variations in all their detail, there is no end.

I am the Atman that dwells in the heart of every mortal creature: I am the beginning, the life-span, and the end of all.

I am Vishnu: I am the radiant sun among the light-givers: I am Marichi, the wind-god: among the stars of night, I am the moon.

I am the Sama Veda: I am Indra, king of heaven: of sense-organs, I am the mind: I am consciousness in the living.

I am Shiva: I am the Lord of all riches: I am the spirit of fire: I am Meru, among the mountain peaks.

Know me as Brihaspati, leader of the high priests, and as Skanda, the warrior-chief. I am the ocean among the waters.

I am Bhrigu, the great seer: among words, I am the sacred syllable OM: I am the vow of japam: I am Himalaya among the things that cannot be moved.

I am the holy fig tree: I am Narada, the godly sage, Chitraratha, the celestial musician, and Kapila among the perfected souls.

Among horses, you may know me as Uchchaishrava, who was brought forth from the sea of nectar: I am Airavata among royal elephants: I am king among men.

Of weapons, I am God's thunderbolt: I am Kamadhenu, the heavenly cow: I am the love-god, begetter of children: I am Vasuki, god of snakes.

I am Ananta, the holy serpent: of water beings, I am Varuna: Aryaman among the Fathers: I am Death, who distributes the fruit of all action.

I am Prahlada, the giant: among those who measure, I am Time: I am the lion among beasts: Vishnu's eagle among the birds.

Among purifiers, I am the wind: I am Rama among the warriors: the shark among fish: Ganges among the rivers.

I am the beginning, the middle and the end in creation: I am the knowledge of things spiritual: I am the logic of those who debate.

In the alphabet, I am A: among compounds, the copulative: I am Time without end: I am the Sustainer: my face is everywhere.

I am death that snatches all: I, also, am the source of all that shall be born: I am glory, prosperity, beautiful speech, memory, intelligence, steadfastness and forgiveness.

I am the great Sama of the Vedic hymns, and the Gayatri among poetic metres: of the months, I am Margashirsha: of seasons, the time of flowers.

I am the dice-play of the cunning: I am the strength of the strong: I am triumph and perseverance: I am the purity of the good.

I am Krishna among the Vrishnis, Arjuna among the Pandavas, Vyasa among the sages, Ushanas among the illumined poets.

I am the sceptre and the mastery of those who rule, the policy of those who seek to conquer: I am the silence of things secret: I am the knowledge of the knower.

O Arjuna, I am the divine seed of all lives. In this world, nothing animate or inanimate exists without me.

There is no limit to my divine manifestations, nor can they be numbered, O foe-consumer. What I have described to you are only a few of my countless forms.

Whatever in this world is powerful, beautiful or glorious, that you may know to have come forth from a fraction of my power and glory.

But what need have you, Arjuna, to know this huge variety? Know only that I exist, and that one atom of myself sustains the universe.

Iran: Islamic Poetry

Poetry is powerful. When words are guided by the pen of a skillful hand, they can be like a swift arrow which can transcend time and culture, penetrate the mind, pierce the heart, and capture the emotions. Through the centuries, the uniqueness of Islamic poetic style has captivated the attention of European and Western culture because of its blend of spiritual, emotional, and intellectual depth.

Prior to the 1500s, endemic in Islamic literature was didactic writing using odes and lyrics, used primarily as religious guidelines and intellectual material for society. Supreme poets such as Firdausi, Rumi, Sa'di, and Hafiz were masters in this era. Of these names, Hafiz is considered the "king of lyric" and "master of ghazals." In order to examine Islamic poetry before the sixteenth century, Islamic philosophy, literary forms, poetic styles, and Hafiz, the supreme Persian poet, must be considered.

Having originated in the seventh century with the Prophet Muhammad (570–632 CE) and the revelation of the Koran, its membership numbers more than 1.2 billion. The Islamic religion is considered to be the second largest religion in the world. Followers of the Islamic faith consist of nearly fifty Muslim countries, extending from northwestern Africa to Indonesia with a growing number of converts in Europe, India, China, the United States, and other parts of the Americas.

When the patriarch father of the Arabic and Hebrew people, Hazrat Abraham, prayed with his oldest son, Ishmael, he said, "Muslemin"; in English it means, "Oh Lord, make us submissive unto Thee." Thus word *Islam* means submission to the Will of God, and a Muslim is one who submits to His divine authority. Descending from the family of Abraham, Muhammad was given to meditation, especially after his marriage to Khadijah. He was said to have visited a cave on a small mountain not far from Mecca where he devoted himself to meditation for one full month each year. Concerned with the apostasy and immorality among his people, Muhammad meditated for Divine guidance. God honored his request by revealing to Muhammad, the Koran. As a result of his obedience, it is believed that the Prophet Muhammad experienced a complete and final revelation of the Will of God through the Koran.

Through the transcribing of the Koran, Islamic literature was birthed. Consisting of 114 surahs (chapters), the Koran was revealed over a twenty-two year period to the Prophet who served as Allah's (God's) messenger. The surahs were codified after Muhammad's death. They are considered the highest and most sacred form of literature, for it is, *kalam*, the word of God. It is generally held that the language, grammatic forms, and linguistic methods used in the Koran are without parallel among any Arabic literature. Both women and men read and recited the surahs. After the death of Muhammad, the Koran was codified: accounts of his teachings, life and practices were also written and kept for followers to use as guidelines for their devotion. The *Sunnah* is the narrative reports of the words and deeds of Muhammad. They were collected and used as textual sources, and the *Hadith* is a literary work comprised of the personal recollections of those who knew Mohammed. Although classified as literature, six sections of the Hadith traditions are considered authoritative and have the same effects as laws. Both the Sunnah and the Hadith are also highly regarded in Islamic literature. Between the eighth and tenth centuries, the *Shariah* was developed. This was Islamic law that set forth the system of ethics and laws to stipulate and guide the daily lives of its followers. Thus the Koran and other sacred religious materials provided the foundation of Islamic literature

Islamic dominance grew between two periods, AD 634–642 and 700–732. During these eras, there were the influences that affected the formation of Islamic literature. First, as result of political domination and cultural amalgamation, there were changes in the philosophical ideologies in the Arabo-Islamic empire. The contact with non-Muslim Arabs and other nationalities expanded. Because of its intellectual brilliance and prolific literature, Greece was at one time the rival of Persia (Iran). Consequently, there was a major Greek influence on logic and reasoning, especially among the intellectuals. Islamic writers became tolerant of other ideologies, and these influences were reflected in the literature. As a result, works of non-Islamic writers were promoted, such as al-Akhtal, the poet, and John of Damascus. Second, after Alexander's conquest of the Middle East, a dualistic philosophy of Persia metaphysic ideologies from India, dogma from Christianity, Hellenism from Greece, and Mysticism permeated Islam. Syrians were interested in Plato's wisdom and Aristotle's logic. Muslim thinkers and writers began to devote attention to literary topics concerning the soul, intelligence, and immortality. Additionally, in Persia, as a result of the Arabic influence, the ode and lyric emerged. Many great poets, such as Daqiqi, used monorhymes. Although monorhymes were characteristic of Persian literature, Firdausi used rhyming couplets and made them a basis of the Persian epic. Other great poets like Sana'i and Rumi also adapted this technique. Finally, one of the greatest influences on Islamic culture and literature was held by the Sufi movement. *Sufism* was a mystic belief that one must have knowledge of and a union with God, which was to be based upon a personal experience conceived to be adopted as a way of life supported by unselfish love and dedication. Thus, the Sufi movement combined asceticism and devotional love to God and His Divine will. By the twelfth century orders and centers had developed. Practice became infused in the daily lives, poetry, and devotional readings of the people.

In Iran, during the seventh century under Sasanian shahs, the majority of literature was comprised in the form of religious books containing Zoroastrian teachings and the Magian Code of the Zoroastrian. Prose and poetry were literary traditions. Having individuals serve as court poets had been commonplace for centuries. The poets celebrated the triumphs of the rule through odes and panegyric. Poets were rewarded with jewels or perhaps female slaves of their own. The poetry was carried and shared from one court to another. Often the artist recited his work orally. In this case, the meter and rhyme were important. Prose, on the other hand, was less preferable because it was more difficult to use. In the written format of the language, there was no system of punctuation to mark pauses, beginnings, and endings of sentences.

The qasida was the most common type of poetry. The qasida was presented in an eulogistic style to describe a person or event. As a general rule, except for the Muhammadan court, there were strict requirements to those who dealt with literature about which style of literature was suited for each class and community of people. Poets were vigorously trained to commit certain notable events to memory. Then, they selected and analyzed appropriate linguistic style. Next it was important to decide on a meter. And ultimately, the theme was committed to verse. In the traditional style, two halves of the opening lines must rhyme, and all the lines at the end must repeat the first line.

By the thirteenth century, from the qasida, another poetic form had emerged. This was the ghazal. The original Arabic meaning is "a lover's exchange." Many of the qasidas and great ghazals in Persian and Arabic have been ascribed to Sa'di of Shirz, an Iranian poet who lived in the thirteenth century. Two of his most notable works are *Bustan* and *Gulistan*. A student of Sa'di, Shamsu'd-Din Muhammad Hafiz has been acknowledged as the supreme Persian poet. Hafiz studied the work of Sa'di and was greatly influenced by him, even though he had lived one hundred years before Hafiz. He is better known in the Western world as Hafiz of Shiraz. Both he and Sa'di lived in Shiraz, a city located in southern Iran. Shamsu'd-Din Muhammad Hafiz, did not have an easy life. His father, Baha'u'd-Din, was a wealthy merchant who migrated from Isfahan to Shiraz which was a striving cultural center in the southern region of Iran. However, economic conditions and good fortune changed. By the time of Baha'u'd-Din's death, his estate was in disarray, and the family was left in poverty. Hafiz had to work to take care of himself, but he managed to attend school and receive a solid traditional religious education. He was very devoted to his religious studies. Demonstrating his devotion and self-discipline, Hafiz committed the entire Koran to memory and could recite it without error. He was admired for his mental agility and educational achievements. Therefore, the name Hafiz is used to refer to those who know and recite the sacred Islamic scripture.

After having memorized the Koran, Hafiz began to compose and recite poetry. However, he met with little success, until according to legend, on a hill north of Shiraz, while keeping a vigil at the Shrine of Baba Kuhi, Hafiz was visited by Imam' Ali. Ali gave him many revelations concerning mystical things and told Hafiz that the gift of poetry and the keys of all knowledge were his. Hafiz felt that he had been given mysterious heavenly food and precious blessings. Hafiz's admirers referred to him as one who had the tongue of the unseen and who was also able to interpret mysteries. Hafiz served as a court poet. He enjoyed the patronage of rulers. His work was multifaceted, and his fame during his lifetime extended from the Far East, India, and Mesopotamia. He witnessed the rise and fall of several dynasties and the transfer of power through blood and war. Hafiz was not always in a favorable relationship with each of the ruling families, and his writing reflected current events. He made references to loss of freedom under religious hypocrisy and censorship. Hafiz's life did not always meet with success and praise. However, he only enjoyed limited fame during his lifetime. A turning point in Hafiz's career came under the liberal-minded sultanate of Shah Shojg, son of the previous austere and orthodox ruler, Mubariz al-Din. During the reign of Shah Shoja, Hafiz composed his most mature work, and his fame spread. His works were widely received; he used proverbial expressions, the simple colloquial language of the people to express his thoughts and feelings. Some of his critics say that his work sometimes appears mystical, and at other times, it appears erotic. Sometimes, it is serious, spiritual, and then, conversely, worldly. At times, he found himself excluded from social circles, ostracized, misunderstood, unappreciated by his friends; and rejected by his beloved.

Hafiz began to perfect his own poetic style. During his lifetime, the longer panegyric court poetic forms known as qasida had been replaced by the ghazel. The ghazal, a short poem sometimes consisting of five to twelve lines, had become a predominant, well-established poetic style. Sometimes they were comprised of six to fifteen couplets which were linked by a common theme or symbolism. Each line is an identical meter called a *beyt*. The beyts are comprised of a couplet or two hemistich of equal length. Except in the first beyt, the same end-rhyme is repeated through the ghazel. Hafiz is credited with mastering the use of the ghazel instead of the qasida (ode) in panegyrics. Hafiz's work has been set apart because of his ability to depart from formalism and give conventional subjects a freshness and subtlety. He was bilingual, writing both in Persian and Arabic. Considered as one of the finest lyric poets, Hafiz composed approximately 500 ghazals during the fourteenth century.

By the seventeenth century, long after his death, as a result of expanded trade between the East and West, Hafiz's fame had reached Europe. In the Islamic world, his name has been known for centuries. His work has been translated and interpreted by both poets and artists who have tried to capture the spirit and feelings of Hafizian poetry. However, there have been problems associated with the translations of Hafizian works. These range from an understanding of Sifu imagery which greatly influenced the style and underlying religious ideology of Hafiz. The Sifis felt that a true disciple will follow the Path of love in total submission to the Beloved. Common topics in Hafiz's writings are the Beloved, rose petal, and nightingale. He may have been literally speaking of a romantic love for an individual or of a deeper spiritual love and devotion. However, some feel that he wrote of the rose petal as not merely a rose itself but perhaps to point to its aesthetic beauty which he is unable to attain. He also frequently wrote of the nightingale who held the rose petal. The possession of the rose petal heightened the agony of his love. The Beloved is sometimes interpreted as the king or ruler who is loved by his countrymen. These may have been symbolic or real.

In summary, prior to the fifteenth century, endemic in Islamic literature was didactic writing which was used as religious guidelines and intellectual material for society. Islamic poetry was predominantly characterized by the use of ode and lyric forms. Poets, such as Firdausi, Rumi, Sa'di, and Hafiz, were supreme masters in their era. Just as William Shakespeare is highly regarded by Westerners, the name Hafiz is known in the Islamic world. Because of his poetic charm and linguistic agility, Hafiz is considered the "king of lyric" and "master of ghazals." His work has transcended generations because of his ability to intrigue audiences, demonstrate the evolution of poetic expression, and transmit mystical, spiritual, secular emotions, and ideologies of his society.

Hafiz (AD 1300?–1388)

I Cease Not from Desire

I cease not from desire till my desire
Is satisfied; or let my mouth attain
My love's red mouth, or let my soul expire.
Sighed from those lips that sought her lips in vain.
Others may find another love as fair;
Upon her threshold I have laid my head,
The dust shall cover me, still lying there,
When from my body life and love have fled.

My soul is on my lips ready to fly,
But grief beats in my heart and will not cease,
Because not once, not once before I die,
Will her sweet lips give all my longing peace.
My breath is narrowed down to one long sigh
For a red mouth that burns my thoughts like fire;
When will that mouth draw near and make reply
To one whose life is straitened with desire?
When I am dead, open my grave and see
The cloud of smoke that rises round thy feet:
In my dead heart the fire still burns for thee;
Yea, the smoke rises from my winding-sheet!
Ah, come, Beloved! for the meadows wait
Thy coming, and the thorn bears flowers instead
Of thorns, the cypress fruit, and desolate
Bare winter from before thy steps has fled.
Hoping within some garden ground to find
A red rose soft and sweet as thy soft cheek,
Through every meadow blows the western wind,
Through every garden he is fain to seek.
Reveal thy face! that the whole world may be
Bewildered by thy radiant loveliness;
The cry of man and woman comes to thee,
Open thy lips and comfort their distress!
Each curling lock of thy luxuriant hair
Breaks into barbèd hooks to catch my heart,
My broken heart is wounded everywhere
With countless wounds from which the red drops start.
Yet when sad lovers meet and tell their sighs,
Not without praise shall Hafiz' name be said,
Not without tears, in those pale companies
Where joy has been forgot and hope has fled.

Light in Darkness

High-nesting in the stately fir,
The enduring nightingale again
Unto the rose in passionate strain
Singeth: "All ill be far from her!

"In gratitude for this, O rose,
That thou the Queen of Beauty art,
Pity nightingales' mad heart,
Be not contemptuous of those."

I do not rail against my fate
When thou dost hide thy face from me;
Joy, wells not of propinquity
Save in the heart once desolate.

If other men are gay and glad
That life is joy and festival,
I do exult and glory all,
Because her beauty makes me sad.

And if for maids of Paradise
And heavenly halls the monk aspires,
The Friend fulfils my heart's desires,
The Tavern will for heaven suffice.

Drink wine, and let the lute vibrate;
Grieve not; if any tell to thee,
"Wine is a great iniquity",
Say, "Allah is compassionate!"

Why, Hafiz, art thou sorrowing,
Why is thy heart in absence rent?
Union may come of banishment,
And in the darkness light doth spring.

O Ask Not

O love, how have I felt thy pain!
    Ask me not how—
O absence, how I drank thy bane!
    Ask me not how—

In quest, throughout the world I err'd.
And whom, at last, have I preferr'd?
    O ask not whom—

In hope her threshold's dust to spy,
How streamed down my longing eye!
    O ask not how—

Why bite my friends their lips, despleas'd?
Know they what ruby lip I seiz'd?
    O ask not when—

But yester-night, this very ear
Such language from her mouth did hear—
    O ask not what—

Like Hafiz, in love's mazy round,
My feet, at length, their goal have found,
    O ask not where.

Iraq: *Gilgamesh*: Background

Widely known as the first great heroic narrative, *Gilgamesh* is based upon myths and legends about the historical figure of Gilgamesh, a king of the ancient Babylonian city of Uruk around 2700 BC. The text details the adventures of the hero-king Gilgamesh and his companion Enkidu and includes several biblical parallels, the most notable of which is the digression concerning a great flood and its lone survivor. In addition, the epic is remarkable for its exploration of a wide range of humanistic concerns: the nature of heroism and the concept of hubris; the inherent conflict between nature and civilization; the divinity in humanity and the human-like nature of the gods; happiness, love, grief, and loneliness as manifestations of the human condition; and the human search for literal or figurative immortality. The cultural context of *Gilgamesh* remains obscure, but it lends the poem an immediacy found only in the most enduring works of world literature. The earliest versions of the story, like those of many other surviving epics, were first transmitted orally. According to Mesopotamian tradition, a scholar-priest of Uruk, Sinleqqiunninni, first "authored" the epic, collecting and organizing some of the tales into a written, linear narrative some time between 1600–1400 BC. However, what is called the Standard Version of the epic has been culled from several additional written sources. The most complete surviving text, which has been adapted from a set of twelve partially damaged, cuneiform-inscribed clay tablets dating from the seventh century BC was found in the ruins of Assurbanipal's library at Nineveh, Assyria; other older fragments were discovered at Assur and Babylon, among other sites, after the Nineveh tablets. Recent discoveries throughout Mesopotamia give archaeologists hope that the entire epic will eventually be restored.

Selected Bibliography

Tigay, Jeffrey H. *The Evolution of the Gilgamesh Epic.* Philadelphia: U of Pennsylvania P, 1982.

Gilgamesh

Prologue

Gilgamesh King in Uruk

I will proclaim to the world the deeds of Gilgamesh. This was the man to whom all things were known; this was the king who knew the countries of the world. He was wise, he saw mysteries and knew secret things, he brought us a tale of the days before the flood. He went on a long journey, was weary, worn-out with labour, returning he rested, he engraved on a stone the whole story.

When the gods created Gilgamesh they gave him a perfect body. Shamash the glorious sun endowed him with beauty, Adad the god of the storm endowed him with courage, the great gods made his beauty perfect, surpassing all others, terrifying like a great wild bull. Two third's they made him god and one third man.

In Uruk he built walls, a great rampart, and the temple of blessed Eanna for the god of the firmament Anu, and for Ishtar the goddess of love. Look at it still today: the outer wall where the cornice runs, it shines with the brilliance of copper; and the inner wall, it has no equal. Touch the threshold, it is ancient. Approach Eanna the dwelling of Ishtar, our lady of love and war, the like of which no latter-day king, no man alive can equal. Climb upon the wall of Uruk; walk along it, I say; regard the foundation terrace and examine the masonry: is it not burnt brick and good? The seven sages laid the foundations.

1

The Coming of Enkidu

Gilgamesh went abroad in the world, but he met with none who could withstand his arms till he came to Uruk. But the men of Uruk muttered in their houses, "Gilgamesh sounds the tocsin for his amusement, his arrogance has no bounds by day or night. No son is left with his father, for Gilgamesh takes them all, even the children; yet the king should be a shepherd to his people. His lust leaves no virgin to her lover, neither the warrior's daughter nor the wife of the noble; yet this is the shepherd of the city, wise, comely, and resolute."

The gods heard their lament, the gods of heaven cried to the Lord of Uruk, to Anu the god of Uruk: "A goddess made him, strong as a savage bull, none can withstand his arms. No son is left with his father, for Gilgamesh takes them all; and is this the king, the shepherd of his people? His lust leaves no virgin to her lover, neither the warrior's daughter nor the wife of the nobel." When Anu had heard their lamentation the gods cried to Aruru, the goddess of creation, "You made him, O Aruru, now create his equal; let it be as like him as his own reflection, his second self, stormy heart for stormy heart. Let them contend together and leave Uruk in quiet."

So the goddess conceived an image in her mind, and it was of the stuff of Anu of the firmament. She dipped her hands in water and pinched off clay, she let it fall in the wilderness, and noble Enkidu was created. There was virtue in him of the god of war, of Ninurta himself. His body was rough, he had long hair like a woman's; it waved like the hair of Nisaba, the goddess of corn. His body was covered with matted hair like Samuqan's, the god of cattle. He was innocent of mankind; he knew nothing of the cultivated land.

Enkidu ate grass in the hills with the gazelle and lurked with wild beasts at the water-holes; he had joy of the water with the herds of wild game. But there was a trapper who met him one day face to face at the drinking-hole, for the wild game had entered his territory. On three days he met him face to face, and the trapper was frozen with fear. He went back to his house with the game he had caught, and he was dumb, benumbed with terror. His face was altered like that of one who has made a long journey. With awe in his heart he spoke to his father: "Father, there is a man, unlike any other, who comes down from the hills. He is the strongest in the world, he is like an immortal from heaven. He ranges over the hills with wild beasts and eats grass; he ranges through your land and comes down to the wells. I am afraid and dare not go near him. He fills in the pits which I dig and tears up my traps set for the game; he helps the beasts to escape and now they slip through my fingers."

His father opened his mouth and said to the trapper, "My son, in Uruk lives Gilgamesh; no one has ever prevailed against him, he is strong as a star from heaven. Go to Uruk, find Gilgamesh, extol the strength of this wild man. Ask him to give you a harlot, a wanton from the temple of love; return with her, and let her woman's power overpower this man. When next he comes down to drink at the wells she will be there, stripped naked; and when he sees tier beckoning he will embrace her, and then the wild beasts will reject him."

So the trapper set out on his journey to Uruk and addressed himself to Gilgamesh saying, "A man unlike any other is roaming now in the pastures; he is as strong as a star from heaven and I am afraid to approach him. He helps the wild game to escape; he fills in my pits and pulls up my traps." Gilgamesh said, "Trapper, go back, take with you a harlot, a child of pleasure. At the drinking-hole she will strip, and when he sees her beckoning he will embrace her and the game of the wilderness will surely reject him."

Now the trapper returned, taking the harlot with him. After a three days' journey they came to the drinking-hole, and there they sat down; the harlot and the trapper sat facing one another and waited for the game to come. For the first day and for the second day the two sat waiting, but on the third day the herds came; they came down to drink and Enkidu was with them. The small wild creatures of the plains were glad of the water, and Enkidu with them, who ate grass with the gazelle and was born in the hills; and she saw him, the savage man, come from far-off in the hills. The trapper spoke to her: "There he is. Now, woman, make your breasts bare, have no shame, do not delay but welcome his love. Let him see you naked, let him possess your body. When he comes near uncover yourself and lie with him; teach him, the savage man, your woman's art, for when he murmurs love to you the wild beasts that shared his life in the hills will reject him."

She was not ashamed to take him, she made herself naked and welcomed his eagerness; as he lay on her murmuring love she taught him the woman's art. For six days and seven nights they lay together, for Enkidu had forgotten his home in the hills; but when he was satisfied he went back to the wild beasts. Then, when the gazelle saw him, they bolted away; when the wild creatures saw him they fled. Enkidu would have followed, but his body was bound as though with a cord, his knees gave way when he started to run, his swiftness was gone. And now the wild creatures had all fled away; Enkidu was grown weak, for wisdom was in him, and the thoughts of a man were in his heart. So he returned and sat down at the woman's feet, and listened intently to what she said. "You are wise, Enkidu, and now you have become like a god. Why do you want to run wild with the beasts in the hills? Come with me. I will take you to strong-walled Uruk, to the blessed temple of Ishtar and of Anu, of love and of heaven: there Gilgamesh lives, who is very strong, and like a wild bull he lords it over men."

When she had spoken Enkidu was pleased; he longed for a comrade, for one who would understand his heart. "Come, woman, and take me to that holy temple, to the house of Anu and of Ishtar, and to the place where Gilgamesh lords it over the people. I will challenge him boldly, I will cry out aloud in Uruk, 'I am the strongest here, I have come to change the old order, I am he who was born in the hills, I am he who is strongest of all.' "

She said, "Let us go, and let him see your face. I know very well where Gilgamesh is in great Uruk. O Enkidu, there all the people are dressed in their gorgeous robes, every day is holiday, the young men and the girls are wonderful to see. How sweet they smell! All the great ones are roused from their beds. O Enkidu, you who love life, I will show you Gilgamesh, a man of many moods; you shall look at him well in his radiant manhood. His body is perfect in strength and maturity; he never rests by night or day. He is stronger than you, so leave your boasting. Shamash the glorious sun has given favours to Gilgamesh, and Anu of the heavens, and Enlil, and Ea the wise has given him deep understanding. I tell you, even before you have left the wilderness, Gilgamesh will know in his dreams that you are coming."

Now Gilgamesh got up to tell his dream to his mother, Ninsun, one of the wise gods. "Mother, last night I had a dream. I was full of joy, the young heroes were round me and I walked through the night under the stars of the firmament, and one, a meteor of the stuff of Anu, fell down from heaven. I tried to lift it but it proved too heavy. All the people of Uruk came round to see it, the common people jostled and the nobles thronged to kiss its feet; and to me its attraction was like the love of woman. They helped me, I braced my forehead and I raised it with thongs and brought it to you, and you yourself pronounced it my brother."

Then Ninsun, who is well-beloved and wise, said to Gilgamesh, "This star of heaven which descended like a meteor from the sky; which you tried to lift, but found too heavy, when you tried to move it it would not budge, and so you brought it to my feet; I made it for you, a goad and spur, and you were drawn as though to a woman. This is the strong comrade, the one who brings help to his friend in his need. He is the strongest of wild creatures, the stuff of Anu; born in the grass-lands and the wild hills reared him; when you see him you will be glad; you will love him as a woman and he will never forsake you. This is the meaning of the dream."

Gilgamesh said, "Mother, I dreamed a second dream. In the streets of strong-walled Uruk there lay an axe; the shape of it was strange and the people thronged round. I saw it and was glad. I bent down, deeply drawn towards it; I loved it like a woman and wore it at my side." Ninsun answered, "That axe, which you saw, which drew you so powerfully like love of a woman, that is the comrade whom I give you, and he will come in his strength like one of the host of heaven. He is the brave companion who rescues his friend in necessity." Gilgamesh said to his mother, "A friend, a counsellor has come to me from Enlil, and now I shall befriend and counsel him." So Gilgamesh told his dreams; and the harlot retold them to Enkidu.

And now she said to Enkidu, "When I look at you you have become like a god. Why do you yearn to run wild again with the beasts in the hills? Get up from the ground, the bed of a shepherd." He listened to her words with care. It was good advice that she gave. She divided her clothing in two and with the one half she clothed him and with the other herself; and holding his hand she led him like a child to the sheepfolds, into the shepherds' tents. There all the shepherds crowded round to see him, they put down bread in front of him, but Enkidu could only suck the milk of wild animals. He fumbled and gaped, at a loss what to do or how he should eat the bread and drink the strong wine. Then the woman said, "Enkidu, eat bread, it is the staff of life; drink the wine, it is the custom of the land." So he ate till he was full and drank strong wine, seven goblets. He became merry, his heart exulted and his face shone. He rubbed down the matted hair of his body and anointed himself with oil. Enkidu had become a man; but when he had put on man's clothing he appeared like a bridegroom. He took arms to hunt the lion so that the shepherds could rest at night. He caught wolves and lions and the herdsmen lay down in peace; for Enkidu was their watchman, that strong man who had no rival.

He was merry living with the shepherds, till one day lifting his eyes he saw a man approaching. He said to the harlot, "Woman, fetch that man here. Why has he come? I wish to know his name." She went and called the man saying, "Sir, where are you going on this weary journey?" The man answered, saying to Enkidu, "Gilgamesh has gone into the marriage-house and shut out the people. He does strange things in Uruk, the city of great streets. At the roll of the drum work begins for the men, and work for the women. Gilgamesh the king is about to celebrate marriage with the Queen of Love, and he still demands to be first with the bride, the king to be first and the husband to follow, for that was ordained by the gods from his birth, from the time the umbilical cord was cut. But now the drums roll for the choice of the bride and the city groans." At these words Enkidu turned white in the face. "I will go to the place where Gilgamesh lords it over the people, I will challenge him boldly, and I will cry aloud in Uruk, 'I have come to change the old order, for I am the strongest here.' "

Now Enkidu strode in front and the woman followed behind. He entered Uruk, that great market, and all the folk thronged round him where he stood in the street in strong-walled Uruk. The people jostled; speaking of him they said, "He is the spit of Gilgamesh." "He is shorter." "He is bigger of bone." "This is the one who was reared on the milk of wild beasts. His is the greatest strength." The men rejoiced: "Now Gilgamesh has met his match. This great one, this hero whose beauty is like a god, he is a match even for Gilgamesh."

In Uruk the bridal bed was made, fit for the goddess of love. The bride waited for the bridegroom, but in the night Gilgamesh got up and came to the house. Then Enkidu stepped out, he stood in the street and blocked the way. Mighty Gilgamesh came on and Enkidu met him at the gate. He put out his foot and prevented Gilgamesh from entering the house, so they grappled, holding each other like bulls. They broke the doorposts and the walls shook, they snorted like bulls locked together. They shattered the doorposts and the walls shook. Gilgamesh bent his knee with his foot planted on the ground and with a turn Enkidu was thrown. Then immediately his fury died. When Enkidu was thrown he said to Gilgamesh,

"There is not another like you in the world. Ninsun, who is as strong as a wild ox in the byre, she was the mother who bore you, and now you are raised above all men, and Enlil has given you the kingship, for your strength surpasses the strength of men." So Enkidu and Gilgamesh embraced and their friendship was sealed.

2

The Forest Journey

Enlil of the mountain, the father of the gods, had decreed the destiny of Gilgamesh. So Gilgamesh dreamed and Enkidu said, "The meaning of the dream is this. The father of the gods has given you kingship, such is your destiny, everlasting life is not your destiny. Because of this do not be sad at heart, do not be grieved or oppressed. He has given you power to bind and to loose, to be the darkness and the light of mankind. He has given you unexampled supremacy over the people, victory in battle from which no fugitive returns, in forays and assaults from which there is no going back. But do not abuse this power, deal justly with your servants in the palace, deal justly before Shamash."

The eyes of Enkidu were full of tears and his heart was sick. He sighed bitterly and Gilgamesh met his eye and said, "My friend, why do you sigh so bitterly?" But Enkidu opened his mouth and said, "I am weak, my arms have lost their strength, the cry of sorrow sticks in my throat, I am oppressed by idleness." It was then that the lord Gilgamesh turned his thoughts to the Country of the Living; on the Land of Cedars the lord Gilgamesh reflected. He said to his servant Enkidu, "I have not established my name stamped on bricks as my destiny decreed; therefore I will go to the country where the cedar is felled. I will set tip my name in the place where the names of famous men are written, and where no man's name is written yet I will raise a monument to the gods. Because of the evil that is in the land, we will go to the forest and destroy the evil; for in the forest lives Humbaba whose name is 'Hugeness,' a ferocious giant." But Enkidu sighed bitterly and said, "When I went with the wild beasts ranging through the wilderness I discovered the forest; its length is ten thousand leagues in every direction. Enlil has appointed Humbaba to guard it and armed him in sevenfold terrors, terrible to all flesh is Humbaba. When he roars it is like the torrent of the storm, his breath is like fire, and his jaws are death itself. He guards the cedars so well that when the wild heifer stirs in the forest, though she is sixty leagues distant, he hears her. What man would willingly walk into that country and explore its depths? I tell you, weakness overpowers whoever goes near it: it is not an equal struggle when one fights with Humbaba; he is a great warrior, a battering-ram. Gilgamesh, the watchman of the forest never sleeps."

Gilgamesh replied: "Where is the man who can clamber to heaven? Only the gods live for ever with glorious Shamash, but as for us men, our days are numbered, our occupations are a breath of wind. How is this, already you are afraid! I will go first although I am your lord, and you may safely call out, 'Forward, there is nothing to fear!' Then if I fall I leave behind me a name that endures; men will say of me, 'Gilgamesh has Men in fight with ferocious Humbaba.' Long after, the child has been born in my house, they will say it, and remember." Enkidu spoke again to Gilgamesh, "O my lord, if you will enter that country, go first to the hero Shamash, tell the Sun God, for the land is his. The country where the cedar is cut belongs to Shamash."

Gilgamesh took up a kid, white without spot, and a brown one with it; he held them against his breast, and he carried them into the presence of the sun. He took in his hand his silver sceptre and he said to glorious Shamash, "I am going to that country, O Shamash, I am going; my hands supplicate, so let it be well with my soul and bring me back to the quay of Uruk. Grant, I beseech, your protection, and let the omen be good." Glorious Shamash answered, "Gilgamesh, you are strong, but what is the Country of the Living to you?"

"O Shamash, hear me, hear me, Shamash, let my voice be heard. Here in the city man dies oppressed at heart, man perishes with despair in his heart. I have looked over the wall and I see the bodies floating on the river, and that will be my lot also. Indeed I know it is so, for whoever is tallest among men cannot reach the heavens, and the greatest cannot encompass the earth. Therefore I would enter that country: because I have not established my name stamped on brick as my destiny decreed, I will go to the country where the cedar is cut. I will set up my name where the names of famous men are written; and where no man's name is written I will raise a monument to the gods." The tears ran down his face and he said,

"Alas, it is a long journey that I must take to the Land of Humbaba. If this enterprise is not to be accomplished, why did you move me, Shamash, with the restless desire to perform it? How can I succeed if you will not succour me? If I die in that country I will die without rancour, but if I return I will make a glorious offering of gifts and of praise to Shamash."

So Shamash accepted the sacrifice of his tears; like the compassionate man he showed him mercy. He appointed strong allies for Gilgamesh, sons of one mother, and stationed them in the mountain caves. The great winds he appointed: the north wind, the whirlwind, the storm and the icy wind, the tempest and the scorching wind. Like vipers, like dragons, like a scorching fire, like a serpent that freezes the heart, a destroying flood and the lightning's fork, such were they and Gilgamesh rejoiced.

He went to the forge and said, "I will give orders to the armourers; they shall cast us our weapons while we watch them." So they gave orders to the armourers and the craftsmen sat down in conference. They went into the groves of the plain and cut willow and box-wood; they cast for them axes of nine score pounds, and great swords they cast with blades of six score pounds each one, with pommels and hilts of thirty pounds. They cast for Gilgamesh the axe "Might of Heroes" and the bow of Anshan; and Gilgamesh was armed and Enkidu; and the weight of the arms they carried was thirty score pounds.

The people collected and the counsellors in the streets and in the market-place of Uruk; they came through the gate of seven bolts and Gilgamesh spoke to them in the market-place: "I, Gilgamesh, go to see that creature of whom such things are spoken, the rumour of whose name fills the world. I will conquer him in his cedar wood and show the strength of the sons of Uruk, all the world shall know of it. I am committed to this enterprise: to climb the mountain, to cut down the cedar, and leave behind me an enduring name." The counsellors of Uruk, the great market, answered him, "Gilgamesh, you are young, your courage carries you too far, you cannot know what this enterprise means which you plan. We have heard that Humbaba is not like men who die, his weapons are such that none can stand against them; the forest stretches for ten thousand leagues in every direction; who would willingly go down to explore its depths? As for Humbaba, when he roars it is like the torrent of the storm, his breath is like fire and his jaws are death itself. Why do you crave to do this thing, Gilgamesh? It is no equal struggle when one fights with Humbaba, that battering-ram."

When he heard these words of the counsellors Gilgamesh looked at his friend and laughed, "How shall I answer them; shall I say I am afraid of Humbaba, I will sit at home all the rest of my days?" Then Gilgamesh opened his mouth again and said to Enkidu, "My friend, let us go to the Great Palace, to Egalmah, and stand before Ninsun the queen. Ninsun is wise with deep knowledge, she will give us counsel for the road we must go." They took each other by the hand as they went to Egalmah, and they went to Ninsun the great queen. Gilgamesh approached, he entered the palace and spoke to Ninsun. "Ninsun, will you listen to me; I have a long journey to go, to the Land of Humbaba, I must travel an unknown road and fight a strange battle. From the day I go until I return, till I reach the cedar forest and destroy the evil which Shamash abhors, pray for me to Shamash."

Ninsun went into her room, she put on a dress becoming to her body, she put on jewels to make her breast beautiful, she placed a tiara on her head and her skirts swept the ground. Then she went up to the altar of the Sun, standing upon the roof of the palace; she burnt incense and lifted her arms to Shamash as the smoke ascended: "O Shamash, why did you give this restless heart, to Gilgamesh, my son; why did you give it? You have moved him and now he sets out on a long journey to the Land of Humbaba to travel an unknown road and fight a strange battle. Therefore from the day that he goes till the day he returns, until he reaches the cedar forest, until he kills Humbaba and destroys the evil thing which you, Shamash, abhor, do not forget him; but let the dawn, Aya, your dear bride, remind you always, and when day is done give him to the watchman of the night to keep him from harm." Then Ninsun the mother of Gilgamesh extinguished the incense, and she called to Enkidu with this exhortation: "Strong Enkidu, you are not the child of my body, but I will receive you as my adopted son; you are my other child like the foundlings they bring to the temple. Serve Gilgamesh as a foundling serves the temple and the priestess who reared him. In the presence of my women, my votaries and hierophants, I declare it." Then she placed the amulet for a pledge round his neck, and she said to him, "I entrust my son to you; bring him back to me safely."

And now they brought to them the weapons, they put in their hands the great swords in their golden scabbards, and the bow and the quiver. Gilgamesh took the axe, he slung the quiver from his shoulder, and the bow of Anshan, and buckled the sword to his belt; and so they were armed and ready for the journey. Now all the people came and pressed on them and said, "When will you return to the city?" The counsellors blessed Gilgamesh and warned him, "Do not trust too much in your own strength, be watchful, restrain your blows at first. The one who goes in front protects his companion; the good guide who knows the way guards his friend. Let Enkidu lead the way, he knows the road to the forest, he has seen Humbaba and is experienced in battles; let him press first into the passes, let him be watchful and look to himself. Let Enkidu protect his friend, and guard his companion, and bring him safe through the pitfalls of the road. We, the counsellors of Uruk entrust our king to you, O Enkidu; bring him back safely to us." Again to Gilgamesh they said, "May Shamash give you your heart's desire, may he let you see with your eyes the thing accomplished which your lips have spoken; may he open a path for you where it is blocked, and a road for your feet to tread. May he open the mountains for your crossing, and may the nighttime bring you the blessings of night, and Lugulbanda, your guardian god, stand beside you for victory. May you have victory in the battle as though you fought with a child. Wash your feet in the river of Humbaba to which you are journeying; in the evening dig a well, and let there always be pure water in your water-skin. Offer cold water to Shamash and do not forget Lugulbanda."

Then Enkidu opened his mouth and said, "Forward, there is nothing to fear. Follow me, for I know the place where Humbaba lives and the paths where he walks. Let the counsellors go back. Here is no cause for fear." When the counsellors heard this they sped the hero on his way. "Go, Gilgamesh, may your guardian god protect you on the road and bring you safely back to the quay of Uruk."

After twenty leagues they broke their fast; after another thirty leagues they stopped for the night. Fifty leagues they walked in one day; in three days they had walked as much as a journey of a month and two weeks. They crossed seven mountains before they came to the gate of the forest. Then Enkidu called out to Gilgamesh, "Do not go down into the forest; when I opened the gate my hand lost its strength." Gilgamesh answered him, "Dear friend, do not speak like a coward. Have we got the better of so many dangers and travelled so far, to turn back at last? You, who are tried in wars and battles, hold close to me now and you will feel no fear of death; keep beside me and your weakness will pass, the trembling will leave your hand. Would my friend rather stay behind? No, we will go down together into the heart of the forest. Let your courage be roused by the battle to come; forget death and follow me, a man resolute in action, but one who is not foolhardy. When two go together each will protect himself and shield his companion, and if they fall they leave an enduring name."

Together they went down into the forest and they came to the green mountain. There they stood still, they were struck dumb; they stood still and gazed at the forest. They saw the height of the cedar, they saw the way into the forest and the track where Humbaba was used to walk. The way was broad and the going was good. They gazed at the mountain of cedars, the dwelling-place of the gods and the throne of Ishtar. The hugeness of the cedar rose in front of the mountain, its shade was beautiful, full of comfort; mountain and glade were green with brushwood.

There Gilgamesh dug a well before the setting sun. He went up the mountain and poured out fine meal on the ground and said, "O mountain, dwelling of the gods, bring me a favourable dream." Then they took each other by the hand and lay down to sleep; and sleep that flows from the night lapped over them. Gilgamesh dreamed, and at midnight sleep left him, and he told his dream to his friend. "Enkidu, what was it that woke me if you did not? My friend, I have dreamed a dream. Get up, look at the mountain precipice. The sleep that the gods sent me is broken. Ah, my friend, what a dream I have had! Terror and confusion; I seized hold of a wild bull in the wilderness. It bellowed and beat up the dust till the whole sky was dark, my arm was seized and my tongue bitten. I fell back on my knee; then someone refreshed me with water from his water-skin."

Enkidu said, "Dear friend, the god to whom we are travelling is no wild bull, though his form is mysterious. That wild bull which you saw is Shamash the Protector; in our moment of peril he will take our hands. The one who gave water from his water-skin, that is your own god who cares for your good name, your Lugulbanda. United with him, together we will accomplish a work the fame of which will never die."

Gilgamesh said, I dreamed again. We stood in a deep gorge of the mountain, and beside it we two were like the smallest of swamp flies; and suddenly the mountain fell, it struck me and caught my feet from under me. Then came an intolerable light blazing out, and in it was one whose grace and whose beauty were greater than the beauty of this world. He pulled me out from under the mountain, he gave me water to drink and my heart was comforted, and he set my feet on the ground."

Then Enkidu the child of the plains said, "Let us go down from the mountain and talk this thing over together." He said to Gilgamesh the young god, "Your dream is good, your dream is excellent, the mountain which you saw is Humbaba. Now, surely, we will seize and kill him, and throw his body down as the mountain fell on the plain."

The next day after twenty leagues they broke their fast, and after another thirty they stopped for the night. They dug a well before the sun had set and Gilgamesh ascended the mountain. He poured out fine meal on the ground and said, "O mountain, dwelling of the gods, send a dream for Enkidu, make him a favourable dream." The mountain fashioned a dream for Enkidu; it came, an ominous dream; a cold shower passed over him, it caused him to cower like the mountain barley under a storm of rain. But Gilgamesh sat with his chin on his knees till the sleep which flows over all mankind lapped over him. Then, at midnight, sleep left him; he got up and said to his friend, "Did you call me, or why did I wake? Did you touch me, or why am I terrified? Did not some god pass by, for my limbs are numb with fear? My friend, I saw a third dream and this dream was altogether frightful. The heavens roared and the earth roared again, daylight failed and darkness fell, lightning flashed, fire blazed out, the clouds lowered, they rained down death. Then the brightness departed, the fire went out, and all was turned to ashes fallen about us. Let us go down from the mountain and talk this over, and consider what we should do."

When they had come down from the mountain Gilgamesh seized the axe in his hand: he felled the cedar. When Humbaba heard the noise far off he was enraged; he cried out, "Who is this that has violated my woods and cut down my cedar?" But glorious Shamash called to them out of heaven, "Go forward, do not be afraid." But now Gilgamesh was overcome by weakness, for sleep had seized him suddenly, a profound sleep held him; he lay on the ground, stretched out speechless, as though in a dream. When Enkidu touched him he did not rise, when he spoke to him he did not reply. "O Gilgamesh, Lord of the plain of Kullab, the world grows dark, the shadows have spread over it, now is the glimmer of dusk. Shamash has departed, his bright head is quenched in the bosom of his mother Ningal. O Gilgamesh, how long will you lie like this, asleep? Never let the mother who gave you birth be forced in mourning into the city square."

At length Gilgamesh heard him; he put on his breastplate, "The Voice of Heroes," of thirty shekels' weight; he put it on as though it had been a light garment that he carried, and it covered him altogether. He straddled the earth like a bull that snuffs the ground and his teeth were clenched. "By the life of my mother Ninsun who gave me birth, and by the life of my father, divine Lugulbanda, let me live to be the wonder of my mother, as when she nursed me on her lap." A second time he said to him, "By the life of Ninsun my mother who gave me birth, and by the life of my father, divine Lugulbanda, until we have fought this man, if man he is, this god, if god he is, the way that I took to the Country of the Living will not turn back to the city."

Then Enkidu, the faithful companion, pleaded, answering him, "O my lord, you do not know this monster and that is the reason you are not afraid. I who know him, I am terrified. His teeth are dragon's fangs, his countenance is like a lion, his charge is the rushing of the flood, with his look he crushes alike the trees of the forest and reeds in the swamp. O my Lord, you may go on if you choose into this land, but I will go back to the city. I will tell the lady your mother all your glorious deeds till she shouts for joy: and then I will tell the death that followed till she weeps for bitterness." But Gilgamesh said, "Immolation and sacrifice are not yet for me, the boat of the dead shall not go down, nor the three-ply cloth be cut for my shrouding. Not yet will my people be desolate, nor the pyre be fit in my house and my dwelling burnt on the fire. Today, give me your aid and you shall have mine: what then can go amiss with us two? All living creatures born of the flesh shall sit at last in the boat of the West, and when it sinks, when the boat of Magilum sinks, they are gone; but we shall go forward and fix our eyes on this monster. If your heart is fearful throw away fear; if there is terror in it throw away terror. Take your axe in your hand and attack. He who leaves the fight unfinished is not at peace."

Humbaba came out from his strong house of cedar. Then Enkidu called out, "O Gilgamesh, remember now your boasts in Uruk. Forward, attack, son of Uruk, there is nothing to fear." When he heard these words his courage rallied; he answered, "Make haste, close in, if the watchman is there do not let him escape to the woods where he will vanish. He has put on the first of his seven splendours but not yet the other six, let us trap him before he is armed." Like a raging wild bull he snuffed the ground; the watchman of the woods turned full of threatenings, he cried out. Humbaba came from his strong house of cedar. He nodded his head and shook it, menacing Gilgamesh; and on him he fastened his eye, the eye of death. Then Gilgamesh called to Shamash and his tears were flowing, "O glorious Shamash, I have followed the road you commanded but now if you send no succour how shall I escape?" Glorious Shamash heard his prayer and he summoned the great wind, the north wind, the whirlwind, the storm and the icy wind, the tempest and the scorching wind; they came like dragons, like a scorching fire, like a serpent that freezes the heart, a destroying flood and the lightning's fork. The eight winds rose up against Humbaba, they beat against his eyes; he was gripped, unable to go forward or back. Gilgamesh shouted, "By the life of Ninsun my mother and divine Lugulbanda my father, in the Country of the Living, in this Land I have discovered your dwelling; my weak arms and my small weapons I have brought to this Land against you, and now I will enter your house."

So he felled the first cedar and they cut the branches and laid them at the foot of the mountain. At the first stroke Humbaba blazed out, but still they advanced. They felled seven cedars and cut and bound the branches and laid them at the foot of the mountain, and seven times Humbaba loosed his glory on them. As the seventh blaze died out they reached his lair. He slapped his thigh in scorn. He approached like a noble wild bull roped on the mountain, a warrior whose elbows are bound together. The tears started to his eyes and he was pale, "Gilgamesh, let me speak. I have never known a mother, no, nor a father who reared me. I was born of the mountain, he reared me, and Enlil made me the keeper of this forest. Let me go free, Gilgamesh, and I will be your servant, you shall be my lord; all the trees of the forest that I tended on the mountain shall be yours. I will cut them down and build you a palace." He took him by the hand and led him to his house, so that the heart of Gilgamesh was moved with compassion. He swore by the heavenly life, by the earthly life, by the underworld itself: "O Enkidu, should not the snared bird return to its nest and the captive man return to his mother's arms?" Enkidu answered, "The strongest of men will fall to fate if he has no judgement. Namtar, the evil fate that knows no distinction between men, will devour him. If the snared bird returns to its nest, if the captive man returns to his mother's arms, then you my friend will never return to the city where the mother is waiting who gave you birth. He will bar the mountain road against you, and make the pathways impassable."

Humbaba said, "Enkidu, what you have spoken is evil: you, a hireling, dependent for your bread! In envy and for fear of a rival you have spoken evil words." Enkidu said, "Do not listen, Gilgamesh: this Humbaba must die. Kill Humbaba first and his servants after." But Gilgamesh said, "If we touch him the blaze and the glory of light will be put out in confusion, the glory and glamour will vanish, its rays will be quenched." Enkidu said to Gilgamesh, "Not so, my friend. First entrap the bird, and where shall the chicks run then? Afterwards we can search out the glory and the glamour, when the chicks run distracted through the grass."

Gilgamesh listened to the word of his companion, he took the axe in his hand, he drew the sword from his belt, and he struck Humbaba with a thrust of the sword to the neck, and Enkidu his comrade struck the second blow. At the third blow Humbaba fell. Then there followed confusion for this was the guardian of the forest whom they had felled to the ground. For as far as two leagues the cedars shivered when Enkidu felled the watcher of the forest, he at whose voice Hermon and Lebanon used to tremble. Now the mountains were moved and all the hills, for the guardian of the forest was killed. They attacked the cedars, the seven splendours of Humbaba were extinguished. So they pressed on into the forest bearing the sword of eight talents. They uncovered the sacred dwellings of the Anunnaki and while Gilgamesh felled the first of the trees of the forest Enkidu cleared their roots as far as the banks of Euphrates. They set Humbaba before the gods, before Enlil; they kissed the ground and dropped the shroud and set the head before him. When he saw the head of Humbaba, Enlil raged at them. "Why did you do this thing? From henceforth may the fire be on your faces, may it eat the bread that you eat, may it drink where you drink." Then Enlil took again the blaze and the seven splendours that had been Humbaba's: he gave the first to the river, and he gave to the lion, to the stone of execration, to the mountain and to the dreaded daughter of the Queen of Hell.

O Gilgamesh, king and conqueror of the dreadful blaze; wild bull who plunders the mountain, who crosses the sea, glory to him, and from the brave the greater glory is Enki's!

3

Ishtar and Gilgamesh, and the Death of Enkidu

Gilgamesh washed out his long locks and cleaned his weapons; he flung back his hair from his shoulders; he threw off his stained clothes and changed them for new. He put on his royal robes and made them fast. When Gilgamesh had put on the crown, glorious Ishtar lifted her eyes, seeing the beauty of Gilgamesh.

She said, "Come to me Gilgamesh, and be my bridegroom; grant me seed of your body, let me be your bride and you shall be my husband. I will harness for you a chariot of lapis lazuli and of gold, with wheels of gold and horns of copper; and you shall have mighty demons of the storm for draft-mules. When you enter our house in the fragrance of cedar-wood, threshold and throne will kiss your feet. Kings, rulers, and princes will bow down before you; they shall bring you tribute from the mountains and the plain. Your ewes shall drop twins and your goats triplets; your pack-ass shall outrun mules; your oxen shall have no rivals, and your chariot horses shall be famous far-off for their swiftness.

Gilgamesh opened his mouth and answered glorious Ishtar, "If I take you in marriage, what gifts can I give in return? What ointments and clothing for your body? I would gladly give you bread and all sorts of food fit for a god. I would give you wine to drink fit for a queen. I would pour out barley to stuff your granary; but as for making you my wife—that I will not. How would it go with me? Your lovers have found you like a brazier which smoulders in the cold, a backdoor which keeps out neither squall of wind nor storm, a castle which crushes the garrison, pitch that blackens the bearer, a water-skin that chafes the carrier, a stone which falls from the parapet, a battering-ram turned back from the enemy, a sandal that trips the wearer. Which of your lovers did you ever love for ever? What shepherd of yours has pleased you for all time? Listen to me while I tell the tale of your lovers. There was Tammuz, the lover of your youth, for him you decreed wailing, year after year. You loved the many-coloured roller, but still you struck and broke his wing; now in the grove he sits and cries, "kappi, kappi, my wing, my wing." You have loved the lion tremendous in strength: seven pits you dug for him, and seven. You have loved the stallion magnificent in battle, and for him you decreed whip and spur and a thong, to gallop seven leagues by force and to muddy the water before he drinks; and for his mother Silili lamentations. You have loved the shepherd of the flock; he made meal-cake for you day after day, he killed kids for your sake. You struck and turned him into a wolf; now his own herd-boys chase him away, his own hounds worry his flanks. And did you not love Ishullanu, the gardener of your father's palm-grove? He brought you baskets filled with dates without end; every day he loaded your table. Then you turned your eyes on him and said, 'Dearest Ishullanu, come here to me, let us enjoy your manhood, come forward and take me, I am yours.' Ishullanu answered, 'What are you asking from me? My mother has baked and I have eaten; why should I come to such as you for food that is tainted and rotten? For when was a screen of rushes sufficient protection from frosts?' But when you had heard his answer you struck him. He was changed to a blind mole deep in the earth, one whose desire is always beyond his reach. And if you and I should be lovers, should not I be served in the same fashion as all these others whom you loved once?"

When Ishtar heard this she fell into a bitter rage, she went up to high heaven. Her tears poured down in front of her father Anti, and Antum her mother. She said, "My father, Gilgamesh has heaped insults on me, he has told over all my abominable behaviour, my foul and hideous acts." Anu opened his mouth and said, "Are you a father of gods? Did not you quarrel with Gilgamesh the king, so now he has related your abominable behaviour, your foul and hideous acts?"

Ishtar opened her mouth and said again, "My father, give me the Bull of Heaven to destroy Gilgamesh. Fill Gilgamesh, I say, with arrogance to his destruction; but if you refuse to give me the Bull of Heaven I will break in the doors of hell and smash the bolts; there will be confusion of people, those above with those from the lower depths. I shall bring up the dead to eat food like the living; and the hosts of dead will outnumber the living." Anu said to great Ishtar, "If I do what you desire there will be seven years of drought throughout Uruk when corn will be seedless husks. Have you saved grain enough for the people and grass for the cattle?" Ishtar replied, "I have saved grain for the people, grass for the cattle; for seven years of seedless husks there is grain and there is grass enough."

When Anu heard what Ishtar had said he gave her the Bull of Heaven to lead by the halter down to Uruk. When they reached the gates of Uruk the Bull went to the river; with his first snort cracks opened in the earth and a hundred young men fell down to death. With his second snort cracks opened and two hundred fell down to death. With his third snort cracks opened, Enkidu doubled over but instantly recovered, he dodged aside and leapt on the Bull and seized it by the horns. The Bull of Heaven foamed in his face, it brushed him with the thick of its tail. Enkidu cried to Gilgamesh, "My friend, we boasted that we would leave enduring names behind us. Now thrust in your sword between the nape and the horns." So Gilgamesh followed the Bull, he seized the thick of its tail, he thrust the sword between the nape and the horns and slew the Bull. When they had killed the Bull of Heaven they cut out its heart and gave it to Shamash, and the brothers rested.

But Ishtar rose up and mounted the great wall of Uruk; she sprang on to the tower and uttered a curse: "Woe to Gilgamesh, for he has scorned me in killing the Bull of Heaven." When Enkidu heard these words he tore out the Bull's right thigh and tossed it in her face saying, "If I could lay my hands on you, it is this I should do to you, and lash the entrails to your side." Then Ishtar called together her people, the dancing and singing girls, the prostitutes of the temple, the courtesans. Over the thigh of the Bull of Heaven she set up lamentation.

But Gilgamesh called the smiths and the armourers, all of them together. They admired the immensity of the horns. They were plated with lapis lazuli two fingers thick. They were thirty pounds each in weight, and their capacity in oil was six measures, which he gave to his guardian god, Lugulbanda. But he carried the horns into the palace and hung them on the wall. Then they washed their hands in Euphrates, they embraced each other and went away. They drove through the streets of Uruk where the heroes were gathered to see them, and Gilgamesh called to the singing girls, "Who is most glorious of the heroes, who is most eminent among men?" "Gilgamesh is the most glorious of heroes, Gilgamesh is most eminent among men." And now there was feasting, and celebrations and joy in the palace, till the heroes lay down saying, "Now we will rest for the night."

When the daylight came Enkidu got tip and cried to Gilgamesh, "O my brother, such a dream I had last night. Anu, Enlil, Ea and heavenly Shamash took counsel together, and Anu said to Enlil, 'Because they have killed the Bull of Heaven, and because they have killed Humbaba who guarded the Cedar Mountain one of the two must die.' Then glorious Shamash answered the hero Enlil, 'It was by your command they killed the Bull of Heaven, and killed Humbaba, and must Enkidu die although innocent?' Enlil flung round in rage at glorious Shamash, 'You dare to say this, you who went about with them every day like one of themselves!' "

So Enkidu lay stretched out before Gilgamesh; his tears ran down in streams and he said to Gilgamesh, "O my brother, so dear as you are to me, brother, yet they will take me from you." Again he said, I must sit down on the threshold of the dead and never again will I see my dear brother with my eyes."

While Enkidu lay alone in his sickness he cursed the gate as though it was living flesh, "You there, wood of the gate, dull and insensible, witless, I searched for you over twenty leagues until I saw the towering cedar. There is no wood like you in our land. Seventy-two cubits high and twenty-four wide, the pivot and the ferrule and the jambs are perfect. A master craftsman from Nippur has made you; but O, if I had known the conclusion! If I had known that this was all the good that would come of it, I would have raised the axe and split you into little pieces and set up here a gate of wattle instead. Ah, if only some future king had brought you here, or some god had fashioned you. Let him obliterate my name and write his own, and the curse fall on him instead of on Enkidu."

With the first brightening of dawn Enkidu raised his head and wept before the Sun God, in the brilliance of the sunlight his tears streamed down. "Sun God, I beseech you, about that vile Trapper, that Trapper of nothing because of whom I was to catch less than my comrade; let him catch least, make his game scarce, make him feeble, taking the smaller of every share, let his quarry escape from his nets."

When he had cursed the Trapper to his heart's content he turned on the harlot. He was roused to curse her also. "As for you, woman, with a great curse I curse you! I will promise you a destiny to all eternity. My curse shall come on you soon and sudden. You shall be without a roof for your commerce, for you shall not keep house with other girls in the tavern, but do your business in places fouled by the vomit of the drunkard. Your hire will be potter's earth, your thievings will be flung into the hovel, you will sit at the cross-roads in the dust of the potter's quarter, you will make your bed on the dunghill at night, and by day take your stand in the wall's shadow. Brambles and thorns will tear your feet, the drunk and the dry will strike your cheek and your mouth will ache. Let you be stripped of your purple dyes, for I too once in the wilderness with my wife had all the treasure I wished."

When Shamash heard the words of Enkidu he called to him from heaven: "Enkidu, why are you cursing the woman, the mistress who taught you to eat bread fit for gods and drink wine of kings? She who put upon you a magnificent garment, did she not give you glorious Gilgamesh for your companion, and has not Gilgamesh, your own brother, made you rest on a royal bed and recline on a couch at his left hand? He has made the princes of the earth kiss your feet, and now all the people of Uruk lament and wail over you. When you are dead he will let his hair grow long for your sake, he will wear a lion's pelt and wander through the desert."

When Enkidu heard glorious Shamash his angry heart grew quiet, he called back the curse and said, "Woman, I promise you another destiny. The mouth which cursed you shall bless you! Kings, princes and nobles shall adore you. On your account a man though twelve miles off will clap his hand to his thigh and his hair will twitch. For you he will undo his belt and open his treasure and you shall have your desire; lapis lazuli, gold and carnelian from the heap in the treasury. A ring for your hand and a robe shall be yours. The priest will lead you into the presence of the gods. On your account a wife, a mother of seven, was forsaken."

As Enkidu slept alone in his sickness, in bitterness of spirit he poured out his heart to his friend. "It was I who cut down the cedar, I who levelled the forest, I who slew Humbaba and now see what has become of me. Listen, my friend, this is the dream I dreamed last night. The heavens roared, and earth rumbled back an answer; between them stood I before an awful being, the sombre-faced man-bird; he had directed on me his purpose. His was a vampire face, his foot was a lion's foot, his hand was an eagle's talon. He fell on me and his claws were in my hair, he held me fast and I smothered; then he transformed me so that my arms became wings covered with feathers. He turned his stare towards me, and he led me away to the palace of Irkalla, the Queen of Darkness, to the house from which none who enters ever returns, down the road from which there is no coming back.

"There is the house whose people sit in darkness; dust is their food and clay their meat. They are clothed like birds with wings for covering, they see no light, they sit in darkness. I entered the house of dust and I saw the kings of the earth, their crowns put away for ever; rulers and princes, all those who once wore kingly crowns and ruled the world in the days of old. They who had stood in the place of the gods like Anu and Enlil, stood now like servants to fetch baked meats in the house of dust, to carry cooked meat and cold water from the water-skin. In the house of dust which I entered were high priests and acolytes, priests of the incantation and of ecstasy; there were servers of the temple, and there was Etana, that king of Kish whom the eagle carried to heaven in the days of old. I saw also Samuqan, god of cattle, and there was Ereshkigal the Queen of the Underworld; and Belit-Sheri squatted in front of her, she who is recorder of the gods and keeps the book of death. She held a tablet from which she read. She raised her head, she saw me and spoke: 'Who has brought this one here?' Then I awoke like a man drained of blood who wanders alone in a waste of rushes; like one whom the bailiff has seized and his heart pounds with terror."

Gilgamesh had peeled off his clothes, he listened to his words and wept quick tears, Gilgamesh listened and his tears flowed. He opened his mouth and spoke to Enkidu: "Who is there in strong-walled Uruk who has wisdom like this? Strange things have been spoken, why does your heart speak strangely? The dream was marvellous but the terror was great; we must treasure the dream whatever the terror; for the dream has shown that misery comes at last to the healthy man, the end of life is sorrow." And Gilgamesh lamented, "Now I will pray to the great gods, for my friend had an ominous dream."

This day on which Enkidu dreamed came to an end and he lay stricken with sickness. One whole day he lay on his bed and his suffering increased. He said to Gilgamesh, the friend on whose account he had left the wilderness, "Once I ran for you, for the water of life, and I now have nothing." A second day he lay on his bed and Gilgamesh watched over him but the sickness increased. A third day he lay on his bed, he called out to Gilgamesh, rousing him up. Now he was weak and his eyes were blind with weeping. Ten days he lay and his suffering increased, eleven and twelve days he lay on his bed of pain. Then he called to Gilgamesh, "My friend, the great goddess cursed me and I must die in shame. I shall not die like a man fallen in battle; I feared to fall, but happy is the man who falls in the battle, for I must die in shame." And Gilgamesh wept over Enkidu. With the first light of dawn he raised his voice and said to the counsellors of Uruk:

Hear me, great ones of Uruk,
I weep for Enkidu, my friend,
Bitterly moaning like a woman mourning
I weep for my brother.
O Enkidu, my brother,
You were the axe at my side,
My hand's strength, the sword in my belt,
The shield before me,
A glorious robe, my fairest ornament;
An evil Fate has robbed me.
The wild ass and the gazelle

That were father and mother,
All long-tailed creatures that nourished you
Weep for you,
All the wild things of the plain and pastures;
The paths that you loved in the forest of cedars
Night and day murmur.
Let the great ones of strong-walled Uruk
Weep for you;
Let the finger of blessing
Be stretched out in mourning;
Enkidu, young brother. Hark,
There is an echo through all the country
Like a mother mourning.
Weep all the paths where we walked together;
And the beasts we hunted, the bear and hyena,
Tiger and panther, leopard and lion,
The stag and the ibex, the bull and the doe.
The river along whose banks we used to walk,
Weeps for you,
Ula of Elam and dear Euphrates
Where once we drew water for the water-skins.
The mountain we climbed where we slew the Watchman,
Weeps for you.
The warriors of strong-walled Uruk
Where the Bull of Heaven was killed,
Weep for you.
All the people of Eridu
Weep for you Enkidu.
Those who brought grain for your eating
Mourn for you now;
Who rubbed oil on your back
Mourn for you now;
Who poured beer for your drinking
Mourn for you now.
The harlot who anointed you with fragrant ointment
Laments for you now;
The women of the palace, who brought you a wife,
A chosen ring of good advice,
Lament for you now.
And the young men your brothers
As though they were women
Go long-haired in mourning.
What is this sleep which holds you now?
You are lost in the dark and cannot hear me.

He touched his heart but it did not beat, nor did he lift his eyes again. When Gilgamesh touched his heart it did not beat. So Gilgamesh laid a veil, as one veils the bride, over his friend. He began to rage like a lion, like a lioness robbed of her whelps. This way and that he paced round the bed, he tore out his hair and strewed it around. He dragged off his splendid robes and flung them down as though they were abominations.

In the first light of dawn Gilgamesh cried out, "I made you rest on a royal bed, you reclined on a couch at my left hand, the princes of the earth kissed your feet. I will cause all the people of Uruk to weep over you and raise the dirge of the dead. The joyful people will stoop with sorrow; and when you have gone to the earth I will let my hair grow long for your sake, I will wander through the wilderness in the skin of a lion." The next day also, in the first light, Gilgamesh lamented; seven days and seven nights he wept for Enkidu, until the worm fastened on him. Only then he gave him up to the earth, for the Anunnaki, the judges, had seized him.

Then Gilgamesh issued a proclamation through the land, he summoned them all, the coppersmiths, the goldsmiths, the stone-workers, and commanded them, "Make a statue of my friend." The statue was fashioned with a great weight of lapis lazuli for the breast and of gold for the body. A table of hard-wood was set out, and on it a bowl of carnelian filled with honey, and a bowl of lapis lazuli filled with butter. These he exposed and offered to the Sun; and weeping he went away.

4

The Search for Everlasting Life

Bitterly Gilgamesh wept for his friend Enkidu; he wandered over the wilderness as a hunter, he roamed over the plains; in his bitterness he cried, "How can I rest, how can I be at peace? Despair is in my heart. What my brother is now, that shall I be when I am dead. Because I am afraid of death I will go as best I can to find Utnapishtim whom they call the Faraway, for he has entered the assembly of the gods." So Gilgamesh travelled over the wilderness, he wandered over the grasslands, a long journey, in search of Utnapishtim, whom the gods took after the deluge; and they set him to live in the land of Dilmun, in the garden of the sun; and to him alone of men they gave everlasting life.

At night when he came to the mountain passes Gilgamesh prayed: "in these mountain passes long ago I saw lions, I was afraid and I lifted my eyes to the moon; I prayed and my prayers went up to the gods, so now, O moon god Sin, protect me." When he had prayed he lay down to sleep, until he was woken from out of a dream. He saw the lions round him glorying in life; then he took his axe in his hand, he drew his sword from his belt, and he fell upon them like an arrow from the string, and struck and destroyed and scattered them.

So at length Gilgamesh came to Mashu, the great mountains about which he had heard many things, which guard the rising and the setting sun. Its twin peaks are as high as the wall of heaven and its pops reach down to the underworld. At its gate the Scorpions stand guard, half man and half dragon; their glory is terrifying, their store strikes death into men, their shimmering halo sweeps the mountains that guard the rising sun. When Gilgamesh saw them he shielded his eyes for the length of a moment only; then he took courage and approached. When they saw him so undismayed the Man-Scorpion called to his mate, "This one who comes to us now is flesh of the gods." The mate of the Man-Scorpion answered, "Two thirds is god but one third is man."

Then he called to the man Gilgamesh, he called to the child of the gods: "Why have you come so great a journey; for what have you travelled so far, crossing the dangerous waters; tell me the reason for your coming?" Gilgamesh answered, "For Enkidu; I loved him dearly, together we endured all kinds of hardships; on his account I have come, for the common lot of man has taken him. I have wept for him day and night, I would not give up his body for burial, I thought my friend would come back because of my weeping. Since he went, my life is nothing; that is why I have travelled here in search of Utnapishtim my father; for men say he has entered the assembly of the gods, and has found everlasting life. I have a desire to question him concerning the living and the dead." The Man-Scorpion opened his mouth and said, speaking to Gilgamesh, "No man born of woman has done what you have asked, no mortal man has gone into the mountain; the length of it is twelve leagues of darkness; in it there is no light, but the heart is oppressed with darkness. From the rising of the sun to the setting of the sun there is no light." Gilgamesh said, "Although I should go in sorrow and in pain, with sighing and with weeping, still I must go. Open the gate of the mountain." And the Man-Scorpion said, "Go, Gilgamesh, I permit you to pass through the mountain of Mashu and through the high ranges; may your feet carry you safely home. The gate of the mountain is open."

When Gilgamesh heard this he did as the Man-Scorpion had said, he followed the sun's road to his rising, through the mountain. When he had gone one league the darkness became thick around him, for there was no light, he could see nothing ahead and nothing behind him. After two leagues the darkness was thick and there was no light, he could see nothing ahead and nothing behind him. After three leagues the darkness was thick and there was no light, he could see nothing ahead and nothing behind him. After four leagues the darkness was thick and there was no light, he could see nothing ahead and nothing behind him. At the end of five leagues the darkness was thick and there was no light, he could see nothing ahead and nothing behind him. At the end of six leagues the darkness was thick and there was no light, he could see nothing ahead and nothing behind him. When he had gone seven leagues the darkness was thick and there was no light, he could see nothing ahead and nothing behind him. When he had gone eight leagues Gilgamesh gave a great cry, for the darkness was thick and he could see nothing ahead and nothing behind him. After nine leagues he felt the north wind on his face, but the darkness was thick and there was no light, he could see nothing ahead and nothing behind him. After ten leagues the end was near. After eleven leagues the dawn light appeared. At the end of twelve leagues the sun streamed out.

There was the garden of the gods; all round him stood bushes bearing gems. Seeing it he went down at once, for there was fruit of carnelian with the vine hanging from it, beautiful to look at; lapis lazuli leaves hung thick with fruit, sweet to see. For thorns and thistles there were haematite and rare stones, agate, and pearls from out of the sea. While Gilgamesh walked in the garden by the edge of the sea Shamash saw him, and he saw that he was dressed in the skins of animals and ate their flesh. He was distressed, and he spoke and said, "No mortal man has gone this way before, nor will, as long as the winds drive over the sea." And to Gilgamesh he said, "You will never find the life for which you are searching." Gilgamesh said to glorious Shamash, "Now that I have toiled and strayed so far over the wilderness, am I to sleep, and let the earth cover my head for ever? Let my eyes see the sun until they are dazzled with looking. Although I am no better than a dead man, still let me see the light of the sun."

Beside the sea she lives, the woman of the vine, the maker of wine; Siduri sits in the garden at the edge of the sea, with the golden bowl and the golden vats that the gods gave her. She is covered with a veil; and where she sits she sees Gilgamesh coming towards her, wearing skins, the flesh of the gods in his body, but despair in his heart, and his face like the face of one who has made a long journey. She looked, and as she scanned the distance she said in her own heart, "Surely this is some felon; where is he going now?" And she barred her gate against him with the cross-bar and shot home the bolt. But Gilgamesh, hearing the sound of the bolt, threw up his head and lodged his foot in the gate; he called to her, "Young woman, maker of wine, why do you bolt your door; what did you see that made you bar your gate? I will break in your door and burst in your gate, for I am Gilgamesh who seized and killed the Bull of Heaven, I killed the watchman of the cedar forest, I overthrew Humbaba who lived in the forest, and I killed the lions in the passes of the mountain."

Then Siduri said to him, "If you are that Gilgamesh who seized and killed the Bull of Heaven, who killed the watchman of the cedar forest, who overthrew Humbaba that lived in the forest, and killed the lions in the passes of the mountain, why are your cheeks so starved and why is your face so drawn? Why is despair in your heart and your face like the face of one who has made a long journey? Yes, why is your face burned from heat and cold, and why do you come here wandering over the pastures in search of the wind?"

Gilgamesh answered her, "And why should not my cheeks be starved and my face drawn? Despair is in my heart and my face is the face of one who has made a long journey, it was burned with heat and with cold. Why should I not wander over the pastures in search of the wind? My friend, my younger brother, he who hunted the wild ass of the wilderness and the panther of the plains, my friend, my younger brother who seized and killed the Bull of Heaven and overthrew Humbaba in the cedar forest, my friend who was very dear to me and who endured dangers beside me, Enkidu my brother, whom I loved, the end of mortality has overtaken him. I wept for him seven days and nights till the worm fastened on him. Because of my brother I am afraid of death, because of my brother I stray through the wilderness and cannot rest. But now, young woman, maker of wine, since I have seen your face do not let me see the face of death which I dread so much."

She answered, "Gilgamesh, where are you hurrying to? You will never find that life for which you are looking. When the gods created man they allotted to him death, but life they retained in their own keeping. As for you, Gilgamesh, fill your belly with good things; day and night, night and day, dance and be merry, feast and rejoice. Let your clothes be fresh, bathe yourself in water, cherish the little child that holds your hand, and make your wife happy in your embrace; for this too is the lot of man."

But Gilgamesh said to Siduri, the young woman, "How can I be silent, how can I rest, when Enkidu whom I love is dust, and I too shall die and be laid in the earth. You live by the sea-shore and look into the heart of it; young woman, tell me now, which is the way to Utnapishtim, the son of Ubara-Tutu? What directions are there for the passage; give me, oh, give me directions. I will cross the Ocean if it is possible; if it is not I will wander still farther in the wilderness." The wine-maker said to him, "Gilgamesh, there is no crossing the Ocean; whoever has come, since the days of old, has not been able to pass that sea. The Sun in his glory crosses the Ocean, but who beside Shamash has ever crossed it? The place and the passage are difficult, and the waters of death are deep which flow between. Gilgamesh, how will you cross the Ocean? When you come to the waters of death what will you do? But Gilgamesh, down in the woods you will find Urshanabi, the ferryman of Utnapishtim; with him are the holy things, the things of stone. He is fashioning the serpent prow of the boat. Look at him well, and if it is possible, perhaps you will cross the waters with him; but if it is not possible, then you must go back."

When Gilgamesh heard this he was seized with anger. He took his axe in his hand, and his dagger from his belt. He crept forward and he fell on them like a javelin. Then he went into the forest and sat down. Urshanabi saw the dagger flash and heard the axe, and he beat his head, for Gilgamesh had shattered the tackle of the boat in his rage. Urshanabi said to him, "Tell me, what is your name? I am Urshanabi, the ferryman of Utnapishtim the Faraway." He replied to him, "Gilgamesh is my name, I am from Uruk, from the house of Anu." Then Urshanabi said to him, "Why are your cheeks so starved and your face drawn? Why is despair in your heart and your face like the face of one who has made a long journey; yes, why is your face burned with heat and with cold, and why do you come here wandering over the pastures in search of the wind?"

Gilgamesh said to him, "Why should not my cheeks be starved and my face drawn? Despair is in my heart, and my face is the face of one who has made a long journey. I was burned with heat and with cold. Why should I not wander over the pastures? My friend, my younger brother who seized and killed the Bull of Heaven, and overthrew Humbaba in the cedar forest, my friend who was very dear to me, and who endured dangers beside me, Enkidu my brother whom I loved, the end of mortality has overtaken him. I wept for him seven days and nights till the worm fastened on him. Because of my brother I am afraid of death, because of my brother I stray through the wilderness. His fate lies heavy upon me. How can I be silent, how can I rest? He is dust and I too shall die and be laid in the earth for ever. I am afraid of death, therefore, Urshanabi, tell me which is the road to Utnapishtim? If it is possible I will cross the waters of death; if not I will wander still farther through the wilderness."

Urshanabi said to him, "Gilgamesh, your own hands have prevented you from crossing the Ocean; when you destroyed the tackle of the boat you destroyed its safety." Then the two of them talked it over and Gilgamesh said, "Why are you so angry with me, Urshanabi, for you yourself cross the sea by day and night, at all seasons you cross it." "Gilgamesh, those things you destroyed, their property is to carry me over the water, to prevent the waters of death from touching me. It was for this reason that I preserved them, but you have destroyed them, and the *urnu* snakes with them. But now, go into the forest, Gilgamesh; with your axe cut poles, one hundred and twenty, cut them sixty cubits long, paint them with bitumen, set on them ferrules and bring them back."

When Gilgamesh heard this he went into the forest, he cut poles one hundred and twenty; he cut them sixty cubits long, he painted them with bitumen, he set on them ferrules, and he brought them to Urshanabi. Then they boarded the boat, Gilgamesh and Urshanabi together, launching it out on the waves of Ocean. For three days they ran on as it were a journey of a month and fifteen days, and at last Urshanabi brought the boat to the waters of death. Then Urshanabi said to Gilgamesh, "Press on, take a pole and thrust it in, but do not let your hands touch the waters. Gilgamesh, take a second pole, take a third, take a fourth pole. Now, Gilgamesh, take a fifth, take a sixth and seventh pole. Gilgamesh, take an eighth, and ninth, a tenth pole. Gilgamesh, take an eleventh, take a twelfth pole." After one hundred and twenty thrusts Gilgamesh had used the last pole. Then he stripped himself, he held up his arms for a mast and his covering for a sail. So Urshanabi the ferryman brought Gilgamesh to Utnapishtim, whom they call the Faraway, who lives in Dilmun at the place of the sun's transit, eastward of the mountain. To him alone of men the gods had given everlasting life.

Now Utnapishtim, where he lay at ease, looked into the distance and he said in his heart, musing to himself, "Why does the boat sail here without tackle and mast; why are the sacred stones destroyed, and why does the master not sail the boat? That man who comes is none of mine; where I look I see a man whose body is covered with skins of beasts. Who is this who walks up the shore behind Urshanabi, for surely he is no man of mine?" So Utnapishtim looked at him and said, "What is your name, you who come here wearing the skins of beasts, with your cheeks starved and your face drawn? Where are you hurrying to now? For what reason have you made this great journey, crossing the seas whose passage is difficult? Tell me the reason for your coming."

He replied, "Gilgamesh is my name. I am from Uruk, from the house of Anu." Then Utnapishtim said to him, "if you are Gilgamesh, why are your checks so starved and your face drawn? Why is despair in your heart and your face like the face of one who has made a long journey? Yes, why is your face burned with heat and cold; and why do you come here, wandering over the wilderness in search of the wind?"

Gilgamesh said to him, "Why should not my cheeks be starved and my face drawn? Despair is in my heart and my face is the face of one who has made a long journey. It was burned with heat and with cold. Why should I not wander over the pastures? My friend, my younger brother who seized and killed the Bull of Heaven and overthrew Humbaba in the cedar forest, my friend who was very dear to me and endured dangers beside me, Enkidu, my brother whom I loved, the end of mortality has overtaken him. I wept for him seven days and nights till the worm fastened on him. Because of my brother I am afraid of death; because of my brother I stray through the wilderness. His fate lies heavy upon me. How can I be silent, how can I rest? He is dust and I shall die also and be laid in the earth for ever." Again Gilgamesh said, speaking to Utnapishtim, "It is to see Utnapishtim whom we call the Faraway that I have come this journey. For this I have wandered over the world, I have crossed many difficult ranges, I have crossed the seas, I have wearied myself with travelling; my joints are aching, and I have lost acquaintance with sleep which is sweet. My clothes were worn out before I came to the house of Siduri. I have killed the bear and hyena, the lion and panther, the tiger, the stag and the ibex, all sorts of wild game and the small creatures of the pastures. I ate their flesh and I wore their skins; and that was how I came to the gate of the young woman, the maker of wine, who barred her gate of pitch and bitumen against me. But from her I had news of the journey; so then I came to Urshanabi the ferryman, and with him I crossed over the waters of death. O, father Utnapishtim, you who have entered the assembly of the gods, I wish to question you concerning the living and the dead, how shall I find the life for which I am searching?"

Utnapishtim said, "There is no permanence. Do we build a house to stand for ever, do we seal a contract to hold for all time? Do brothers divide an inheritance to keep for ever, does the flood-time of rivers endure? It is only the nymph of the dragon-fly who sheds her larva and sees the sun in his glory. From the days of old there is no permanence. The sleeping and the dead, how alike they are, they are like a painted death. What is there between the master and the servant when both have fulfilled their doom? When the Anunnaki, the judges, come together, and Mammetun the mother of destinies, together they decree the fates of men. Life and death they allot but the day of death they do not disclose."

Then Gilgamesh said to Utnapishtim the Faraway, "I look at you now, Utnapishtim, and your appearance is no different from mine; there is nothing strange in your features. I thought I should find you like a hero prepared for battle, but you lie here taking your ease on your back. Tell me truly, how was it that you came to enter the company of the gods, and to possess everlasting life?" Utnapishtim said to Gilgamesh, "I will reveal to you a mystery, I will tell you a secret of the gods."

5

The Story of the Flood

"You know the city Shurrupak, it stands on the banks of Euphrates? That city grew old and the gods that were in it were old. There was Anu, lord of the firmament, their father, and warrior Enlil their counsellor, Ninurta the helper, and Ennugi watcher over canals; and with them also was Ea. In those days the world teemed, the people multiplied, the world bellowed like a wild bull, and the great god was aroused by the clamour. Enlil heard the clamour and he said to the gods in council, 'The uproar of mankind is intolerable and sleep is no longer possible by reason of the babel.' So the gods agreed to exterminate mankind. Enlil did this, but Ea because of his oath warned me in a dream. He whispered their words to my house of reeds, 'Reed-house, reed-house! Wall, O wall, hearken reed-house, wall reflect; O man of Shurrupak, son of Ubara-Tutu; tear down your house and build a boat, abandon possessions and look for life, despise worldly goods and save your soul alive. Tear down your house, I say, and build a boat. These are the measurements of the barque as you shall build her: let her beam equal her length, let her deck be roofed like the vault that covers the abyss; then take up into the boat the seed of all living creatures.'

"When I had understood I said to my lord, 'Behold what you have commanded I will honour and perform, but how shall I answer the people, the city, the elders?' Then Ea opened his mouth and said to me, his servant, 'Tell them this: I have learnt that Enlil is wrathful against me, I dare no longer walk in his land nor live in his city; I will go down to the Gulf to dwell with Ea my lord. But on you he will rain down abundance, rare fish and shy wild-fowl, a rich harvest-tide. In the evening the rider of the storm will bring you wheat in torrents.'

"In the first light of dawn all my household gathered round me, the children brought pitch and the men whatever was necessary. On the fifth day I laid the keel and the ribs, then I made fast the planking. The ground-space was one acre, each side of the deck measured one hundred and twenty cubits, making a square. I built six decks below, seven in all, I divided them into nine sections with bulkheads between. I drove in wedges where needed, I saw to the punt-poles, and laid in supplies. The carriers brought oil in baskets, I poured pitch into the furnace and asphalt and oil; more oil was consumed in caulking, and more again the master of the boat took into his stores. I slaughtered bullocks for the people and every day I killed sheep. I gave the shipwrights wine to drink as though it were river water, raw wine and red wine and oil and white wine. There was feasting then as there is at the time of the New Year's festival; I myself anointed my head. On the eleventh day the boat was complete.

"Then was the launching full of difficulty; there was shifting of ballast above and below till two thirds was submerged. I loaded into her all that I had of gold and of living things, my family, my kin, the beast of the field both wild and tame, and all the craftsmen. I sent them on board, for the time that Shamash had ordained was already fulfilled when he said, 'In the evening, when the rider of the storm sends down the destroying rain, enter the boat and batten her down.' The time was fulfilled, the evening came, the rider of the storm sent down the rain. I looked out at the weather and it was terrible, so I too boarded the boat and battened her down. All was now complete, the battening and the caulking; so I handed the tiller to Puzur-Amurri the steersman, with the navigation and the care of the whole boat.

"With the first light of dawn a black cloud came from the horizon; it thundered within where Adad, lord of the storm was riding. In front over hill and plain Shullat and Hanish, heralds of the storm, led on. Then the gods of the abyss rose up; Nergal pulled out the darns of the nether waters, Ninurta the war-lord threw down the dykes, and the seven judges of hell, the Annunaki, raised their torches, lighting the land with their livid flame. A stupor of despair went up to heaven when the god of the storm turned day-light to darkness, when he smashed the land like a cup. One whole day the tempest raged, gathering fury as it went, it poured over the people like the tides of battle; a man could not see his brother nor the people be seen from heaven: Even the gods were terrified at the flood, they fled to the highest heaven, the firmament of Anu; they crouched against the walls, cowering like curs. Then Ishtar the sweet-voiced Queen of Heaven cried out like a woman in travail: 'Alas the days of old are turned to dust because I commanded evil; why did I command this evil in the council of all the gods? I commanded wars to destroy the people, but are they not my people, for I brought them forth? Now like the spawn of fish they float in the ocean.' The great gods of heaven and of hell wept, they covered their mouths.

"For six days and six nights the winds blew, torrent and tempest and flood overwhelmed the world, tempest and flood raged together like warring hosts. When the seventh day dawned the storm from the south subsided, the sea grew calm, the flood was stilled; I looked at the face of the world and there was silence, all mankind was turned to clay. The surface of the sea stretched as flat as a roof-top; I opened a hatch and the light fell on my face. Then I bowed low, I sat down and I wept, the tears streamed down my face, for on every side was the waste of water. I looked for land in vain, for fourteen leagues distant there appeared a mountain, and there the boat grounded; on the mountain of Nisir the boat held fast, she held fast and did not budge. One day she held, and a second day on the mountain of Nisir she held fast and did not budge. A third day, and a fourth day she held fast on the mountain and did not budge; a fifth day and a sixth day she held fast on the mountain. When the seventh day dawned I loosed a dove and let her go. She flew away, but finding no resting-place she returned. Then I loosed a swallow, and she flew away but finding no resting-place she returned. I loosed a raven, she saw that the waters had retreated, she ate, she flew around, she cawed, and she did not come back. Then I threw everything open to the four winds, I made a sacrifice and poured out a libation on the mountain top. Seven and again seven cauldrons I set up on their stands I heaped up wood and cane and cedar and myrtle. When the gods smelled the sweet savour, they gathered like flies over the sacrifice. Then, at last, Ishtar also came, she lifted her necklace with the jewels of heaven that once Anu had made to please her. 'O you gods here present, by the lapis lazuli round my neck I shall remember these days as I remember the jewels of my throat; these last days I shall not forget. Let all the gods gather round the sacrifice, except Enlil. He shall not approach this offering, for without reflection he brought the flood; he consigned my people to destruction."

"When Enlil had come, when he saw the boat, he was wrath and swelled with anger at the gods, the host of heaven, 'Has any of these mortals escaped? Not one was to have survived the destruction.' Then the god of the wells and canals Ninurta opened his mouth and said to the warrior Enlil, 'Who is there of the gods that can devise without Ea? It is Ea, alone who knows all things.' Then Ea opened his mouth and spoke to warrior Enlil, 'Wisest of gods, hero Enlil, how could you so senselessly bring down the flood?

Lay upon the sinner his sin,
Lay upon the transgressor his transgression,
Punish him a little when he breaks loose,
Do not drive him too hard or he perishes;
Would that a lion had ravaged mankind
Rather than the flood,
Would that a wolf had ravaged mankind
Rather than the flood,
Would that famine had wasted the world
Rather than the flood,
Would that pestilence had wasted mankind
Rather than the flood.

It was not I that revealed the secret of the gods; the wise man learned it in a dream. Now take your counsel what shall be done with him.'

"Then Enlil went up into the boat, he took me by the hand and my wife and made us enter the boat and kneel down on either side, he standing between us. He touched our foreheads to bless us saying, 'In time past Utnapishtim was a mortal man; henceforth he and his wife shall live in the distance at the mouth of the rivers.' Thus it was that the gods took me and placed me here to live in the distance, at the mouth of the rivers."

6

The Return

Utnapishtim said, "As for you, Gilgamesh, who will assemble the gods for your sake, so that you may find that life for which you are searching? But if you wish, come and put it to the test: only prevail against sleep for six days and seven nights." But while Gilgamesh sat there resting on his haunches, a mist of sleep like soft wool teased from the fleece drifted over him, and Utnapishtim said to his wife, "Look at him now, the strong man who would have everlasting life, even now the mists of sleep are drifting over him." His wife replied, "Touch the man to wake him, so that he may return to his own land in peace, going back through the gate by which he came." Utnapishtim said to his wife, "All men are deceivers, even you he will attempt to deceive; therefore bake loaves of bread, each day one loaf, and put it beside his head; and make a mark on the wall to number the days he has slept."

So she baked loaves of bread, each day one loaf, and put it beside his head, and she marked on the walls the days that he slept; and there came a day when the first loaf was hard, the second loaf was like leather, the third was soggy, the crust of the fourth had mould, the fifth was mildewed, the sixth was fresh, and the seventh was still on the embers. Then Utnapishtim touched him and he woke. Gilgamesh said to Utnapishtim the Faraway, I hardly slept when you touched and roused me." But Utnapishtim said, "Count these loaves and learn how many days you slept, for your first is hard, your second like leather, your third is soggy, the crust of your fourth has mould, your fifth is mildewed, your sixth is fresh and your seventh was still over the glowing embers when I touched and woke you." Gilgamesh said, "What shall I do, O Utnapishtim, where shall I go? Already the thief in the night has hold of my limbs, death inhabits my room; wherever my foot rests, there I find death."

Then Utnapishtim spoke to Urshanabi the ferryman: "Woe to you Urshanabi, now and for ever more you have become hateful to this harbourage; it is not for you, nor for you are the crossings of this sea. Go now, banished from the shore. But this man before whom you walked, bringing him here, whose body is covered with foulness and the grace of whose limbs has been spoiled by wild skins, take him to the washing-place. There he shall wash his long hair clean as snow in the water, he shall throw off his skins and let the sea carry them away, and the beauty of his body shall be shown, the fillet on his forehead shall be renewed, and he shall be given clothes to cover his nakedness. Till he reaches his own city and his journey is accomplished, these clothes will show no sign of age, they will wear like a new garment." So Urshanabi took Gilgamesh and led him to the washing-place, he washed his long hair as clean as snow in the water, he threw off his skins, which the sea carried away, and showed the beauty of his body. He renewed the fillet on his forehead, and to cover his nakedness gave him clothes which would show no sign of age, but would wear like a new garment til he reached his own city, and his journey was accomplished.

Then Gilgamesh and Urshanabi launched the boat on to the water and boarded it, and they made ready to sail away; but the wife of Utnapishtim the Faraway said to him, "Gilgamesh came here wearied out, he is worn out; what will you give him to carry him back to his own country?" So Utnapishtim spoke, and Gilgamesh took a pole and brought the boat in to the bank. "Gilgamesh, you came here a man wearied out, you have worn yourself out; what shall I give you to carry you back to your own country? Gilgamesh, I shall reveal a secret thing, it is a mystery of the gods that I am telling you. There is a plant that grows under the water, it has a prickle like a thorn, like a rose; it will wound your hands, but if you succeed in taking it, then your hands will hold that which restores his lost youth to a man."

When Gilgamesh heard this he opened the sluices so that a sweet-water current might carry him out to the deepest channel; he tied heavy stones to his feet and they dragged him down to the water-bed. There he saw the plant growing; although it pricked him he took it in his hands; then he cut the heavy stones from his feet, and the sea carried him and threw him on to the shore. Gilgamesh said to Urshanabi the ferryman, "Come here, and see this marvellous plant. By its virtue a man may win back all his former strength. I will take it to Uruk of the strong walls; there I will give it to the old men to eat. Its name shall be "The Old Men Are Young Again'; and at last I shall eat it myself and have back all my lost youth." So Gilgamesh returned by the gate through which he had come, Gilgamesh and Urshanabi went together. They travelled their twenty leagues and then they broke their fast; after thirty leagues they stopped for the night.

Gilgamesh saw a well of cool water and he went down and bathed; but deep in the pool there was lying a serpent, and the serpent sensed the sweetness of the flower. It rose out of the water and snatched it away, and immediately it sloughed its skin and returned to the well. Then Gilgamesh sat down and wept, the tears ran down his face, and he took the hand of Urshanabi; "O Urshanabi, was it for this that I toiled with my hands, is it for this I have wrung out my heart's blood? For myself I have gained nothing; not I, but the beast of the earth has joy of it now. Already the stream has carried it twenty leagues back to the channels where I found it. I found a sign and now I have lost it. Let us leave the boat on the bank and go."

After twenty leagues they broke their fast, after thirty leagues they stopped for the night; in three days they had walked as much as a journey of a month and fifteen days. When the journey was accomplished they arrived at Uruk, the strong-walled city. Gilgamesh spoke to him, to Urshanabi the ferryman, "Urshanabi, climb up on to the wall of Uruk, inspect its foundation terrace, and examine well the brickwork; see if it is not of burnt bricks; and did not the seven wise men lay these foundations? One third of the whole is city, one third is garden, and one third is field, with the precinct of the goddess Ishtar. These parts and the precinct are all Uruk."

This too was the work of Gilgamesh, the king, who knew the countries of the world. He was wise, he saw mysteries and knew secret things, he brought us a tale of the days before the flood. He went a long journey, was weary, worn out with labour, and returning engraved on a stone the whole story.

7

The Death of Gilgamesh

The destiny was fulfilled which the father of the gods, Enlil of the mountain, had decreed for Gilgamesh: "in nether-earth the darkness will show him a light: of mankind, all that are known, none will leave a monument for generations to come to compare with his. The heroes, the wise men, like the new moon have their waxing and waning. Men will say, 'Who has ever ruled with might and with power like him?' As in the dark month, the month of shadows, so without him there is no light. O Gilgamesh, this was the meaning of your dream. You were given the kingship, such was your destiny, everlasting life was not your destiny. Because of this do not be sad at heart, do not be grieved or oppressed; he has given you power to bind and to loose, to be the darkness and the light of mankind. He has given unexampled supremacy over the people, victory in battle front which no fugitive returns, in forays and assaults from which there is no going back. But do not abuse this power, deal justly with your servants in the palace, deal justly before the face of the Sun."

The king has laid himself down and will not rise again,
The Lord of Kullab will not rise again;
He overcame evil, he will not come again;
Though he was strong of arm he will not rise again;
He had wisdom and a comely face, he will not come again;
He is gone into the mountain, he will not come again;
On the bed of fate he lies, he will not rise again,
From the couch of many colours he will not come again.

The people of the city, great and small, are not silent; they lift up the lament, all men of flesh and blood lift up the lament. Fate has spoken; like a hooked fish he lies stretched on the bed, like a gazelle that is caught in a noose. Inhuman Namtar is heavy upon him, Namtar that has neither hand nor foot, that drinks no water and eats no meat.

For Gilgamesh, son of Ninsun, they weighed out their offerings; his dear wife, his son, his concubine, his musicians, his jester, and all his household; his servants, his stewards, all who lived in the palace weighed out their offerings for Gilgamesh the son of Ninsun, the heart of Uruk. They weighed out their offerings to Ereshkigal, the Queen of Death, and to all the gods of the dead. To Namtar, who is fate, they weighed out the offering. Bread for Neti the Keeper of the Gate, bread for Ningizzida the god of the serpent, the lord of the Tree of Life; for Dumuzi also, the young shepherd, for Enki and Ninki, for Endukugga and Nindukugga, for Enmul and Ninmul, all the ancestral gods, forbears of Enlil. A feast for Shulpae the god of feasting. For Samuqan, god of the herds, for the mother Ninhursag, and the gods of creation in the place of creation, for the host of heaven, priest and priestess weighed out the offering of the dead.

Gilgamesh, the son of Ninsun, lies in the tomb. At the place of offerings he weighed the bread-offering, at the place of libation he poured out the wine. In those days the lord Gilgamesh departed, the son of Ninsun, the king, peerless, without an equal among men, who did not neglect Enlil his master. O Gilgamesh, lord of Kullab, great is thy praise.

Asian Music

Asian music is obviously complex. One way of appreciating this complexity is to consider this musical expression from the point of view of its form and instrumentation,which vary from country to country. A solo instrument or voice is the preference of Southwest Asia. The instruments of choice are bowed lutes, end-blown flutes, plucked lutes, and vase-shaped drums. Persia's (Iran's) classical music features the *dastgah*, a suite made up of several *gushe* (rhythmic formulas), improvisation being the guiding principle. A classical performance includes the *tar* (long-necked and plucked lute), *sitar* (smaller long-necked lute), *kemanche* or *kamaniah* (bowed lute), and *santir* (dulcimer). Similarly, Turkey's classical performance is the *fasil*, a compositional suite. Significant instruments are the *darabukka* (vase shaped drum with a single head), *kanun* (trapezoid, plucked zither), *kemanche*, *saz* (long-necked, plucked lute), *zurna* (conical double-reed instrument), *dawul* (double-headed drum), and the Arabic lute. Arabic music feature the *ud* (lute), *darabukka*, and the western violin. The human voice is also a favorite instrument. The classical form, the *maqamat*, involves the performance of complex melodic music.

The music of India, in South Asia, reveals northern and southern preferences, with the more difficult forms performed in the south. Instruments of choice are the *vina* (large lute with gourd resonators), *mrdangam* (large, double headed, laced instrument played with the bare fingers), and the transverse flute, as well as the human voice. In the north, the *sitar*, transverse flute, *shanai* (double reed pipe), *tabla* (small single drums), *tambura* (long-necked string instrument), and *sarod* figure prominently as does the human voice. The difference between northern and southern music is the repertoire performances for vocal and instrumental music that are specific to the North.

A unique characteristic of the music of Southeast Asia is the use of the bronze gong. The Burmese ensemble called a *saing-waing* is a circle of small, tuned bronze kettles; the player makes the musical sound by striking the kettles with small mallets. The *patt-waing* also hangs in a circle, but it consists of small, tuned drums. This ensemble also includes the *na* (wooden clappers and bells) and the *saung* (harp).

Two types of ensemble distinguish classical music in Thailand, Cambodia, and Laos. They are *piphat*, basic instrumentation and *mahori*, string instruments. The gong circle is the *khawng wong*, and the *ranat* (xylophone) is a supporting instrument. In Hindu-Islamic cultures, ensembles of gong-chimes dominate. Larger gong-chime ensembles are *gamelans*, and *gamelan sekati* is the Muslim version used for specific festivities.

In East Asia, musicians pay more attention to tradition; thus Chinese music is virtually the same as it was when Confucius lived. China, Korea, and Japan basically use ceremonial music, preferring such instruments as the small, bowed lutes, plucked lutes, and plucked zithers. They use their instruments also for dramatic plays. Chinese operas are sometimes referred to as Peking operas. The Japanese prefer to use their instruments in the performance of Noh. It is this immense variety which keeps Asian music continually vibrant.

Archetype, Myth, Culture: The Symbolic Structure of the Human Psyche

One hundred years ago, in the study of dreams, Sigmund Freud and his followers first investigated the unconscious aspects of psychic experience. They found in the remembered traces of dream life the symbolic language of a split consciousness. Freud also discovered that if he left his patients to "free associate" from the symbolic elements in their dreams, they often revealed key psychological determinants of their illnesses. Inevitably, for Freud this symbolic language illuminated evidence of a repressed infantile sexuality.

Sometime around 1910, Carl Jung, Freud's hand-picked successor, began to see dream symbolism, less as a tool of repression and more as a window on the infinite. He shifted from a personal and biographical to a universal and mythological approach to the symbols of the psyche. Comparing the dreams of his patients to his wide reading in world myth and religion, Jung noticed the commonality of dream images and situations found in all peoples and cultures and expressed not only in dreams but in fairy tales, myths, literature, popular culture, film, song, and art.

Drawing on his clinical experience and on studies of comparative mythology such as James Frazer's the *Golden Bough* (1910), Jung felt that certain images universally reside in the human unconscious: water, for example, symbolizing purification, fire symbolizing passion, spring meaning rebirth and change, or winter representing death. In the conscious expression of art, literature, and religion, these unconscious energies are given form. For Jungian psychology, the symbolic narratives of myth are guides to human healing, to bridging the gap between conscious individuality and largely unconscious collective psyches. The common cultural hero myths are simultaneously external stories of adventure and internal quests for psychic unity.

In his book the *Hero With a Thousand Faces*, Jungian folklorist Joseph Campbell retells the hero's narrative as a universal "monomyth," with its own structure. Campbell identifies the pattern as one of separation-initiation-return; he illustrates this narrative structure in a wide variety of world myths. For example, Jason leads the Argonauts past the clashing rocks and into a sea of marvels. Here they face countless dangers and monsters until they win the Golden Fleece. With the help of the fleece's power, Jason is able to return to his kingdom and reclaim his rightful throne from a usurper. The hero's initiation typically begins an event: something happens, a crisis or inciting incident, to lift the hero out of the realm of the ordinary. It may be a herald from another world. Moses, for example, hears God in a burning bush; Athena appears to Telemachus, pushing him out into the world to find his father; a ghost appears to Hamlet; witches to Macbeth; and Joan of Arc hears her "voices." Wizards, like Gandalf, in Tolkien's *Lord of the Rings* or Merlin, in *Le Morte D'Arthur* summon Frodo and Arthur to the hero's journey. Aladdin discovers a magic lamp. In other narratives, a crisis precipitates the call: a tornado in the *Wizard of Oz*, war and desolation in *Star Wars*, the selling of Joseph into slavery, or the stampede that kills Mufasa in the *Lion King*. The call may also be a personal crisis of faith. Young Prince Gautama, the future Buddha, raised in luxury and in isolation from the sight of sickness, suffering, and death, loses his innocence and, like other heroes, must quest to reconcile his desires, dreams, and ideals with the realities of the human condition. For the Buddha, as for Joseph or Hamlet, or Luke Skywalker, the call to adventure is also an archetypal Fall from Paradise.

Just as seekers of wisdom need spiritual mentors and philosophical guides, Campbell notes the presence of the helper archetype who often appears at the beginning of the hero's quest. This outside source of strength may be represented in a physical object. The hero may, for example, be given an amulet—Dorothy's red shoes, Arthur's sword, Excalibur, the Ring of Power in the *Lord of the Rings*, or Roy Hobbs' bat "Wonderboy" in Bernard Malamud's the *Natural*. More often, however, the supernatural helper is a wise guide: Athena, Obi Wan Kenobi, Merlin, or any of Disney's spiritual helpers like Jiminy Cricket, the wise baboon Rafiki in the *Lion King*, or Grandmother Willow in *Pocohantas*. For Campbell, these figures are the psyche's response to the dangers the ego faces in crossing the threshold into the realm of the unconscious.

Even with supernatural help, the hero's journey is a perilous undertaking, comprised of a series of encounters with danger and difficulty that Campbell refers to as a "road of trials": the labors of Hercules or Psyche, the duels with dragons or pagan knights in the legends of chivalry, the struggles of Moses to free the Hebrews from Egyptian captivity, or Dorothy Gale's efforts, not only to reach Oz, but then to return with the witch's broom. These trials are always both physical and spiritual tests of physical courage and resourcefulness as well as tests of faith, character, and endurance. The dragons are internal, in Jungian terms, and projected into the psychic landscape of the narrative. These unknown regions, whether desert, jungle, or deep sea, according to Campbell, allow projection of unconscious content. Thus, the dragons and giants of myth can be seen as projections of the ego's rage or pride or lust e.g., the archetypal temptresses (Delilah, Dido, or Duessa in Spencer's Fairie Queene).

In many of these mythic cultural narratives, the hero's internal demons succeed at first and lead him astray. Campbell represents this nadir as the trial of the soul. The hero is isolated, weak, often sexually spent and physically restrained. Odysseus is Calypso's sexual prisoner, Joseph is thrown into Potiphar's jail, Samson is chained and blind in Gaza, Joan of Arc is on trial in an English prison, Spenser's Red Crosse Knight is locked in Orgoglio's dungeon, Dorothy Gale awaits her fate in the castle of the Wicked Witch. Even in the belly of the whale, hope must win out over despair. The hero must experience hell to see heaven. Psychologically, the process is twofold. The hero, imprisoned by the boundaries of his limited ego, must have the old identity stripped away. He must be reduced to nothing—Samson shorn of his hair, Joseph of his coat, Joan of her armor. Like King Lear before the pelting storm, without kingdom, friends, family, wealth, or youth, the hero must find meaning in the face of the natural essence of humanity. The death of the old ego prepares for the rebirth of the new, unified ego.

The hero's ultimate triumph over both the internal and external limitations of the ego is never just an end in itself; it prepares the way for Campbell's final themes of return, reconciliation, and reunion. Unlike so many of today's "anti-heroes" who avoid the dual responsibilities of family and social commitment, the heroic archetype models social as well as personal integration. Thus Odysseus and Beowulf return to their kingdoms to rule in wisdom and peace, Joseph is reconciled to his brothers, father, and tribe, generous in his newly acquired powers, and Dorothy returns from Oz with new-found wisdom about the meaning of "home." For Campbell, the hero's journey is always an internal one of psychic healing and an external one of increased social responsibility. Political leaders, like Arthur or Simba, must learn to rule; spiritual leaders like Buddha or Jesus must teach; and romantic heroes must commit to love and family.

By returning from the realm of myth and adventure into the world of human potentiality, the hero completes what Campbell sees as a primary function—the unification of one's personal and limited consciousness with what Jung refers to as the collective unconscious. Heroic narratives, then, are today, as they have always been, stories a culture tells of its world view, a source of narrative stability, hope and inspiration as it seeks to understand and interpret the world.

Appendix A: Additional Biographies and Backgrounds

Euripides (485–404?/406? BC)

Not much is known about Euripides' personal life; his birth and death dates are conjectured. Most literary historians cite 485 BC as his birth date and death date as 404 or 406 BC. Euripides was born in Salamis, an island in the Saronic Gulf, of humble parents—neither rich nor poor. His mother sold vegetables but was not a shopkeeper. Records also indicate that Euripides was married, possibly two times and had three sons—one who produced some of his father's plays posthumously. Euripides died in Macedonia, having been invited there for two years as the guest of King Archelaus who prided himself on having distinguished Greeks in his court.

Although Euripides was considered one of the three great tragedians, he did not enjoy great popularity during his brief lifetime. Historians cannot explain why he won so infrequently the Dionysian Festivals unless his criticism of Athenian society, its public policy and social values and politics offended the people. Athenian officials did not like Euripides' drama because it forced them to rethink their mistakes and values in fighting the Peloponnesian Wars (431–404 BC). Furthermore, the plays' focus on women at a time and in a society where women were second-class citizens made the playwright anachronistic. Another reason is that the dramatist changed the focus of the dramatic events from gods to humans. Euripides thought the values and will of humans were just as important as those of the gods. But more importantly, the playwright believed that these gods were an innate part of humans instead of an ethereal, esoteric, supernatural outsider. Therefore, his humans are real and fallible, so in order to solve dilemmas, Euripides relied on Aeschylus' idea of using the skene. Women as the central focus of his plays did not help his popularity. The successful Aristophones showed his disapproval of Euripides' ideas in his satire the *Frogs*. Euripides also made innovative structural changes, especially in his use of a prologue and epilogue. The dialogic verse (or speeches by the actors) was separated by lyrical odes sung by the chorus. One criticism of this technique is that the speeches often seen unrelated, or distantly related, to the main action. Sometimes a solo sung by an actor came before a scene of dialogue.

The Euripidean dramas and approximate production dates which exist are *Cyclops* (satyric, ca. 438); *Alcestis* (438); *Medea* (431); the *Children of Heracles* (430–?427); *Hippolytus* (428); *Andromache* (ca. 426); *Hecuba* (ca. 424); the *Suppliants* (422–?420); *Electra* (ca. 413); *Helen* (412); *Iphigenia Among the Taurians* (ca. 411); *Ion* (412–?410); the *Phoenician Women* (411–409); *Orestes* (408); the *Bacchae* (406–405); *Iphigenia at Aulis* (406–405); *Rhesus* (unknown date). Even if the Athenians did not acclaim Euripides with many prizes and even if literary critics debate his rank, the fact that eighteen or nineteen of his ninety-two plays survive attests to his worth as a playwright.

Selected Bibliography

Coldewey, John C., and W.R. Streitberger. *Drama: Classical to Contemporary*. Upper Saddle River, NJ: Prentice Hall, 1998.

Foley, Helen P. *Ritual Irony: Poetry and Sacrifice in Euripides*. Ithaca, NY: Cornell UP, 1985.

Jacobus, Lee A. *The Bedford Introduction of Drama*. 3rd ed. Boston: Bedford, 1997

Medea

If the theme of tragedy is the sufferings and disasters experienced by humans, then Euripides' *Medea* is the epitome of tragedy. Euripides attributes people's sufferings and disasters to their nature, more particularly ignorance, unbridled passions, irrational emotions, limitless greed, and ambition—all of which cause cruelty and/or people's inhumanity to each other. Any of these traits can be considered Medea and Jason's tragic flaw. Most view as the catalyst in this powerful drama the fact that the sorceress is rejected by her loved one—the one for which she had forsaken family and country.

Euripides' powerfully intense drama was first presented to the Athenians in 431 BC at the Dionysian Festival. Euripides, like other Greek writers, draws upon the vast literary storehouse of Greek history, myths and legends. Although Medea begins with the myth of Jason and his quest for the Golden Fleece, the focus of the play is on Medea, a female whose self-worth is not dependent upon the men in her life, especially her father, brother, and husband. It is Jason who needs her sorceress powers to obtain the Golden Fleece. In a society where women were considered socially inferior, a theme focusing on this fiercely independent woman, fully developed as a character, is a major Euripidean innovation.

The themes of sexual jealousy, unrequited love, abandonment, infanticide, and lustful vengeance are emotionally challenging. Medea's fiery temperament is evident from the moment she enters the stage, albeit she a pitiful sight as she pleads her case before the chorus women and audience. By the time she requests amnesty from Creon, the audience, knowing more about her motives, does not deem her as pitiful.

However, Medea is to be pitied at the beginning of her relationship with Jason; her passion is so powerful that she kills her father and brother to help her new-found love—a stranger—escape with the Golden Fleece. If Medea is pitied, what is one to feel for Jason, a male who abandons his wife and children for a younger woman? The Greek audience understands Jason's decision in the context of Greek law. He is concerned with his children's welfare since Medea is not a citizen of Corinth. By marrying the King of Corinth's daughter, Jason insures Medea and their children's safety and security. As Jason's concubine, Medea would be afforded some royal status because children of an alien mother would not be allowed Athenian citizenry. Lee Jacobus calls her Asiatic. Hans Henny Jahnn, Ivan Van Sertima, and William McDonald assert that Medea is Black. Even Herodotus, a Greek historian, records in 5 BC that Medea and the people of Medea's hometown, Colchis, located in Black Africa, were black-skinned and had wooly hair.

This powerfully intense drama, with all of its complexities, has seduced audiences, playwrights, and patrons of the arts since it won last prize at the Dionysian Festival in Athens. Alexander the Great produced the play in the fourth century. Seneca, a Roman playwright (AD 60) and Pierre Corneille, French dramatist (AD 1606–1684) wrote their own versions. Hans Henry Jahnne, a German poet, did an adaptation in 1926, making Medea an older Black woman. In 1956, Countee Cullen used a Black actress in his prose rendering consisting of twenty-eight lyrics. A Japanese all-male Kabuki version of *Medea* was performed in New York in 1986 with Yokio Ninagawa as director. *Medea*, by Euripides, with its complexities of themes, is the universal play. It transcends time, generations, gender, race, and culture.

Selected Bibliography

Baker, Houston. *A Many Colored Coat of Dreams: The Poetry of Countee Cullen.* Detroit: Broadside, 1974.

Corti, Lillian. *The Myth of Medea and the Murder of Children.* Westport, CT: Greenwood, 1998.

Jacobus, Lee A. *The Bedford Introduction to Drama.* 3rd ed. Boston: Bedford, 1997.

Jahnn, Hans Henny. *Medea in Dramen, I.* Frankfurt: Band, 1963.

McDonald, William P. "The Blackness of Medea." *College Language Association Journal* 19 (1975): 20–37.

Sertima, Ivan Van, ed. *Black Women in Antiquity.* 1984. New Brunswick, NJ: Transaction, 1992.

Geoffrey Chaucer's *The Miller's Tale*

Geoffrey Chaucer's description of the Miller in the "General Prologue" allows the reader to anticipate the Miller's behavior as well as the type of tale he tells. Although he apologizes for his behavior because he is drunk, the Miller insists on telling his story. The tale itself is a fabliau, a genre cultivated in Medieval France. The fabliau was written to burlesque the behavior and values of courtly decorum. The humorous stories are usually indecent and focus on bourgeois, middle, or lower class character and situations.

"The Miller's Tale" centers around an old, jealous husband who is deceived by his young wife with younger, more attractive lovers. One of the suitors is also a victim of deceit. The outcome of the practical jokes is predictable, though unrealistic; the story ends with a semblance of poetic justice. Two motifs are combined in "The Miller's Tale." One is that old husbands who marry young wives should expect negative consequences. The other is that young men should be aware of attempting to be too clever when they are involved in an illicit relationship. These motifs allow the development of a plot which exposes the weakness and gullibility of human nature. Demonstrating refined sensibilities, Chaucer, the pilgrim/narrator, asks not to be held responsible for the bawdy tale of the Miller, defending his need to record everyone's story as accurately as he can.

Geoffrey Chaucer's
The Nun's Priest's Tale

On initial reading, "The Nun's Priest's Tale" may appear merely as a narrative of talking birds and beasts. However, the tale is enriched and enjoyment increased if readers can appreciate Chaucer's plot, style, vocabulary, structure, and characterization. The genre to which this tale belongs is the *fable* in which animals are given physical and moral attributes of men and women and in which readers are expected to learn a lesson from the words and actions of the characters which readers can apply to their lives. In "the Nun's Priest's Tale," readers learn to be alert, to be on guard, especially against flatterers, and to remain silent. Authors continue to use the animal fable to convey a moral or political message. Of ancient origins, the animal fable was familiar to Chaucer's audience. In "The Nun's Priest's Tale," Chaucer preserves the framework of the animal fable. The birds and animals are the major characters, and this is stressed by their being given names, while the human characters remain anonymous. The action primarily concerns the animals Chaunteleer, Pertelote, and Russell. Chaunteleer and Pertelote are birds. They live in a farm yard, roost on a beam in a coop, eat corn, crow, and mate frequently. On the other hand, Russell is a fox who lurks in the vegetable plot, is the enemy of the poultry, and at the first opportunity, seizes Chaunteleer and runs off with him. The exception to normal animal behavior is the capacity of the animals to converse in human speech. In style, structure, and characterization, Chaucer changes the basic animal fable to make it something other than a simple fable. Whatever moral readers accept, the humor, joy, and elegance of the tale will remain the chief attraction.

The Ramayana

Of even greater antiquity than the *Mahabharata,* the *Ramayana* as a narrative, is believed to have been recited by storytellers from the early days of the Aryan occupation of northern India. One-third the length of the *Mahabharata,* this epic poem was composed in Sanskrit by Valmiki in the fourth century BC.

Like the Greek epic, the *Odyssey,* the *Ramayana* is also the story of the trials, adversities, and final triumph of one family. It is a tender story of love and devotion between husband and wife, father and son, and brothers. Rama, the prince of Ayodhya, is banished from the kingdom for fourteen years by his stepmother, Queen Kaikeyi, because she wants her son to be crowned the next king. Rama is followed into exile by his devoted wife, Sita, and younger brother, Lakshmana. While in exile, they wander through the forests of central and southern India; they visit important hermitages, protect the sages from the attacks by the demons, and live a peaceful life. Towards the end of their term, Sita is abducted by the demon king of Lanka (Sri Lanka), Ravana. At the head of a large army, Rama defeats Ravana and rescues Sita and then returns to Ayodha to begin his glorious rule. Primitive and subhuman characters embody positive traits of loyalty, friendship, and self-sacrifice, whereas the material and scientific development of Ravana's kingdom leads to negative traits of drunkenness, greed, violence, and sensuality.

The *Mahabharata,* moreso than the *Ramayana,* has become one of the primary Hindu scriptures. Rama is worshiped as an incarnation of Vishnu, god in the form of Preserver. Rama and Sita, as ideal man and woman, set the standards for social behavior to this day. Their story is recited and re-enacted throughout India during the Dassehra-Diwali festivities every fall.

Appendix B: Yoruba, Egyptian, and Greco-Roman Gods and Goddesses

Yoruba Gods and Goddesses

In Yoruba religion, there is a kind of informal hierarchy or pantheon of gods in which a single Creator rules over the cosmos by means of hundreds of minor gods or *Orishas*, each with a specific role or sphere of activity.

God	Association
Olorun (or Olodumare)	Owner of the Heavens" or "The Almighty or Supreme Spirit"; the Creator of all things; the omniscient, the life-giver, ultimate judge of mankind; though the supreme deity, he is regarded as an abstract, distant, detached spirit and hence is not seen as playing a spiritual role in the day-to-day activities of the individual—such specific roles' being left to the Orishas.
Obatala (or Orishala or Orisa-n la)	Though sometimes represented with his wife, Obudua, as independent of or as superior to Olorun, Obatala is frequently shown as being the implementer of Olorun's creative work, finishing up and filling out the details; sometimes, Oluron and Obatala are considered one and the same; the god responsible for shaping or designing the human form, in contrast to the work of Olorun, which is to breathe life into these forms; often considered king of the Orishas.
Obudua	Copartner and wife to Obatala; co-creator of all that is, second only to Olorun; as powerful as her husband; sometimes regarded, with Olorun and Obatala, as one of the points of a trinity.
Ogun	God of war, hunt, and blacksmiths; some consider him the most important of the Orishas; associated with agreements, oaths, and contracts (and hence courts, in which litigants swear to be truthful by appealing to the name of this god); god of fearsome, terrible revenge, particularly as a result of deceiving a companion on an agreement.
Shango (or Sango, Sayoe)	God of thunder and lightning; depicted as having four wives representing the four major rivers in Nigeria; probably achieved importance in the Yoruba psyche because he was identified with the frequently violent rain storms and tornadoes which strike West Africa; despite his popularity, he is not considered the most powerful god.
Eshu (or Baba)	Since the Yorubas have no concept of an evil god, Eshu has wrongly been likened to Satan; Eshu is merely mischievous; sometimes deemed the guardian of houses and villages; the god of *Ifa* (which is the highly complex science of divination, often based on the number 4), which many consult before making major life decisions.

A Common Myth

According to oral tradition, the high god, Olorun (Olodumare), asked Orishala to descend from the sky to create the first Earth at Ile-Ife. Orishala was delayed and his younger brother, Oduduwa, accomplished the task. Shortly afterwards, sixteen other orisha came down from heaven to create human beings and live on Earth with him. The descendants of each of these deities are said to have spread Yoruba culture and religious principles throughout the rest of Yorubaland.

Egyptian Gods and Goddesses

The Nile River plays an important part in Egyptian mythology, in that creatures which appear near or live in the Nile became associated with many of the Egyptian gods and goddesses. The striking fertility of the Nile, in contrast to the barren condition of the surrounding desert, is also a basic theme of a mythology which extends over 3,000 years.

In this system, the pharaoh, himself a god, mediates between humans and the sun god Ra; and hence, the pharaoh is said to be the son of Ra and consequently associated with the God Horus.

The many divinities of ancient Egypt and the myths about them were not just important to the Egyptians but had great influence on the mythologies of many later civilizations. During the 1300's BC, the pharaoh Amenhotep IV chose Aton as the only god of Egypt. Aton had been a little-known god worshiped in Thebes. Amenhotep was so devoted to the worship of Aton that he changed his own name to Akhenaton. Although the Egyptians stopped worshiping Aton after Akhenaton died, some scholars believe that the worship of this one divinity lingered among the people of Israel, who had settled in Egypt, and became an important part of the religion that was developed by their leader Moses. These scholars have suggested that the Jewish and Christian belief in one God may come from the cult of Aton. Further, there is overwhelming evidence to suggest that the Greeks copied a great number of their deities from the Egyptians and that philosophers such as Socrates and Plato had studied in the Egyptian mystery schools. Hence, much of Greco-Roman religion and thought very likely is influenced by Egypt.

God	Association
Nun	Chaos, the original ocean from which all plants and animals have been germinated; the abstract Father of the Gods; sometimes represented up to his waist in water, with his arms up, to support all of the other gods, who have come from him
Atum	Sometimes associated with Ra, the great sun god; the rising and setting sun; represented with a man's head, wearing the dual crown of the pharaohs; was said to have fathered the first divine couple, without the aid of a wife
Ra	The Sun God; creator of Shu and Tefnet, who later gave birth to Geb and Nut, who in turn parented Osiris and Isis, Set and Nepthys—the eight great gods; generated mankind and all other living creatures from his tears
Khepri	"Scarab (beetle)"; he who becomes; god of transformation, by which life renews itself; represented either as a scarab-faced man or a man decapitated by an insect
Shu	He who "raises" or "holds up"; supports the sky, like the Greek figure Atlas, who probably is derived from Shu; the god of air; represented as a human wearing an ostrich feather
Anhur	Possibly associated with memory, and hence representative of the past; also associated with the creative mind; perhaps the origin of the Greek God Mercury

Geb	The Earth god, shown lying under the feet of Shu; assumed to be the father (and Nut, the mother) of the Osirian gods
Osiris	At first, a nature god, in command of the vegetation which dies at harvest and is reborn in spring at the time of planting; later, worshiped throughout Egypt as god of the dead; very likely the source of the Greek God of the Dead, Hades or Pluto.
Set	Originally, Osiris' evil brother; later, the personification of evil, eternally opposed to good; was rough and wild, with white skin and red hair; likely associated with the Greek Prometheus, the fire giver and with the Hebraic Satan
Horus or Hor	Title given to the pharaoh in power; a sun god, often represented as a falcon or a falcon-headed god
Harakhtes	The sun in its daily course between the eastern and western horizon
Harmakhis	The spiritual rather than physical rising sun; resurrection
Anibis	Conductor of souls to the Afterlife; fourth son of Ra; invented funeral rites and bound up the mummy of Osiris to protect it from corruption; like Anhur, probably associated with the Greek God Hermes, in his mystical (rather than external) function
Upuaut	"He Who Opens the Way"; Wolf-headed or jackal-headed god; sometimes worshiped as a god of the dead, but more likely represents the transition between life and death; possibly the origin of the Roman God Janus, who is said to have had several faces
Thoth	Like Anhur and Anibis, probably associated with the Greek God Hermes, in his capacity as messenger of the Gods; sometimes worshiped as the moon god, or god of the lower or concrete mind; often represented with the head of a bird, frequently an Ibis; keeper of the divine archives and patron of history; a divine scribe and god of knowledge and writing.
Ptah	Creator of Ra, hence of everything, including the images or concepts of the gods for people to worship
Bast or Bastet	Daughter of the sun god Ra often depicted as a cat
Buto	Cobra goddess who protected the pharaoh by spitting poison on his enemies or burning them merely by her look; queen of all of the goddesses; symbol of the pharaoh's total power over the lands; possibly associated with the Greek figure, Medusa, who not only had snakes growing from her head but who could turn men into stone with but a glance
Hathor	Goddess of joy and love; consort of Horus; the cow, her sacred animal; later identified with Isis; responsible for the souls of humans and has foreknowledge of the destiny of a newly-born baby; because of this foreknowledge, often identified with the Greek Fates
Isis	Consort of Osiris; considered the model of the ideal woman, wife, and mother; goddess of medicine and of agriculture
Mayat	Goddess of truth, justice, unity, and order; often identified with the feather, which is sacred to her; shown as a woman with one feather in her hair; responsible for the belief that when humans die, their heart is weighed against a feather, to determine the individual's spiritual purity
Nepthys	Wife of Seth (Set?)
Nut	Creator of darkness; wife of Geb and mother of Isis, Osiris, Set, and Nepthys
Renenet	Goddess of children and protector of children at birth; goddess of good fortune and riches
Sekhment	Goddess of war; associated with the lioness, with a heart like the spirit of the desert; called the mighty one and, like Buto, brings destruction to the enemies of Ra; consort of Ptah; regarded as the eye of Ra; possibly the origin of the Greek Athena

Tauret	Like Renenet, considered the goddess of childbirth, depicted with the body of a hippopotamus, the legs of a lion, the breasts of a woman, the tail of a crocodile; protector of pregnant women
Tetnut	Goddess of moisture, rain, dew; said to share her soul with Shu; symbol of creation; protector of Ra and the pharaoh; has the head of a lion and wears a solar disk as a headdress

Common Egyptian Myths

1. At the beginning of time, before the earth, sky, gods, or men had been created, the sun god lived alone in the watery mass of Nun which filled the universe. The sun god created by himself two other gods whom he spat out of his mouth, the god Shu who represents air, and the goddess Tefnut, who represents moisture. Shu and Tefnut then had two children, Geb, the earth god and Nut, the goddess of the sky, who had four children. These were Osiris and his consort Isis, and Seth and his consort Nepthys. These nine gods together made up the Great Ennead of Heliopolis, the most important group of gods in the Egyptian Pantheon.
2. In the beginning Geb and Nut were one. Then Shu split them apart. Geb became the earth and Nut became the sky. Ra is reborn every morning. Human beings were created differently from gods and goddesses. The gods and goddesses wept, and from their tears human beings sprang.
3. The sun ages over the course of the day. Every morning the sun is a newborn baby. The sun grows older with every passing minute. By noon the sun is a full grown adult. In the afternoon the sun gets older and at sunset, the sun dies to be born again in the new morning. At the death of the sun, as night came, the sun was said to travel in the underworld through the night before rebirth in the morning.

Greco-Roman Gods and Goddesses

The Olympians: The "Twelve"

Of the many major and minor gods in the Olympian dynasty, the most important are the TWELVE, a group chosen by the Greeks themselves as the key figures in the Olympian group and the basis for most of their religious observances. Greek law is also to some extent derived from the concept of the TWELVE, and Greeks in both court proceedings and in ordinary conversation took their oath "by the Twelve." The divinities constituting this group were:

God\Goddess	Association
Zeus (Jupiter, Jove)	Leader of the Olympians, god of lightening, and representative of the power principle.
Hera (Juno)	Wife of Zeus and goddess of marriage and domestic stability.
Poseidon (Neptune)	God of the sea. Often called "the earth shaker," possibly because the Greeks attributed earthquakes to marine origin.
Hades (Pluto, Dis)	God of the Underworld and presider over the realm of the dead. Also connected with the nature myth by his marriage to Persephone (Proserpine), who spent half of her time on earth (the growing season) and half in the underworld (the winter period). Hades does not represent death itself, that function being relegated to a lesser divinity Thanatos.
Pallas Athena, Athena (Minerva)	Goddess of wisdom, but also associated with many other concepts from warfare to arts and crafts. Her birth was remarkable, since she sprang fully-armed from the forehead of Zeus. She was the patron goddess of Athens and to the Athenians represented the art of civilized living.
Phoebus Apollo	Son of Zeus and Leto, daughter of the Titans Krios and Phoebe. Son-god, archer, musician, god of truth, light, and healing. Represented the principle of intellectual beauty. At the temple dedicated to him at Delphi, the oracle divulged in cryptic language the will of the gods.
Artemis (Cynthia, Diana)	Twin sister of Apollo, virgin goddess of the moon, the chase (hunt) and the caste (chastity).
Aphrodite (Venus)	Daughter of Zeus and Dione in one version; in another, supposed to have risen from the waves (sea foam). Goddess of love and physical beauty.
Hephaestus (Vulcan)	Lame blacksmith god who forged the thunderbolts of Zeus. The much deceived husband of Aphrodite.

Hermes	Son of Zeus and Maia (ma'ya), daughter of Atlas. Messenger and general handyman of Zeus; god of commerce, traders, travelers, and thieves. Depicted as wearing winged sandals and winged hat.
Ares (Mars)	Son of Zeus and Hera; god of war.
Hestia (Vesta)	Virgin sister of Zeus, goddess of the hearth and home. Served in Rome by the sacred sisterhood of the Vestal virgins. Later replaced among the TWELVE by Dionysus.
Dionysus (Bacchus)	God of wine, son of Zeus and the mortal woman Semele. Like Demeter, connected with the principle of fertility and, like Persephone, represented the nature myth by dying in the autumn and being reborn in the spring. The Eleusinian mysteries were dedicated to all three fertility deities and the festivals of Dionysus were periods of wild, bacchaenic rejoicing. Since plays were usually performed at these festivals, Dionysus also became the god of the theatre. Represented the ecstatic principle, as opposed to the intellectual principle signified by Phoebus Apollo.

	Lesser Olympians
Demeter (Ceres)	Sister of Zeus and goddess of agriculture. Mother of Persephone and symbol of fertility.
Eros (Cupid)	Eternal child of Hephaestus and Aphrodite, spirit of love whose mischievous darts have caused many of the world's troubles.
Pan	Son of Hermes, woodland god with goat-like horns and hooves, player of pipes and supervisor of rustic gaieties.
Nemesis	Avenging goddess, the principle of retribution.
Hebe	Goddess of youth and cupbearer of the gods.
Iris	Goddess of the rainbow and sometimes, like Hermes, messenger of the gods.
Hymen	God of the marriage festival.
The Three Graces	Aglaia (Splendor), Euphrosyne (Mirth), and Thalia (Good Cheer)
The Nine Muses	Spirits of learning and the arts, as follows: CLIO—history; THALIA—comedy (Shares name with one of the Graces) MELPOMENE—tragedy; TERPSICHORE—dance ERATO—love poetry; CALLIOPE—epic poetry EUTERPE—lyric poetry; POLYHYMNIA—sacred poetry
The Erinyes (Furies)	Tisiphone, Megaera, Alecto: represented the pangs of conscience and relentlessly hounded wrongdoers
The Three Fates	Spirits who allotted to each person a destiny: CLOTHO—spun the thread of life LACHESIS—wove it into a pattern which determined the kind of life to be led ATROPOS—cut it, terminating existence

Appendix C: Morgan State University

Morgan State University
STUDENT EVALUATION FORM[1]

FOR OFFICIAL USE ONLY ( ) Insert Teacher Code Number	
	Name of Teacher
	Hegis Code, Course Number and Section Number
	Semester and Year

* * * * * *

I. DIRECTIONS: Listed below are a number of statements about the instructor, the course, the text and other readings, and the examinations. Please indicate, by circling the number on the appropriate line, the extent to which you agree or disagree with the statement (*SD* = Strongly Disagree, *D* = Disagree, *U* = Uncertain, *A* = Agree, and *SA* = Strongly Agree)

	SD (1)	D (2)	U (3)	A (4)	SA (5)
A. *The Instructor's Ability to Transmit Knowledge Clearly*					
1. Is well organized	1	2	3	4	5
2. Clearly interprets abstract ideas and theories	1	2	3	4	5
3. Gives explanations which are clear and to the point	1	2	3	4	5
4. Makes good use of examples and illustrations	1	2	3	4	5
B. *The Instructor's Ability to Relate the Subject Matter to the Course Objectives and Textbook*					
1. Makes it clear how each topic fits into the course	1	2	3	4	5
2. Adds to the understanding of the required reading rather than merely repeating it	1	2	3	4	5

	SD (1)	D (2)	U (3)	A (4)	SA (5)
3. Spends an appropriate amount of time relating text and lecture materials	1	2	3	4	5
4. When appropriate, relates the material of the course to other areas of knowledge	1	2	3	4	5
C. *The Instructor's Ability to Motivate Students*					
1. Is aware when students are having difficulty in understanding a topic and changes his approach or offers additional explanations	1	2	3	4	5
2. Is stimulating and interesting to listen to	1	2	3	4	5
3. Stimulates my curiosity and makes me want to learn more about the subject	1	2	3	4	5
4. Gives me new viewpoints or appreciations	1	2	3	4	5
D. *The Instructor's Sensitivity to the Needs of Students*					
1. Is personally interested in the students in the class	1	2	3	4	5
2. Welcomes questions from the students	1	2	3	4	5
3. Is available for individual help	1	2	3	4	5

* * * * * *

II. OPTIONAL: If you desire, please answer the following questions:

A. How and in what ways has the formal written work of the course been helpful to you, either by its nature or through comments made on work returned, or both? Are the grades just, and does the grading "system" seem reasonable to you? What improvements could be made in these respects?

B. Please make any summary or additional suggestions or comments either in favor of the course as it is or toward its possible improvement, or both.

[1]Based on the *University of Minnesota Student Evaluation Form*

DEPARTMENT OF ENGLISH and LANGUAGE ARTS

Course Syllabus

Humanities 201

THE FRESHMAN ENGLISH —HUMANITIES— WRITING PROFICIENCY EXAMINATION PROGRAM

Facts That You Should Know

1. The Freshman English—Humanities—Writing Proficiency Examination Program is a five stage, General Education Requirement which every Morgan student must satisfy in order to be eligible for graduation. A student must pursue the five stages of the Program in the following order:

STAGE 1:	English	101
STAGE 2:	English	102
STAGE 3:	Humanities	201
STAGE 4	Humanities	202
STAGE 5	Writing Proficiency Examination	

2. Students may not advance to any stage of the Program until they have satisfied all of the preceding stages. Students found in violation of the sequence will be removed from a given stage (course or examination) until they have satisfied all of the prerequisites of that stage.
3. Through placement testing, the University will determine the level at which students are to enter the Program. Students must enter the Program at the prescribed level and move forward in proper sequence. They are exempted from all courses that precede the level to which they are assigned.
4. Students may meet the course and examination requirements of the Program in the following ways:

   A. Advanced Placement Exemption:

   As a result of placement testing by the University, students may be exempted from any of the stages of the program. If these students are to be exempted from any of the stages of the Program by placement testing, they will be notified of such exemption or advanced placement at the time of their matriculation at Morgan. Students exempted from any one or more of these stages will receive credit, but no grade, for the course.

B. Transfer Credit:

The transcript of students bringing transfer credit from other institutions will be evaluated to determine if those credits meet any of the requirements of the Program. If students are to be exempted from any of the five stages of the Program, they will be notified of such exemption at the time of matriculation at Morgan. No transfer credit is accepted for the Writing Proficiency Examination, and students transferring to Morgan with the A.A. degree should arrange to take the Examination during their first semester at Morgan.

C. Regular Course Enrollment:

Students may satisfy any of these stages by enrolling and receiving a passing grade in the relevant course.

D. Proficiency Testing:

Students may satisfy the requirement for English 101 and 102 and Humanities 201 and 202 through proficiency tests. Students desiring to pursue credit through proficiency testing should apply in the English Office (Holmes Hall 202) by the end of the third week of classes of the semester in which they seek to be tested.

5. Passing grades in Humanities 201 and 202 are "A," "B," "C," and "D."
6. Students may satisfy the Writing Proficiency requirement by enrolling and receiving a passing grade in English 350 (Writing Practicum). Students who fail the Writing Proficiency Examination should also enroll in that course.
7. Students should take the Writing Proficiency Examination in their junior year (after passing Humanities 202) and should register for that Examination in the Office of the English Department well before the date on which the Examination is scheduled. By no means should students wait until their senior year to take the Examination.

Class Attendance Policy

Students are expected to attend every class. In the event of unavoidable absence, the student will submit written, official verification of the reason for the absence. Students should submit the written, official verification upon their return; the instructor will make the final determination as to the validity of the excuse. The student is responsible for all work, whether or not he/she is present. If a student accumulates more unexcused absences than the number of hours for which the class meets weekly, the student will receive an "F" for the course.

Exit Examination

Beginning in Fall, 1995, each student in a Freshman English or Humanities course will need to pass a Departmental exit examination in order to pass the course.

Procedures and Requirements

1. Classes meet three hours a week.
2. Students should note that the indicated readings, including related introductory and auxiliary materials, are to be completed before the class periods in which they are to be taken up.
3. Written reports *will be assigned* on outside reading and on *field experiences* in art, film, dance, music, and drama; and there will be music selections from at least three different cultures.
4. In addition to completing a number of requirements (as outlined by the instructor, in writing, at the beginning of the course), students will write a minimum of one documented essay in the course, which essay will constitute 10–20 percent of the final grade (the percentage to be specified by the instructor at the beginning of the semester). In addition, all of the major examinations will have an essay component.

Required Texts

Humanities in the Ancient and Pre-Modern Worlds

Objectives

The general objectives of this course are to make students articulate members of the intellectual community, interested in the ideas and literary forms reflective of ancient and transitional cultures; to make students aware of the personal, social, artistic, and literary values of these cultures; and to make students constantly alert and receptive to opportunities to improve and enlarge their experiences in the humanities.

Specifically, students

1. will become articulate concerning the humanities, observing the communication standards required of Morgan students:
   a. students will become more proficient in research skills and write clearer, more effective documented essays.
   b. students will write clearly structured essay-type examinations that are focused and effectively supported.
2. will recognize in literature the forms, themes, and movements of the humanities.
3. will develop a keen understanding of the relationship between cultural movements and historical facts.
4. will acquire literary skills, being able
   a. to recognize distinctions among literary forms.
   b. to distinguish specifically among the genres or modes: drama, lyric, and narrative.
   c. to differentiate various modes of presentation within each of the above categories.

HUMANITIES 201

Ancient and Transitional

Introduction — 2 weeks

Drama — 3 weeks
*Aristotle's "Poetics"; *Oedipus Rex* or *Antigone*
Everyman
Japanese Noh Play or Other Asian Drama
Ozidi (African Drama)

Lyrics — 2 weeks
*Catullus
*Egyptian Poetry
*Indian, Chinese, Japanese (Haiku), and Islamic Lyrics (one lyric from at least two of the four cultures)
*Psalms
Sappho
Solomon, "Song of Songs"

Narrative — 5 weeks
**Bhagavadgita* (or other selection from the *Mahabharata*) or *Ramayana*
*Chaucer, "General Prologue"; "The Pardoner's Tale" or "The Miller's Tale" or "The Nun's Priest Tale" or "The Wife of Bath's Tale"
*Creation Folk Tales and Myths (African, Greek [Hesiod], and Hebraic [Genesis])

*Dante, Selected Cantos from the *Divine Comedy*
Gilgamesh
*Homer, Excerpts from *Odyssey* or *Iliad*; or Virgil, *Aeneid*
*"Job"
Plato, "The Apology" (emphasizing the possible connection with Egyptian wisdom teaching)
Popul Vuh (Mayan epic: journey through the underworld)
**Sundiata*

Supportive Visual Arts and Music

In addition to studying the above literary texts, the class will have multi cultural experiences in the visual arts and music.

Notes

The term *ancient* refers to the world-wide classical era; the term *transitional*, to linkages between ancient and modern cultures.

The asterisked selections are core or required items.

Index

A

B

C

D

E

F

G

H

I

J

K

L

M

N

O

P

Q

R

S

T

U

V

Y

Z

Figure 1. Wall Painting.
Found in the Tomb of Huy, Viceroy of Nubia, at Gurnet Murai.
Photograph © Erich Lessing/Art Resource, NY.

Figure 2. Temple Relief.
Limestone; H. 37 cm, W. 33.5 cm. From Deir el-Bahri, Mortuary Temple of Mentuhotep II, Middle Kingdom, Eleventh Dynasty, c. 2000 BC.
Courtesy of PhotoDisc, Inc.

Figure 3. Wooden Statue Depicting King Tutahkamun Guarding the Burial Chamber.
New Kingdom, Eighteenth Dynasty. Cairo Museum.
Photo courtesy of Steven Beikirch.

Figure 4. Gold Burial Mask of King Tutahkamun.
New Kingdom, Eighteenth Dynasty. Cairo Museum.
Photo courtesy of Steven Beikirch.

Figure 5. Canopic Shrine of King Tutahkamun.
Depicting King Surrounded by the Protective Figures of Isis, Nephthys, Neith, and Seiket. New Kingdom, Eighteenth Dynasty. Cairo Museum.
Photo courtesy of Steven Beikirch.

Figure 6. Canopic Shrine of King Tutahkamun.
Close-up of the Goddess Seiket. New Kingdom, Eighteenth Dynasty.
Cairo Museum
Photo courtesy of Steven Beikirch.

Figure 7. Canopic Chest of King Tutahkamun.
Showing Human Headed Stoppers for the Hollowed-out Chambers Below. New Kingdom, Eighteenth Dynasty. Cairo Museum.
Photo courtesy of Steven Beikirch.

Figure 8. Wooden Statue of Anubis, the Jackal-Headed God, thought to Judge the Dead; Tutahkamum Collection.
New Kingdom, Eighteenth Dynasty. Cairo Museum.
Photo courtesy of Steven Beikirch.

Figure 9.
Throne of King Tutahkamun.
New Kingdom, Eighteenth Dynasty.
Cairo Museum
Photo courtesy of Steven Beikirch.

Figure 10. Game-Box (Senet) and Stand, Found in the Annex of King Tutankhamun's Tomb. New Kingdom, Eighteenth Dynasty. Cairo Museum.
Photo courtesy of Steven Beikirch.

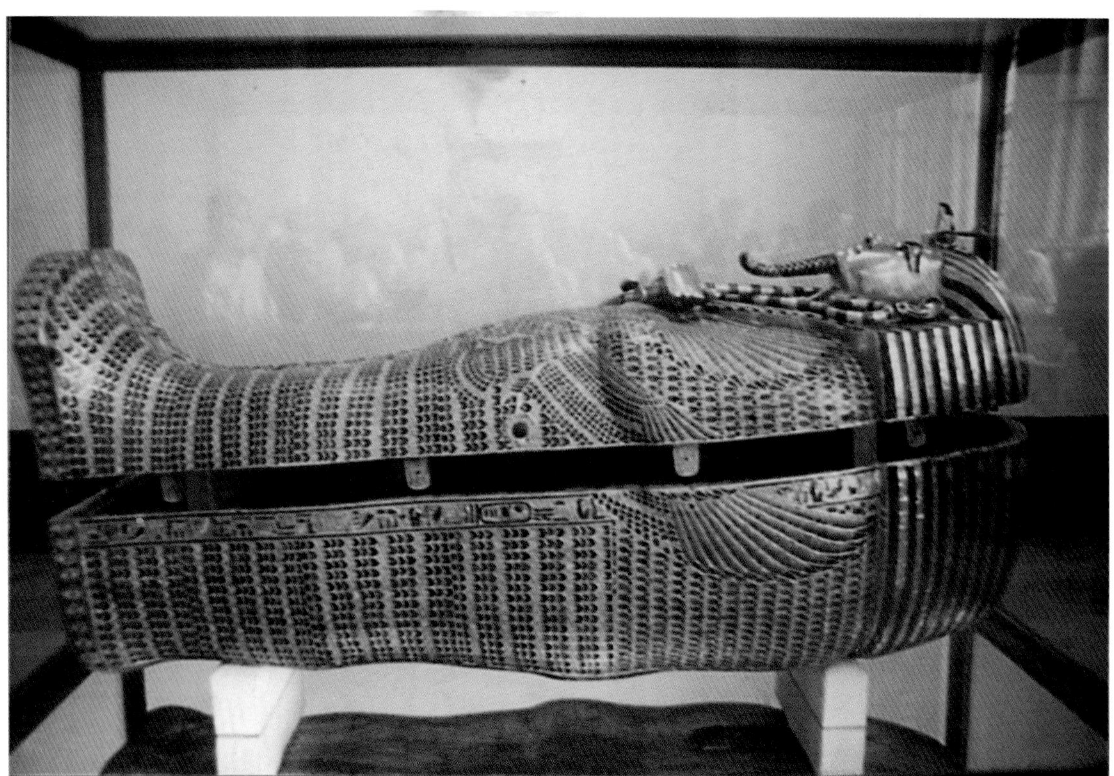

Figure 11. King Tutankhamun's Guilded and Inlaid Second Coffin.
New Kingdom, Eighteenth Dynasty. Cairo Museum
Photo courtesy of Steven Beikirch

Figure 12. Wall Painting Depicting the Falcon-Headed God Osiris in the Temple of Osiris Located at Abydos.
New Kingdom, constructed by Seti I, c. 1300 BC.
Photo courtesy of Steven Beikirch

Figure 13. Queen Nofretari guided by Isis.
Painted bas-relief. Tomb of Nofretari, Valley of the Queens, Thebes. Nineteenth Dynasty, c. 1301–1238 BC.
Giraudon/Art Resource, NY.

Figure 14. Horus as the Falcon-Headed God.
Granite. Egyptian, Late Period, c. 50 BC.
Photo courtesy of Steven Beikirch.

Figure 15. Madonna and Child with Saint John the Baptist and Saint Peter
—by Cimabue.
National Gallery of Art, Washington, DC.

Figure 16. Seated Buddha.
Kushana, c. 50 BC–320 AD.
Borromeo/Art Resource, NY.